A.—[Sketched by A. R. Waud.]

CIVIL WAR MACON

CIVIL WAR MACON

The History of a Confederate City

by
Richard W. Iobst, Ph.D.

MERCER UNIVERSITY PRESS

1979   1999

TWENTY YEARS OF PUBLISHING EXCELLENCE

ISBN 0-86554-634-7
MUP/H474

© 1999 Mercer University Press
6316 Peake Road
Macon, Georgia 31210-3960
All rights reserved

First Edition.

∞The paper used in this publication meets the minimum
requirements of American National Standard for Information
Sciences—Permanence of Paper for Printed Library Materials,
ANSI Z39.48-1984.

Library of Congress Cataloging-in-Publication Data

Iobst, Richard W. (Richard William), 1934-
    Civil War Macon / by Richard W. Iobst. —1st ed.
        p. cm.
Includes bibliographical references and index.
ISBN 0-86554-634-7 (alk. paper)
        1. Macon (Ga.)—History—19th century. 2. Macon (Ga.)—
Social life and customs—19th century.
3. Georgia—History—Civil War, 1861-1865. 4. United States—
History—Civil War, 1861-1865—Social aspects.   I. Title.
f294.m2I53   1999
975.8'513—dc21   99-22455
                                        CIP

CONTENTS

In memory of my son,
Richard William Iobst III

ILLUSTRATIONS AND CREDITS

(between pages 252 and 253)

1. Railroad Station, Macon, Georgia. On the second floor of this building were the headquarters of General Marcus J. Wright, commanding the Post of Macon in 1864 Marcus J. Wright Papers, P-1044, photograph of the Railroad Station, at Macon, Georgia (see *Macon Telegraph*, 13 August 1864, Southern Historical Collection, Wilson Library, The University of North Carolina at Chapel Hill.

2. Eugenius A. Nisbet. From a portrait painted from life. Courtesy of Mrs. Fitzallen Yow Eldridge, Sylva, North Carolina.

3. Defenses of Macon, 1864 from Thomas Yoseloff, ed., "The Official Atlas of the Civil War", 1958, Plate CXXXV-4 (135) from the original in possession of Major General William T. Sherman.

4. Brown's Hotel, 1876. Courtesy of the Middle Georgia Archives, Washington Memorial Library, Macon, GA.

5. Cotton Factory, Macon, GA., ca. 1876. Courtesy of the Middle Georgia Archives, Washington Memorial Library, Macon, GA.

6. Macon Armory, 1865. Courtesy of the Middle Georgia Archives, Washington Memorial Library, Macon, GA.

7. Residence of William B. Johnston, Macon, GA. Today the building is known as the Hay House. Courtesy of the Middle Georgia Archives, Washington Memorial Library, Macon, GA.

8. Confederate States Laboratory, ca. 1870's. Courtesy of the Middle Georgia Archives, Washington Memorial Library, Macon, GA.

9. Confederate States Laboratory, ca. 1912. Courtesy of the Middle Georgia Archives, Washington Memorial Library, Macon, GA.

10. Wesleyan Female College, 1876. Courtesy of the Middle Georgia Archives, Washington Memorial Library, Macon, GA.

11. Railroad Depot, Macon, Georgia ca. 1876. Courtesy of the Middle Georgia Archives, Washington Memorial Library, Macon, GA.

12. Samuel S. Dunlap House. Used as Stoneman's headquarters on 30 July 1864. The house is now used as the Superintendent's Residence at the Ocmulgee National Monument. Courtesy of The Ocmulgee National Monument, Macon, GA.

13. Schofield Iron Works, ca. 1876. Courtesy of the Middle Georgia Archives, Washington Memorial Library, Macon, GA.

14. Group of unidentified Confederate soldiers from Macon. Courtesy of the Middle Georgia Archives, Washington Memorial Library, Macon, GA.

15. Hendley Varner Napier, ca. 1862. Ocmulgee Rangers (Company A, 19th Georgia Cavalry; then 10th Confederate Cavalry). Courtesy of the Middle Georgia Archives, Washington Memorial Library, Macon, GA.

16. Mrs. Selina Shirley Poe. Led the women of Macon in support of Confederate soldiers and their families. Courtesy of the Middle Georgia Archives, Washington Memorial Library, Macon, GA.

17. Brigadier General Edward Dorr Tracy, Jr., ca. 1863. Department of Mississippi and East Louisiana. Macon's highest ranking Confederate officer. Courtesy of the Middle Georgia Archives, Washington Memorial Library, Macon, GA.

18. Simri Rose in Masonic dress, ca. 1860. Courtesy of the Middle Georgia Archives, Washington Memorial Library, Macon, GA.

19. William E. Brice, ca. 1861. Member of the Thomson Guards. Courtesy of the Middle Georgia Archives, Washington Memorial Library, Macon, GA.

20. Railroad car shed, Macon, GA. Courtesy of the Middle Georgia Archives, Washington Memorial Library, Macon, GA.

21. Telegraph and Messenger Building, ca. 1876, Macon, Georgia. Courtesy of the Middle Georgia Archives, Washington Memorial Library, Macon, GA.

22. Fort Hawkins as it might have appeared during the war. Courtesy of the Middle Georgia Archives, Washington Memorial Library, Macon, GA.

23. Blind Asylum, ca. 1876. Used as a hospital, known as the Blind Asylum Hospital, during the war. Courtesy of the Middle Georgia Archives, Washington Memorial Library, Macon, GA.

24. Washington Block (built in 1857) ca. 1879. Mulberry Street from Second Street, Macon, Georgia. Courtesy of the Middle Georgia Archives, Washington Memorial Library, Macon, GA.

25. Stephen Collins, Mayor of Macon 1864-1866. Courtesy of the Middle Georgia Archives, Washington Memorial Library, Macon, GA.

26. Ovid G. Sparks, Mayor of Macon 1858-1860, 1863. Courtesy of the Middle Georgia Archives, Washington Memorial Library, Macon, GA.

27. Methven S. Thomson, Mayor of Macon 1860-1862. Courtesy of the Middle Georgia Archives, Washington Memorial Library, Macon, GA.

28. John J. Gresham, Mayor of Macon 1843-1847 and civic leader during the war. Courtesy of the Middle Georgia Archives, Washington Memorial Library, Macon, GA.

29. Joseph Clisby, ca. 1860, photograph of a drawing. Courtesy of the Middle Georgia Archives, Washington Memorial Library, Macon, GA.

30. William W. Carnes, ca. 1862, in Confederate Uniform. Courtesy of the Middle Georgia Archives, Washington Memorial Library, Macon, GA.

31. Dr. Stanford E. Chaille, 1868, Surgeon in charge of the Ocmulgee Hospital. Courtesy of the Middle Georgia Archives, Washington Memorial Library, Macon, GA.

32. Private L.W. Hunt, Macon Guards (Company C, 8th Georgia Regiment). Courtesy of the Middle Georgia Archives, Washington Memorial Library, Macon, GA.

33. Bibb County Courthouse, ca. 1860s with Macon Gas Company on right. (Copied from: Ballou's Pictorial Drawing-Room Companion). Courtesy of the Middle Georgia Archives, Washington Memorial Library, Macon, GA.

34. Howell Cobb as Secretary of the Treasury in the Buchanan Administration. Hargrett Rare Book and Manuscript Library, University of Georgia Libraries.

35. Howell Cobb, Jr., after the war. Hargrett Rare Book and Manuscript Library, University of Georgia Libraries.

36. Major John Addison Cobb. Hargrett Rare Book and Manuscript Library, University of Georgia Libraries.

37. Colonel Horace Capron, Massachusetts Commandery. Military Order of the Loyal Legion and the US Army Military History Institute.

38. Major General James H. Wilson, Massachusetts Commandery. Military Order of the Loyal Legion and the US Army Military History Institute.

39. Colonel Robert H.G. Minty, Massachusetts Commandery. Military Order of the Loyal Legion and the US Army Military History Institute.

40. Major General George M. Stoneman, Massachusetts Commandery. The Loyal Legion and the US Army Military History Institute.

41. General Joseph E. Johnston. Massachusetts Commandery Military Order of the Loyal Legion and the US Army Military History Institute.

42. Brigadier General Felix Robertson. Massachusetts Commandery, Military Order of the Loyal Legion and the US Army Military History Institute.

43. Colonel Smith D. Atkins. Massachusetts Commandery, Military Order of the Loyal Legion and the US Army Military History Institute.

44. Camp Oglethorpe, Macon Georgia. Federal prisoners spending their leisure time. Massachusetts Commandery, Military Order of the Loyal Legion and the US Army Military History Institute.

45. Prisoners digging escape tunnels at Camp Oglethorpe, Macon, Georgia. Massachusetts Commandery, Military Order of the Loyal Legion and the US Army Military History Institute.

46. Gov. Joseph Brown's message to the citizens of Macon to take up arms in defense of the city.

47. Remains of Confederate breastworks, 1955, in Vineville, near Pio Nono Avenue. UDC Cross of Honor recipients, L to R: Frank C. Jones, George M. Nottingham, Jr., and Val Sheridan. Courtesy of the Middle Georgia Archives, Washington Memorial Library, Macon, GA.

48. Nathan Campbell Munroe, Jr. Courtesy of Mark Patterson, private collection.

49. Mrs. Nathan Campbell Munroe, Jr. Courtesy of Mark Patterson, private collection.

ACKNOWLEDGMENTS

The research and writing of this book began with an idea from my friend and fellow laborer in the study of Confederate history, Bill Elliot of Macon. It was furthered by the urging of my Mother, Marguerite B. Scull, whose kind encouragement kept me working on the manuscript at times when I would probably have abandoned the project.

Willard Rocker, Chief of Genealogy; Peer Ravnan, Archivist of the Middle Georgia Archives; and Muriel McDowell and Anne Rogers, Genealogy Librarians at the Genealogy and Historical Room and Middle Georgia Archives of Macon's Washington Memorial Library, spent countless hours steering me to newspaper files, to the records of the Confederate Ordnance Facilities in Macon, filmed by the National Archives and housed in the library, and to many manuscript and photograph collections.

I also wish to thank the staff of the Hargrett Rare Book and Manuscript Library of the University of Georgia Library for their permission to research the voluminous Howell Cobb Collection and other collections which present a detailed view of life in Macon during the period, as well as a thorough account of the military actions on Dunlap's Hill and Major General James H. Wilson's successful capture of the city in late April, 1865.

Janie C. Morris, Research Services Librarian; William R. Erwin, Senior Reference Librarian; and Jason Tomberlin of the Special Collections Library, Duke University, helped me find materials, especially in the John McIntosh Kell Collection, which contains the letters of Nathan C. Munroe, Jr., a prominent Maconite of the period, and his daughter Julia Blanche Kell, wife of Captain Kell. Munroe's letters contain much information about life in Macon during the war years. The information contained at Duke concerning the Reserve Artillery of the Army of Tennessee sent to Macon to aid in its defense when Lieutenant General John B. Hood led that army in an abortive invasion of Tennessee after the fall of Atlanta, was invaluable since much of the successful defense of Macon in the November engagement was because of well-handled and well-placed artillery.

My thanks are also given to John White, an Archivist with the Southern Historical Collection in the Louis Round Wilson Library of the University of North Carolina at Chapel Hill, who helped me find a number of manuscripts in his fine depository.

Linda M. Matthews, Head, Special Collections, and her staff in the Special Collections Division of the Robert W. Woodruff Library, Emory University, Atlanta, showed me numerous materials in their care as did the staff of the

Georgia Department of Archives and History, also in Atlanta. The wartime Letter book of Georgia Governor Joseph E. Brown as well as the Letter books of the Georgia Adjutant General Henry C. Wayne, were especially useful.

Ms. Sylvia Flowers, Archaeologist, and Guy LaChine, Chief Ranger at the Ocmulgee National Monument, in Macon gave me valuable insights into the two Battles of Dunlaps Hill, a portion of which occurred on the monument grounds, as well as kind permission to use a photograph of the Superintendent's residence which served, during the period, as the residence of Captain Samuel S. Dunlap, and was an objective of both the raid led by Major General George M. Stoneman in July, 1864, and the second effort to capture Macon under Brigadier General Hugh J. Kilpatrick and his subordinate, Colonel Smith D. Atkins, in the following November.

Much credit for the chapter about Camp Ogelthorpe is due to my close friend, Alan Marsh, Supervisory Park Ranger at Andersonville National Historic Site, for the many documents he furnished me concerning the Camp, used as a prisoner of war camp for officers during the war.

John M. Stockbridge, Director of the Planning Department of Athens-Clarke County, Georgia, spent a delightful day with me showing me the many graves in Oconee Hill Cemetery which I had missed on an earlier expedition, especially those of the parents of Howell Cobb. He also drove me through the historic district of Athens to show me the homes of Howell Cobb and other leaders of the time.

Macon's Confederate hospitals were made far more real to me through an unpublished manuscript entitled "James Mercer Green: Southern Gentleman, Confederate Surgeon," prepared by Dr. Ian A. Cameron, then of Macon and currently a resident of Halifax, Nova Scotia. Dr. Cameron has graciously permitted me to use his manuscript, which he presented as a speech before many organizations in the Macon and Middle Georgia area.

No set of acknowledgments for this book would be complete without thanking the staffs of the National Archives and the Library of Congress in Washington who allowed me to use the many rich collections in their care.

Dr. Richard J. Somers and his staff in the Archives of the U;.S. Army Military History Institute, Carlisle Barracks, Pennsylvania proved indispensable in steering me toward many fine collections which presented the Federal side of the raids against Macon in 1864 and 1865. The librarians of the Library in the Institute have more rare military histories under their care than any other depository that I visited. The photographic section of the Institute furnished me with a number of photographs of Federal and Confederate officers involved in the two battles of Macon.

I also wish to thank Dr. and Mrs. John M. Coski of The Museum of the Confederacy in Richmond who spent a long day providing much research information which I have used in the preparation of this book. Dr. Coski, who is the Historian for the Museum, also provided my Mother and me with a detailed map of how to leave Richmond heading to North Carolina with a bare minimum of traffic.

In Knoxville, Nick Wyman, Unit Head of Special Collections, and his staff in the Special Collections Library of the University of Tennessee, Knoxville, were very supportive in their efforts to provide me with much valuable information about Tennesseeans who fought at Macon in 1864.

The staff of the Delaware Historical Society in Wilmington made the diaries of James H. Wilson available to me, especially the diary for 1865 which details Wilson's invasion of Georgia and the events which occurred during and after his capture of Macon.

Ms. Carrie K. Holthouser, President of the Western North Carolina Civil War Round Table read the entire manuscript. Her gracious comments, based upon a thorough knowledge of the period, greatly add to the accuracy of the book. Carrie also helped proofread the galley-proofs. However, any errors in the galleys should be attributed to me. Thanks are also due to Dr. Peter S. Carmichael of the Department of History at Western Carolina University for reading portions of the manuscript and giving me the benefit of his wisdom in Civil War matters. I also owe a tremendous debt of gratitude to Mr. Bill Elliot and Mr. Mark Patterson of Macon, two students of their city's Confederate history, who read the manuscript and helped to keep it accurate. Mark also furnished unpublished photographs of the period, especially the portrait of Nathan Campbell Munroe, Jr. My appreciation is also extended to Dr. Charles Kellum of Macon who furnished me information concerning one of his ancestors who served as a guard at Camp Ogelthorpe, and to Ms. Fitzellen Elldridge of Sybra, North Carolina, for permission to publish a portrait of her ancestor, Eugenia A. Nesbit.

Others in Macon who helped in my research include Mrs. Marvia Mitchell, Cemetery Specialist in charge of Macon City Cemeteries, who graciously helped me find information concerning the reinterments of John B. Lamar and General Edward Dorr Tracy, Jr. after the war. I also owe a great debt of gratitude to my friend, John T. Pellew of Macon who allowed me to use his copy of the rare volume edited by Mary Wright Stock, *Shinplasters and Homespun: The Diary of Laura Nisbet Boykin*. Without their help much valuable information would have been unavailable to me.

Bill Kirwan, Chief Librarian, and his staff at Hunter Memorial Library, Western Carolina University, permitted me to use the many excellent secondary works on Civil War history housed there. These works, listed in the bibliography, furnished me with numerous insights into the study of the war in Macon and Middle Georgia.

I also owe a tremendous debt to Nelda Reid, Director of Learning Resources, and Dianne J. Lindgren and Shirley Orr, Library Assistants, at Southwestern

Community College for permitting me unlimited access to an excellent microfilm reader, and for securing a number of significant collections on microfilm through the interlibrary loan process. Without the microfilm reader it would have been impossible to complete my research.

Patri Woods, Library Assistant at the Haywood County Public Library in Waynesville also allowed me to secure a great many valuable items through interlibrary loan. Without these materials my stay away from my office in Cullowhee would have been far more prolonged.

No summary of those who supported the preparation of this book would be complete without thanking Dr. Scott Nash, former Managing Editor of the Mercer University Press, Jon P. Peede, former Editor, and the current Editor, Dr. Marc Jolley, for their encouragement and patience as the work of research and writing stretched into a period of over two years. I hope I have not disappointed them.

Last, but certainly not least, I wish to thank my wife, Mary, and my son Carl for their help in untangling the mysteries of our computer, and in taking with good grace my long absences in doing the research for this project. They have also supported me in other ways too numerous to mention.

As is always the case, any mistakes made in the preparation of the manuscript are mine alone.

Richard W. Iobst
Cullowhee, North Carolina
December 1998

Introduction

This is the story of Macon, Georgia, during the period 1860-1865. It is a story of excitement, determination, and human triumph and failure. In a sense, it is the story of the urban population of the Lower South as these people faced the greatest test of wills and self-sacrifice in American history.

Macon, founded in 1823 as a frontier settlement in the heart of the rapidly-expanding cotton belt of the Lower South, was from the first an important town. Located almost in the geographical center of Georgia, the town grew rapidly. By 1860 it was an integral part of the Lower South Industrial Complex which would play such an important role in the desperate war which was destined to begin the following year. In that year the town included 5,042 white people, twenty-one freedmen, and 3,069 slaves. The County of Bibb, of which Macon was the county seat, contained a population of 8,838 whites, eighty-four freedmen, and 7,030 slaves. This concentration of people made Macon the fifth largest city in Georgia.

When the war began the citizens of Macon determinedly supported the Southern cause, even offering troops to defend South Carolina before the actual start of hostilities.When the news of the secession of South Carolina arrived in late December 1860, the event was received with wild enthusiasm. At noon on Friday, 20 December the moment when the South Carolina Ordinance of Secession went into effect, the church bells in Macon began to peal. One of the volunteer units, the Jackson Artillery, fired a 100-gun-salute in honor of the occasion. At 7:00 P.M. the bells rang again, and another 100-gun-salute was fired. Numerous bonfires illuminated the streets, and many homes were illuminated. A procession of 1,500 people led by a band, marched through the streets to Macon's principal hotel, the Lanier House, where they heard fiery speeches by some of the city's leading secessionists.

Dramatic events quickly followed. When Georgia seceded on 19 January 1861, Hermione Rose Walker scribbled in her diary that "Today the secession ordnance was signed, half-past twelve o'clock. I have been to the greatest popular demonstration every known in Macon. I got so excited I was half wild and am not sure but I screamed- Joined the noise with the rest."[1]

Early in the morning of 12 April 1861, Confederate troops under the command of General Pierre G.T. Beauregard fired on Fort Sumter. When the news reached Macon the attack was celebrated by a salute of seven guns.

---

[1] Hermione Rose Walker diary, 21 Jan. 1861, Hermione Rose Walker Papers, SHC.

During the war that followed Macon was the scene of intense activity. The city became the site of numerous manufacturing activities. including a sword manufacturing enterprise, and other similar activities. Three very important Confederate ordnance facilities were located there. These consisted of the Confederate States Arsenal, located in the Findlay Iron Works, which manufactured cannon tubes of various calibers, with their accompanying carriages. The Arsenal also produced a variety of other war materials including shoes, saddles, shells for ordnance of different sizes, revolving pistols, knapsacks, cartridge box belts, Columbiad carriages from oak timber, and flannel for cartridge bags. The most popular weapons included twelve-pound bronze-barreled Napoleons and ten- to thirty-pound iron-barreled Parrot guns. The Arsenal was commanded by Colonel Richard M. Cuyler. A Confederate States Armory, temporarily housed in the old depot of the Macon and Western Railroad, rented from the city, manufactured gun stocks, rifle barrels, and pistols. During its peak production the Armory, commanded by Colonel James H. Burton, manufactured 1,500 gun stocks a month. Much of this production went to the Richmond Armory which assembled the rifles. Burton attempted to complete a massive, new Armory, which remained unfinished at the end of the war. The last facility was the Confederate States Central Laboratory, led by the noted Irish-born chemist, John W. Mallet, and housed in a number of buildings in the central section of the city. It produced shells and bullets for the Confederate armies, and conducted experiments to determine the proper size bullets for .54, .58, and .69 caliber rifles. Mallet also performed a noteworthy contribution by testing shells to determine the charge of powder needed to burst them with certainty.The Laboratory also prepared complete sets of gun-metal gauges for small-arms bullets. Mallet, like Burton, constructed an elaborate new Laboratory complex, but the sudden collapse of the Confederacy in the Spring of 1865, also found it unfinished.

Macon was also a center for the raising and training of troops. The several military companies in the city at the beginning of the war soon left, but other units were raised to take their places. Macon's Camp Ogelthorpe, although initially established for troops who fought in the Mexican War, soon became a center of activity. According to some accounts, Macon furnished more troops for the Confederacy in proportion to its general population than any other community in the South.

Macon was an important transportation hub served by a number of railroads. Possibly no single line played a more important role in the Confederate War effort than the Macon and Western Railroad which became the lifeline for the Army of Tennessee during the Atlanta Campaign of 1864. Troops were sent to the front on this road, and men wounded on such bloody battlefields as Shiloh, Chickamauga, Lookout Mountain, Missionary Ridge, Resaca, Kennesaw Mountain, Peachtree Creek, the Battle of Atlanta, Ezra Church, and Jonesboro, came to Macon to be treated in the hospitals there. When Dr. Samuel H. Stout, Medical Director of the Army of Tennessee removed most of the Atlanta hospitals to Macon early in July 1864, as Sherman's three armies approached Atlanta, Macon became an important hospital center, although some hospitals were located there earlier. Many of the men who died in these hospitals were buried in the city's major cemetery, Rose Hill.

Macon was also the site of Camp Ogelthorpe, an important prisoner of war camp which held captured Federal officers. There, many brave men suffered and died, especially in 1864. As in nearby Andersonville, the principal prisoner of war camp in the Confederacy for enlisted men by 1864, few prisoners managed to escape.

During 1864, Macon became the headquarters for the Georgia Reserves led by Major General Howell Cobb. Cobb, one of the most important Southerners to be active in the leadership of the Federal Government during the Nineteenth Century, had served as Georgia's Governor, in the Federal House of Representatives, and as Secretary of the Treasury in President James Buchanan's Cabinet. He and his brother, Thomas R. R. Cobb, played a crucial role in establishing the Confederate Government which Howell Cobb served for a time as President of the Confederate Congress. In a very real sense, the history of Macon during the last year of the War is part of Cobb's biography. Wealthy planter that he was he could have sat out the conflict in some safe haven, possibly on one of his plantations in then-remote Southwest Georgia. But, instead, he chose to serve in the field, first with the Army of Northern Virginia, then as Commander of the District of Florida, and, finally, in Macon. Although he was not a trained soldier, Cobb helped to defeat a cavalry raid led by the division of Major General George M. Stoneman, although a portion of his success was due to Stoneman's timidity and ineptness. Stoneman and many of his men were captured by Confederate cavalry led by Brigadier General Alfred Iverson, Jr., aided by local militia units, at the Battle of Sunshine Church in nearby Jones County in August, 1864.Cobb was also able to repel Federal cavalry commander Hugh Judson Kilpatrick and his subordinate, Smith D. Atkins when a brigade of cavalry under their command assaulted Macon on November 20, 1864. In the end, he probably would have ably defended Macon, a city which he loved so well, if he had not received a communication informing him of a preliminary surrender of General Joseph E. Johnston's Army of Tennessee to Major General William T. Sherman. This agreement was part of an arrangement between the two generals known as the Sherman-Johnston Convention which surrendered all Confederate forces in Georgia and the Carolinas. Cobb received quick paroles for his men and even helped Wilson by urging the Confederates to accept their defeat without further bloodshed. Although President Andrew Johnson did not pardon him, Cobb was paroled and allowed to travel anywhere he wished.

Macon, in short, was a very important city during the period. A history of the contribution of cities in the Lower South Industrial Complex to the Confederate war effort would be incomplete without a discussion of affairs in Macon during that tumultuous time.

Chapter 1

The Eve of War: Macon in 1860

Macon is located at the head of navigation on the Ocmulgee River in the center of the State of Georgia. In 1860, on the eve of the Civil War, Macon was a very diverse community. Although the city tended to be homogeneous in its thinking, its population included people from many different states and many countries, especially from Europe. It was, moreover, a business community dedicated to supplying the surprisingly sophisticated needs of its citizens, of the cotton planters who grew the short staple upland cotton, which provided the principal foundation of wealth for the antebellum South in general, and for the people of Middle Georgia in particular. This amazing diversity would serve Macon well in the desperate struggle that was to come.

John C. Butler, an early historian of Macon and Bibb County wrote, "In the history of America, and more particularly of the Southern States, the [Antebellum] period of which we now write, was the most remarkable for general prosperity. It was the golden era of the Southern States. Wealth and happiness abounded. All commercial institutions, agricultural and mechanical industries were in a thriving condition.... This period the augmenting glory of the South may be compared to the brilliant and peculiar one of Athens, when under the administration of Pericles, that was the 'eye and light of Greece, and was the most splendid and prosperous in Grecian annals'."[1]

Perhaps Butler's comments were a bit overblown but Macon was certainly prosperous. In 1860, the thriving town on the Ocmulgee included 5,042 white people, 21 freedmen, and 3,069 slaves. Bibb County, of which Macon was the county seat, contained 8,838 whites, 84 freedmen, and 7,030 slaves. This concentration of people, large for the time, made it the fifth largest city in Georgia. Although there were a number of wealthy people in the community, the population included many occupations. There were workmen, watchmakers,

---

[1] John C. Butler, *Historical Record of Macon and Central Georgia*, with Foreword by Spencer B. King, Jr., Ph.D. (Macon: J.W. Burke Co., 1958) [Reprint] 218-19, hereafter cited as Butler, Historical Record.

goldsmiths, carpenters, laborers, teachers, preachers, and many others.[2] The *Macon Directory for 1860* listed many occupations, businesses, and trades. Adams and Reynolds operated a cotton warehouse at the corner of First and Poplar Streets, J.B. Allgood was listed as a "negro dealer" with his place of business located at the corner of Fifth and Plum Streets. Mrs. E.A. Anderson kept a boarding house on the corner of Cherry and Fifth Street. Carriage dealer J.W. Babcock was located on Mulberry and First Streets. T.W. Brantley was listed as Sheriff of Bibb County. John T. Boifeuillet served as Treasurer of the Southwestern Railroad. Eliphalet E. Brown was the proprietor of Brown's Hotel on the corner of Fourth and Plum Streets.[3]

Many businesses were listed in the *Directory*. These included slave depots operated by G.H. Noel, G.F. Stubbs, and W.R. Phillips. The many cotton buyers included Robert Coleman, S.F. Dickinson, B. Elliott, James Graybill, E. Price, John Hollingsworth, A. Lesueur, and E.A. Wilcox. A cotton mill, operated by the Macon Manufacturing Company, was located on the corner of Lamar and Oglethorpe Streets. There were people who dealt in ambrotypes, daguerreotypes, and tintypes; there were auctioneers, editors, druggists, painters, iron fence makers, carriage dealers, sculptors, lawyers, two marble works, gun manufacturers, and ice dealers. There were three iron works in Macon. One was operated by Robert Findlay and Sons at the corner of Congress and Oglethorpe Streets; another by Thomas C. Nisbet on Cotton Avenue. Another was the business owned by Schofield and Brother on Fifth Street north of the Passenger Depot.[4]

The community included a total of ten sawmills, six carriage houses, two dentists' offices, five manufacturers of machinery, four printing houses, one cotton gin, four blacksmiths, and two saddlery and harness shops. Although the roads were bad, the railroads were excellent. They included the Central Railroad which ran from Macon to Savannah, the Macon and Western whose final destination was Atlanta, and the South Western which ran lines to Albany and Columbus.[5]

---

[2] 1860 Georgia Population Schedules, Appling, Baker, Baldwin, Banks, Berrien and Bibb Counties, Microcopy No. M-653, Roll No. 111, hereafter cited as Georgia Population Schedules, Bibb County, 1860.

[3] Mears and Company, comps., *The Macon Directory for 1860 Containing The Names of the Inhabitants A Business Directory and an Appendix of much useful information* (Macon: Andrews Book & Job Printing Office, 1860) 15-16, 18, 20, 22.

[4] Ibid. The author gathered his information from a number of pages in the Directory. The best account of the Findlay Iron Works is Robert S. Davis, Jr., Cotton, Fire, & Dreams: *The Robert Findlay Iron Works and Heavy Industry in Macon, Georgia 1839-1912* (Macon: Mercer University Press, 1998).

[5] Morton Ray McInvale, "Macon, Georgia: The War Years, 1861-1865," (Ph.D. diss., Florida State University, 1973) 3.

The Georgia Central Railroad, whose president, Richard R. Cuyler, supervised the operation of the line from his office in Savannah, ran a distance of 191 miles, with a thirty-seven-mile long branch to Milledgeville and a branch to Eatonton which had a length of fifty-nine miles.

The South Western Railroad operated lines to Albany, with branches to Butler, and Fort Gaines, Georgia, and Eufaula, Alabama. Cuyler was also president of this line, whose headquarters were also located in Savannah. John T. Boifeuillet of Macon, as noted above, served as Treasurer of this line.

The third railroad to operate out of Macon was the Macon and Western which ran for a distance of 103 miles to Atlanta. President Isaac Scott oversaw the operations of the line from his office at Macon.[6]

Perhaps the vitality of Macon's business community was shown by a correspondent for the *Americus Republican* who visited the thriving town on the Ocmulgee early in April, 1860. He observed, "The different Factories and Machine shops were all in full blast-the sound of the hammer may be heard in every direction. Quite a number of large business houses have been erected there within the past twelve months. The shelves of the merchants seemed filled with splendid, beautiful stocks of goods. Macon is rapidly improving, and the day is not far distant when it will be the city. She has the means and the will, and these two combined, will accomplish anything."

John W. Burke, Agent for the Methodist Book Depository on Cotton Avenue, headed a prosperous book store and was a "clever gentleman to deal with." W.W. Parker and Company operated a dry goods store in the Masonic Building a few doors below the Methodist Depository. In the spring of 1860, the firm sold a full line of spring goods, primarily ladies' dress goods. As the visitor proceeded down Cotton Avenue he passed J.T. Schreiner and Sons who dealt in jewelry and piano fortes, the ancestors of today's pianos. Next was the establishment of E.J. Johnston and Company whose stock-in-trade was sewing machines. For crockery and oil lamps the shopper could find a good selection at Bolshaw and Herzog's, located at 11 Cotton Avenue. Bolshaw and Herzog's had a competitor in Robert P. McEvoy's store which sold crockery and glassware. The firm of Carhart and Curd sold hardware and cutlery, while E. Saulsbury sold ready-made goods. His competitor, C.H. Baird, under the *Macon Telegraph* Office, also sold ready-made clothing. Baird also offered fancy cassimeres and vests. B.A. Wise's business, located on Cherry Street, sold cutlery and house furnishing goods.[7] D.C. Hodgkins and Son manufactured guns at the corner of Mulberry and North Third Streets. Ovid G. Sparks, the Mayor of Macon at the beginning of the war was a commission merchant together with his

---

[6] The Macon Directory for 1860, pp. 100-101.

[7] Article in the Americus Republican reprinted in the *Macon Daily Telegraph*, 7 Apr. 1860.

partner, Thomas Hardeman, Jr. Their business was located on the corner of Third and Poplar Streets.[8]

The secret of Macon's vitality, as in communities across America, was found in its people. William Thomas Jenkins, writing in his Doctoral Dissertation for the University of Georgia entitled "Ante Bellum Macon and Bibb County, Georgia," quoted another writer, Walter A. Harris, "Macon's society did not originate in the old south along the Atlantic Coast, but was brought in from other states. There was no tradition of aristocracy such as that found in Virginia or South Carolina. He suggested that leadership in founding and leading Macon during the antebellum period came from men who were from Connecticut such as O.H. Prince and Edward D. Tracy, or men like Jerry Cowles who came to Macon from New York. These men became lawyers, speculators, bankers, and promoters rather than planters. They created a business and legal society rather than one controlled by planters. Although some of them became planters, their main interest was in business, law, transportation, and trade. These were the leaders that set the pace and made Macon what she had become in 1860."[9]

This leadership included Assistant US Marshall Thomas L. Ross, who owned $13,500 in real estate and $8,000 in personal property. He was born in North Carolina. Mayor Sparks was born in Georgia, made his living as a warehouse and commission man, and owned $12,000 in real estate and $51,000 in personal property. Robert P. McEvoy, another prominent Macon leader, was a thirty-three-year-old merchant with real estate valued at $8,800 and personal property with a worth of $13,300. Dudley W. Hammond, born in South Carolina, was a fifty-four-year-old physician worth $45,000 in real estate and $26,080 in personal property. His fellow physician, Andrew Pye, forty, was worth $6,750 in real property, and $37,200 in personal property. Azel R. Freeman, sixty-seven, on the other hand, was Secretary and Treasurer of the Macon Gas Company. Born in New Jersey, his worldly goods were valued at $35,000 in real estate and $18,000 in personal property. The thirty-five year-old David Wills, the new Presbyterian Minister, hailed from Pennsylvania. John T. Napier was a wealthy planter with $20,000 in real property and $39,200 in personal property. James M. Armstrong was a twenty-seven-year-old Methodist minister, while Eliphalet E. Brown, the forty-five-year-old proprietor of Brown's Hotel came from Connecticut. He was worth $60,000 in real estate (the value of the hotel) and $20,000 in personal property.[10]

---

[8] The Macon Directory for 1860, 71, 89.

[9] William Thomas Jenkins, "Ante Bellum Macon and Bibb County, Georgia," (Ph.D. diss., University of Georgia, 1966), 389.

[10] Georgia Population Schedules, Bibb County, 1860.

The wealthiest citizen in Macon, John Basil Lamar, brother-in-law of Secretary of the Treasury Howell Cobb, was a native-born Georgian who at 47 controlled $213,000 worth of real estate in Macon and Bibb County and a personal estate, much of it in slaves, valued at $283,000, a tremendous sum which would run into many millions of dollars in today's currency. Lamar also served as trustee for his sister, Mary Ann Cobb's property in Bibb County which was valued at $68,000 in real estate and $205,170 in personal property. The Roman Catholic Priest, twenty-six-year-old Father Thomas O'Reilly, by contrast, was worth $3,000 in real estate and $300 in personal property, and was born in Ireland. Attorney Washington Poe, sixty, was somewhere between Lamar and O'Reilly, with a net worth of $26,150 in real estate and $25,000 in personal property. Judge Asa Holt, owner of the home which is today known as the "Cannon Ball House" and one of Macon's best-known citizens, was a seventy-year-old planter from North Carolina who was worth $40,000 in real estate and $160,000 in personal property. The leaders of the prominent Nisbet Family, James A. Nisbet, forty-seven, an attorney worth $25,000 in real estate and $10,000 in personal property and the 56-year-old Eugenius A. Nisbet, his brother and partner, worth $30,000 and $30,000 in each category had more influence in the community than their wealth might suggest.[11]

Not only were these people influential, but the trades and professions represented are interesting and go far to describe the sophisticated nature of the city in which they lived. The occupations of Maconites included attorneys; physicians; dentists; school teachers; music teachers; ministers; planters; traders; merchants; harness makers; governesses; baggage masters; dyers; railroad car builders; editors and publishers; land agents; washers and ironers; Justices of the Peace; railroad treasurer; daguerreotype makers, known as "daguerres;" draftsman; boot and shoemakers; watchmen; gunsmiths; gas fitters; railroad contractors; builders; brick masons; sheriff; policemen; firemen; blacksmiths; and others far too numerous to list here.[12]

Macon's cosmopolitan nature may also be explained by the diversity of the states and countries of much of its population. States included South Carolina, Tennessee, Kentucky, Virginia, North Carolina, Maryland, Delaware, Ohio, Indiana, Illinois, Michigan, Pennsylvania, New Jersey, New York, Connecticut, Massachusetts, New Hampshire, Vermont, Maine, Rhode Island, and California. Foreign countries were Canada, England, Ireland, Scotland, France, Holland, and Switzerland. The then-independent German States were well represented by Hess-Darmstadt, Hanover, Bavaria, Brunswick, Baden, Rhinefelt, Prussia, and Wurttemberg. Even Scandinavia was represented by Sweden.[13]

---

[11] Ibid.
[12] Ibid.
[13] Ibid.

Some of the building mentioned by the report for the *Americus Republican* involved V. Pierce's design for a proposed enlargement of the town's largest hotel, the Lanier House, located on Mulberry Street near Second. Plans called for the building to be carried over an alley to the south and covering the next lot. The whole would be raised one story. This would make a "very long and imposing" four story front. The windows would also be improved through the addition of lintels. The reporter for the *Macon Daily Telegraph* noted, "the renovation of the old favorite Hotel will add thirty-five rooms to its capacity, and make it among the largest public houses in the South. The Lanier House was considerably improved in all its departments last fall, and it is now one of the best and most comfortable hotels we know of in any Southern interior town."[14]

By early June, final plans for the renovation were complete and work on the Lanier House extension had begun. The front of the building would be extended by sixty feet, with the addition of forty-eight rooms, thirty of them large "family" rooms. Two stores, a barber shop, and a bathing room, would also be added. The building would have a total front on Mulberry Street of 135 feet "which will be masticated." The front was decorated with iron cornices and caps, and would have a balcony, so popular in the period, running its entire length. An observatory, or cupola, twenty-four feet high with a base of fourteen feet was located on top. The management assured the public that the entire building "will be well ventilated and be furnished in the finest and most fashionable style."[15]

Another large building project, constructed in 1860, involved a "Carriage Repository" built by L.D. Wilcoxon and Company, which was nearly completed by early September. The 180-foot-long, thirty-three-foot-wide building, located on Second Street, would hold "with ease" 200 carriages and buggies, and would be the largest store house in the city, with the exception of the establishment of J.W. and W.A. Ross.[16]

Not to be outdone, Thomas C. Nisbet, a member of one of the most prominent families in Macon, purchased the site of the Macon Steam Mill, and was building a foundry out of granite. Plans called for the new foundry to connect with Nisbet's already large manufacturing facilities on Cotton Avenue, then the heart of the business section.[17] The *Daily Telegraph* reporter boasted, as was the custom of this expansionary time, "Macon is behind no city in the South in the number and character of her foundries and machine shops, of which she has three, viz:- Findlay's, Nisbet's and Schofield's. All of which

---

[14] *Macon Daily Telegraph*, 29 Feb. 1860.

[15] Ibid., 4 June 1860.

[16] Ibid., 4 Sept. 1860.

[17] Ibid., 7 Sept. 1860.

manufacture yearly, an immense amount of steam engines, boilers, mill gearing &c., which will compare favorable with those manufactured in any other shop in the United States."[18]

At the close of 1860, Macon had become a large and prosperous community. One hundred and two thousand bales of cotton were shipped over the railroads. The first bales were shipped over the Southwestern Railroad by W.R. Phillips of Twiggs County, to the firm of Coats and Woolfolk in Macon. The number of stores and large homes was rapidly growing. Besides a number of large public buildings, including the new City Hall, there were seventeen new stores constructed during the year, together with sixty-seven new homes. The increase of travel to Macon called for additional hotel accommodations. The Granite Hall underwent large additions, and a new hotel, the Stubblefield House, was almost finished. The Lanier House, as mentioned elsewhere in this chapter, received a large addition and other improvements.

The Georgia Methodist Conference established a large book store, known as a "Book Depository," at the corner of Mulberry and Second Streets, under the supervision of Reverend J.W. Burke and a board of directors. Four job printing offices did a large business, and, according to John C. Butler, "Every railroad company, bank, factory and corporate company was thriving and paying remunerative dividends upon the stock invested."[19]

Macon's business community shone brightly when the Belgian Fair opened on 12 December 1860. Many people from out-of-town gathered to view a large assortment of Belgian and Southern products and "articles of innumerable description." Businesses in such cities as Charleston and Baltimore sent handsome merchandise to the Fair Grounds at Camp Oglethorpe where the exhibition was held. Baltimore alone sent $50,000 worth of goods. The exhibition from Belgium was very large, displaying an extensive number of ornamental and interesting articles. Since the Cotton Planters' Fair, an annual event in Macon, was in session at the time, the combined fairs lasted for two weeks, with many successful displays and operations. Historian Butler wrote, "It was the grandest and longest display ever made in the State, and in variety the largest that had been made in the South. From the political agitations that prevailed throughout the country for six months and that was now shaking the prosperous system of Southern institutions, the planters were resolved upon the establishment of 'direct trade' with Europe."[20]

At 9:00 A.M. on the twelfth, a special train carrying Governor Joseph Emerson Brown and the Legislature arrived from Milledgeville, hosted by Richard R. Cuyler. The group was received at Camp Oglethorpe by the Jackson

---

[18] Ibid.

[19] Butler, *Historical Record*, 223-224.

[20] Ibid., 222-223.

Artillery which greeted them with a fifteen-gun-salute. During the evening the Macon Battalion paraded under its leader, Captain Robert A. Smith. The unit, Butler noted, "elicited great admiration by their brilliant and soldierly appearance."[21]

All of this business activity was fueled by money from Macon's banks. These consisted of the Bank of Middle Georgia on Third Street near Mulberry, incorporated on 18 February 1856, and operated by President Isaac Scott and Cashier A.H. Powell. The firm was funded by $125,000 in capital stock. President E. Bond's Manufacturer's Bank, which employed G.W. Hardie as Cashier, did business on the Southwest corner of Second and Cherry Streets.[22]

Macon's post office, administered by Postmaster Dr. Ed L. Strohecker, did business on Second Street near Mulberry.[23] One of the most significant building projects involved the construction of a new city hall. On 26 May 1860, the Bibb County Bar Association recommended that the Inferior Court unite with the City Council to build a new city hall, "which will answer the purpose of a City Hall and Court House." The building, which had to be substantial, should be convenient to the business part of the city.[24] The Inferior Court took the first step towards carrying out the suggestion by appointing John Jones Gresham as a one-man-committee to meet and confer with a committee of the City Council to erect the building. The *Daily Telegraph* commented, "We hope the Council will appoint a Committee immediately and take such other steps in the matter as will cause the erection of the building at any early day."[25]

On 3 July 1860, Alderman Abel Harrison moved that a committee of three be appointed to confer with Gresham. Acting on Harrison's motion, the Council appointed Mayor Sparks, Harrison, and William P. Goodall to the committee.[26]

Following this action, Sparks called a special meeting of Council on 9 August 1860, in which he asked them to consider purchasing the Patton and Collins cotton warehouse for use as both a city hall and a city market. Alderman Harrison offered a resolution approving the action of the Mayor, and authorizing him to obtain a title to the property immediately.[27]

The committee met on 15 August and thoroughly examined the Patton and Collins Warehouse. The building, and particularly some nearby sheds which came with the property, was in much better condition than they expected. They

---

[21] Ibid., 222.

[22] Ibid., 97.

[23] *The City Directory for 1860*, 97.

[24] *Macon Daily Telegraph*, 29 May 1860.

[25] Ibid., 3 Jul. 1860.

[26] Macon City Council Minutes, July 3, 1860, Book D, p. 397, microfilm, Washington Memorial Library, Macon.

[27] Ibid., 9 Aug. 1860, 399.

reported that the premises lent itself to the building of new stalls for the City Market. They observed, "The space that can be used at present in the New Market extends from the door on the South East Side to the end of the house on Poplar Street including one hundred and twenty two feet in length and forty five feet in width. The improvements necessary for the occupancy of the upper story of the building can easily be made for the reception and accommodation of the Council (with Hall, Mayor & Clerks offices) by the first or fifteenth of November." The committee recommended that the improvements be started immediately, to assure their completion by the specified time. The committee also decided to lease part of the building to Thomas T. Wyche, a cotton merchant, for business purposes, on the condition that he allow the Council to control the upper and lower stories of the building, and whatever sheds were needed to make the improvements needed for the Market. Wyche only needed a counting room, a place to exhibit his cotton, and enough space in the sheds to allow him to store cotton. Furthermore, he only needed the space in the City Hall until 1 January 1861, when he planned to make other arrangements. The committee explained the unusual arrangements because it was in the best interest of the City which needed the money Wyche would pay in rent. The rent, in turn, could be used to improve the building, without interfering in the operation of the Market. No one, the committee argued, could possibly be injured by the arrangement, especially because of the money which would be brought into the Treasury. There would be, the committee argued, ample room for a Market, a room for a City Hall, and a Council Chamber, Mayor and Clerk's offices, and even enough room to house an organization known as the "Andrew Jackson Artillery," one of the militia units which were growing more numerous as war loomed. After much discussion, the Council adjourned and agreed to meet on 21 August, when final action would be taken.[28]

On 21 August, in a called Council meeting, the Aldermen agreed to rent Wyche a portion of a shed until 1 January 1861, provided he agreed to give possession of the shed to the city at that time.[29]

In an effort to soothe the feelings of some Maconites who were concerned with Council's arrangement with Wyche, a reporter for the *Daily Telegraph* wrote, "we will state that the building...will be put into immediate repairs for the purpose of a City Hall, and Council will hold its meetings there in a short time. Owing to the fact that the lease of the sheds will not expire until January next, the old market house will be used until that time. Don't be impatient, but 'wait for the wagon.'"[30]

---

[28] Ibid., 16 Aug. 1860, 401-403.

[29] Ibid., 21 Aug. 1860, 403.

[30] *Macon Daily Telegraph*, 3 Sept. 1860.

Council soon appointed Aldermen Abel Harris, C.H. Rodgers, and J.T. Boifeuillet to a committee which would hire a draftsman to make a design showing improvements needed on the building, and report back at its next meeting.[31]

The group made its report on 25 September urging the adopting of a renovation plan prepared by a Mr. Melcher. The report was adopted. At the same meeting, the Jackson Artillery, slated to share the building with the City Government, notified Council of its plans for an armory on the ground floor.[32] As the year drew to a close, work progressed on the project.[33]

In 1860, (and throughout much of the Nineteenth Century) Macon was governed by a City Council composed of a Mayor, a Mayor Pro Tempore, and six Alderman. The Mayor, elected for a term of one year, presided over meetings of the Council, and served on a number of important committees appointed by Council. He received a salary of $1,000 a year. The Mayor Pro Tem and members of the Council, all elected for one-year terms, received no salary. Macon had a Clerk and Treasurer, also elected for a term of one year. His salary, due to the significance of his office, was $1,200 a year. Other officials were appointed by Council for one-year terms. These included the Overseer of the Public Hands with a salary of $900; a Chief Marshal, also salaried at $900; a Deputy Marshal with a salary of $800; a Bridge Keeper who collected tolls from persons crossing the single bridge, known as the "City Bridge," who earned $850; the Clerk of the Public Market, $500; the Guard House Keeper whose annual salary was $300; the Keeper of the Magazine, $200; a sexton who supervised burials in Rose Hill and Oak Ridge Cemeteries, both owned by the City, who worked for fees; and a City Physician at $600. The Physician had to furnish all medicine at his own expense. Council committees included Finance, Streets, Public Property, Fire Department, Market, Pumps, Gas, and Rose Hill.[34]

The officials elected by qualified voters on 10 December 1859, included Ovid G. Sparks as Mayor; Dr. Gabriel Harrison, Mayor Pro Tem; Richard Curd, Clerk and Treasurer; and Aldermen J.V. Grier, C.H. Rodgers, William P. Goodall, Thomas A. Harris, J.T. Boifeuillet, and Thomas Dougherty. Appointed officials were John B. Cumming, Chief Marshal; Deputy Marshal George D. Lawrence; James Richardson, Bridge Keeper; S. Worran, Clerk of Market; William P. Anderson, Guard House Keeper; D.C. Hodgkins, Keeper of

[31] Council Minutes, 4 Sept. 1860, 404-405.

[32] Ibid., 25 Sept. 1860, 409.

[33] Ibid., 16 Oct. 1860, 415.

[34] Ibid., Dec. 14, 1859, 365-366; Dec, 20, 1859, 367.

the Magazine; and A. Brydie, Sexton. On 3 January 1860 Dr. A.P. Collins was appointed City Physician.[35]

In September 1860, Mayor Sparks was forced to resign because of poor health and heavy business engagements. An election to fill the vacancy was ordered on 22 September.[36] The Democratic candidate, Dr. Methvin Thomson, was elected with a vote of 377, a majority of twenty-nine over his opponent, Dr. Gabriel Harrison, Macon's Mayor Pro Tem, who had 348 votes. Joseph Clisby's *Macon Daily Telegraph*, a Whig paper, observed, "To be beaten by so popular a candidate as Dr. Thomson, is no discredit to Dr. Harrison, who is also a most esteemed and estimable gentleman, but not so long a resident in, or so largely identified with the prosperity of the city."[37]

Macon's police force, never large in the Antebellum Period, numbered a captain, a lieutenant, and six men until the organization of the Minute Men of Macon in November 1860. The latter group, created as a result of the sectional crisis which came to a head by the election of Abraham Lincoln to the presidency, created a need for a larger police force. Other reasons for the enlargement of the force included expansion of the city limits and the town's growing population. Under the new arrangement, the captain and the lieutenant headed an expanded force of twelve men. All of the force was armed, with two men to guard the City Magazine where arms and ammunition was stored. After 12 November 1860, the City Council ordered the Guard House bell to be rung each evening at 8:00.[38] Then, on 13 November 1860, the Council increased the regular police force to thirty, but with no mounted patrols.[39] But, on 1 January 1861, the aldermen decided not to keep a larger police force due to the lack of money to support them. This action led to the establishment of a City Watch of ten men which would patrol the community from 9:00 P.M. until after sunrise. At least twice a week, the entire city was patrolled. Each member of the Watch would be paid $40 a month with horses furnished by the men. The force consisted of two squads of five men each.[40]

The Fire Department consisted of Chief Engineer George S. Obear and George W. Price as Assistant Engineer. The force included three Engine Companies and one Hook and Ladder Company. Engine Company No. 1, known as the Protection Fire Company, had fifty members with 700 feet of leading hose; Engine Company No. 2, the Ocmulgee Engine Company, located on Second Street near Cherry, included sixty-five men with 650 feet of hose, and

---

[35] Ibid., Dec. 10, 1859; 365-366; Jan. 3,1860, 370.
[36] *Macon Daily Telegraph*, 12 Sept. 1860.
[37] Ibid., 24 Sept. 1860.
[38] Council Minutes, 10 Nov. 1860, 420, 422.
[39] Ibid., 13 Nov. 1860, 422.
[40] Ibid., 1 Jan. 1861, 434-435.

Engine Company No. 3, consisted of sixty members and sixty feet of hose. This latter company was situated on Third Street near Mulberry. The Hook and Ladder Company, known as Hook and Ladder Company No. 1, had thirty-seven members. The department owned two trucks with all the necessary hooks and ladders. During 1859 there were seven fires in Macon and seven alarms. Two of the conflagrations, authorities believed, were caused by incendiaries.[41]

Masonic Lodges in Macon consisted of Macon Lodge No. 5; Constantine Chapter No. 4; and Franklin Lodge No. 2. Other organizations which fell under this general category were the Sons of Temperance Sons of Malta Altoona Lodge No. 2, and the Sons of Temperance's Tomachici Division which met at Temperance Hall every Friday night.[42]

The total value of real estate was $4,717,551. The value of personal property, much of it in slaves, was $10,279,574 for a total of $14,997,125. The community generated $7,650 in state taxes, $2,295 in school taxes, and included thirteen schools with an enrollment of 370 pupils. The agricultural produce of Bibb County yielded an average of twelve bushels of corn per acre and 600 pounds of cotton (one bale) per acre. In 1860 the average yield of wheat per acre was ten bushels.[43]

Macon contained a Methodist Episcopal Church with a membership of 300 people and a valuation of $500 in its physical plant. Another Methodist Episcopal Church boasted 200 members with a building worth $400. The Baptist Church with Reverend Sylvanus Landrum as pastor, was located on Second Street between Cherry and Poplar Streets. Its congregation numbered 400 with a sanctuary valued at $400. A Primitive Baptist Church included 100 members with a value of $400. The Presbyterian Church, situated on Mulberry Street at the corner of First Street, had no regular pastor, but the pulpit was supplied every Sabbath. The Protestant Episcopal Church, on Fourth Street near Walnut, was led by Reverend Henry K. Rees; and the Catholic Church, led by Reverend Thomas O'Reilly, was situated on Fourth Street near Poplar. The Methodist Church, under Reverend J.R. Armstrong, was built on the corner of Arch and Oglethorpe. Reverend Patello's Methodist Church (colored) was located on New Street near Wharf. The Young Men's Christian Association, which held church services, had a membership of 300 with a building, situated on Mulberry Street near Second, worth $1,000.[44]

In addition to the taxes collected locally for the schools, Bibb County drew an annual appropriation of $2,500 from the State Treasury for public education.

---

[41] Ibid., 10 Jan. 1860, 375-376; *The City Directory for 1860*, 98.

[42] *The City Directory for 1860*, 99.

[43] *Social Statistics for Bibb County*, Social Statistics- 1860 Georgia, Appling Thru Worth Microcopy No. T-1137.

[44] Ibid.; *The City Directory for 1860*, 100.

It also received an annual sum of $6,000 for the support for the Academy for the Blind. For the purposes of taxation, lands and houses and lots were the only types of property known as Real Estate. Personal property included slaves, merchandise, live stock, notes, accounts, and money. Lawyers, doctors, dentists, and daguerreotype artists [makers of photographs] were taxed, as well as banks and railroads. Each individual received a tax exemption of $300 on furniture. A poll tax was collected on each male white citizen between the ages of twenty-one and sixty. The Macon Free Academy had a fund from which $1,000 was appropriated on an annual basis to support the school. In addition, the city gave an annual appropriation of $1,000 to the Academy.[45]

The principal colleges included Wesleyan Female College under Reverend John M. Bonnell and the Home Institute led by Miss E.M. Melville and Miss E.J. Gay, with Herman L. Scheiner as Professor of Music. Other schools, included the Southern Reform Medical College led by Dr. L. Bankston as President and Dr. James Mercer Green's Academy for the Blind. Nathan C. Munroe, Jr. served as Treasurer of the latter institution and Robert A. Smith filled the office of Secretary.[46]

Newspapers in Macon in 1860 included the weekly and semi-weekly *Georgia Citizen* whose proprietor was L.F.W. Andrews. Simri Rose and Company's weekly *Journal and Messenger,* and Joseph Clisby's *Georgia Telegraph* were two of the most important newspapers in the City. Other papers consisted of the *Baptist Champion* issued semi- monthly by its proprietor, Joseph Walker; the *Christian Index,* a weekly under E.W. Warren; and the weekly *American Republic* under the leadership of J. Russel and Company.[47]

Macon could boast a gas works, known as the Macon Gas Company under President Joseph M. Boardman; a magnetic telegraph office on Cherry Street near Third Street, with J.C. Butler as Superintendent; and an olympic club which played baseball at Camp Oglethorpe every Saturday evening.[48]

Culture in such a community as Macon, was certainly not neglected. On 17 December 1858, Professors Hasslocher and Waldau, assisted by the Macon Harmonic Society, presented a "Grand Vocal and Instrumental Concert." Sir John Stevenson, a prominent vocalist of the time, sang "The Harp that once thro' Tara's Hall," and the Society presented the solo and chorus from the "Miserere," from Verdi's fine opera "IL Trovatore."[49]

---

[45] *Social Statistics for Bibb County.*
[46] *The City Directory for 1860,* 101.
[47] Ibid.
[48] Ibid., 100.
[49] Newspaper clipping, n.d., Lewis Neale Whittle Papers, Middle Georgia Archives, Microfilm, Washington Memorial Library, from original in Lewis Neale Whittle Papers, Southern Historical Collection, UNC.

Ralston's Hall, the principal theater in Macon, was leased by its owner, Mr. Ralston, to the owner of a theater company, W.G. Fleming. Fleming presented Miss Maggie Mitchell, a comedienne, during the short theater season in March, 1860. In describing the abilities of Miss Mitchell, the *Macon Telegraph* reported, "Miss Maggie Mitchell is becoming a favorite with the Macon Theater-goers. She was again greeted by a large audience last night [9 March 1860]. Of the acting we can say but little from personal observation, except that the few moments we remained in the hall made us wish to linger longer. Mr. Fleming's Company is deserving the increasing patronage it receives. To-night Miss Maggie appears as the French Spy, which is esteemed as one of her best personations." Fleming was described as a talented actor- who, as manager, "strictly adheres to every propriety in the drama, that would render it unexceptionable to any audience."[50]

During the same month, Ralston's Hall saw operatic performances of "Ernani" (19 March), "Lucia di Lammermor" (20 March), and "Il Trovatore" (21 March).[51]

Ralston's Hall was remodeled in 1859. After the renovation, the facility seated about 1,000 people "in a comfortable manner, with full opportunity for every one to witness whatever may be passing before them on the stage."[52] George W. Scattergood, a native of Macon who attended a local institution, the Polhill School operated by B.M. Polhill, a locally-renowned educator, saw a performance of Bumsey and Newcomb's Minstrels at Ralston's in September, 1860. He observed the beauty of the theater which contained a new dropped curtain, "which is far superior to the former one in beauty."[53]

Scattergood enjoyed other amusements. These included hunting, especially for robins and opossums. He also went to the Fair Ground to see the ball club play ball. Sometimes he rode about town, especially going by the Wesleyan Female Seminary to see the girls, but also just to ride around Macon. On occasion he drove around the Macon Reserve, a park-like area in the vicinity of modern Central City Park. Young Scattergood also enjoyed watching the militia drill and hearing numerous political speeches.[54] Scattergood's account of his activities on 7 October 1860, gives the flavor of the times. He observed, "Yesterday evening after school I went home with Geo. Ernest. When we got

---

[50] *Macon Daily Telegraph*, 10 Mar. 1860.

[51] Ibid., 6 Mar. 1860.

[52] *Georgia Journal and Messenger*, 16 Nov. 1859.

[53] George W. Scattergood, Jr., journal, Sept. 19, 1860, George W. Scattergood, Jr., Journal, 1860, Typescript in Middle Georgia Archives, Washington Memorial Library, Macon.

[54] Ibid., Jan. 23, Apr. 24, 25, May 4, June 12, 25, Sept. 10, 18, 24, 28, Oct. 8, 24, 1860.

there, we went to the Sugar cane bed, and commenced the sugar mill business with our teeth for the rollers. We eat [sic] a few stalks, perhaps eight or ten between us. After supper we went opossum hunting. We rambled up Rock Creek, gathering muscadines, as we went, until the dog treed across the creek; then we crossed it, but did not get the Opossum, for no sooner had we got part of the way, than the dog stopped barking, and directly came up to us. Then we went farther up the creek, and crossed into Mr. Ernest's New Grounds, as they are called; we came about three quarters of a mile, when the dog treed again. Our light went out, but was soon lighted, we then proceeded to the tree, and went through the usual process; when we got it, we were astonished to find so small [a] one, and holding it down to the dog, which treed it, another dog rushed forward, and would have torn it into pieces had we not jerked it in time away."[55]

All of this prosperity had its dark sides, however. One of these was the state of its public health. When a family friend died in the fall of 1859, Anne Tracy Johnston, wife of William B. Johnston, wrote to her brother, Edward Dorr Tracy, Jr. "The providences of God are certainly most mysterious & to me it has certainly been proven that Earth is not our abiding place. I often think of that large company of dear ones in that other land waiting to receive us, we will certainly not be strangers in a strange land, & these many losses of dear friends wean us, & make us more willing to tread that dark valley through which they have gone before. Perhaps it is as I grow older these things impress me more."[56]

Occasionally, such diseases as smallpox, yellow fever, and typhoid fever came to Macon. Such was the case in February, 1860, when many contracted smallpox. Anne Johnston described the disease as it hit the Johnston household to her brother, Edward,

"I had no hesitation in remaining upon my own premises, & taking care of the rest of my servants, preventing them being carried to the Pest House unnecessarily & sharing the entire isolation to which we were all subjected until the period for infection was past. We all most wonderfully escaped[,] particularly Adline & George, neither of whom had been vaccinated & who were both exposed night & day for 8 days George actually sleeping with his brother after he was broken out. Poor little Fred died at the pest house, indeed the mortality has been & always is very great. John Baxter has had charge of our cases, &

---

[55] Ibid., Oct. 8, 1860.

[56] Anne Tracy Johnston to Edward Dorr Tracy, Jr., Macon, 11 Nov. 1859, Tracy-Steele-Johnston Family Correspondence, Middle Georgia Archives, Washington Memorial Library, Macon, hereafter cited as Tracy-Steele-Johnston Family Correspondence. Edward Dorr Tracy, Jr., a young Huntsville, Alabama attorney, had married into the prosperous Steele Family of Huntsville.

deserves the highest praise for his care, judgement, & calmness he certainly should succeed if merit meets with its reward. He remained at home 21 days after the negroes were removed rather uncomfortable most of the time as we had the old kitchen burned & all my kitchen furniture- & Adeline & George for 10 days really very sick from vaccination which kept us watching each moment for the development of small pox."[57]

Only a month later Mrs. Johnston reported her son Edward Tracy Johnston, was sick with scarlet fever. She noted, "Now I have grown to be a fatalist & think we must do all in our power to render life pleasant & satisfactory."[58]

Macon's streets were generally unpaved muddy thoroughfares where hogs and mules wandered everywhere. The sidewalks were poor at best.[59] Cows wandered around the streets. They ate shrubbery, shade trees, and even gardens. When Macon's City Council considered a bill to restrict the turning loose of cattle within the city limits in February 1861, the *Daily Telegraph's* reporter noted that the cattle were "ever on the watch for a tender bud or twig, or an open garden gate, and are scarcely baffled by any kind of a latch in making their way into forbidden premises."[60]

On 18 July 1860, Sexton Brydie proudly told the *Daily Telegraph* that there had not been a single death in the city since 5 July. Taking his cue, the *Telegraph* reporter observed, "This statement shows a state of health enjoyed by few cities of the same population as Macon. Indeed, the excessive heat of the weather and various other causes have contributed to swell the weekly bills of mortality of a large number of our cities to an alarming extent."[61]

Unfortunately, many people did die in Macon and Bibb County during 1860. Diseases which killed people then were measles, inflammation of the stomach, apoplexy, bronchitis, scrofula, spasms, old age, dropsy, consumption, typhoid fever, teething, died at birth, erysipelas, pneumonia, inflammation of the bowels, blue disease, congestive chills, affliction of the brain, diarrhea, bowel complaint, whooping cough, and others. Of course, some people died by being run over by the railroads, by being poisoned with laudanum, or even by being shot. Others succumbed to accidental shootings, accidental burnings, killed by stabbing, and others. Heart attacks were known by the term "affection of heart."

---

[57] Anne Tracy Johnston to Edward Dorr Tracy, Jr., Macon, 12 Feb. 1860, Ibid.

[58] Anne Johnston to Mrs. Ellen Steele Tracy, Macon, 13 Mar. 1860, Ibid. Ellen Steele Tracy was the wife of Edward Dorr Tracy, Jr.

[59] McInvale, "Macon, Georgia: The War Years," 3-4.

[60] *Macon Daily Telegraph*, 6 Feb. 1861.

[61] Ibid., 18 Jul. 1860.

Some simply died of the cold, probably hypothermia. One Bibb County resident was even killed by a mule.[62]

Slavery was another evil of the time, one which by the numbers given earlier in this chapter, was commonplace. In the city of Macon alone there were 3,069 slaves. Some of these were owned by such well-known figures as Seth Cason who owned thirty-seven, Thomas L. Ross an owner of ten, Washington Poe with eight, John B. Lamar with fifteen, John B. Lamar as Trustee for his sister, Mary Anne Cobb with ten, Asa Holt who owned twenty-six, Eugenius A. Nisbet with twenty-five, Stephen Collins as owner of nineteen, Simri Rose who was the owner of six, and William B. Johnston, owner of the Johnston Mansion, eighteen. Some of the slaves were owned by industries. The Macon and Western Railroad Company owned six, and the Georgia Central Railroad owned twelve.[63]

Several dealers sold slaves. These included G.H. Noel at the corner of Poplar and Second Streets, G.F. Stubbs, whose business was located on Fourth Street at the corner of Poplar; and W.R. Phillips, with a business on Poplar Street at the corner of Third.[64]

The slave codes in Macon were very strict. A master could be punished if his slave violated the law. If a slave was imprisoned, his owner had to pay a certain fee to free him. Blacks could not drink alcoholic beverages. They were not allowed to hold public meetings without a permit from the Mayor and four Aldermen. When slaves were punished for some infraction of the law, they were taken to a secluded place in the city by the marshal or police officers to receive their punishment. The Market House was used as a place to execute public sentences. But the law also gave certain protections to slaves, usually because of their monetary value. If white persons employed a black without the permission of his owner they could be fined twenty dollars. A slave owner could not hire out his slaves without getting a ticket or badge which detailed the particular employment.

The lives of free blacks were closely regulated. They could not remain longer than five days in the city without going before the Clerk of the City Council to

---

[62] Federal Mortality Census Schedules, 1860-1880 and related indexes, in the custody of the Daughters of the American Revolution, Microcopy, Roll 8, 1860, Georgia, Index and Schedules, Appling-Worth Counties, Bibb County, p. 27, Washington Memorial Library, Macon. Laudanum was a painkiller made of opium mixed with whiskey.

[63] Georgia Population Schedules Bibb County; 1860 Slave Schedules Georgia Appling through Butts Counties. Microcopy M-653. Eighth Census (1860) Slave Inhabitants, Georgia, Volume 1:70. The numbers given were those owned within the Macon city limits.

[64] The Macon Directory for 1860, 93.

name his guardian. The guardian could then be held responsible for any action the free black would take. When a free black came to Macon he had to pay $50 to the City Treasurer within thirty days or be confined in jail. The law also had great power through an ordinance which stipulated that free persons of color who might be suspected of having a bad or suspicious character could be ordered to leave town within five days or be imprisoned. This was the reason that there were only eighty-four free blacks in Bibb County, and only twenty-two in Macon, in 1860.[65]

But, despite these evils, Macon was a thriving place in 1860. In summarizing the city during that year, William Thomas Jenkins described Macon as a place where "A settled and somewhat sophisticated way of living had developed. Good transportation...had made Macon an important inland trading center. Schools and colleges, although not up to later standards, were in operation. Business was in an excellent state of prosperity. Churches were thriving. Attention was being given to city and county improvements in roads, sanitation, and public buildings. People had more time to give to good works, and the city and county had produced its share of state leaders in politics, law, and medicine."[66] The thriving city on the Ocmulgee, in short, only a little more than a generation after its founding as a frontier town in 1823, had, by 1860, assumed its place as a prominent city of the Antebellum South.

---

[65] McInvale, "Macon, Georgia: The War Years," 6-8; Georgia Population Schedules Bibb County.

[66] Jenkins, "Ante Bellum Macon and Bibb County, Georgia," 388.

Chapter 2

Preparing for War:
The Volunteer Companies

Nineteenth Century militia units, especially in the South, were not only military units composed of citizen-soldiers, but they were social entities as well. The militia units in Macon were no exception. An examination of their activities during 1860, the year before the war began, furnishes us with a glimpse into the military/social lives of the Macon men who marched off to war in the spring of 1861.

In 1860 there were no less than five organized military companies in Macon. They were the Macon Volunteers whose armory was located on Mulberry Street near Second Street. Organized in 1825, it was the oldest militia company in Macon. Its captain was a man who was highly regarded in the community, Captain Robert A. Smith. The unit held regular meetings on the first Friday in January, April, July, and October. Its regular parades were conducted on 8 January, 22 February, 23 April, 17 June, and 4 July, with drill meetings on every Tuesday night. The second-oldest company, the Bibb County Cavalry was organized in 1834 and reorganized in 1857. It was led by Captain E. Fitzgerald. The third-oldest company, the Floyd Rifles, was organized in 1841. Captain Thomas Hardeman, another Maconite who was highly esteemed by his fellow citizens, led his men in regular meetings on the first Friday in January, April, July, and December, with regular parades on 8 January, 22 February, 1 May, and 4 July. The two remaining units were both organized in 1859. One of these, the Jackson Artillery, commanded by Captain Theodore Parker, listed a number of prominent Macon men as officers. These included First Lieutenant John T. Boifeuillet, Second Lieutenant George A. Dure, Third Lieutenant John B. Cumming, and Ensign E.G. Jeffers. The fifth unit, the Macon Guards, organized in 1859, was commanded by Captain Joel R. Griffin.[1]

---

[1] *The Macon Directory,* 97-8. But the *Macon Daily Telegraph* noted that the Jackson Artillery was not organized until January 8, 1860.

Macon's militia units were organized in conformity with the laws of the State, but all company officers were nominated at an annual election. According to Captain Smith of the Macon Volunteers, "Such nomination is intended to express the feeling of members towards their officers." If a commissioned officer failed to get a nomination he resigned his commission. The company members felt it was good to have annual nominations to approve or disapprove the actions of their officers. Smith felt that "A good officer is gratified & encouraged by it, an incompetent or faithless one is easily removed by it." The bylaws of the Macon Volunteers called for a nomination of all the commissioned officers, and an election of all the non-commissioned officers should be held at the first quarterly meeting in each year. If a vacancy occurred by death or resignation the corps would fill the same with a vote of a majority of the members present. One of the other bylaws provided for a Quartermaster and a Finance Committee consisting of three members which would be appointed by the officer commanding, on each annual first quarterly meeting of the Corps. Smith recommended that the offices of Secretary and Treasury should be consolidated because one person could serve in both capacities. "I need not say to you," Smith told a friend, Captain George M. Harvey, "that a rigid enforcement of your Bye Laws is indispensable to your own success as a commanding officer and equally is indispensable to your own success as a commanding officer and equally to the prosperity of your corps." It was necessary to conduct weekly drills in that portion of William J. Hardee's famous book, *Hardee's Tactics*, known as the School of the Soldier. Monthly drills or parades were also important."[2]

The frequent parades of these units kindled the military spirit among the citizens, and gave the part-time soldiers an opportunity to interact with the people of Macon. Lieutenant George Ross, of the Floyd Rifles, led the men on parade and drill on the morning of Monday, 12 March 1860. Although the unit marched in blustering wind and dust which blew in everyone's eyes, the men marched to the Fair Grounds to fire at a target. A silver goblet provided by the commissioned officers in the unit was won by private John A. Nelson of East Macon. His three shots averaged 4.40 inches in the target.[3] Later in March, Lieutenant Ross, who was described as "one of the finest looking men in the city, and an active officer," led the Rifles for drill in front of Findlay's Foundry.

---

[2] Capt. Robert A. Smith to Capt. George M. Harvey, Macon, 1 Jan. 1859, George M. Harvey Papers, 1859-1865, Photocopy, the Southern Historical Collection, Louis R. Wilson Library, The University of North Carolina at Chapel Hill. Future citations from this collection will be followed by SHC. Harvey was commander of a newly-organized volunteer company known as the Newnan Guards, located in Newnan, Georgia.

[3] *Macon Daily Telegraph,* 13 Mar. 1860.

Before the men stacked their arms at the conclusion of their evolutions, they gave Maconites "a proof that Macon has reason to be proud of her military."[4]

Not to be outdone, the Macon Guards, commanded by Captain Joel R. Griffin, paid the people of East Macon a visit on 12 March. The citizens turned out in large numbers to witness the men at drill. The firm of Messrs. Lane and Company "complimented the corps by giving them a glass or two of wine to wash down the intolerable dust."[5]

Captain Robert A. Smith's Macon Volunteers even held a drill in the Zouave exercise. The *Daily Telegraph* noted, "We did not witness any of their movements, our engagements at the time, carrying us in a different part of the town. We presume the question will not again be asked: Where were the Macon Volunteers?"[6]

One of the most elaborate parades held in the early spring of 1860, was a joint operation given by the Jackson Artillery and the Macon Guards. Captains Parker and Griffin formed their companies at their armories on the afternoon of 28 March, and marched them to the open space in front of the Courthouse. There, the units formed into a battalion, and, led by Captain Parker, marched up Mulberry Street, keeping time to the music of the New Orleans Brass Band, which had been hired for the occasion. The companies halted before the Wesleyan Female College, "to allow the young ladies to admire their martial bearing and gay feathers, as also to hear a few pieces played by the band." The companies then marched up College Street, and then went to the Blind Asylum. Leaving that point to the left, they marched to the old Macon and Western Railroad Station, and fired three rounds from the brass cannon. However, as the men returned to the business district, they heard a fire alarm as they were half way down Cotton Avenue. They proceeded at double quick time, and reached the scene of the fire just in time to offer their assistance, which, fortunately, was not needed. Just before the battalion was dismissed, a pair of horses attached to a carriage filled with ladies who were watching the parade, became frightened at the sound of the drum. The panicked animals ran some distance down Cherry Street, but were stopped after almost hitting a man who was crossing the street. Shortly after the fire, a carriage horse ran away with his buggy near Hardeman and Sparks' Warehouse. After rushing down the street for several blocks, the horse finally struck the buggy against a lamp post, and demolished both the buggy and the post.[7]

---

[4] Ibid., 24 Mar. 1860.
[5] Ibid.
[6] Ibid., 23 Mar. 1860.
[7] Ibid., 29 Mar. 1860.

In early March the Macon Volunteers entertained the Macon Guards at a collation furnished by Sergeant Woodruff of the Volunteers at his unit's armory.[8] The Bibb County Cavalry, captained by E. Fitzgerald, tried to go through their evolutions in the streets, but, the many vehicles constantly passing through, impeded the free movements of their horses, so they went to Camp Oglethorpe, where they drilled until dusk. The *Daily Telegraph* observed, "We like to see a body of cavalry- and more especially with full ranks now, when shortly each corps may have to stand on its own merits."[9]

Camp Oglethorpe, which was destined to play an important role in the war, was located at the foot of Seventh Street, near the southwest commons of the city. Named, for Georgia's founder, General James Oglethorpe, it was laid out under an act of the Georgia General Assembly in 1843 as a parade ground for the Georgia Volunteer Companies in Macon. The camp was situated in an old field which contained ten acres. In 1851, when Macon's City Council, wanted to use the grounds for holding a State Fair, the mayor and council, realizing the land belonged to the volunteer companies, asked their permission to use it to hold the fair of the Southern Central Agricultural Association. This request was granted. For their part, the military companies petitioned the city to manage and control that part of Seventh Street which ran though Camp Oglethorpe upon the same terms which allowed them to use the surrounding property for an encampment. This petition was received and granted.[10]

The Camp was large enough to permit an encampment of 75–100 companies of cavalry, infantry, and artillery, at one time, and still have enough ground to hold a review of all the troops. It occupied a high level plateau, within seventy-five yards of the tracks of the Macon and Western Railroad. The land was well-watered with springs and branches on three sides of it. By 1860 the grounds were well-kept, fenced, and provided with buildings for commissary stores.[11]

One of the most colorful and interesting ceremonies held by the military early in 1860, was the presentation of a flag to the Jackson Artillery. The banner, prepared by F.S. Bloom and several other prominent Maconites, was placed on exhibit at W.W. Parker and Company.[12] Made of heavy yellow silk, the flag was decorated with the arms and motto of Georgia, with the words "Jackson Artillery," above, and "Macon, Georgia" below on a blue scroll. On the other side it showed "a beautiful view of an artillery encampment at West

---

[8] Ibid., 7 March 1860.

[9] Ibid., 23 Mar. 1860.

[10] Ibid., 20 Mar. 1860.

[11] Ibid., 11 Apr. 1860.

[12] Ibid., 15 Mar. 1860. The donors included Lewis N. Whittle, L.M. Lamar, W.B. Parker, J.B. Ross, P.E. Bowdre, I.H. Taylor, Albert Mix, R. Collins, E. Alexander, Phil Tracy, Ovid G. Sparks, J.M. Boardman, and T.R. Bloom. Ibid., 17 Mar. 1860.

Point, and a flag staff in the foreground with the stars and stripes, waving from it." This side, too, had a scroll above which bore the name of the company, and below, the date of its organization: "January 8th, 1860." The flag was carried on an oaken staff which was surmounted with the axe and spear. The *Daily Telegraph* described the banner as "a very beautiful thing, and does credit to the taste which devised it, and the liberality of the donors."[13]

Plans called for the unit to parade for the first time completely equipped and in full uniform. Judge Philemon "Phil" Tracy was scheduled to speak on behalf of the Jackson Artillery, and Captain Parker planned to receive the flag for his men. The ceremony was scheduled to take place in front of the Lanier House at 4:00 P.M. on 16 March 1860.

The flag was presented before a large crowd while the "Star Spangled Banner" was played. The unit then drilled and saluted their new emblem. The eighty-five men who turned out for the ceremony, were dressed in the US regulation army uniform. Judge Tracy made a stirring speech and Captain Parker responded with appropriate remarks. The unit then went to Terpsichorean Hill where they enjoyed an elegant collation.[14]

In commenting on the occasion, John Jones Gresham wrote his friend, young Huntsville, Alabama, attorney, Edward Dorr Tracy, Jr., "Phil made a speech yesterday upon the presentation of a flag to the Artillery Co. and it was said to have been a very happy effort."[15]

During April the activities of the various military organizations continued. The Macon Volunteers held a target practice at Camp Oglethorpe on 5 April at which the shooting was not as accurate as it should have been because their muskets "were in bad order." When the reporter from the *Daily Telegraph* arrived at the camp he was greeted with the "gay plumes of the military, and simultaneous reports of muskets rang" in ears. The field of contestants was narrowed to five men, one of whom, Private Josiah Bass, a young Macon attorney, won the prize- a handsome silver pitcher. His shooting covered a target area of five and a half inches. He was given some competition by Sergeant Tobe Conner, whose target range was six and a half inches. After the competition ended Captain Smith "gave the citizens an opportunity of judging of the efficiency of his Company, by drilling them till dark in front of the Lanier House."[16]

On 10 April the Floyd Rifles held a joint parade with two fire companies, Ocmulgee Fire Company No. 2 and Young America No. 3. Lieutenant George

---

[13] Ibid., 14 Mar. 1860.

[14] Ibid., 17 Mar. 1860.

[15] John Jones Gresham to Edward Dorr Tracy, Jr., Macon, 17 Mar. 1860, Tracy-Steele-Johnston Family Correspondence.

[16] Ibid., 6 Apr. 1860.

W. Ross of the Floyd Rifles, led the three organizations. Afterwards, the participants went to the Rifles' Armory to enjoy drinks served from an enormous punch bowl.[17]

The Macon Volunteers invited the ladies of Macon to view an evening parade and drill at Camp Oglethorpe on the afternoon of 23 April to celebrate the company's thirty-fifth anniversary.[18] On the morning of the 23rd, the men marched to Camp Oglethorpe with full ranks, including some veterans of the Seminole Wars, among them was the distinguished Macon publisher and donor of Rose Hill Cemetery, Simri Rose, "who marched in the front rank as lightly to the sound of the drum and fife as the youngest member of the corps." During the morning, the men shot for prizes, the first of which was won by Private Markwalter. After the competition the men dined at Brown's Hotel, a meal which was followed by a number of speeches. During the afternoon the Volunteers paraded for the ladies. Upon their return to the city Private Bates presented a prize to Josiah Bass, obviously the best shot in the company.[19]

Four companies, the Floyd Rifles, the Macon Guards, the Bibb County Cavalry, and the Jackson Artillery, turned out for a large drill on 1 May. After the parade the company ate at Benton's Spring Garden. The Macon Guards, commanded by Captain Griffin, "made a fine appearance," and Captain Fitzgerald's Bibb County Cavalry "had a beautiful turn-out," and afterwards had their meal at Camp Oglethorpe. The Jackson Artillery, commanded by Lieutenant Boifeuillet, impressed the spectators with the thunder of their artillery.[20] After the parade, the Macon Guards visited the village of Vineville, marching through the small community, to a place where they could engage in one of their favorite employments [next to marching], target shooting. Second Corporal Thomas Hodgkins won the first prize, while the second prize was claimed by Sergeant John McManus. The company dined at the home of First Lieutenant Lucius M. Lamar. During the meal several speeches were made by members of the company.[21]

The Bibb County Cavalry, after the parade, went to Camp Oglethorpe, and exercised shooting and cutting at the head and the ring (using the saber while on horseback). The riding, according to a reporter from the *Daily Telegraph*, "may be classed as good, bad and indifferent." Sergeant Leonidas Lamar won the prize for his performance in both shooting and the use of the saber. The men then ate a large dinner furnished by their lieutenants and catered by Charles H. Freeman. Late in the afternoon, the company returned to the city and engaged in a number

[17] Ibid., 10 Apr. 1860.
[18] Ibid., 23 Apr. 1860.
[19] Ibid., 24 Apr. 1860.
[20] Ibid., 2 May 1860.
[21] Ibid., 3 May 1860.

of rapid cavalry evolutions on Mulberry Street. They then "cordially accepted" an invitation by the Proprietor of the Lanier House, Mr. Logan, to join him in a glass of wine.[22]

Sometimes, the men were invited by volunteer companies from other communities to participate in encampments. This was the case with the Macon Guards, who were invited by the Governor's Guards of Fort Valley, to attend a four-day-encampment with them at Fort Valley. It would be the first encampment of the Guards.[23] Upon learning of the plans for the encampment, a reporter for the *Daily Telegraph* wrote, probably with his tongue in his cheek, "We will...put in a word of advice to the young ladies of Fort Valley and the surrounding country, who anticipate being present and joining in the festivities of the occasion; we would advise them to steel their hearts or they will be stolen by some of our boys. We have known such things to happen in days 'lang syne'." The reporter understood that many men and women of Macon planned to visit the encampment, and that "The presence of the ladies of our city may act as a counter check upon the boys, which may make them behave themselves, or otherwise the hearts of our fair Houston county friends might fare badly."[24]

In preparation for the encampment, the Guards paraded on June 1, accompanied by a "spirit stirring drum," and the "shrill music of the wry-necked fife," of the Macon Brass Band. The most interesting feature of the parade was the first appearance of two of the Pioneers, a newly-formed part of the Macon Guards, who were clad in huge bear skin caps, called shakos, leather aprons, and gauntlets. These men were armed with a short rifle, an axe, and a sword.[25]

On the evening of 5 June the Macon Guards, en route to Fort Valley, were accompanied to the depot of the Macon and Southwestern Railroad by the Macon Volunteers and the Jackson Artillery. As the cars moved out of the car shed, the Guards were greeted by a peal of musketry from the Volunteers and the roar of the only cannon the Jackson Artillery owned, a twelve-pounder Napoleon. A crowd of Maconites cheered the men, who were in high spirits, as the cars rolled toward the south.[26]

A reporter who visited the encampment wrote, "Macon is a growing city-her Military progressive and her daughters handsome; and doubtless the latter exercises a powerful and beneficial influence over the former."[27]

During the encampment, held at Camp Powers on the outskirts of Fort Valley, the men enjoyed themselves thoroughly, because such events were

---

[22] Ibid.
[23] Ibid., 11 May 1860.
[24] Ibid., 20 May 1860.
[25] Ibid., 2 June 1860.
[26] Ibid., 6 June 1860.
[27] Ibid., 31 May 1860.

largely social occasions, although there were interludes of drill.[28] The Camp was situated on the edge of the small town, about 350 feet from a hotel known as the Planter's House. When the Macon Guards arrived they were formally welcomed by the Governor's Guards of Milledgeville, whose captain, John T. Griffin, made an appropriate speech. Lieutenant Hill responded on behalf of the Macon Guards. The ninety-five men of the Guards stowed away their equipment and marched, at 5:00 P.M. to the sounds of an "excellent band of music, the martial strains of which enliven our streets and give decidedly a spirited and war-like odor to the very atmosphere we breath." The men from Macon presented an imposing spectacle in their full dress uniforms with hats made of bear skin, with the hair left on. The party [for that was the highlight of Nineteenth century militia gatherings] was augmented by a barrel of lager beer. The men feasted at a 120-foot-long table with over 600 other men from various Georgia militia units. A ball was held on the night of 8 June, the night before the men left, at Smith's Hall in Fort Valley.

On Saturday morning the Guards were escorted to the railroad depot by the Governor's Guards. As the train started, a parting volley was fired as a salute, and the Guards left "in high glee and full spirits, expressing feelings of the deepest satisfaction on their visit and association in the pleasant and sweet little village, Fort Valley."[29]

The men returned to Macon, full of experience in drill, accuracy in target practice, and with "any quantity of mementoes in the shape of curls, billet-doux, &c., testifying to his gallantry in the Court of Cupid."[30]

Their train arrived on the morning of 9 June where they were met by the Jackson Artillery who escorted the Guards to their armory; there the Guards disbanded to return briefly to their homes, "some to receive the fond caresses of wives, and others who were not blessed in this particular, to receive the congratulations of affectionate mamas on their safe return from the seat of war." The Guards reassembled at the Jackson Artillery Armory, and were escorted by their hosts to H.N. Ells and Company for a dinner where many speeches were made and toasts drunk. It was an appropriate ending to a successful encampment.[31]

The Guards, being a social as well as a military organization, passed resolutions thanking the Governor's Guards, Captain Griffin, and the ladies of Fort Valley and Houston County for their hospitality. They also thanked their sponsors, F.S. Bloom, E.L. Strohecker, and others who paid their railroad fare,

---

[28] Ibid., 8 June 1860.

[29] Ibid., 13 June 1860.

[30] Ibid., 9 June 1860. It was customary for young women to cut off their curls and give them to young men of their choosing in such encampments.

[31] Ibid., 11 June 1860.

and also Virgil Powers, the General Superintendent of the Southwestern Railroad. They also expressed their appreciation to their escorts, the Macon Volunteers and the Jackson Artillery, for the kindnesses shown to them.[32]

Later in the month, the Bibb County Cavalry planned to parade at Camp Oglethorpe, and try their hands at target shooting, for the prize of a silver ice pitcher presented by W.J. McElroy. The unit planned to have dinner on the grounds after the contest.[33]

One of the finest encampments held by the Macon militia units during 1860 took place at Chalybeate Springs near Talbotton in West Georgia. The Macon Volunteers, the unit which attended this camp, left Macon on Monday morning, 18 June.[34] Arriving at the hamlet of Geneva in the early afternoon, the men ate, and proceeded by stage to Talbotton. When they arrived at Collingsworth Institute near Talbotton they were met by the Scott Rifles who escorted them into the small West Georgia community. Private Jack Brown of the Scott Rifles made a welcoming speech in front of Richards Hotel in which he offered them the hospitalities of the village. Captain Smith replied for the Volunteers. After the speech-making the men ate at the hotel as the guests of Mr. Richards. They then drilled for an hour and a half, leaving Talbotton at 7:00 P.M. When they reached Chalypeate Springs later that night, they were greeted by sky-rockets, and another meal prepared by their host, Dr. Lightner at their camp, named for the doctor. The next morning began with drill, while they waited for more volunteers to arrive.[35]

On 21 June the Volunteers engaged in Zouave drill at a dress parade. A highlight of the drill was presented by a group of the Volunteers known as the "Tap Squad," who went through the manual of arms by the tap of a drum without a single spoken command. Early on the following morning, 22 June, the Volunteers returned by stage to Talbotton, and were treated to wine and cigars by Jack Brown who was elected an honorary member of the company. The Volunteers camped at Camp Miller, named for their host in Talbotton. After a few hours' rest, they turned out for another dress parade in the evening. An outdoor supper was ruined when a heavy rain "destroyed our hopes and ruined our pleasures as far as the ladies go," but supper was served indoors. Camp was struck at midnight, and the unit returned to Macon where they were met by the Floyd Rifles who took them to their Armory for punch and pitchers of lemonade.[36] Of course, the men did everything they could to increase the

---

[32] Ibid., 15 June 1860.

[33] Ibid., 30 May 1860.

[34] Ibid., 18 June 1860.

[35] Ibid., 22 June 1860.

[36] "Simon" in Ibid., 26 June 1860. For a brief account of the return of the Volunteers see Ibid., 25 June 1860.

martial fervor of the public. When one of their number married they all attended the wedding ceremony.[37]

Occasionally they accompanied the remains of a deceased member. Such was the case when Dr. James Dean, son of prominent Maconite, James Dean, died at Indian Springs on 8 August 1860. His remains were brought to Macon on 9 August and interred in Rose Hill Cemetery with full military honors by his unit, the Floyd Rifles.[38]

The men celebrated anniversaries of historical events with parades, such as the anniversary of the Battle of Bunker Hill. On 16 June the Bibb County Cavalry celebrated that important first major engagement of the American Revolution with a parade through the streets of Macon.[39]

All of the military companies paraded on 4 July to celebrate Independence Day. In announcing the parade, a reporter for the *Daily Telegraph* noted, "We understand that during the day the Volunteers and Guards design drilling by tap of the drum. This is a new feature in military tactics, or at least it has never been practiced by our military companies, and will consequently be viewed with interest by a large number of citizens." He added that Macon was proud of her military.[40]

On occasion, new fashions in military dress had the effect of increasing the martial ardor of the people. On 31 July a reporter for the *Daily Telegraph*, walking on Mulberry Street in front of the Lanier house at a late hour, saw a group of men surrounding a figure, "who from his fantastic dress, we thought was either a Japanese, a Chinese, a Sioux Indian, or one of the last importation from Africa." As the reporter drew closer he saw it was one of the Macon Volunteers dressed in the uniform of the Macon Volunteer Zouaves. The uniform, made of bright cloth and in a strange fashion, presented "a picturesque and graceful appearance." At this time, the Volunteers included twenty or thirty Zouaves, all active young men, well drilled. The reporter ended with an ominous note, "it would not surprise us if they did not take up the gauge of battle thrown down by the Chicago Zouaves in a short time; and if they do, we are satisfied they will reflect honor on themselves and the city from whence they hail."[41]

---

[37] Ibid., 16 June 1860.

[38] Ibid., 10 Aug. 1860.

[39] Ibid., 18 June 1860.

[40] Ibid., 4 July 1860. The reporter was, of course, wrong when he said that the tap drill had not been practiced by any of Macon's military companies because the Volunteers had exhibited their skills at this exercise during the encampment at Chalybeate Springs in June. See above, Ibid., 26 June 1860.

[41] Ibid., 2 Aug. 1860.

Even in 1860, as if to herald the approach of the war, some Georgia firms advertised military equipment to the volunteers. T.B. Marshall and Brother of Savannah offered tents, marquees, and awnings to the military companies, as well as tarpaulins. D.C. Hodgkins and Son advertised guns and sporting goods in their store on Mulberry Street in Macon.[42]

Arms of improved design were filtering in to some of Macon's volunteer companies. In September the Bibb County Cavalry received a new and improved revolver which fired five rounds without stopping to load, and was self-cocking. A reporter for the *Daily Telegraph* reported the weapon was the same one adopted by the US cavalry. The Bibb County unit also received new sabers and holsters as well as a new cap similar to one worn by members of the Jackson Artillery. The arms were furnished by the US Government as part of a quota system which allocated arms from Federal arsenals and armories to each state based upon population.[43] The Macon Volunteers also received new arms from the Federal Government in September. These were Minie muskets of an improved design. To celebrate their good fortune, the Volunteers held a parade followed by target practice. A small prize was won by Private T.J. Shinholser who fired three shots which averaged three and a half inches, into the bull's eye. The Jackson Artillery also obtained a supply of new muskets which would take the place of their former arms- sabers. The Artillery also obtained heavy ordnance and were now thoroughly equipped to do service in the field.[44]

In October efforts were made to reorganize the military system in Georgia. A reporter for the *Daily Telegraph* observed, "Georgia has no military organization, or none worthy of the name. And although every other man is a Colonel or a Major,...there is little or no military pride and spirit in the State." Certain communities, however, had volunteer companies to whom the people looked with confidence in case of unexpected trouble, either internal or external. These companies, however, were not numerous. They were mostly confined to the larger cities, Savannah, Augusta, Macon, Atlanta, and Columbus, although a few served in some of the smaller towns. Unfortunately, the State could not call into the field more than 2,000 men. The editor of the *Daily Telegraph* urged the State to increase the number of military companies which might take the field in case of an emergency. He pointed out that "The military spirit can only be fostered by giving the people a good military organization and making them familiar with the weapons, rules and arts of war; and it should be remembered, that with a people situated as we of the South are military spirit is nearly synonymous with patriotism. The absence of one is usually very good evidence of the absence of the other." Arms should be provided for 50,000 men, together

---

[42] Ibid. 19 Apr. 1860; 3 May 1860.
[43] Ibid., 7 Sept. 1860.
[44] Ibid., 10 Sept. 1860.

with the manufacture of powder and weapons of war. A militia organization should be established for each county in the state by drafting a sufficient number of volunteers with at least one company of infantry of not less than seventy men, and one company of cavalry or artillery of not less than thirty-eight men. The only way for all white men between twenty-one and forty-five to avert service would be to pay a tax into the military fund of their home county. "The subject," the editor continued, "is of such importance, that it should receive the earnest attention of all who have the interest, the safety and the honor of the State and the South at heart."[45]

None of these articles had the desired effect. It remained for the election of Lincoln to solidify public sentiment throughout Georgia, and to cause Governor Joseph E. Brown to recommend a reorganization of the Georgia militia, especially the creation of new volunteer companies. In his message, the Governor also recommended "that a commutation tax sufficient to raise a military fund ample for the support of the system be collected from those who do not perform military duty."[46]

To add to the pressure on the Governor to reorganize the militia, a Military Convention with representatives from sixty-seven militia companies, met in Milledgeville in November 1860, shortly after Lincoln's election. This group unanimously adopted a resolution calling for immediate secession, and "cheerfully" offered their services to the Governor whenever needed.[47]

The Convention urged Georgia's leaders to appropriate one million dollars as a military fund for the current political year. They also recommended the establishment of an armory in Georgia for the manufacture of arms and munitions. The militia should be organized as a force upon the same pattern as the US Army with various branches of service, direct procurement of arms, accouterments, ammunition and stores, which were sufficient for a large army. All arms would be placed under a chief of ordnance whose task involved the safekeeping and distribution of the arms and equipment. All armories would be placed under the ordnance department, together with foundries, arsenals, and arms factories. Each artillery company would be furnished with a battery of six rifled cannon, together with all the necessary equipment needed to wage war. The cavalry would be furnished with a revolver and a carbine. Another

---

[45] Ibid., 17 Oct. 1860. See also the article, "Military System for Georgia," in the same issue and Ibid., 19 Oct. 1860.

[46] "Annual Message of Governor Joseph E. Brown, to the Georgia Legislature. Assembled November 7, 1860," in Ibid., 12 Nov. 1860.

[47] John B. Lamar to Howell Cobb, Telegram, Milledgeville, 12 Nov. 1860, Howell Cobb Papers, 1860, Hargrett Library, The University of Georgia, Athens, hereafter cited as Cobb Papers with appropriate year.

resolution consisted of generating interest in making uniform military cloth, hats, buttons, and other items.[48]

Reaction to the action of the Military Convention was generally positive. However, the Floyd Rifles formally endorsed the stand of their delegation in opposing the authority of the Convention to issue political sentiments. But, the Rifles intended to offer their services to the Governor, if needed. A set of resolutions adopted in Macon explained the firm determination of the men "to maintain Georgia's honor, and protect Georgia's rights at any cost and at every sacrifice."[49]

Despite the opposition of the Rifles, the Macon Guards endorsed the action of the Convention, tendered their services to Governor Brown, and adopted a blue cockade to be worn upon the left breast as an addition to their uniform.[50]

When the cadets of the Georgia Military Institute in Marietta, arrived in Macon, en route to Milledgeville, they were received at the Depot of the Macon and Western Railroad by Captain Smith and the Macon Volunteers. When Major Ellison Capers, who led the cadets, responded to Smith's opening remarks, his speech was cheered by the large crowd of people gathered to welcome the group. The cadets and Volunteers breakfasted at Brown's Hotel, and then formed a battalion under Smith to march into Macon. Later, the cadets, led by Capers, performed Infantry and Light drill in a way that excited the crowd. The youthful soldiers-to-be also demonstrated their prowess at bayonet exercise. After the cadets left for Milledgeville on the Georgia Central Railroad, the Volunteers paraded for an hour on Mulberry Street, showing the people their good condition and finely-honed drilling skills. A reporter for the *Daily Telegraph* called the cadets "an ornament to the State," who reflected "credit upon the Superintendent and other officers of the Institute."[51]

When Abraham Lincoln was elected President on 7 November 1860, a large meeting convened in Macon's Concert Hall to organize a company of minute men. Attorney Washington Poe, one of Macon's leading citizens, presided over the enthusiastic gathering.[52] Joel R. Branham was elected chairman of an Association of Minute Men, and a resolution was passed that the group "will neither sanction or approve in its action, any violation of the Constitution or the laws of Georgia."[53] The Minute Men organized into a company known as Minute Men Company No. 1 with George G. Griffin as captain, three lieutenants, four sergeants, four corporals, two quartermasters, and a secretary

---

[48] *Macon Daily Telegraph*, 17 Nov. 1860.

[49] Ibid., 19 Nov. 1860.

[50] Ibid., 24 Nov. 1860.

[51] Ibid., 21 Nov. 1860.

[52] Ibid., 7 Nov. 1860.

[53] Ibid., 14 Nov. 1860.

and treasurer. The group was distinguished by the wearing of a blue cockade, a symbol which was required by their constitution. Those who did not wear the emblem were subject to a fine of one dollar.[54] The cockades were worn as the badges of distinction in a group which quickly enrolled 500 members.[55]

The organization of the Minute Men was noticed by at least one enterprising merchant, William Belden, who advertised "Minute Men's Glazed Caps," lettered according to the Constitution of the Association.[56]

The editor of the *Daily Telegraph* disapproved of the impromptu organization of the Minute Men, believing the volunteer companies, organized under the laws of Georgia, were sufficient. A reporter for the paper commented, "The most important matters just now, are arms and discipline. The day of bush fighting and Indian warfare is past, and the value of training has been demonstrated on a thousand fields." He assured his readers, "There is yet time to get arms enough from the Federal Government, to furnish an army of thousands, and we most earnestly recommend our friends not to rely on revolvers and fowling pieces, but to take advantage of the discipline and arms, which will best fit them for quelling insurrection, or punishing invasion."[57]

Despite this attitude, the paper continued to give careful attention to the activities of the impromptu group. On 23 November one of its reporters wrote about a procession of Minute Men scheduled for that evening. The men planned to leave their rendezvous at the Bibb County Court House at 7:30 P.M. and march to Concert Hall carrying torches and accompanied by musicians. There, plans called for them to be addressed by Judges Phil Tracy and Clifford Anderson. The paper noted that there were then over 600 Minute Men in town. These citizen soldiers were organized into four companies: Company A, led by Captain B.F. Ross; Company B under Captain George G. Griffin; Company C, commanded by Captain Adderhold; and Company D, under the leadership of Captain William T. Massey. There were, according to this account, other companies in the unincorporated portion of Bibb County.[58] Dr. George G. Griffin was formally elected Surgeon of the Macon Volunteers. In announcing the appointment, the *Macon Telegraph* asserted: "In our opinion, this appointment is made in the nick of time, as we have no doubt that the Doctor's service will be brought into requisition at an early day- not, however, to bandage and splinter broken limbs, but to heal broken hearts."[59]

---

[54] Ibid., 16 Nov. 1860.

[55] Ibid., 17 Nov. 1860.

[56] Ibid., 19 Nov. 1860.

[57] "Constitutionalist," in Ibid., 12 Nov. 1860.

[58] Ibid., 23 Nov. 1860.

[59] Ibid., 12 June 1860. Griffin was a physician.

That evening, between six and seven hundred Minute Men turned out for the parade. The four companies met at the Court House at 7:00, and marched in column to Concert Hall at 7:30. All of them were "able-bodied and soldier-like." As reported earlier, the line was lighted up by many transparencies with appropriate mottoes, and Bengal lights, explosive pyrotechnics, and the cheers of the people. Two flags, each twelve feet long, and bearing the old colonial devices of Georgia- a rattlesnake in coil and the motto 'noli me tangerre [Don't tread on me]' were carried by the men. On the reverse of one of the flags was the motto "Resistance to Lincoln is obedience to God!" On the other was the motto, "Secession and Death, rather than Submission and Dishonor." Judges Phil Tracy and Clifford Anderson, and Joel R. Branham made appropriate speeches. The *Daily Telegraph's* reporter described the scene: "Every countenance beamed with animation and high resolve, and cheer after cheer shook the hall."[60]

The Minute Men scheduled a meeting at Concert Hall on the night of November 30 to which they invited the ladies. Judge Eugenius A. Nisbet and Washington Poe planned to speak. The *Daily Telegraph* pronounced both these men as "able and experienced men [who] take strong secession ground, and will give satisfactory reasons for the faith that is in them."[61]

In rural Bibb County, a public meeting was held in East Macon precinct [the modern Cross Keys area of Macon]. Well-known Macon physician Dr. James Mercer Green presided over the meeting, and Dr. James A. Damour was asked to serve as Secretary. The highlight of the gathering was an address by Judge W.T. Massey who made a "forcible and pointed speech disrobing the hideous abolition monster of its garments, and [presented] it in all its monstrous deformities to the gaze of the world." The meeting resulted in the organization of Minute Men with Samuel S. Dunlap elected Captain and L.D. Wimberly, First Lieutenant.[62] On 28 November Misses Sallie and Julia Holman, daughters of George Holman, presented a beautiful flag, with fifteen stars on one side and an inscription to the "MM" battalion on the other. However Dr. Damour, acting for the organization, declined the flag.[63]

As the Secession Convention of Georgia in January 1861, began, Macon's military companies organized into a battalion known as the "Independent Volunteer Battalion of Macon." The units, which were formerly in the First Regiment, First Brigade, Eighth Division of Georgia Militia, continued, however to train and elect their officers as separate company units.[64]

---

[60] Ibid., 26 Nov. 1860. For additional information see Ibid., 24 and 28 Nov. 1860.
[61] Ibid., 30 Nov. 1860.
[62] Ibid., 26 Nov. 1860.
[63] Ibid., 28 Nov. 1860.
[64] Ibid., 3 Jan. 1861.

Joel R. Branham, "a man of considerable military attainments, together with a clear head and great firmness of character," was suggested as the battalion's Lieutenant Colonel.[65] But a private in the Macon Guards, disagreed, believing that each man should vote for his own candidate. This anonymous individual believed that Macon was home to a good many military-minded men, such as Captain B.F. Ross, Colonel Washington Poe, Colonel Nathan Bass, Captain Robert A. Smith, and others who should be considered.[66]

Shortly after Governor Brown ordered the Georgia Militia to seize Fort Pulaski on 4 January 1861, the Macon Volunteers held an election for officers at their armory. Captain Smith was reelected Captain; with A.G. Butts as First Lieutenant; George S. Jones, Second Lieutenant; C.H. Freeman, Third Lieutenant; George W. Hardie, Ensign; and Robert A. Atkinson, First Sergeant.[67]

Parades became more frequent, and such military supplies as knapsacks, kegs of powder, and other munitions, passed through the streets on drays "as if they were the most innocent things in the world."[68] Judge Eugenius A. Nisbet pushed for the appointment of Macon physician, Dr. Henry K. Green, as surgeon in chief of the military forces of Georgia.[69] Judge Phil Tracy also urged the Governor to appoint Dr. Green to that post, and asked for the appointment of Dr. George Griffin of Macon as one of the assistant surgeons for the new Georgia army which was about to be raised.[70] The people of Macon subscribed $800 to buy suitable military cloth to uniform the volunteer companies while they paraded as a battalion. The city's women came forward and agreed to make the cloth with the stipulation that every man who accepted a suit be ready to go "when the hour of peril comes."[71]

That peril would soon come, and the people of Macon would be tested more severely than they had ever been tested before.

---

[65] Ibid., 11 Jan. 1861.

[66] "Private of the M.G.," in Ibid., 12 Jan. 1861.

[67] Ibid., 7 Jan. 1861.

[68] Ibid., 15 Jan. 1861. See also Ibid., 16 Jan. 1861.

[69] Eugenius A. Nisbet to Governor Brown, Macon, 11 Jan. 1861, in Incoming Correspondence of the Governor, Record Group 1-1-5, Box 41 in Georgia Department of Archives and History, Atlanta, hereafter cited as GDA&H.

[70] Phil Tracy to Governor Brown, Macon, 16 Jan. 1861, in Ibid., Box 48.

[71] *Macon Daily Telegraph*, 10 Jan. 1861.

Chapter 3

Macon in the Secession Crisis

During the secession crisis of 1860-1861, Macon citizens held the view that the Southern states should stay in the Union and work within the American political system. Therefore, when the Bibb County Democratic Party met at the Bibb County Court House on 7 February 1860, to choose delegates to the State Convention scheduled to be held at Milledgeville on 14 March; the purpose of the meeting involved the selection of delegates to the National Democratic Convention in Charleston. Thomas R. Bloom presided over the meeting as chairman while W.C.M. Dunson served as secretary. The delegates selected Phil Tracy, Oliver A. Lochrane, Joel R. Griffin, T. R. Bloom, and Lewis N. Whittle as delegates to the State Convention from Bibb County. During the meeting, speeches were made by such Macon luminaries as Colonel Nathan Bass, Thomas C. Nisbet, James A. Nisbet, Dr. Joel Branham, Lewis N. Whittle, Judge Oliver A. Lochrane, John J. Gresham, John B. Lamar, William C. Wilson, and Captain Z.T. Conner.[1]

While this attitude of pro-Union feelings continued in the spring of 1860, there was a feeling among Maconites that the Northern people were not martial, that, if war came, they would not really be willing to fight. The *Macon Daily Telegraph* felt that Northerners "are the last ones who would make a martial demonstration. They are willing to do their part in speaking, in threatening, in writing, in distributing floods of incendiary documents, in making prayers, in fact in doing the wind work, but when they are asked to shoulder their muskets, to leave their homes, their wives and children, and risk their lives in a fanatical foray, they will desert." After all, the paper asserted, "They all know that John Brown was once a live man- they now know he is a dead man, and as long as they remember his bloody martyrdom, they will not risk the charms of a rope from our [Governor] Joe Brown or the Alabama governor." If the South, or, for that matter, any state in the Union, were determined to leave the Union, all that

---

[1] Bibb County Democratic Meeting, Macon, 7 Feb. 1860, in Cobb-Erwin-Lamar Collection, Hargrett Library, The University of Georgia, hereafter cited as Cobb-Erwin-Lamar Collection.

was necessary was to cut the cord, "and there is not power enough in the General Government or all the States, to unite the parts, and it is all gammon and nonsense to talk otherwise." After all, the paper felt, how many men in Georgia would volunteer to go to Rhode Island and try and force her back into the Union if she should secede, "not one hundred." The paper continued in a like vein by saying that none of the followers of William Lloyd Garrison, Horace Greeley, Wendell Phillips, or Henry Ward Beecher would invade Georgia to force her back into the Union if she should secede. The paper concluded, "This thing of risking one's life for a principle, and a wrong one at that, is easy to talk about, but it's hard to practice."[2]

Many Maconites believed, as did John J. Gresham, on the eve of the National Democratic Convention, that the military was in the ascendancy in the spring of 1860. Writing on 17 March 1860, at the close of the Georgia Democratic Convention in Milledgeville, Gresham could see little hope of a peaceful solution of the slavery question. Possibly Stephen A. Douglas, the flamboyant Senator from Illinois, could steer the ship of state to a peaceful solution of the controversy. After all, Georgia's apparent favorite son for the presidential nomination, Secretary of the Treasury Howell Cobb, had been abandoned by the delegates at the State Convention.[3]

Cobb's brother-in-law, John B. Lamar, believed that friends of Stephen A. Douglas had manipulated the delegates to the Georgia Democratic Convention "to clear the field," as Lamar declared, "of any obstruction in the way of a man or a principle, for his behoof." Lamar believed that, whatever happened to the Democrats at Charleston, would be the fault of the Douglas people. There was, Lamar felt, a strong reaction to the way Cobb's presidential candidacy as Georgia's favorite son was handled by the Milledgeville delegates.[4]

Cobb considered himself to be the heir apparent of President James Buchanan, although he never received a formal endorsement from the Pennsylvanian. His friends mismanaged the March Convention, and Cobb retired from serious consideration as a presidential candidate in 1860.[5] Commenting on Cobb's defeat, Lamar observed, "Numbers...[of Cobb's enemies] begin to suspect that instead of having gained anything at the March Convention, they were there used as tools by the secret friends of Douglas to clear the field of any

---

[2] *Macon Daily Telegraph,* 4 Feb. 1860.

[3] John J. Gresham to Edward Dorr Tracy, Jr., Macon, 17 Mar. 1860, in Tracy-Steele-Johnston Family Correspondence.

[4] John B. Lamar to Cobb, Macon, 5 Apr. 1860, Cobb Papers, 1860. Cobb was married to Mary Ann Lamar Cobb, Lamar's sister.

[5] Roy Franklin Nichols, *The Disruption of American Democracy,* New York: The Macmillan Company, 1948, 278, hereafter cited as Nichols, *Disruption of American Democracy.*

obstruction in the way of a man or a principle, for his behoof. And that whatever may betide at Charleston they have a clear field now & will be held responsible."[6]

Cobb, for his part, wrote Lamar expressing his desire to run for the US Senate from Georgia after his term as Secretary of the Treasury in Buchanan's Cabinet, and after he moved to Macon. He confided, "The more I think of it the more I am satisfied that it will be greatly to my interest in every respect to move to Macon."[7]

On May 19, 1860, a Democratic meeting in Macon elected delegates to go to Milledgeville in June to attend a reconvened meeting of the March State Convention. The plan of the Democrats, whose party was now a sectional instead of a national party because of the Charleston Convention, planned to hold their own convention in another city where they could nominate a candidate of their own choosing. The Macon meeting chose John B. Lamar, Joel Branham, Alex Spear, Phil Tracy, and Edwin L. Strohecker, all of whom had promoted the candidacy of Cobb, to represent Macon and Bibb County at the reconvened State Convention.[8] Cobb responded with happiness when he learned that Lamar would be a delegate to the June Convention, after all his brother-in-law, Lamar, was one of his strongest supporters.[9] The Cobb supporters in Bibb County now turned to Vice President John C. Breckinridge as their candidate for the presidency.[10]

In late June former Georgia Governor Herschel V. Johnson spoke in Macon in support of Douglas during a political gathering chaired by Nathan Bass. John A. Cobb confided to his father that Johnson "had a good crowd but most of them were against him." Whenever Johnson mentioned Breckinridge's name almost every man in the audience applauded. This angered the former Georgia governor. Johnson spoke for an hour and a quarter, a short address for that period, although he had enough material to make a long speech. The younger Cobb stated, "You may know that he did not get through for he never was known to make as short a speech before." Johnson, who planned to run for governor, said he would run even if he got only five votes in the State. That night he was hung and burned in effigy, with a paper pinned on his breast with the words "Gov Johnson" on his chest, and the phrase "the [Benedict] Arnold of Georgia," on his back. John Cobb told his father that Johnson had attacked

---

[6] Lamar to Cobb, Macon, 5 Apr. 1860, Cobb Papers, 1860.

[7] Cobb to Lamar, Washington, 24 Apr. 1860, Ibid.

[8] John A. Cobb to Howell Cobb, Macon, 19 May 1860, Cobb Papers, 1860.

[9] Cobb to Lamar, Washington, 22 May 1860, Ibid.

[10] For an account of the Baltimore Convention which nominated Breckinridge as the Southern candidate for President and Senator Joseph Lane of Oregon for Vice President see Nichols, *Disruption of American Democracy,* 313-322.

the elder Cobb several times during the speech, saying "that if a certain prominent man from Georgia had stood any chance to have been nominated there would have been no secession [from the national Democratic ticket] from Georgia." The younger Cobb noted, "The people here feel sorry for Johnson & his presence creates the feeling like that of the corpse of some distinguished man was passing through the city."[11]

As the time for the presidential election slowly drew near many people in Macon showed little interest in politics. As Dr. James Mercer Green informed John B. Lamar, they "have lately been taken with a most violent attachment to business." Other prominent Democrats talked of the uselessness of engaging in partisan struggles, while all the county officials "seem to be seized with a most praiseworthy & zealous devotion to their official duties." Many thought that it would be foolish to anger the Douglas wing of the party so that Douglas and his followers would oppose them in the January elections. Herschel V. Johnson continued to attack Cobb and his followers "with the virulence of a hydrophobic dog." Johnson, Green felt, "seems to run riot in his deep double dyed concentrated hatred of everything patriotic & Southern." The actions of some of the Douglas supporters, men like Whig Representative Alexander H. Stephens and his half-brother and political ally, Linton, were going around the State making speeches attacking Cobb and his followers. The comments of some of the Douglas people certainly did not help the growing sectional feeling in Georgia which was fomented by the approaching presidential election. Such comments as Johnson's statement during a speech at Indian Springs in Butts County when he said, "there was only one thing worse than Breckinridge & that was Hell," did nothing to pour oil on troubled waters. Green, who was one of Cobb's most faithful supporters, and who feared Georgia might go for Douglas, hoped that Lamar [who was away on business in New York] would soon return to Macon and help Breckinridge carry the State.[12]

The fervor caused by the approaching election even caused some of the Blacks in Macon to cluster around the doors of the hall where speeches were in progress, so they could hear some of the speeches. This tendency concerned the Editor Joseph Clisby of the *Daily Telegraph*, who like many Southern whites feared a slave insurrection. He described the scene: "They do not congregate in sufficient number to make an unlawful assembly, but scatter themselves around-some at the Hall door and some in the streets where it is very easy to hear what is said within, when the windows and doors are open." Possibly this unusual conduct on the part of Blacks, Clisby reported, "should be looked after by the city officers."[13]

---

[11] John A. Cobb to Howell Cobb, Macon, 30 June 1860, Cobb Papers, 1860.

[12] Dr. James Mercer Green to John B. Lamar, Macon, 3 Sept. 1860, Ibid.

[13] *Macon Daily Telegraph*, 8 Sept. 1860.

While many in Macon might have pretended to have little interest in the upcoming presidential election, this was probably only a front that they were putting up. Many of the people, who appeared calm, feared the election of the Republican contender. A relative of Lewis N. Whittle wrote to the Macon attorney on September 29, that Breckinridge was much like his relative, Aaron Burr, because "he has no patriotism, if he had he would withdraw [from the race]. Douglas, too, did not seem patriotic to this writer, but he was "the smartest of them all." Unfortunately, he confided "I fear Lincoln is to be the man."[14]

When, in late October, Douglas came to Macon, the Douglas supporters, "what few there are," went to great lengths to prepare for his visit. John A. Cobb, who was staying with his uncle, John B. Lamar in Macon, wrote his mother that fiery Georgia Senator Robert Toombs planned to come to Macon and make a speech on the night of Wednesday, 31 October, in an attempt to counterbalance Douglas' address. Douglas' speech was scheduled for the afternoon.[15]

Douglas's arrival was accompanied by the firing of cannon, rockets, and a good deal of noise from the crowds who were there to greet him. He was accompanied by his wife, Adele, and his friend and supporter, Alexander H. Stephens who introduced him to the crowd at the depot. Both Stephens and Douglas made speeches in which they took a strong stand "against disunion for existing grievances or on account of Lincoln's election."[16]

When Lincoln was elected President on 7 November a strong feeling that secession was the only solution for Georgia began to pervade Macon. When Howell Cobb's brother, Thomas R. R. Cobb made a fiery speech in favor of secession at Milledgeville, John B. Lamar returned to Macon hoarse from "applauding & hallooing." He told his nephews John and Lamar that it was the finest speech he had ever heard, and advised "Uncle Tom not to publish it- but to go all over the state & speak it." To add to the fire eating speeches being made in and near Macon, Francis Bartow of Savannah and Senator Toombs both spoke in Macon in favor of secession on the night of 13 November. Both of the men made fine speeches, according to Lamar Cobb, but Bartow's was the best. All of this prompted young Cobb to tell his Mother, "I am for secession— dissolution—disunion or whatever else you may call it- now & forever." Both John B. Lamar and his nephew John began wearing blue cockades on the left of

---

[14] C.D.Whittle to Lewis N. Whittle, Milbank, VA., 29 Sept. 1860, Microfilm, Lewis N. Whittle Papers, Middle Georgia Archives, Washington Memorial Library, Macon.

[15] John A. Cobb to his mother, Macon, 28 Oct. 1860.

[16] *Georgia Journal and Messenger*, 7 Nov. 1860. For a lengthy account of Douglas' visit see the *Macon Daily Telegraph*, 1 Nov. 1860.

their hats, an emblem which denoted secession. Lamar hoped that a report he had heard about Vice President Breckinridge being for submission to the Republicans was false. "If it is true," he told his Mother, "he is not the man I thought he was." Uncle John told his nephews that "Resistance to oppression is obedience to God." This was pretty strong language, but Lamar went even further when he told his nephews that, if Georgia submitted to Lincoln and did not secede he would sell his property and go to either South Carolina where his father came from or to Paris, France. Young Lamar felt that he "should hate very much to stay a day [in] a disgraced state: & am not prepared to say that I will." The young man was prepared to stand by any state which seceded if Lincoln or anyone else tried to keep her in the Union. He planned to "battle for her as long as my arm can be raised from my side if she calls for assistance."[17]

As soon as the results of the election became known Macon's leaders held a public meeting to adopt measures for the public welfare, measures which would lead to secession. Attorney Washington Poe presided over the meeting. He urged calm, advising firmness and determination. Poe appointed a committee of ten to draft a report. The members of the Committee included Samuel T. Bailey, Robert A. Smith, Charles J. Harris, Lewis N. Whittle, John B. Lamar, Joel R. Branham, Edward L. Strohecker, J.H.R. Washington, James Mercer Green, and T. R. Bloom. The committee prepared a lengthy report which was read by Captain Smith, who strongly supported secession. The report concluded with three resolutions, the first of which urged Bibb's delegation to the General Assembly to introduce a bill "for the speedy call of a Convention of the people of the State, to take such action and devise such measures as will protect themselves and families from impending ruin." The second resolution requested the introduction of a bill to purchase enough good rifles to supply every man who was subject to military duty. The final resolution recommended that every citizen of Georgia organize and arm themselves as fast as possible "for their protection against impending dangers." The committee also recommended the adoption of resolutions, including the appointment of a Committee of Safety and the organization of Minute Men. The resolutions were adopted, together with the entire report.[18]

By mid-November a kind of panic seized Macon. The banks closed down, and no cotton could be sold. This prompted John B. Lamar, who managed the plantations for his brother-in-law, to write Howell Cobb on November 19, that he had over 700 bales of cotton in Hardeman and Sparks' Warehouse which temporarily could not be sold. To make matters worse, more cotton was coming in daily, the secession feeling was growing stronger, and the Legislature was calling on everyone who could to frame a bill calling for a secession convention.

---

[17] Lamar Cobb to his mother, Macon, 14 Nov. 1860, Cobb Papers, 1860.
[18] Butler, *Historical Record*, 231-235.

Some prominent Maconites, led by Judge Eugenius A. Nisbet, wanted to select candidates who would seek a compromise with Lincoln and the Republicans. But many more candidates wanted to elect delegates who would vote for secession without thought of compromise. Even while plans for a convention were moving ahead, secession sentiments were intensifying among the people. Preparations were being made to raise Georgia's colonial flag with the rattlesnake and the pine tree. Lamar told Cobb that the people were pushing for secession "far in advance of their representatives."[19]

Lamar wanted Cobb to resign his post as Secretary of the Treasury as soon as possible. At least he should send his wife to Macon immediately, either by steamer from Baltimore, or overland by easy stages through Richmond, Columbia, and Augusta. Since Mary Ann was expecting another child it would be well if she came to Macon to stay in Lamar's home, "the Bear's Den." Besides, the climate in Macon during November was more pleasant than in Washington.[20]

At the same time, Lamar wrote Colonel David Barrow, a wealthy planter who was closely allied both socially and politically with the Cobbs, to send copies of the most recent secession speeches of Robert Toombs, Thomas R. R. Cobb, Francis Bartow, and Henry R. Jackson for publication in the Macon newspapers. After all, the *Daily Telegraph*, whose editor, Clisby, favored compromise with the Lincolnites, was publishing Alexander H. Stephens' most recent anti-secession speech in three installments on a daily basis "on the principle that it is the only one that has been reported."[21]

Also toward the end of the pivotal month of November, a report reached James A. Nisbet that his kinsman, Thomas C. Nisbet, had applied to Lincoln for a position with the Federal Government. Although, James treated the report "with the contempt it deserved," since "our blood for generations is too Southern not to fire up at such a suggestion, and therefore it produced only indignation." Unfortunately, the report was gaining credence among some Maconites. James felt that such news was "defamatory of any Southern man to be placed in the attitude of asking or taking office of an administration, as foreign in every particular to the South as the Russian Autocracy, and as hostile as was that of George III to the colonies." Thomas assured his kinsman he would vote only for secession candidates for the convention. He had been a secessionist in the crisis of 1850, and was one now. He assured James, and the readers of the *Daily Telegraph*, that "I have never applied for any office, nor have I ever

---

[19] Lamar to Cobb, Macon, 19 Nov. 1860, Ibid.

[20] Ibid.

[21] Lamar to Colonel David Barrow, Macon, 21 Nov. 1860, Colonel David C. Barrow Papers, Correspondence May 1860-Mar. 1865, Ms. 69, Hargrett Library, The University of Georgia, Athens, hereafter cited as Barrow Papers.

entertained an idea of accepting an office from any man, living or dead, and I would see every office in the government closed forever, before I would accept it from an administration hostile not only to our institutions, but to the best interest of the whole country." [22]

The secession feeling was so high in Macon by early December that even visitors were impressed by it. Henry Ruffner Morrison, a Virginian who was visiting Macon, noted that the facilities in Macon were numerous and favorable for spreading secessionist sentiments throughout all of the cotton states. He wrote his father, "The telegraphic dispatches which are daily & almost hourly transmitted from State to State and from Capital to Capital together with the intercommunication between States by committees and by friendly conference, leaves no room for false conclusions." No intelligent man could close his eyes to what was going on throughout South Carolina, Georgia, and the Gulf States. This led Morrison to the reluctant conclusion that "The Union must be dissolved. No power on earth can prevent it under existing circumstances." Popular sentiment in Macon, Morrison concluded, was overwhelming for secession. The whole mass of intelligent people were calling for it. Georgia would secede, and South Carolina was already pledged "to resume her sovereignty." In fact, the Palmetto State, would leave the Union within thirty days. Representatives from South Carolina had addressed a large gathering in Macon on 1 December.

Secession sentiment was also growing in Alabama and Florida. Morrison confided to his Father, "It is impossible to give you any adequate idea of the state of feeling in the South. It is not the mad outburst of passion nor the aimless desire for revolution which most of the Northern press denounce as a vile characteristic of Southern 'fire-eaters'." Every minister in Macon was calling for secession. On the night of 1 December a public meeting was held at Concert Hall with one of the largest crowds the young Virginian had ever seen. The gathering was called by the people of all political parties for the purpose of discussing the issues before the country. Judge Nisbet, when called upon for his advice, spoke of his strong attachment to the Union. He told of the sadness he felt now that he "was forced to abandon all hope of perpetuating that Confederacy which has done so much for the amelioration of the race." The elderly jurist and statesman showed such deep emotion as to cause a sympathetic feeling to pass through the audience. Even "many a manly cheek. was moistened with a tear." For a moment Morrison, who was present, felt that there was still hope, that love of the Union was still present in Macon. But his hopes were dashed a few moments later when a resolution was proposed which declared the "unalterable determination of Georgia" to leave the Union. Not one

---

[22] James A. Nisbet to Thomas C. Nisbet, Macon, 24 Nov. 1860, in *Macon Daily Telegraph*, 26 Nov. 1860.

voice in the crowd was raised in opposition. Morrison observed the scene: "The universal shout of applause which rose from the vast crowd & the waving of handkerchiefs by the throng of ladies who crowded the lobbies, showed most unanswerably that the Rubicon is nearly crossed." When Georgia Senator Alfred Iverson, Sr. was discovered among the spectators, he was called to the podium amid the wildest enthusiasm. Iverson made a speech filled with a tirade of abuse of the Federal Government, dwelling on the future glories of the nascent Southern republic. He told his listeners he was on the way to Washington to assume his position as Senator from Georgia, but he would be ready to meet any "emergency" with the full conviction that he would soon turn his back forever upon the national capital, and hoped the day was now at hand to seal the end of the present Union. That, he assured the people, "would be the proudest day of his life." Soon, Iverson friend, Senator Robert Toombs, a leader "of the same stripe" as Iverson, would speak in Macon. As Morrison expressed it, "With influences like these, brought to bear upon [the] public mind, the disunion sentiment must be strengthened." Morrison closed, with almost an afterthought, "The fair is attracting large numbers of persons to the city."[23]

Much of the secession sentiment revolved around John B. Lamar, Macon's wealthiest citizen, who was doing all he could to speed Georgia's departure from the Union. Mary Ann Cobb, Lamar's younger sister, recently arrived in Macon from Washington, wrote her husband that the Bear's Den was filled with secession documents- including hundreds of copies of Toombs' speeches having arrived on the morning of 10 December. She had sent a bundle of them to Dr. James Mercer Green's office, and then sent men to take additional bundles of them to the Fair for distribution in packages. These included not only Toombs' speeches, but those of Thomas R. R. Cobb and Henry Benning, a prominent resident of Columbus. A meeting of secessionists was planned for that evening at the Bear's Den. Cobb's wife, quite a secessionist herself, told him that Judge Nisbet was forced to "confess his true sentiments" before he was allowed to present his name as a candidate for a seat in the approaching convention. She explained to Cobb, as if it were necessary, "Everything looks revolutionary here."[24]

---

[23] Henry Ruffner Morrison to his Father, Macon, 2 Dec. 1860, in *Civil War Times Illustrated Collection*, USAMHI, hereafter cited as *Civil War Times Illustrated Collection*. Morrison was referring to the Southern States Cotton Exposition then in progress at Camp Oglethorpe.

[24] Mary Ann Cobb to her husband, Macon, 10 Dec. 1860, Cobb Papers, 1860. Lamar used his home to distribute copies of many secession speeches, and even secession sermons, throughout Macon, Bibb County, and Middle Georgia. See A.B. Seals to Lamar, Atlanta, 12 Dec. 1860; William Flinn to Lamar, Milledgeville, 12 Dec. 1860; Henry Jackson to Lamar, Savannah, 12 Dec. 1860; L.F.W. Andrews to

Resigning his cabinet post in early December, Cobb prepared to leave for Macon. He indicated an interest in giving a secession speech in Macon; wanted his brother Thomas to meet him in Columbia, South Carolina; and desired an appointment as a commissioner from Georgia to South Carolina.[25]

Lamar passed on Cobb's plans to Colonel David Barrow, and asked the latter's support in securing Cobb's appointment as a commissioner from Georgia to South Carolina. Cobb arrived in Macon by train on the night of 18 December and immediately scheduled a speech for Thursday, 20 December.[26]

On Friday, 7 December, Thomas R. R. Cobb, upon the invitation of the local Minute Men, made a four-hour-long secession speech in Macon which strongly affected the opinions of his listeners. Lamar wrote Cobb to tell him of the speech and to inform him about a Bibb County meeting planned for Friday, 14 December to elect delegates to the Georgia Convention. Lamar planned to be one of the candidates.[27] Commenting on her brother-in-law's remarks, Mary Ann Cobb wrote her husband in early December that Thomas Cobb's speech "electrified" the people of Macon. She noted a conversation between two women who heard the speech: "one said 'well he spoke 5 hours'. 'Yes said the other-and if had spoken 75 hours I could have listened without being tired'."[28]

The meeting, mentioned by Lamar, was held at the Bibb County Court House. It was called to order by Judge W. T. Massey, who made a motion nominating Dr. Edwin L. Strohecker as Chairman. Leading secessionist Dr. James A. Damour, served as Secretary. Strohecker explained the objects for which the gathering had convened, and then turned the floor over to Dr. Joel Branham who moved that the delegates selected should be nominated by acclamation. Captain Robert A. Smith objected, and Charles Rogers made a substitute motion, which was adopted, that the name of each delegate should be balloted for, and the men who received the three highest votes should be declared elected. The names of John B. Lamar, Washington Poe, and Judge Eugenius A. Nisbet were submitted to the meeting, and were elected unanimously. Judge Clifford Anderson also received a large vote, although

---

Lamar, Macon, 14 Dec. 1860; John H. Seals to Lamar, Milledgeville, 15 Dec. 1860; S. Rose & Co., to Lamar, Bill, 15 Dec. 1860; and John H. Seals to Lamar, Atlanta, 21 Dec. 1860, all in Ibid.

[25] Cobb to his wife, Washington, 10 Dec. 1860, Ibid. It was common for states to send commissioners to other states during the secession crisis of 1860-1861. This was done to pass along information, and observe conditions among the people of different Southern States.

[26] Lamar to Colonel David Barrow, Macon, 13 Dec. 1860, Barrow Papers. James M. Smyth to Lamar, Telegram, Augusta, 18 Dec. 1860, Cobb papers, 1860. *Georgia Journal and Messenger*, 19 Dec. 1860.

[27] Lamar to Cobb, Macon, 11 Dec. 1860, Ibid, Cobb papers, 1860.

[28] Mary Ann Cobb to her husband, Macon, Dec. 1860, Ibid.

everyone knew he had repeatedly declined to accept the nomination, even if it were urged upon him. Dr. Strohecker, Dr. James Mercer Green, and Colonel James A. Nisbet were appointed a committee to notify Nisbet, Poe, and Lamar of their nomination. After a motion by James Nisbet to ask the Chairman to appoint an Executive Committee of the secession party in Bibb County, the meeting adjourned.[29]

On 10 December another meeting was held in Macon, chaired by Judge Asa Holt with James C. Rodgers as Secretary. The purpose of the meeting was to continue to support the Federal Government, "if it could be faithfully administered and executed, according to the designs of its founders." But the group condemned some of the Northern States for refusing to enforce the Fugitive Slave Law, and their enactment of laws which obstructed Federal marshals and others in their official duties of apprehending escaped slaves. The gathering believed that the Northern States were refusing to abide by the US Constitution, which, in the eyes of Macon's leaders, was "the common bond of Union." Therefore, many Maconites felt that they were no longer bound to remain in the Union because other states had violated the compact, a document entered into through the voluntary consent of free, sovereign, and independent States. After all, Macon's leaders believed, the Federal Government had certain powers, while the others were "reserved to the several States or the people thereof." Since events had proceeded this far, the people attending the meeting wanted a provisional government for a Southern Confederacy, or "the US of the South," to take effect and operate on a future specified day, but as soon as possible. They wanted their action to be sent to the conventions of the various Southern states, many of which were in the process of organizing.[30]

On 20 December 1860, South Carolina became the first State to secede from the Union. At noon, on Friday, 21 December, the hour when the South Carolina Ordinance of Secession went into effect, the bells in Macon began to peal, and the Jackson Artillery fired a 100-gun-salute in honor of the occasion. At 7:00 in the evening the bells ran again, and another salute of 100 guns was fired. Bonfires illuminated the streets, and many homes were lit. Captain B.F. Ross and his Minute Men assembled at the Court House, and were formed into line with banners and transparencies. The unit led a procession of 1,500 people, preceded by a band. They marched to the Lanier House where they heard brief but fiery speeches by Judge Clifford Anderson, Judge Phil Tracy, Captain Robert A. Smith, Colonel A.M. Speer, a Captain Barbiere of Tennessee,

---

[29] *Georgia Journal and Messenger*, 19 Dec. 1860. Bibb County's delegates to the Georgia Secession Convention were Poe, Nisbet, and Lamar. See Butler, *Historical Record*, 243.

[30] Ibid. Macon's papers, at this time, were filled with news of meetings in all of the counties surrounding Bibb: Jones, Houston, Monroe, and Crawford.

Colonel James A. Nisbet, and Captain L. B. Branham. From there, the crowd marched to the home of Judge Eugenius A. Nisbet, and called him out to make "a very happy response." The group then marched up the hill to Wesleyan Female College to hear warm Southern rights speeches by Reverends F. Forster and W. C. Bass, remarks which were answered by the crowd who gave rousing cheers for the ministers and for the young ladies of the college. As the procession returned to downtown Macon, they also cheered as they passed the residences of Captain B. F. Ross and Thomas A. Harris, both of which were "brilliantly illuminated." The crowd then cheered in front of the *Macon Daily Telegraph* office, and then marched to John B. Lamar's home. Lamar was ill, but Howell Cobb, who was staying at the "Bear's Den," responded for him. They then went to the home of Colonel Washington Poe, who spoke to them, and was greeted with a round of applause for his efforts. Afterward, the procession proceeded to Concert Hall where the Minute Men were dismissed after giving three cheers for Captain Ross.[31]

In late December the speeches and processions continued, all of them designed to push the cause of the secessionists.[32] All of this led the *Georgia Journal and Messenger* to insert a note of caution. The paper, after admitting an honest difference of opinion existed concerning the secession of Georgia, urged its readers to avoid "everything like bitterness of feeling and intolerance of spirit" which should be avoided. After all, the article continued, "In exercising the prerogatives of American freemen, let us not forget the amenities and courtesies due to a common brotherhood."[33]

This appeal fell on deaf ears as far as John B. Lamar was concerned. He worked tirelessly to secure his election to the Georgia Convention, scheduled to begin in January. On December 24 he went with Phil Tracy to attend a political meeting at Pumpkin Hollow, a small settlement near Macon. Early on the following day, Christmas day, accompanied by Howell Cobb, Jr., Tracy attended a barbecue in the Warrior Precinct of Bibb County. The indefatigable secessionist had spent most of the 24th drumming up recruits for Macon's volunteer companies. When, during the course of his activities on the 24th, Lamar asked Lewis N. Whittle to attend the barbecue with him, the latter responded with amazement, "Go to a barbecue on Christmas Day. I would as soon think of going on Sunday!!" Lamar came home heartily disgusted with Whittle, and determined to go to the barbecue himself. He returned home at 10:00 A.M., said good morning to everyone, sat before the fire for a few minutes, and then left to join the Minute Men in another procession. Lamar felt that Joseph Clisby, Editor of the *Daily Telegraph* and a man who supported the

---

[31] *Macon Daily Telegraph*, 24 Dec. 1860.

[32] Ibid., 25 Dec. 1860.

[33] *Georgia Journal and Messenger*, 26 Dec. 1860.

Union to the last, was "the most disconsolate man he ever saw- he looks as if he had lost his last friend." Mary Ann Cobb confided to her husband, who was in Clarksville, Georgia, making a speech, that she wished Clisby and "his printing press, young wife and all were in Yankee land- where they might sing Hozannas [sic] to 'the Union' to their heart's content- without molestation."[34]

When Major Robert Anderson moved his garrison from Fort Moultrie to Fort Sumter in Charleston Harbor on 26 December it took the secessionists in Macon by surprise as it did the rest of the Lower South. Mary Ann told her husband, "A large sum of money would be paid now for Anderson's scalp." All of the volunteer companies in the City volunteered their services to Governor Francis Pickens of South Carolina. The 60 Minute Men from Pumpkin Hollow, although they had never drilled, also offered their services. They planned to march in a unit to the polls on election day decorated with blue cockades and red sashes. John Addison Cobb's unit, the Macon Volunteers, had been offered to Governor Pickens, and had been accepted.[35]

When the news of Major Anderson's action reached Macon, the Floyd Rifles, Macon Guards, Jackson Artillery, and Macon Volunteers met to ascertain the feelings of the men concerning the crisis. All of the units decided to offer their services to South Carolina. Even the Bibb Cavalry and the Minute Men wanted to rush to the defense of South Carolina. However, Governor Pickens told them he would call upon them if necessary.[36]

A reporter for the *Daily Telegraph* tried to put the best face on the steadily deteriorating state of affairs in Charleston Harbor when it explained to its readers that Major Anderson's act was not necessarily an act of hostility, although people would probably see it that way. Unfortunately, "nothing but the most conciliating course on the part of the government can prevent immediate war- a war which will assuredly involve all the Slave States." The reporter believed that coercion was absurd, and hoped the idea would be abandoned by the North and the incoming Lincoln Administration. He concluded with news of "The intense excitement which pervades Macon since the receipt of this news, and the almost universal desire to rush to the rescue, shows that South Carolina will lack nothing for the triumphant indication of her rights and her territory from the assaults of an invading foe."[37]

During December, Macon's volunteer companies became even more active than before. On the afternoon of 11 December the entire Macon Battalion, 250 strong, handsomely uniformed and equipped, marched to the Fair Ground, and

---

[34] Mary Ann Cobb to her Husband, Macon, 25 Dec. 1860, Cobb Papers, 1860.

[35] Mary Ann Cobb to her Husband, Macon, 28 Dec. 1860, Ibid.

[36] *Macon Daily Telegraph*, 28 Dec. 1860.

[37] Ibid, 28 Dec. 1860.

went through a number of military drills until sunset. The Jackson Artillery, complete with four cannon, joined in the practice.[38]

As January came, events moved swiftly toward the secession of Georgia. When Governor Brown seized Fort Pulaski guarding the mouth of the Savannah River, in early January, the Minute Men passed a resolution approving of the action, and pledged to support him "at any sacrifice, and at all hazards."[39] A rumor circulated throughout the city that the Minute Men would be immediately placed on a war footing.[40]

As the time for the Convention approached large numbers of delegates passed through Macon on their way to Milledgeville. Many others came through as observers. A reporter for the *Journal and Messenger* predicted that Milledgeville would be crowded during the next few days. Moreover, he believed, an ordinance of secession would be passed. He felt that "Georgia must, therefore, look now rather to her own safety and interests and those of her Southern Confederates, than to a longer continuance in the Union."[41]

On the morning of 15 January ten cars crowded with people went from Macon to Milledgeville. Mary C. Nisbet of Macon confided to her friend, Mary Jones that she thought the secession ordinance would be passed on Saturday, 19 January an act which she wanted to witness. Showing she had the bravado felt by many Southerners at the time, the young Macon woman had "no idea that we shall have war; if so, but one or two battles, and then peace we shall have on our own terms."[42]

A reporter for the *Journal and Messenger* described the convention as consisting "of men of ripe age, experience and influence. Comparatively few young men are members of this important body. With few exceptions, all seemed deeply impressed with the fearful responsibility of their trust." Many spectators attended the meetings, and the hotels and private homes of Milledgeville were filled to overflowing. The reporter noted, "Never ...was the proverbial hospitality of the citizens of Milledgeville more fully tested."[43]

On 18 January Cobb wired his son John from Milledgeville, "Secession resolution passed by thirty five majority we will go out tomorrow." In a telegram to another of his sons, Lamar, on 19 January, Cobb exclaimed,

---

[38] Ibid., 12 Dec. 1860. For other information concerning parades and appearances by Macon's military units in late December, 1860, see Ibid., 29 and 31 Dec. 1860.

[39] Ibid., 7 Jan. 1861.

[40] Ibid., 11 Jan. 1861.

[41] *Georgia Journal and Messenger*, 16 Jan. 1861.

[42] Mary C. Nisbet to Mary Jones, Macon, 17 Jan. 1861, in Robert Manson Myers, ed., *The Children of Pride*, Yale University Press: New Haven and London, 1972, 642.

[43] *Georgia Journal and Messenger*, 23 Jan. 1861.

"Ordinance passed by a majority of one hundred and nineteen." The vote in favor of secession was 208 to 89 opposed. John C. Butler described the Bibb delegation as a distinguished group which enjoyed high esteem among the county delegations. He concluded, "The names of Washington Poe, Eugenius A. Nisbet and John B. Lamar, are inseparably associated among the most honored in the history of Macon, and are among the purest recorded in the galaxy of the State."[44]

During the Convention Judge Nisbet offered what were probably the two most important resolutions adopted by the group. One of these called for the secession of Georgia from the Union, and urged the cooperation of the Convention with other states to form a Southern Confederacy. The second resolution called for the appointment of a committee of seventeen "to report an ordinance to assert the rights, and fulfill the obligation of the State of Georgia to secede from the Union."[45]

When the news of Georgia's secession reached Macon on Saturday, 19 January the event was greeted by the thunder of a 119-gun-salute by the cannon of the Jackson Artillery. The people were startled from their normal routine by "the heavy thunders that belched forth from the guns." When the first cannon fired an electrical current seemed to pervade the air. Maconites shouted, "The Ordinance has passed." The *Daily Telegraph* reported "in an instant the city was alive with every manifestation of joy."[46]

The *Journal and Messenger* took a more philosophical view. After all, the paper reported, whatever differences of opinion might have existed before in regard to the need for taking the radical step of seceding from the Union, "now that it is consummated, all will yield a ready acquiescence and heartily unite in building up the great and vital interests of our beloved State."[47]

Not to be outdone, Joseph Clisby, editor of the *Daily Telegraph*, the *Journal and Messenger's* principal competitor, editorialized, "The Empire State of the South will now take her position at the head of the secession column, and devote her vast talents, influence and power, to the work of building up an independent Southern Confederacy- a white man's Republic."[48]

Mary Ann Cobb wrote her husband that preparations were underway for a torchlight parade by the Minute Men, the firing of guns, ringing of bells, and a

---

[44] Cobb to John A. Cobb, Telegram, Milledgeville, 18 Jan. 1861, Cobb Papers, 1861. Cobb to Lamar Cobb, Telegram, Milledgeville, 19 Jan. 1861, Ibid. John S. Bowman, ed., *The Civil War Almanac*, New York: Gallery Books, 1983, p. 43, hereafter cited as Bowman, *Civil War Almanac*. Butler, *Historical Record*, 243.

[45] Ibid., 240.

[46] *Macon Daily Telegraph*, 21 Jan. 1861.

[47] *Georgia Journal and Messenger*, 23 Jan. 1861.

[48] *Macon Daily Telegraph*, 19 Jan. 1861.

group of young ladies who planned to sit on a balcony somewhere in Macon to sing a song known as "the Southern Marsellaise," which they had been practicing all week. Included in plans for the celebration was the illumination of houses and a general celebration of great magnitude. She concluded happily, "Hurrah It has come sooner than I expected."[49]

Hermione Rose Walker confided to her diary that "Today the secession ordnance was signed, half-past twelve o'clock. I have been to the greatest popular demonstration ever known in Macon. I got so excited I was half wild and am not sure but I screamed- Joined the noise with the rest."[50]

Plans for Macon's formal observance of Georgia's secession included a parade organized by Judge Clifford Anderson, Chairman of the Committee of Arrangements. Plans called for the procession, led by Captain B.F. Ross, to form at the Court House. The order of march included (1) the Jackson Artillery; (2) the Macon Volunteers; (3) the Macon Guards; (4) the Floyd Rifles; (5) Company A of the Minute Men; (6) Company C of the Minute Men; (7) Company B of the Minute Men; (8) the Macon Fire Department; (9) the Mayor and Aldermen; and (10) the citizens. The parade would begin with the firing of a signal gun at 6:00 P.M. A chorus, organized for the occasion and composed of both men and women, would sing a song when the parade reached Dr. Emerson's house, which was located on Mulberry Street, opposite the Lanier House. The parade route continued up Mulberry to College Street and on to the Academy of the Blind. The route continued through High, Spring, Orange, New, Oak, First, Plum, Fourth, Walnut, and Second Streets back to Mulberry Street where it would end.[51]

The *Daily Telegraph* urged the people to turn out en masse, and do everything possible to make Macon's secession celebration the grandest display ever seen in Georgia's history. "Then," the paper asserted, "with a strong pull,

---

[49] Mary Ann Cobb to her Husband, Macon, 18 Jan. 1861, Cobb Papers, 1861. Also see *Macon Daily Telegraph*, 19 Jan. 1861. The committee of arrangements for the celebration included such Macon leaders as Clifford Anderson, A.G. Butts, Lamar Cobb, J.H. Lamar, L.M. Lamar, F.S. Bloom, W.H. Ross, Henry N. Ells, Richard Freeman, W.W. Parker, J. Kenan, George G. Griffin, and J.W. Adderhold. The song would be sung by a choir of men and women from the balcony of Dr. Emerson's house. See *Macon Daily Telegraph*, 21 Jan. 1861.

[50] Hermione Rose Walker diary, 21 Jan. 1861, Hermione Rose Walker Papers, SHC. However, on the 19th, the day the secession ordinance was actually passed, she wrote "Today is one which will be well remembered by our people. Georgia declared herself out of the union. I am glad and sad. I am angry with myself." Ibid., 19 Jan. 1861.

[51] *Macon Daily Telegraph*, 19 Jan. 1861.

a long pull, and a pull altogether, we'll start on our happy journey in this Southern Land of Canaan."[52]

Some changes in parade arrangements did occur. The event did not start until 8:00 P.M., and moved from the Court House up Mulberry Street to Dr. Emerson's balcony, adjoining Granite Hall, where a choir of thirty young *women* sang a patriotic ode. Their singing was accompanied by cheers by the enthusiastic crowd. The shouts of the excited people sounded through the center of the City. After the song, the parade moved on until it reached the home of Judge James Nisbet where the people expected a speech. Instead of remarks, the Judge furnished the crowd with a bowl of punch which was "about the size of a barrel." After partaking of Nisbet's donation the crowd proceeded along the street where each house was brilliantly illuminated. When the immense throng reached Wesleyan Female College, it halted and responded to the waving of handkerchiefs by the college girls with long, loud cheers. Another halt was made at the Brown House where the people were entertained by appropriate songs sung by an Atlanta theatrical group known as Messrs. Barnes and Wright. The songs were "received with such shouts as only Macon men can give." The *Daily Telegraph* related that during the event "The clamors of party strife were hushed, and we can scarcely hope to see such a universal illumination in our city for many years to come."[53]

Numerous bonfires burned throughout the streets, while rockets and balloons were sent up to the sky. The *Journal and Messenger* called the affair "the most imposing and brilliant pageant we have ever witnessed, and worthy of the inauguration of a young Republic."[54]

Perhaps Conway D. Whittle of Milbank, Virginia, best expressed the feelings of most Southerners toward secession in a letter to his brother Lewis in Macon: "Whether Virginia has or has not what is termed 'the right' to withdraw herself from that Union is not the question. It does not enter into the question so far as the citizen is concerned. It is enough for him she has withdrawn and that act on her part withdraws him."[55]

On 22 January the Jackson Artillery, sixty men with a full battery of four six-pounders and two twelve-pounder howitzers, and a full complement of Minie muskets, received orders to leave for the Georgia coast. At the appointed time on 24 January the company marched to the Georgia Central depot accompanied by

---

[52] Ibid., 21 Jan. 1861.

[53] Ibid., 22 Jan. 1861.

[54] *Georgia Journal and Messenger*, 23 Jan. 1861. John A. Cobb wrote his brother Lamar, "Great excitement here, nearly every house in the city illuminated." John A. Cobb to Lamar Cobb, 21 Jan. 1861, Cobb Papers, 1861.

[55] Conway D. Whittle to Lewis N. Whittle, Milbank, Va., 8 Feb. 1861, Lewis N. Whittle Papers, SHC, hereafter cited as Whittle Papers.

the Macon Volunteers, the Floyd Rifles, and the Macon Guards. Crowds cheered the men as they passed. A reporter for the *Daily Telegraph* related, the enthusiasm "plainly showed the strong hold that the Jackson Artillery has upon the hearts of our citizens, particularly the ladies, many of whom could not refrain from tears. When the Band struck up the 'Girl I left behind me'," the men began their journey to "that soul-inspiring air of 'Dixie's Land', the parting adieus of near friends, and the exulting huzzahs of thousands, being reverberated back from the gas-light dome of the old depot, plainly and to tyrants that there is a people who never say die." As the train left the volunteer escort fired a parting salute to the men.[56]

When the men reached Savannah they were escorted to Gibbon's Hotel by the Chatham Artillery, and then served dinner at the Marshall House. From Savannah, the men took the steamer *St. John* for the trip to their ultimate destination, St. Simons Island.[57]

About the time the company left, a Jackson Artillery Fund was established for the men and their families. The firm of Carhart and Curd contributed $100 to the fund on 24 January followed by a second donation by Jackson Deloache of $50.[58]

After the secession of Georgia, the volunteer companies of Macon took center stage in the life of Macon. By 1 February 1861, the community had raised six companies, with a new organization, the Rutland Guards, joining the already-established units. In fact, so many volunteer companies were organizing that Georgia Assistant Adjutant General William Magill notified Captain Thomas Hardeman of the Floyd Rifles on 2 February, that Governor Brown had limited the number of rifles issued to each company to sixty. Unfortunately, although tents were being manufactured, none were currently on hand.[59]

While the infantry companies needed tents and rifles, the Floyd rifles were looking for two thirty-two-pounder cannon to complete their battery. The unit had left in late January to defend the Georgia coast at St. Simons Island.[60]

---

[56] A.G. Butts to John B. Lamar, Macon, 22 Jan. 1861, Cobb Papers, 1861; *Macon Daily Telegraph*, 25 Jan. 1861. See also *Georgia Journal and Messenger*, 30 Jan. 1861.

[57] *Macon Daily Telegraph*, 29 Jan. 1861 and 28 Jan. 1861.

[58] Ibid. See also Ibid., 28 Jan. 1861.

[59] List of volunteer companies in the state of Georgia, Adjutant Generals Letter Book, 1 Feb. 1861, 22 Dec. 1860-18 Feb. 1861, p. 4, GDA&H, hereafter cited as Adjutant Generals Letter Book with appropriate dates. The state had 158 volunteer companies by 1 February, Ibid. William Magill to Capt. Thomas Hardeman, Milledgeville, 2 Feb. 1861, Ibid., 491.

[60] *Macon Daily Telegraph*, 9 Feb. 1861. *Georgia Journal and* Messenger, 23 Jan. 1861; T.R. Bloom to Howell Cobb, Macon, 13 Feb. 1861, Cobb Papers, 1861.

By mid-February, Maconites organized still another volunteer company, the Gresham Rifles, with forty members. This unit, commanded by Captain M. R. Rogers, included J. H. Pickett as First Lieutenant and W. H. Shaw as Second Lieutenant. Still another organization, the Lewis Volunteers, led by Captain George W. Hardie, a veteran of the Macon Volunteers, was looking for recruits. The *Daily Telegraph* reported Hardie to be "a kindly, high-toned gentleman-of pure moral and religious principles, who, while he will make good soldiers of his corps, will look after their health, comfort and general welfare with scrupulous vigilance." On 15 February 1861, the Gresham Rifles offered their services to Governor Brown.[61]

Military parades were the order of the day, and crowds gathered to watch the men march through the streets. On Washington's Birthday, 22 February, Captain Smith's Macon Volunteers paraded with full ranks, making one of "the finest displays that they have made in years." At 10:00 A.M. the unit went to the Fair Grounds to shoot for a silver cup, with B. Pope Freeman winning the prize. The cup was presented by Private Joel R. Branham, Jr. who made a speech to fit the occasion.[62]

While troops paraded, efforts were underway to recruit even more men. A Military Committee, chaired by B.F. Ross, was organized for the purpose of raising additional units. This group offered to accept the first two companies raised under a proclamation by Governor Brown. First Lieutenant Robert Atkinson of the Georgia Army, a graduate of the Georgia Military Institute, helped by opening a recruiting office in Macon. A public meeting, sponsored by Mayor Methvin S. Thomson, was held at City Hall in mid-February, "to consider of the mode and manner in which the number of men required by the Governor to be furnished by Bibb county shall be raised." At the same time no more six months units would be accepted, reflecting the belief of many in authority that the war which might come at any moment would be protracted.[63]

The war would come sooner for some because another detachment of recruits left Macon on Saturday, 16 February, on the Georgia Central Railroad bound for Savannah.[64]

Men of influence attempted to secure military appointments for their friends and relatives. John B. Lamar and Washington Poe wrote the Governor requesting a commission in the Georgia Army for their friend Charles M. Wiley, formerly a cadet in the Georgia Military Institute and then an officer in one of the

---

[61] *Macon Daily Telegraph*, 15 Feb. 1861.

[62] *Macon Daily Telegraph*, 16, 20, 23 Feb. 1861; 23 Feb. 1861. The Macon Guards, Floyd Rifles, and Bibb County Cavalry also paraded. See also *Georgia Journal and Messenger*, 27 Feb. 1861.

[63] *Macon Daily Telegraph*, 17 Feb. 1861; 25 Feb. 1861; 15 Feb. 1861.

[64] Ibid., 18 Feb. 1861.

Macon volunteer companies.[65] Maconite C. B. Cole wrote Howell Cobb requesting a position for his son George in the Confederate Army.[66] Even Cobb's son, John, urged his father to "use your influence" to secure an appointment for his friend, Lieutenant Robert H. Atkinson.[67]

In March, the number of men volunteering for twelve months became so great that it was difficult to furnish them with muskets and uniforms. A newly-organized company, the Independent Volunteers, needed five or six hundred dollars to purchase uniforms.[68]

During the period before war actually began it was not easy to offer a volunteer company for Confederate service. The experience of Dr. James A. Damour of Macon and his tender of the Independent Volunteers is a case in point. On 2 March Thomas J. Berry, the Acting Assistant Adjutant General of Georgia, wrote Damour, then a lieutenant in Captain J.W. Adderhold's Macon Independent Volunteers and a First Lieutenant in the First Regiment of the Georgia Army, that newly-installed President Jefferson Davis could not accept volunteers except through a call on their respective governors. If Davis made such a call Governor Brown would accept the services of the needed men and offer them to Davis.[69] A few days later Berry informed Damour that no equipment was available, not even knapsacks, to outfit the many volunteers offering their services to the State. However, the men would be equipped by the Confederate Government if Davis called on Brown for their services.[70] Damour wrote Confederate Secretary of War Leroy Pope Walker on 4 March that he had learned the Confederate authorities planned to accept volunteer companies for a period of not less than twelve months. Under these terms, Damour offered the services of the Independent Volunteers to the Confederacy.[71] Assistant Secretary of War S. S. Scott, replied on March 6, informing Damour that the company must secure the consent of the State of Georgia before being accepted by the Confederacy.[72] Scott soon sent another letter to Damour citing part of the first

---

[65] John B. Lamar and Washington Poe to Governor Brown, Macon, 16 Feb. 1861, Box 37, GDA&H.

[66] C.B. Cole to Cobb, Macon, 25 Feb. 1861, Cobb Papers, 1861.

[67] John A. Cobb to his Father, Macon, 28 Feb. 1861.

[68] *Macon Daily* Telegraph, 5 Mar. 1861.

[69] Thomas J. Berry to Dr. James A. Damour, Milledgeville, 2 Mar. 1861, Adjutant Generals Letter Book, II, 18 Feb. 1861-25 Apr. 1861, 92.

[70] Thomas J. Berry to Damour, Milledgeville, 8 Mar. 1861, Ibid., p. 160. See also Damour to Brown, Macon, 8 Mar. 1861, Incoming Correspondence of the Governor.

[71] Damour to Leroy Pope Walker, Macon, 4 Mar. 1861, Letters Received by the Confederate Secretary of War, March-May 1861, Microfilm, Roll 2, p. 712, National Archives and Records Administration (NARA).

[72] S.S. Scott to Damour, Montgomery, 6 Mar. 1861, in Letters Sent by the Confederate Secretary of War, Roll 1, p. 29, NARA.

section of An Act to Provide for the Public Defense. This portion stated: "The President is hereby authorized to employ the militia, military & naval forces of the C.S. & to ask for & accept the services of any number of volunteers not exceeding one hundred thousand, who may offer their services, either as cavalry, mounted riflemen, artillery or infantry, in such proportion of these several arms as he may deem expedient, to serve for twelve months after they shall be mustered into service, unless sooner discharged." Under this act the consent of the state was not needed, but, as of early March 1861, Davis hadn't made the call indicated under this act. However, when he did, Scott explained, the Confederate Government would accept the company's services.[73] Damour replied to these letters on 9 March assuring the Secretary he would ask Governor Brown for permission to offer the company to the Confederacy, but Walker had to order the unit into action.[74]

Scott, acting for Walker, answered Damour on 11 March that the Independent Volunteers should offer their services to Brown so the unit could be part of the complement of 2,000 troops which the Confederate War Department had recently made on Georgia.[75] Damour thanked Secretary Walker for his answer, and added, "The cause which they have espoused will never have cause to blush when the history of Southern Independence is being perused."[76] Desirous of entering the army as an officer, Damour replied to Scott's 11 March letter on the 17th that he would join the Confederate Army for the term of three years even if the Independent Volunteers were not accepted by Brown, and listed Howell Cobb, Thomas R. R. Cobb, Eugenius A. Nisbet, and A. H. Kenan as references. Damour's efforts were finally successful when, on 18 March Georgia Adjutant General Henry C. Wayne, wrote Adderhold accepting the Independent Volunteers for the War.[77] Finally, assured of a Confederate commission, Damour resigned as a candidate for an officer's slot in the Independent Volunteers.[78]

---

[73] S.S. Scott to Damour, Montgomery, 7 Mar. 1861, Ibid., p. 32.

[74] Damour to Walker, Macon, 9 Mar. 1861, in Letters Received by the Confederate Secretary of War, March-May 1861, Microfilm, Roll 2, p. 720.

[75] Scott to Damour, Montgomery, 11 Mar. 1861, Letters sent by the Confederate Secretary of War, Microfilm, Roll 1, p. 45, NARA.

[76] Damour to Walker, Macon, 15 Mar. 1861, C.S. Sec. of War, Ltrs. Recd., Roll 1, p. 72.

[77] Damour to Walker, Macon, 17 Mar. 1861, in Confederate Secretary of War, Letters Received., Roll 1, p. 88. See also J.J. Hooper, Private Secretary to Walker, Montgomery, 22 Mar. 1861, Confederate Secretary of War, Letters Sent, Roll 1, p. 63. Henry C. Wayne to Adderhold, Milledgeville, 18 Mar. 1861, Adjutant Generals Letter Book, II, p. 314. Once the unit was officially accepted by the State it would soon be transferred to the Confederacy.

[78] *Macon Daily Telegraph*, 26 Mar. 1861.

Some were more fortunate than the untrained Damour in securing military appointments. As early as 30 January John McIntosh Kell was appointed a lieutenant in the naval service of Georgia by Adjutant General Wayne. The appointment provided Kell with the same pay and allowances he had received as a lieutenant in the US Navy.[79]

Wayne commissioned another prominent Maconite, Leroy Napier, Jr., a graduate of the US Military Academy at West Point, to the captaincy of the Bibb County Cavalry on 23 March.[80]

Even Howell Cobb, anxious to fight if a war should come, wrote his wife from Montgomery, where he served as President of the newly-organized Confederate Senate, "Tell the Col [John B. Lamar] & the boys that the Georgia regiment for Pensacola has been ordered to Macon to organize- and that I would give freely five hundred dollars to beat Jim Ramsey for Col."[81]

A.M. Rowland of the Jackson Artillery was more fortunate than Cobb in securing an immediate commission with the Confederate Army. Rowland was commissioned as a First Lieutenant, and his fellow-Maconite, Campbell Tracy, was commissioned as Second Lieutenant.[82]

Even as Damour tried to secure Confederate acceptance of the Independent Volunteers, the *Daily Telegraph* asserted that the unit had already been accepted by the Confederacy, but needed money to purchase uniforms. The paper also queried: "Cannot the ladies of Macon present this gallant corps with an appropriate flag? What say they?"[83]

Flags were, of course, very important to Civil War units, as well as to outfits in all American Wars. The quality of the flag was also very significant. Writing to his Uncle John on 13 March John A. Cobb asked him to buy a flag for the Macon Volunteers. Possibly Lamar would give the citizens of Macon "a sample of his eloquence, by making a speech in presenting it." When Lamar ordered a flag for the Macon Volunteers, John A. Cobb wanted to know if the emblem was made of silk, pointing out that "Flags for that purpose are generally made of silk." After young Cobb told several members of the company about the flag they expressed pleasure to learn that they would soon get one

---

[79] John McIntosh Kell to his Mother, Macon, 30 Jan. 1861, Kell Letters, Duke University.

[80] Wayne to Leroy Napier, Jr., Milledgeville, 23 Mar. 1861, Adjutant Generals Letter Book, Feb. 18, 1861-Apr. 25, 1861, p. 369; *Macon Daily* Telegraph, 18 Mar. 1861.

[81] Cobb to his Wife, Montgomery, 28 Mar. 1861, Cobb Papers, 1861.

[82] *Macon Daily Telegraph*, 25 Mar. 1861.

[83] *Macon Daily Telegraph*, 11 Mar. 1861.

because they had been waiting a long time for such an emblem.[84] Lamar replied he had an artist working on a design. On one side was a wreath of the cotton plant in the center of which was the inscription "Macon Volunteers April 23, 1825." On the reverse was the coat of arms of Georgia, the triple columns, with a Confederate flag on each side partially opened. Over the arch were seven stars, and at the base, the date 19 January 1861, when Georgia seceded. The silk was a deep blue with a fringe. Including a mahogany staff and a brass spear head the cost was $65, a large sum for the time.[85] Plans called for the flag to be presented by one of John A. Cobb's sisters on 23 April the anniversary of the company's organization in 1825.[86]

Two Macon tailors, Mr. Kennedy on Cherry Street, and Mr. Peters, on Mulberry Street, offered to make uniforms for the Independent Volunteers and Nathan C. Munroe, Jr. gave $50 to aid families of members of the Jackson Artillery who needed assistance. On 19 March Joseph Clisby of *The Daily Telegraph* appealed for money to help the families of the Jackson Artillery.[87]

While these efforts were underway, the men prepared to go to fight a war which many in Macon thought was inevitable. The Floyd Rifles, the Macon Volunteers, and Brown's Infantry continued to drill.[88] Mary Ann Cobb wrote her husband as a proud mother would, "The drum & fife are sounding....It is the parade afternoon of the 'Macon Volunteers'[.] John & Lamar paraded themselves before me 'armed cap a pied' in their undress uniform- far more comfortable looking then their full dress uniform." Her small daughter, Sarah, was concerned that "The soldiers will all get wet." The mother added: "What a comfortable idea she has of soldiering."[89]

Maconites contributed to the Confederate war effort in other ways. The city quickly became a rendezvous for troops from different parts of the State. In late March, Governor Brown ordered a number of volunteer companies to meet at Macon on 2 April. The Governor wanted Isaac Scott, President of the Macon and Western Railroad, to make arrangements so that the expense of their trip might be paid in one lump sum from the State Treasury. The Governor expected Scott to offer a reduced rate for their train fare because the troops were "to enter

---

[84] John A. Cobb to John B. Lamar, Macon, 13 Mar. 1861, 16 Mar. 1861, Cobb Papers, 1861.

[85] Lamar to John A. Cobb, Savannah, 19 Mar. 1861, Ibid.

[86] Lamar to John A. Cobb, Savannah, 20 Mar. 1861, Ibid. For a detailed description of the flag see Ibid.

[87] *Macon Daily Telegraph*, 21 Mar. 1861; 20 Mar. 1861; 19 Mar. 1861.

[88] Ibid., 9, 23, and 29 Mar. 1861.

[89] Mary Ann Cobb to her Husband, Macon, 29 Mar. 1861, Cobb-Erwin-Lamar Collection.

the active service of our common country."[90] Also in late March, Brown ordered Brown's Infantry and the Independent Volunteers to prepare to go to Pensacola to help defend that city.[91]

While the drilling of companies, the rendezvousing of troops, the presentation of flags, and the commissioning of officers continued, the business community in Macon was offering books, weapons, and other items to the now thoroughly combative people of Macon. In early January 1861, the Methodist Bookstore offered a *Confederate States Almanac*, a pamphlet of 176 pages, including, besides the usual calendar, all the facts associated with the history, government and resources of the Confederate States. Boardman's Bookstore, not to be outdone by one of its rivals, advertised a new supply of such military books as *Hardee's Tactics, Scott's Tactics, Cooper's Tactics, Cavalry Tactics,* and *Mahone's Treatise on Field Fortifications.*[92] Still another bookstore, J. J. & S. P. Richards, on Cotton Avenue, sold Colonel Henry Wager Halleck's monumental *Elements of Military Art and Science; or Course of Instruction in Strategy, Fortification, Tactics of Battles, &c., Embracing the Duties of Staff, Infantry, Cavalry, Artillery and Engineers, Adapted to the use of Volunteers and Militia,* published in New York by D. Appleton and Company.[93]

The firm of Schofield and Brother, which usually manufactured steam engines, circular saw mills, mill and gin gearing, sugar mills, brass and iron castings of all kinds, gas and water pipes, iron fronts for buildings, iron planers, lathes of all sizes, and all kinds of machinist's tools, now began to manufacture shot and shell. These included ammunition for guns ranging in size from ten-inch rifled cannon to six-pounders. If workmen could be found, the firm had the capability of turning out fifty tons of ammunition a month. The partners were building a thirty by sixty foot one-story brick blacksmith shop, "and cannot fail of success."[94]

Master machinist for the South Western Railroad, T. B. E. Elfe, made a beautiful scabbard of black walnut for a cavalry sword, which promised "to be an excellent substitute for steel."[95] Swords were manufactured by D. C. Hodgkins and Son of Macon, who had a small supply of the 1850 pattern sabers used by the US Cavalry. In a letter concerning swords to foundry man Christopher D. Findlay of Macon, Adjutant General Wayne noted, "It does not make much

---

[90] Brown to Isaac Scott, Milledgeville, 29 Mar. 1861, Governor's Letter Book Jan. 1, 1847-Apr. 23, 1861, p. 804. See also *Macon Daily Telegraph*, 30 Mar. 1861.

[91] *Macon Daily Telegraph*, 28 Mar. 1861.

[92] Ibid., 11 Feb. 1861.

[93] Ibid., 26 Feb. 1861.

[94] Ibid., 15 Feb. 1861.

[95] Ibid., 15 Feb. 1861. Walnut is a hard wood which is often used for gunstocks and cabinet work.

difference what sword you have, as officers in battle are rarely even given an occasion to use them. If there is reason to apprehend much annoyance from cavalry a strong weapon, to resist saber cuts, is necessary." Wayne assured Findlay that "If only the bayonet is to be met, a light straight sword is sufficient. The matter however does not lie in the weapon but in knowing how to use it and skill in handling it."[96] The importance of music to military unit was not ignored. John C. Schreiner and Sons advertised such martial musical instruments as drums and fifes.[97]

The merchants of Macon, concerned about the future of their city in the new nation and worried about what the coming of war might do to their businesses, met in late February to discuss the commercial future of their "cherished" city. Macon possessed, in terms of locality, health, wealth, and intelligence, superior advantages as a great commercial center of the new Southern Confederacy. The meeting could see no reason why her trade and population could not double in five years, "unless we should have war-which Heaven forbid!"[98]

Unfortunately, Heaven would not oblige the merchants in averting war.

---

[96] Henry C. Wayne to Christopher D. Findlay, Milledgeville, 25 Feb. 1861, Adjutant Generals Letter Book, 25 Feb. 1861; 18 Feb. 1861–25 Apr. 1861, p. 34.

[97] Ibid., 30 Mar. 1861.

[98] *Georgia Journal and Messenger*, 20 Feb. 1861.

Chapter 4

And the War Came:
Military Preparations Continue

With the advent of April 1861, the tempo of patriotic feeling in Macon expressed itself even more strongly than earlier in the year. Doctor Griggs, a Macon physician, offered his services free of charge to the families of men who left for military duty. Master Machinist Elfe announced that men who quit the employ of the Southwestern Railroad to go to the defense of Georgia would have preference in employment when they returned.[1]

As April 2, the date for the rendezvous of military companies from around the State in Macon, drew near, the possibility of war became more apparent. On the night of April 1, the volunteers poured into Macon on all of the railroads which served the City. The eighty members of the Quitman Guards of Forsyth were greeted by Captain Adderhold and a detachment of his company who escorted them to their quarters. Other units, the Newnan Guards of Newnan, the Southern Guards of Columbus, the Etowah Infantry from Etowah, the Southern Independents of Bainbridge, the Ringgold Infantry who hailed from Ringgold, Atlanta's Gate City Guards, Perry's Southern Rights Guard, the Walker Light Infantry and the Oglethorpe Light Infantry, both from Augusta, joined such Macon units as the Floyd Rifles and the Macon Volunteers in camp.[2]

Mary Ann Cobb told her husband, still in Montgomery, that Macon was full of military companies, and the election for company officers was in full swing. No friend to Governor Brown, she related that the Governor and Adjutant General Wayne were also in Macon. The Governor had caused some dissatisfaction among the soldiers by not having furnished quarters and provisions for them before they arrived, forcing Georgia officials to buy food on a daily basis until supplies ordered from Savannah could arrive. Another cause for discontent was Brown's rule of allowing the officers only to vote for the candidates for company office, while not extending the same privilege to the men.

---

[1] *Macon Daily Telegraph*, 1 Apr. 1861.

[2] Ibid., 2 Apr. 1861.

Electioneering was especially intent for the Georgia Regiment. Lieutenant Ramsay, an officer in one of the volunteer companies, seemed to have the edge over the other candidates. Governor Brown, who stayed at the Lanier House, was greeted by the firing of muskets, and entertained with a band which serenaded him in front of the hotel. Plans called for Brown to review the troops on the afternoon of 3 April. The parade was held on 4 April because of a delay caused by the election of Ramsay as colonel of the Georgia Regiment. The morning of the fourth was cloudy and showery, which threatened to cause many people to stay at home instead of coming to watch the review.[3]

While in camp, two of the Macon units, the Brown Infantry and the Independent Volunteers, were organized as a battalion by order of Adjutant General Wayne.[4] A committee of Macon citizens supported the volunteer companies by serving them a daily lunch of hams, beef tongues, and other items.[5]

On 5 April the Brown Infantry of Macon and the Walker Light Infantry of Augusta struck their tents for the trip to Pensacola where they were going to guard that important point. They marched to the depot escorted by the Oglethorpe Light Infantry and the Independent Volunteers. At the depot Captain Smith of the Brown Infantry drew his men up in front of the Brown House for a flag presentation and a patriotic speech by Captain Thomas Hardeman, Jr. The banner was sewn by Mrs. C. Rogers of Macon. When the time for departure drew near Captain Smith made a brief speech, and, after receiving the flag, marched his men to the cars. The scene was filled with sorrow because suddenly mothers, sisters, and friends realized that they would part with their friends and loved ones. War was coming closer to being a reality to the people of Macon.[6] The next days were filled with departures, preparations for flag presentations, and tenders of service to the State.[7]

The prelude to war ended when Confederate troops stationed in and around the city of Charleston, fired on Major Robert Anderson and his men in Fort Sumter early in the morning of 12 April. The fort capitulated to Confederate forces on the following day. On 15 April President Abraham Lincoln issued a call for 75,000 troops to crush the young Confederacy.[8] The war had begun. The

---

[3] Mary Ann Cobb to her Husband, 3, 4 Apr. 1861, Cobb Papers, 1861.

[4] Henry C. Wayne, General Orders No. 2, Adjutant General's Office General Orders, Book 1, p. 14, GDA&H, hereafter cited as Adjutant Generals Order Book.

[5] *Macon Daily Telegraph,* 4 Apr. 1861.

[6] Ibid., 6 Apr. 1861.

[7] Ibid., 8, 9 Apr. 1861; Mary Ann Cobb to Howell Cobb, Jr., Macon, 9 Apr. 1861, Cobb Papers, 1861; Henry C. Wayne, General Orders No. 5, 10 Apr. 1861, Adjutant Generals Order Book, No. 1, pp. 16-17; Lucius M. Lamar to Governor Brown, Macon, 11 Apr. 1861, Brown, Incoming Correspondence of the Governor, Box 37.

[8] Bowman, ed., *Civil War Almanac,* 50-51.

attack was celebrated in Macon by a detachment of the Jackson Artillery, commanded by Lieutenant Boifeuillet, which fired a salute of seven guns on the evening of 12 April.[9]

Some Maconites, however, were more thoughtful. Macon businessman Nathan C. Munroe, Jr. wrote his daughter that Lincoln and his administration were just posturing. Munroe believed that the call the President made "for troops in Virginia[,] Kentucky and Tennessee [would] result in their secession very soon carrying with them all the slave holding states" Munroe believed that the Confederacy would then be so powerful that the Congress which Lincoln had called to meet on 4 July 1861, would be "more ready to advise peace than to urge war measures."[10] A week later Munroe wrote that the excitement in Macon was tremendous, including the military preparations and the departure of soldiers, with constant news coming from Charleston. This filled "the public mind with an anxiety which is painfully exciting." The elderly businessman noted the enthusiasm "which pervades the public mind- & with what eagerness the young and even men of more mature manhood rush to the Battlefield." He also pointed out that six companies had been raised in Macon with a total of about 500 men. This departure had made an impact upon the community, "and made it necessary to organize a new company for home protection from the middle aged & old men- it is called the Silver Greys." Munroe believed there would soon be a great battle, probably in the vicinity of Washington, in which, he felt, "we shall be Victorious." But he also felt the battle would be bloody "and many will fall a sacrifice on the alter of patriotism to sustain the just cause of our beloved country."[11]

Indeed, the martial spirit in Macon was very great during the spring of 1861. When the Macon Guards called for further volunteers at an enthusiastic meeting held on 12 April fifty-seven men enlisted.[12]

The following days were filled with the return of troops and their departure for areas where, the Confederate Government believed, there would soon be action. On the morning of 15 April the main body of the Jackson Artillery returned to Macon from their duty at St. Simons Island for a week's leave. They were welcomed by Captain Hardeman, ate breakfast at the Brown House, and were escorted to their armory by the Macon Volunteers and the Floyd Rifles.[13]

Other units were called away. Captain Lucius Lamar's Macon Guard, with seventy men, left on the evening of 16 April for duty at Tybee Island near

[9] *Macon Daily Telegraph*, 13 Apr. 1861.

[10] Nathan C. Munroe to Bannie Kell, Macon, 16 Apr. 1861, Kell Letters, DU.

[11] Same to same, Macon, 23 Apr. 1861, Ibid.

[12] *Macon Daily Telegraph*, 13 Apr. 1861.

[13] *Georgia Journal and Messenger,* 17 Apr. 1861; Nathan C. Munroe to his daughter, Macon, 16 Apr. 1861, Kell Letters.

Savannah.[14] On 18 April Governor Brown ordered the Macon Volunteers and the Floyd Rifles to leave for Norfolk, Virginia. Clifford Anderson, judge and fire eater who had organized some of the Macon celebrations connected with the secession of Georgia, and was a member of the Floyd Rifles, left with them. Robert S. Lanier, father of the future Georgia poet and musician Sidney Lanier, law partner and brother-in-law of Anderson, was an honorary member of the Macon Volunteers. He confided to his brother William, "[I] regret I cannot go with them." Lanier observed that the war movement "is assuming gigantic proportions," but he hoped it would not get beyond all control, and that the matter [the dispute between the North and the South] "may yet soon be settled."[15]

When the Macon Volunteers left they received the flag purchased in Savannah by John B. Lamar. Mary Ann Lamar Cobb, daughter of Howell and Mary Ann Cobb, presented the banner through her brother Lamar, a member of the unit, in front of the Lanier House. Lamar Cobb made "a beautiful address," followed by a brief speech by Captain Robert Smith. Ensign Isaac waved the flag over the heads of the company, and "invoked their aid in its defense on the battle field." The two units, 66 men in the Volunteers and eighty men in the Floyd Rifles, went home to say good-bye to their families, and went to the depot late in the evening, escorted by the Bibb Cavalry, dismounted for the occasion, and the Jackson Artillery, with a band. A crowd of 2,000 people marched with them. The occasion was a solemn one since hardly a word was spoken. "All hearts were full," a reporter for the *Daily Telegraph* commented, and the press of 5,000 people to see them off was immense. When the long train left the station it bore away "the hope and pride of so many sad and fond hearts left behind."[16]

Commenting on Macon's contributions to the Confederate war effort by the third week in April, the *Daily Telegraph's* reporter boasted, "Macon has done nobly. Enough of our fighting population are away for a time." The Bibb County Cavalry, not yet called by the Governor, planned to go into service as a mounted patrol immediately, presumably in the vicinity of Macon, until they received a permanent assignment.

---

[14] Nathan C. Munroe, Jr., to Bonnie Kell, Macon, 16 Apr. 1861, Kell Letters; *Macon Daily Telegraph*, 17 Apr. 1861.

[15] Robert S. Lanier to William Lanier, Macon, 19 Apr. 1861, Cobb Papers, 1861. See also *Macon Daily Telegraph*, 20 Apr. 1861, and Lamar Cobb to John A. Cobb, Macon, 19 Apr. 1861, Cobb Papers, 1861.

[16] *Macon Daily Telegraph*, 22 Apr. 1861. The 85 men of the Columbus Light Guards left for Virginia on the same train. Ibid. For reaction by the Volunteers to the flag presentation see Robert S. Lanier, R. Atkinson, and Jackson Barnes to John B. Lamar, Macon, 26 Apr. 1861, Cobb Papers, 1861.

The Macon Volunteers, the Floyd Rifles, the Columbus Light Guards, and the Spalding Grays were the first four companies sent from Georgia to Virginia.[17] Other units passed through Macon during the following days, and other companies were raised in Macon.[18]

All of these volunteers prompted a movement to supply them with many items which the Government did not provide. There was also concern over the condition of the loved ones they left behind. In late April, Captain Hardeman reported that $2,000 was subscribed for the Floyd Rifles, and $600 for their families. Captain Smith noted that about $1,600 was raised for his men.[19] The committee headed by Mayor Thomson advertised for contributions to help support soldier's families.[20] On 27 April the women of Macon organized the Ladies Soldiers Relief Society with Mrs. Washington Poe as President; Mrs. Thomas Hardeman, Jr. as Vice President; Miss Julia Wrigley as Secretary; and Miss M.E. Bass as Secretary. The purpose of the organization was "To make clothing and such other necessary articles as may be needful for the soldiers who have been or may be called into the service of the country." Although a small number of ladies met initially, a much larger gathering soon met at the armory hall of the Macon Volunteers.[21]

By early May the work of the Society began to bear fruit. The women quickly received financial contributions from various groups in the City, and promised to furnish each of Macon's soldiers stationed at Pensacola, Florida, with a cap, shirt, pair of pants, and shoes. Their first objective was to outfit Captain John B. Cumming's Sparks Rifles, and then supply other Macon soldiers posted in the West Florida city.[22]

Prospective contributors were urged to make their donations through Mrs. Miriam Dessau at her dress shop on Mulberry Street between 8:00 and 9:00 A.M. each working day. Those ladies who sent for work were required to send a written order, or the work could not be delivered. By 7 May the Society had procured a new home, the Concert Hall.[23]

By early July the organization had 250 members, although only eighty of them were active. The ladies began to knit socks, caps, pants, and under

---

[17] Governor Brown to Captains Thomas Hardeman, Jr., Robert A. Smith, *et als.*, Milledgeville, 23 Apr. 1861, GLB, 1847-1861, p. 1.

[18] Eugenius A. Nisbet to Governor Brown, Macon, 24 Apr. 1861, Brown, Incoming Correspondence of the Governor, Box 41; *Macon Daily Telegraph*, 22, 23, 26, 30, 1861; *Georgia Journal and Messenger*, 1, 2 May 1861.

[19] *Georgia Journal and Messenger*, 24 Apr. 1861.

[20] *Macon Daily Telegraph*, 30 Apr. 1861.

[21] Ibid.; Ibid., 6 July 1861.

[22] Ibid., 1, 2 May 1861.

[23] Ibid., 7 May 1861.

garments "sufficient in number for our every brother in arms from this county."[24] By 9 July the Society made 78 coats, 306 pants, 576 shirts, 431 drawers, 110 havelocks, 248 towels, 226 handkerchiefs, in all 1,975 articles. They began sending clothing to the Floyd Rifles at Norfolk; Brown's Infantry and the Independent Volunteers at Pensacola; and to the Macon Guards, Central City Blues, Macon Volunteers, and the Sparks Guards. The group was also preparing sheets, pillow cases, gowns, towels, bandages, lint, and lemons, pot wines, and jellies for the Macon companies.[25]

John A. Cobb wrote his uncle from the camp of the 29th Battalion, Georgia Volunteers near Sewell's Point, Virginia, "The Ladies Relief Society sent us on some handkerchiefs, & towels which were very acceptable for we were about running out of them."[26]

Some of the funds used by the Society in its work came from raffling such items as a watch at the jewelry store of E.J. Johnston and Company, and receiving funds from concerts held for the benefit of the Society.[27] The Society's account book for 1861-1863 is filled with money paid to purchase and ship items for the soldiers. On 19 July 1861, Miss Wrigley paid $162.49 for 295 1/4 yards of cashmere for making soldiers items.[28] On 24 July the group bought flannel from M. Landauer and Brother of Macon for $238.[29] The Society purchased flannels, buttons, socks, caps, kerseys, jeans, rice, hospital supplies, sheeting, cutting patterns, thread, osnaburgs, and many other items. Some of the expenditures involved paying for the packing of boxes of clothing, postage, and drayage.[30]

Other sources supported Macon's volunteers. One of the most important was Macon's City Council. On 25 September 1860, the Jackson Artillery petitioned the Council to establish an armory in the newly-completed City Hall.[31] When State authorities ordered the Jackson Artillery to St. Simons Island, the Council voted to continue paying the salaries of Chief Marshal John B. Cumming and

[24] *Macon Daily Telegraph*, 6 July 1861.

[25] Ibid., 9 Jul. 1861.

[26] John A. Cobb to John B. Lamar, Camp near Sewell's Point, Va., 10 Jul. 1861, Cobb Papers, 1861.

[27] *Macon Daily Telegraph*, 1, 3 June 1861.

[28] J. Rhodes Browne to Miss Julia Wrigley, Receipt, Macon, 19 July 1861, Ladies Aid Society Account Book 1, Southern Womens Collection, Eleanor Brockenbrough Library, The Museum of the Confederacy, Richmond, Va., hereafter cited as Account Book 1.

[29] M. Landauer and Brother to...., Macon, 24 Jul. 1861, Ibid.

[30] Examination of the Ladies Aid Society Account Book 1 by the author. Account Book 2 continues the record of the work of the Ladies Soldiers Relief Society almost to the end of the war.

[31] Council Minutes, 25 Sept. 1860, Book D, 1854-1862, p. 409.

policemen Kent and Arnold, all members of the unit, to their families during their absence.[32] As if in repayment for this generous action, the company commander, Captain George A. Dure, offered his men for the protection of Macon in May 1861, "So long as we are not under orders from Governor Brown."[33] Over a year later, on 16 May 1862, the Council authorized Mayor Thomson to loan the City cannon to the unit.[34]

The Council appropriated funds to pay for uniforms and other essential equipment. Even before Georgia seceded, on 8 January 1861, Alderman John S. Jones moved to appropriate $300, later increased to $400, to help buy serviceable uniforms for the military companies in Macon.[35] Later in January, and again on 5 February 1861, the Council refused to appropriate funds to buy uniforms for another company, the Minute Men, because war had not yet begun. The matter was instead referred back to the Finance Committee.[36] However, after war broke out, the aldermen gave $1,000 to the Macon Volunteers and Floyd Rifles, when they were ordered to the front. Mayor Ovid G. Sparks also appointed a committee of four Council members and four citizens to raise funds to aid soldiers' families. A few weeks later, on 14 May the Council raised $300 to buy medicines for members of three other companies: the Macon Guards, Independent Volunteers, and Brown Infantry.[37]

As the War continued and victory continued to elude the Confederacy, the Council continued to raise money for the troops.[38] On 18 June a town meeting decided to appoint a committee of five to supervise the preparation of clothing for the volunteers.[39] The members of this committee were William T. Massey, E. J. Johnson, J. M. Jones, A. G. Bostick, and E. C. Grier.[40] After the Bibb County Inferior Court voted to levy a special tax , not to exceed $15,000, to support the soldiers and their families, the Council agreed to go along with the idea. On 23 July City notes for $15,000 were issued to buy supplies for the soldiers, especially those who had suffered as a result of the Battle of Manassas.[41] Mayor Sparks received Council's authorization to borrow $2,300 on August 6,

---

[32] Ibid., 22 Jan. 1861, p. 442.

[33] Ibid., 14 May 1861, pp. 470-471.

[34] Ibid., 16 May 1862, p. 564.

[35] Ibid., 8 Jan. 1861, p. 440.

[36] Ibid., 29 Jan. and 5 Feb. 1861, pp. 443-444. The Council based its refusal on the supposition that the money had not yet "been called for" by the companies. See Ibid., 5 Feb. 1861, p. 444.

[37] Ibid., 20 April 1861, p. 465; Ibid., 14 May 1861, p. 470.

[38] Ibid., 28 May, 18 and 25 June 1861, pp. 476, 479-481.

[39] Ibid., 18 June 1861, p. 481.

[40] *Macon Daily Telegraph*, 29 June 1861.

[41] Council Minutes, 3 and 23 July 1861, pp. 483, 487-488. See also *Georgia Journal and Messenger*, 26 June 1861.

to help soldiers' families left destitute, "and which has been used by the city for other than the purpose contemplated."[42]

In August 1861 a committee went to the Manassas Battlefield in Virginia, for the purpose of providing funds and supplies to the Macon troops who had fought and suffered there. During the trip the members gave $20 to the Macon Guards, but expended $448 in traveling expenses.[43]

Wealthy individuals also raised money for uniforms and equipment. Foremost among these was the wealthy planter-politician and Howell Cobb's brother-in-law, John B. Lamar. A reporter for the *Daily Telegraph* announced on June 1, that Lamar was getting up complete uniforms for the Macon Volunteers in which two of his nephews, John A. and Lamar Cobb served.[44] The men were measured for their new clothing on June 6.[45] When the uniforms arrived in early July, the company passed a resolution thanking Lamar "for his most acceptable and serviceable present of a uniform presented to each member of the corps."[46] The resolution was sent to Lamar by Alex M. Speer the Secretary of the Volunteers on 6 July with the hope of the men that "you may be long spared in honor & health to bless our common country."[47]

When Lamar learned that Howell Cobb, busy raising the Sixteenth Georgia Infantry Regiment, wanted a sword made, and a uniform, Lamar obliged. The wealthy Maconite also contacted the Macon firm of Claghorn and Smith about manufacturing cartridge boxes for Cobb's Regiment. The firm had 1,000 on hand, but had promised them to someone in Savannah. Claghorn and Smith charged $4.50 to manufacture each cartridge box, with a belt and a bayonet sheath. Cobb also needed $1,000 to outfit his regiment, and additional money to buy two horses for himself. .[48]

As the spring of 1861 gave way to a tense summer, troops continued to pass through Macon bound for the theaters of war. In early July the Quitman Grays of Quitman County, Georgia, the Houston Volunteers from Perry, and the Lee Volunteers of Starkville, all passed through the city. The eighty-seven

---

[42] Council Minutes, 6 Aug. 1861, p. 489.

[43] Ibid., 27 Aug. 1861, p. 493.

[44] *Macon Daily Telegraph*, 1 June 1861.

[45] John A. Cobb to his mother, Camp Lee near Norfolk, Va., 6 June 1861, Cobb Papers, 1861.

[46] *Georgia Journal and Messenger*, 17 July 1861.

[47] Alex M. Speer to Lamar, Sewells Point, Va., 6 July 1861, Cobb Papers, 1861.

[48] Lamar to Cobb, Macon, 30 June 1861, Ibid. See also Cobb to Lamar,..., 30 June 1861, Ibid. Lamar to Cobb, Macon, 2 July 1861, Ibid. Cobb to Lamar, . . . , 30 June 1861, Ibid.

members of the Ramah Guards, organized at Ramah Church, near Gordon in Wilkinson County, followed them on 14 July.[49]

There were also parades, whenever the men had time to participate in one. A new unit, the Volunteer Cadets, composed of the youth of the City, paraded on 17 July. One of Macon's favorite units, the Jackson Artillery, marched with only thirty members on the evening of 18 July. On the following evening the Macon Guards (Reserve), composed of older men who planned to stay and defend the city, if necessary, paraded.[50]

The Battle of Manassas, fought on 21 July 1861, was the first large-scale engagement of the war. Fought near Manassas Junction, Virginia, the fight had a profound effect upon the people of Macon. Although it was a Confederate victory, the Southern losses were fearful, amounting to 387 killed, 1582 wounded, and thirteen missing.[51] It was the first time in the war that any of Macon's men were killed or wounded in battle. It was, in short, the time when war became not merely parades, artillery salvos, and posturing, but the real thing. It brought reality to the people that the war would not be a bloodless affair with a quick victory in sight for the South. The news of the battle was slow in getting to Macon. However, the interest of the people was so great that a dense crowd gathered before the Telegraph Office, and patiently waited. The *Daily Telegraph* office was also crowded with people eager for news. On 22 July a large crowd gathered in front of the Telegraph Office. During the following day, the excitement increased, with the streets filled with people concerned about the safety and condition of the Macon Guards, a unit which had seen much fighting in the battle. Leonidas Lamar, the son of Judge Henry Lamar of Macon, was among the dead. Altogether, six members of the Guards were killed and fourteen wounded.[52]

Writing to his nephew John on 25 July John B. Lamar observed "As grievous as this news was [the casualties suffered by the Macon Guards] it was a relief to the community in their awful suspense. The people of Macon take a deep interest in the welfare of her volunteers. It is manifested in every way & every day." The women showed this concern by making winter clothing for all of Macon's soldiers. Therefore, the action of the people when they thought the Guards had suffered heavy losses at Manassas showed a feeling that make Lamar

---

[49] *Macon Daily Telegraph*, 2 July 1861; 15 Jul. 1861.

[50] Ibid., 18 Jul. 1861; 19 Jul. 1861; 20 Jul. 1861.

[51] Bowman, *Civil War Almanac*, p. 60.

[52] *Macon Daily Telegraph*, 24 Jul. 1861; 25 Jul. 1861; 13 Aug. 1861; Lillian S. Henderson, comp., *Roster of the Confederate Soldiers of Georgia, 1861-1865*, in six volumes (Georgia: Longino and Porter, 1959-1964) 935-941.

"think well of human nature." Everybody was eager to go to the field or do anything in their power to help the wounded.[53]

When news of the losses suffered by the Macon Guards arrived in Macon, a committee was appointed to go to Manassas to administer to the wounded. This committee included Mayor Thomson, Captain B.F. Ross, L.C. Plant, Captain George A. Dure, and Ovid G. Sparks. A number of others, John B. Ross, Henry N. Ells, Dr. E.L. Strohecker, Dr. J. Dickson Smith, Dr. L.F.W. Andrews, John T. Brown, John C. Butler, and Jerry Cowles, offered to go as doctors and nurses. The Soldiers Relief Society sent boxes of carded lint, cotton and bandages with the Committee.[54] The ladies also procured a new supply for shoes for the Guards, and worked to provide them with new uniforms.[55] The Soldiers Relief Society quickly appealed for money from the ladies of Macon to help the wounded.[56]

When the committee returned to Macon, Dr. J. Dickson Smith reported the wounded were all under good medical treatment. Many of them were housed at private homes in the vicinity of the battlefield, and were given every comfort. The committee also visited the Sparks Guards, and found them in good health. They also visited Major Thomas Hardeman's Battalion, finding them in good health, and anxious to fight again. Smith reported, "Upon the whole our Macon boys are nobly doing their duty and are highly worthy [of] all the confidence we may repose in them."[57]

Another side of war was revealed to many Maconites when some of them received trophies from the battlefield. Henry N. Ells returned from his trip with the Committee with a Fire Zouave's cap which had a bullet hole in it "just above the visor." He also brought the spear head of a flag staff, a number of letters and envelopes taken from Federal dead, a cartridge box, fragments of conical shells, and flattened musket balls of all kinds. One Maconite, T.R. Bloom, obtained an artillery sword captured from a private in Colonel William T. Sherman's Brigade. Some received buttons cut off the coats of the Zouaves; and such bizarre trophies as a memento of the New York Fire Zouaves in the form of "part of the moustaches and side whiskers taken from one of them, whom he captured during the fight."[58]

---

[53] Lamar to John A. Cobb, Macon, 25 Jul. 1861, Cobb Papers, 1861. For another article concerning supplies for the Macon Guards see the *Macon Daily Telegraph*, 16 Aug. 1861.

[54] Ibid., 24 Jul. 1861. See also Council Minutes, 27 Aug. 1861, p. 493.

[55] *Macon Daily Telegraph*, 2 Aug. 1861.

[56] Ibid., 25 July 1861.

[57] Ibid., 13 Aug. 1861. A long article on the wounded of the Macon Guards appeared in the *Macon Daily Telegraph* on 6 Aug. 1861.

[58] *Macon Daily Telegraph*, 5 Aug. 1861; 16 Aug. 1861; 3 Aug. 1861.

On a more patriotic note, someone suggested that a monument be erected in Macon to honor those men killed at First Manassas. The *Daily Telegraph's* reporter commented, "Let it stand like the Battle Monument at Baltimore, an imperishable record of public gratitude to these martyrs for the liberty of their country."[59]

As the summer of 1861 passed the citizens of Macon prepared for a long war. In early August Captain Lucius M. Lamar's Macon Guards advertised for twenty-five recruits, promising that uniforms and equipment would be furnished.[60] A new unit, composed mostly of Irish and known as the Lochrane Guards in honor of Judge Oliver A. Lochrane, was organized with seventy members. Jackson Barnes served as captain with James Meara and D. Dunfry as lieutenants.[61] The Guards left for Virginia on August 29. Before they departed, Miss Monroe of Macon presented them with a beautiful flag during a ceremony at Concert Hall. The usual speeches were given beginning with "a chaste and patriotic address" by Colonel Lewis N. Whittle. His remarks were followed by a response made by Captain Barnes. A third speech was presented by Judge Lochrane who donated $1,000 to the company.[62] Lieutenant Stubbs of the Central City Blues returned to Macon to get a few more recruits. The Blues served in Western Virginia with the twelfth Georgia Regiment in General Henry R. Jackson's Brigade, in General William W. Loring's Army. In an effort to entice men to serve with him, Stubbs called the country they would campaign in "one of the most healthy and romantic countries in the world." Still another unit, the Rutland Guards, commanded by Captain J. W. Stubbs, marched out of Macon and camped at the school house near the home of Reverend Richard Cain, on the Hawkinsville Road, eight miles from Macon, while they waited for the authorities to muster them into the service. They left Macon on 27 August bound for Camp Stephens, near Griffin, Georgia.[63]

One of the most interesting units raised in Macon during the summer of 1861 was the German Artillery, an all-German unit officered by Captain F. H. Burghard, and Lieutenants J. H. King, N. Biuswanger, and F. Herzog. Burghard was an experienced artillerist who was thoroughly drilled in the German states. He had seen much service in Europe, having been wounded on several occasions. Some dozen or so of the men were also experienced artillerists.[64]

---

[59] Ibid., 8 Aug. 1861.

[60] Ibid., 9 Aug. 1861. See also articles in *Macon Daily* Telegraph, 16, 20 Aug. 1861.

[61] Ibid., 10 Aug. 1861.

[62] Ibid., 30 Aug. 1861; *Georgia Journal and Messenger,* 4 Sept. 1861.

[63] *Macon Daily Telegraph*, 12 Aug. 1861; 22 Aug. 1861; 28 Aug. 1861.

[64] Ibid., 23 Aug. 1861.

September saw the organization of several other companies. Among them were the Thomson Guards, named for Mayor M. S. Thomson, and composed of members of the Young America Fire Company, No. 3. Another, the Lamar Infantry, was named for one of its benefactors, John B. Lamar. Other supporters included such prominent men as Lewis N. Whittle and T.R. Bloom. T. W. Brantley was captain of the outfit, with F. W. Johnston as First Lieutenant, John A. McManus served as Second Lieutenant, and John H. Dunlap was Third Lieutenant. Still another unit organized in September was the Ross Volunteers. The officers of this unit included Captain R.F. Woolfolk, First Lieutenant A. F. Redding, and Second Lieutenant S. H. Gates.[65]

By mid-September Macon and Bibb County had furnished the Confederate Army with the Jackson Artillery, Brown Infantry, Independent Volunteers, Macon Guards, Floyd Rifles, Macon Volunteers, Sparks Guards, Central City Blues, Rutland Guards, Bibb Greys, and Lochrane Guards. The raising of these units caused the *Daily Telegraph's* reporter to exclaim, "Bibb, with a voting population of 18,000, has now a thousand men in the field, and in a pinch could turn out a thousand more; not all of them so light of foot or supple in the joints as the dear fellows who have gone, but still good, steady-going soldiers for all that- men who could stand their hand with the Hessians at the bayonet, and hit the mark as long too though they had to squint at it through spectacles." The paper believed that two or three more companies could be supplied from Macon, so that the permanent strength of the community in the army would be about 1,200 men.[66]

In addition to the volunteer companies who left for the field as Confederate soldiers, the Bibb County militia, 700 men, mustered at Camp Oglethorpe, led by Colonel J. Van Valkenburg, commander of the 50th Regiment of Georgia Militia, in early August.[67] This was only a prelude to a review of the unit by Brigadier General G. R. Hunter of the Georgia militia on 10 September. Five hundred men paraded before General Hunter, Colonel Raines, and Brigade Inspector Major G. W. Persons. Van Valkenburg and his staff were also present. The regiment paraded through the streets of Macon before large crowds. Many called for the General to make a speech, which he did, "paying glowing tribute to the efficiency and proficiency of the 50th Regiment and its officers."[68]

The coming of October saw such units as the Lamar Infantry the Ross Volunteers, and the Thomson Guards go to Camp Oglethorpe for training.[69] The month also saw the organization of the Napier Artillery which had a complete

[65] Ibid., 12 Sept. 1861; 21, 23 Sept. 1861.

[66] Ibid., 17 Sept. 1861.

[67] *Georgia Journal and Messenger*, 14 Aug. 1861.

[68] *Macon Daily Telegraph*, 11 Sept. 1861.

[69] Ibid., 1, 8, 9 Oct. 1861.

battery of six and twelve-pounder brass cannon. Its commander was Captain Leroy Napier, Jr.[70] Still another unit, the Huguenin Rifles, raised in the Warrior District of Bibb County, attracted much attention as the men marched through Macon to Camp Oglethorpe. The company was accompanied by a large cavalcade of wagons and carriages. On the morning of 30 September Colonel E. D. Huguenin, for whom the company was named, was introduced to the men by their commander, Captain Cicero A. Tharpe. Huguenin then made "an eloquent and patriotic" speech to the unit, after which the men greeted him with three cheers.[71]

Some of these units, like the Huguenin Rifles, trained at other places.[72] Others, such as the Thomson Guards, were escorted to the Georgia Central Depot with the German Artillery, Floyd Rifles, and the Reserve Guard of the Macon Volunteers as escorts.[73]

So great was the response to the calls for volunteers during this period that, by the end of October, Bibb County had raised seventeen companies, all but three of which were in the service by 29 October. So good was this record that the *Daily Telegraph* had every right to exclaim, "we are of opinion that no county of equal population in the Southern States, can show as good a record.– These seventeen companies are believed to muster about 1,375 rank and file."[74]

Through the fall of 1861 men continued to leave for the Georgia coast or for the major concentration points for Confederate troops.[75]

While the recruits for field service kept coming in, two companies were organized for home defense. The *Journal and Messenger* urged every man, old and young (including ministers) to arm themselves and prepare to defend the City in case of an attack.[76]

In February, 1862, the *Daily Telegraph* urged every male citizen in Macon and Bibb County between the ages of sixteen and sixty to drill. "Every place of business," the paper exclaimed, "should be closed at three o'clock in the afternoon, and then every man would have an opportunity of drilling. Let us commence this thing at once."

As detachments of the Macon Volunteers and the Floyd Rifles paraded in celebration of the anniversary of the Battle of New Orleans in January, 1862.[77]

---

[70] Ibid., 16 Oct. 1861.

[71] Ibid., 1 Oct. 1861.

[72] Ibid., 3 Oct. 1861.

[73] Ibid., 5 Oct. 1861.

[74] Ibid., 29 Oct. 1861.

[75] This is based upon a careful examination of the *Macon Daily Telegraph* and the *Georgia Journal and Messenger* for the period.

[76] *Georgia Journal and Messenger*, 13 Nov. 1861.

[77] *Macon Daily Telegraph*, 9 Jan. 1862.

efforts continued to supply the men with money, uniforms, and equipment. John B. Lamar spent $980 for seventy uniforms for the Macon Volunteers (for $14.00 apiece). He also purchased pants, caps, trimming for caps, sashes, flax thread for the caps, six officers' uniforms, and fifty pairs of socks for a total expenditure of $1,210.75. His supplier was the firm of E. Winship, a dealer in ready-made clothing and gentlemen's' furnishing goods, whose place of business was located at the corner of Cotton Avenue and Cherry Street.[78]

During the spring and summer of 1861, the Soldiers Relief Society and other groups continued to support the men. The men who volunteered owned but few acres of cotton, and only a few slaves, but they expected their more affluent fellow-townsmen to furnish them with supplies to arm and support them.[79]

Fund raising activities continued in the hot summer months. The Juvenile Soldiers' Relief Society, a junior version of the parent organization, made arrangements to hold a fair at Concert Hall in early August.[80] A raffle was held at the Lanier House later in the month during which "The largest, latest, and most accurate map of Virginia ever published" was raffled off, and the money raised placed in a fund for the benefit of the Macon Guards.[81] Requests for such items as money, blankets, sheets, pillows, and even rice, teas, sugar, cologne, lozenges, flax seed, arrow root, brandy, wine, blackberry cordial, and other items appeared in the newspapers.[82]

The firm of Cleghorn and Smith sold Captain T. W. Brantley of the Lamar Infantry, $468 worth of supplies including haversacks, canteens with strap, and 7 dozen cap fronts and straps on October 18.[83] In late October General Rutherford of Macon donated 50 bushels of wheat to soldiers' families, while Major Alexander Smith of Houston County, gave 15 bushels of corn for the same purpose.[84]

The State, of course, was doing what it could to support state troops. D. W. K. Peacock, Agent of the Georgia Commissary Department reported he had received 6,522 sacks of flour, 689 barrels of flour, 356 boxes of candles, 1,875 bushels of peas, 1,795 bushels of corn meal, 3,321 pounds of bacon, nine hogsheads of sugar, ninety-eight barrels of syrup, eighty boxes of soap, fourteen

---

[78] E. Winship to Lamar, Bill, Macon, 21 Oct. 1861. See above for information concerning Lamar's efforts to furnish the unit with full uniforms.

[79] *Macon Daily Telegraph*, 30 May 1861.

[80] *Georgia Journal and Messenger,* 7 Aug. 1861.

[81] *Macon Daily Telegraph*, 24 Aug. 1861.

[82]Ibid., 16, 24 Aug. 1861.

[83] Cleghorn and Smith to T.W. Brantley, Bill, 18 Oct. 1861, Cobb Papers, 1861.

[84] *Macon Daily Telegraph*, 29 Oct. 1861.

barrels of lard, and 1,336 pounds of beef in the month of January 1862. Large amounts of these supplies were sent to the Georgia State Troops.[85]

Groups of Maconites continued to hold meetings to raise money to outfit and supply volunteers. During such a meeting, held at City Hall on 15 February 1862, the Inferior Court was asked to take immediate action to give whatever money might be needed to fit out and equip all the volunteers from Bibb County. The Court appointed a military committee composed of a number of the leading citizens to supervise, outfit, and equip all volunteers; fix the amount of money needed for this purpose; receive the money from the Court; and spend it for the support of the volunteers. The meeting passed other resolutions, including the raising of a soldier's tax under authority of an act, passed by the Georgia Legislature, to support indigent families of Bibb County volunteers. The resolution stated all of these people were entitled to receive a comfortable support during the absence of their fathers, husbands, sons, and brothers. Extra taxes for this purpose would be raised by the Court as often as the soldiers' families needed the money. Another resolution thanked Mayor Thomson for spending the money to help the merchants of Macon. Still another, thanked the Ladies Soldiers Relief Society for their valuable services, and ask them to continue the work.[86]

All of this support was needed because in February and March, 1862, other companies were organized in Macon and Bibb County. These included the Whittle Guards of Rutland District, the Gresham Rifles, the Macon Invincibles, and the Southern Right's Guards.[87]

When 875 men turned out for a parade on 4 March and 146 of them volunteered for the war, it saddened a reporter for the *Daily Telegraph* to report, "It was a frightful sight to see the number of grey and bald headed men in the ranks, who refused to confess to overage...men between sixty and eighty should be more careful of themselves." Unfortunately, there were young men of twenty to twenty-six watching the parade. Some of them pleaded over age and some physical infirmity, "to whom five pounds of meat at a dinner is a small allowance, and who could have whipped a platoon on parade if they had only laid out their strength." But Macon and Bibb County, by early March 1862, could boast that there were only 600 men left in the county who might be subject to a draft, of whom 400 were heads of families. The county, with a vot-

---

[85] Ibid., 4 February 1862.

[86] Ibid., 17 Feb. 1862. The committee included Benjamin F. Ross, T.R. Bloom, William S. Holt, William Holmes, Thomas Bagby, James A. Nisbet, William B. Johnston, P.E. Bowdre, Methvin S. Thomson, J.H. Jossey, and Lewis N. Whittle.

[87] Ibid., 18, 27 Feb., 28 Mar. 1862. The Whittle Guards had fifty-two men and the Gresham Rifles numbered seventy men. The numbers of troops in the other companies was unavailable.

ing population of only 1,700 white men over the age of twenty-one, had furnished 1,500 men to the Confederate Army.[88]

In mid-March an additional company, Company C, was organized by the Macon Volunteers for home defense as a "home guard." Plans called for the organization of these men under proper officers. The authorities intended to equip them with military equipment in the Armory of the Macon Volunteers. This material included new arms and uniforms.[89] Another company, the Juvenile Company, organized in late March, 1862, consisted of forty-three youths between the ages of twelve and sixteen. Presumably this group also planned to serve as a home guard.[90]

Many Maconites wrote the Secretary of War asking for various things relating to military affairs. Sometimes the petitioners asked for the appointment of a prominent officer to higher rank. Thomas Hardeman, Jr., and other officers of the Second Georgia Battalion, wrote President Davis recommending the promotion of Captain Robert A. Smith, formerly commander of the Macon Volunteers and now the captain of Company D in the Battalion, to the rank of Colonel to raise a regiment for the war. Hardeman noted that Smith "has been a commissioned officer of the volunteer forces of Georgia since 1847," and deserved the appointment.[91]

Occasionally, a prominent leader wanted a friend who had raised a company of troops to be allowed to enter Confederate service. When Captain John B. Cumming raised a company of volunteers for Confederate service, Eugenius A. Nisbet petitioned Secretary of War Walker for his request to be granted. Nisbet also petitioned for Captain C.D. Anderson's company from Fort Valley to receive the same privilege.[92] In his reply, written on 14 May 1861, John Tyler, one of Walker's assistants, said that the two companies would be accepted.

---

[88] Ibid., 5 Mar. 1862. The Macon Volunteers and the Floyd Rifles had recruited so many men that they were able to organize two companies in each unit. These were the Macon Volunteers, Companies A and B, and the Floyd Rifles, Companies A and B. Ibid., 9 Jan. 1861, 5 Mar. 1862 and Capt. H.P. Westscott to Governor Brown, Telegram, Macon, 17 Feb. 1862, GLB 1861-1865, p. 202. The Whittle Guards trained at Camp Stephens near Griffin, and became part of the Tenth Georgia Battalion with Major J.E. Rylander as commander. This battalion later guarded prisoners at Camp Oglethorpe. Statement of J.H. Woodward, donated by Dr. Charles Kellum, Macon, Georgia, Personal Collection.

[89] *Macon Daily Telegraph*, 14 Mar. 1862.

[90] Ibid., 20, 21 Mar. 1862.

[91] Thomas Hardeman, Jr. and others to President Davis, Georgia Barracks near Norfolk, 5 Feb. 1862, Confederate Secretary of War, Letters Received, Roll 27, Jan.-Feb. 1862, NARA.

[92] Eugenius A. Nisbet to Walker, Macon, 10 May 1861, Ibid., Roll 2, Mar.-May 1861.

However, he added "The rule, however, ... is this–when a sufficient number of companies from a state come to be thus presented for the war, they will be thrown into Regimental organization, but not be drawn into service until they can be thus organized into regiments."[93]

Pulaski S. Holt also wanted a Confederate commission because he had raised five or six companies for the war. The men were not equipped, but Holt planned to uniform them at his own expense, and raise other companies to make up a regiment of infantry, or a battalion of cavalry, if he received a commission. His references included such dignitaries as Confederate Senator Benjamin H. Hill, Eugenius A. Nisbet, Colonel Alfred H. Colquitt, and Major Thomas Hardeman, Jr.[94]

Charles E. Nisbet, W. W. Parker, and C.F. Stubbs wanted to raise a troop of horse for the war, to include not more than 200 men, they assured Secretary of War Randolph that they would furnish all the horses, horse equipment, and complete uniforms for the officers and men. They would even furnish each man with a Navy revolver, "and a carbine, or Maynard rifle, or some other approved cavalry arm." They needed arms or wagons. The troop, the trio assured the secretary, would be raised in a few days, and be ready to take the field "at once." The interesting part of their plan was to fit and equip their men to fight a guerrilla war rather than service as regular cavalry.[95]

One of the most interesting efforts made by a Macon citizen during the first year of the war was made by Lieutenant Henry N. Ells, who raised the Napier Artillery, a company with a full battery of four brass six-pounders, two brass twelve-pounder howitzers, six caissons, an artillery wagon, and a forge. Ells had spent $9,500 to have a New Orleans foundry make the cannon and other equipment. The battery was scheduled for shipment by 19 November 1861, complete with tents and uniforms. Ells wanted acting Secretary of War Judah P. Benjamin to accept the unit for the war, and wanted it sent to the Georgia coast. The ambitious Ells wanted to buy "a very superior lot of horses" for the battery.[96]

In his reply, Benjamin enclosed a circular which noted that when artillery companies furnished their own guns for the war, the Government would pay for them, and equip the batteries, including horses, when they were ordered to take the field. However, the officers of the Quartermaster's Department had to buy the

---

[93] John Tyler to Nisbet, Montgomery, 14 May 1861, Confederate Secretary of War, Letters Roll 1, Vol. 1, p. 325.

[94] P.H. Holt to Leroy Pope Walker, Macon, 5 June 1861, Confederate Secretary of War, Letters Received, Roll 3, June 1861.

[95] Charles E. Nisbet, W.W. Parker, and C.F. Stubbs to George M. Randolph, Macon, 15 Apr. 1862, Ibid., Roll 64, Feb.-Dec. 1862.

[96] Lieut. Henry N. Ells and others to Benjamin, Macon, Oct. 1861, *OR*, Ser. 2, vol. 3, 731.

horses and equipment. If Ells purchased them the Confederacy would repay him at fair market value. The Government would select a camp of instruction, acting on the recommendation of the company, and the men would be permitted to drill and prepare for battle. On these terms the company would be mustered into service as soon as it was ready.[97]

By mid-May 1862, Ells had enlisted seventy-five or eighty men in the Napier Artillery, and scheduled an election of officers to take place on 15 May. The unit, camped in Macon, was then in State service. Ells, who called his unit, the "finest and best equipped battery in C. S." with a full complement of seventy-two well-drilled horses, wanted to know to whom they should report after the full complement of 150 was raised. The battery included four six-pounders and two twelve-pounder howitzers, with a battery wagon and forge. The battery even included a blacksmith and a saddle and harness maker.[98]

On 15 May Randolph telegraphed Ells to apply to General Alexander R. Lawton to muster in the company, "and report by letter to General R E Lee."[99] In a letter which followed, Randolph explained that the company could be mustered in with seventy men, and brought up to its full complement later with conscripts.[100]

So many men volunteered that soon prominent Maconites began to seek exemptions for men who were needed to perform important functions at home. Eugenius A. Nisbet urged Confederate Secretary of War Leroy Pope Walker to exempt David Craig, a member of Captain Ross's company in Major Thomas Hardeman's Second Georgia Battalion, stationed near Norfolk, Virginia. Before his enlistment, Craig worked as a machinist for Schofield and Brother. Nisbet explained that "workmen of this sort are exceedingly difficult [to] get." Walker obliged and ordered Craig's discharge on October 10.[101]

---

[97] Judah P. Benjamin, Acting Secretary of War, to Lieut. Henry N. Ells and others, Richmond, 31 Oct. 1861, Secretary of War, Letters Sent, Roll 3, Vols. 3-4, Sept. 17, 1861-Feb. 18, 1862, p. 207.

[98] Capt. Henry N. Ells to George W. Randolph, Macon, 12 May 1862, Confederate Secretary of War, Letters Received, Roll 45, Feb.-Dec. 1862.

[99] Randolph to Ells, Richmond, 15 May 1862, Telegram, Telegrams Sent by the Confederate Secretary of War 1861-1865, Chapter IX, Vol. 34, Sept. 13, 1861-Mar. 21, 1863, NARA.

[100] Randolph to Ells, Richmond, 21 May 1862, Confederate Secretary of War, Letters Sent, Roll 4, Vol. 6, Feb. 18-May 23, 1862.

[101] Eugenius A. Nisbet to Leroy Pope Walker, Macon, 4 Oct. 1861, Confederate Secretary of War, Letters Received, Roll 11, Sept.-Oct. 1861, NARA. Walker to Confederate Adjutant and Inspector General's Office, Richmond, 10 Oct. 1861, endorsement, Ibid.

Schofield later asked Nathan Bass, a member of the Confederate Congress representing the Macon District, to obtain the discharge of two mechanics.[102] The manufacturers had a large contract with the Confederate Government to make shot and shell, and to make machinery for the Confederate Arsenal at Augusta. It was very difficult, Schofield assured Benjamin, to get mechanics to work in the machine shop. One of the men, John Strye in Captain Ross's Floyd Rifles, was stationed near Norfolk. The other, George Strye, was in the Thompson Guards, under Captain Van Valkenburg. Strye's unit was stationed at Brunswick, Georgia.[103]

When Virgil Powers, President of the Southwestern Railroad, wrote Secretary of War Randolph in April 1862, he wanted to know if there would be any exemptions under the Conscript Act for railroad employees. "If not," Powers observed, "I fear we will have great difficulty in keeping our Road in operation as a large proportion of the employees of this coy [company] are subject under the law & unless specially exempted nearly all of them will volunteer within the [next] thirty days." The company employed thirteen "engine runners" [engineers] on the payroll, but with the firm's present small business, not more than three or four of these individuals would remain.[104]

Former US Congressman, Eugenius A. Nisbet asked Secretary of War Benjamin to discharge James Harvey of the Lochrane Guards, assigned to Phillip's Georgia Legion. Harvey, "an expert shoemaker," could make shoes for the volunteers from Macon and Bibb County. Nisbet explained that shoes were "scarcer than men" in Macon.[105] Other prominent Maconites, including Oliver A. Lochrane, Mayor Thomson, Lewis N. Whittle, Isaac Scott, J. B. Ross, T.R. Bloom, Nathan C. Munroe, William B. Johnston, and Ed L. Strohecker, as well as Congressman Bass, petitioned Benjamin for Harvey's release. Harvey, who was then stationed with his unit at Hardeeville, was badly needed at home, not only to make shoes but to care for his family.[106]

Another prominent Macon citizen, Judge Oliver A. Lochrane, asked Governor Brown to exempt Macon and Bibb County from a draft. The jurist explained "So many companies have left here in case of fire or other trouble we

---

[102] Nathan Bass to Judah P. Benjamin, Richmond, 22 Jan. 1862, Confederate Secretary of War, Letters Received, Roll 23, Jan. 1862.

[103] Schofield and Brother to Nathan Bass, Macon, 18 Jan. 1862, enclosed in Ibid. The letter was received at the War Department on January 22, 1862, but there is no record of any action taken.

[104] Virgil Powers to Randolph, Macon 24 Apr. 1862, Ibid., Roll 150, Apr. 1862.

[105] Eugenius A. Nisbet to Benjamin, Macon, 14 Oct. 1861, Ibid., Roll 13, Oct. 1861.

[106] Oliver A. Lochrane and others to Benjamin, Macon, 10 Jan. 1862, Ibid., Roll 23, Jan 1862.

can scarcely hope to meet or act successfully with what we have got some eighteen companies have gone and I know you will look to the necessity of maintaining a force in the cities sufficient to act promptly for protection." So many Maconites had volunteered under the volunteer system that Macon and Bibb County should not be called upon to furnish even more. Besides, Lochrane explained, "We feel the defeats of the last few days too much, worse might have been anticipated under the stand still policy we have been pursuing."[107]

James A. Nisbet, a judge and law partner of his brother, Eugenius, petitioned Governor Brown and Adjutant General Wayne to exempt Macon Gas Company President George A. McIlhenny because he "cannot be spared, as there is nobody to take his place."[108]

A number of prominent leaders petitioned Secretary of War George W. Randolph on 2 May to exempt the superintendent, the engineer, two weavers, two spinners, three sizers, and five carders and card strippers as well as fifteen workers in the mill owned by the Macon Manufacturing Company. The facility, which manufactured brown sheetings, shirtings and drills, had 130 hands who faced conscription. It produced 4,000 yards of goods per day, and the Confederacy would suffer if production was even partially stopped. The committee, which included such Macon leaders as John Jones Gresham; Thaddeus G. Holt; Nathan C. Munroe, Jr.; James D. Carhart; and William B. Johnston, quickly received the exemptions.[109]

Occasionally people did not share the loyalty expressed by some of their neighbors toward the young Confederacy. Some of them wanted to leave and go north. Mrs. Emma C. Wood, wife of a Northerner named Seth G. Wood, who was engaged in the furniture business in Macon with his uncle Grenville Wood, wanted to join her husband who had gone north. She was a life-long resident of Macon and the daughter of Commissary Henry Clark of the Twentieth Georgia Regiment. In a letter to Secretary of War Benjamin in which she asked for a permit to go north in a flag of truce steamer, she explained that her Mother's family was well known to Major Thomas Hardeman, Jr. Her husband was also a friend

---

[107] Oliver A. Lochrane to Governor Brown, Macon, 14 Feb. 1862, Incoming Correspondence of the Governor, Box 38, GDA&H. The defeats mentioned certainly included the capture of Roanoke Island, North Carolina in which a number of Georgians were casualties. Other defeats at this time were the capture of Forts Henry and Donelson in Tennessee. The "stand still policy" referred to was an oblique criticism of Confederate President Davis who favored a defensive policy which involved defending every inch of ground in the Confederacy.

[108] James A. Nisbet to D.C. Campbell, Macon, 28 Feb. 1862, Ibid., Box 41.

[109] John Jones Gresham and others to George W. Randolph, Macon, 2 May 1862, Confederate Secretary of War, Letters Received, Microfilm, Roll 48, Apr.-Aug. 1862; George W. Randolph to John Jones Gresham, Richmond, 12 May 1862, Confederate Secretary of War Letter Book, Roll 4, Microfilm, Vol. 6, p. 442, NARA.

of George W. Ross of the Floyd Rifles and Captain Robert A. Smith and Lieutenant A.G. Butts of the Macon Volunteers. Writing the letter from S. C. Newton's Atlantic Hotel in Norfolk, Virginia, she noted "I am an entire stranger here with the exception of the members of those companies I have mentioned. I am unable to come [to Richmond] myself for I have a little child with me not old enough to walk and I expect soon to become a mother again." She plaintively explained that she needed her "husband's care and attention," and was all alone with no one to advise or direct her, "no earthly friend; but I have a Father in Heaven and I pray that he may influence you in my behalf."[110]

Another disloyal Maconite, James Melcher, a carpenter and a Northerner by birth, was brought before Mayor Thomson and the City Council on the charge that he spoke treasonable "sentiments." The investigation lasted for hours, and ended when Melcher was found guilty. The Mayor and Council ordered him to leave Macon in five days. Both Melcher's prosecutor, Major John Rutherford, and his defense attorney, Colonel Lewis N. Whittle, spoke eloquently for their respective causes.[111]

So much concern was expressed about the disloyalty of some Macon citizens that a public meeting was held on 9 August urging the Mayor and City Council to pass a resolution instructing the Clerk of Council to place a loyalty oath to the Confederacy in a blank book, to be kept at the mayor's office in City Hall. Furthermore, the people of Macon were told, through the newspapers, to come forward and take a loyalty oath within a prescribed time. The names of those individuals who did not take the oath would be published at a later date. The oath, the wording of which showed the depth of emotion expressed by many Maconites at the time, stated: "I do most sincerely and solemnly swear before Almighty God, without mental reservation of any kind, that I do, in good faith and forever, renounce all allegiance to, and citizenship in the United States of America; that I will support and defend the Constitution of the Confederate States of America; and that I will in all things demean myself as a true and faithful citizen of the said Confederate States; and I do promise that I will endeavor to discover, and will report any and every unfaithful person of whom I may obtain reliable intelligence, So help me God." However, a substitute motion was made by Reverend J. Knowles and after some debate was adopted. This resolution resulted in the appointment of a committee to carry out the administering of a revised oath.[112]

---

[110] Emma C. Wood to Judah P. Benjamin, Norfolk, 13 Mar. 1862, Confederate Secretary of War, Letters Received, Microfilm, Roll 76, Feb.-May 1862, NARA.

[111] *Macon Daily Telegraph*, 27 Jul. 1861.

[112] Ibid., 10 Aug. 1861. The committee included such notables as Colonel J.H. Josey, W.D. Williams, Dr. James Mercer Green, Honorable Thaddeus G. Holt, T.R. Bloom, and E.E. Grier.

The Committee met at Concert Hall in August, and adopted a much simpler loyalty oath which renounced allegiance to the United States and stated, "I will support and defend the Constitution of the Confederate States of America; and that I will in all things demean myself as a true and faithful citizen in the said Confederate States."[113]

With all of these men in uniform there would be sadness too, even before the major armies were ready to fight to settle the issue. While Maconites mourned the death of some of their sons at the Battle of First Manassas, it was equally hard to bear when other young men died in the fall of 1861 and in early 1862. William Allen, a member of the Jackson Artillery, was killed by falling between the cars on his way to Savannah on the Georgia Central Railroad in September. His body was returned to Macon and buried in Rose Hill Cemetery with full military honors.[114] In early October, Lieutenant John M. Stubbs, a promising young Macon attorney who had enlisted in the Central City Blues died. A reporter for the *Daily Telegraph*, which would soon not have ink enough to record the names and deeds of the dead, stated that Stubbs "has met a glorious death and enrolled his name on the records of imperishable fame."[115]

When seven Macon soldiers were killed by the falling in of the magazine and by the explosion of a shell during an artillery barrage at Pensacola, Florida in late November, 1861, their bodies were brought to Macon and buried in Rose Hill Cemetery with full military honors. Over a thousand people attended the funerals, and heard a sermon preached by Reverend David Wills, Pastor of Macon's Presbyterian Church. An eyewitness recorded, "the funeral wagon was decorated with flowers, they being white mostly, and loops of crape, and that drawn by six horses with a small Confederate flag attached to their head, each man, according to military law, after being shrouded was wraped [sic] in a flag. I never witnessed such a scene before." The bodies were escorted by a guard furnished by the Reserve City Guards, the Macon Guards, Number Two, The Young America Fire Company, and the Floyd Rifles Number Two, and a portion of the Napier Artillery.[116] The *Journal and Messenger*, commented on Reverend Wills' remarks, saying his "Address [was] marked with good sense and

[113] *Georgia Journal and Messenger*, 21 Aug. 1861.

[114] *Macon Daily Telegraph*, 21 Sept. 1861.

[115] Ibid., 8 Oct. 1861.

[116] L.V. Ellis to Cousin Wyse, Macon, 1 Dec. 1861, in Civil War Miscellany, Middle Georgia Archives, Genealogy and Archives Room, Washington Memorial Library, Macon. The names of six of the men were Andrew Micklejohn and Thomas Champion, both of the Brown Infantry; George W. Bramely, H. Crawford, George Haggerty, and J.L. Berry. The funeral was held at the new City Hall. *Georgia Journal and Messenger*, 27 Nov. 1861.

sound judgment, and was appropriate and well timed." Wills "paid handsome and well deserved tribute to the dead."[117]

On 18 March 1862, Mr. Cook, a member of the Gresham Rifles, died at Camp Stephens of pneumonia. In mid-April fifteen carloads of sick soldiers came to the Floyd House, a hospital set up by the Soldiers' Relief Society. Another Maconite, Private Oliver W. Crenshaw of Company A, Macon Volunteers, died of consumption in late March, and was buried with full military honors. A detachment of Company B, Macon Volunteers, fired a salute over his grave.[118]

The first year of the war had proved especially active for the men who left, and for those who attempted to gain exemptions for those they felt needed to stay at home. Although the war had not yet reached Macon, the people of Macon were definitely *in* the war. But, for those left behind, life continued almost as usual during the first year of war.

---

[117] *Georgia Journal and Messenger*, 4 Dec. 1861.
[118] Ibid., 19 Mar. 1862, 14 Apr. 1862, 1 Apr. 1862.

Chapter 5

Life in Macon During the
First Year of the War

During the first year of conflict life continued almost as usual. Since Macon was nearly in the geographic center of the Confederacy, the initial fighting was far away in Northern Virginia, Tennessee, Kentucky, Missouri, and on the coast of Georgia and the Carolinas. A feeling of security, therefore, was felt by most Maconites. Besides, it looked as if the Confederacy might achieve its independence quickly, and life as people knew it, would not have to change at all.

In May 1861, soon after the war began, Mary Ann Cobb was packing to leave Macon and return to her home in Athens because summers in Macon were hot and humid. Before she left, however, she had to go to the dentist, and then proceed with two men to her son Lamar's office and pack up his law books because he was away in the army. She even planned to remove his carpet in case of fire, acting upon the advice of her brother, John, and her son, Lamar. At 4:00 P.M. she renewed her visiting, going as far as Vineville. She was tired. She was the mother of twelve children and she felt depressed because the war had taken some of her sons to distant points in Virginia. Possibly, she wrote, the war was ordained by God "simply for the good of all concerned."[1]

As the first spring of the war advanced, Macon business leaders scheduled a meeting on 12 June to call for subscriptions of cotton and other produce to help pay for the war.[2] During the meeting 1,165 bales of cotton were subscribed, although the Bibb County cotton crop in 1860 was 5,020 bales.[3] By mid-June a committee chaired by Pulaski T. Holt, was appointed by Macon leaders to procure subscriptions of cotton and other produce for the use of the Confederacy.[4]

---

[1] Mary Ann Cobb to her husband, Macon, 9 May 1861, Cobb Papers, 1861.

[2] *Macon Daily Telegraph*, 8 June 1861.

[3] Ibid., 13 June 1861.

[4] Ibid., 19 June 1861.

Early in June Robert S. Lanier wrote his brother-in-law and law partner, Judge Clifford Anderson, then with the Confederate Army in Virginia, that his servant, Mary, had improved from an illness, and was prepared to go and work in the Lanier House, Macon's leading hotel which was owned by Lanier. It was almost impossible, Lanier confided, to hire Blacks upon any terms, and Lanier was unable to dispose of another slave, Georgia Ann. There simply was no demand for hired hands in Bibb County, although another slave, Dave, was working in the country. Besides, everything was quiet in Macon, although Lanier had heard of some cases of typhoid fever in the city, and an outbreak of scarlet fever in East Macon Precinct.

Lanier did not believe things were working out satisfactorily for Lincoln and his cabinet. There seemed to be a lack of unity in the Northern war effort. Meanwhile, the secession feeling in Maryland was increasing, despite Lincoln's efforts to quell it. Lanier was encouraged by the refusal of the three months' volunteers in the Federal Army to extend their term of service. Besides, Virginia and Tennessee were much stronger than the people of the Lower South supposed. He ended his letter with an injunction to Anderson not to eat too much fried meat because "it will breed disease."[5]

Another individual who found nothing of interest transpiring in Macon was J.M. Boardman who reported to Anderson "We have had very hot weather for a few days past, and day before yesterday the first shower in a long time. It is showering all round and we hope the impending drought is well over."[6]

In early July Wesleyan Female College held its annual commencement exercises. The young ladies of the college planned to perform the popular operetta, "The Flower Queen," and donate the proceeds to the Soldiers' Relief Society.[7]

The arts were very popular in Macon throughout the war, and especially during the first year. Their role in sustaining the morale of the people by creating a badly-needed diversion cannot be underestimated. It also illustrates the fact that Macon was a diversified city with a strong interest in culture and the arts. Its citizens were not about to give up these enjoyments on account of the war. Most of the entertainment was presented in Wesleyan Female College, the Concert Hall, and Ralston's Hall. The first facility was located where the current Macon Post Office is, on the corner of College Street and the latter two buildings were located downtown in the center of the city. On 24 April 1861, the *Journal and Messenger's* reporter described a "literary entertainment of a

---

[5] Robert S. Lanier to Clifford Anderson, Macon, 11 June 1861, Clifford Anderson Papers, Reel 1, Microfilm, SHC, hereafter cited as Anderson Papers.

[6] J.M. Boardman to Anderson, Macon, 26 June 1861, Ibid.

[7] *Georgia Journal and* Messenger, 3 July 1861; *Macon Daily Telegraph*, 2 July 1861.

very agreeable character," presented by the young women of the Adelphean Society of Wesleyan College. Although the aftershocks of the news of the attack on Fort Sumter and the coming of the war prevented a large attendance, the compositions read by the students "were uniformly good and generally well delivered." The accompanying music was "excellent," and the audience showed its appreciation by applause and by showering bouquets onto the stage. The reporter asserted, "The scene presented within the spacious hall: its walls hung with garlands, vieing in loveliness with the graceful group upon the stage, budding into cultivated womanhood, presented a most pleasant contrast to the entire outer world- its din of war and bloody strife."[8]

As the spring of 1861 wore on and the war continued with no immediate end in sight the entertainments became more patriotic with the proceeds of many performances donated to the Soldier's Relief Society. A concert, probably presented in Concert Hall, featured a new national song with music written by Professor Schreiner of Schreiner's Music Store.[9] In early July, Schreiner directed a Soldier's Concert by Macon's German Singing Society and the Macon Cornet Band at Ralston's Hall.[10]

Messrs. Couturier and Reeves of Charleston presented an entertainment for the relief of Confederate soldiers in September. Half of the proceeds were given to the Soldier's Relief Society. The concert featured Couturier, who spoke several passages of "Hamlet" and another production, "The Lady of Lyons" in "a very effective manner." The passages from "Hamlet" featured dialogue between Hamlet and Polonius.[11]

Another group, the Atlanta Amateurs, performed on the night of 8 September. Their appearance featured a tableau, popular at the time, presenting "The Union as it was," which, according to the *Daily Telegraph*, was well done. A native of South Carolina in the audience cried out "Georgia has seceded thank God, and so has South Carolina." Receipts for the two presentations were $400.[12]

On 25 September another tableau, this one given at Ralston's Hall by young ladies to aid the Soldiers' Relief Fund, was a success. Because of a crowded house, the tableau netted $200. The *Journal and Messenger* reporter exclaimed, "God bless our patriotic little girls in their labors of love."[13]

October was the season of concerts in Macon, and that month in 1861 was no exception. One of Macon's many volunteer companies, the German Artillery,

[8] *Georgia Journal and Messenger*, 24 April 1861.

[9] *Macon Daily Telegraph*, 20, 27, May 1861.

[10] Ibid., 2 July 1861.

[11] Ibid., 2, 4 September 1861.

[12] Ibid., 9 September 1861; *Georgia Journal and Messenger*, 11 September 1861.

[13] *Georgia Journal and Messenger*, 25 September 1861.

which had received orders to leave for the Georgia coast on October 24, had received $1100 from the Soldier's Relief Society to help purchase their arms and equipment. The men learned that the Society's treasury was empty, and therefore planned to give a concert at Ralston's Hall for the benefit of the Society. Their efforts would be aided by the Manager of the Atlanta Amateurs, Billy Barnes, who planned to sing several songs.[14]

Another group, Fitz's Panopticon of the South, presented a mechanical exhibition of life including moving figures which represented scenes in the "Revolution of 1861." These included, of course, the bombardment of Fort Sumter. A matinee performance was scheduled for families and schools, when all children would be admitted for fifteen cents.[15]

On 25 October an exhibition at Concert Hall featured a variety of entertainments: tableaux, charades, comic songs, music, and singing. A representation of a minor victory by Colonel Ambrose R. Wright and his Georgians over a Federal force on Hatteras Island at Chicamicomico in the fall of 1861, known as "the Chicamicomico Races," was also presented. The price of admission was fifty cents, all of it scheduled for the relief of the soldiers.[16]

At the end of the month a concert was presented during which the instrumental music was provided by Messrs. Czurda, Mathews, and Branham. A singer named Branham sang such songs as "Hiawatha and his Bridges return Home," and the "Death of Minnehaha."[17]

By mid-November 1861 Macon had its own Amateur Club, the "Resident Amateur Club," which planned to present its first patriotic program at Ralston's Hall on Thursday, 21 November.[18]

Not to be outdone, a group known as "The Confederate Minstrels," performed at Ralston's on Saturday night, 23 November. Every member of the group was from South Carolina, a heroic state in the eyes of Maconites because it was the first state to secede from the Union.[19]

Another performance featured a popular black performer named Blind Tom who planned to perform at City Hall, known to Maconites as the "New City

---

[14] *Macon Daily Telegraph*, 16 October 1861.

[15] Ibid., 17 October 1861. A panopticon is a building so arranged that all parts of the interior are visible from a single point.

[16] Ibid., 25 October 1861. The Chicamicomico Races alluded to an engagement on Hatteras Island in North Carolina where a Georgia unit nearly destroyed a party of Federal troops. The name originated when the Federals escaped only by running as fast as they could.

[17] Ibid., 29 October 1861.

[18] Ibid., 19 November 1861.

[19] Ibid., 23 November 1861.

Hall," in late November.[20] Tom, described by the *Daily Telegraph* as a "prodigy," was a "wonderful embodiment of musical taste and skill–unrivaled memory, unequaled initiative faculties, in a blind negro boy, eleven years old!" A pianist, Tom would attract audiences in Macon throughout the war years.[21]

During the first year of the war the people of Macon were also treated to tableau vivants [living pictures] and charades by living actors and actresses which afforded "innocent and amusing recreation for the citizens" and afforded "assistance to the patriotic and indefatigable Soldiers' Relief Society."[22] They also attended performances by the Queen Sisters of Charleston who presented patriotic songs and entertainments,[23] and an address by Colonel William Napier of Milledgeville who spoke about the war.[24]

When the ladies determined to raise $5,000 in Bibb County to support the building of a gunboat—the *C.S.S. Georgia*—in Savannah, they not only sent their jewelry, silver plates, engravings, and paintings to be raffled or sold with the proceeds applied to the project, but they sponsored a concert held in Macon in late March where the proceeds were donated to the fund.[25]

Another aspect of Macon life during the war years was presented by the business community. Macon's businessmen, always quick to make a profit, began to manufacture many items for the war soon after the outbreak of hostilities. These included such entrepreneurs as J. C. Thornton who, as early as May 1861, produced a Bowie knife for war and camp service. It boasted a blade fourteen inches long with a guard and a convenient sheath. While Thornton was producing his knives, E. J. Johnston and Company were manufacturing regulation swords, which the *Daily Telegraph* assured its readers, "are beautiful and serviceable weapons." D.C. Hodgkins and Sons were busily manufacturing percussion caps.[26]

A sword produced by E.J. Johnston, was designed for President Davis. By late June, it was completed and placed on exhibition at the Johnston store before it was sent to Richmond on 25 June.[27] The weapon was handsomely though plainly ornamented, and bore the inscription "General Jefferson Davis, first President of the Confederate States." On the other side it was inscribed, "Presented by Messrs E.J. Johnston & Co."[28] Early in 1862, Johnston

---

[20] Ibid.

[21] Ibid., 28 November 1861.

[22] Ibid., 19 October 1861.

[23] Ibid., 3, 4 March 1862.

[24] Ibid., 7, 10 March 1862.

[25] Ibid., 18, 20 March 1862.

[26] Ibid., 21 May 1861.

[27] Ibid., 25 June 1861.

[28] Ibid., 26 June 1861.

exhibited a service sword which had a phoenix rising from its ashes on the blade. The inscription included the letters "US" below the phoenix, and "C.S." above, which represented the birth of the Confederacy from the ashes of the old Union. The sword was manufactured for the officers of the 8th Georgia Regiment who planned to present it to their colonel, E.W. Chastain."[29]

Fine swords were also produced by the firm of William J. McElroy and Company. McElroy also made knives, brass mountings for swords, guns, and light ornamental brass castings of all kinds at his shop on Third Street.[30]

While Johnston and McElroy were producing their swords, the firm of Morse's Rifles and Pistols made a new type of double rifle which doubled the destructive power of the rifle. It could be loaded five or six times a minute at the muzzle. Morse boasted that he could "convert every old rifle and musket in the country into an arm of precision, and with his plan of loading, a most important contribution might be added to our means of defence."[31]

Other Macon businesses offered many types of war materiel. The firm of W.C. Kennedy sold military goods, blue and gray cloths, gold and silver lace, buttons, and tailor trimmings.[32] John N. Kein and Company sold soldiers' blankets made of two-ply woolen carpeting[33]. A new supply of *Hardee's Tactics*, with the addition of a *Manual for Colt's Pistol,* cloth-bound and illustrated, in two volumes for $2.50, was sold at J. W. Burke's Methodist Bookstore. Burke also merchandised fine lithograph maps of the "Seat of War" for $3.00 apiece.[34] These included, of course, a map of the "Battles on Bull's Run," showing the battlegrounds of 18 and 21 July, "with the locality of all the troops in the field marked down and explained." The map was made from actual observation by Solomon Bamberger, and was lithographed by Messrs. West & Johnson.[35]

The list of articles offered for sale in Macon during the first year of the war is almost endless. Military caps of different styles, "furnished on short notice," were sold by C. B. Stone. The music store of John C. Schreiner and sons sold snare drums, wood drums, bass drums, all of different sizes, together with a "good assortment of fifes.[36] Seven shooter pistols were sold at E. Feuchtwangers, whose business was located on Cherry Street near Second Street, "next door to Mrs. Bulkey's Millinery Establishment."[37] Tent cloth and mili-

---

[29] Ibid., 18 March 1862.

[30] Ibid., 11 February, 7 August 1862.

[31] Ibid., 20 June 1861.

[32] Ibid., 6 August 1861.

[33] Ibid., 9 August 1861.

[34] Ibid., 12 August 1861.

[35] Ibid., 17 September 1861.

[36] Ibid., 12 August 1861.

[37] Ibid., 13 August 1861.

tary duck were produced by the Ocmulgee Mills at Seven Islands on the Ocmulgee River in Butts County.[38] The *Daily Telegraph* described the tent cloth manufactured by the Ocmulgee Mills as "a fabric which in strength, durability and water-proof qualities leaves nothing to be desired."[39] The firm of E. Winship advertised such military goods as 350 yards of blue broad cloth, 400 pairs of service pants, 250 hickory shirts, jackonets, draws, half hose, and 2,000 yards of gray jeans.[40]

A machinist, W. A. Rines, who worked at Findlay's Foundry, produced a new conical shell. The taper of the shell was of chilled iron and the point was fabricated of steel. Guaranteed to penetrate both brick and earthen forts, the advent of the shell sounded like a death knell to brick fortifications such as Fort Pulaski. The advertisement revealed that "the sharp point of this projectile will obviate all possibility of its glancing off from any surface however hard or oblique."[41]

Nathan Weed's company sold hardware, iron, tin plate, knives of solid steel with black walnut handles, blacksmith's bellows, pruning knives, hubs, spokes, and felloes. Weed also sold iron of all sizes, English iron of all sizes, horse shoe iron, cast and plough steel, cut and wrought nails, agricultural implements, carriage materials, builders' hardware, mechanics tools, curriers tools, black-smith's tools, hoes, and axes. The business also dealt in, shovels, spades, hand hammers, plow lines, bar steel, axles, traces, well buckets, and butcher knives.[42]

Weed also made steel pikes, fourteen inches long, with an appendage which served both as a Bowie knife, and a hook to unhorse cavalry or "pull the enemy to you- removed at pleasure, or made firm." Weed suggested that, since the pikes were "an effective weapon...our cause would not be seriously injured by having ten or twelve regiments armed with them."[43]

One Maconite, Professor Jean Ferri, even gave lessons in the use of Bowie knives. He guaranteed that his pupils would "have no wounded bones, and cartilages are no obstruction to his knives." Ferri gloomily assured his potential customers that "the artery is always reached at every cut and severed, and the enemy breathes out his life gently there, in less than twenty seconds." Through

---

[38] Ibid., 3 July 1861.

[39] Ibid., 20 July 1861.

[40] Ibid., 18 July 1861. Jackonets referred to jackets made of a lightweight cotton fabric.

[41] Ibid., 12 November 1861.

[42] Ibid., 7 Feb 1862; Nathan Weed, Advertisement on bill to John B. Lamar, Macon, 30 December 1861, Cobb Papers, 1861.

[43] Ibid., 21 February 1862.

the use of the Bowie knife the battlefield would be "deprived of half its terrors, and, therefore, "war becomes a more rational enjoyment.[44]

By March, 1862, there were six machine shops in Macon, which might employ five hundred men altogether. These shops had motive power and all the needed machinery and tools for working in iron. Several of the shops had foundries attached to them. Macon was a healthy, central location, with good railroad communications to all points of the compass. It was in the interior of the Confederacy and, therefore, secure against the approach of Federal armies, and yet no important government contract, and no considerable amount of government work had been done in Macon by the end of the first year of war. Since, by March 1862, much of Tennessee was captured by the Federals, the Confederate authorities should turn their attention to Macon to develop war manufacturing facilities.[45]

There were other businesses in Macon during the first year of war, businesses which played no direct part in the war effort. The 24 December 1861 issue of the *Daily Telegraph* included notices for blacks to hire, oysters, beef, vegetable burning oil, Christmas presents, salt, sugar, syrup, flour, meal, cider vinegar, fireworks and toys, cotton goods, molasses, leather, smith's tools, sundries, new music, drugs and medicines, feathers, apples, and many other items.[46]

Soon after the war began Jacob Dinkter advertised his Ice Cream Saloon which sold ice cream, cakes, and confections. The establishment also catered excursion parties, picnics, and weddings.[47]

The firm of N. S. Prudden and Company, located across Mulberry Street from the Lanier House, sold staple and fancy dry goods.[48]

O'Donnell and Wippler's Restaurant, located under Ralston's Hall on Third Street, featured oysters, fish, and wild game.[49] Dr. M. A. Schlosser, who claimed he could cure permanently all foot diseases, was endorsed by Dr. E. L. Strohecker and Walter C. Hodgkins. Schlosser, whose office was located in Room No. 9 of the Lanier House, claimed that he had served as Surgeon Chiropodist to two famous European rulers of the nineteenth Century, Emperor Napoleon III of France and King Ludwig II of Bavaria.[50]

Another Macon physician, Dr. Hammond, successfully performed an operation on a black male slave of a Mrs. Lockett of Clinton, Georgia. The

---

[44] *Macon Daily Telegraph*, 13 August 1861.

[45] Ibid., 18 March 1862.

[46] Ibid., 24 December 1861.

[47] Ibid., 15 April 1861.

[48] N.S. Prudden and Company to John B. Lamar, Bill, Macon, 11 June 1861, Cobb Papers, 1861.

[49] *Macon Daily Telegraph*, 9 September 1861.

[50] Ibid., 5 October 1861.

surgery involved the repair of a strangulated inguinal hernia, considered "one of the most critical and dangerous operations in Surgery."[51]

The civilian tone of the City during the first year of the war can be followed by studying the correspondence of John B. Lamar whose letters often made it seem as if the war were far away from Macon during that early period. On 4 May 1861, he paid $2.00 to Editor Joseph Clisby to send the *Daily Telegraph* to Howell Cobb, then in Montgomery.[52] At the end of May, Lamar, who was often sick, informed his sister that he was walking about, but was still taking medicine for jaundice and was still weak from a bout with fever.[53] Mary Ann, deeply worried about her brother, wrote on 27 June that she had read in the *Daily Telegraph* that there was a good deal of sickness in Macon. Since she had not received a reply to an earlier letter she confessed "my fears have become almost unsupportable."[54]

Later in the summer Lamar noted that two gallons of gin in Macon cost $2.00, and a demijohn of the liquor was valued at $4.00. However, Belgian gin could not be purchased in Macon at any price by August 1861, possibly because of the increasingly extensive blockade placed by the Federals along the Southern coast.[55] Lamar's nephew, John A. Cobb, wanted him to buy horses for Howell Cobb because of the difficulty of finding horses in Athens.[56]

Because the summer of 1861 was very wet, the cotton crop would be a small one. By 31 August Lamar wrote John A. Cobb that "no one ever knows any more of how a cotton crop is going to turn out until it has turned out, than he does of the price it will command afterward." It didn't look as if the cotton would bloom to make a boll by the usual date of 10 September. Lamar lamented "if the blooms dont hurry they will be too late. There are precious few just now." The crop on his Swift Creek Plantation in Bibb County looked poor. There were, of course, deaths in Macon that summer. Lamar noted that Henry G. Lamar, whose son Leonidas had been wounded at the Battle of First Manassas, died on 30 August. The death of his son "preyed on him & caused his death," Lamar believed. Another Lamar friend, Jimmy Ray died on the morning of 31 August. The cause of his death was old age since he was between ninety and one-hundred years old. However, Lamar noted, "Macon is very healthy."[57]

By early November, Lamar noted that the cotton crop was turning out better than he had thought, but the unusual wet weather would cause the quality to be

---

[51] Ibid., 3 December 1861.

[52] Lamar to Joseph Clisby, Macon, 4 May 1861, Cobb Papers, 1861.

[53] Lamar to Mary Ann Cobb, Ibid., 28 May 1861.

[54] Mary Ann Cobb to Lamar, Athens, GA., 27 June 1861, Ibid.

[55] Lamar to Mary Ann Cobb, Macon, 9 August 1861, Ibid.

[56] John A. Cobb to Lamar, Athens, 18 August 1861, Ibid.

[57] Lamar to John A. Cobb, Macon, 31 August 1861, Ibid.

poor. Fortunately he had plenty of bread and meat for another year, and had laid up supplies of salt, bagging, rope, and clothes for the slaves. Even though salt cost $12.00 a sack on the Macon market by early November, Lamar had shrewdly purchased it in the spring for $1.25. Since he had acquired 200 bushels he had saved between $250 and $2400, and all the other supplies in the same proportion. Lamar had about 800 pounds of wool, which would make half of the cloth for slave clothing. He could get shoes at some price. The plantations could do without bagging, rope, and twine. Since he had packed seed cotton away in pens and let it lay, the English would send him bagging. Salt was another story, it was essential. Lamar hoped that "enough will be made on the long line of our coast during the year" to ensure a supply of the precious commodity. His hopeful mood ended with the statement, "Verily, verily providence has our beloved country in charge, state & Confederate, the evidence is that we get along tolerably well in spite of our rulers."[58]

Times were so good in November that Lamar was able to purchase 172 yards of jeans for his slaves at sixteen cents a yard from the Macon firm of Ross and Seymour on 8 November.[59]

On 9 November Lamar shipped uniforms of blue broadcloth to Cobb and to nephews, Lamar and John.[60] Nearly three weeks later he wrote Cobb asking his help in securing a position for Dr. James Mercer Green with a military hospital, preferably one of the Georgia Hospitals in Richmond. After all, Green was Lamar's physician, and "the best physician we have in Macon, as he is the only physician who attends me, when I am sick." Moreover, he tended members of the Cobb Family when they were in Macon.[61] As if to prove a point, Lamar paid Green for medical services on the same day, 27 November for treating himself, Mary Ann Cobb, and two slaves.[62]

The war, however, did impact the Cotton Planters' Convention which met in the Council Chamber of Macon's new City Hall on 12 November. Presided over by Howell Cobb, the meeting was "not largely attended due to war."[63]

When Mary Ann Cobb made tentative plans to come to Macon for Christmas, Lamar assured her he had plenty of food, even if she brought many servants. "All that I have will belong to you & your children & Andrew when I peg out," he assured her, "& I should like for you to enjoy some of it beforehand." Two rooms his sister used in her visits to Macon would be available for this visit. To make matters easier, he planned to use his library as a

---

[58] Lamar to Howell Cobb, Macon, 3 November 1861, Ibid.

[59] Ross and Seymour to Lamar, Macon, 8 November 1861, Ibid.

[60] Lamar to Mary Ann Cobb, Macon, 9 November 1861, Ibid.

[61] Lamar to Cobb, Macon, 27 November 1861, Ibid.

[62] Green to Lamar, Macon, 27 November 1861, Ibid.

[63] *Macon Daily Telegraph*, 20 November 1861.

bedroom throughout the winter. As for food, he had twenty-six young geese, twenty-one ducks, and thirteen turkeys in the yard, and his servant, Henry, planned to get six additional turkeys on the following day. More ducks would arrive from his Sumter County Plantation soon. These items, in addition to the spare ribs and back bones available during hog killing time, should feed everyone well. However, he might not be in Macon to greet her when she came because he had to go to Sumter County and attend to his plantations there. His niece Mary Ann [one of Mrs. Cobb's daughters] should bring her French books so she could study that language. Little Andrew Jackson Cobb had his flag staff, made of a broom handle, which he could attach another flag to and play at mustering troops.[64]

Ten days later Lamar wrote that he had twenty-eight turkeys, twenty-six geese, and twenty ducks "raising their voices in the lot daily, seeming to call on them to come along with their ma." He was disappointed when he and his servant Henry went to the depot of the Macon and Western Railroad and did not find the Cobbs on the train. Thereupon, bachelor that he was, he returned home, drew up a seat by the fire, and read the last chapters of 1st Samuel in his French bible until time for bed. He confided that it "bothered my brain to know who wrote the two books of Samuel, they were written by more than one person." Lamar was happy that the ladies of Macon were fixing up a Christmas tree for a grand Christmas celebration with everyone contributing whatever they could to it. There was an admittance fee at the door which would go to the Soldiers' Relief Society. Everyone who went in could draw a prize from the tree by the number of his ticket. The children of Macon were anxious to see the "Santa Claus doings on a big scale." In a burst of humor Lamar wrote, "he puts nothing in our stockings this Christmas but carries everything to the tree for distribution. The old chap is in favour of the Southern Confederacy I suppose & wishes to aid the cause in his way."[65]

That Christmas of 1861, before the war really impacted Macon, was a happy one. Even the weather cooperated to raise the spirits of everyone. The editor of the *Daily Telegraph* noted that a friend told him "so fair a Christmas as we had day before yesterday, has not been seen in Macon since the year of grace, 1839." The day was beautiful, the temperature mild, the sky cloudless, and the "sun as bright and dazzling as that luminary ever gets to be."[66]

Mary Ann Cobb wrote her husband from Macon on 8 January 1862, that Thomas Cobb, their youngest child, had an attack of fever, but was better. The three older children walked with their Uncle John on the east bank of the Ocmulgee "sometimes as far as the 'Mound'. Their son, Andrew Jackson

---

[64] Lamar to Mary Ann Cobb, Macon, 12 December 1861, Cobb Papers, 1861.
[65] Lamar to Mary Ann Cobb, Macon, 22 December 1861, Ibid.
[66] *Macon Daily Telegraph*. 27 December 1861.

Cobb, she reported, "gets a little tired and bleats occasionally when he has to ascend or descend a hill or rugged place much to the amusement of his sisters. One of Macon's physicians, Dr. Roosevelt, was attending to Eliza Cobb who had a bilious attack during the Christmas season. The child, however, was quickly getting well under Roosevelt's homeopathic treatment. The doctor himself was recovering from a severe attack of inflammatory rheumatism "and today," Mary Ann wrote, "while telling me of his acute suffering I told him I had been quite a victim of neuralgia." Whereupon, Roosevelt told Mrs. Cobb he could give her a medicine which would give her immediate relief.[67]

But, despite occasional frightening attacks of illness, Macon was so quiet that Mary Ann confided to her husband a few days later that the "'War' and the 'Camp' seem further off from here than at Athens."[68]

Since the new year was so warm and pleasant, Mary Ann decided to stay for a time in Macon. By late January her daughter, Mary Ann, was going to school three days a week (one hour in the afternoon) to a French teacher who taught in her home on Walnut Street near John B. Lamar's house. Little Mary Ann studied intermediate French while her uncle continued his studies of that language and read every day in his French bible. He also read the novel *Gil Blas* in French, and did well although he only studied French for five weeks before the war during an extended trip to New York.[69]

In late March the weather was so beautiful that the three youngest Cobb children played in their uncle's flower garden.[70] Two days later she talked of giving $20.00 for herself and her three daughters to the Gunboat Fund. She called the ship, which became the *C.S.S. Georgia*, "a second Merrimac."[71]

By the end of the month things were so quiet that all she could confide to Cobb was that she had been to Vineville to bring Olivia, one of her servants, with her baggage back to the "Bear's Den." "Hotspur," a horse, was sick with kidney problems, forcing Lamar to send for a black horse doctor, famous in Macon for his work with horses.[72]

There were other happenings in Macon during the first year of war. Deaths were a common occurrence in a day when medicine was in its infancy. On 25 May 1861 Eugenia A. Nisbet, daughter of Judge Eugenius A. Nisbet, died at the

---

[67] Mary Ann Cobb to her husband, Macon, 8 January 1862, Ibid. The Mound referred to was probably the Great Temple Mound, one of the featured attractions in the modern Ocmulgee National Monument.

[68] Mary Ann Cobb to her husband, Macon, 11 January 1862, Ibid.

[69] Mary Ann Cobb to her husband, 20 January 1862, Ibid.

[70] Mary Ann Cobb to her husband, 17 March 1862, Ibid.

[71] Mary Ann Cobb to her husband, 20 March 1862.

[72] Mary Ann Cobb to her husband, Macon, 27 March 1862.

age of sixteen.[73] Another child of a prominent Maconite, Marion Preston Rose, daughter of Simri Rose, an 1859 graduate of Wesleyan Female College, and a member of the Baptist Church passed away aged twenty.[74]

Prominent businessman Thomas Hardeman, Sr. died at his home in Vineville on Sunday, 11 August 1861. His funeral, conducted by Methodist pastor Dr. Mann, was held at the Methodist Church on the twelfth. His passing was of such import that the business houses in the city closed, and he was buried with Masonic honors.[75]

Destruction of a different kind hit the city frequently during the period. Fires were commonplace, especially in a community where most of the structures were built of wood. Early in the morning of 19 April a fire was discovered in Granite Hall on Mulberry Street. One part of the main floor was occupied by the dry goods dealer, N. S. Prudden, who managed to save most of his merchandise, although much of it was damaged. The other section of the building was occupied by Miss Murphy's millinery establishment. A portion of her goods was also saved. Another business located in the building, Grannis' General Agency Office, lost only part of its effects. The second and third floors of the building were operated as a hotel by B.F. Dense. Dense saved some of his furniture. The building, owned by J. C. Dunham of Eatonton, cost $20,000, but only $5,000 in insurance had been taken out by Dunham through the Augusta Insurance and Banking Company. Dense's furniture was insured for $2,000 by the same company, and Prudden had insurance covering $6,000 of his losses. A reporter for the *Daily Telegraph* deplored the loss of one of the city's landmarks because "Mulberry Street may be marred in its fair proportions for some time to come."[76]

During the fire the boarders in Dense's hotel lost most of their clothing and other property. Through the efforts of George S. Obear and his firemen the adjoining stores of R. P. McEvoy and John L. Jones, although in great danger, were saved, although Jones quickly removed his merchandise. The *Journal and Messenger*'s reporter related that Dense would be able to start his business again having obtained several rooms besides those he occupied, in an adjoining building, over the McEvoy store. The paper joined its rival in lamenting the loss of the Granite Hall, a building which "was among our best constructed and most beautiful buildings- nearly new." Its destruction "presents a melancholy void in the center of the most beautiful block in our city." The paper blamed the destruction on an "incendiary."[77]

---

[73] *Georgia Journal and Messenger*, 29 May 1861.

[74] Ibid., 26 June 1861.

[75] Ibid., 14 August 1861.

[76] *Macon Daily Telegraph*, 19 April 1861.

[77] *Georgia Journal and Messenger*, 24 April 1861. See also Ibid., 1 May 1861.

Another spectacular fire occurred early on Saturday morning 25 May in a row of wooden buildings on Cotton Avenue, opposite the City Hall. The fire burned half a block on Macon's most important business thoroughfare.[78] Occupied by several tenants, the structures consisted of eight one-story wooden tenements which were used as grocery and provision stores. The rear portions of the buildings were occupied as living quarters. Henry Abel, in whose store the fire began, lost most of his goods. The tenement occupied by Krutz's Bakery also burned. The fire spread quickly because many of the buildings were old, and of little value. The *Journal and Messenger's* writer hoped "that the owners of the property will rebuild with an eye to the benefits now conferred on it by the location of the new City Hall."[79]

During the period there were other spectacular fires in Macon. One of these took place late on Monday night, 17 June when a fire broke out in a small wooden building in the rear of the Arch Street Methodist Church. The building was quickly burned, and the flames spread to the church which also was destroyed. The church, a new building, was brick. Its loss, the *Journal and Messenger's* correspondent noted, "will be a very serious loss to the large and worthy congregation which has been in the habit of worshiping" there.[80]

One of the most destructive fires during the summer of 1861, happened late on Sunday night, 30 June when a fire broke out on the south side of Cotton Avenue near Cherry Street, on the second story of a building owned by a Mr. Youngblood. The blaze burned the provision and grocery stores of Wheeler and Wilbur, Bearden and Gaines, and McCallie and Jones. It also consumed a one-story wooden building used by W. B. Heath as a barroom which was crushed by the falling of a brick wall. Another one-story brick store on the corner, occupied by the business of Messrs. Cherry, escaped destruction. The buildings which burned were two story brick tenements, built years before, and of only moderate value. Much of the property was owned by G. J. Blake and J. B. Ross. Most of the goods in the stores were saved. Wheeler and Wilbur's lost from $500 to $800 in merchandise; Bearden and Gaines lost about $7,000, while McCallie and Jones lost much of their inventory, but were covered by insurance. Ross and Blake suffered considerable loss. The property consumed included thirty-five to forty hogsheads of bacon, a large amount of pickled pork, lard, molasses, and spirits. The fire did not spread outside of the block where it started due to the strenuous efforts of the fire companies.[81]

Not all of the buildings destroyed by fire during 1861-1862 were businesses. In mid-August the roof of a wooden stable owned by Mrs. Robert Findlay

---

[78] *Macon Daily Telegraph*, 27 May 1861.

[79] *Georgia Journal and Messenger*, 29 May 1861.

[80] Ibid., 19 June 1861.

[81] Ibid., 3 July 1861. See also *Macon Daily Telegraph*, 2 July 1861.

caught fire, but local residents put it out before the fire companies arrived. This fire, started by incendiaries, according to the *Daily Telegraph's* reporter, caused the paper to urge that "Vigilant efforts should be made to ferret out the incendiaries, and if caught, they should be made an example of."[82]

Another stable, located on Poplar Street on the property of Mrs. Evans, was destroyed in early October. Unfortunately, two horses, belonging to J. P. Harvey, were burned to death in the blaze.[83]

Only a week later a one-story house owned by a Mrs. Morris and located on Oak Street, was burned. The fire bells "by a continual ringing roused many of [the] citizens from their slumbers." Although the fire companies came quickly, the building, worth about $1,200, was completely consumed.[84]

Still another house burned on 22 January 1862. The building, a large and fine two story wooden building owned by John L. Burge and located in East Macon, had been unoccupied for several months. Despite the energy shown by the fire companies which fought the conflagration, the building and its outhouses were completely destroyed. The loss in property was $1,500.[85] Fortunately, an adjoining cotton warehouse, owned by the firms of Lightfoot and Flanders and O. F. Adams, was saved by the black citizens of the neighborhood who heroically fought the blaze.[86] This bravery prompted the owners of the building to return the "sincere thanks of the Fire Companies and citizens of Macon, for their prompt assistance in saving our Ware House from conflagration."[87]

The warehouse next to the Freight Depot of the Georgia Central Railroad in East Macon was not so fortunate. The building, which was used by both the Central and South Western Railroads to smoke bacon for their hands, lost its roof, and part of the meat was charred. The blaze was caused by the accidental falling of a piece of bacon into the fire, which spread to a nearby post and on into the roof. The loss was small, 20,000 pounds of bacon, while over 60,000 pounds of it was saved. Although the hoops and staves of several barrels of lard were burned, the lard was also saved.[88]

Another factor which played a key role in the life of the people was religion. Church services were held as usual, of course, but there was an increased call upon God to bring a quick victory to the Confederacy. As early as 15 February 1861, prayer meetings were held in the Presbyterian, Episcopal, Methodist, and Baptist churches for the Confederacy and the army. The pastors of these churches

---

[82] *Macon Daily Telegraph*, 12 August 1861.
[83] *Georgia Journal and Messenger*, 9 October 1861.
[84] *Macon Daily Telegraph*, 16 October 1861.
[85] Ibid., 23 January 1862.
[86] Ibid., 24 January 1862.
[87] Ibid.
[88] Ibid., 24 February 1862.

urged their parishioners to pray that the approaching war might be averted, and that if it did start the people of Georgia might be ready to meet the crisis "with the faith and patience and determination of patriots and christians."[89]

On 7 April 1861 officers and soldiers of the new Confederate Army attended the service of the Methodist Church in military fatigue dress. Some were from Augusta, and all of them were on their way to Pensacola, Florida, where it was thought fighting would soon occur. Reverend Dr. L. Pierce illustrated his sermon by the circumstances around him, and Reverend Dr. J. E. Evans, the Presiding Elder, alluded to the soldiers in the congregation, and invited those who were members of a Christian church to participate in the Sacrament of Holy Communion. Many accepted the invitation and came forward.[90]

The Georgia Conference of the Methodist Church met in Macon on Wednesday, 1 May, and elected as its president, Dr. Lovic Pierce. Fewer delegates than usual were present because the war had begun, but much discussion occurred involving the Sabbath School issue and the happiness of the children.[91]

As the war continued, its influence over Macon's religious community grew. Reverend David Wills, the Presbyterian minister, planned to repeat his discourse upon the relations of Christianity to war before the Fifth Georgia Regiment.[92]

As time passed, religion played a major role in strengthening the resolve of the people to continue the struggle for their independence. When Macon observed a national fast day on 19 June the city wore the aspects of a Sabbath. Stores were closed, and deeply solemn services were held in the churches which were filled with serious and devout people. The *Journal and Messenger,* commenting on the day, noted, "Let the same pious and trustful spirit exhibited by our community on Thursday last, continue to pervade our land, we need not fear 'what man can do unto us'. Our enemies will be scattered like chaff before the wind. 'Trust in the Lord, and keep your powder dry', is a maxim eminently suited to these times of peril."[93]

Unfortunately, some of this feeling did not reach the soldiers in the field, a fact which prompted Captain Robert A. Smith to write to his friend, Reverend John W. Burke in mid-August. Smith believed that "if ever there was a time when men ought to pray everywhere- it is at such a time as this." He believed that when a civil war raged between people who were the descendants of the fathers of constitutional liberty, everyone should "give themselves to serious

---

[89] Ibid., 15 February 1861.

[90] *Georgia Journal and Messenger*, 10 April 1861.

[91] Ibid., 8 May 1861.

[92] *Macon Daily Telegraph*, 10 May 1861.

[93] Ibid., 26 June 1861.

prayer." The people of Macon should pray as one man for the success of the Confederacy. "How can we who are in the field fight successfully," he confided, "unless our friends at home support us by their prayers?" Smith believed that "without God we can do nothing."[94]

Sometimes, even in the first year of the war, some of Macon's ministers expressed interesting views. During a national fast day, observed on 7 March 1862, Mary Ann Cobb attended services at the Baptist Church. As she left she met the pastor, Reverend Samuel Boykin, who asked about her husband. Boykin added, "when you write to the Gov [Cobb] tell him the people are beginning to think the President is a traitor!" Mary Ann was startled by Reverend Boykin's statement. Although she had heard and read of abuse heaped on Davis "in every shape and form," she had never heard the word traitor attached to the President. She looked at the minister with surprise. Boykin continued, "the President is not enough of a secessionist- and if he does not look sharp he will be hoisted out of the Presidency and Mr. [Robert] Toombs put in his place." This disturbed Mary Ann, who replied, "Well then…you would rather have a rash man than a safe one." Boykin, who surprised her with his militant fervency, replied that the people wanted someone who would go ahead "and whip the Yankees." Fortunately, another minister, Reverend Warren, entered the conversation, with a defense of Davis, saying "he believed he was a good Christian gentleman and would do right." He then stepped up to Mary Ann and observed, "You are right- we might get a rash man over us who would know nothing about directing the war- and I don't want anybody…but our President to have charge of the Military Affairs."[95]

The first year of war in Macon was relatively peaceful, but things would soon change. Although fighting did not swirl about the City for another two years, the war would soon come to Macon in other ways.

---

[94] Robert A. Smith to Rev. John W. Burke, Sewell's Point, Va., 14 August 1861, Civil War Miscellany, Box 1, Middle Georgia Archives, Washington Memorial Library, Macon.

[95] Mary Ann Cobb to her husband, Macon, 8 March 1862, Cobb Papers, 1862.

Chapter 6

The War Comes to Macon:
Military Hospitals

At first hospital work in Macon consisted of sending hospital supplies to the sick and wounded Georgia soldiers in the field. On 31 August 1861, a meeting was held in Macon to organize the Georgia Hospital Relief Society. John Jones Gresham, Lewis Neal Whittle, and Dr. Joel Branham joined the pastors of the churches and the Soldiers' Relief Society to serve as the Central Hospital Committee of Georgia. Judge Eugenius A. Nisbet served as Chairman and his brother, James T. Nisbet was Secretary.[1]

In early September Reverend W. J. Hard of Augusta, collected supplies to support the Georgia Hospital in Richmond, part of the Chimborazo Hospital, located on Chimborazo Hill next to the James River on the eastern side of Richmond.[2] In mid-September, W. T. Massey raised money to send nurses to sick soldiers among the Georgia troops stationed at Sewall's Point, Virginia. This money was specifically given to the members of the Jackson Artillery, many of whom were sick at the time.[3]

It was not until the spring of 1862, that Mayor Thomson announced that "Macon must become a general hospital, if need be, for the general reception and nurture of the wounded and the sooner the required preparation can be made, the better." The Mayor believed that Macon's public building would furnish hospital space, and the ladies of the city would provide "that untiring care that soothes and makes tolerable the pillow of affliction."[4]

By the spring of 1862, wounded men were coming into Macon, primarily as a result of the Battle of Shiloh, and money was raised to support nearly 1,000

---

[1] *Macon Daily Telegraph*, 3 September 1861. The best general study of Confederate hospitals is Horace H. Cunningham, *Doctors in Gray; the Confederate Medical Service*, Baton Rouge: Louisiana State University Press, 1958.

[2] Ibid., 5 September 1861. Hard served as Agent for the Fourth Congressional District of Georgia, to collect supplies throughout Middle Georgia.

[3] Ibid., 11 September 1861.

[4] Ibid., 4 March 1862.

soldiers, housed in Macon, many of them in the City's first hospital, the Floyd House.[5]

Dr. William H. Doughty of Augusta, Surgeon in charge of the Floyd House Hospital, arranged his facility into different wards. There were few deaths, although there were many serious cases of pneumonia.[6] Doughty soon established rules for the hospital. All visitors, except relatives of the soldiers or ministers of the Gospel, had to report at the office, and were not allowed to bring food to the patients, until after it was inspected by Dr. S. S. Douglas, the Hospital Steward, and found to conform to the diet prescribed in each case. Servants could not bring articles unless they had an order addressed to Assistant Surgeon W. H. Elliott or Dr. Douglas. The hospital would accept volunteer nurses, if needed, subject to the control and direction of the Surgeon. Visiting hours were from 10:00 A.M. until 6:00 P.M.[7]

A reporter for the *Daily Telegraph* visited the hospital in July and found it neat, clean, with good order prevailing in all its departments. He noted, "The rooms, bed, bedding, and patients are all kept clean. The patients receive the best of attention. The Hospital is divided into two wards—one under the charge of Dr. W. H. Doughty, and the other under Dr. Elliott—both of whom are clever gentlemen." The sick were rapidly getting well, and everything that could be done for them was accomplished. The reporter praised the hospital, exclaiming, "In the magnitude and system of its general arrangement, this Hospital is not excelled by any." However, the facility needed dried fruit and cordials, which, it was hoped, the women would supply.[8]

During July and August 1862, the Floyd House Hospital experienced only five deaths out of a total of some 200 to 250 patients treated. Three of these were brought into the facility in a dying condition. Two hundred and forty-four patients were treated in August alone, with only three deaths.[9] Part of the low mortality was due to the attention of the people of Macon who contributed chickens, vegetables, wine, sundries, butter, and tomatoes.[10]

As early as May, 1862, the hospital treated an average of 113 patients every day. The staff included the steward, five cooks, fifteen nurses, one ward master,

---

[5] Ibid., 15 April 1862. The best account of Macon's Confederate hospitals Dr. Ian A. Cameron's "James Mercer Green: Southern Gentleman, Confederate Surgeon, unpublished Mss., pp. 6-7. Macon, 23 May 1997, hereafter cited as Cameron, "James Mercer Green." The author is deeply indebted to Dr. Cameron for permission to use his manuscript.

[6] *Macon Daily Telegraph*, 1 May 1862.

[7] Ibid., 6 May 1862.

[8] Ibid., 21 July 1862.

[9] Ibid., 6 September 1862.

[10] Ibid., 8 August 1862.

and seven launderers. On 10 May the hospital received 1,775 rations; on June 11, 1,491 rations; on June 21, 1,658 rations; and on 1 July 1,318 rations. During the period 1-10 September there were 155 men in the hospital. This number increased to 177 on 11-20 September. By 31 October the sick numbered 184.[11]

In November 1862, Mrs. T. H. Plant of Macon wrote to J. C. Balthrop of Tennessee about the death of his son, G. J. Balthrop. She visited the young soldier's ward nearly every day for several months, and was attracted to him because of his intense suffering and by "his quiet uncomplaining manner." She saw the young man twice a day. His wound was in the right lung, and he was given every attention that could be given. His nurse, a Mr. Dunbar, attended him constantly, and his doctor thought he might recover until he found that his ribs were separated by the ball which had wounded him. "He was perfectly conscious till the last moment," Mrs. Plant wrote, "[Balthrop] was visited several times by Mr. Warren, the Baptist Minister, and although he could not converse very freely on account of his wound–still he enjoyed seeing Mr. W. Said he felt perfectly ready and willing to die, that he could put his whole trust in his Savior. His suffering was very great and towards the last he prayed that he might be taken from this world of suffering." She added that young Balthrop "died perfectly happy and quietly on the 9th. of November Calling on those around him to meet him in Heaven."[12]

The nurses and matrons who served the Floyd House Hospital, then known as the "General Hospital," had to have both experience and tact in management. Their duties included administering medicine and food to the sick; and preserving cleanliness and order about the sick beds. Chief Surgeon Doughty noted that their most essential quality was "a quiet, gentle manner. With an effective organization of this character, the mortality from disease would be materially reduced, and the welfare of our heroic soldiers promoted in every respect."[13]

---

[11] Entries for May, June, July, and September 1862, Macon General Hospital Account Book, GDA&H, hereafter cited as Macon General Hospital Account Book. During the period 21-30 September there were 191 men in the hospital. Other numbers for the period included 161 for 1-10 October; 128 for 11-20 October; and 1,657 for 21-30 October. Ibid.

[12] Mrs. T.H. Plant to J.C. Balthrop, Macon, 13 November 1862, in Tennessee Civil War Letters (Typescript), Records of East Tennessee, Civil War Records, vol. 3, p. 104, Mrs. John Trotwood Moore and others, Historical Records Survey Transcription Unit Division of Women's and Professional Projects Works Progress Administration, Nashville, Tenn. The Historical Records Survey, 1 June 1939, in 3 vols., 2, p. 104, in Division of Manuscripts, UT.

[13] Dr. William H. Doughty in *Macon Daily Telegraph*, 11 December 1862.

The hospital needed two elderly women as Chief Matrons to "superintend the domestic economy of the house, receive and prepare nourishment for the sick." Their pay was set at $100 a month, plus board. Two competent women were also needed as assistant matrons to oversee the laundry and clean the clothing and bedding of the sick. Their pay was established at $35.00 a month plus board. Thirty dollars a month and board was offered for two ward matrons to serve as nurses.[14]

By early 1863, Dr. James Mercer Green had assumed control of the Macon hospitals. Green, a graduate of Jefferson Medical College in Philadelphia, came to Macon in 1837, soon after his graduation. He set up a practice in the growing frontier town, and was elected to the City Council in 1846. His wife, Sarah Virginia Prince, whom he married in 1846, was orphaned as a child when her parents were both drowned at sea in a ship wreck on the coast of North Carolina in 1837. Washington Poe, Postmaster of Macon, an able attorney, and one of the City's leading citizens, had adopted all three Prince children. The Greens became the parents of seven children. In 1851, Green began a project to provide an educational facility for the two hundred and twenty blind children in Georgia. His efforts resulted in the establishment of the Georgia Academy for the Blind in 1852. During the war the facility occupied a building erected for the purpose in 1858 on a site between College and Orange Streets. The Greens built their beautiful home on Poplar Street.

In 1853, Green joined his brother, Kollick, and their friend Philemon Tracy as editors of the *Georgia Telegraph*. His reputation as a physician was enhanced in 1855 when he published a treatise entitled "Enlargement of Bronchial Glands simulating Aortic Disease." Active in the secession movement as a member of a group located in Charleston, South Carolina, and known as the "1860 Association," Green became a leader in the movement in Macon to promote secession.[15]

In the fall of 1861, Green failed to secure a permanent position with the Georgia Hospitals. He explained his failure to Howell Cobb, observing "I feel convinced that it is in my power to [be] of great service to hundreds of our poor sick & dying soldiers who are too often treated as if they were paupers instead of the owners of the medicines & supplies so munificently sent from Georgia for their relief."[16]

---

[14] Dr. William H. Doughty in Ibid.

[15] Cameron, "James Mercer Green," pp. 1-6. The Poes adopted the Prince children because Mrs. Selina Shirley Poe was Mrs. Prince's sister.

[16] James Mercer Green to Howell Cobb, Richmond, 21 December 1861, Cobb Papers, 1861.

When he arrived in Macon early in 1863, Green became Chief Surgeon of the Floyd House Hospital.[17] Cobb, who was then commanding Confederate forces in Florida, wanted Green to join him there but Green demurred feeling he should stay in Macon because his wife had developed a heart ailment. However, he assured Cobb, "If in the course of a month or two my wifes [sic] health should improve so much as to allow me to leave her I will make application to be ordered to report to you."[18]

In the spring of 1863, Macon's hospital facilities were increased when the Ladies' Soldiers' Relief Society, an offshoot of the Ladies' Aid Society, held a meeting in Concert Hall, over Messrs. Mix and Kirtland's Store to organize a permanent Wayside Home in Macon.[19] By mid-June the ladies had established the Wayside Home, which occupied a "large and well arranged house near the depot," and were calling for meat, flour, meal, poultry, eggs, butter, and vegetables. Sick or wounded soldiers, or those who could not pay their hotel bills, were permitted to rest at the home, free of charge, when passing through Macon. Surgeons were kept in attendance to care for the sick and wounded.[20]

It cost nearly $1,500 a month to operate the facility, part of which was raised by a Grand Exhibition by the pupils of B. M. Polhill's School. Maconites could enjoy the Exhibition, which included declamation, dialogue, and tableaux, for a $1.00 admission fee.[21] The Exhibition was a success, with the hall being crowded "with the elite of the town."[22]

The Wayside Home continued to receive support, especially in the matter of lower prices for food, and more money to purchase supplies.[23] Some of the money came from a lecture delivered by a Colonel Gordon at Ralston's Hall on 13 November. The title of Gordon's address was "What will he do with it?" Peculiar as the title was, the affair netted the Wayside Home $379.50.[24]

Hospital facilities in Macon were greatly expanded in September 1863, when hundreds of sick and wounded soldiers were sent down after the bloody Confederate victory at Chickamauga on 19-20 September. James Mercer Green urged the use of the Blind Academy as a hospital,[25] a call which was supported by the Post Commandant at Macon, Colonel D. Wyatt Aiken. Aiken wrote Governor Brown on 24 September that hospital room was needed for the sick

---

[17] John A. Cobb to his Father, Macon, 11 March 1863, Cobb Papers, 1863.

[18] James Mercer Green to Howell Cobb, Macon, 28 March 1863, Ibid.

[19] *Macon Daily Telegraph*, 8, 13, May 1863.

[20] Ibid., 16 June 1863.

[21] Ibid., 26 June 1863.

[22] Ibid., 30 June 1863.

[23] Ibid., 27 October 1863.

[24] Ibid., 13, 16 November 1863.

[25] Cameron, "James Mercer Green," p. 7

and wounded who were being sent to Macon by the hundreds. In order to make room for the wounded, Aiken wanted Brown to remove the dozen inmates of the Academy to Milledgeville.[26] Brown replied there was no place in Milledgeville where the children could be taken care of, therefore Aiken had to find other quarters for them in Macon.[27]

By November 1863, the Blind Asylum—or Academy, the terms were used interchangeably throughout the war years—cost $8,022.22 a year to operate, including salaries. The students housed there numbered 24.[28] When the building was taken over for hospital purposes, the Superintendent, Reverend W. D. Williams, bought a large building in Fort Valley for $1,000, and removed the children to that place.[29]

It was well that the Confederacy obtained the Blind Academy for a hospital. After the Battle of Chickamauga Macon was inundated with sick and wounded men. By 24 September several hundred men were sent down from the overcrowded hospitals in Atlanta. One hundred and fifty of them were lodged in the City Hall which was converted into another hospital known as the "City Hall Hospital."[30] Calls were made upon the citizens to supply food due to temporary shortages caused by the arrival of so many men.[31] Chairman R. W. Crawford of a group known as the "Aid Committee for Relief of Wounded of [General Braxton] Bragg's Army," appealed for planters to share their food with the soldiers hospitalized in Macon.[32] The Arch Street Baptist Congregation, who met at City Hall because their church was destroyed by fire, was forced to meet at a house near the site of their former sanctuary.[33]

A reporter for the *Daily Telegraph* described the Floyd House Hospital as being in "admirable order, and far more comfortable, in point of cleanliness, than formerly." Dr. A.M. Few, Chief Surgeon, kept the floors clean from spittle and other defilement, while the beds and cots were clean. The second and third stories of the building were occupied by 300 sick and wounded soldiers, and these floors were filled to capacity. Conditions were so bad that 180 of the slightly wounded were sent to Milledgeville and Eatonton on the invitation of the city governments of those communities to make room for several hundred

---

[26] Colonel D. Wyatt Aiken to Governor Brown, Telegram, Macon, 24 September 1863, GLB 1861-1865, p. 548.

[27] Brown to Aiken, Telegram, Milledgeville, 24 September 1863, Ibid.

[28] *Georgia Journal and Messenger*, 25 November 1863. The sum asked to support the institution for the following year was $12,000. Ibid.

[29] Ibid., 9 December 1863.

[30] *Macon Daily Telegraph*, 24 September 1863.

[31] Ibid., 24, 25 September 1863.

[32] Ibid., 26 September 1863.

[33] Rev. Thomas T. Christian in Ibid., 28 September 1863.

more men expected to arrive in Macon on 28 or 29 September. The total sick and wounded in Macon by the end of September was about 900 men. These were housed at the Blind Academy Hospital, the Bibb County Court House [which had also been turned into a hospital, the City Hall Hospital, and the Floyd House Hospital. Unfortunately, the Court House was not suitable, according to Dr. Whitehead, Chief Surgeon of the Confederate Hospitals in Macon during the absence of Dr. Green, therefore these men were transferred to the Blind Academy Hospital. Part of the Court House would then be transferred to the teachers of the Macon Free School.

The City Hall and City Council Chamber were prepared for a hospital and were being furnished with a supply of bunks and bedding sufficient to accommodate 150 men. The citizens of Macon and the Confederate Commissary Department provided hams, beef, turkey, chickens, and vegetables. The men were permitted to eat what they wished, except for those who were very ill.[34]

Dr. Stanford E. Chaille, a surgeon in the Provisional Army of the Confederate States [P.A.C.S.], who arrived in Macon during the crisis, quickly wrote Dr. Samuel Hollingsworth Stout, Medical Director of the Army of Tennessee, to tell him that Dr. Green needed two assistant surgeons. Chaille was ordered to Macon by General Bragg upon the request of General P. G. T. Beauregard, then commanding the Department of South Carolina, Georgia, and Florida.[35]

In early November 1863, Green informed Stout that one of his subordinates, Acting Assistant Surgeon Collins, was doing his job well. He was keeping his wards "remarkably clean, & under careful surveillance will make a very useful officer." The men who were sent to Eatonton, Fort Valley, Americus, and Butler because of overcrowding in Macon were carefully attended to by the doctors in these places who were contracted to care for them. Few men were dying in Macon too, and although Green had thirty cases of hospital gangrene, none had died because of it, except two who died from complications caused by a combination of hemorrhage and gangrene. "I am very happy to say," Green wrote, "that the gangrene has entirely ceased & I have no new cases." To add to

---

[34] Ibid., 28 September 1863.

[35] Dr. Stanford E. Chaille to Dr. Samuel H. Stout, Macon, 7 October 1863, Samuel H. Stout Papers, Correspondence 1847-1863, Box 1, Special Collections Division, Woodruff Library, Emory University Library, hereafter cited as Stout Correspondence, Emory University. The same letter may be found in the Samuel H. Stout Papers, microfilm, Reel 2, SHC.

Green's euphoria over the success of the hospitals under his charge, forty-nine men were sent back from the hospitals to the Army.[36]

Towards the end of November Stout decided to send an officer to Macon to open another hospital. Green assured his superior that he would be happy to help the officer. Since he had served as a physician in Macon for over twenty years he could smooth his way.

In the matter of granting leaves of absence Green displayed less enthusiasm. He noted Surgeon Douglas had more authority in that area than he did, and assured Stout he was cautious about granting such leaves. Many men who had families nearby had asked him for leaves. In those cases where he could give them he did so sparingly. "It really seems very hard," he confided to Stout, "to refuse this privilege to a good soldier who has been a year or two from home, & who is within half a days ride of his family." However, if such authority was properly used, Green believed, it would limit the number of desertions. An incident concerning the issuance of passes occurred when one of the men who had received such a hospital pass was arrested by an officer and returned to the hospital. The arresting officer threatened to send the pass to General Bragg. Although Green had never received an order to the contrary, he wanted Stout to tell Bragg what had happened. After all, though Green never expected to meet the commander of the Army of Tennessee, he "should be sorry to be known to him only in a bad light." Green felt the order was too harsh, and Congress should pass a law forcing surgeons to grant such leaves.[37]

On the following day, Green told Stout that a rumor that he was being superseded as Chief Surgeon of the Macon hospitals was false. Stout must consider Green as Surgeon of the Post of Macon. However, if Stout decided to send "an independent officer here, I will afford him every facility in my power."[38]

The pressure on Macon's hospitals increased in late November 1863, when 500 additional wounded were sent from Atlanta to Macon. This news prompted the *Daily Telegraph* to exclaim, "People must help to feed the men- all who desire to aid in this good work are requested to send cooked provisions to the General Hospital [Floyd House] and the City Hall building [City Hall Hospital]."[39] Because of these additional wounded, Green worked to secure 250 additional beds in the Macon hospitals.[40]

---

[36] Green to Stout, Macon, n.d., Stout Correspondence, Emory University. For additional information concerning hospital operations in Eatonton see Green to Stout, Macon, 18 November 1863, Ibid.

[37] Green to Stout, Macon, 25 November 1863, Stout Correspondence, Emory.

[38] Green to Stout, Macon, 26 November 1863, Ibid.

[39] *Macon Daily Telegraph*, 30 November 1863.

[40] Green to Stout, Macon, 7 January 1864, Samuel H. Stout Papers, Microfilm, Reel 1, SHC.

Early in 1864 one of Macon's more important hospitals, the Blind Academy Hospital, changed its name to the Ocmulgee Hospital. Since the facility was located on a high bluff next to the Ocmulgee River, Green believed this new name would be more appropriate.[41] The building, situated upon a square of ground at the river was rented from the State of Georgia for $2,700 a year, and could be secured for the duration of the war. However, since so many additional wounded were coming to Macon, additional buildings had to be erected. It was imperative that this expansion should be accomplished before the spring and summer campaigns of 1864. Therefore, Dr. Chaille, Ocmulgee's Surgeon in Charge, planned an expansion which would accommodate 300 additional men, and, in an emergency, up to 100 more. Instead of an additional ward, it would be better, Chaille believed, to have only five for greater security from fire, and to provide better ventilation for the buildings. The existing five buildings should be extended, Chaille thought, from 80 to 100 feet, "which the nature of the ground will readily admit of."[42]

Work continued slowly on the expansion. In early April 1864, Chaille hoped it would be completed in six weeks. It wasn't easy, he assured Stout, to keep the Quartermaster, the carpenters, the lumber man, the shingle man, and the railroad men all working efficiently. Progress was so slow that Chaille decided not to take a twelve-day-leave which he had received over two weeks earlier. He felt "This Hospital will probably be badly needed by May 15th and I am sure it will require my daily presence here to effect its completion." Another problem he faced was the lack of surgeons. Earlier, he had received orders to send five medical officers to Andersonville Prison, including one of his two Assistant Surgeons, Dr. P. H. Wright. Chaille hoped that he would receive a replacement for Wright since that officer "was given me by you on my special application he is an old student of mine, & a good officer."[43]

While workmen slowly expanded the Ocmulgee Hospital, Macon's doctors faced other problems. On 14 March Green made the rounds of the hospitals under his charge, and noticed that Mrs. Hallmark, the Principal Matron of the Floyd House Hospital, had invented a method for dyeing the hospital's white coverlets. She dipped the cloth in a strong infusion of red oak bark or black jack, then in a solution of copperas. Finally, she placed the coverlets in a solution of potash. Green believed that clean lye would do as well. The color varied according to the different strength of the oak bark infused, and of the solutions of

---

[41] Green to Stout, Macon, 29 January 1864, Stout Correspondence, Emory.

[42] Chaille to Stout, Macon, 2 February 1864, Ibid.

[43] Chaille to Stout, Macon, 3 April 1864, Ibid.

copperas and soda. The color achieved was "all of a pleasant warm colour, & far better than the white, or the dirty black left by the oak bark & copperas."[44]

By the beginning of April the Macon hospitals were well-run facilities. The *Daily Telegraph's* reporter observed that the Floyd House Hospital was a model for some hotels. The Ocmulgee Hospital, under Dr. Chaille's leadership, with his two able Assistant Surgeons, Drs. P. H. Wright and F. Walker, "is another deserving mention." The Ocmulgee Hospital had a splendid garden spot laid out, but could not grow vegetables due to a shortage of seeds. The reporter urged people to bring in cabbage, turnip, onion, beet, and bean seeds.[45]

One problem which surfaced in the spring of 1864, was the theft of property in the Ocmulgee Hospital. Dr. George F. Cooper, then Surgeon in Charge during the absence of Dr. Chaille, explained that Hospital Steward Powell made his reports for several weeks by deducting the property in use from the entire amount received. The Steward, Cooper believed, planned to take an accurate inventory of all the property which he neglected. Upon being questioned, the Steward explained he knew some property was missing, but Cooper was not told of this until the day the items were found missing. The angry Cooper lashed out against the thieves of whom he believed some example should be made. But Powell was also guilty because he was aware of the shortfall and did not report it for several weeks. Cooper wanted Green's opinion about whether charges and specifications should be made.[46]

Another difficulty involved the lack of medical officers in the Macon hospitals. The Floyd House Hospital was entitled to four Assistant Surgeons, but had only two. Although three assistant surgeons were authorized for the City Hall Hospital, only two were on duty. The Blind School Hospital, with three authorizations, had only two on duty. Only one assistant surgeon was on duty at the Ocmulgee Hospital, although Surgeon Chaille's time "is very much taken up with the progress of his building, & overlooking their proper construction." At this time [15 May 1864] the Macon Hospitals held 800 men.[47]

The situation was worsened by Sherman's approach to Marietta and Atlanta during the Atlanta Campaign. Green believed that, through the use of tents, the Macon hospitals could accommodate 600 to 1,000 more. He also made more hospital space available in Macon by sending five or six hundred men to Guyton on the Georgia Central Railroad, and an additional six hundred and thirty for

---

[44] Green to Stout, Macon, 14 March 1864, Stout Correspondence, Emory. Copperas is a ferrous sulfate which, when mixed with water, has a copperish color.

[45] *Macon Daily Telegraph*, 1 April 1864.

[46] Dr. George F. Cooper to Green, Macon, 11 May 1864, Stout Correspondence, Emory.

[47] Green to Stout, Macon, 15 May 1864, Ibid.

treatment in Columbus. He wanted permission to send more sick and wounded to the West Georgia city.[48]

Efforts were made to alleviate the problems concerned with the increase of patients at Macon. One of the problems which would remain with the Macon hospitals during the terrible summer of 1864, was the matter of transporting the men from the Macon and Western Railroad Depot to the hospitals. Fortunately, the omnibus owned by the firm of Greer and Masterson furnished transportation to five hundred men in May, working in some cases until after midnight. Unfortunately, many seriously wounded men lay in the car shed from four to six hours while awaiting transportation.[49] In an effort to solve this difficulty, Green issued an appeal through the *Daily Telegraph* for additional transportation for the wounded.[50]

The problem of enough tents was largely solved when Howell Cobb, then commanding in Macon, ordered Post Quarter Master Major John L. Morgan to turn over the tents he had on hand to Dr. Green.[51] Because of Cobb's action, Green obtained fifty-seven tents, and expected to borrow two hundred more. Chaille also assured Green that, when his present buildings were completed, and Green furnished him with more tents, he would be able to receive six hundred men at the Ocmulgee Hospital. The Floyd House Hospital could also be increased to serve 380 or 400 more men for a total of 1,650 men in the Macon hospitals. Unfortunately, Green believed that he couldn't occupy any additional buildings "with out the disagreeable resort of impressing," but he felt, "this must be done if necessary."[52]

Green tried to solve the problem of procuring additional hospital space by carefully searching for such facilities throughout Macon. He found two buildings which might be used. One of these, the old Planters Hotel and the row of stores beneath it would accommodate 350 men. The Brown House Hotel would receive perhaps 250 more. Green informed Cobb and other leaders that "With these two buildings we might be enabled to get over the present emergency.[53] Green also wanted to impress the Wesleyan Female College as a hospital.[54]

Green also turned to Colonel Aiken for additional space. There were 1,133 beds available for hospital use, with 1,003 patients to fill them. But Green had

[48] Green to Stout, Macon, 22 May 1864, Ibid.

[49] *Macon Daily Telegraph*, 24 May 1864.

[50] *Macon Daily Telegraph*, 25 May 1864.

[51] Lamar Cobb to Maj. John L. Morgan, Macon, 25 May 1864, Howell Cobb Letter Book, 1864-1865, UGA, p. 86.

[52] Green to Stout, Macon, 30 May 1864, Stout Correspondence, Emory.

[53] Green to Cobb, Macon, 31 May 1864, Cobb Papers, 1864. See also *Macon Daily Telegraph*, 30 May 1864.

[54] Cameron, "James Mercer Green," p. 10.

320 more patients coming down from Atlanta by the evening of 3 June. The anguished Green wrote, "What shall be done with these men shall our brave sick & wounded lie on the floor or be turned into the streets- every one almost will answer no." Green believed that double the present amount of hospital space would soon be needed, and urged Aiken to consult with Judge Nisbet about the best way of handling the matter.[55]

On 18 June 1864, Judge Oliver A. Lochrane, presiding judge of the Bibb Superior Court, dissolved a bill of injunction which would have prevented Green from using the Planters Hotel as a hospital. Lochrane, however, prohibited Green from using the stores underneath the hotel until Stout sent a telegram stating that the sick men were sent to Macon and the medical authorities needed the stores for hospital space. Green, thereupon, wrote Stout, "Please oblige me then by sending at once a telegraphic order that you intend to send me 1000 sick & wounded men, & to make proper provision for them. If a battle has occurred or is imminent please state that." In the meantime, Green planned to continue to make out requisitions for hospital space. Green suffered a major defeat in this area, however, when Lochrane denied him the use of the Female College. Green needed this building, and told Stout "as it is of immense importance for us to get it, I hope you will at once procure authority from Genl. [Joseph E.] Johnston, the War Dept. Or other authority that we can compel its impressment." The angry doctor wanted some of the people of Macon "to have some little of the burdens of the war as well as all its profits." "It is disgusting," he continued, "to see the contemptuous indifference & even hatred that many of these wealthy foreigners & yankees & some disloyal men of Southern birth have to everything concerning the soldiers, hospitals &c. I desire most sincerely to be able to learn some of these men their duties to the Govt. that protects them."[56] Macon's hospitals during June were doing well despite the lack of enough space. A visitor described the facilities as neat and clean, especially "Ocmulgee on the riverbank," which was "well arranged and [the] most comfortable institution of the kind in this portion of the country."[57] Another observer noted that Dr. S. P. Green, in charge of Ward No. 1 at the Floyd House Hospital, conducted his ward like "clock work." The space was

---

[55] Green to Aiken, Macon, 3 June 1864, Eugenius A. Nisbet Letters, 1862-1864, Manuscript Department, Duke University, hereafter cited as Nisbet Letters, DU.

[56] Green to Stout, Macon, 18 June 1864, Stout Correspondence, Emory. For an account of business profits in Georgia during the War see Mary A. DeCredico, *Patriotism for Profit Georgia's Urban Entrepreneurs and the Confederate War Effort*, The University of North Carolina Press: Chapel Hill and London, 1990.

[57] T.J.A. Louisiana, in *Macon Daily Telegraph*, 2 June 1864.

neat, rations were well prepared, nurses were kind and attentive, and the women of Macon were always on hand distributing delicacies to the sick and wounded.[58]

Another visitor wrote that City Hall Hospital was operated under the supervision of Dr. L. L. Saunders and was located on the block of buildings formed by Cotton Avenue on the west, and First Street on the east. It faced the open space formed by the diagonal direction of Cotton Avenue, as it ran in the heart of Macon. The building was described as "a large square bldg., two stories in height, and built on the style of Grecian architecture, and is very commodious." The main floor housed the offices of Dr. Saunders, the matron, the dispensary, and the room occupied by the regular officers of the Hospital. On the same floor, and on the second floor, were two very large and well ventilated rooms, which were then filled with the sick and wounded. Altogether, the Hospital contained five wards. The Chief Ward Master was Uriah Kellog; the Chief Cook, John Smith; George Elder served as mailman; Sam Wheeler as Chief Cook; and "Old Aunt Peggy the head laundress."[59]

There were some who wanted to help the hospitals. A businessman, S. Davis Tonge of Bainbridge, Georgia, for instance, wanted to furnish forty-two bales of cotton he had stored in Americus for use in his factory. Since the factory was closed because the male operatives between the ages of seventeen and fifty were conscripted into the army, this material could be sent to Dr. Green for use in pillows and mattresses. The Macon Cotton Factory could run the raw cotton through machinery which removed the lint, and made the fiber more buoyant and useful as bedding.[60]

The beleaguered Green had other problems besides the lack of hospital space. One of these difficulties was comparatively minor. All women who visited the City Hall Hospital were directed to come at exactly 8:30 A.M. and leave their food on the shelves on the ground floor, until a special committee composed of women assigned them wards in which to distribute food.[61]

Other problems were more serious. One of these involved a group of doctors on duty at the Ocmulgee Hospital who wanted to use the room assigned as an office for the officer of the day, as a mess room. The room was fairly large, fifteen by thirty feet, and was large enough to mess in and still provide space for the officer of the day. The officers, Drs. P. Henry Wright, William Love, and others, planned to furnish their own servant, food, and furniture and, if allowed to use the room, would not interfere with the operation of the hospital. The men did

---

[58] Ibid., 23 June 1864.

[59] Ibid., 6 July 1864.

[60] S. Davis Tonge to Green, Bainbridge, GA., 13 June 1864, Stout Correspondence, Emory.

[61] Ibid., 28 May 1864.

not wish to lose their commutation money paid to them for quarters.[62] As Chief Surgeon for the Ocmulgee Hospital, Dr. Chaille, urged Stout to grant the request, explaining the application was only for the right to eat in the Hospital. The applicants planned to pay all expenses, and added, "I cannot think that a room assigned to the officer of the day, and used as Mess Room could be considered as quarters furnished by the government, to all those messing therein." After all, the Richmond medical authorities allowed medical officers to mess in their hospitals.[63]

Chaille was able to present the Medical Director of the Army of Tennessee with better news. The improvements to the Ocmulgee Hospital were nearly complete, except repairs to the four buildings erected before he came to Macon. These structures were being renovated with plank roofing, and were being shingled, and properly prepared to receive patients. The carpenters who worked on the new buildings were finishing their work. Chaille could accommodate 400 patients, having had as many as 471. He would not, however, be able to take care of more than 550; "which last number," he wrote, "I will be able to accommodate after this week." However, he explained, "I shall never report my capacity over 500 which is as many as I can properly accommodate." On another, even more pleasant front, he informed Stout "Two weeks ago a second Miss Chaille made her appearance in the Confederacy, and with her mother is doing as well as could be expected."[64]

When Sherman crossed the Chattahoochee and began the siege of Atlanta, Macon became second only to Richmond, as a hospital center when Medical Director Stout and his assistant Dr. L. M. Bemiss, ordered the removal of some of the Atlanta Hospitals to Macon. These included the Fair Ground Hospital, the Polk Hospital, and the Brown and Grant Hospitals. Plans called for the movement to begin at 5:00 A.M. on 7 July with the removal of the hospital furniture. Those sick and wounded who could not stand the long railroad journey to Macon would be housed in the Medical College, Institute, and Empire Hospitals which would continue to operate in Atlanta. Plans called for the furnishing of tents to make up the anticipated lack of space in Macon's hospital facilities.[65]

Because so many tents were set up as hospital facilities in the vicinity of the Vineville Academy Hospital in Vineville, E. N. Corey, Medical Inspector for

---

[62] P. Henry Wright, William Love, and others to Stout, Ocmulgee Hospital, Macon, 13 June 1864, Ibid.

[63] Chaille to Stout, Ocmulgee Hospital, Macon, 20 June 1864, Ibid.

[64] Ibid.

[65] Dr. L.M. Bemiss for Dr. Samuel H. Stout to Dr. J.P. Logan, Atlanta, 6 July 1864, Samuel H. Stout Papers, Manuscripts Department, Tulane University Libraries, hereafter cited as Stout Papers, Tulane.

the Army of Tennessee, inspected the rapidly-expanding tent hospitals. He urged the Medical Inspectors Office for the District of Virginia, Tennessee, and Georgia, to instruct medical officers to follow a plan for tent hospitals. The tents had to be pitched in wards of twenty-two tents to each ward set in two parallel rows with a space of ten feet between each tent. The street which lay between the rear of the tents must be twenty feet wide. The street in front and on both sides of the wards had to be fifty feet wide. Medical officers also had to insist upon a more systematic plan for their cooking and washing departments so they could be policed more effectively. Medical officers had to use a type of sink known as the box sink for toilet purposes and change them every morning.[66]

Stout adopted Corey's plan and instructed surgeons in charge of hospital encampments to arrange their facilities in accordance with his suggestions.[67]

The impact of so many sick and wounded soldiers on Macon prompted William Blackshear to write his wife, "The wounded are bearing down upon us by thousands." Despite this, most people in Macon remained hopeful that Sherman would be defeated at Atlanta.[68]

Laura Nisbet Boykin scribbled in her diary that "Our quiet city becomes . . . the great receiving Hospital for the wounded." She noted that public buildings were impressed, and the streets crowded with ambulances, carriages and wagons, "bearing their freight of mutilated men." The very air the people inhaled "betokens," she wrote, "in its impurity, the presence of disease and death." When she went to the depot of the Macon and Western Depot she observed thousands of men being lifted from the straw-covered floors of the cattle-cars, and in the hospitals. These scenes burned into her memory "with the red-hot iron of wrath against our oppressors, and in anguish of spirit we cry out. 'How long, O Lord! How long'; But we endeavor to possess our souls in patience. It is the baptism of blood, which we are undergoing, before the Confederacy can take a place in the community of nations."[69]

During the afternoon of 27 June a freight train brought eighty to one-hundred wounded to Macon. Arriving at 4:00 P.M., the men were laid on the ground below the freight house. Those who could walk the half mile to the hospital did. A single ambulance carried the remainder. However, as late as 8:00 P.M., a

---

[66] E.N. Corey to Medical Inspectors Office, District of Va., Tenn., and Ga., Macon, 14 July 1864, Stout Correspondence, Emory. Hospital facilities located in tents were known as "Hospital Encampments."

[67] Stout to Surgeons in Charge of Hospital Encampments, Macon, 15 July 1864, Ibid.

[68] William Blackshear to his wife, "The Retreat," 22 July 1864, Blackshear Papers.

[69] Laura Nisbet Boykin diary, 15 August 1864, in Mary Wright Stock, ed., *Shinplasters and Homespun The Diary of Laura Nisbet Boykin*, Rockville, Md., Printer, nd, p. 3, hereafter cited as Boykin Diary.

dozen men still lay on the ground below the freight house, groaning in agony. Even as late as 9 July Green wrote Stout, "The wounded and sick from the Atlanta hospitals came pouring in yesterday, three trains having arrived during the day. It is a great pity and some reflection upon the benevolent and public spirit of Macon that so many of these poor, weary fellows should be compelled to totter to the hospitals, on foot, under a scorching sun, when there are numbers of private vehicles which could be devoted to that purpose for an hour or so during the day. The time has come when Macon…must bare her arms to lift the burden imposed by God and humanity."[70]

Fortunately, by 22 July the car shed on the railroad across from the Brown House was converted into Stout Hospital and many wounded were moved there awaiting transportation to the other hospitals. The railroad station houses were quickly filled to overflowing with the wounded. Throughout the long, hot days in late July and August, the sick and wounded arrived, awaiting transportation to one of the hospitals.[71]

The sudden influx of so many wounded men created problems in Macon. Dr. Stout appealed to the people for labor, material of all kinds, lumber, straw, and wagon and ambulance transportation. The hospitals needed to be expanded and hospital encampments established. He urged Maconites, "unitedly and at once, [to] devote a few days to the laudable business of providing for the braves now defending your homes, who may soon be at your doors, stricken by disease and the missiles of the enemy."[72] The suffering of so many men who lacked people to care for them prompted Stout to request the conscription of two hundred Blacks to serve in the hospitals in and about Macon.[73]

The Macon hospitals, by the summer of 1864, included the Floyd House (Macon General Hospital), located in the Floyd House, at the corner of Mulberry and Third Streets; the Bibb County Academy, on Academy Square, occupying the block bounded by Walnut, Ocmulgee, First, and Second Streets; and Ocmulgee Hospital, located near Walnut Street on the riverbank. Other hospitals were located in the old passenger station at the corner of Fourth and Plum Streets [Stout Hospital]; City Hall; the Bibb County Court House; the Male Academy; the Macon Volunteers Armory; Ells' Saloon; the Macon Hotel; and elsewhere.[74]

---

[70] Richard W. Iobst, "The Sacrifice of 600 Men," unpublished Mss., p. 7, Middle Georgia Archives, Washington Library, Macon, hereafter cited as Iobst, "Sacrifice of 600 Men."

[71] Ibid., p. 8.

[72] *Macon Daily Telegraph*, 22 July 1864.

[73] Stout to Major Rowland, Enrolling Officer, Macon, 26 July 1864, Stout Papers, Emory.

[74] Iobst, "Sacrifice of 600 Men," p. 6.

The activities of the Macon Hospitals in 1864 can be best understood by examining the record of Ocmulgee Hospital. This hospital, one of the largest hospitals in Macon, was established on 11 December 1863 under Chief Surgeon Dr. E.J. Roach as an appendage to the Floyd House Hospital. It began to receive patients on 21 January 1864 and on 22 January Surgeon Roach was relieved, and replaced by Dr. Chaille. Chaille arrived on 27 January and the name, as noted above, was changed to Ocmulgee Hospital on 27 January. When Federal General George M. Stoneman attacked Macon on 30 July his three-inch ordnance rifles threw shells into part of the hospital, but no one was injured because many of the wounded were removed to Vineville, although the hospital did not close.[75]

When it was first opened the hospital consisted of the brick building and bath house, and two small wards (1 and 2), the mess hall and the drug store (which was then used as a kitchen). The hospital could then provide beds for only eighty patients. When it was completed in July 1864, the facility operated in thirty buildings and a number of other structures. These included one two-story brick building and one small frame building used as a bath house. Both of these buildings were owned by the City of Macon. Eight wards were located in separate buildings with two other wards in a portion of other buildings. A barracks to house , a baggage room with a carpenters shop attached, a drug store, a mess hall, a building which contained kitchens, store room, etc.; a buttery; a laundry, a house and yard; a dead house, a building for general purposes, a stable, and seven latrines. All of these were built and operated by the Confederacy. The ten wards had a capacity of 243,660 cubic feet which accommodated 304 patients, although under normal conditions, the facility provided beds for 250 patients and about 60 attendants. By adding tents the number of patients might be increased to 500. Plans also called for the addition of a guard house and a lavatory when materials became available. Chaille wanted a portion of the hospital yard to be set aside for a gymnasium.[76]

Many of the patients admitted to the Ocmulgee Hospital during the summer of 1864 were suffering from wounds made by Minie balls. These projectiles hit the men in such places as their elbows, the right side of the face, legs, thighs, arms, and other areas of the body. The doctors used chloroform, dispelling some views that this drug was reserved for the use of officers. It was common in the Ocmulgee Hospital, as elsewhere, to amputate an arm or a leg when the bone was shattered, and, therefore, could not be repaired using the medical knowledge available at the time. Most of these men were reported as "doing well" after the surgery. However, such diseases as gangrene and diarrhea greatly weakened the

---

[75] Chaille to Stout, Ocmulgee Hospital, Macon, 26 February 1865, Ocmulgee Hospital Record Book, p. 295, NARA. See above, pp. 111-12, 117.

[76] Ibid., p. 297.

patients and caused some deaths. Private E. S. Watson of the 15th Mississippi Regiment was wounded in the lower third of his left leg by a Minie ball on 13 May 1864. He arrived at Ocmulgee Hospital on July 9, and was operated on by Dr. Chaille on 15 July. Unfortunately, gangrene had destroyed the skin and part of the anterior section of both sides of his leg as far as the knee joint. Chaille was forced to amputate the lower third of the leg using chloroform. Watson died of diarrhea on 20 July five days after his surgery. Chaille's medical notes told the grim story: "little hope was entertained of this operation, amputation was deemed but chance." Another patient, Sergeant Thomas O'Barr of the 31st Alabama Regiment, was wounded by a Minie ball which entered the outside of the upper third of his left leg. The ball passed through between the fibula and tibia bones, fracturing the tibia. Chaille, using chloroform, performed a circular operation on the lower third of O'Barr's left thigh on 24 July. However, the stump did badly from the beginning, becoming gangrenous. To make matters worse, O'Barr suffered constantly from diarrhea and a sick stomach to such an extent that he could retain no food. He died on 30 July 1864. Another unfortunate patient, William M. Murray, a corporal in the 54th Virginia Regiment, was wounded by a Minie ball which fractured his right leg. Although doctors performed a circular operation in middle third of the thigh, Murray died on the morning of 14 July. One of the reasons for his death was the fact that he was admitted in a delirious and dying condition.

Sometimes the wound left the patient permanently crippled. Private H. E. Franklin of the 38th Tennessee Regiment, was wounded when a Minie ball fractured the upper third of his right femur. Franklin's wound was infected with gangrene when he entered the hospital, but the gangrene was arrested. He did well, but his limb was crooked and shortened by several inches.[77]

Yet, despite these deaths, the death rate in the Ocmulgee Hospital was very small in proportion to those who lived. One hundred and forty-two men lived after surgery, while only twenty-six died. This was a percentage rate of eighty-four percent who lived, and only sixteen percent who died, a tribute to the Hospital's surgeons and staff.[78]

Some of the men merely had to have minor surgery. Private E.G. Taylor, Company D, 66th Georgia Regiment, had deformed and abnormal nails removed. Another private received a gunshot wound to the left lobe of his brain.

---

[77] Examination of various cases admitted to Ocmulgee Hospital by the author in Notes of Surgical Cases, Ocmulgee Hospital, July-August 1864, Chapter VI, Vol. 755, Medical Department, NARA.

[78] Ibid.

After an operation performed by Assistant Surgeon Love, the man lived. Most of the cases were gunshot wounds received in the fighting around Atlanta.[79]

Some of them were not so fortunate. Private A. Edwards of Christopher Findlay's Macon Arsenal Battalion died of pneumonia on 13 March 1864. Another private, John Folender, Company E. Bernands Battalion, died of diphtheria on 8 May 1864. Folender's effects were turned over to his mother before he died. According to hospital records, "He left no Government clothing of any kind."[80]

The doctors of Ocmulgee Hospital performed twenty-two surgical operations in March 1864. In June 1864, the facility had a total of 600 beds available for patients. During the same month eighteen detailed soldiers were employed in the facility. By July 1864, it contained 550 patients. By September, 1864, the hospital was supported by eleven medical officers. Among the items on hand to treat the patients were forceps, stethoscopes, arrow root, lint, tea, muslin, sewing needles, vials, soap, acaciae, and cinnamon. Another article with which the hospital was well-stocked was "18 2/3 dozen" bottles of whiskey. Other supplies included blank books, pencils, pens, matches, locks and keys, knives and forks, plate scales, quill pens, and soap.[81]

One of the patients in Ocmulgee, Carroll Henderson Clark of Company I, 16th Tennessee Regiment, was wounded in the arm during the Battle of Atlanta on 22 July 1864. On the following day he was placed in a railroad car and sent to Macon, and placed in Ocmulgee Hospital "where a great many wounded & sick were sent." In the bunk next to him was a Missouri soldier who lost both an arm and a leg in the fighting of 22 July. Clark suffered a great deal with gangrene, and was given morphine to enable him to sleep. A great deal of pus collected below the wound, and his arm, hands, and fingers were terribly swollen. One of the doctors said that his arm had to be amputated. Clark protested by crying and begging to be permitted to risk the gangrene. He got someone to take him to the railroad depot where he took a train for Dawson, Georgia, where he was taken into the home of a Mr. Leek, who refugeed from Dalton, and whom he evidently met while in North Georgia. When he arrived at the Leek residence, Clark was in bad shape, so Leek called in his family physician, a Dr. Roushenburg, who examined his arm. Roushenburg visited

---

[79] Ocmulgee Hospital Records, in 2 books, Book 1, pp. 1, 15, Special Collections, Emory University.

[80] Ibid., Book 2, pp. 7, 10.

[81] Ibid., Book 1, pp. 8-9; Book 2, pp. 9, 16, 17, 31, 47, and 51.

Clark often, regularly administering morphine to relieve the pain. At the right time he lanced the arm, and it began to heal immediately.[82]

Nineteen percent of the Confederate wounded were struck in the chest or abdomen. These wounds were considered very serious. Abdominal wounds were generally believed fatal because of the probability of hemorrhage or infection. About twelve percent of the men received wounds in the head, face, and neck. Most of the wounds, about sixty-five percent, were located in the arms and legs.

The use of anesthetics was connected to another pressing problem. Since most of the drugs used as anesthetics came from Europe, they were in short supply because of the intensive Federal blockade. Therefore, the supply of opiates, ether, and chloroform were never sufficient, and the culture of opium in the South, despite the best efforts of the Medical Department, only had limited success. There was greater progress, however in the use of other drugs and their substitutes. Some of the Macon surgeons made effective use of Southern herbs in the preparation of medicines. Other surgical substitutes like cotton rags for sponges, scrapings from old clothes and sheets for lint bandages, cotton, flax, and horsehair ligatures and sutures were always in short supply.[83]

Sometimes, even the surgeons became ill. Dr. W. H. Cunningham, an Assistant Surgeon assigned to the Vineville Hospital, wanted to be relieved from his duties because he was seized with a violent inflammation of the bone in October 1863. By 28 August 1864, he petitioned Medical Director Stout for relief so he could go to Montgomery, Alabama.[84]

Macon was also the place where an examining board to examine sick and inefficient men in the unorganized militia of the state met. The duty of the board was to determine those who were physically able to be sent to the front. However, the board was disbanded by General Gustavus W. Smith, Commander of the First Division, Georgia Militia under Special Order No. 92.[85] Brown demurred telling Smith that his command was organized at the Governor's direction, "and is not in any manner subject to your control, your order

---

[82] E.N. Haston, "Carroll Henderson Clark, My Grandfather's Diary of the War," *Spencer Times*, nd, Manuscript Department, University of Tennessee Library, Knoxville.

[83] Iobst, Sacrifice of 600 Men, pp. 8-9.

[84] Dr. W.H. Cunningham to Stout, Vineville near Macon, 28 August 1864, Samuel H. Stout Papers, Microfilm, Reel 2, SHC.

[85] Andrew J. Hansell, A.D.C. to Governor Brown, Macon, 6 September 1864, GLB 1861-1865, p. 691.

disbanding it cannot be respected. You command the first Division Georgia Militia in service, but not the militia of the state."[86]

Macon's hospitals continued to support the Army of Tennessee during the fall of 1864. On 11 October Major G. R. Fairbanks was authorized to impress for the use of the hospitals six hundred cords of wood belonging to John H. Brantley, Jr. at Coley's Station on the Brunswick Railroad.[87]

Later in October, Dr. Chaille urged Stout to approve a requisition of three comforts to each bed for Ocmulgee Hospital, which could accommodate 600 patients, and "has repeatedly accommodated over 700." Chaille had 927 comforts on hand, but needed 873 more.[88] Dr. Johnson Gore, Surgeon in Charge of the Macon Hospitals in the absence of Dr. Green, asked Stout to approve Chaille's request.[89]

As November approached Macon's hospitals were challenged by a new danger, the Sherman invasion. Whether they would survive this new emergency remained to be seen at the end of October.

---

[86] Brown to Smith, Milledgeville, 7 September 1864, Ibid. See also Ben C. Gancey, A.D.C. to General Wayne, to M.C.E. Bennet, Milledgeville, 17 September 1864, Adjutant General's Letter Book, August 15-October 24, 1864, p. 266.

[87] Howell Cobb, Special Orders No. 112, Macon, 11 October 1864, Howell Cobb Special Orders 1865, p. 76.

[88] Chaille to Stout, Macon, 20 October 1864, Stout Papers, Microfilm, Reel 2, SHC.

[89] Johnson Gore to Stout, Macon, 20 October 1864, Ibid.

Chapter 7

Camp Oglethorpe:
Macon as a Depot for Federal Prisoners

It was not long after the beginning of the war that the Confederate authorities began to look closely at Macon as the site for a prison. Its location in the middle of Georgia, one of the most easily defended states in the Confederacy, its size, and excellent rail connections caused the Confederate Government to give the city serious attention. This view, however, was not shared by many Maconites. As early as 25 October 1861, the *Daily Telegraph's* reporter exclaimed, "We understand that the Secretary of War has telegraphed to Governor Brown, to know if five hundred Hessians could be accommodated with lodgings in this city. Would not the Penitentiary at Milledgeville be a better place?"[1]

The Battle of Shiloh, 6-7 April 1862, in which many Federal troops were captured, caused the authorities to take a closer look at Macon as the site for a prisoner of war camp. When some prisoners arrived in Macon in late April, Captain W. L. Calhoun, commanding prisoners in Macon, ordered to send prisoners to Milledgeville, wired Governor Brown, "I have orders...to carry prisoners to Milledgeville, and will be compelled to do so unless that order is countermanded by proper authority."[2] Brown replied that there was no prison room, provisions, arms, or guard for them in Milledgeville, and directed Calhoun to "Have the prisoners stopped at Atlanta."[3] Brown telegraphed one of his principal aides, Colonel Lewis N. Whittle of Macon, on 25 April, "See that the prisoners are stopped at Macon, or sent back to Atlanta."[4] Several days later Brigadier General John H. Forney asked Brown to make accommodations for 800 prisoners which he had sent from overcrowded Cahaba Prison in Alabama to

---

[1] *Macon Daily Telegraph*, 25 October 1861.
[2] Capt. W.L. Calhoun to Brown, Telegram, Macon, 22 April 1862, GLB 1861-1865, p. 270.
[3] Brown to Calhoun, Telegram, Milledgeville, 22 April 1862, Ibid.
[4] Brown to Whittle, Telegram, Milledgeville, 25 April 1862, Ibid., p. 268.

Macon.[5] In his reply, Brown told Forney that he had no supplies for prisoners at Macon, and urged him to seek higher authority to provide for the prisoners.[6]

The news that 800 prisoners would arrive in Macon in early May posed a problem for the local authorities. One observer noted, "Our City fathers are at their wits end to know what to do with them." Plans called for the men to be temporarily housed in the City Market House when they reached Macon.[7]

When it learned of plans to send hundreds of prisoners to Macon the *Daily Telegraph's* editor opined "This surely is an elephant of immense magnitude— the state of the provision market and the accommodations for such guests, taken into the account." Mayor Thomson was determined to place the prisoners in the Market House, and he called on Colonel Jones, commandant of the post, to furnish him men for guard duty. The B Companies of both the Macon Volunteers and Floyd Rifles joined the Thomson Guards in performing this duty.[8] On the following day, 3 May a reporter for the paper put it even more bluntly, "At a time when it is difficult to feed our own population, we are to be *blessed* with the presence and custody of 900 prisoners of war. We have no place to hold them—no food to give them—nobody whose time can well be spared to guard them—nor, except in the mere matter of hostages for the safety of our own prisoners in Lincoln's dominions, can we conceive of any object in holding them as prisoners."[9] Besides, the expense alone would prohibit Maconites from allowing prisoners to be housed in their midst. After all, a writer for the paper complained, "The expense attending their subsistence and safe keeping is not short of a thousand dollars per day, and is a good deal more than that of the same number of effective troops in the field."[10]

The City Council decided the matter at a meeting on 2 May when it decided not to place the new arrivals in the Market House, but would transfer them to the Fair Ground [Camp Oglethorpe]. Mayor Thomson was directed to have the

---

[5] General John H. Forney to Brown, Telegram, Mobile, 30 April 1862, Ibid., p. 283.

[6] Brown to Forney, Telegram, Milledgeville, 2 May 1862, Ibid. For additional information concerning where the prisoners should be sent see Governor John Gill Shorter of Alabama to Brown, Telegram, Montgomery, 24 May 1862, GLB 1861-1865, p. 303; Brown to Shorter, Telegram, Milledgeville, 26 May 1862, Ibid.; and Adjutant General Henry C. Wayne to General Alexander R. Lawton, Telegram, Milledgeville, 26 May 1862, Ibid.

[7] Julia P. Jones to Mary Ann Cobb, Macon, 2 May 1862, Cobb-Erwin-Lamar Collection. A reporter for the *Macon Daily Telegraph* reported on May 2, that 886 prisoners from Cahaba were scheduled to come to Macon.

[8] *Macon Daily Telegraph*, 2 May 1862. Both B companies, as noted in an earlier chapter, were reserve units.

[9] Ibid., 3 May 1862. Italics are authors.

[10] Ibid., 13 May 1862.

buildings there cleared and fitted up as soon as possible to receive them. The cotton stored there was removed to another warehouse. The Council also disallowed privileges granted before the war to the volunteer companies for the use of the camp.[11]

Therefore, when the men arrived in Macon they were taken to Camp Oglethorpe, after some delay. A *Daily Telegraph* writer described them as "not fine looking soldiers: we noticed several boys of tender years, and many of pale and sickly appearance. The majority of them hail from Iowa; the balance consisting of Missourians, Indianians, Illinoisans, and a few Tennesseeans." A large crowd gathered near the South Western Railroad Depot to witness their arrival.[12]

Camp Oglethorpe, as it appeared to the prisoners, was fifteen to twenty acres in size. The area was enclosed by a picket fence. A fine grove of pine trees, which provided "a most beautiful shade," was located at the northwest corner of the enclosed area. The structures erected inside of the enclosed area included three large weather-boarded frame buildings; and two small frame buildings, one used for a doctor shop, the other for a cook house for the prison hospital. The best building on the grounds was used as a hospital. It consisted of a row of stalls made for horses in time of fairs. These were the only structures in the area. There was a spring in the camp which never ran dry, but the water it provided was not of the best quality. A well had been dug in the center of the grove. Chaplain F. F. Kiner, a lieutenant in the 14th Iowa Infantry, captured at Shiloh, wrote he had never seen "a stronger stream in a well;...1400 men supplied themselves from it daily and never exhausted it." This large supply of water enabled the prisoners to wash themselves regularly.[13]

The *Daily Telegraph's* reporter, in an excellent piece of Confederate propaganda, informed his readers, "The prisoners are much pleased with their locality and treatment at Camp Oglethorpe, and the officer who brought them is so well satisfied with the place that he says he shall bring on a thousand more. We hope not. If it were left with us, we would put every one of them, officers excepted, on parole and send them out of the country."[14]

Rations during May 1862, included one pound of flour or meal per day; three quarters of a pound of pork; some rice, sugar, molasses, rye for coffee, and a

[11] City Council Minutes, 2 May 1862, Book P, pp. 561-62.

[12] *Macon Daily Telegraph*, 5 May 1862.

[13] F.F. Kiner, *One Year's Soldiering Embracing the Battles of Fort Donelson and Shiloh, and the Capture of two hundred officers and men of the Fourteenth Iowa Infantry, and their confinement six months and a half in Rebel Prisons*, E.H. Thomas, Printer: Lancaster, Iowa, 1863, p. 98, in Hugh Weedon Mercer Papers, Folder 1, Emory University.

[14] *Macon Daily Telegraph*, 6 May 1862.

small portion of hard soap. The men could exercise by walking, playing ball, and generally moving around.[15] Despite the seeming comforts of their new home, Dr. Hinkle, the surgeon hired to attend the prisoners, reported between two and three hundred of the men were on the sick list. The prevailing illnesses included diarrhea, dysentery, bronchitis, and pneumonia. Hinkle asked the people to send old mattresses, coverlets, bagging, and carpeting for use in the prison hospital.[16]

Orders arrived from Richmond on 22 May discharging the privates included in the first batch of prisoners. These men took the oath for parole on the 24th, and left for the North after staying at Camp Oglethorpe for less than three weeks. One hundred and five officers, many of whom were sickly, remained.[17] Those discharged spoke very favorably of conditions at the camp, and were happy at being paroled. They, however, had no wish to be exchanged. Nearly twenty men had died during May, the first month of the prison's operation.[18]

Despite the seemingly good conditions at Camp Oglethorpe, Quartermaster J. B. Dorr of the 12th Iowa Regiment complained to Iowa Governor Samuel J. Kirkwood that the prisoners at Montgomery, Alabama, and Camp Oglethorpe should be exchanged because "These men are receiving less than one-fourth rations of a private in the US Army, and are subjected to all the hardships and indignities which venomous traitors can heap upon them. They are without money or clothing...."[19]

More prisoners, 636 in all, arrived in Macon on Saturday, 31 May. These included eighty commissioned and 320 non-commissioned officers, a few marines, and, according to a writer for the *Daily Telegraph*, "a small suspicious looking crowd in citizens dress, who appear to be somewhat exclusive in their associations, and may be bridge-burners, or guilty of other misdemeanors, which entitled them to public protection." The general appearance of the men, however, appeared to be superior to those who arrived in early May.[20]

Prison life in Macon was still fairly good as the spring of 1862 turned into summer. The men were allowed to shoot marbles, toss horse-shoes, and manufacture bone jewelry. The people of Macon purchased several thousand dollars worth of the jewelry and allowed the prisoners to buy rancid pork for

---

[15] Kiner, *One Year's Soldiering*, 100-101.

[16] *Macon Daily Telegraph*, 7 May 1862. See also Ibid., 13 May 1862.

[17] Morton R. McInvale, "'That Thing of Infamy', Macon's Camp Oglethorpe During the Civil War," in *The Georgia Historical Quarterly*, LXIII, Summer, 1979, No. 2, pp. 279-80, hereafter cited as McInvale, "'That Thing of Infamy'."

[18] *Georgia Journal and Messenger*, 4 June 1862.

[19] J.B. Dorr to Gov. Samuel J. Kirkwood, Nashville, Tenn., 11 June 1862, O.R., Series II, 4:133.

[20] *Georgia Journal and Messenger*, 4 June 1862.

forty cents a pound. The officers also purchased tomatoes, onions, peaches, and other food. However, they could only rarely buy potatoes. Lieutenant Kiner wrote that the Confederates kept bringing prisoners into the camp during the summer until the number reached 1,200 or 1,400. These included men from over 140 different regiments. The guards took away the prisoners' cooking utensils, except what was sufficient for a small number of men. The nights were always cold, and the men lay in the open without covering, getting sicker. Diseases became more fatal. As time went on their flour rations changed to corn or rice meal. The corn meal was unsifted and of the coarsest kind, usually with pieces of cob ground in it, and whole grains of corn. In an effort to obtain more cooking utensils the men gathered up old pieces of tin or sheet iron, or pieces of flat iron, and made plates and pans. A tablespoon of salt was issued to each man every seven days. However, they could buy it from the people of Macon at the rate of ten cents per spoonful, or for $100 a sack. The cakes they ate contained neither salt nor soda. When they ate dinner they arranged their plates upon boards stuck up on four sticks, or maybe on the ground. To supplement their meat ration, the men ate maggots. Because of the scarcity of potatoes, which cost from twenty to twenty-five cents a quart, or eight dollars a bushel, the men ate only five bushels during the summer. They could buy second-rate beef for fifteen cents a pound. Cattle heads and hoofs were purchased by the piece. Flour might be obtained at $40.00 a barrel; meat cost forty to fifty cents per pound and sugar from thirty-five to fifty cents per pound. Tea cost $140 per sack, although coffee and tea could usually not be obtained at any price. Clothing cost $8.00 for a good wool hat, while coarse shoes went for $8.00 to $12.00 a pair. Calf boots might be purchased for from $25.00 to $40.00 a pair.[21]

During the summer 400 to 500 men appeared for medicine at sick call. Later in the summer, the mortality became very great. One to seven men died each day, the others looked like nothing more than living skeletons. Many fell over dead in the prison yard; others died sitting against a tree or anywhere. Many of them died in bed in the hospital. Kiner believed that, of the men captured at Shiloh, 200 died in Macon. In an effort to aid the sick the prisoners themselves served as nurses. Every morning a fresh set of nurses went into the hospital to relieve those that went on duty the previous day.[22]

Some of the guards were kindhearted and showed sympathy to the men. Some of them were very ignorant, although the officers had their men under control at all times. Punishments of prisoners included staking, which consisted of laying a man down on his face and driving forked sticks across each ankle and wrist, and one across his neck. His limbs were extended, forcing him to lie

[21] Kiner, *One Year's Soldiering*, 100-103, 106-110; McInvale, "'That Thing of Infamy'," 281, 285.

[22] Kiner, *One Year's Soldiering*, 113, 115.

motionless for hours at a time. For small offenses, the guards would stake prisoners down or tie them with their backs to a tree for several days at a time, releasing them only at mealtimes. Under these conditions some escaped, but most were recaptured, and would be incarcerated in the Bibb County Jail where they nearly starved. Some of the men who were caught were staked down for a day or two, and then released into camp with a pair of shackles which consisted of iron bands around each ankle, connected by a short chain which allowed them to walk by taking very short steps. They would have to wear these implements for weeks.[23]

These conditions prompted Lieutenant Henry W. Mays, 9th Kentucky; and Lieutenants N. J. Camp and George W. Brown, 23d Missouri, to attempt an escape on 1 June. They boldly passed by the sentries, and walked through Macon singing "Dixie." Slipping into the river swamp they reached the Ocmulgee River, found a small boat, and began their trip by using a tin plate and canteen for paddles. The following morning found them twenty-five miles down the river. They hid themselves all day and at night, and, having made wooden paddles from a tree, resumed their journey. Toward morning they came across some men in a boat whom they believed were hunting for them. To their joy, they discovered they were three other prisoners who escaped several days before disguised as Confederate soldiers. These men were well-equipped, having about their waists a bag with flour, dried peaches, and files. They had salt in their boots. The two boats kept together while traveling over 300 miles by night with oars muffled with Spanish moss. On 11 June they reached Hawkinsville, where three small steamers were tied up. They passed by these vessels without being seen. As they went down the Ocmulgee to the Altamaha River they saw people on the riverbanks, and greeted them with cheers for Jefferson Davis. When questioned, they said they were messengers from the Confederate President. At last, on 17 June they reached Wolf Island in Altamaha Sound. On the next day they arrived at Sapelo Island which they found deserted. On the following day, 18 June they were picked up by the steamer *Wamsutta*, which transferred them to the steamer *Florida* in St. Simons's Sound. Once again they transferred to another ship, this time the *Massachusetts*, which carried them to Fortress Monroe.[24]

The first commander of the camp, Major Hardee, remained in command until 20 May 1862.[25] According to Kiner he was "a perfect gentleman." [26]His successor, Major J. E. Rylander, commander of the 10th Georgia Battalion, ran

---

[23] Ibid., 121, 122, 124.

[24] J. Robley Dunglison to Col. E.S. Sanford, Baltimore, 6 July 1862, OR, Ser. II, 7:142-143.

[25] McInvale, "'That Thing of Infamy'," p. 282.

[26] Kiner, *One Year's Soldering*, 121.

Camp Oglethorpe from May until November when his command left for Virginia, and was replaced by the First Georgia Regiment.[27] Kiner described Rylander as "cruel and tyrannical, presumptuous and overbearing."[28]

James Pike of Company A, 4th Ohio Cavalry, a prisoner at Camp Oglethorpe, described life under Rylander in 1862. An officer named Cory was kept tied up for three days by his wrists to a tree until his toes just touched the ground. His offense consisted of helping to kill a yearling calf which had entered the camp. A Floridian and two Kentuckians, all political prisoners, were held in the Bibb County Jail on quarter rations for forty-two days. Their offense was to escape from the prison. Under Rylander's administration the men were confined in bad quarters; the dead were left unburied for days; some were left unburied entirely. The prisoners were denied medical attention; chaplains were not allowed to preach to them or even pray for them. Pike recited a whole litany of offenses committed by his captors: "our men and officers were shot without cause; an insane man was shot at Macon...for no offense; we were compelled to bury men in river banks where their bodies were liable to be washed out; we were beaten with clubs...we were fed on foul and unwholesome diet, frequently left without any rations two or three days at a time, and our exchange was delayed as long as possible; we were kept confined in camp surrounded by swamps, as the rebels said, that we all might die." He soberly concluded, "I find it impossible to enumerate all the hardships put upon us, but have enumerated such as were the most intolerable."[29]

The City Council, not wanting to bury those prisoners who died in Rose Hill and Oak Ridge Cemeteries, selected a ridge southwest of the camp to bury deceased federal soldiers.[30] On 27 June the Aldermen expressed their concern over the sanitary conditions prevailing at the camp, and, fearing for the health of the city, ordered the burial of dead animals, or throwing them into the river three miles below Macon.[31]

From the summer of 1862 until the spring of 1864, not much information is available concerning Camp Oglethorpe. On 7 October 1862, about half of the 1,300 prisoners in the Camp left the stockade. The remainder departed for Richmond on the following day. Only twenty Federal officers, all of them sick, remained.[32] In early January 1863, an observer noted that there were seventy-

---

[27] McInvale, "'That Thing of Infamy'," p. 282.

[28] Kiner, *One Year's Soldiering*, 121.

[29] James Pike, "Eleven Months among the Rebels," Murfreesborough Tenn., March 22, 1863, excerpt in *O.R.*, Ser. II, 5:419.

[30] Council Minutes, 20, 27 June 1862, Book P, pp. 569, 571.

[31] Ibid., 27 June 1862, p. 571.

[32] McInvale, "'That Thing of Infamy'," pp. 282-283.

three officers confined in the prison. These held the rank of brigadier general on down.[33]

When Sherman's armies drove south from Chattanooga in May 1864, Macon resumed its role as a prison camp. Adjutant and Inspector General Samuel Cooper telegraphed Cobb on 2 May to make provisions for the safe keeping of federal officers to be sent from Andersonville Prison to Macon.[34] Lucy Barrow informed her father that the authorities were determined to make Oglethorpe a depot for commissioned officers. Reserve forces, based in Macon under Cobb, guarded between 150 and 200 prisoners by 4 May.[35]

When a *Daily Telegraph* reporter learned that 1,400 officers had arrived by 11 May he wrote the camp was not, "in many respects, a good selection, and we are sorry so many prisoners should be quartered in Macon, but perhaps we may as well bear the burden as any other community, and perhaps may not have to bear it long."[36]

Perhaps the writer was exaggerating the number a bit, because he reported on 18 May that twenty-seven carloads had arrived on the morning of 17 May and were incarcerated in the stockade. This number included a good many men captured at Plymouth, North Carolina by General Robert F. Hoke on 20 April including their commander, Brigadier General Henry W. Wessells. A total of 1,000 officers were in the prison.[37]

In an effort to prevent escapes, Cobb issued Special Orders No. 16 which directed that a commissioned officer should be detailed each day as Officer of the Guard for the prisoners. This official would not leave the camp while on duty, and until regularly relieved. His responsibilities included visiting the guards at least twice during the night and once at midnight. The prisoners had to be confined within the line of sentinels, and were required to be accompanied by a guard when visiting the sinks or the stream for washing. Further directives forbade prisoners to talk with the guard or any one else; and only two prisoners were allowed with each sentinel. The guards, for their part, could not talk with the prisoners or permit prisoners to talk to each other or any one else, except the Officer of the Guard. That official had to examine all persons who had anything

---

[33] *Macon Daily Telegraph*, 12 January 1863.

[34] Samuel Cooper to Cobb, Telegram, Richmond, May 2, 1864, Cobb Papers, 1864.

[35] Lucy Barrow to David C. Barrow, Macon, 4 May 1864, Barrow Papers, Hargrett Library, University of Georgia. For a brief evaluation of the competence of the reserves to guard the prisoners at Macon see Maj. Thomas P. Turner to Gen. John H. Winder, 25 May 1864, in *O.R.*, Ser. II, Vol. 7:168.

[36] *Macon Daily Telegraph*, 11 May 1864.

[37] *Macon Daily Telegraph*, 18 May 1864; Richard W. Iobst, *The Bloody Sixth: The Sixth North Carolina Regiment Confederate States of America* (Gaithersburg, Md., Butternut Press, 1987) 197.

to sell to the prisoners to determine if they had any letters or anything else that they might pass on to the prisoners. If nothing was found they could go into the compound and sell their merchandise. No more than one person was allowed to enter the prison at the same time. The prisoners could not receive presents or speak to the visitors. No alcoholic beverages were allowed in the compound. Finally, anyone "attempting to escape may be shot."[38]

Since it was necessary to provide a commander for the prison and troops to guard it, Cobb issued Special Orders No. 22, placing the prisoners under Colonel D. Wyatt Aiken, a South Carolinian who commanded the post. The reserve troops guarding the prisoners would continue to perform their duties.[39] The camp commandant was Major Thomas R. Turner. He turned over his post on 18 May to Captain W. Kemper Tabb of Maryland. Tabb was considered to be a cruel commander. He sold an imprisoned captain's watch and other effects and kept the money. When the officer complained to him, Tabb had him bucked. Tabb also broke up several church services in which the prisoners prayed for Abraham Lincoln.[40] However, Tabb showed some mercy when he asked General John H. Winder, then commanding the Department of Henrico at Richmond, to send money to some of the prisoners which had been taken from them at Libby Prison.[41]

Prisoners continued to pour into Camp Oglethorpe during the last days of May. On 20 May five hundred arrived,[42] to be followed by 800 more on the 23rd. Many of these came from the battlefields of Virginia where Grant and Lee were engaged in some of the most desperate fighting of the war in the region between the Rapidan and Richmond.[43] Some of the prisoners came from Florida, where the Confederates had won a major victory at Olustee on 20 February. This number included their commander, General Truman Seymour.[44]

Captain George C. Gibbs was placed in command of Camp Oglethorpe on 25 May by order of the War Department.[45] By the spring of 1864, the prison consisted of a three-acre open field surrounded by a twelve-foot-high wooden fence with an outside walk for sentries four feet from the top which ran entirely

---

[38] Howell Cobb, Special Orders No. 16, Macon, 8 May 1864, Howell Cobb Special Orders 1865, 14-15.

[39] Howell Cobb Special Orders No. 22, Macon, 14 May 1864, Ibid., 18.

[40] McInvale, "'That Thing of Infamy'," 283.

[41] W. Kemp Tabb to Gen. John H. Winder, Macon, 23 May 1864, O.R., Ser. II, Vol. 7:158.

[42] *Macon Daily Telegraph*, 21 May 1864.

[43] Ibid., 24 May 1864.

[44] Pope Barrow to Lucy Barrow Cobb, Macon, 24 May 1864, Cobb Papers, 1864.

[45] John Withers, A.A.G., Special Orders No. 121, Richmond, 25 May 1864, O.R., Ser. I, 39, Pt. 2, 625.

around the fence. The walk was protected on the outside by a railing. Sentries were posted at intervals of about ten yards, and could see the entire compound from the walk. At the northwest corner of the prison, near the gate, and also on the east side, the Confederates placed two twelve-pounder brass cannon that could sweep the camp. In early July they placed three other cannon on a little hill in the rear of the camp. About ten feet from the stockade ran a line of boards nailed to posts, or picket fence, called the "dead line" because the guards were ordered to shoot anyone who touched it. Because there were only a few buildings within the enclosure, prisoners were allowed to build whatever shelters they could from scrap lumber and other materials brought into the prison for that purpose. In 1864, the buildings included a large shell of a building and four rude sheds or rather roofs set on posts ten feet high. The sanitary conditions were always inadequate, although never as bad as Andersonville. The stream, described earlier in this chapter, still flowed through the camp for sixty feet in 1864, but there never was enough water, and lice plagued the prisoners everywhere. Some twenty feet of this stream, before it entered the sink, was used for bathing and washing clothes. The stream could not be used for drinking or cooking because the waste water from some factories located just above the prison ran into it. Water was procured from several tubs which were set in the slope of ground at the roots of a tree. They were filled with water furnished by a spring in the bank. A well at the other end of the enclosure also furnished the prisoners with water. However, because a thousand men had to be supplied, the supply was entirely inadequate. A row of men always stood, one behind the other, bathing themselves and washing their clothes. The volume of water was less than the amount which would flow through a tub two inches in diameter. The prisoners, who had lice both in their clothes and in their quarters, were always infested with vermin.

The available shelter in 1864 was similar to that of 1862, The two principal buildings were formerly used at County and State fairs. One of these structures was nearly 100 feet long and about thirty-five feet wide. It had a floor. The other building had been used as a stable for cattle and hogs. It was very filthy. The building with the floor was used as a hospital. There were a few pine and oak buildings in the stockade which furnished some shelter from the sun. Between three and four hundred men found quarters in these buildings. The others lay in the open. After awhile the guards provided this latter group with boards, and some poles and rude roofs were built which helped to keep the sun and rain off the men. However, there were no sides, ends or floors around these shelters. Even these shelters did not provide shelter for all the men. Others lived in the open air.[46]

---

[46] Edward D. Jervey, ed., "Ten Weeks in a Macon Prison, 1864: A New England Chaplain's Account, *The Georgia Historical Quarterly*, LXX, Winter, 1986, No. 4,

On 10 June orders were issued by Cobb to send fifty Federal officers to Charleston on a special mission.[47] One of the prisoners, Louis R. Fortescue, confided to his diary that the object of this was "to prevent our forces from destroying the city by shells. The Rebels threatened some time ago to put our prisoners in the city if our forces persisted in shelling the place."[48]

Luther G. Billings of the 3d New York Cavalry served on the Federal ship *Water Witch,* on duty with the South Atlantic Blockading Squadron. His ship was captured by a Confederate naval expedition in Ossabaw Sound on 3 June 1864. When he arrived at Macon in early June he was invited to join Captain Gibbs, whom Billings described as inebriated, to have a drink. Gibbs exclaimed, "Better take it, Gunboats–it's the last chance you will have while you are in this country!" As Billings was pushed through the large gates, he and his companions were surrounded by a "crazy" mob of ragged men, who saluted the new arrivals with the cry of "fresh fish," the prisoners' name for newly-arrived captives. Billings described the men as "ragged, unwashed and unshaven, with rags or dirty parts of undergarments barely covering them, with repulsive unhealed wounds, sores, and such large wolfish eyes! We could not realize that this mob of brutalized savages was comprised of the bravest officers who ever led their troops into the thick of battle." Some of the men had been prisoners for fifteen months. They were captured in battle, and only had the clothes on their backs. In the crowd of men there was not one pair of blankets or any bed or bedding. Some of the prisoners had dug oven-like caves in the dirt, and had burrowed into them like animals. Others walked restlessly back and forth like caged animals, until, exhausted and weak from lack of proper food, they fell down anywhere and slept.

A constant murmur of hundreds of voices hung over the camp which was broken occasionally by the challenge of a sentry or a shrill cry of distress. The restless crowd was never still, never quiet. There was no hospital and no medicines. The sick died and lay where they had died until the dead wagon with its four mules and black drivers came in the night and morning and removed the corpses "like piled wood in the shallow trench under the cool pine trees that

---

670-671, 680-681, hereafter cited as Jervey, ed., "Ten Weeks in a Macon Prison, 1864;" Luther G. Billings, "Only Yesterday," typescript, n.d., p. 57, LC., hereafter cited as Billings, "Only Yesterday." A.O. Abbott, *Prison Life in the South: at Richmond, Macon, Savannah, Charleston, Columbia, Charlotte, Raleigh, Goldsborough, and Andersonville* (New York: Harper & Brothers, Publishers, 1865) 61.

[47] Howell Cobb, Special Orders No. 41, Macon, 10 June 1864, Howell Cobb Special Orders 1865, p. 32.

[48] Louis R. Fortescue diary, 1863-1864, n.d., p. 77, SHC. See also Samuel Cooper to Cobb, Telegraph, Richmond, June 1864, Cobb Papers, 1864.

whispered the only sympathy or sorrow they were to excite." The deaths became very numerous. Many died from scurvy, although fresh vegetables and fruits were available.

Billings spent his first night sleeping on the ground. The following morning he was assigned to a company and squad. The 1,500 officers in Camp Oglethorpe in the late spring and summer of 1864, were later increased to 2,300. General Truman Seymour was the senior officer there, and theoretically in command. The men were divided into companies of 100, with each company under the command of a ranking officer. These units were then sub-divided into squads of ten. The chief commissary was issued rations, and then issued them to the captains of each company. He, in turn, sub-divided the rations into tenths and the tenths divided among the men.

Rations, by 1864, consisted of five pints of corn meal (including the ground cobs), two tablespoonfuls of beans; two tablespoonful of rice (which contained weevils), two tablespoonfuls of sorghum, one of salt, and three ounces of rancid bacon. This food had to last each man for five days, but most men ate it in four days or less. No utensils were available, so the men improvised pieces of bark, old strips of cloth, or anything they could find. Each company was issued one axe, three mess kettles, and three covered skillets or "Dutch ovens." Five men could carry a supply of wood on their backs from the woods along the riverbank. Meals were eaten at any time. The usual repast consisted of a paste made of corn meal mixed with water and a little salt, which the men fried like cakes. The bacon was used to grease the skillet. The rice and beans were usually mixed and stewed together. The men were allowed to buy extra cooking utensils, and even vegetables. Sometimes they purchased small onions and blackberries. On occasion they bought extra bacon.[49]

Roll call was held at 9:00 A.M. A company of the guard was brought in, and deployed across the yard near its center, while half a dozen men were sent through one half of the camp to drive the prisoners across this line. When one side of the compound had been emptied, an opening was made, and all the prisoners were counted through it. The guard who drove them out was required to see that no one stayed in their quarters. This procedure usually took from an hour and a half to three hours because the guards were usually not satisfied with the first count. Later in the summer the men were divided into divisions, and counted much more quickly.

Amusements consisted of classes in German, French, Logic, Rhetoric, Butler's Analogy, and some higher mathematics. Preaching took place on Sundays by one of the chaplains among the prisoners. There were two Sunday services, one at 11:00 A.M. and another at 7:00 P.M. Prayer meeting was held on Thursday night, and prayer and conference meetings on Saturday night. The

---

[49] Billings, "Only Yesterday," 57-62.

meetings were generally well-attended. Other amusements included such sports as cricket, wicket, baseball, and sword exercise (without the swords). More sedentary activities consisted of cards, dominoes, and checkers.[50]

There were instances when the guards murdered prisoners. One of the murders was witnessed by Luther Billings who was cooking dinner at 11:00 o'clock one night. On his way to the stream for water he noticed a man right behind him. Suddenly, a shot rang out and the man fell over. The bullet struck the man in the right side of his chest and ranged upward. Billings saw he was dying, and asked him what he had done. He replied, "Nothing," since he was at least thirty feet from the dead line. Billings, angered at what he had seen, shook his fist at the guard, who was placidly reloading his rifle, shouting "You cowardly murderer, if you want to kill Yankees why don't you go to the front?" The guard replied with an oath "I'll kill you, too." Billings believed he would have done so if the other guard had not approached, alarmed at the shot, and prevented him. By this time the mortally wounded prisoner was dead. Billings became even more incensed when he learned the guard had been promoted to corporal. "Probably promoted," the former paymaster observed, "for this act of gallantry!"[51]

Camp Oglethorpe contained two classes of prisoner. The first were those whose spirits were broken by their sufferings. This group suffered from the diseases of the camp. Since they lacked the will, their deaths swelled the number of those who died. The other group was impatient of confinement, wanted to be exchanged, or to escape by any means. They constantly began rumors of exchange or trying to escape and go home. When they rebelled at their captivity, they began a new disease called "homesickness," which caused hundreds to die. After a week's confinement, Billings was approached by Captain J. A. Kellogg of a Wisconsin Infantry Regiment, who asked him to join in an escape attempt. The former paymaster agreed, and was informed that a tunnel organization composed of fifty prisoners had started to dig a tunnel. Since only three could work at a time in the confined atmosphere, they wanted more to join them. Billings and two of his friends joined the effort. They dug a funnel-shaped shaft about four feet across at the bottom and at the top just wide enough to allow a man to push through, the passage was about six feet deep. About three inches from the top the men had mortised sockets in the dirt to hold pieces of board, then laid old sacking on top of the board, and scattered dirt beaten down hard on the sacking. They hid the cracks with a slight sprinkle of dirt, completing the disguise. When the dirt was removed at the edges the sacking might be lifted up, the board removed, and the entrance opened. After this the top was replaced and the workers were concealed. During the work on the tunnel, two men

---

[50] A.O. Abbott, *Prison Life in the South*, 67-68.

[51] Billings, "Only Yesterday," 64-65.

slipped into the shaft, after which another man replaced the cover. This left a small space for air. A number of men sat around talking, or playing a game. Others wandered listlessly about to sound the alarm if anything suspicious occurred. If a guard approached those at the tunnel entrance quickly replaced the cover, so that the workers, who promised not to shout even if they died a slow death by suffocation, were buried inside.

Digging proceeded slowly. As the tunnel grew longer, the men became hardened to the work. They disposed of the dirt excavated by taking out small quantities at night and putting some of it into the little stream. Some they scattered on the heaps of refuse. The who carried the refuse away favored the prisoners and never told on them. Through these efforts the tunnel was finally completed. However, because a second tunnel had been started, the men waited to break out of theirs so they would not give the other one away. The plan was to push down the Ocmulgee River to the Altamaha, and then on to the sea at Darien. In order to accomplish their escape, the men bought an old boat from one of the , which he agreed to hide below the bridge. They also obtained a tracing map of the river which showed all the towns and villages on its banks. Planning to travel at night, they decided to fill the boat with water and swim beside it, floating along with the current when they approached houses. All of these plans were dashed, however, when Billings and his fellow prisoners noticed activity among the guards. The four twelve-pounders mounted on platforms which commanded the inside of the stockade, were loaded with canister and trained on the lower part of the compound. Then the guards moved in and loaded their muskets with ball cartridges. Forming a line across the stockade from the dead line to the dead line the guards slowly moved forward, driving the men like sheep before them. At last the prisoners were penned together in the lower right hand corner of the stockade. While the guards stood at the ready, Gibbs, flanked by his aides, walked to the mouth of the tunnel Billings and his companions had dug, and directed a working party of Blacks to break it in and follow the excavation to the stockade. Gibbs went immediately to the second tunnel and did the same, after which the guards marched out again. Gibbs had an order posted saying that if any more tunnels were dug, all the trees would be cut down and the sheds removed, thus taking away the only shelters the men enjoyed. Although Billings and his friends began a new tunnel, their hearts were not in it. Besides, Gibbs prevented other tunnels by digging a deep ditch all around the outside of the stockade. Billing's tunnel was discovered because a Captain Silver of a Pennsylvania Cavalry regiment had been paid $1,000 dollars in gold and his freedom for information concerning escape attempts.[52]

---

[52] Billings, "Only Yesterday," 66-74.

Jacob Heffelfinger of the 36th Pennsylvania Infantry, recorded in his diary that three tunnels were discovered, all on 27 June. According to Heffelfinger, Gibbs not only threatened to cut the trees down and destroy the sheds, but also intended to remove the bunks from the sheds. Despite this discovery, Heffelfinger reported, several men actually escaped from the prison during the night of 26 June by crawling through a ditch used as a sink. Although fired on by the guards, they ran into river swamp. Bloodhounds were set upon their trail the following morning, but the men managed to elude them.[53]

The very thought of a prison escape consumed Gibbs with anxiety. He even used the very possibility of such an event to seek higher rank. In a letter to Adjutant General Samuel Cooper, on 16 June 1864, Gibbs elaborated upon his role as prison commandant, "It is plain that any officer who is expected to command this military prison, the most important in the Confederacy, as being composed of officers only, must be of rank to command at least the officers of the guard furnished him....In the event of attempt outbreak or other trouble I...ask who commands the prison guard?...Most of these officers are known to be intelligent, some fearless, many desperate, and all are of more or less notoriety–I had almost said distinction. The question is still unsettled, who commands the prison guard, myself or the lieutenant colonel of 'reserves' or 'militia'? Having had some military experience as colonel of a regiment in the field, I hope I may be excused for expressing strongly my disinclination to serve under such officers." He also noted that the prison was still without a medical officer or a quartermaster.[54]

Gibbs repeated his request to Cooper on 26 June noting his perplexity: that "who, in the event of revolt among the prisoners here, commands the force to quell it, myself or the officer commanding that part of the Georgia Reserves from which my guard is drawn? The contingency referred to is not unlikely-has once occurred and is again threatened. There is more danger to the railroads, wires, and bridges in this section of country, particularly in the direction of Atlanta, in the 1,400 prisoners (officers) here than in 20,000 enlisted men in Andersonville,

---

[53] Jacob Heffelfinger Diary, January 1, 1864-July 4, 1865, June 27-28, 1864, Civil War Times Illustrated Collection, USMHI, hereafter cited as Heffelfinger Diary. The order to remove the bunks was rescinded on 29 June. Ibid. Heffelfinger was captured at the Battle of the Wilderness on 5 May 1864.

[54] Gibbs to Cooper, C.S. Military Prisons, Macon, 16 June 1864, *O.R.*, Ser. II, Vol. 7:372-373. Gibbs, a North Carolinian, had served as Colonel of the Forty-second North Carolina for nearly two years in the Second Army Corps, Army of Northern Virginia. His request for promotion was strongly endorsed by Brigadier General W.M. Gardner, Commanding the Post at Richmond, and by his former corps commander, Lieutenant General Richard S. Ewell, at this time commanding the Department of Richmond, Ibid., 373.

especially when it is remembered that my guard is supplied by a regiment not 400 strong, imperfectly armed, and almost entirely without discipline or drill." The matter was finally settled when Gibbs was appointed to his old rank as Colonel.[55] Despite earlier actions taken by the City Council to bury the dead beyond the City limits south of Macon, some of the dead were still being buried in the woods about a quarter of a mile behind the prison camp. Chaplain Henry S. White, a prisoner in the stockade, wrote the men were placed in plain coffins, with their clothes on, and buried respectably. He described the scene: "A detail of our own officers connected with the hospital as nurses or attendants usually went and buried the dead. We did not wish the rebels to touch the sacred forms of our martyred dead."[56]

Life continued as usual during late June. On the 29th two new pumps were installed in the prison, enabling the prisoners to use three good wells of water besides the spring. On 2 July six officers from Sherman's Army, then approaching Atlanta, were brought into camp.[57]

On 4 July, as the Confederate officers were conducting the usual roll call, a captain of German descent named Herzog displayed a tiny US flag, and began singing the "Star Spangled Banner" as he waved it above his head. The result was electric when all the prisoners who could joined in the song, and enthusiastically rallied around Herzog and burst into tears. A spontaneous celebration followed with Chaplain Dixon of the 14th Connecticut, leading the men in prayer, followed by everyone singing the song "America," led by Captain Ives of Rhode Island. This was followed by a magnificent speech by Colonel LeGrange. Another song followed, then a fiery speech from Billings' friend Captain Kellogg. Many other speeches were then given. However, while Colonel Thorpe of the 1st New York Dragoons spoke, the officer of the day entered and said that Gibbs had ordered that there should be no more speeches.[58]

The men reluctantly complied with the order, but not until the officer who brought it threatened to have the howitzers fire on them. However, before the prisoners dispersed, they gave rousing cheers for the flag, Abraham Lincoln, General Grant, and the Emancipation Proclamation. During the meeting the little flag was waving over the prisoners' heads held by an officer perched in the framework of the building. For dinner, Heffelfinger had a good cabbage soup. During the evening of the 4th all the prisoners were jubilant, improvising fireworks out of boards and pitch-pine trees. They also made mock elephants and giants which they placed around the yard.[59]

---

[55] Ibid., 418-419.

[56] Jervey, ed., "Ten Weeks in a Macon Prison, 1864," 698.

[57] Heffelfinger diary 29, June and 2 July, 1864.

[58] Billings, "Only Yesterday," 75-76; Heffelfinger diary, 4 July, 1864.

[59] Billings, "Only Yesterday," 76; Heffelfinger diary, 4 July, 1864.

A number of men successfully escaped during the spring and summer of 1864. One of them passed out of the yard by hiding himself in a box on the sutler's wagon.[60] A number of others escaped when they were allowed to work as blacksmiths and in other occupations in the city. Aaron Eugene Bachman of the First Pennsylvania Cavalry wrote, "We went into the war for the Union cause and not to work for the Rebels, but we did all we could to keep from starving, and made for home as soon as we could see our way clear, although a number of these were recaptured. Some of these men married the girls working in the Macon Cotton Factory.[61]

Some were not so fortunate in their escape attempts. In early July a prisoner dashed up the street leading from the prison. He was fired upon by two guards who missed. However, one of the balls passed through the siding of a kitchen, one hundred and fifty yards in front of the fleeing man, seriously injuring a black man owned by James Gates. The prisoner was finally chased down at the railroad tracks and recaptured.[62] Another officer who attempted to escape disguised as a black laborer, was discovered when his white skin was visible through his open shirt.[63]

On one occasion a prisoner persuaded a black peddler, allowed in the enclosure to sell dewberries, to let him hide under the immense tin tub in which he brought his berries. The peddler left the compound and drove his wagon into his shed, and the prisoner came out of hiding after nightfall and began his escape. Unfortunately, he ran into a detachment of the Provost Marshall's guard, who noticed the blackberry stains on his clothing, and took him into custody. Although he was closely questioned, he did not tell how he had escaped. After returning the prisoners to the compound the guard questioned the peddler who drove the berry cart, accusing him of duplicity in the escape. Although he was promised immunity if he confessed, the peddler denied resolutely having any knowledge about the attempted escape. He was hung from a tree because he kept his silence.[64]

General John H. Winder, Commandant of Confederate Prisoners, informed Cooper from his headquarters at Camp Sumter—Andersonville Prison—that Camp Oglethorpe was not secure and would take great expense and labor to make it so. It was not in a good location since it was located within a few hundred yards of three important railroad depots and a number of very large workshops. Escaped prisoners, Winder believed, would probably burn all of

---

[60] Heffelfinger diary, 5 July, 1864.
[61] Aaron Eugene Bachman, "My Experiences As A Union Soldier in the Civil War," Mss., p. 49, USMHI.
[62] *Macon Daily Telegraph*, 2 July 1864.
[63] Ibid., 21 July 1864.
[64] Billings, "Only Yesterday," 79-80.

these facilities. Furthermore, Winder noted, the prison was "in a large town, which renders an inefficient guard more inefficient. He added, "It is in an unhealthy locality, to which our troops ought not to be exposed."[65]

These escapes and near escapes prompted Cobb to order Colonel George W. Lee, commanding the Reserve camp, known as Camp Rescue, to send five hundred men to relieve the three hundred sent there earlier. These five hundred Reserves would remain at Camp Oglethorpe.[66] When news spread in Macon of the approach of Stoneman and his raiders in late July, Cobb ordered Colonel John B. Cummings, Commanding the Fifth Regiment, Georgia Reserves, the unit which provided guards for the prison, to detail one hundred men with a complement of officers from his command to remove the Federal officers to Charleston. Plans called for the removal of the prisoners in detachments. The first would start on 27 July at 5:00 P.M.[67] Cobb issued the order despite the argument put forward by General Sam Jones, then commanding in Charleston, to General Cooper, that sending 600 officers from Macon would complicate negotiations to exchange those now there. However, Jones assured Cooper, "If the prisoners must be sent from Macon allow me to exercise some discretion as to where they shall be confined." Jones also needed additional troops to guard them.[68]

Colonel Gibbs also used this opportunity to urge the release of Federal chaplains because "they give a great deal of trouble." Robert Ould, Confederate Agent of Exchange, agreed and assured Gibbs that Secretary of War Seddon had ordered their unconditional release, presumably without being exchanged.[69]

When the prisoners learned the news of the transfer they washed their clothes, prepared corn pone, and packed their haversacks. The first detachment began the move to Charleston early in the morning of 27 July and the exodus continued the following day. The men marched to the depot of the Georgia Central Railroad and began the trip to Charleston.[70] Chaplain White described the scene as one which was "full of joy." The Confederates, he explained, "gave

---

[65] Gen. John H. Winder to Cooper, Andersonville, 18 July 1864, O.R., Ser. II, 7:472.

[66] Capt. R.J. Hallett for Cobb to Col. George W. Lee, Macon, 25 July 1864, Cobb Papers, 1864. See also Hallett to Lee, Macon, 25 July 1864, Howell Cobb Letter Book, 1864-1865, p. 176.

[67] R.J. Hallett, A.A.G., for Cobb to Col. John B. Cummings, Headquarters Georgia Reserves, Macon, 27 July 1864, Howell Cobb Letter Book 1864-1865, p. 179.

[68] Gen. Sam Jones to Cooper, Adams' Run, S.C., 26 July 1864, *OR*, Ser. II, 7:502.

[69] Col. George C. Gibbs to Seddon, Telegram, Macon, 29 July 1864, with endorsement by Colonel Robert Ould, Richmond, 29 July 1864, *OR*, Ser. II, 7:511. Ould assured Seddon that "The chaplains and surgeons have been ordered to Richmond to be sent through the lines by flag of truce." Ibid.

[70] Abbott, *Prison Life in the South*, 84.

us to understand that it was for exchange." Two days later another six hundred prisoners left Macon. Their captors marched them in the night to the depot, where trains were waiting to take them to Savannah. They left at night and did not arrive in Gordon until 8:00 A.M.[71]

Despite the fact that the prisoners left in late July, Stoneman and those officers in his division who were captured with him at Sunshine Church, were incarcerated at Camp Oglethorpe for a time. However, Cobb wrote to Seddon on 12 August asking him to close Camp Oglethorpe and establish no more prison camps near Macon.[72]

After this, until near the end of the war the role of Camp Oglethorpe as a prisoner of war stockade ended. On 11 August the *Daily Telegraph* announced "82 prisoners came down from Atlanta on August 10."[73]

On 1 October 1864, Dr. J. McCurdy, Assistant Medical Director of the 14th Army Corps, wrote to US Surgeon General Joseph K. Barnes that he had charge of the sick and wounded prisoners at Macon in late August-early September 1864, complaining that because a number of officers had suffered so long with chronic and scorbutic diarrhea, scurvy, ulceration of the bowels, and kindred afflictions, efforts should be made to secure their release immediately. McCurdy complained, "The wretched condition of those helpless officers beggars description." Most of them had been confined to their beds from four months to a year, with their bowels moving from one to three times an hour. They had been packed into crowded apartments, and had eaten coarse, and often sour meal and a little bacon. He concluded: "These men have been prisoners more than a year, have no money, scarcely any articles of clothing, &c., and too feeble to sit erect while using the bedpan."[74]

The travails of the imprisoned Federal officers at Macon finally ended when Adjutant General Cooper telegraphed General John H. Winder at Andersonville on September 5, "Take immediate measures for sending the prisoners at Andersonville and Macon to Charleston and Savannah."[75]

The very site of Camp Oglethorpe has been lost. The Georgia State Fair was never again held there. That event was moved to several locations before it was permanently established at Central City Park in 1870. The site of the stockade was taken over by the Macon and Brunswick Railroad, and most of the prison and fairgrounds structures were removed until the area was only a barren area of

---

[71] Jervey, ed., "Ten Weeks in a Macon Prison, 1864," 700.

[72] Cobb to Seddon, Telegram, Macon, 12 August 1864, *OR*, Ser. II, 7:585-586.

[73] Macon Daily Telegraph, 11 August 1864.

[74] Dr. J. McCurdy to Col. Joseph K. Barnes, Youngstown, Ohio, 1 October 1864, OR, Ser. II, Vol. 7, 908.

[75] Cooper to Winder, Telegram, Richmond, 5 September 1864, Ibid., Ser. II, Vol. 7, 773.

track next to Seventh Street. Today, the Southern Railway Company's Brosnan Yards occupy the site where thousands of men suffered and hundreds of them died.[76]

---

[76] McInvale, "'That Thing of Infamy'," 290.

Chapter 8

Macon as an Ordnance Center:
The Arsenal

On 8 April 1864, the Confederacy's Superintendent of Ordnance, the Pennsylvania-born West Point graduate Brigadier General Josiah Gorgas reviewed the achievements of the past three years:

It is three years today since I took charge of the Ordnance Department of the Confederate States at Montgomery–three years of constant work and application. I have succeeded beyond my utmost expectations. From being the worst supplied of the Bureaus of the War Department it is now the best. Large arsenals have been organized at Richmond, Fayetteville, Augusta, Charleston, Columbus, Macon, Atlanta and Selma, and smaller ones at Danville, Lynchburgh and Montgomery, besides other establishments. A superb powder mill has been built at Augusta. The credit of which is due to Col. G.W. Rains. Lead smelting works were established by me at Petersburgh, and turned over to the Nitre and Mining Bureau....A cannon foundry established at Macon for heavy guns, and bronze foundries at Macon, Columbus, GA., and at Augusta; a foundry for shot and shell at Salisbury, N.C.; a large shop for leather work at Clarksville, Va.; besides the Armories here [Richmond] and at Fayetteville, a manufactory of carbines has been built up here; a rifle factory at Ashville [sic] (transferred to Columbia, S.C.); a new and very large armory at Macon, including a pistol factory, built up under contract here and sent to Atlanta, and thence transferred under purchase to Macon; a second pistol factory at Columbus, Ga;- All of these have required incessant toil and attention, but have borne such fruit as relieves the country from fear of want in these respects. Where three years ago we were not making a gun, pistol nor a sabre, no shot nor shell (except at the Tredegar Works) a pound of powder- we now make all these in quantities to meet the demands of our large armies. In looking over all this I feel that my three years of labor have not been passed in vain.[1]

One of the main reasons Gorgas had met with such success was his almost uncanny ability to choose superb subordinates who could find substitutes for materials not easily available in the beleaguered South, and to seek out scarce and needed supplies. The most brilliant of these individuals included Colonel Richard Matthei Cuyler of Savannah, a member of an important family of railroad developers in Georgia; Colonel James Henry Burton, formerly chief engineer of the Royal Small Arms Factory at Enfield, England, known as the Enfield Works; and Colonel John William Mallet, Superintendent of Confederate Laboratories with headquarters at the Confederate States Central Laboratory in Macon.[2]

In late April 1862, Federal forces captured Fort Pulaski which protected the mouth of the Savannah River below Georgia's major city, Savannah. With this threat, the Savannah Ordnance Office prepared to move to the interior city of Macon. In preparation for the move Captain Smith Stansbury, Gorgas' assistant in the Ordnance Office at Richmond, wrote to Captain Richard M. Cuyler, in charge of the Ordnance operations in Savannah, "Colonel Gorgas instructs me to write to you that he entirely approves of your removal of stores to Macon. He is entirely satisfied that in the event of the fall of Savannah you will act for the best."[3]

Gorgas directed Cuyler to "organize the Depot of repairs and constructions at Macon," and ordered the transfer of all tools, materials, and stores not needed at Savannah to Macon. The Laboratory established as part of the Arsenal at Savannah would also be removed to the City on the Ocmulgee River.[4]

Richard Matthei Cuyler, born in Savannah in 1825, was the son of Richard Randolph Cuyler and his wife, Mississippi Gordon, daughter of Ambrose Gordon and his wife, Elizabeth Meade. She was the sister of William Washington Gordon, founder and first president of the Georgia Central

---

[1] Josiah Gorgas, Journal, 8 April 1864, in Sarah Woolfolk Wiggins, ed., *The Journals of Josiah Gorgas 1857-1878* (Tuscaloosa and London: The University of Alabama Press, 1995) 97-98.

[2] Frank E. Vandiver, *Ploughshares into Swords: Josiah Gorgas and Confederate Ordnance* (Austin: University of Texas Press, 1952) ix.

[3] Captain Smith Stansbury to Captain Richard M. Cuyler, Richmond, 19 April 1862, Letters Received, Arsenal, 1862, Records of Confederate Ordnance Establishments at Macon, Georgia, Box 3197, Records of the Arsenal at Macon, Georgia, Military Records Group 109, NARA, Microfilm, hereafter cited as Letters Received, Arsenal, 1862.

[4] Gorgas to Cuyler, Richmond, 25 April 1862, Ibid.

Railroad.[5] The younger Cuyler served for twenty years as an officer in the US Navy, but resigned his commission in 1860. In 1861 he was appointed head of the Savannah Arsenal. After the war he lived in Baltimore, but died of apoplexy in Fishkill, New York, on 18 May 1879. He was buried in Laurel Grove Cemetery in Savannah.[6]

As preparations for the move continued, Cuyler inquired about mechanics available to work in the new facility. The owners of the Findlay Iron Works in Macon, the people to whom Cuyler posed the question, answered they had only a few mechanics in their employ. These included C. Parker, William Wallace, James Mitchell, D. Hogan, and men by the name of Gibon and O'Connell, all machinists, and Thomas Lackee, striker. Besides these, the Findlays had a black machine blacksmith, a black molder, and a black engineer. There were, the Findlays asserted, several other fine machinists available, including some in the 2nd Georgia Battalion which was preparing to leave for Goldsboro, North Carolina. These men could be retained in Macon. Besides these, Cuyler could "safely rely on getting–from forty to fifty mechanics around Macon." He would, however, have to move quickly to engage their services.[7]

In May, 1862, Cuyler rented the factory of James N. and Christopher D. Findlay at the head of Third Street in Macon. The lease included the machinery then in the shops, although the Confederate Government purchased all materials and hand tools then in the shop. Cuyler reported "Neither the large stock of patterns nor the office furniture was leased or purchased, but simply allowed to remain at the Arsenal the property of the Messrs Findlay."

Cuyler removed the foundry from the lower part of the machine shop to a building erected for the purpose. He also supervised the construction of a carpenter and wood machinery shop together with a wheelwright shop and a steam hammer room. A number of sheds were also built on the property. The Findlay's blacksmith shop was also enlarged, and many new forges added. Many machines were added to the shops. The Arsenal soon rented the upper story of a harness shop on Cherry Street owned by the firm of Little, Smith and Company. Cuyler also acquired an arms repair shop from the firm of D.C. Hodgkins and Sons who had leased the property from the owner. The Government bought machinery and most of the tools owned by the Hodgkins firm. The Ordnance Bureau also rented a warehouse on Second Street from James J. Snider. Another facility, a warehouse on Cherry Street, was rented from the firm of Harris and Dease. Still another facility was rented from swordmaker

---

[5] Robert Manson Myers, *The Children of Pride* (new Haven: Yale University Press, 1972) 1502.

[6] *Savannah Morning News*, 24 May 1879.

[7] James N. and Christopher D. to Cuyler, Macon, 28 April 1862, Letters Received, Arsenal, 1862.

E.J. Johnston. This consisted of the old Presbyterian Church on Fourth Street which Johnston used as a warehouse.[8]

On 1 September 1863, Cuyler petitioned the Mayor and City Council to rent a lot southwest of Findlay's Foundry, to build a bombproof for proving heavy guns. The petition was approved on 22 September and terms for the rental were set at $1,000 per year. Both parties reserved the right to remove the bombproof, and all improvements placed on the property.[9]

Although a railroad track was extended to Findlay's Foundry for use by the Arsenal,[10] and a few new buildings were erected for Laboratory and other purposes as noted above,[11] most of the buildings erected for Arsenal purposes were temporary.[12] No attempt was made by the Confederate Government, as in the case of the Armory and Laboratory, to build a completely new Arsenal. Nevertheless, the Arsenal was an impressive operation. At the end of the war a reporter for the *Daily Telegraph* wrote the facility was an "extensive establishment in splendid condition," which had "ample machinery for the fabrication of a great many patterns of small arms, cannon etc, and it is hoped that the government will not only preserve it intact, but enlarge and make it one of its chief instruments in the production of the essential material of war."[13]

Cuyler shipped a large number of ordnance supplies from Savannah including uncut cannon balls, lint, bullet molds, steel, musket balls, brass fuse plugs, gun carriage bolts, tin straps for six and twelve-pounder cannon, musket caps, pistol caps, rifled shell, ammunition boxes, and many other items.[14] Cuyler, anxious to begin work as soon as possible, received a list of men subject to the new Confederate Conscription Act from D.C. Hodgkins and Sons.[15] All of this activity was accelerated by Gorgas who wanted the Macon Arsenal placed in operation as soon as possible, partly because he wanted twelve

---

[8] Cuyler to Major W. McBurney, Chief Ordnance Officer, Cavalry Corps, Military Division of the Mississippi, Macon, 10 May 1865, on file in Genealogy and Archives Room, Washington Memorial Library, hereafter cited as Cuyler Letter, 10 May 1865.

[9] Council Minutes, 1, 22 September 1863, Book E, pp. 33, 35.

[10] Gorgas to Cuyler, Richmond, 30 July 1862, Letters Received, Arsenal, 1862.

[11] Gorgas to Cuyler, Richmond, 16 April 1864, Ibid.

[12] Gorgas to Cuyler, Richmond, 28 April 1863, Ibid.

[13] *Macon Daily Telegraph*, 19 May 1865. The writer of the article either had his tongue in his cheek when he wrote these words or expressed a naivete not usually found in the post-Confederate South.

[14] A.T. Cunningham to Cuyler, Ordnance Office, Savannah, 5 May 1862, Letters Received, Arsenal, 1862, vol. 4.

[15] D.C. Hodgkins and Sons to Cuyler, Macon, 2 May 1862, Ibid. The list included Walter C. Hodgkins, John C. Hodgkins, George F. Barrett, Richard A. Magill, John B. Peyton, J. B. Shelverton, and B.F. Cawley.

four-gun batteries manufactured quickly. The Pennsylvanian, however, cautioned Cuyler to operated the Arsenal's Laboratory on a "limited scale."[16]

The Arsenal began to function when Cuyler took charge of the facility on 10 May. As one of his first actions, the new superintendent, asked for a detachment of troops to be sent to Macon to guard the Arsenal. Although watchmen were already in place, a guard for such an important establishment seemed indispensable.[17] In the meantime, Cuyler wired General Alexander R. Lawton, commanding in Savannah, "Can you furnish me with detachment of twenty five or thirty men & one officer for guard purposes, temporary. I have applied to Richmond for a company."[18] The *Daily Telegraph's* writer proudly announced the inception of the new facility by saying that the Findlay Iron Works "have been transferred to the control of the Confederate Government during the war, and will hereafter be known as the 'Macon Arsenal', Capt. R.M. Cuyler, commanding."[19]

Even before Cuyler officially took over the newly-transferred Arsenal, serious efforts began to collect brass bells to be melted down in the local foundries and used for cannon. The *Daily Telegraph* asked for bells in the City, except from the new City Hall which was used to give fire alarms, "as a patriotic offering to the Confederacy, to be cast into cannon." Planters might contribute their old field bells. Columbus, Georgia, might be used as an example because in that city the women appealed for old brass andirons, knobs, keys, belt buckles, and even bright and shiny cooking utensils.[20] Such prominent Macon women as Mrs. H. B. Troutman, Mrs. H. M. Colquit, Mrs. Amelia Ross, Mrs. Dr. Robert Collins, Mrs. S. D. Howard, Mrs. T. R. Bloom, Mrs. S. A. Weed, and Mrs. Thomas Hardeman, Sr., appealed for brass. On 21 March 120 pounds of the metal came in, some of it from fire sets and valuable brass kettles. A reporter for the *Daily Telegraph* appealed, "Men of Macon take hold and get up a first rate field battery right here in Macon by our own founders."[21] Several days later, however, the paper urged the people to send no more brass because "We have been advised that the household brass is unfit for ordnance, on account of the zinc used in its composition."[22] Despite this, the paper called for church bells to be cast into cannon on 3 April. Macon's Christ Episcopal Church planned to

---

[16] Gorgas to Cuyler, Richmond, 7 May 1862, Ibid.

[17] Cuyler to Gorgas, C.S. Arsenal, Macon, 9 May 1862, Records of Ordnance Establishments at Macon, Georgia, Box 3192, Telegrams Sent, Arsenal, 1862-65, Microfilm, hereafter cited as Telegrams Sent, Arsenal, 1862-1865.

[18] Cuyler to General Alexander R. Lawton, Telegram, Macon, 9 May 1862, Ibid.

[19] *Macon Daily Telegraph*, 16 May 1862.

[20] Ibid., 19 March 1862. See also Ibid., 20 March 1862.

[21] Ibid., 22 March 1862.

[22] Ibid., 27 March 1862.

donate its 226-pound bell soon.[23] The *Daily Telegraph* pursued this theme on 4 April, urging the people to fit up a complete field battery of four six-pounder rifled cannon and two twelve-pounder howitzers, "at our own expense, and let them be the property of Macon forever."[24] Soon, the congregation of the Primitive Baptist Church announced their plans to donate their church bell, which weighed 900 pounds.[25]

During May, Cuyler continued to ask for the brass bells of the Macon churches to be melted down to make cannon tubes. This request included the bell of the Mulberry Street Methodist Church whose pastor, Reverend J. E. Evans, promised to furnish the bell when Cuyler called for it.[26] The wardens and vestry of Christ Episcopal Church on Walnut Street unanimously voted to offer their bell to Cuyler.[27] Cuyler replied on 23 May, "The generous tender of your Church Bell for the use of the Government is gratefully accepted. I will at once report the fact to the Chief of Ordnance." However, the Church should keep its bell until it was called for.[28] The bell was not needed until early October 1863, when Cuyler sent a messenger to take it down and bring it to the Arsenal. He promised to replace the bell "at the end of the war if desired."[29] As late as October 1863, Cuyler offered to pay "Fair prices...for old copper, brass and zinc, delivered at this Arsenal, or at Albany [Georgia]."[30]

During May 1862, the first month of its operation in Macon, the new Arsenal became the center of much activity. Cuyler obtained two anvils on 14 May from Savannah.[31] He notified Gorgas on the 16 May that 400 guns with ammunition had arrived at Savannah and should be forwarded to Corinth, Mississippi, then being besieged by Federal troops.[32] Cunningham, in the

---

[23] Ibid., 13 April 1862.

[24] Ibid., 4 April 1862.

[25] Ibid., 5, 10 April 1862.

[26] Rev. J.E. Evans, Mulberry Street Methodist Church, Macon, to Cuyler, 12 May 1862, Letters Received, Arsenal, 1862.

[27] J.L. Jones, Secretary, Christ Episcopal Church, to Cuyler, Macon, 21 May 1862, Christ Church Records, Correspondence, 1862-1863, Washington Library, hereafter cited as Christ Church Records, 1862-1863.

[28] Cuyler to J.L. Jones, Macon, 23 May 1862, Ibid. See also Rev. Oliver J. Hart and Calder W. Payne, comps., *The History of Christ Church Paris Macon, Georgia March 5, 1862-March 5, 1975* (Macon: Omnipress, Inc., 1974) 42.

[29] Lieut. Col. Richard M. Cuyler to J. L. Jones, Macon, 7 October 1863, Christ Church Records.

[30] *Macon Daily Telegraph*, 22 October 1863.

[31] Cuyler to A.T. Cunningham, Telegram, Macon, 15 May 1862, Telegrams Sent, Arsenal, 1862-65.

[32] Cuyler to Gorgas, Telegram, Macon, 16 May 1862, Ibid. Cuyler had already ordered Cunningham to send the guns, 20 cases with 20 to the case, to Corinth,

meantime, was shipping many articles from the Savannah Arsenal to Macon.[33] Another opportunity arose when Gorgas ordered Cuyler to accept all the revolvers the firm of Griswold and Gunnison in Griswoldville, near Macon, could produce during an eight-month period.[34] However, when Cuyler wrote asking for an order the firm explained they could not deliver more than a specimen of their revolvers within the next two months. After that they expected to finish and deliver from fifty to sixty revolvers a week on a regular basis. Griswold and Gunnison assured the Superintendent "we shall endeavor to make an article that will stand your thorough tests and of as good workmanship as the hands we have and can procure can give them."[35]

When Cuyler sent D.C. Hodgkins, the Superintendent of his Armory Department, to Griswoldville in July 1862, to examine the Griswold and Gunnison factory, he found twenty-two machines running, worked by twenty-four hands, twenty-two of whom were slaves. One hundred revolvers were under fabrication. The barrels were forged from ordinary one inch square bar iron. The cylinders were cut from ordinary round bar iron. Hodgkins wrote, "I cannot approve of this process but the proprietors feel confident they will stand the required test." Hodgkins showed the foreman how to case harden the revolvers, and how to temper the springs and trim the steel without using acids. He also taught the firm's managers how to blue the revolvers. "I also enjoined on them the importance of having high polish on [the] inside [of] the barrel," he reported, "to prevent the roll stripping, and reducing the liability to foul." However, Gunnison should use more experienced mechanics, especially to assemble the revolvers. Hodgkins also thought it was necessary to subject each pistol to a thorough proofing and close examination.[36]

In early August, 1862, the firm produced five weapons per day, all designed for the cavalry service. A reporter for the *Daily Telegraph* examined a revolver which he described as "the first fruit of the skill and inventive ingenuity in elaborating machinery and tools for the purpose of men who had never seen a pistol shop, or a single tool or piece of machinery for making them."[37]

Cuyler to A.T. Cunningham, Telegram, Macon, 16 May 1862, Ibid. See also Cuyler to Gorgas, Telegram, Macon, 20 May 1862, Ibid.

[33] A.T. Cunningham to Cuyler, Savannah, 19 May 1862, Letters Received, Arsenal, 1862.

[34] Gorgas to Cuyler, Richmond, 19 May 1862, Ibid. Gorgas insisted the revolvers "must stand the usual tests, and be of good workmanship."

[35] Griswold and Gunnison to Cuyler, Griswoldville, GA., 29 May 1862, Ibid.

[36] D.C. Hodgkins to Cuyler, Armory Department, Macon Arsenal, 16 July 1862, Ibid.; *Daily Telegraph*, 5 August 1862.

[37] *Daily Telegraph*, 6 August 1862.

In October, 1862, Cuyler ordered Lieutenant R. Milton Cary, Acting Ordnance, Artillery and Ordnance Inspecting Officer, to inspect twenty-two revolving pistols manufactured by Griswold and Gunnison after the model of the "Colts Navy Pistol." Cary took each pistol apart, and carefully inspected each part. The weapons were then subjected to a powder proof by being fired separately using fifty-four grams of powder and two bullets. Cary then adjusted the cylinders of those pistols which passed this test, and fired them, some with one bullet and some with two bullets. During this test, Cary charged the cylinders to their utmost capacity. The barrels of three of the pistols burst. Another weapon was discarded because of a defect in casting the base, and a second pistol was rejected because of a broken hand spring, a third for a busted tube, and a fourth because of a broken ramrod catch. The firm planned to repair the last three so they could pass inspection.[38]

Lachlan H. McIntosh, Georgia's Chief of Ordnance, assured Cuyler he would give him a large number of military supplies including cartridge boxes, waist belts, cap pouches, knapsacks, and many other items. The list included "a large lot of pikes awaiting the orders of the Confederate Government."[39]

During May, Cuyler purchased many kinds of material to equip his new Arsenal. The list included coal, coke, iron, lead, copper, and brass. The iron was purchased from the firm of Elliot and Russell of Rome, Georgia. It included two carloads, 32,000 pounds more or less, at $60.00 for a ton weighing 2,240 pounds. Elliot and Russell agreed to send Cuyler one car load of iron, about 16,000 pounds, a week. E.G. Walker and Company of Chattanooga, Tennessee, contracted to sell 8,000 bushels of mixed coal at fifteen cents a bushel at the mines, 16,000 bushels of coke at eighteen cents a bushel, and 2,800 bushels of fine coal at eleven cents per bushel. The firm planned to load it on the cars at the mines, and Cuyler would have to pay for transportation to Macon. One of Cuyler's agents, W. W. McDowell, told him that Walker would not make either a written or verbal contract except on the basis that if the miners raised the price of coal to him he would have to make a corresponding raise. Fortunately, Cuyler could cancel the order at any time he wanted to. McDowell also contracted with Dr. John W. Lewis of Cartersville, Georgia, for 500 tons of hot blast charcoal at $60 a ton of 2,240 pounds. Unfortunately, Major Mark A. Cooper of the Etowah Iron Works was supplying large amounts of iron for the ironclads under construction at Wilmington and Charleston. Because of the great scarcity of coal and the small number of men at work at his mill, Cooper could not supply Cuyler's needs for five or six weeks. Cooper would work in Cuyler's

---

[38] Lieutenant R. Milton Cary to Cuyler, Macon, 14 October 1862, Letters Received, Arsenal, 1862. For additional test results of pistols manufactured by Griswold and Gunnison see also Cary to Cuyler, Macon, 22 October 1862, Ibid.

[39] Lachlan H. McIntosh to Cuyler, Milledgeville, 20 May 1862, Ibid., 1862.

order at a price of ten cents per pound, and would load the cars at his Etowah mill. Another iron maker, Horace Ware of the Shelby Iron Manufacturing Company at Columbiana, Shelby County, Alabama, promised to write Cuyler concerning the amount his firm could furnish, time of delivery, and price. McDowell cautioned Cuyler about Ware with the words "watch him–as he has the reputation of being tricky."[40] Elliott and Russell acted promptly by sending two carloads of pig iron to the Macon Arsenal on May 21.[41]

Cuyler continued to obtain materials from other sources. One of these, Schofield and Brother of Macon, informed him they had a four wheel dray, which had only been used once, for sale.[42] Cunningham shipped cartridge bags and buckshot from Savannah.[43]

The list of contractors with whom Cuyler had accounts included Samuel J. Gustin, Macon; Little and Smith, Mallett Beck and Company, and Captain John McReady, all of Savannah; Grenville Wood and John W. Lewis of Cartersville; O. W. Massey of Macon; R. M. Everitt of McDonough, Georgia; Mallett Beck and Company, Reynolds and Company and Thomas C. Nisbet of Macon; J. C. and J. E. Denham of Eatonton, Georgia; S. E. Jordon of Perry, Georgia; Dixie Iron Works of Macon; and others.[44] James Stewart, a Government Assistant Medical Purveyor, wrote Cuyler offering his services to buy chemicals for the Arsenal's laboratory.[45]

In July 1862, Jerry Cowles wanted a contract to furnish iron, using President Isaac Scott of the Macon and Western Railroad as a reference.[46] Gorgas placed a condition on the sale when he learned Cuyler was planning to purchase a building for laboratory purposes. Possibly small arm and field ammunition might be stored there, or was it too close to other buildings to serve as a storage facility for ammunition? At any rate, Gorgas ordered "If the building can be used for other purposes besides a laboratory purchase it. A small laboratory will

---

[40] W. W. McDowell to Cuyler, Macon, 21 May 1862, Ibid. Cuyler wanted to purchase iron from the Tredegar Works in Richmond because the rolling mills at Etowah were so buy fulfilling Government contracts. He wrote: "I shall find trouble in building the carriages for the twelve four gun batteries ordered unless I get the iron from the Tredegar Works." Cuyler to Gorgas, Macon, 2 June 1862, with endorsement by Gorgas, Ibid.

[41] Elliott and Russell to Cuyler, Rome, GA., 21 May 1862, Ibid.

[42] Schofield and Brother to Cuyler, Macon, 23 May 1862, Ibid.

[43] A.T. Cunningham to Cuyler, Savannah, 23 May 1862, Ibid.

[44] List of Contractors, Macon, 1863, Accounts with Contractors, Armory, 1863, Chapter IV, Vol. 76, Records of Ordnance Establishments at Macon, Georgia, Microfilm, NARA.

[45] James Stewart to Cuyler, Macon, 16 July 1862, Letters Received, Arsenal, 1862.

[46] Gorgas to Cuyler, Richmond, 8 July 1862, Ibid.

accommodate all you need to do."[47] When Cuyler made arrangements to lease the factory of D. C. Hodgkins and Company, Gorgas approved it as well as the purchase of the firm's machinery and tools. He, however, cautioned Cuyler to take great care in the manufacture of arms in order to produce a reliable weapon, directing the thorough testing of the barrels, locks, and springs because "Very few country made arms have proved serviceable." It was also essential to have ample space for storing materials as well as a magazine for powder.[48] Several weeks later, Gorgas urged Cuyler to stick to the general plan for the temporary buildings of the Arsenal, and build a furnace for remelting scrap iron "in as inexpensive a manner as is compatible with the work."[49]

Cuyler was beset with other problems. Major J.E. Rylander, commanding Camp Oglethorpe, had to turn down a request for tents to house the Arsenal Guard because he did not have enough for his own men.[50] He needed a good blacksmith to take charge of the Arsenal's Blacksmith Shop, but couldn't immediately obtain one.[51] Cuyler was more fortunate in fulfilling his need for a machinist who was experienced in building gun carriages. He hired a man named Tomlinson who had several years experience at Old Point Comfort, Virginia.[52]

Cuyler, in fact, was so desperate for mechanics that he wired Gorgas about Private Mitchell of Co. H, Twelfth Georgia Regiment, who was home on furlough. Mitchell was "a machinist," Cuyler wrote, "whom I want dreadfully."[53] Writing Gorgas regarding the services of Private J. G. Eckman, another member of the same company who was home on furlough from the Richmond Arsenal, Cuyler plaintively asked, "Can I keep him? The only way I can get machinists is to steal them."[54]

In an effort to obtain more equipment, Cuyler directed Lieutenant H. L. Ingraham in the Ordnance Office at Savannah, to order Master Machinist Atkinson to go to Savannah and superintend the moving to Macon of the steam hammer of the Georgia Central Railroad and a large lathe. Atkinson must also select other pieces of machinery from the Georgia Central Railroad which might be useful, together with the necessary shafting and belting. Cuyler especially needed a small lathe to help in the casting of twelve and six-pounder shot, shell,

---

[47] Gorgas to Cuyler, Richmond, 22 May 1862, Ibid.

[48] Gorgas to Cuyler, Richmond, 27 May 1862, Ibid.

[49] Gorgas to Cuyler, Richmond, 28 June 1862, Ibid.

[50] Major J.E. Rylander to Cuyler, Camp Oglethorpe, 31 May 1862, Ibid.

[51] Gorgas to Cuyler, Richmond, 4 June 1862, Ibid.

[52] Gorgas to Cuyler, Richmond, 8 July 1862, Ibid.

[53] Cuyler to Gorgas, Telegram, Macon, 12 July 1862, Telegrams Sent, Arsenal, 1862-65.

[54] Cuyler to Gorgas, Telegram, Macon, 15 July 1862, Ibid.

and shrapnel. The shells had to be fitted with a new type of fuse known as the Borrman Fuse.[55]

Sometimes, Cuyler received help from his colleague, Armory Superintendent James H. Burton. Matthew Fortson, one of Burton's machinists, helped Cuyler to set up a fan-blower. Burton also promised to send one or two more mechanics in a couple of days.[56] Occasionally, Burton asked Cuyler for help. On 14 July 1862, for instance, the former official sent Armory Foreman W. D. Lotz to look for any old or new sheet metal to make a flue for the Armory boiler.[57] Occasionally, Burton wanted other things. In early July Cuyler asked Gorgas if he might allow Burton to use one of the Arsenal buildings for gun stocking machinery.[58]

As time went on, Cuyler was tasked to provide many items with little time to make them. Sometimes he had to repair arms which had been misused.[59] He always needed some item to keep his operation going. These included saddle blankets, although a substitute might be made of Brussels carpet; "which answer the purpose admirably." This type of carpet might be purchased from the firm of Freeman and English who made carriages on Cherry Street between Second and Third Streets.[60] Nails were always needed to build buildings, additions to buildings, and to fabricate other items needed in the manufacture of cannon and accouterments. The Arsenal also needed workmen, sheet tin, rope, lime, and shot gun caps.[61] Gorgas directed Cuyler to collect old lead and keep it, if not needed, subject to order. The lead might be found in window weights, old lead pipes, and lead roofing. All of this, Gorgas ordered, "to be done quietly by means of agents and without advertising."[62]

Even the Macon City Council gave Cuyler trouble. The City wanted the Confederate Government to pay for dray licenses if the Confederacy hauled equipment to and from the Arsenal. Mayor Thomson wrote that "drays from Savannah are here fulfilling a governmental contract for individual benefit

---

[55] Cuyler to Lieutenant H.L. Ingraham, Macon, 10 June 1862, Letters Received, Arsenal, 1862.

[56] Burton to Cuyler, Macon, 12 July 1862, Letters Received, Arsenal, 1862.

[57] Burton to Cuyler, Macon, 14 July 1862, Ibid.

[58] Cuyler to Gorgas, Telegram, Macon, 5 July 1862, Telegrams Sent, Arsenal, 1862-1865.

[59] Col. J.E. Jones, Fiftieth Regiment GA. Militia, to Cuyler, Macon, 7 June 1862, Ibid.

[60] Christopher D. Findlay to Cuyler, Macon, 22 June 1862, Ibid.

[61] Major Hermann Hirsch to Cuyler, Savannah, 25 June 1862, Ibid; Cuyler to John R. Hamlet, Telegram, Macon, 25 June 1862; Cuyler to Cunningham, Telegram, Macon, 1 July 1862, Ibid.; Cuyler to Humphries, Telegram, Macon, 2 July 1862, Ibid; and Cuyler to Major Marcus H. Wright, Telegram, Macon, 2 July 1862, Ibid.

[62] Gorgas to Cuyler, Richmond, 7 June 1862, Letters Received, Arsenal, 1862.

[therefore] it will be necessary for the owner to comply with the license ordinance of the city."[63]

The following August, Thomson complained about the amount of powder stored in the Arsenal facilities because it posed a danger to the city, arguing, "So long as the plea of necessity existed or may exist, our people would risk as much as any for the advancement of our cause, but I respectfully submit that such risks should not be incurred, even by the Government a day longer than they can be avoided."[64]

By early June requests poured in for cannon and accouterments. Gorgas urged Cuyler to make bronze field guns, both six-pounder and twelve-pounder howitzers. Drawings would be furnished to enable the Arsenal to manufacture 3-inch rifled cannon, six-pounder iron guns, and the popular iron twelve-pounder howitzer.[65] Cuyler also wanted to produce a Sharps Shooting Rifle of .577 caliber with the groove turned in thirty inches. The rifle, which had a twenty-six-inch barrel, would cost $8.25 for materials and $42 in labor costs to produce.[66]

Cuyler and Gorgas were always interested in experimenting with the manufacture of the most up-to-date arms. On 31 August 1862, Gorgas sent his subordinate the drawings of the English Whitworth gun. He wanted the Macon Arsenal to duplicate the weapon, when its steam hammers were completed.[67] First Lieutenant Charles Colcock Jones, Jr., commanding the Chatham Artillery in Savannah, wanted one hundred and fifty belts for artillery short swords which Lieutenant Colonel George W. Rains had furnished from the Augusta Arsenal.[68] General John C. Pemberton, defending the strategic Confederate stronghold at Vicksburg, Mississippi, needed ten thousand pounds of cannon powder.[69] When siege carriages for twenty-four-pounders were needed, Cuyler was able to furnish them from the Savannah Office.[70]

As the war continued the need to produce cannon, rifles, ammunition, and other munitions greatly increased. The Arsenal, in short, manufactured far more items than simply cannon and gun carriages. Sometimes, the Arsenal did not

---

[63] Mayor Thomson to Cuyler, Macon, 12 June 1862, Ibid.

[64] Thomson to Cuyler, Macon, 18 August 1862, Ibid.

[65] Gorgas to Cuyler, Richmond, 4 June 1862, Ibid.

[66] Walter C. Hodgkins to Cuyler, Macon, 5 June 1862, Ibid. For the results of windage tests on the rifle see Hodgkins to Cuyler, Macon, 20 June 1862, Ibid.

[67] Gorgas to Cuyler, Richmond, 31 August 1862, Ibid.

[68] First Lieutenant Charles Colcock Jones, Jr. to Cuyler, Savannah, 21 June 1862, Ibid.

[69] First Lieutenant Ingraham to Cuyler, Telegram, 10 June 1862, Telegrams Sent, Arsenal, 1862-65. See also Cuyler to Gorgas, Telegram, Macon, 23 June 1862, Ibid.

[70] Cuyler to Gorgas, Telegram, Macon, 14 June 1862, Ibid.

have the capability of producing items immediately. On 5 July 1862, Cuyler wired Major M.M. Slaughter in Columbus that the Arsenal could not produce cavalry equipment for some time.[71] But, Cuyler continued to produce many other items quickly and efficiently. In late July he was ready to furnish ammunition to the Macon Light Artillery if General Hugh Mercer, Commanding the Military District of Georgia, authorized the issue.[72] He wired Gorgas on 26 August that he had a battery ready to send to Abingdon, Virginia, no later than 1 September but could not supply saddle cloths for the horses.[73] Occasionally Gorgas wanted Cuyler to repair rifles which had become unserviceable.[74] By 20 September 1862, Gorgas ordered Cuyler to "Repair everything that will shoot and where the barrels are not too much injured cut them off and make carbines of them."[75]

Cuyler, however, wanted to produce primarily cannons. Although he wanted to make ten-inch Columbiads, especially for coast defense, Gorgas wanted him to emphasize the manufacture of smaller cannon because he did not believe the Macon Arsenal had the capability to band large guns. First, Cuyler should band a few twenty-four-pounder smoothbores. This was necessary to test the metal in a casting of moderate size. After the Arsenal's machinists cast these, they might cast a couple of eight-inch Columbiads. If these were cast and banded successfully, the Arsenal might begin to manufacture ten-inch Columbiads, which, Gorgas wrote, "the Dept is very anxious to see effected, but, which you cannot yet undertake." After all, the iron which Cuyler proposed to use, had as of late October 1862, only been cast in small amounts.[76]

The Ordnance Department, however, didn't want any bronze guns produced except for the very popular twelve-pounder Napoleon, although Cuyler could make a number of twenty or thirty-pounder Parrott guns whenever possible.[77] Gorgas also wanted Cuyler to fabricate field shell and spherical case shot using paper fuses.[78]

Cuyler received instructions to pack each package and box of cartridges with a due proportion of caps. Such attention to detail would "prevent a serious waste of musket & rifle percussion caps."[79] On 3 November Gorgas directed

---

[71] Cuyler to Maj. M.M. Slaughter, Telegram, Macon, 5 July 1862, Ibid.

[72] Cuyler to General Hugh Mercer, Telegram, Macon, 25 July 1862, Ibid.

[73] Cuyler to Gorgas, Telegram, 26 August 1862, Ibid.

[74] Gorgas to Cuyler, Richmond, 12 September 1862, Letters Received, Arsenal, 1862.

[75] Gorgas to Cuyler, Richmond, 20 September 1862, Ibid.

[76] Gorgas to Cuyler, Richmond, 21 October 1862, Ibid.

[77] Gorgas to Cuyler, Order, Richmond, 29 October 1862, Ibid.

[78] Colonel T.S. Rhett to Cuyler, Richmond, 21 October 1862, Ibid., Reel 1191.

[79] Gorgas to Cuyler, Circular, Richmond, 29 October 1862, Ibid.

Cuyler to suspend the construction of all siege carriages until further orders, although the Arsenal was to continue making 10-inch shot as needed. All ten-pounder Parrott shells were needed in Richmond.[80]

In November Gorgas issued Order No. 104 which directed the Macon Arsenal to produce 60,000 rounds of small arms ammunition and 300 to 500 rounds of field artillery ammunition every month. To complicate the matter, however, Cuyler could only expect to receive 60,000 pounds of lead a month because that was "was all that can be depended on from the Nitre and Mining Bureau. Cuyler had to make up any deficiencies through his own contracts.[81]

On 10 November Gorgas ordered an increase in the amount of small arms ammunition to 10,000 rounds per day, and an increase in the amount of field ammunition to 100 to 125 rounds a day.[82] On the following day, Cuyler received directions to discontinue the casting of all field guns except the ever-popular light twelve-pounder Napoleons.[83] Two months later, Gorgas directed Cuyler to "make every exertion to produce Napoleon guns as rapidly as possible. Please to report what number you can turn out in a period of ninety days."[84] Moreover, if General Pierre G. T. Beauregard, commanding the Department of South Carolina, Georgia, and Florida with headquarters in Charleston, wanted Cuyler to recast bronze guns of different sizes into twelve-pounder Napoleons, the Superintendent should do so.[85]

Later, on 6 February 1863, Gorgas issued a circular directing that the production of ammunition for twelve-pounder Howitzers and twelve-pounder Napoleons would be proportionally increased together with the ammunition for the various rifled field pieces.[86] There was also a need to fill requisitions for carriages for eight-inch Columbiads.[87]

In early November, Cuyler received orders to send arms to Major J. L. Brent at Vicksburg for forwarding across the Mississippi to General Richard Taylor's

---

[80] Gorgas to Cuyler, Order, Richmond, 3 November 1862, Ibid. See also Gorgas, Circular, Richmond, 30 October 1862, Ibid.

[81] Gorgas, Order No. 104, Richmond, November 1862, Ibid.

[82] Gorgas to Cuyler, Richmond, 10 November 1862, Ibid.

[83] Gorgas to Cuyler, Order, Richmond, 11 November 1862, Ibid.

[84] Gorgas to Cuyler, Richmond, 19 January 1863, Box 3191, Microfilm, Orders and Circulars Received, Arsenal, 1862-63, NARA.

[85] Captain Thomas L. Bayne, Richmond, to Culyer, 12 November 1862, Letters Received, Arsenal, 1862.

[86] Gorgas to Cuyler, Circular, Richmond, 6 February 1863, Orders Received, Arsenal.

[87] Gorgas to Cuyler, Richmond, 8 February 1863, Ibid.

forces in Louisiana. There was a note of urgency in this because it was important "to get them over as early as possible."[88]

The demands upon the Macon Arsenal grew even greater as the war continued, and the stress of supplying large armies in the field began to affect the Confederacy's ability to manufacture arms and munitions. Sometimes the work involved weapons much more complex than twelve-pounder Napoleons. On 24 November 1862, First Lieutenant R. Milton Cary, temporarily commanding the Macon Arsenal in the absence of now Lieutenant Colonel Cuyler, prepared to send ten siege carriages for 4.62-inch rifle guns.[89]

By mid-December, Gorgas wanted shells for ten, twenty, and thirty-pounder Parrott guns and shells for three-inch rifle guns to be sent to Richmond immediately.[90] On 18 December Cuyler received instructions to send through Major Marcus H. Wright, Superintendent of the Atlanta Arsenal, 400 rounds of twenty-pounder Parrott ammunition for General Sterling Price's Army in the Trans-Mississippi Department.[91]

On occasion Cuyler caught up with the demands from the field. By 3 January 1863, Major Bayne informed him that no more arms were needed by General Taylor's command, and that the Macon Arsenal did not need to send any additional arms for repair to Richmond.[92] A week later, Gorgas ordered the manufacture of canister for field guns stopped, "there being large quantities reported in store with the armies in the field."[93]

But, as Grant's campaign against Vicksburg heated up in early 1863, General John C. Pemberton's army needed more ammunition. Accordingly, Gorgas ordered 25,000 rounds of assorted small arms ammunition to be sent to Pemberton on January 29.[94] Other western armies also needed more ammunition as Federal forces pushed further into the Western Confederacy in the early months of 1863. General Braxton Bragg's command in Middle Tennessee needed 100,000 rounds of assorted small arms ammunition, primarily .69 and .577 caliber, on 9 January.[95]

---

[88] Captain Thomas L. Bayard [for Gorgas], Order 115, Richmond, 5 November 1862, Ibid.

[89] Lieutenant R. Milton Cary to Colonel T.S. Rhett, Inspector of Ordnance, Macon, 24 November 1862, Ibid.

[90] Thomas L. Bayne [for Gorgas] to Cuyler, Richmond, 16 December 1862, Ibid.

[91] Gorgas to Cuyler, Richmond, 18 December 1862, Ibid.

[92] Thomas L. Bayne to Cuyler, Richmond, 3 January 1863, Ibid.

[93] Gorgas to Cuyler, Richmond, 10 January 1863, Ibid.

[94] Gorgas to Cuyler, Richmond, 29 January 1863, Ibid. See also Military Storekeeper Richard Lambert to Major F.C. Humphreys, Ordnance Officer at Columbus, GA., Macon, 30 January 1863, Letters sent by Richard Lambert, Military Storekeeper, Box 3191, Orders and Circulars Received at the Arsenal, 1862-64..

[95] Gorgas to Cuyler, Richmond, 9 January 1863, Ibid.

There were deficiencies to be filled in the District of Georgia, too. These were especially evident in the equipment of light batteries. Hanleiter's Battery needed a forge, Bomar's Battery required a battery wagon, Martin's Battery suffered from the lack of a harness for the forge and battery wagon, and a number of deficiencies existed in the areas of spare harness and cutting and entrenching tools. There was also a shortage of ammunition for the twelve-pounder howitzers in Martin's and Hanleiter's Batteries.[96]

In late February, Gorgas directed "the most rigid attention must be exercised in reference to calibre of bullets for rifled arms" because complaints were constantly received from the field "that the cartridges for the Enfield rifles are found too large."[97]

Gorgas also wanted to know the number of firearms of all kinds on hand in Macon, and how many the Ordnance Department could issue to the field by 15 April. Monthly reports were also required after that date.[98]

In March 1863, other problems arose. One of these concerned the charges for eight and ten-inch Columbiads. The eight-inch Columbiad could not be filled with a charge of powder over ten pounds, while the charge for the ten-inch Columbiad had to be less than fifteen pounds.[99] Cuyler also was told to manufacture ten-pounder and twenty-pounder banded Parrott guns, especially the twenty-pounder variety because they were "especially needed."[100]

During the spring of 1863, Cuyler continued to produce revolving pistols, knapsacks, cartridge box belts, Columbiad carriages from oak timber, and flannel for cartridge bags,[101] On 21 April he was ordered to send, through Colonel Phil Stockton, Commander of the Arsenal in Jackson, Mississippi, 3,000 sets of infantry accouterments to General Edmund Kirby Smith's Trans-Mississippi Department.[102] The amount spent for many of these items was listed in the monthly "Estimate of funds required at Macon Arsenal Georgia" for April, 1863, which included $15,000 needed to manufacture infantry accouterments, knapsacks, cavalry equipment, canteens, leather, wood, and navy revolvers; $15,000 for payrolls at the Arsenal and the Arsenal Armory; $590 for the rent of

---

[96] Thomas L. Bayne [for Gorgas], to Cuyler, Richmond, 4 February 1863, Ibid.

[97] Gorgas to Cuyler, Circular, Richmond, 24 February 1863, Ibid.

[98] Gorgas to Cuyler, Richmond, 4 March 1863, Ibid.

[99] Gorgas to Cuyler, Richmond, 16 March 1863, Ibid..

[100] Gorgas to Cuyler, Richmond, 18 March 1863, Ibid.

[101] Gorgas to Cuyler, Richmond, 16 April 1863, Ibid.; Cuyler to Gorgas, Telegram, Macon, 20 April 1863, Telegrams Sent, Arsenal, 1862-65; Thomas L. Bayne [for Gorgas] to Cuyler, Richmond, 20 April 1863, Orders and Circulars Received, Arsenal, 1863; Gorgas to Cuyler, Richmond, 16 April 1863, Ibid; and Gorgas to Cuyler, Richmond, 18 April 1863, Ibid.

[102] Gorgas to Cuyler, Richmond, 21 April 1863, Ibid.

the Arsenal; $62.50 for the rent of the Arsenal Armory; $62.50 for the rent of the warehouse; contingent expenses, $10,000; $10,000 for infantry accouterments; $15,000 for knapsacks; $2,000 for other cavalry equipment; $2,000 to buy canteens; $20,000 for the purchase of leather; $5,000 for wood; and $6,000 needed for the purchase of navy revolvers.[103]

The list for June, 1863, included $10,000 for the manufacture of artillery harness; $5,000 for the manufacture of infantry accouterments; $7,000 to buy pine lumber; $6,000 needed to produce Colt's Revolvers [the Confederate imitation of the famous sidearm]; $1,000 for wood; $12,000 for knapsacks; $15,000 for leather; $7,000 for shingles; $30,000 to pay for hired men; $590 for the monthly rental of the machine shop; $666 for rental of the harness shop; and $10,000 for contingent expenses.[104]

Another of Cuyler's problems related to personnel matters. In mid-June 1862, not long after the Arsenal relocated to Macon, five of the workmen in the Armory Department walked off the job. Although Walter C. Hodgkins, Armory Superintendent, told them that such activities would not be allowed, on 16 June they claimed the right to strike whenever they pleased, without asking for permission. Three of the men, George F. Barrett, Richard A. Magill, and I. B. Shelverton left the facility against Hodgkins' orders. Hodgkins therefore adopted regulations to prevent a recurrence of the action, and told Cuyler that he considered it "such a mark of disrespect and insubordination that I will not allow them to renew work...while I have the establishment in charge."[105] Two days later, Hodgkins informed his chief that the men had returned, admitted they were wrong, and promised to obey the rules and regulations of the Armory in the future.[106]

The possibility that some of his workers would be conscripted under the Conscription Act of April 1862, posed another difficulty. Cuyler asked Gorgas on 18 October for authority to deal with the problem. The problem was acerbated because many employees worked in the Arsenal to escape service in the field, and then deserted their jobs. Gorgas replied that "conscripts will be

---

[103] Richard Lambert, Military Storekeeper, to H.W. Hall, "Estimate of funds required at Macon Arsenal Georgia during the month of April 1863," Macon, 25 March 1863, Lambert, Letters Sent, Arsenal.

[104] Richard Lambert, Military Storekeeper, to H.W. Hall, Macon Arsenal, "Estimate of funds required at Macon Arsenal during the month of June 1863," Macon, 27 May 1863, Ibid.

[105] Walter C. Hodgkins to Cuyler, Macon, 16 June 1862, Letters Received, Arsenal, 1862.

[106] Hodgkins to Cuyler, Macon, 18 June 1862, Ibid.

enrolled and detailed and treated as deserters if they leave the Government employment."[107]

Cuyler had to occasionally deal with the Confederate authorities to secure exemptions for some of his employees. When it seemed that one of his key employees, Christopher D. Findlay, would be conscripted, he wrote Lieutenant Colonel John B. Weems, Commandant of the Camp of Instruction at Macon, to inform him that when the agreement was reached to lease the Findlay Foundry it was agreed that one of the owners should be permanently employed in the Arsenal. Findlay was employed as Purchasing Agent and Corresponding Clerk, but was liable to be drafted because of the Conscript Law. Although Findlay had served as a commissioned officer in the Confederate Army, he did not like the idea of being enrolled. Besides, his services were indispensable. The matter was referred to Secretary of War Seddon who directed Findlay's permanent deferment.[108]

In mid-December 1862, when Gorgas inquired about exemptions for Ordnance officers, clerks, draftsmen, superintendents, and others permanently employed on a fee or salary basis, Assistant Secretary of War and former Associate Justice of the US Supreme Court John A. Campbell replied that these officials were exempt by law. "No enrollment of such officers is necessary," Campbell noted, "& no order from the Department is necessary for their protection.." All that was needed was a certificate from Gorgas which indicated that their position and exemption was proper. However, persons who were employed as laborers or employed temporarily, or used in occasional service which did not constitute part of the Ordnance Department, needed a special order to ensure their exemption.[109]

By February 1863, when the matter of securing exemptions was becoming a problem, Gorgas, to ensure the validity of the exemption of men employed at the Macon Arsenal, directed Cuyler to appoint an officer to examine the credentials of all Arsenal employees to determine their exemptions from military service.[110] Furthermore, officers employed at the Arsenals had to be employed on duties appropriate to their rank, and could not be forced to perform duties not connected with their profession, except when the public interest would be better served when they could be used for these duties occasionally.[111]

---

[107] Gorgas to Cuyler, Richmond, 29 October 1862, Ibid.

[108] Cuyler to Lt. Col. John B. Weems, Macon, 1 December 1862, Secretary of War Letters Received, October-December 1862, Microfilm, Roll 41, no. 1261.

[109] John A. Campbell to Gorgas, Richmond, 16 December 1862, Letters Received, Arsenal, 1862.

[110] Gorgas to Cuyler, Richmond, 12 February 1862, Ibid., 1863.

[111] Gorgas to Cuyler, Richmond, 18 February 1863, Ibid.

As inflation increased throughout the Confederacy Gorgas directed Cuyler to pay fixed wages to his men at the rates which they received on 31 March 1863.[112] A month later Gorgas sent a circular to all the Ordnance establishments directing the reduction of the number of clerks employed by the Ordnance Bureau. Preference would be given to those persons exempt from military duty.[113]

Desertion was also a problem. On 4 June 1863, Cuyler wired Lieutenant A. T. Cunningham, Ordnance Officer in Savannah, to arrest a deserter named Michael Boas. Boas had stolen items from the Arsenal and fled to Savannah. He was five feet ten inches tall, had black hair and eyes, was of a dark complexion, and looked "like a Bowery Boy."[114] Another deserter, James Reynolds, went to Savannah and might, because he was a British citizen, "try to get protection from [the] British Counsel."[115]

Sometimes personnel problems were even more serious. Arsenal Laboratory Superintendent T. C. Donner related an incident which underscored some of Cuyler's production problems. On 5 September 1862, the pan which contained the lubricating and anti-fouling mixture used in munitions production was overturned four times. Donner told the men working with the pan that he would severely whip the next person who overturned it. On the following morning the pan was again upset, this time upon a pile of cartridges ruining about two hundred of them. Donner, who had found his previous threats to whip personnel effective, was convinced that this repetition of the offense was intentional. He therefore took a light, slender cowskin whip from his office, and went to the dipping table. When he saw what had happened he became satisfied that the accident was not intentional, but because he had promised a whipping he felt obligated to administer it. He whipped a child who was operating the dipping table, trying to make the blows "as slight as possible." On 8 September the child's father, enraged when he heard of the whipping, and accompanied by a friend, came to Donner. After hearing Donner's version of the incident they left "declaring that they were perfectly satisfied." At the same time the men came to see him one of the other employees, Martin Beammon, brought two other boys to Donner's office for fighting. Since Donner had expressly forbidden fighting, he began to think of using his whip again. When one of the boys started to run out of the building, Donner grabbed the cowskin, "which was within reach at that moment," and pursued the boy. He had nearly overtaken him, had aimed one blow at him, and was about to catch him when he realized that the fear of being

---

[112] Gorgas to Cuyler, Richmond, 1 March 1863, Ibid.

[113] Gorgas, Circular, Richmond, 27 April 1863, Ibid.

[114] Cuyler to Lt. A.J. Cunningham, Macon Arsenal, 4 June 1863, Telegrams Sent, Arsenal, 1862-1865.

[115] Cuyler to Cunningham, Macon, 29 June 1863, Ibid.

punished might have caused the youth to run. The hotheaded Donner stopped his pursuit and returned to his office. Later in the day the boy's father, a Mr. Bagley, came to Donner with a whip in his hand, and accompanied "by several gentlemen," whom Donner did not know. During the ensuing argument Donner admitted that he had struck at Bagley's son, and could have struck him again if he had overtaken him before stopping the pursuit. Bagley left, promising to attack Donner when he left the building at the end of the day. Some of Bagley's friends urged him to attack Donner at once, but the enraged father replied that Donner was "in his own house." At 6:00 P.M., as the boys were being dismissed, Donner saw Bagley walking up and down the street with his whip. Donner evidently left by a different route because he supposed Bagley still intended to whip him. Although Donner felt intimidated for a time, nothing happened as a result of his encounter with Bagley.[116]

On 3 June 1863 Cuyler informed Major Marcus H. Wright in Atlanta that he was paying his conscripts full mechanic's wages.[117] However, personnel problems were equaled by those relating to constant shortages of different kinds of material needed to accomplish the mission of supplying the armies in the field with ordnance materials. The procurement of materials and the manufacture of some items was, however, not a problem. In June Cuyler had no trouble in obtaining some of these items, including copper. Writing to Lieutenant Colonel J.R. Waddy, Chief of Ordnance in Charleston, Cuyler noted, "I have plenty [of] material for bronze guns."[118] Storekeeper Richard Lambert was able to buy 517 pounds of the precious metal for $310.50 from the firm of William Battersly and Company of Savannah on 30 June.[119] The casting of the very popular twelve-pounder Napoleon cannon was also not a problem. Cuyler telegraphed Col. A. J. Gonzales on 28 April that the Arsenal was casting one "every other day from now on."[120] Another area which did not present any difficulties was the production of sand bags needed for the fortifications around closely-besieged Charleston. Cuyler could obtain these at the rate of 10,000 a day for $2.15

---

[116] T.C. Donner to Cuyler, Macon, 9 September 1862, Letters Received, Arsenal, 1862.

[117] Cuyler to Maj. Marcus H. Wright, Macon, 3 June 1863, Telegrams Sent, Arsenal, 1862-1865.

[118] Cuyler to Lt Col J.R. Waddy, Macon, 2 June 1863, Ibid.

[119] Richard Lambert to William Battersly and Company, Macon, 30 June 1863, Letters Sent, Arsenal, 1863.

[120] Cuyler to Capt. A. J. Gonzales, Macon, 28 April 1863, Telegrams Sent, Arsenal, 1862-1865. Gonzales was Chief of Artillery and Ordnance for the Department of South Carolina, Georgia, and Florida.

apiece. He could send from eight to 10,000 of them to Major William H. Echols of the Corps of Engineers at the South Carolina city.[121]

But the difficulty to obtain some items did slow production. Lead was one of the most important of the ever-scarce items the shortage of which constantly plagued the Confederate war effort. As early as 3 April 1862, over a month before the Arsenal officially began its Macon operation, Lieutenant Ingraham of the Savannah Arsenal was in Macon collecting lead in every shape and from every source. A reporter for the *Daily Telegraph* pleaded, "The crisis is upon us-we cannot pass thro-the fiery ordeal with any hope of ultimate success without lead. As everything is staked upon the present issue at arms with the enemy, it is devoutly to be hoped that every pound and every ounce of lead that can be spared in Macon and its vicinity will be immediately placed in charge of Lieut. Ingraham."[122] Cuyler, who felt the scarcity of lead acutely, wired Gorgas on 1 September 1862, that he would be out of lead in two days, and could not find any of the precious commodity anywhere.[123] In June 1863, Cuyler needed lead for ammunition.[124] He informed Rains in Augusta on 22 April 1863, that he had stopped operations at his laboratory "for want of small grain cannon, rifle & musket powder," and needed a supply at once.[125] In the spring of 1863 shortages also developed in Cuyler's supply of linseed oil.[126] Another commodity which Cuyler needed was beeswax because there was "none to be bought in Macon."[127] By September 1863, after Federal General William S. Rosecrans maneuvered Bragg out of copper-rich southeastern Tennessee, Cuyler asked Gorgas for permission to melt down 6-pounder guns for rifle shell bases because he could not get copper. This shortage would force him to stop making projectiles to help defend Charleston, which was then closely besieged.[128]

Despite these problems the people of Macon showed great pride in the Arsenal. As early as January 1863, Confederate Ordnance Inspector General Benjamin Huger stated that the Government works under construction in Macon would permanently employ about 1,800 workers. With their families, it would

---

[121] Richard Lambert to Maj. William H. Echols, Macon Arsenal, 4 August 1863, Lambert, Letters Sent, Arsenal.

[122] *Macon Daily Telegraph*, 3 April 1862.

[123] Cuyler to Gorgas, Telegram, Macon, 1 September 1862, Telegrams Sent, Arsenal, 1862-1865.

[124] *Macon Daily Telegraph*, 16 June 1863.

[125] Cuyler to Rains, Telegram, Macon, 22 April 1863, Telegrams Sent, Arsenal, 1862-1865.

[126] Cuyler to Capt. Eccles, A.Q.M., Charlotte, N.C., Telegram, Macon, 4 June 1863, Ibid.

[127] Cuyler to Capt. J.T. Trezevant, Charleston Arsenal, Telegram, Macon, 27 June 1863, Ibid.

[128] Cuyler to Gorgas, Telegram, Macon, 19 September 1863, Ibid.

mean a population increase of about 9,000.[129] On 12 June 1863 a battery of twelve-pounder bronze Napoleons passed through the streets of Macon bound for the field. A *Daily Telegraph* reporter observed, "Guns beautifully shaped, and carriages and caissons thoroughly made and handsomely painted."[130]

When Virginian E. Taliaferro arrived for duty at the Macon Arsenal in the fall of 1863, he wrote his father about his pleasant situation. His responsibilities included the management of the employees, but his duties were "at least very agreeable and congenial with my tastes." Macon was as expensive a place to live in as Richmond, and Taliaferro might have to accept his Father's offer of financial assistance. But the city on the Ocmulgee was also a beautiful town, and, Taliaferro noted, "there are a great many very handsome residences around the environs." His associates were very pleasant, in fact, one of them was an old college friend of his. He liked the people, but he desired promotion. His working hours were long, from 8:00 A.M. until 6:00 P.M., except for a period of an hour and a half for lunch. His wife "employs herself" with her books and needle work during the day, and at night Taliaferro gave her a French lesson. Then the two of them read from a book of history or travel for an hour, after that he read to her some book of poetry or romance. The Taliaferros attended Christ Episcopal Church, and appreciated the services.[131]

A few days later he wrote his sister, Mrs. Beverly R. Wellford of Gloucester, Virginia, that he was still only a First Lieutenant in the Regular Army, but had served temporarily as a Captain for over fifteen months. He wanted her to help him to secure the temporary rank of Major in the Provisional Army. "Besides," he told her, "there are here at this Arsenal already four captains on ord. Duty & no major, and I am the ranking captain." He added, "These facts shd [should] be brought out."[132]

On 10 January 1864, Taliaferro finally received his long- coveted promotion to the temporary rank of Major for service with volunteer troops, and was ordered to report to Cuyler for service with local troops at the Macon Arsenal.[133]

The effort to raise an Arsenal battalion, led by Christopher D. Findlay, began on 9 March 1863, when Findlay was asked by Cuyler, Colonel James H. Burton, Superintendent of the Macon Armory, and then-Captain John W. Mallett, Superintendent of the Laboratory, to raise a company to guard the

---

[129] *Macon Daily Telegraph*, 13 January 1863.

[130] Ibid., 13 June 1863.

[131] E. Taliaferro to his Father, Macon, 20 October 1863, White-Wellford-Taliaferro-Marshall Papers, 1743-1797, Microfilm, Reel 1, SHC, hereafter cited as Taliaferro Letters.

[132] E. Taliaferro to his Sister, Macon, 23 October 1863, Ibid. He also told her "I am quite pleasantly situated here & have very agreeable associates." Ibid.

[133] James A. Seddon to E. Taliaferro, Richmond, 10 January 1864, Ibid.

ordnance works at Macon. He received authority from Secretary of War Seddon to raise the company which would be under the orders of then-Major Cuyler.[134] On 3 September of that year, Secretary of War Seddon received an application from Colonel D. Wyatt Aiken, commanding the Post at Macon, to raise a battalion of exempted men and non-conscripts organized in local companies, including some from the ordnance facilities.[135] Later, Findlay wrote Captain W.L. Winder, on his father's staff at Americus, Georgia, that he wanted to increase his command to a regiment and guard prisoners at the prison about to be established near Americus. Findlay told Winder, "In point of drill and discipline we claim to be far superior to any troops in this state- the men have a thorough knowledge of guard duty- and are in every respect fine soldiers."[136]

During the fight to protect Macon from Stoneman and his raiders, then-Lieutenant Colonel Mallet commanded two infantry companies from the Arsenal, and one company from the Armory. Together, these companies formed a battalion.[137]

Work at the Arsenal was suspended during the period 9-13 July 1863, when fire destroyed a building next to the repair shop. [138]Sometimes the work was slowed by illness. During August 1863, half of Cuyler's workforce was sick, prompting him to report to Gorgas on 27 August, "Can furnish two 8 inch Columbiads with carriages by 1st October, if no accident & not too much sickness."[139]

Through it all, Cuyler continued to produce artillery. On 28 August 1863, he reported that six Napoleons were ready, but no carriages were available for

---

[134] Maj. Christopher D. Findlay to Capt. W.L. Winder, Macon, 19 December 1863, Letters Received, Confederate Secretary of War, Microfilm, Roll 126, December 1863-April 64, NARA.

[135] Seddon to Col. D. Wyatt Aiken, Richmond, 3 September 1863, Secretary of War, Letters Sent, Vol. 12, April 21-September 18, 1863, NARA. See also Col. D. Wyatt Aiken to Seddon, Macon, 25 August 1863, Secretary of War, Letters Received, Roll 80, December 1862-December 1863, NARA. J.H. Hart annotated this letter for Assistant Secretary of War John A. Campbell on September 7, "permission to increase Cuyler's co to a battn. Withdrawn." Ibid.

[136] Findlay Letter 19 December 1863. Findlay entered service in May, 1861, as a lieutenant in the 8th Georgia Regiment.

[137] James H. Burton to Gorgas, Macon, 2 August 1864, Letters Sent Armory, 1863-1865, Roll 9, Microfilm, NARA, hereafter cited as Letters Sent, Armory, 1863-1865. Two of these companies were under Findlay, although Mallet was in overall command.

[138] Cuyler to Gorgas, Telegram, Macon, 9 July 1863, Telegrams Sent, Arsenal, 1862-1865.

[139] Cuyler to Gorgas, Telegram, Macon, 27 August 1863, Ibid.

them.[140] A few days later he wired Colonel Wright in Atlanta that he had three six-pounders ready to send, but they lacked carriages. He could also send four pieces of field artillery which was ready for the field, except he had no horses to pull it.[141] A month later he telegraphed Gorgas that a battery of twelve-pounders was completed with another ready on 4 October.[142]

The production of Napoleons continued unabated during the fall of 1863. On 2 November, Cuyler announced that another battery of Napoleons was ready, but he did not know where to send it. He informed Gorgas that "Genl [William H.C.] Whiting at Wilmington [is] in want of it."[143] On 18 November he wired Gorgas that he had another battery of Napoleons ready, presumably to send to Charleston.[144] The following day he notified Colonel H. Oladowski, Bragg's Chief of Ordnance, trying to secure enough artillery to press the Confederate siege of Chattanooga, "I have a battery of napoleons for you. Col Gorgas asks if you will see that it be given to Major Waddell at Decatur."[145]

At first, in the spring of 1863, the Arsenal produced twelve-pounders for the Army of Mississippi or for the defense of Charleston. It was not until November 1863, that four Macon twelve-pounders were sent to Bledsoe's Missouri Battery in the Army of Tennessee. After that, twelve-pounders were sent regularly to Bragg's Army.[146]

At the end of September Cuyler asked Gorgas for funds needed to buy such items as knapsacks, navy revolvers, wood, hides, to pay hired men, and to rent the machine shop and foundry, the warehouse and armory, a harness shop, a lot adjoining the Arsenal with a house on it, and a four-acre lot from the city to build a rolling mill and a proving ground; and money for a new warehouse to store materials awaiting distribution. He also needed money for contingencies. The total amount required was $109,312.[147]

A month later the financial needs of the Arsenal included money for knapsacks, Navy revolvers, wood, hides, pine lumber, oak lumber, the payroll, and rental money for a number of facilities including a machine shop and foundry, warehouse and armory, harness shop, a lot adjoining the Arsenal with a

---

[140] Cuyler to Humphreys, Commanding Arsenal, Columbus, Telegram, Macon, 28 August 1863, Ibid.

[141] Cuyler to Wright, Telegram, Macon, 1 September 1863, Ibid.

[142] Cuyler to Gorgas, Telegram, Macon, 30 September 1863, Ibid.

[143] Cuyler to Gorgas, Telegram, Macon, 2 November 1863, Ibid.

[144] Cuyler to Gorgas, Telegram, Macon, 18 November 1863, Ibid.

[145] Cuyler to Col. Hypolite Oladowski, Telegram, Macon, 19 November 1863, Ibid.

[146] Larry J. Daniel, *Cannoneers in Gray: the Field Artillery of the Army of Tennessee* (Tuscaloosa: University of Alabama Press, 1984) 76, 109.

[147] Richard Lambert to Gorgas, Macon, 28 September 1863, Lambert, Letters Sent, Arsenal.

house on it, a four-acre lot from the city for the rolling mill, houses for slaves, a proving ground, and a new warehouse for stores for distribution. Cuyler also needed $10,000 for contingencies. The total amount needed for November, 1863, was $87,812.[148]

The availability of funds was always a problem for Cuyler beginning with the summer of 1863. On 2 July he informed Gorgas he had bought 800 bales of cotton to send to Europe to obtain crucial materials, but did not have sufficient funds to buy more. He wanted William B. Johnston, the Confederate Depository in Macon to advance him $300,000 because it was advisable to buy the cotton at once before the price went up.[149] Johnston could give him the money if Secretary of the Treasury Christopher G. Memminger authorized it. Four thousand bales of cotton would cost $800,000.[150]

In August 1863, Cuyler directed Lambert to write Richmond to see if his estimate for funds for July and August 1863, was received. What money the Arsenal had on hand at that time was needed to buy cotton. "Over that," Lambert wrote, "I won't have sufficient [funds] to pay the hands employed at the end of this month."[151] As late as March, 1864, Cuyler complained about the lack of funds. He wanted Gorgas to have Depository Johnston turn over $241,000 to him. After all, Cuyler observed, "He has cart loads."[152]

The wages of workman at the Arsenal by the end of 1863, were good, even by the standards of a Confederacy racked by inflationary pressures during the third autumn of the war. Cuyler paid salaries in a descending scale. First class mechanics, including moulders, pattern makers, blacksmiths, and machinists commanded $5.50 a day. Detailed soldiers worked on piece work, but could not make more than $225 a month. Carriage makers earned $5.00 a day, carpenters brought in $4.75, tanners received a salary of $5, helpers earned $3.50, laborers from $2.00 to $3.00. Despite these salaries the workers came close to striking in mid-December 1863. Fortunately, Cuyler observed, "most of the foremen behaved well & induced their men to send me a respectful petition which I forwarded." Even his "refractory" moulders "repented," and were back at work by December 18.[153]

---

[148] Lambert to Gorgas, Macon, 28 October 1863, Ibid.

[149] Cuyler to Gorgas, Telegram, Macon, 2 July 1863, Telegrams Sent, Arsenal, 1862-1865.

[150] Cuyler to Gorgas, Telegram, Macon, 4 July 1863, Ibid.

[151] Lambert to Maj. Edward B. Smith, Assistant Chief of Ordnance, Macon, 14 August 1863, Letters Sent, Arsenal, 1863.

[152] Cuyler to Gorgas, Telegram, Macon, 5 March 1864, Telegrams Sent, Arsenal, 1862-1865.

[153] Cuyler to Cunningham, Telegram, Macon, 18 December 1863, Ibid.

Despite shortages of lead, money, and other commodities, Cuyler had a fairly large number of munitions on hand on 1 January 1864. These included twenty-three six-pounder bronze guns; two six-pounder iron guns; one 6-pounder iron gun (an old English gun); fourteen twelve-pounder bronze howitzers; one twenty-four-pounder siege gun; one 10-pounder Parrott gun; four 3-inch bronze rifle guns; and one twenty-four-pounder siege gun. His supply of carriages was also fairly sizable. These encompassed one twenty-pounder Parrott gun carriage; nine six-pounder gun carriages; four eight-inch siege gun carriages and limbers; three ten-inch Columbiad carriages; three ten-inch Columbiad chassis; four eight-inch Columbiad carriages; four eight-inch Columbiad chassis; one twenty-four-pounder siege gun carriage and limbers; nine caissons; thirty-two field limbers; six battery wagons; ten field forges; one garrison gin; one card sling; twenty-eight sponge buckets; twenty-eight tar buckets; twenty wooden water buckets; ten fire buckets; and four mallets. Other minor items included 185 gunners' gimblets; eleven gunners haversacks; 181 trail handspikes; and 211 shod handspikes.[154]

The spring of 1864 saw much activity at the Arsenal. On 22 April Cuyler told Lieutenant Colonel J.M. Kennard, Chief of Ordnance at Demopolis, Alabama, that one of the latter's ten-pounder Parrott guns burst while being tested that morning. This was the first time, Cuyler observed, it had happened. A new one was being manufactured.[155] In early May, Cuyler asked for authority to equip sixty recruits to help guard prisoners at Andersonville.[156]

When Sherman pressed towards Atlanta in June 1864, Cuyler did what he could to supply the Atlanta Arsenal.[157] The Arsenal was producing material of all kinds, especially in the area of twelve-pounder Napoleons; nine-inch siege guns, Parrott guns, bronze twelve-pounder Napoleons; and bronze six-pounders. The facility also made carriages for six-pounders, twelve-pounders; and Parrotts. Caissons in stock included those for twelve-pounder Napoleons and for Parrotts. Cuyler also had limbers, battery wagons, spare wheels, field forges, bucket sponges, lanyards, gunstocks, nose bags [for horses], vent covers, hot shot forks, hot shot tongs, hot shot ladles, and artillery harness. The Arsenal also had ammunition for rifled cannon, ten-inch Columbiads, thirty-two-pounders,

---

[154] Inventory of Ordnance and Ordnance Stores on Hand at the Arsenal January 1, 1864, Microfilm, Chapter IV, Vol. 59 1/2, NARA.

[155] Cuyler to Lt. Col. J.M. Kennard, Telegram, Macon, 22 April 1864, Telegrams Sent, Arsenal, 1862-65.

[156] Cuyler to Gorgas, Telegram, Macon, 10 May 1864, Ibid.

[157] Cuyler to Lt. Col. H. Oladowski, Telegram, Macon, 30 June 1864, Ibid.

Parrotts, six-pounder shells, twenty-four-pounder canister, twelve-pounder canister, and even shells for ten-inch mortars.[158]

In July 1864, as the siege of Atlanta began, Cuyler was caught up in events at Macon's back door, and, with new pressures upon him, did what he could to supply General Joseph E. Johnston's Army of Tennessee, as well as Governor Brown's State forces. On 12 July he informed Brown of orders he received to hold 5,000 rifles for the State troops. Of these, 1,000 Enfield Rifles were ready for issue. Although Johnston wanted 1,000 Austrian rifles, Cuyler planned to hold them for the State forces.[159] Possibly Captain Humphreys could help Cuyler to arm the Georgia militia more quickly by sending the guns captured from the Federals, or using those of killed and wounded Confederates. If this could be done, Cuyler wanted them sent to Macon immediately.[160]

When the Governor issued a proclamation calling for exempted men to help defend Atlanta, Cuyler complained that "Many negro mechanics will be thrown out of employment if tanners go. Great loss will result & supplies of leather at least here will stop."[161]

The Macon Arsenal did send a trainload of twelve-pounder Napoleon and ten-pounder Parrott shells and .58 caliber cartridges to Oladowski on 21 July. Unfortunately, Cuyler did not have any twelve-pounder howitzer carriages in Macon, but thought he could get some from the Augusta Arsenal.[162]

Cuyler was also called upon to send cannon to guard the huge Andersonville Prison. The artillery included eight twelve or twenty-four-pounder howitzers with ammunition. Cuyler called upon Lieutenant Colonel J.C. Moore, commanding the Savannah Arsenal, for ammunition for the cannon.[163] However, over a month later the guns had not been delivered, a fact which probably upset the nervous General John Henry Winder, Superintendent of Confederate Prisons East of the Mississippi. Besides, Colonel Geroge W. Rains at Augusta, who had cannon, had not even sent them to Macon for transfer to Andersonville.[164]

As Sherman's siege of Atlanta continued, Wright sent his Arsenal Laboratory and hands to Macon to work under either Mallett or Cuyler, both

---

[158] Richard Lambert, "Return of Ordnance Stores Received, Issued and Remaining on Hand, at Macon Arsenal, GA.," Macon, 30 June 1864, Lambert Letters Sent, Arsenal, 1864.

[159] Cuyler to Brown, Telegram, Macon, 12 July 1864, Telegrams Sent, Arsenal, 1862-1865. See also Cuyler to Capt. W.D. Humphreys, Depot Ordnance Officer, Atlanta, Telegram, Macon, 12 July 1864, Ibid.

[160] Cuyler to Capt. W.D. Humphreys, Telegram, Macon, 23 July 1864, Ibid.

[161] Cuyler to Brown, Telegram, Macon, 15 July 1864, Ibid. See also Cuyler to Gen. Henry C. Wayne, Telegram, Macon, 15 July 1864, Ibid.

[162] Cuyler to Lt. Col. H. Oladowski, Telegram, Macon, 21 July 1864, Ibid.

[163] Cuyler to Col. George W. Rains, Telegram, Macon, 18 July 1864, Ibid.

[164] Cuyler to Rains, Telegram, Macon, 23 August 1864, Ibid.

now promoted to the rank of colonel. Wright wanted either officer to use the men, writing "The former [Mallet] can get to work soon, but his special work will stop. It will take Col. Cuyler some time to put up buildings, but operatives would not have so far to go to work with him."[165]

With the coming of August 1864, the demands made upon Cuyler by Lt. Col. John B. Hood and his hard-pressed army increased. One of these requests involved sending Blacks to work on the Atlanta fortifications. When Hood inquired about the availability of such labor, Cuyler responded "I have no negroes engaged on public buildings. Have referred your telegram to Cols Mallet & Burton who have a large number."[166] Later on the same day, Cuyler informed Hood that Mallet would send his Blacks, and, while Burton did not consider the order addressed to him, he would send his if ordered.[167]

Colonel Marcus J. Wright, who came down to Macon from Atlanta and who ranked all three Macon Ordnance officers, was concerned about the flow of supplies to Hood. In an effort to speed up the flow of ordnance materials to the beleaguered Army of Tennessee, he ordered Lieutenant Colonel J. A. deLagnel, commanding the Columbus Arsenal, to take command of the entire ordnance force at Macon "with reference to supplying Genl Hoods Army, continuing as much as possible the routine of the commands."[168] While this might have seemed like a slap in the face to Cuyler, Burton, and Mallet, the exigencies of the times demanded some centralized control that was closer to Macon than Richmond. At any rate, Cuyler did not have many guns mounted to send to anyone. On 16 August he reported the only guns in Macon mounted were two twelve-pounder Napoleons and four six-pounders. All of the latter were at Camp Oglethorpe to help guard prisoners. The nearest supply of cannon was the Arsenal at Demopolis, Alabama.[169] Hood, despite his need for all the arms and munitions he could get, had permitted Cobb to keep the two twelve-pounders for local defense because there were rumors that another raid on Macon was imminent.[170]

With Sherman's defeat of Hood and occupation of Atlanta, the Ordnance facilities at Macon were controlled by events more than ever before. When the fall of Atlanta appeared imminent, Cuyler, Burton, and Mallet decided to ship

---

[165] Col. Marcus H. Wright to Gorgas, Telegram, Macon, 21 July 1864, Ibid.

[166] Cuyler to Hood, Telegram, Macon, 2 August 1864, Ibid.

[167] Cuyler to Hood, Telegram, Macon, 2 August 1864, Ibid.

[168] Col. Marcus H. Wright to Lt. Col. J.A. deLagnel, Telegram, Atlanta, 4 August 1864, Ibid. Gorgas, of course, approved Wright's action.

[169] Cuyler to Maj. J.O. Dawson, Commanding Post of Columbus, Telegram, Macon, 16 August 1864, Ibid.

[170] Cuyler to Lt. Col. J.M. Kennard, Chief of Ordnance, Atlanta, Telegram, Macon, 29 August 1864, Ibid.

all stores, not immediately needed in the field, to Savannah for safekeeping.[171] Hood, in early September, soothed Cuyler's anxieties by saying Macon was as safe as any other place to keep arms and ammunition in view of the dangers to the Lower South caused by Sherman's capture of Atlanta.[172] However, a month later, on 4 October Cuyler ordered his surplus stores and spare machinery sent to Savannah to remove it farther from Sherman.[173]

During the fall of 1864, Cuyler became involved in a ticklish situation between Governor Brown and General Cobb. The issue involved the refusal of the Governor to surrender 1,000 rifles which Cuyler had lent to the Georgia Militia during Sherman's siege of Atlanta, and which were stored in the Arsenal for safekeeping. When Colonel Kennard wanted the arms sent to the Army of Tennessee, then at Lovejoy's Station on the Macon and Western Railroad below Atlanta, Brown refused to give them up. Cuyler refused to be the middle man in the matter, saying he had to have higher authority before he sent the arms to Kennard. He assured the harried Kennard that either Gorgas or President Davis would have to authorize the transfer, and wired Gorgas to that effect.[174] Cuyler telegraphed Gorgas for instructions.[175] He also wired Brown saying he told Kennard of the Governor's refusal, asking Brown, "Do you still refuse. It is perhaps of vital important that the arms be sent."[176]

The matter was referred to the Bibb Superior Court for adjudication, but before a decision was obtained, Cobb compromised with Brown by promising to return the arms when the Militia reassembled. Cuyler, in the meantime, took 1,000 other arms stored in the Arsenal and sent them to the Army of Tennessee.[177]

During October, Cuyler supported Cobb and General Gustavus W. Smith, commanding the Second Brigade of Georgia Militia, to move on Atlanta from Lovejoy's Station in an effort to regain control of the latter city.[178]

When Sherman's troops approached Macon on 17 November during the March to the Sea, Cuyler collected ordnance materials to defend the city. He telegraphed Rains to send 10,000 pounds of small grain cannon powder and

---

[171] Cuyler to Gorgas, Telegram, Macon, 2 September 1864, Ibid.

[172] Cuyler to Gorgas, Telegram, Macon, 8 September 1864, Ibid.

[173] Cuyler to Lt. Col. John W. Mallet, Telegram, Macon, 4 October 1864, Ibid.

[174] Cuyler to Lt. Col. J.M. Kennard, Telegram, Macon, 28 September 1864, Ibid.; Cuyler to Gorgas, Telegram, Macon, 28 September 1864, Ibid.

[175] Cuyler to Gorgas, Telegram, Macon, 28 September 1864, Ibid.

[176] Cuyler to Brown, Telegram, Macon, 28 September 1864, Ibid.

[177] Cuyler to Gorgas, Telegram, Macon, 3 October 1864, Ibid.

[178] Cuyler to Maj. L.L. Butler, Telegram, Macon, 7 October 1864, Ibid; Cuyler to Gorgas, Telegram, Macon, 13 October 1864, Ibid.; Cuyler to Gorgas, Telegram, Macon, 18 October 1864, Ibid.

5,000 pounds of musket and rifle powder to Macon. He also needed 10,000 one-inch fuses, half of them timed at three seconds and the balance equally divided between two, four, and five seconds. Cobb needed them immediately.[179]

He also asked Military Storekeeper T. M. Bradford at Milledgeville to send General Wayne, then opposing Sherman's Right Wing at Gordon, 10,000 .69 caliber cartridges. Bradford should keep 50,000 cartridges in Milledgeville and send the balance of the ammunition to Savannah for safekeeping.[180]

After Sherman's troops passed Macon, Cuyler reinstalled the Arsenal machinery, which had been dismantled preparatory to sending it to Savannah, and resumed operations at the Arsenal Laboratory and the arms repair and harness shops. He returned only that machinery which was needed to perform essential tasks. Some of the Arsenal stores were sent for safekeeping to Columbia, South Carolina, and some remained in Savannah.[181]

The remainder of the Arsenal's history may be briefly told. Cuyler continued to operate the facility, but was hampered because he had to reestablish it after the close call to Macon posed by the near approach of Sherman's Right Wing. On 5 January 1865, a month and a half after Sherman's force had passed, he told Gorgas that the Arsenal would be "in full operation in three (3) days."[182] When part of Johnston's army passed through Macon in early February to oppose Sherman, then marching through South Carolina, Cuyler asked Lieutenant Colonel J.C. Moore, commanding the Selma Arsenal, to furnish artillery harness, especially horse collars, for the artillery.[183]

As the end approached Cuyler was beset by another problem. General Beauregard ordered the tracks removed from the Brunswick Railroad, a key connection between Macon and the Lower South. Because Sherman's troops had destroyed large sections of the Georgia Central Railroad, an important artery for the Arsenal to procure supplies, Cuyler telegraphed Gorgas on 20 February 1865, that "This Arsenal will certainly stop without use of said road."[184] In an effort to prevent the tearing up of the track, he asked Beauregard to suspend his

---

[179] Cuyler to Rains, Telegram, Macon, 17 November 1864, Ibid.

[180] Cuyler to T.M. Bradford, Telegram, Macon, 20 November 1864, Ibid. Many Confederate leaders believed that Savannah was safe. This attitude was fostered by Sherman who brilliantly confused all of his opponents in the Lower South concerning his movements. See also Cuyler to Wayne, Telegram, Macon, 20 November 1864, Ibid.

[181] Cuyler to Gorgas, Telegram, Savannah, 2 December 1864, Ibid. Once again, Sherman's movements continued to confuse Confederate leaders.

[182] Cuyler to Gorgas, Telegram, Macon, 5 January 1865, Ibid.

[183] Cuyler to Lt. Col. J.C. Moore, Telegram, Macon, 1 February 1865, Ibid.

[184] Cuyler to Gorgas, Telegram, Macon, 20 February 1865, Ibid. See also Cuyler to Beauregard, Telegram, Macon, 20 February 1865, Ibid. Beauregard ordered the track removed to keep Federal forces from using the road.

orders until he heard more details. Cuyler felt that if the road were destroyed, he could not "keep up Arsenal supplies for want of coal."[185] In fact, the breakdown of Georgia's railroad lines had paralyzed the Macon Arsenal which could send no arms forward "for want [of] transportation." Cuyler had been able to send 1,500 rifles to Augusta for General Daniel H. Hill's forces, but had no arms in his possession by the end of February.[186] Despite these problems the resourceful Cuyler, like his counterparts, Burton and Mallet, would continue to produce war materials until the end.

---

[185] Cuyler to Beauregard, Telegram, Macon, 20 February 1865, Ibid.

[186] Cuyler to Capt. O.T. Gibbes, Ordnance Officer, Augusta, Telegram, Macon, 28 February 1865, Ibid.

Chapter 9

Macon as an Ordnance Center:
The Armory

The Confederate States Armory in Macon was guided from its inception by the second in the triumvirate of outstanding ordnance officers chosen by Gorgas to head up the Government ordnance works in the Middle Georgia city. The man Gorgas selected to head Armory operations in Macon was James Henry Burton. Burton was born of English parentage in Shannondale Springs, Jefferson County, Virginia, on 17 August 1823. He received his education at Westchester Academy, Westchester, Pennsylvania, and entered a Baltimore machine shop as an apprentice at the age of sixteen. In 1844 he was hired by the Federal Arsenal at Harper's Ferry, Virginia, and was appointed foreman the following year. He later became master-armorer, a position he held until 1854. Burton went to England in 1855, and received an appointment as chief engineer of the Royal small-arms factory at Enfield, where he worked until 1860.

Returning to Virginia in that year, Burton was commissioned a lieutenant colonel in the Ordnance Department of Virginia by Governor John Letcher, and appointed head of the Virginia State Armory. He also received directions to order machinery for the Tredegar Iron Works at Richmond. After the capture of Harper's Ferry, Burton was placed in charge of the removal of that machinery to Richmond, manufacturing muskets there for Virginia. Burton supervised the loan of the machinery to the Confederacy. Muskets made in Richmond by Burton were stamped with his initials on the stock (J.B.). Burton soon received a commission as Lieutenant Colonel in the Confederate Ordnance Bureau, and was placed in command of the Richmond Armory. In January, 1862, he was commissioned Superintendent of Armories. In the summer of 1862, he was ordered to go to Atlanta to establish a permanent Government Armory, and finally, after some effort, chose Macon as the site for the important facility. Burton was connected with a number of important arms enterprises including a partnership in the firm of Spiller and Burr, the Alexander carbine, the McNeill carbine, the S.C. Robinson Company, and others.[1]

As early as March 1861, two months after Georgia seceded, Macon merchant T. R. Bloom wrote John B. Lamar, "I understand as Bills will be introduced into the Convention to locate a manufactory of arms & an Armory, now it strikes me this is a very important move for our State as absolutely necessary in the present state of affairs....There is no reason why we should not encourage the manufacturing of everything of the kind at home."[2]

On 22 May 1861, a reporter for the *Daily Telegraph* described a company organized to manufacture artillery, small arms, laboratory stores, and projectiles. Located in Macon, the firm was directed by its Acting Superintendent, Thomas E. McNeill. It offered ten thousand shares of stock at one hundred dollars a share to provide the needed capital. Nothing immediately came of the effort, however.[3] It was not until early June, 1862, that Josiah Gorgas directed Burton to locate an armory in the area around Atlanta. Burton went to that city and began to examine the region for a site. He found it difficult to find a location which provided the needed facilities. The planned armory needed a level tract for the erection of the necessary buildings; a large supply of water from a running stream to provide water for the operation of steam engines and for other purposes, and proximity to a railroad, with the means of connecting the line to the armory with a siding. Burton was disappointed by the country around Atlanta which "is so broken and rolling that it is almost impossible to find an acre of perfectly level ground." He had found, however, a suitable site, high and commanding, bordered on one side by the Macon and Western Railroad, and immediately outside of the Atlanta city limits. A good supply of water was furnished from a stream of spring water two or three hundred yards away. Used as a race track of a mile in circumference before the war, the site included between forty and fifty

---

[1] William B. Edwards, "Civil War Guns, The Complete Story of Federal and Confederate Small Arms: Design, Manufacture, Identification, Procurement, Issue, Employment, Effectiveness, and Postwar Disposal," p. 206, file in Genealogy and Archives Room, Washington Memorial Library, Macon. Burton was 5 feet 7 inches in height, had a high forehead, hazel eyes, a Roman nose, a small, round chin. His face was oval, his hair black, and his complexion fair. Andrew Johnson, Pardon Papers of James Henry Burton, Washington, D.C., 4 October 1865, James Henry Burton Papers, Microfilm, Washington Memorial Library, Macon, Microfilm, hereafter cited as Burton Papers. The originals are in the Yale University Library. For an excellent account of the relationship of Burton with the Spiller and Burr Company see Matthew W. Norman, *Colonel Burton's Spiller & Burr Revolver: An Untimely Venture in Confederate Small-Arms Manufacturing* (Macon: Mercer University Press, 1996). Shannendale Springs is now located in West Virginia.

[2] T.R. Bloom to John B. Lamar, Macon, 20 March 1861, Cobb Papers, 1861.

[3] *Macon Daily Telegraph*, 22 May 1861.

acres. Captain Marcus H. Wright was renting the property, and building a number of temporary buildings on it for a laboratory. The owner, a resident of Barnwell, South Carolina, wanted to sell the land for $15,000, and Burton had talked to Wright about sending an agent to discuss the matter with the owner. It was necessary to buy a few additional acres next to the site to secure the water supply. Burton wanted Gorgas' approval for the purchase because it was the only parcel of land in the area that answered the purpose.

Burton had also visited Macon, and felt that city provided a number of advantageous sites, and was also a better place to live than Atlanta, yet it also had its disadvantages. It was farther away from the coal-producing areas of the Confederacy, a fact which raised the price of coal an additional $2.00 per ton more than in Atlanta because of the transportation. But building would be cheaper in Macon because of the vast supply of lumber in the surrounding forests. After considering all factors, Burton believed that the supply of lumber was the best point for locating the Armory, aside from the safety issue. "Macon is certainly a safer point than Atlanta," he told Gorgas, "but at present there would seem to be no doubt as regards the safety of the latter place, notwithstanding the late attack upon Chattanooga, from which point the enemy have now retired without having accomplished anything of value to them." Chattanooga, Burton believed, was a very important place because, without it, the entire supply of coal would be cut off to points to the south. Burton showed great vision when he observed that because immense stores were placed in Atlanta, "no doubt the enemy would be glad to reach this point in order to capture or destroy them if possible." Burton also learned that only one shop in the Atlanta area could build stock machines. The Government might buy the shop for $20,000, along with all the machines and fixtures it held.[4]

A few days later, Burton was invited to visit Macon by several important Maconites. The result of that visit, coupled with what Burton believed to be "the prevailing feeling manifested by the people generally of this place [Atlanta] towards the Govt. Through its agents," caused him to decide to locate the Armory in Macon. The people of Macon really wanted the facility, while some in Atlanta seemed to have the opposite feeling. One of Macon's leading citizens, William B. Johnston, rode around the city with Burton and examined the ground with reference to the needs of the proposed armory. Macon, Burton decided, offered superior advantages with respect to eligible sites. He had found one which provided him with everything he needed. The tract belonged to the City of Macon, well within the city limits. It was high enough to be healthy,

---

[4] Burton to Gorgas, Atlanta, 11 June 1862, Box 3198, Vols. 20, 29, and 31, Letters Sent Macon Armory, Georgia 1862-65, Microfilm, NARA, hereafter cited as Letters Sent Armory, 1862-65. The reels used by the author may be found in the Washington Memorial Library, Macon.

was well-watered, and was located next to a railroad. In short, it was perfect. There was, however, another reason for locating the Armory in Macon. Burton observed, "The citizens, Mayor and Council very properly anticipate advantages to be derived from the location of so large a Govt. establishment in it, have determined to do a most liberal act in order to secure these advantages." The Macon City Council offered to donate thirty acres of land for the Armory if it was located there. Since the land was worth about $1,000 an acre, Burton believed the Maconites were sincere. Besides, the objections to locating the facility in Atlanta were increasing. There were several thousand soldiers in hospitals there, and the price of food was escalating. Flour cost from $20 to $23 per barrel, and salt was $50 a sack with proportionate prices for other items. This caused Burton to fear that mechanics who worked in the Armory could not live in Atlanta on the wages they would receive. There was also difficulty in obtaining houses for workers because of the large numbers of people refugeing in Atlanta from coastal Georgia. Furthermore, there were few facilities for building houses, and no materials. For these reasons, Burton urged Gorgas to accept the Macon offer. Fortunately, Burton had kept all the stock-making machines on the railroad cars, so they could be sent at once to Macon. Burton concluded his recommendations to Gorgas saying "I confess that I am disappointed in Atlanta as a location for the Armory....Speculation in real estate seems to be the sole object in view by the citizens of this place, and hence the indifference manifested towards the establishment of manufacturing, and other enterprizes [sic] of industry. This state of things must change before Atlanta can become a thriving city."[5]

Burton wanted to know the exact terms upon which the Macon City Council was willing to rent temporary quarters for the Armory in the old depot of the Macon and Western Railroad. The facility could be adapted for the manufacture of small arms, and Burton wanted to lease the structure for a period of one to two years. He also wanted to alter the building by inserting windows in the walls and substituting windows for the existing wide doors in the side of the structure, "so as to fit it for use as a workshop." He also wanted the right to erect temporary structures and a steam engine while reserving the right to remove these items when the new facility was completed.[6]

On the same day, the City Council voted to rent the premises to Burton for $1,000 a year, payable semi-annually, this included some of the brick buildings west of the City Bridge currently occupied by soldiers' families whom the City agreed to remove.[7] Burton accepted the terms on the following day.[8]

---

[5] Burton to Gorgas, Atlanta, 25 June 1862, Ibid. See also Burton to William B. Johnston, Atlanta, 26 June 1862, Ibid.

[6] Burton to the Mayor and City Council of Macon, Macon, 30 June 1862, Ibid.

[7] Council Minutes, 30 June 1862, Book 5, 1859-1862, pp. 572-573.

The premises included about three acres of level land with several buildings. One of these was a one-story brick building 130 x 33 feet, formerly used as a depot for freight; a two-story brick building, 50 x 22 feet which was formerly used as offices; and a wooden building, with dimensions of 150 x 20 feet formerly used as a car shed. The Armory had the use of another one-story brick building about 100 x 33 feet, formerly used as an engine and car house, about a quarter mile away from the other buildings. Captain Cuyler used the old depot building as a magazine for the storage of powder and ammunition. Cuyler and Burton decided that the former officer should have the use of the outer brick building for his purposes so that Burton could use the old depot building for the setting up of his stock machinery.[9]

Announcing the conversion of the old Macon and Western Depot, the *Journal and Messenger* noted, "The erection of extensive buildings has been commenced and we understand that a portion of the necessary machinery is now in readiness to be put into operation whenever they are completed. This will be quite an improvement in the recent use to which these premises have been appropriated."[10]

Now that arrangements had been made to establish the Armory in Macon, and temporary buildings were secured, Burton wrote Major W. S. Downer, Superintendent of the Richmond Armory, to obtain certain machines to manufacture small arms. He also wanted to set the pay of workers. Machinists would be paid $2.00 to $3.00 a day; pattern makers, $2.50 to $3.00; millwrights from $2.50 to $3.00; and the best carpenters, $2.00 to $2.50. Living was cheaper in Macon than in Richmond, so lower wages could be paid. Machines to manufacture gunstocks were badly needed, especially the pulleys for stock machines. Burton did not need shafting because he could procure this from an armory in Holly Springs, Mississippi. He assured Downer that "Every effort will be made to supply you with stocks at the earliest moment possible." He also promised to prepare a list of tools needed as soon as possible.[11]

Burton showed much energy in preparing the Armory for operation. On 5 July he asked Cuyler for one of his buildings in which to place gun stocking machinery.[12] He sent an agent named Lotz to Richmond to purchase a globe

---

[8] Burton to Mayor Methvin S. Thomson, Macon, 1 July 1862, Letters Sent, Armory, 1862-65; *Georgia Journal and Messenger*, 2 July 1862.

[9] Burton to Gorgas, Macon, 23 August 1862, Ibid.

[10] *Georgia Journal and Messenger*, 16 July 1862.

[11] Burton to Maj. W.S. Downer, Atlanta, 3 July 1862, Letters Sent, Armory, 1862-65. One of the major tasks of the Macon Armory was to manufacture gunstocks for rifles fabricated at the Richmond Armory.

[12] Cuyler to Gorgas, Macon, 5 July 1862, Letters Sent Arsenal, 1862.

valve for a steam engine and a lift pump for the engine well.[13] Burton also commissioned his Master Builder, Jeremiah Fuss, to select tools needed in the Armory from the firms of Carhart and Hurd and Nathan Weed in Macon.[14]

In order to buy tools, he secured $1,000 in ordnance funds from Cuyler.[15] However, this was only a temporary measure. Burton, in short, was strapped for funds as he developed Armory operations in Macon. He asked Wright for a loan of $10,000 from his budget, promising to repay him as soon as he received an allocation of $50,000 from Gorgas.[16] As late as 24 July he reported to Gorgas that he still had not received the draft for $50,000 although he had issued a warrant for that sum on 30 June. If Gorgas did not assign a Military Store Keeper and Paymaster, through whom funds could be channeled, to the Armory soon he could not employ clerical help because he had no funds to pay them.[17] On the following day he wrote to Gorgas asking to be reimbursed for his private funds which he used before receiving money from the Government.[18] He then wrote to B.C. Pressley, Confederate Assistant Treasurer, based in Charleston, asking to draw on him for the $50,000.[19] He later informed Pressley that he wanted Confederate Treasury small change notes in the total amount of $1,000, and only $9,000 in $10 notes.[20] Fortunately, Gorgas appointed Lieutenant Charles Selden, Jr. as Paymaster and Military Storekeeper for the Armory in late September, thus providing an official to handle allocated funds. This provided a temporary solution for Burton's financial problems.[21]

He also needed materials to alter the temporary facilities to make them suitable for Armory purposes. To this end, he wrote Wright to send the window glass needed to alter the doors in his temporary quarters. He also needed 10,000 shingles to cover a boiler and an engine house.[22] He later wrote William F. Smith, whom he had sent to Atlanta to buy machinery and materials, that he needed 110,000 shingles for the engine house and boiler and for other

---

[13] Burton to C.S. Ordnance Department, Macon, 5 July 1862, Letters Sent Armory, 1862-65.

[14] Burton to Carhart and Hurd, Macon, 9 July 1862, Ibid.; Burton to Nathan Weed, Macon, 9 July 1862, Ibid.

[15] Burton to Cuyler, Receipt, Macon, 11 July 1862, Burton Papers.

[16] Burton to Wright, Macon, 15 and 17 July 1862, (2 letters), Letters Sent, Armory, 1862-65.

[17] Burton to Gorgas, Macon, 24 July 1862, Ibid.

[18] Burton to Gorgas, Macon, 25 July 1862, Ibid.

[19] Burton to B.C. Pressley, Macon, 5 August 1862, Ibid.

[20] Burton to B.C. Pressley, Macon, 11 August 1862, Ibid.

[21] Burton to B.C. Pressley, Macon, 1 October 1862, Ibid.

[22] Burton to Wright, Macon, 11 July 1862, Ibid.

construction.[23] He also needed timber and carpenters. Burton added, "I have decided to make my machine shop building two stories instead of one story only as originally contemplated."[24]

Throughout the summer of 1862, Burton continued to contract for supplies to repair the old Macon and Western Depot and begin work on the new Armory. He inquired whether LeRoy Napier could furnish 12,000 hard brick, and engaged the firm of Ross and Seymour of Macon to supply window glass for the planned renovations. The price for glass was $8.00 a box. He asked John C. Peck of Macon to furnish him with four or five carpenters to begin renovations. He ordered a platform scale, which weighed 1600 pounds, from Carhart and Curd in Macon.[25]

Burton asked Gorgas for help in making arrangements to haul the large amount of machinery and materials needed by the Armory. One of his problems was that there was no quartermaster at the Post of Macon. Because of this, machinery was piling up at the Macon and Western Depot, and the railroad agents were pushing Burton to move it.[26]

He soon learned that Captain H. C. Cunningham, Assistant Quartermaster at the Post, was available to help with the movement of machinery from the depot. On 17 July Burton informed Cunningham of eight or ten car loads of machinery at the depot which needed to be moved to the Armory. "Please inform me," he told Cunningham, "when you can commence hauling it and what number of drays you can design to the work."[27] When Cunningham failed to respond, Burton asked Colonel Jack Brown, Post Commander, to impress ten drays and teams to move what was by 19 July thirty car loads of machinery.[28] When Brown did not respond immediately, Burton, who had also asked for a guard to be placed at the Armory, wrote, "I trust you will in future arrange to give me the assistance required and agreed upon;" and angrily told the Post Commander, "otherwise my operations will be greatly retarded."[29] Brown promised to send a

---

[23] Burton to William F. Smith, Macon, 22 July 1862, Ibid. For Smith's appointment see Burton to Wright, Macon, 12 July 1862, Ibid. See also Burton to William F. Smith, Macon, 12 July 1862, Ibid. For more information concerning the procurement of shingles for Armory renovations see Burton to Capt. William F. Bacon, Macon, 21 August 1862, Ibid.; and Burton to William F. Smith, Macon, 29 August 1862, Ibid.

[24] Burton to Wright, Macon, 11 July 1862, Ibid.

[25] Burton to LeRoy Napier, Macon, 22 July 1862, Ibid; Burton to Ross and Seymour, Macon, 22 July 1862, Ibid.; Burton to John C. Peck, Macon, 22 July 1862, Ibid.; Burton to Carhart and Curd, 24 July 1862, Ibid.

[26] Burton to Gorgas, Macon, 12 July 1862, Ibid.

[27] Burton to H.C. Cunningham, Macon, 17 July 1862, Ibid.

[28] Burton to Col. Jack Brown, Macon, 19 July 1862, Ibid.

[29] Burton to Jack Brown, Macon, 26 July 1862, Ibid.

hundred men on 28 July to unload twenty car loads of machinery, and a number of car loads of lumber.[30] Burton also had problems getting labor to remove materials at the Southwestern Railroad Depot.[31] Burton was forced to use troops to unload the machinery and lumber because he met with no success in his efforts to hire black laborers even though he was willing to pay their owners $1.00 a day for each man.[32]

Fortunately, some of the machinery was available locally. Burton called upon Schofield and Brother for a cast iron pulley, two iron saddles for boilers, one wrought iron crank shaft for the pump with a crank plate, pin, and pulleys, one wrought iron counter shaft for the pump, one pair of counter hangers for the counter shaft, and other items.[33]

However, Burton was dependent upon Atlanta sources for much of his machinery and parts. He asked E. N. Spiller at the Atlanta Armory for the loan of a set of patterns for a cast iron forge and all of its parts.[34] He wrote W.F. Smith in Atlanta for a main driving belt about sixty feet long and from fifteen to eighteen inches wide for the steam engine which he planned to install.[35]

The new Armory required much material. Burton asked Wright for a barrel or two of sperm oil. He ordered lumber from the firm of Wadley, Jones and Company in Herndon, Georgia, from S. O. Franklin in Terrell, Georgia; and from William F. Smith in Atlanta. He also asked Smith to ship him 10,000 shingles to cover the engine and boiler house. However, when Smith told him that Captain Bacon, the officer assigned to deliver shingles for the Armory, could not secure more than 3,000 "inside of a month," Burton began to look for other sources.[36]

Like his counterparts, Cuyler and Mallet, Burton was beset with a host of things to do before he could begin to manufacture small arms. One of these chores involved gaining possession of the old depot from Cuyler. His letter to Cuyler, written on 22 July revealed Burton's anxiety. He told Cuyler that his time was growing very short for making stocks for rifles. If he couldn't get the

---

[30] Burton to H.W. Bronson, Jr., Freight Agent Macon and Western Railroad, Macon, 28 July 1862, Ibid.

[31] Burton to J.M. Draper, Agent Southwestern Railroad, Macon, 29 July 1862, Ibid.

[32] Burton to Ichabod Davis, Macon, 14 July 1862, Ibid.

[33] Burton to Schofield and Brother, Macon, 14 July 1862, Ibid.

[34] Burton to E.N. Spiller, Macon, 15 July 1862, Ibid.

[35] Burton to W.F. Smith, Macon, 15 July 1862, Ibid.

[36] Burton to Wright, Macon, 15 July 1862, Ibid.; Burton to Wadley, Jones and Company, Macon, 15, 18, 25 July 1862, [three letters], Ibid.; Burton to S.O. Franklin, Macon, 15 July 1862, Ibid; Burton to William F. Smith, Macon, 18 July 1862, Ibid.; Burton to William F. Smith, Macon, 26 September 1862, Ibid. Sperm oil was used to lubricate machinery during much of the 19th Century.

depot soon he would not be "able to supply stocks to the Richmond Armory in time to prevent a suspension of the assembling of muskets at that establishment."[37]

Cuyler removed the powder which belonged to the Arsenal from the depot building on July 25, along with the Arsenal guard who had been protecting it. This, in turn, forced Burton to call upon Colonel Brown for a guard to protect the large amount of Government property already in the temporary Armory facility.[38]

Despite the fact that he had to overcome so many difficulties, no detail seemed too small for the diligent Burton. He asked Gorgas for authority to purchase a horse, a light wagon, and a buggy because he had "so much running about to do that I find it impossible to accomplish what I might if I had some facilities for more rapid locomotion." The wagon was needed to carry light articles and materials to and from the Armory.[39] He even asked Wright for a bell for the use of the Armory. Burton had noticed a large one on the platform of one of the depots in Atlanta which he wanted for his use if Wright didn't need it.[40]

Burton dealt with many problems during the summer of 1862, besides those enumerated above. One of these involved hiring a skilled workforce to make gunstocks and perform the other tasks needed to produce small arms. In mid-July he asked Captain H.N. Ells of the Macon Light Artillery to detail one of his men, William Edge, as a molder. Plans called for Edge to work in the Schofield Foundry. Because he was a good workman, Edge was "essential [to] their bus-iness."[41] On 21 July Burton secured the services of Anthony Murphy of Atlanta as foreman at a starting salary of $3.50 a day to begin with, planning to increase the amount after a month's trial period.[42] Towards the end of July he asked Gorgas to send him John C. Storm, an employee in the Richmond Armory, to work the machine for rough-turning gunstocks.[43] By 15 August Burton employed one detailed man, twenty-one exempts, and twelve men subject to conscription for a total workforce of thirty-four. He also hired a large number of black carpenters and laborers to work on the needed temporary buildings.[44]

---

[37] Burton to Cuyler, Macon, 22 July 1862, Ibid.

[38] Burton to Jack Brown, Macon, 25 July 1862, Ibid. The use of the depot by the Arsenal as a powder magazine delayed the transfer of the facility to the Armory.

[39] Burton to Gorgas, Macon, 12 July 1862, Ibid.

[40] Burton to Wright, Macon, 12 July 1862, Ibid.

[41] Burton to Gorgas, Macon, 19 July 1862, Ibid.

[42] Burton to Anthony Murphy, Macon, 21 July 1862, Ibid.

[43] Burton to Gorgas, Macon, 29 July 1862, Ibid.

[44] Burton to Cuyler, Macon, 21 August 1862, Ibid.

The pay for pattern-makers and first class machinists at the Arsenal was set at $3.00 a day; causing Burton to tell Cuyler that he paid "all men according to their skill and the value of services rendered, but because I give one pattern maker $3.00 it does not follow," he wrote, "that I shall give it to all I employ." He would be glad, however, to cooperate with Cuyler to establish wage scales for different skills.[45]

In late August, Armory workers began to lay a track from the Macon and Western Railroad to the temporary Armory facility. This had been one of the conditions Burton made when he negotiated with the Macon City Council to locate the Armory there. The laying of the line, Burton believed, would not cost much. The only expense involved the cost of materials and labor in laying sills and rails. The grading was completed. The length of the proposed branch rail was about 800 yards, and the estimated cost $3,000 if the track were laid with old flat rails. Because the Armory would require a great deal of wood to operate the necessary steam engines, the tracks could be taken up and used at the new Armory when it was completed. The acquisition of flat rails presented no problem because a large quantity was available at the Navy Yard in Columbus, Georgia. If Burton could obtain twenty-five tons of these rails it would provide enough material to lay the track. Captain H. G. Tyler, Superintendent of the Macon and Western Railroad, promised to lay the track if the Confederacy agreed to pay all damages that might result from accidents on the company's road which resulted from neglect or carelessness from Armory employees in connection with the switch which led to the proposed siding. Burton could see no objection to this because "all owners of private sidings are similarly bound."[46]

Burton contracted with Wadley Jones and Company to provide him with 300 stringers, eighteen feet long, and 6" x 8" in diameter upon which the flat track would be laid. He also wanted to know if the firm could furnish crossties.[47]

Before any work was done on the siding, Burton wrote Mayor Thomson and the City Council asking for permission to lay the temporary track. In his letter

---

[45] Burton to Cuyler, Macon, 21 August 1862, Ibid.

[46] Burton to Gorgas, Macon, 11 August 1862, Ibid. For additional information on Burton's efforts to secure the siding see Burton to Isaac Scott, President, Macon and Western Railroad, Macon, 6 August 1862, Ibid. and Burton to Capt. H.G. Tyler, Superintendent, Macon and Western Railroad, Macon, 22 July 1862, Ibid.

[47] Burton to Wadley Jones and Company, Macon, 26 August 1862, Ibid. Steel tracks were usually laid on wooden stringers at that time because the technology to cast the type of rails used in modern railroads was not available during the Civil War.

he explained that the Confederacy reserved the right to remove the track when the new Armory was completed.[48]

During the summer of 1862, much work was accomplished in renovating the Armory's temporary facilities. When he secured the depot, Burton lowered the entire floor two feet in order to get the interior height needed for his machinery. He also replaced the wide doors in the walls of the building with suitable frames and windows. It was also necessary to erect a long row of posts along the center of the building's length to carry the line of shafting. This was all completed by 23 August and, as Burton told Gorgas, "an excellent shop for the purpose is the result." The machinery for making gunstocks was unpacked, and, to Burton's delight, only one machine was injured in transportation, and that one was repaired. All of the gunstock machines were placed, and much of the shafting to drive them was erected, including the mainline shafting. Plans called for the stock machines to become operative by the end of August, or at least by the time Burton received some gunstocks to work on. The steam engine from Knoxville, along with other machinery, was installed and ready for use. The new boiler from the Reading Works in Vicksburg, Mississippi, was erected, and Armory employees had dug a thirty-foot-deep well for a good supply of water for the steam engines. By late August, a brick boiler and engine house to cover the well were under construction, and plans called for their completion by 26 August. The sixty-one-foot-high brick chimney was finished, and Burton believed he could get up steam to operate the machinery as soon as the boiler house was completed- possibly as early as 26 August. Since he had not received several skilled workers from the Richmond Armory to operate the stock machines, Burton planned to train others. He also intended to manufacture machinery for the new Armory as soon as possible and build a two hundred by thirty-five foot frame building for use as a forging shop to house twelve forges. A third building, one story high, with dimensions of 90' x 33' was needed for use as a store house for guns and other stores and materials. The timber for all these buildings was available at the site. The large building for the machine shop was completely framed, and the brick foundation laid ready for the framing. Workmen would frame the building in a week, and the building would be ready for machinery in three or four weeks. The other two buildings, both smaller and only one story in height, would be ready at about the same time as the large building. The whole area for the temporary facility was surrounded with a strong verticed board fence six feet high. "I have employed, to a great extent, negro carpenters in the framing and erection of buildings," Burton wrote, "and I am pleased to state that I have found their employment very satisfactory indeed."

---

[48] Burton to Mayor Thomson and the Macon City Council, Macon, 29 August 1862, Ibid.

Burton also reported that he had received the machinery from the Holly Springs, Mississippi Arsenal, and from Richmond, and Raleigh, North Carolina, and Armory workers were busy unpacking it, cleaning it, and putting it in order. The Holly Springs machinery was in bad condition due to bad packing, and rough handling in transportation, forcing Armory workers to inventory it. Burton, however, did not foresee any problems in constructing the machinery for the new Armory if the mechanics could be obtained, many of whom were in the Army, although it might be necessary to use some means of selecting them and detailing them for Armory service. Burton had devoted most of his energies to erecting the stock machines as quickly as possible. Now that this was completed, he planned to begin construction of the main works for the new Armory. When the City completed a survey of the site, a site plan would be sent to Gorgas. Burton also intended to forward plans and elevations of the proposed buildings as soon as they were designed. "It gives me much pleasure," he reported, "to state that the utmost good feeling is manifested towards the enterprise I am charged with by the citizens of this city generally, and my experience so far has been satisfactory and I have every reason to believe that the selection of this point as a location for the Armory will be attended with results satisfactory to the Government."[49]

Burton continued to press for such items as bricks and shingles in the early fall of 1862. On 20 September he asked Thomas Knight of Macon to produce 35,000 bricks for the work on the old depot.[50] Shingles remained a problem because Captain Bacon in Atlanta could only let Burton have 30,000 shingles for at least a month. Other arrangements had to be made.[51]

Nearly two months later, the main temporary building was nearly completed, and workmen were erecting the lines of shafting. They were also moving the machinery into the facility, causing Burton to hope that he would have some of the machines operating in a week or ten days. The framing of the Smiths Shop and the store house was progressing satisfactorily. The Reading machinery from Vicksburg was in Macon, but because a number of important parts were missing, the machines were useless until these parts could be replaced. Some machinery from Knoxville had also arrived, but most of it was in the same condition as Reading's. Wright told Burton he had forwarded all of

---

[49] Burton to Gorgas, Macon, 23 August 1862, Ibid. For information about the Reading machinery see Burton to Gorgas, Macon, 22 August 1862, and Burton to Wright, Macon, 27 August 1862, both in Ibid. For additional information about the Holly Springs Arsenal machinery see William S. McElwain to Burton, Macon, 30 August 1862, Burton Papers.

[50] Burton to Thomas Knight, Macon, 20 September 1862, Letters Sent Armory, 1862-65.

[51] Burton to William F. Smith, Macon, 26 September 1862, Ibid.

the machinery from Knoxville. Preparations for the manufacture of gunstocks proceeded smoothly, and Burton planned to make some for the Richmond Armory as soon as possible. He was running the gun stock department extra hours, morning and evening, and planned to send a thousand stocks to Richmond soon. However, the entire operation was hindered because smiths and machinists were hard to get, causing problems which Burton planned to deal with as soon as possible.[52]

With his customary vigor, Burton pushed ahead with the building of the new Armory. On 19 August he accepted the thirty-acre-site offered for the facility by the City of Macon.[53] The thirty- acre- tract initially selected was not suitable for the Armory, and another tract of forty-three acres bounded by the line of the Macon and Western Railroad, Calhoun, Hazel, and Lamar Streets was selected.[54] Since it was necessary to survey the tract, Burton asked Cuyler for the loan of one of his employees to perform the survey.[55]

The new site, which was high and rolling, seemed ideal. The planned buildings, situated on comparatively level ground, would occupy an area of about five acres. A branch which ran parallel to Hazel Street provided a never-failing source of enough water for steam and other purposes. The Armory, moreover, would also control the branch because it ran the entire length of that side of the tract. The highest portion of the land lay along Calhoun Street, and would provide the best site for officers' quarters. Gorgas thought it best to buy Square 49, which contained four acres, from the City at a cost of seven to eight thousand dollars, but the square was worth, Burton wrote, "at least five times that sum." He planned to enclose the entire tract with a temporary but substantial eight-foot-high board fence, and also intended to immediately build one or two frame cottages of four rooms each, at a cost of $1200 to $1500 each. These cottages could be rented for a modest sum to the "Foreman of Labourers" and the "Foreman of Carpenters." Burton planned the buildings to be plain because the number of mechanics available to build them was so small. Due to this labor shortage more elaborate buildings would take too long. He had contracted for three million bricks at a price of $11.00 per thousand delivered at

---

[52] Burton to Gorgas, Macon, 16 October 1862, Ibid.

[53] Burton to Mayor Thomson and the City Council, Macon, 19 August 1862, Letters Sent Armory, 1862-65; *Daily Telegraph*, 28 August 1862.

[54] Council Minutes, 29 August 1862, Book D, p. 591. For information about the deed to convey the land which the City prepared see Burton to Gorgas, Macon, 16 September 1862, Letters Sent, Armory, 1862-65.

[55] Burton to Cuyler, Macon, 28 August 1862, Letters Sent Armory, 1862-65.

the Armory, and expected to have almost a third of these delivered in the fall of 1862. These would be used to make alterations on the temporary facility.[56]

Moving quickly to secure Square 49, Burton formally asked Mayor Thomson for the tract, promising him he would not close or interfere with any of the surrounding streets or thoroughfares.[57] After some deliberation, Council approved the sale on 14 November for $8,010.227.[58]

Anxious to begin building, Burton asked Jeremiah Fuss, his Master Builder, to prepare the necessary plans for the erection of the two cottages. He also told Fuss to plan for two double kitchens, each twenty-six by fifteen feet in size.[59] He also ordered four twelve-inch-square and five-feet-long granite corner stones to mark the boundaries of the new Armory from the firm of Wood and Meador in Stone Mountain, Georgia. One of the dressed faces of each stone was to be cut with the letters "C. S." Burton also ordered seven corner stones nine-inches-square and five-feet-long to be dressed and lettered the same as the others.[60]

When he received the forty-three acres, Burton discovered that Colonel Jack Brown's Regiment of Georgia Volunteers occupied the ground. This prompted him to ask Gorgas for the authority to move Brown and his men to another spot because they were cutting down the trees which Burton wanted to preserve around his planned facility. He complained, "The trees on this tract of land are a very desirable feature, and there is no necessity for their being destroyed in the manner referred to."[61]

Special Orders were issued to First Lieutenant Charles Colcock Jones, Jr. of Savannah's Chatham Artillery, a lawyer in civil life who served as Judge Advocate of his unit, to go to Macon and resolve the matter. Jones found that the only trees there were "straggling" pines and small oaks, "familiarly known as 'scrubby oaks'." Although Brown's men had cleared a parade ground on the east of the encampment, this had been done with the knowledge of the Macon City authorities. Jones, in short, dismissed Burton's complaints as "frivolous

---

[56] Burton to Gorgas, Macon, 16 October 1862, Ibid. For details about Burton's efforts to secure bricks for the temporary Armory facility see Burton to Gorgas, Macon, 23 August 1862; Burton to Mayor Thomson, Macon, 27 August 1862; Burton to Daniel Hartnet, Macon, 15 September 1862; and Burton to William G. Hoge, Macon, 17 September 1862, all Ibid; *Macon Daily Telegraph*, 11 September 1862.

[57] Burton to Mayor Thomson, Macon, 24 October 1862, Letters Sent, Armory, 1862-65.

[58] Council Minutes, 14 November 1862, Book D, p. 607.

[59] Burton to Jeremiah Fuss, Macon, 22 October 1862, Letters Sent Armory, 1862-65.

[60] Burton to Wood and Meador, Macon, 20 September 1862, Ibid.

[61] Burton to Gorgas, Macon, 5 September 1862, Ibid.

and unfounded in fact–and unworthy any further notice on the part of the Government."[62]

Burton penned an angry letter to Mayor Thomson asking if the City authorities had given Brown permission to cut the timber from the area next to the former encampment of the regiment.[63] His anger increased when Thomson replied that no authority was given to Brown to cut down the trees. Thomson noted, interestingly, that the cutting "was all done about the time he [Brown] thought we all belonged to him, and the mischief was done before I knew he had moved."[64]

This response caused Burton to take issue with Jones' report explaining that there were only small pines and oaks left because Brown's men had cut the larger trees down. He concluded a long letter to Gorgas, saying, "I respectfully request and demand a reinvestigation of the subject, whereby the evidence of disinterested witnesses may be secured."[65]

Now that the site was selected Burton began to accumulate other material to build his new facility. He asked Gorgas for permission to buy six mules.[66] He received authorization to purchase the mules at a cost not to exceed $250 each. Burton believed it would cost as much as $600 a pair, or $300 each because the demand in Macon for mules exceeded the supply.[67] He asked John G. White, a wagon maker from Perry, Georgia, to build a half dozen dump carts at a price of $80 apiece. He also wanted a set of running gears for a lumber wagon used for hauling plank, and fitted with a coupling pole.[68] Now that the land for the new Armory was secured, Burton began to collect materials. He ordered a large quantity of lumber for fencing from Wadley, Jones and Company of Herndon, Georgia.[69]

Burton also continued to order shingles for both the projected Armory and the temporary facility.[70] He asked George F. Sweet, Agent for the Copper

---

[62] First Lieutenant Charles Colcock Jones, Jr. to…Savannah, 15 September 1862, Burton Papers.

[63] Burton to Mayor Thomson, Macon, 29 September 1862, Letters Sent Armory, 1862-65.

[64] Mayor Thomson to Burton, Macon, 29 September 1862, Burton Papers.

[65] Burton to Gorgas, Macon, 2 October 1862, Letters Sent, Armory, 1862-65.

[66] Burton to Gorgas, Macon, 3 October 1862, Ibid.

[67] Burton to Gorgas, Macon, 13 October 1862, Ibid. Gorgas wrote Burton giving him the authority to buy the mules on 7 October 1862.

[68] Burton to John G. White, Macon, 4 October 1862; Burton to White, Macon, 9 October 1862; and Burton to White, 13 October 1862, all Ibid.

[69] Burton to Wadley, Jones and Company, Macon, 10 October 1862; Burton to Burton to Wadley, Jones and Company, Macon, 23 October 1862, both Ibid.

[70] Burton to Capt. W.F. Bacon, Assistant Quartermaster, Atlanta, Macon, 16 September 1862, Ibid. See also Burton to Joseph Clisby, Macon, 16 September 1862,

Rolling Works in Cleveland, Tennessee, for a supply of sheet copper suitable for roofing, guttering, and spouting.[71]

Although most of Burton's attention during the summer and fall of 1862 was concerned with the alterations at the temporary Arsenal and the plans to construct a new, permanent facility, he entered into a contract with Macon arms manufacturer Thomas E. McNeill to supply the Confederacy with 20,000 breech-loading carbines of the so-called "Alexander's pattern." He promised to assist McNeill with copies of drawings, sketches, estimates of costs of machinery, and a detailed list of the operations which needed to be performed and the various parts of the carbines during the manufacturing process. Burton planned to superintend and direct the manufacture of a model carbine from the Richmond Armory. In return, McNeill promised to pay Burton $2,000 for his help as soon as the contract was executed and signed, an additional $2,000 after six months, and $1,000 upon delivery of the arms. Burton would also receive $1.50 for each and every complete carbine received by the Confederacy when the arms or parts were delivered.[72]

Burton asked Gorgas to send him a breech-loading carbine of the Alexander's pattern to support his contract with McNeill. He also wanted a model arm of the Sharp's Carbine pattern with the slide working vertically to the axis of the bore.[73] He arranged with the firm of Spiller and Burr to loan McNeill most of their patterns, and furnished the Macon entrepreneur with a sketch of the ground plan for factory buildings.[74]

In early August, Burton furnished McNeill with a partial list of over one hundred machines he would need for the carbine factory. The list included machines for milling barrels; lathes; machines for making gun locks; milling machines; edge milling machines; vertical milling machines; machines for the smithery; a rotary fan blower; a drop hammer; a tilt hammer; furnaces for annealing components; furnaces for casehardening; and tilt hammers for welding barrels.[75]

---

in which Burton asked Clisby, Editor of the *Macon Daily Telegraph*, to insert an advertisement in his paper for "seventy-five thousand best quality pine shingles for which the market price will be paid on delivery." Ibid.

[71] Burton to George F. Sweet, Macon, 24 October 1862, Ibid.

[72] Thomas E. McNeill and James H. Burton, Contract, Macon, 29 July 1862, Burton Papers.

[73] Burton to Gorgas, Macon, 29 July 1862, Letters Sent Armory, 1862-65.

[74] Burton to Gorgas, Macon, October 1862, Burton Papers.

[75] Burton to McNeill, Macon, 4 August 1862, Ibid. Annealing, in this instance, means to heat metals to remove or prevent internal stress. It also means to toughen or temper steel.

During August, Burton worked to obtain some of the Holly Springs Arsenal machinery for McNeill, and received Gorgas' approval to sell McNeill the machinery which Burton did not need in the Armory at the valuation placed upon it when it was purchased by the Confederacy, plus the cost of transporting the items to Macon.[76] The machines were valued at $15,295.[77]

By late October McNeill had not copied any drawings, nor had he used either the Government patterns or the Spiller and Burr patterns. No machine shop was provided, nor did McNeill have a single machinist at work. Only seven months remained before the first delivery of arms was due. This led Burton to report that McNeill "does not possess either the ability or the energy necessary to the due execution of his contract, and as a consequence, it can result in no benefit to the Govt." Burton wanted to annul the contract because nothing good could come of the matter. McNeill disagreed, and tried to force Burton to complete his part of the contract. Burton believed that the matter was a personal one between McNeill and himself. Furthermore, the men who served as McNeill's bondsmen went into the enterprise in good faith, and had, by late October, spent $30,000 of their own money to buy materials such as bar iron and steel. They had also advanced $20,000 to McNeill to direct and manage the enterprise. In short, his backers had lost confidence in McNeill, but were willing to contract with the Confederacy to manufacture breech loading carbines. Burton, however, felt that "The difficulties of getting up such factories at the present time are very great indeed. But when, to these difficulties is added inability upon the part of contractors with the Govt. To make use of the means at their disposal it is...proper for the Govt. to interfere in behalf [of] their own interests." For this reason, he urged Gorgas to stop advancing funds to McNeill because of the unsatisfactory progress he had made up to that time, and the impossibility of his being able to fulfill the contract.[78]

Despite Burton's efforts the contract with McNeill was not annulled at the time.[79] By early December Gorgas appointed Cuyler and Mallet to serve as commissioners to investigate the progress of the McNeill contract.[80]

---

[76] Burton to Gorgas, Macon, 8 August 1862, Letters Sent, Armory, 1862-65; Burton to McNeill and Company, Macon, 18 August 1862, Ibid.

[77] Burton to McNeill, Macon, 19 September 1862, Ibid.

[78] Burton to Gorgas, Macon, October 1862, Burton Papers. See also McNeill to Burton, Macon, 25 October 1862; Burton to Gorgas, Macon, 28 October 1862; and Burton to McNeill, Macon, 28 October 1862, (3 letters), all in Ibid. and Burton to McNeill, Macon, 29 October 1862, Letters Sent Armory, 1862-65.

[79] Burton to McNeill, Macon, 19 November 1862; McNeill to Burton, Macon, 19 November 1862, (2 letters), Burton Papers.

[80] Burton to Cuyler and Mallet, Macon, 4 December 1862, Letters Sent, Armory, 1862-65.

In order to begin the production of gunstocks, Burton began to accumulate supplies of wood. Because he needed a great deal of wood to run his steam engines, he purchased several hundred cords of pine wood on the Macon and Western Railroad in August, and an additional five hundred cords from Thomas L. Shinholser of Macon in mid-September.[81] He arranged with his agent, William F. Smith in Atlanta to secure the round iron for shafting on September 17.[82] He also obtained twenty-five tons of Scotch pig iron from the Holly Springs Armory, part of which stayed in Macon and part of which went to the Richmond Armory to be manufactured into rifle barrels.[83] Burton asked Captain Michaeloffsky, Assistant Quartermaster in Macon, to furnish teams to haul 11,689 pounds of bar iron from the Southwestern Railroad Depot to the Armory.[84]

Burton's correspondence during this period is filled with requests for such items as 5,000 barrels of lime from W. C. Yonge, Superintendent of the Chewacla Lime Company's works at Yongesboro in Russell County, Alabama,[85] to asking for transportation of one hundred cases of gunstocks from the Central Railroad Depot to the Armory.[86] Yet, despite problems relating to the acquisition of building materials,[87] acquiring carts and running gears for a two-horse lumber wagon,[88] and wheelbarrows for excavating earth from the site of the new Armory,[89] Burton pushed ahead with his mission of producing gunstocks and gun barrels, personnel issues, renovating the temporary quarters for the Armory, installing machinery, and building the new Armory.

Although the Confederate Government needed 2,000 gunstocks a month from the Macon Armory, Burton's workforce could produce only 1,500. Even this smaller number was produced because the facility ran extra hours.[90] When the Government wanted stocks for the 1842 model musket Burton informed

---

[81] Burton to H.W. Bronson, Macon, 22 August 1862 and Burton to Thomas L. Shinholser, Macon, 15 September 1862, both in Ibid.

[82] Burton to William F. Smith, Macon, 17 September 1862, Ibid.

[83] Burton to Capt. Michaeloffsky, Macon, 19 September 1862; Burton to Gorgas, Macon, 20 September 1862, both Ibid. Plans called for the rough gunstocks to be finished and fitted with iron fittings in Macon. Of course, some of the pig iron would be used to repair machinery in the Macon Armory. He asked Gorgas on September 6, for seventy tons of pig iron from the Holly Springs Armory use at the Macon Armory. Burton to Gorgas, 6 September 1862, Ibid.

[84] Burton to Capt. Michaeloffsky, Macon, 15 September 1862, Ibid.

[85] Burton to Gorgas, Macon, 4 November 1862, Ibid.

[86] Burton to Capt. Michaeloffsky, Macon, 8 September 1862, Ibid.

[87] Burton to Wadley, Jones and Company, Macon, 1 November 1862, Ibid.

[88] Burton to White, Macon, 3 November 1862, Ibid.

[89] Burton to White, Macon, 10 November 1862, Ibid.

[90] Burton to Gorgas, Macon, 5 November 1862, Ibid.

Gorgas that, if he did this, he would necessarily have to reduce the number of stocks for the model 1855 musket. By 7 November he had orders to repair 2,000 stocks for the model 1855 musket. This was in addition to furnishing finished gunstocks for the Richmond Armory.[91] Possibly because of working overtime, the Armory was able to prepare seven hundred stocks ready for packing by November 15. Burton promised to send stocks to the Richmond Armory as soon as he had 1,000 ready. He assured the anxious Gorgas that his workforce could deliver this number by November 26.[92]

The Armory continued to make 1,500 gunstocks a month in early January 1863, but only because the machinery was run every night until 8:00 P.M. and occasionally on Saturdays.[93] Unfortunately, many of the gunstocks were defective because of the imperfect working of the machinery. Another problem was caused by the employment of inexperienced workmen to operate the machines. Since it was believed that most of the stocks could be made serviceable, Burton and Fuss decided to forward them to the Richmond Armory so that facility could supply the armies in the field. By 23 January 1863, the stock making machines were repaired and adjusted so as to ensure a more defect-free product.[94]

In Burton's report to Gorgas for January 1863 he stated the temporary buildings were completed, and all of the machinery was repaired, placed in good working order, and ready for use. The machine shop was full of good machinery which was propelled by four hundred feet of main line shafting and pulleys. The shop was large enough to employ one hundred and fifty machinists. The Smith's Shop was also completed, and a fan blast and a blast pipe of wood laid down. Eight cast iron forges of a new pattern developed at the Armory were erected and ready to use. The gunstock storehouse was built and in use. All of the frame buildings were whitewashed and presented "a neat appearance." The stock machinery was constantly at work, and regular monthly supplies of stocks were made and sent on to Richmond. By mid-January 1863, Burton planned to send a messenger with 1,008 stocks for rifles and muskets and 432 for carbines to Richmond. The mechanics were building machinery, a project which, Burton

---

[91] Burton to Gorgas, Macon, 7 November 1862, Ibid.

[92] Burton to Gorgas, Macon, 15 November 1862, Ibid.

[93] Burton to Gen. Benjamin Huger, Macon, 7 January 1863, Ibid., hereafter cited as Huger, 7 January 1863 Letter.

[94] Jeremiah Fuss to Burton, Macon, 23 January 1863, Box 3138 Vol. 30, Letters Sent, Master Armorer at the Armory, 1862-65, microfilm NARA. For more information about the problems of producing gunstocks see Burton to Gorgas, Macon, 18 November 1862, Letters Sent Armory, 1862-65.

assured Gorgas, "will be pushed forward as rapidly as the limited force at my command will permit."[95]

Work at the temporary Armory was affected by a fire which occurred in the morning of 12 February 1863.[96] This prompted Burton, some weeks later, to order Fuss to direct the foremen of the different departments to have their employees pick up on a daily basis the discarded waste material thrown about the shops during the manufacturing process and burn it. Fuss was also directed to have a down pipe and a large cock attached to the water tank, and rig up a way to open the cock. Burton also wanted several strong ladders of different lengths built so they would reach the top of the different buildings.[97] Fuss also ordered a guard placed at the Armory during the night.[98]

Burton was deeply concerned about the need to exempt mechanics and other personnel at the Government manufacturing establishments, as well as those contractors who provided materials for arms manufacture, from the terms of the Conscription Act. He wrote Gorgas on 4 September 1862, that "Without some provision it will be impossible for me to carry out satisfactorily the great work entrusted to me, and alike impossible for contractors for arms...to fulfill their contracts." He believed that it would be better to enroll all who might be liable to enrollment, and then exempt those people who were essential to Government operations, and of Government contractors "upon the certificate of some authorized agent or agents of the Govt., or of officers having charge of particular work supplied by contractors, and who would be familiar with the necessities and requirements in each case." This would have the effect of protecting the Government. The authorities should also make provisions for the detailing of mechanics already in the service upon the application of a contractor which was approved by some Government officer or agent. No provision should be made to provide for the hiring of substitutes by mechanics because very few could afford to pay the amount required to procure one. Furthermore, the interest of the Government would be promoted by exempting bondsmen of contractors who were actively engaged in the manufacture of articles contracted for, especially those establishments supported by the Government who manufactured small arms. This would include such firms as Spiller and Burr and McNeill and

---

[95] Burton to Gorgas, Macon, 10 January 1863, Ibid. Hereafter cited as Burton to Gorgas, 10 January 1863 Letter.

[96] Burton to Col. Magill, commanding First GA. Regiment, Macon, 12 February 1863, Letters Sent, Armory, 1862-65.

[97] Burton to Jeremiah Fuss, Macon, 10 March 1863, Ibid.; Jeremiah Fuss to Foremen of Departments, Macon, 10 March 1863, Letters Sent, Master Armorer, 1862-1865.

[98] Jeremiah Fuss to B.F. Perry, Macon, 20 March 1863, Letters Sent, Master Armorer, 1862-65.

Company. Burton told his chief that "I have no doubt but that this subject has been already duly considered by you, but I feel it to be my duty to give you my views upon it, as I am in a position here to observe the results attending the old law of conscription, as well as those of any new laws upon the subject."[99]

Over a month later, Burton announced plans to complete the organization of his official department. He needed someone to serve in the position of Master Armorer who would carry his orders and instructions into effect. Because the work of the Armory would, for some time, be confined to the erection of the new buildings and the construction of machinery, there was no immediate need to have a Master Armorer familiar with the manufacture of arms. Jeremiah Fuss occupied the position of Master Builder for the new Armory, but he was also familiar with the routine of business associated with public armories. Although Fuss received a salary of $1600 a year which was small enough in light of his ability and responsibilities, Burton believed he might be even more useful if he were assigned the duties of Master Armorer. He proposed to appoint Fuss "Acting Master Armorer," which would be a satisfactory arrangement for the present.[100] Fuss became Acting Master Armorer on 1 November. Under the new arrangement he continued to direct and superintend all building operations.[101]

In completing his complement of workers Burton placed an advertisement in the Augusta *Chronicle and Sentinel* and the *Richmond Dispatch* for fifty machinists and several pattern makers, offering as inducements constant employment and the highest current wages.[102]

Because of these efforts Burton could boast that he had 136 employees by 7 January 1863, including forty-five white mechanics, seven white apprentices, five white watchmen and laborers, twenty-three black mechanics and carpenters, and fifty-six black laborers. His managerial staff included himself as Superintendent; First Lieutenant Charles Selden, Jr., Paymaster and Military Storekeeper; Jeremiah Fuss, Acting Master Armorer; Augustus Schwaab, Architect and Engineer; and William Copeland, Master Machinist. His clerks were Henry C. Day, Clerk to the Superintendent, and Daniel E. Stipes, Clerk to the Master Armorer. His foremen included George W. Western, Stock Department; William H. Thornberry, Machine Shop; Oliver Porter, Foreman of Laborers; and B.F. Perry, Foreman of Carpenters.[103]

---

[99] Burton to Gorgas, Macon, 4 September 1862, Letters Sent, Armory, 1862-65.

[100] Burton to Gorgas, Macon, 13 October 1862, Ibid.

[101] Burton to Jeremiah Fuss, Macon, 24 October 1862, Ibid.

[102] Burton to W.S. Jones, Editor, Augusta *Chronicle and Sentinel*, Macon, 20 October 1862; and Burton to Editors of the *Richmond Dispatch*, Macon, 20 October 1862, both Ibid.

[103] Huger, 7 January 1863 Letter.

The employees were well paid. A master machinist made $5.00 a day; the Foreman of the Machine Shop earned $4.50; the Foreman of Stock Machinery was paid $4.00; the Foreman of Carpenters, $4.50; the Foreman of Laborers, $3.75; first class machinists, $4.00; blacksmiths, $4.00; pattern makers, $4.00; millwrights, $4.00; and carpenters, $3.00. All these rates became effective on 1 January 1863.[104]

Unfortunately, the operation of the Armory was hindered because of the great difficulty in obtaining enough competent machinists and blacksmiths. This problem affected the building of machinery needed to produce small arms. Burton could not overcome it because, although he had thirty-five machinists and blacksmiths, he had enough work to keep 170 busy. Secretary of War Seddon refused to grant details of men from the Army when the Confederacy was under pressure from Federal invasions on all sides. If Burton had enough skilled workers he could build the machinery in Macon. However, since he did not, he believed he would have to go to England to purchase it. Contracts might be made with contractors there, he believed, to build much of the necessary machinery. He also felt English sources would have to furnish the large steam engines required for propelling the machinery because there were no factories in the Confederacy which could build them except the Tredegar Iron Works in Richmond which was occupied with military contracts. Burton felt that the machinery for barrel rolling and welding would also have to be bought in England because it had never been made in the Confederacy. He felt that a competent person should be sent to England to enter into contracts for the needed machinery and to obtain glass, hardware, and other materials needed to build the new Armory because they were not available in the Confederacy. In the meantime, the Armory's machine shop could build hammers, power punches, and other items. Besides, Burton believed "The machinery constructed abroad can be run through the blockade with as much facility as other goods and with as little risk of loss; or it can remain in Europe until peace is declared when it will be at once available." Furthermore, the fabrication of the machinery in Europe would be taking place while the building of the new Armory proceeded. The construction of the new Armory would take at least a year, Burton thought, to complete.[105]

Burton had made every effort to obtain skilled workmen, including advertising, but with little success. He wrote General Benjamin Huger, Inspector of Ordnance, that "The demand for this class of labour so greatly exceeds the supply that it is in vain to expect to meet it, and to a great extent this class of mechanics dictate the wages they receive." One of the problems related to

---

[104] Burton to Gorgas, 2 February 1863, Letters Sent, Armory, 1862-65.

[105] Burton to Gorgas, 10 January 1863 Letter.

applications for an increase in wages by Armory employees. This made it imperative to go to England to procure the machinery.[106]

On 30 January Burton prepared a list of machinery which might be acquired in England.[107] Gorgas ordered Burton to estimate the amount of money he would need to deposit upon the contracts for machinery as well as the total sum needed and directed his subordinate to order only such machinery which could not be purchased in the Confederacy. He had to limit his expenditures abroad as much as possible based on a production schedule of 1,200 rifles a week.[108]

Burton noted that he had anticipated Gorgas' instructions in his 30 January letter which, he said, he based on a production schedule of 1,500 rifles per week. This, he explained, was the scale of manufacture stated in Gorgas' instructions. If Gorgas wanted him to revise his estimate on the basis of 1,200 rifles per week, he would do so. However, the reduction to 1,200 rifles a week would not reduce the estimate more than about $25,000. Burton had made as economical an estimate as possible, while keeping in mind the needs of the Armory. He did not see that it could be reduced without leaving out some important machinery, and explained the manner of contracts in England, saying contractors there "will require one third of the contract money to be paid down in advance, and will want to see the whole amount of the contract money secured in England, before they will begin the work." This was the general policy in cases where contracts were made with foreign governments, especially the Confederacy whose future, even as early as February, 1863, was in doubt simply because it had not been officially recognized by foreign powers. Burton wanted Gorgas to give him timely notice if he were selected to go abroad because he had many preparations to make so that the Armory would run smoothly during his absence.[109]

When Gorgas received Burton's letter of the 8th he replied that orders would be given to him as soon as money could be secured to pay the advance. Although the indebtedness of the Confederacy abroad was large, possibly cotton

---

[106] Burton to Huger, 7 January 1863 Letter.

[107] Burton, "List, & estimated cost of machinery for the C.S. Armory Macon, Ga. Proposed to be procured in England: based upon the production of 1500 rifles per week," Macon, 30 January 1863, Burton Papers. The list included two 100-- horsepower beam steam engines ($15,000 for the two); cast iron floor beams and girders, floor plates, stairs for the engine room ($3,500); six high pressure steam boilers, with pipes, connections, and fittings, ($9,000 for all of them); one small pumping engine and pump ($1,500); one large wrought iron tank to contain 30,000 gallons ($2,500); heavy first motion and intermediate shafts, with pedestals and boxes, six pairs of bevel wheels with wooden cogs, for distributing power and a case of iron columns for supporting them ($7,500 for all of this); and many other items. The total estimate for all of the items was $278,013.

[108] Gorgas to Burton, Richmond, 2 February 1863, Burton Papers.

[109] Burton to Gorgas, Macon, 8 February 1863, Ibid.

exports might finance the purchases. It might be beneficial to arrange the purchases through Fraser, Trenholm, and Company, an English firm which handled a number of Confederate transactions, so their extensive credit might be used.[110]

The anxious Burton had an ally in Lieutenant Colonel George W. Rains, commanding the Augusta Arsenal, who had discussed the need to purchase some of the Macon Armory machinery in England with President Davis who "seemed favorably impressed with the suggestion." Rains believed that, with Davis' support, "some action will be taken in the matter."[111]

Events quickly fell into place to expedite Burton's trip. By mid-February he received the authority to use the credit of Fraser, Trenholm, and Company to pay for the machinery.[112] By 21 February Gorgas told Burton that finances should not detain Burton, and Charleston would be the best point to embark.[113]

While plans for the trip materialized, work continued on the new Armory. By 10 January, Burton's workforce had built a good road along the line of the Macon and Western Railroad to divert vehicular traffic which had driven across the Armory grounds. This enabled Burton to enclose the area with a fence. The permanent granite corner stones were planted at the angles to the grounds. Unfortunately, although the work of grading the site had begun, a sufficient workforce could not be employed because of the scarcity of shovels and picks. Burton had entered into a contract for the stone work for the foundations of the Armory buildings and the blasting of the necessary stone had begun. He had also contracted for 5,000 barrels of the best quality lime. The framing of the two cottages on the Armory grounds had been started, and was well advanced. Construction of a siding from the Macon and Western Railroad into the grounds progressed. Burton was receiving proposals for bricks, but found people unwilling to contract for articles scheduled for delivery in the summer of 1863, except on terms which amounted almost to extortion. If he found, he told Gorgas, that he could obtain them in no other way he would have to make them himself. He had entered into a conditional contract to provide roofing slate on the condition that the Government would detail four men from the army whose services were needed by the contractor.[114]

During February, 1863, work continued on the foundations and to secure building materials. Burton contracted with the firm of Wood and Meador of

---

[110] Gorgas to Burton, Richmond, 12 February 1863, Ibid.

[111] Lt. Col. George W. Rains to Burton, Augusta, 12 February 1863, Ibid.

[112] Burton to Gorgas, Macon, 16 February 1863, Letters Sent, Armory, 1862-65.

[113] Gorgas to Burton, Richmond, 21 February 1863, Burton Papers.

[114] Burton to Gorgas, 10 January 1863 Letter. For Burton's efforts to secure exemptions for Welsh slate miners in the Confederate Army see Burton to Enrolling Officer, Selma, AL., Macon, 16 February 1863, Letters Sent Armory, 1862-65.

Stone Mountain, Georgia, for stone on 13 February.[115] Later in the month he sought a contract with Wadley, Jones and Company for framing timber needed for the roofs of the permanent buildings. If a contract was prepared he offered to pay half of the price in seven per cent Confederate bonds.[116]

As he prepared to go to England, Burton did not neglect other aspects of the work on the new Armory. He informed A. Powell, contractor for masonry, that a portion of the excavation for the foundation walls was completed, and he could begin laying masonry at once.[117] However, because Powell was unable to do the work, he contracted with Thomas Alexander. Burton wrote Gorgas, "I think Mr Alexander will push the work on with vigor as he has been accustomed to heavy work on railroads and is a man of means and resources far beyond those of Mr Powell." The contractor for bricks was beginning to make bricks by mid-March. As soon as the man was able to determine the maximum number he could make during the spring and summer of 1863, written contracts would be signed. Because slave-owners generally refused to hire their slaves for work in brick yards, the contractor planned to secure his workforce before he bound himself to produce a certain number. One of the reasons for this hesitation was Burton's wish to have four million bricks made during the coming season.[118]

During March and April, 1863, the final details were worked out for Burton's trip. It was decided that he should leave from Wilmington either aboard the *Cornubia* or the *Giraffe*. He informed Gorgas that he planned to visit Richmond during the middle of March to discuss the plans and elevations of the buildings for the new Armory, and discuss the entire matter with him. He also wanted to talk about shipping cotton to England and using the proceeds of the sale for the purchase of the Armory machinery. He needed large quantities of coal to operate the temporary Armory, and felt he could borrow no more from Cuyler who was nearly out himself. He was also giving out large contracts for lumber for the new buildings, and asked for Gorgas' help in securing rail transportation to bring the coal from Tennessee, and the lumber from points in Georgia. "In view of the important Govt. Works at this point," Burton wrote, "and of the trouble about transportation, I think some special effort should be made by the War Dept. to effect arrangements with the several Railroads leading into Macon for the prompt delivery of materials…necessary to these works."[119]

On 2 April, Gorgas formally directed Burton to go to England, and possibly to France, to buy and contract for the necessary machinery, tools, and other

---

[115] Burton to Wood and Meador, Macon, 13 February 1863, Letters Sent Armory, 1862-65.

[116] Burton to Wadley, Jones and Company, Macon, 17 February 1863, Ibid.

[117] Burton to A. Powell, Macon, 16 February 1863, Ibid.

[118] Burton to Gorgas, Macon, 14 March 1863, Ibid.

[119] Burton to Gorgas, Macon, 10 March 1863, Burton Papers.

materials needed for the new Armory. The necessary funds would be furnished by Major Caleb Huse, Confederate Agent in London, who received instructions to support Burton. Gorgas did not know whether the purchases or contracts should be made in the name of the Confederacy, or in the name of another party and ordered Burton to discuss the matter with James Murray Mason, Confederate Commissioner to England, and Huse. The Chief of Ordnance believed it would be best to operate through a resident of England and have the shipments made to Bermuda as his property. The ownership of the items could change in Nassau. When Burton made contracts he should keep in view that the machinery should be of good workmanship, and be delivered as quickly as possible. It might be best to ship the machinery in sets so the Armory could begin operations without waiting for the entire shipment to arrive. The bayonet-making and lock-making machinery should be sent forward quickly. Huse had received instructions to forward 20,000 Enfield rifles quickly, a number which might be increased to 50,000 if available on good terms. A supply of 20,000 Enfield ramrods should accompany the shipment. Burton was also instructed to use his judgment in selecting steel barrels, Marshall iron, and other materials for armories and arsenals. Huse had already received orders to purchase bullet machines, specification books, and standard instruments for measuring weights and dimensions.

Burton was also directed to buy specimens of the arms of the different European armies which might be copied in the Confederacy. Huse would pay for Burton's contracts, and would have the authority to approve them based upon available funds. Both Gorgas and Seddon had great confidence in Huse, and expected Burton to act in "full consultation" with him. Letters of introduction to Huse, John Slidell—Confederate Commissioner to France—and Mason were includes in Gorgas' letter. Gorgas told Burton that the War Department had great confidence in the latter's knowledge of the resources of England and France, and relied on his ability and energy in accomplishing his mission.[120]

Burton replied that he wanted a letter of credit with authority to draw up to $100,000. Later, he would need an additional $200,000 to pay the remaining two-thirds of the contracts for machinery. He recommended the purchase of a bullet-making machine such as those in use at England's Woolwich Arsenal. Woolwich also contained an excellent shot and shell foundry which had a number of machines for molding shot and shell using unskilled labor.

It seemed necessary to contact Major Norman S. Walker, Confederate Depository at Bermuda, with instructions to facilitate Burton's mission. Burton, for instance, needed commutation money for fuel and quarters at the rate

---

[120] Gorgas to Burton, Richmond, 2 April 1863, Ibid.

of $150 a month. He also wanted authority to buy 4,000 steel shapes for rifle barrels for the Fayetteville Armory.[121]

In April, final arrangements for Burton's trip proceeded smoothly. Secretary of War Seddon agreed to give him a commutation allowance of $150 per month. The Secretary presumed that Burton's trip would not last over three or four months, and noted "This high rate of commutation is allowed to you in consideration of the extraordinary expenses you will be subjected to in connexion with the duties to which you are assigned."[122] The significance of Burtons mission greatly increased when he was directed to purchase munitions for other ordnance facilities, including the ordnance works in Augusta.[123]

In preparation for his trip, Burton ordered Fuss to produce 2,000 gunstocks a month working 10 hours a day. If the stock-making machines broke he directed Fuss to call upon the master machinist to supervise the repairs.[124] He also told Fuss to supervise the laying of the stone foundations of the new Armory buildings. The able Master Armorer had to exercise vigilance to prevent fire and see that the guard was properly set each night.[125]

In early May final arrangements were made for the trip including the appointment of Cuyler as acting superintendent of the Armory on May 7.[126] Captain F. B. Du Barry of the Artillery was assigned as executive officer on May 27.[127]

Burton left Macon for Wilmington on the evening of 6 May, and sailed on the *Giraffe* on 13 May.[128] Arriving in London on June 10, he reported to Mason, and met with Huse on 11 June, because the latter was in Paris on the 10th. During his meetings with the two men he gave them copies of his instructions from Gorgas.[129]

---

[121] Burton to Gorgas, Macon, 13 April 1863, Ibid.

[122] Seddon to Burton, Richmond, 15 April 1863, Ibid. For additional details concerning the financial arrangements for Burton's trip see Capt. Thomas L. Bayne to Burton, Richmond, 25 April 1863; Gorgas to Maj. Norman S. Walker, Govt. Depository, St. Georges, Bermuda, Richmond, 25 April 1863; and Gorgas to Huse, Richmond, April, 1863, all Ibid.

[123] George W. Rains to Burton, 19 April 1863, Ibid.

[124] Burton to Fuss, Macon, 3 April 1863, Letters Sent Armory, 1862-65.

[125] Burton to Fuss, Macon, 8 April 1863, Ibid.

[126] Burton to Cuyler, Macon, 6 May 1863, Ibid.; Cuyler, Order, Macon, 7 May 1863, Chapter IV, Vol. 49, Order Book, Armories, 1862-1865, NARA, hereafter cited as Order Book, Armories, 1862-1865.

[127] Cuyler, Order no 13, Order Book, Armories, 1862-1865.

[128] Burton to Gorgas, Macon, 1 May 1863, Letters Sent Armory, 1862-65; Burton to Seixas, Macon, 5 May 1863, Ibid.; Vandiver, *Ploughshares into Swords*, 174.

[129] Vandiver, *Ploughshares into Swords*, 174.

During the summer of 1863, Burton visited James Davison, Mechanical Manager of the Royal Laboratory at the Royal Arsenal at Woolwich, and advanced 250 pounds sterling for machinery contracted for with the firm of Greenwood and Batley in Leeds. All of the plans and drawings were prepared for the special and most important machines, and instructions left with the contractors. Huse asked Burton to obtain information about the construction of laboratory machinery ordered by Mallet, and for the manufacture of machines for making gun carriages for the Macon Arsenal. Lists of machines and other apparatus used in Woolwich were made. Unfortunately, because Huse could not supply the money, the contracts were not completed. Burton left the papers and other information concerning the machinery with Huse, who promised to buy it when funds became available. The full set of machines needed to make powder barrels cost 1,260 pounds sterling. These powder-making machines were slated to go to Rains in Augusta. However, because of the lack of money, Burton could not buy building materials for the new Armory or for any other ordnance establishment. Huse couldn't even furnish 2,800 pounds for window glass and sheet copper, although Burton did arrange with Fraser, Trenholm, and Company to ship what machinery he bought to Bermuda. He told Major Walker how to receive and store the machinery, and received plans and drawings for a new system of iron plating for ships and shore batteries invented by Charles Lancaster, inventor of the Lancaster Gun who gave Burton a report on experiments made with a nine-pounder field gun which was rifled on the principal of an oval bore, with a picture of the gun mounted.

Burton sent Gorgas a series of blue books on ordnance printed under orders of the British House of Commons, and purchased, with his own money, a three-volume set of a recent edition of the *Aide Memoire to the Military Sciences*, and a relatively new book entitled *Col. Anderson on the Manufacture of Gunpowder*. He bought a pamphlet called *The Nature of the Action of Fixed Gunpowder*, and visited the Government Powder Mills at Waltham Abby upon the invitation of the Superintendent, Colonel Askwith of the Royal Army, who allowed him to view all parts of the works. Askwith generously spent half a day with Burton and explained the entire manufacturing process to him. Askwith even gave him samples of various woods and charcoal used in the manufacturing process, and asked for a general ground plan of the new Armory with the arrangement of the buildings and manufacturing processes.

Invited to visit the Royal Small Arms Factory at Enfield as the guest of Superintendent Colonel W.M. Dixon, Burton saw that preparations were being made there to manufacture 8,000 Whitworth rifles of a hexagonal bore of the barrel with plans to test this principle in the field. However, although the English were willing to sell him samples of the various weapons, he could not purchase them due to lack of funds. He observed the work of the gun makers of Birmingham who admitted the superiority of the system of manufacturing small arms in quantity using machinery. They had formed a joint stock company and planned to construct military rifles using that system. When he visited Birmingham he found the military gun trade sluggish because the United States was not then purchasing British rifles. Burton concluded his official report to Gorgas by acknowledging the kind reception he universally enjoyed and expressed pleasure for "the desire manifested by manufacturers & others to serve the Confederate Government, in their respective specialties." His only regret was that he could not purchase the materials needed because of the lack of funds.[130]

Huse, who strongly supported Burton's mission, finally arranged with Fraser, Trenholm and Company on 28 July 1863 to supply many of Burton's requirements. Greenwood and Batley agreed to provide certain items for building rifle-muskets. In return, they would receive 54,400 pounds or $272,000 from Fraser, Trenholm and Company. Pleased by the speed in which the negotiations were concluded, Burton urged that cotton be sent from the Confederacy to repay the British firm for their quick attention.[131]

Burton sailed from Liverpool for Wilmington on 5 September 1863.[132] However, he did not return to Macon until 14 October.[133] He told Gorgas he would have reported in person at Richmond, but his health was impaired. He resumed his duties on 16 October.[134]

During Burton's absence work continued on the new Armory. Cuyler arranged for the manufacture of 30,000 bricks, and was making efforts to get more from Eufaula, Alabama. The carpenters were doing well, but the stone masons' work proceeded very slowly. Cuyler promised Burton, in a letter of 18 May that "I have much to do but will do all I can to push your work ahead."[135]

Although efforts were made to raise the wages at both the Arsenal and the Armory during the spring,[136] nothing had been done by mid-August. By August the men at both the Arsenal and the Armory were "resorting to every conceivable means of getting away in consequence of the low wages." Cuyler

---

[130] Burton to Gorgas, Macon, 30 October 1863, Letters Sent, Armory, 1862-65. For a detailed list of the prices of material and the machinery Burton bought from Greenwood and Batley see Greenwood and Batley to Burton, "Prices of laboratory machinery (partial list), Albion Foundry, Leeds, England, 10 July 1863, Burton Papers. For additional material on Burton's trip see Burton to Gorgas, Macon, 6 November 1863, and Burton to Col. L.S. Rhett, Macon, 7 November 1863, both Ibid.

[131] For a detailed account of the financial efforts made by Huse see Vandiver, *Ploughshares into Swords*, pp. 175-176.

[132] Ibid., p. 176.

[133] Burton to Gorgas, Macon, 16 October 1863, Letters Sent, Armory, 1862-65.

[134] Cuyler, Order No. 22, Macon, 16 October 1863, Order Book, Armories, 1862-1865.

[135] Cuyler to Burton, Macon, 18 May 1863, Letters Sent, Armory, 1862-65.

[136] Capt. F.B. DuBarry to Fuss, Macon, 29 May 1863, Ibid.

took the position that no one would be allowed to leave unless he had orders to do so. Desertion was prevented only by threats of punishment.[137]

DuBarry did allow the members of the Armory Company to drill from 5:00 until 6:00 o'clock every evening. However, if anyone left his work to drill and failed to appear the foreman of his shop was ordered to dock his pay for the absence.[138]

Some idea of the work done at the Armory during the summer might be formed by Cuyler's estimate of funds needed during the period. The request for wages for arms manufacture was $9,000; materials for the same purpose, $1,500; The erection of new buildings involved $39,000 for wages, and $10,000 for materials. The building of new machinery included wages of $19,000 and materials for $10,000. The total amounted to $178,500. This included $9,000 due from the Confederacy for the previous quarter. Broken down by month, the sums were: July- $69,500; August- $50,000; and September- $50,000.[139]

Not long after he returned, Burton reported the building of the new Armory facilities had slowed during his absence. The main building was only completed for half its length to the top of the first story, and was ready to receive the joists and girders for the second floor. Burton was pushing his workforce to lay them as soon as possible. The workmen had begun to lay the brick on the other half of the building, and were progressing as quickly as the limited number of bricklayers permitted. The main problem, though, was that the bricks had not been delivered in time to lay them in the early summer as planned. The problem was reversed now because the bricks were being delivered rapidly, but there were only thirteen bricklayers available to lay them. Burton needed three times that number to push the work forward. The carpentry work was moving forward more quickly. All the window frames were completed, much of the framing was done for the floors, and the sash and doors would be ready in the fall and winter. The stone foundations were being laid with the entire foundation walls of the main building completed, and progress made in laying the foundation walls of the rear range of buildings. However, the building of these structures had to wait until 1864, although a great deal of grading and filling was done around the buildings and at other places on the premises.

The lumber contractors had generally completed their contracts, and there was no delay resulting from this cause. The slate contractor was behind in his deliveries, but Burton believed he had done his best considering the limited number of slate cutters he had. Although the Government helped him by detailing several miners of Welsh extraction, the delivering of the slate was slowed because cars were unavailable to carry it due to the great demand for

---

[137] Cuyler to Gorgas, Macon, 17 August 1863, Ibid.
[138] Dubarry, Order No. 15, Macon, 15 June 1863, Order Book, Armories, 1862-65.
[139] Cuyler to Gorgas, Macon, 30 June 1863, Letters Sent Armory, 1862-65.

transportation by the quartermasters and other stores for Bragg's Army. The difficulty would remain because by this time Bragg had been virtually pushed out of Tennessee and was drawing most of his supplies from Middle and Southwest Georgia.

The woodworking machinery, which was driven by a fifteen-horsepower steam engine, bought for the purpose, was installed in a building at the new Armory. The black mechanics and laborers employed at the Armory had done their jobs well, but it looked like they couldn't be hired for the following year. The possibility arose that Burton might have to hire them by the month or year after 1 January 1864. That meant they would have to be furnished with food and housing. A frame house of eight rooms for Master Machinist Hiram Herrington and his family was begun. But Burton could not finish the all-important main building before the Spring of 1864, because materials (glass, sheet copper, hardware, slating nails, etc.) were unavailable. He could not buy these items in England as he had hoped because Caleb Huse had no money to buy them.

The building of machinery was slow due to the small number of machinists available, and also because some of the men had been manufacturing shells for cannon needed to defend Charleston. Four machines for making the first boring of barrels were finished; six machines for the first boring of barrels were partly completed; six machines for the second boring were partly finished; three geared punching presses were completed; and a cast iron trough for a small grindstone was ready for operation. Because of the high salaries paid to machinists in the skilled-labor-deprived Confederacy, Burton believed that the machines should be manufactured in England as the cheapest way to get them. For example, the machines necessary to make gunstocks were made in England. Machinery, in short, could be assembled in England at a lower cost than in the South. Although Burton felt the manufacturing facilities available in Macon should produce tools and fixtures, he believed it was too difficult and expensive to make complicated machinery in the Confederacy. The manufacture of machinery was so slow in the South, Burton believed, because of the "present unfortunate condition of the whole country and hence it is almost vain to strive against it. We can only do the best we can [in] the fact of the difficulties and rest content with the result." Wages were high in Macon, but the cost of living continued to rise. This made it necessary to also increase wages. One of the ways to get around the inflation that raged in the city at this time was to permit workmen to buy food at the commissary at Government prices. Burton had been told that it was practiced at some of the Arsenals, and asked Gorgas to consider applying the same system to the Macon Armory.[140] Gorgas agreed and approved the

---

[140] Burton to Gorgas, Macon, 23 October 1863, Ibid.

opening of a provision store at the Arsenal for the sale at cost prices, of provisions for the employees of the several Government facilities in Macon.[141]

During the remainder of 1863 and early 1864, Burton continued to push construction of the new Armory. He tried to supply more bricks by leasing land on which to build a brickyard from the firm of S. M. and B. M. Tufts of Macon,[142] and ordered Fuss to build eight brick-making machines, like those used in the brickyard operated by Mallet at the Laboratory, for use in his brickyard.[143] Burton pursued his plans to lease land from the Tufts throughout January and February 1864. On 27 February he notified Gorgas that he needed a seventeen-acre lot for brickyard purposes adjoining a lot purchased by Mallet for the same purpose. The rent for the property was $150 a year, which Burton considered reasonable. Unfortunately, he felt that the lot operated by Mallet was not large enough to make bricks for both the Armory and the Laboratory.[144]

Burton also initiated plans to buy hogs to feed his workforce.[145] When Isaac Scott told him that C.L. Varner of Cuthbert, Georgia, could furnish him with a large number of hogs at $75 per hundred pounds, he wrote Varner that he would buy 150 good-sized pork hogs, averaging 175 pounds, to make bacon.[146] Anticipating the delivery of the hogs by early January, he directed Fuss to build a suitable pen near the stable on the Armory grounds for them, and also to smoke the meat when ready. The pen had to have troughs for feeding corn to the hogs, with a brick smoke-house nearby, sufficiently large to meet the needs of all three ordnance facilities.[147] When the hogs were not immediately sent, he wrote Varner again, this time expressing a willingness to pay eighty-five cents a pound.[148] Although he made a contract with Varner to supply hogs, he became angry when the latter had filled contracts he had made with Cuyler and Mallet, but had only sent two-thirds of the hogs he had ordered by mid-February. He sent a purchasing agent, John Allen, to Cuthbert to secure the rest;[149] and told Varner that his actions in regard to the Armory were "highly improper...and a breach of contract.[150]

---

[141] Burton, Order No. 25, Macon, December 1863, Order Book, Armories, 1862-65.

[142] Burton to S.M. and B.M. Tufts, Macon, 7 December 1863, Letters Sent, Armory, 1862-65.

[143] Burton to Fuss, Macon, 30 December 1863, Ibid.

[144] Burton to Gorgas, Macon, 27 February 1864, Ibid. See also Burton to S.M. Tufts, Macon, 14 January 1864, Ibid.

[145] Burton to Gorgas, Macon, 4 December 1863, Ibid.

[146] Burton to C.L. Varner, Macon, 23 December 1863, Ibid.

[147] Burton to Fuss, Macon, 28 December 1863, Ibid.

[148] Burton to C.L. Varner, Macon, 2 January 1864, Ibid.

[149] Burton to John Allen, Macon, 13 February 1864, Ibid.

[150] Burton to Varner, Macon, 13 February 1864, Ibid.

In January, 1864, Burton supervised the moving of the machinery, fixtures, and tools of Spiller and Burr's Pistol Factory from Atlanta.[151] Since the pistol-manufacturing firm needed steel for pistol barrels, he asked Gorgas for authority to buy steel from the firm of Thomas Firth and Sons at the Norfolk Works in Sheffield, England.[152]

In an effort to solve his labor problems, at least as far as unskilled labor was concerned, he wrote Editor Joseph Clisby to place an advertisement in the *Daily Telegraph* for 150 Blacks, most of them "Strong able bodied men," with a few women to serve as cooks and washers, promising to pay them "liberal wages," along with subsistence, clothing, and shoes. Slave owners whose slaves were employed at the Armory should give early notice of their plans to rehire them or remove them at the end of the year.[153]

During March and April 1864, the scarcity of black laborers continued to plague Armory operations. Burton was ready to impress as many as 80 black workers by 10 March at salaries of $10 a month plus food and clothing. However, slave owners refused to hire their slaves under those terms.[154] Two weeks later, Burton advertised for 100 able-bodied men at the rate of $25 per month with rations, clothing, shoes, medical attention, and good quarters provided. He urged Slave owners to hire their men, and warned that "Negroes can be impressed–for $11.00 per month with rations and clothing."[155] Even the threat of impressment seemed to have no effect, forcing Burton to confide to Gorgas that "Impressment will have to be resorted to in procuring negro labor." He and Mallet were cooperating in the matter since the latter officer had the same problems connected with his efforts to complete the Laboratory.[156] Through their joint efforts, Mallet was able to hire eighteen laborers, but Burton only obtained one. The two officers bluntly informed Gorgas that "Work of erecting bldgs. in progress must stop unless labor provided for making brick. Armory needs 125 men, laboratory needs 150 men, need to impress blacks asap [as soon as possible]."[157]

The scarcity of black laborers persisted, however. As late at 16 June 1864, Burton wrote General Sam Jones, commanding the Department of South

---

[151] Burton to Hiram Herrington, Master Machinist, Macon, 6 January 1864, Ibid.

[152] Burton to Gorgas, Macon, 6 January 1864, Ibid. By mid-February he expected three tons of steel for pistol barrels and cylinders from Bermuda. Burton to Gorgas, Macon, 12 February 1864, Ibid.

[153] Burton to Clisby, Macon, 7 December 1863, Ibid.

[154] Burton to Gorgas, Macon, 10 March 1864, Ibid.

[155] Burton to Joseph Clisby, Macon, 23 March 1864, Ibid.; *Daily Telegraph,* 5 April 1864.

[156] Burton to Gorgas, Macon, 2 April 1864, Ibid.

[157] Burton and Mallet to Gorgas, Macon, 12 April 1864, Ibid.

Carolina, Georgia, and Florida with headquarters in Charleston, that he needed 120 strong laborers to make bricks.[158] In an effort to solve the problem, Gorgas issued Special Order No. 51 giving Mallet and Burton authority to impress black laborers. Burton wrote Gorgas asking him to use his influence to procure laborers from Jones. "In the meantime," Burton explained, "the best part of the season for brickmaking is passing away and I am without the necessary labor to take advantage of it." Through much effort he had collected a force of brick masons, but because the making of bricks was delayed, he had to reduce the number of masons, and even to suspend the work on the buildings indefinitely.[159]

In order to care for the Blacks, Burton urged the procurement of an Army surgeon and assistant surgeon attached to the military hospitals in Macon. These individuals could care for laborers at all three of the ordnance facilities. Because brick making in hot and humid Middle Georgia was considered unhealthy work during the summer it was imperative to procure doctors quickly.[160]

Another difficulty connected with hiring laborers involved the matter of feeding them. Burton experienced problems in buying meal and rice for rations because meal was $10 a bushel and rice was even more expensive at thirty-five cents per pound. The Commissary Department refused to supply these items, or any other provisions for black laborers, because they were busy making arrangements to supply troops in the field. Although Cuyler's farm, which he used to supply rations to his employees at the Arsenal, could furnish some rations, Burton asked Gorgas to obtain food for Blacks who worked in all of Macon's ordnance establishments. Possibly the officer in charge of the tax in kind in Macon might help with the problem.[161]

With the beginning of 1864, Burton was forced to procure raw material and equipment, both increasingly scarce in the weakening Confederacy, to run the Armory. When Master Machinist Herrington found a fire engine, he offered to pay $5,000 for it.[162] He directed Fuss, on 1 February to organize a company of employees to man the new engine, promising to help him find the men.[163] By late March, Burton had enough men to fight fires, but it was not until December 1864, that the Armory Fire Company was entirely prepared for operations. A complete fire apparatus including a suction engine, hose reel, and 200 feet of leather hose, together with fire axes and torches, was purchased. Burton reported

---

[158] Burton to Gen. Sam Jones, Macon, 16 June 1864, Ibid.
[159] Burton to Gorgas, Macon, 24 June 1864, Ibid.
[160] Burton to Gorgas, Macon, 20 April 1864, Ibid.
[161] Burton to Gorgas, Macon, 19 April 1864, Ibid.
[162] Burton to Hiram Herrington, Macon, 11 January 1864, Ibid.
[163] Burton to Fuss, Macon, 1 February 1864, Ibid.

that fire buckets were always kept filled with water at several places in the workshops. Moreover, a large water tank, framed of wood, was sunk in the center of the quadrangle formed by the buildings at the temporary works. This tank was arranged to receive surface water from the roofs and the grounds around the buildings. The tank contained 22,000 gallons of water, and was usually full. Designed to last for three or four years, the structure was covered with a strong floor in the middle of which was a trapdoor through which the suction pipe could be inserted to draw water. Burton ordered the night watchman to visit and pass through the workshops once an hour throughout the night. In case he gave the alarm plans called for the Fire Company to quickly muster at the Armory.[164]

The problem of procuring raw materials occupied much of Burton's time in the early months of the new year. Although he placed an advertisement in the *Daily Telegraph* for black walnut lumber to make gunstocks,[165] by mid-January, he had only 2,500 gunstocks in store, and found it impossible to obtain walnut lumber to make more. There were a number of reasons for the shortage. During a trip for the purpose to North Georgia Burton found no one willing to undertake a contract, "chiefly in consequence," he wrote Gorgas, "of the proximity of the enemy." No one, of course, wanted Confederate money. Few mechanics of all kinds could be found in the manpower-starved Confederacy, because these individuals had been called into the field. Most of the walnut timber, even in North Georgia was scattered and therefore hard to find.[166] In desperation, Burton sent an agent, C.R. Christian to Monroe, Pike, Upson, and other Georgia counties to arrange with the proprietors of saw mills and the owners of walnut trees to supply the Armory with black walnut plank for gunstocks. The plank must be cut from butt cuts, not over twenty feet long, free of knots, 2 3/8 inches thick, and square-edged.[167]

Another problem arose when the firm of Wood, Meador and Company, under Government contract to provide dressed stone for both the Armory and the Laboratory, needed transportation for four or five hundred bushels of corn to supply food for the horses and mules who hauled the stone at the firm's Stone Mountain facility. Burton issued a certificate asking quartermasters to furnish the necessary transportation.[168]

Burton also kept trying to obtain glass and hardware in England, as well as sheet copper for roofing the new Armory's main building.[169] He was worried that

---

[164] Burton to Gorgas, Macon, 22 March, 28 December 1864, Ibid.

[165] Burton to Clisby, Macon, 11 January 1864, Ibid.; *Daily Telegraph*, 12 January 1864.

[166] Burton to Gorgas, Macon, 16 January 1864, Letters Sent, Armory, 1862-65.

[167] Burton to C.R. Christian, Macon, 9 February 1864, Ibid.

[168] Burton, Certification, Macon, 25 January 1864, Ibid.

[169] Burton to Gorgas, Macon, 4 January 1864, Ibid.

he had not heard from Huse about the purchase of building materials in England, especially glass and copper. The cost of the materials, which he needed "without further delay," was 2,800 pounds sterling.[170]

Throughout it all, Burton continued to push the construction of the new Armory. On 29 December 1863, he wrote Mayor Stephen Collins and the City Council asking for permission to buy parts of Blocks 50 and 52, next to Block 49, to build a siding branching from the main line of the Macon and Western Railroad at a point where the tracks crossed Ash Street. The proposed siding would cross through Block 50, cross Calhoun Street, and pass into the new Armory grounds.[171] The Council agreed to sell the land, amounting to 5.25 acres, for $2,000 an acre, the same price paid for Block 49. Whereupon, Burton asked Gorgas for authority to buy the property. Although it was necessary to build switches, and excavate a great deal of ground, Burton planned to use the earth to fill in the Armory Grounds.[172] Burton also wanted to build a strong platform opposite the Armory buildings on the line of the Macon and Western Railroad to unload heavy stones for coping.[173] To this end, he wrote Isaac Scott, President of the Macon and Western, about the siding and asked him to furnish rails for it.[174]

Much work on the new Armory had been done by the end of January. The front wall of the main building was carried up to the second story, and the walls of the east half carried up to the first story. Eight hundred and eleven perches of stone masonry were laid in the foundation walls of other buildings. Eight frame houses for black quarters, each 40' by 20', were built and the overseer's frame dwelling house was completed. A frame smoke house was finished, and a million bricks hauled to the Armory grounds. The Spiller and Burr pistol machinery, tools, fixtures, and materials were removed to Macon, and initial steps taken to erect the machinery. Eleven hundred stocks for rifle muskets were produced and another 1,584 were sent to the Richmond Armory. Work progressed on a number of machines including two upright jig saws for sawing gunstocks, two machines for buff-griding bayonets, and two machines for the second boring of rifle barrels, all of which were nearly finished, Four machines for the second boring of rifle barrels were completed. A machine for making tubes for friction primers was completed and turned over to the Arsenal. One set

---

[170] Burton to Gorgas, Macon, 4 January 1864, Ibid.
[171] Burton to Mayor Stephen Collins and the City Council, Macon, 29 December 1863, Ibid.; Council Minutes, 29 December 1863, Book E, p. 46.
[172] Burton to Gorgas, Macon, 19 March 1864, Letters Sent Armory, 1862-65.
[173] Burton to Augustus Schwaab, Architect, Macon, 11 March 1864, Ibid.
[174] Burton to Isaac Scott, Macon, 23 March 1864.

of patterns for castings for the brass furnace were finished and a set of patterns for castings for the furnace for heating gun barrels were almost done.[175]

In early February the entire workforce was employed on the main building.[176] Later in the month, 120 workmen were working on the roofs, and Burton was adding to this force almost daily.[177]

In an effort to speed up brick making, Burton ordered each laborer in the brick yard to dig twenty cubic yards of clay per day. When they had dug this amount they were allowed to dig as much as five additional cubic yards a day. However, Burton commented, "Justice to owners requires that the negroes should not be permitted to overwork themselves for the purpose of pecuniary gain."[178]

One of Burton's biggest problems in the spring of 1864, was the difficulty of getting the items he had purchased in England to the Armory. Burton wanted to run the Blockade to bring in the machinery, especially the shafting and driving gear, when Greenwood and Batley were ready to send it, but wanted the heavy machinery to remain in Bermuda because his main building was not ready for it.[179] When three sets of barrel-welding machinery and part of the heavy lines of shafting and fixings arrived in Bermuda in early April, Burton decided there was no place to install the barrel-welding machinery, but he could use the shafting.[180] Although Gorgas wanted the material brought in as soon as possible, none of the first class blockade runners had enough capacity to carry such large amounts of heavy machinery.[181] Besides, no available space was left at the temporary facilities for additional machinery, and none of the permanent buildings were covered to protect the machinery from the elements. Although Gorgas wanted to send additional workmen to Macon to work on the buildings, Burton wrote that it was hard to find housing because Macon was full of refugees. The McNeill Carbine Factory should be moved to Athens into the Cook and Brothers Armory because there would be more room in the Northeast Georgia city to house workmen and their families.[182]

---

[175] Burton to Gorgas, Macon, 1 March 1864, Letters Sent, Armory, 1862-65.

[176] Burton to Gorgas, 3 February 1864, Ibid.

[177] Burton to Maj. E. Taliaferro, Macon, 18 February 1864, Ibid.

[178] Burton to Jeremiah Fuss, Macon, 18 May 1864, Ibid. The laborers received twenty cents a yard for the five additional yards they might dig. It was symptomatic of the time that the black laborers, although badly needed to augment the Confederacy's labor force, were still slaves.

[179] Burton to Gorgas, Macon, 27 February 1864, Ibid.

[180] Burton to Gorgas, Macon, 11 April 1864, Ibid.

[181] N.J. Walker to Burton, St. Georges, Bermuda, 18 April 1864, Burton Papers.

[182] Burton to Gorgas, Macon, 19 April 1864, Letters Sent Armory, 1862-65. For additional information on the scarcity of housing for ordnance workers see Burton to

By 27 May some of the machinery had arrived in Bermuda on the steamers *Queen of Britain* and *Princess Royal*, but the problem of carrying such heavy machinery in blockade runners remained. Major Norman Walker presented another problem [as if Burton did not have enough] when he noted that the climate in Bermuda was so damp that all iron would rust even if it was covered, although much of the machinery was protected to some extent when Walker had it painted with red paint.[183] Burton told Gorgas that the Ordnance Bureau had to "choose between the possibility of injury from rust by leaving the machinery for the present in Bermuda–or the possibility of loss in running the blockade." Even in June, he was hoping to defer the latter danger as long as possible because his buildings were still not ready to receive the machinery. Burton felt it might be preferable to let the machinery remain in England because there could be no advantage in shipping it to Bermuda or Nassau unless it were then shipped to the Confederacy.[184]

He was willing to grant an extension from October to December 1864, to Greenwood and Batley for completing the contract because he feared the machinery would be finished before the building could be ready to receive it. To illustrate his point, Burton wrote Gorgas on 8 June 1864, that "I am meeting with obstacles on all sides in this connection,- want of labor to make bricks-want of RR [railroad] transportation for stone from Stone Mountain,- the supply of roofing slate cut off by the enemy; want of funds with which to purchase additional mules &c&c." Despite these seemingly insurmountable obstacles, he told the Chief of Ordnance he was doing the very best he could under the circumstances. Another problem arose because Huse had not found funds to order the vital machinery for making gunstocks. Burton deeply regretted this because the lost time could not be recovered. Possibly some cotton could be shipped to Fraser, Trenholm and Company to make the payments on the machinery. The amount needed was 9,500 pounds, one-third of which was required immediately, with the balance due when the machinery was completed. The same procedure could be followed in reference to the machinery for Colonel Mallet, and also for Colonel Rains. Possibly, the seemingly-unsuccessful Caleb Huse could be bypassed, and the Macon ordnance officers could deal with Greenwood and Batley directly.[185] Gorgas replied that the contract had been examined, but no contract could be prepared which required the Government to furnish funds abroad within any limited period. Burton's stores would have been ordered long before, except that the Confederacy simply had no money. Replying for Gorgas,

---

Capt. C.P. Bolles, Macon, 9 June 1864; and Burton to Bolles, Telegram, Macon, 10 June 1864, both Ibid.

[183] Walker to Burton, St. Georges, Bermuda, 27 May 1864, Burton Papers.

[184] Burton to Gorgas, Macon, 8 June 1864, Letters Sent, Armory, 1862-65.

[185] Burton to Gorgas, Macon, 8 June 1864, 2nd letter, Ibid.

Major Edwin Smith, wrote, "The only form of contract we can now entertain must look to payment in cotton at Mobile, at (probably) about ten pence per pound."[186]

Huse wrote Burton on 11 June that part of the machinery ordered was underway, including that for Mallet and Rains. The glass and other items for the new buildings were also being prepared for shipment, and would be shipped within ten days.[187] Plans called for the shipment of the machinery in the *Queen of Britain* and the *Princess Royal*. The entire shipment could not be shipped in one vessel because it weighed fifty-nine tons. Burton wanted Major Walker to send him a list of the machinery shipped in each vessel. When he received this information he could decide what parts could be duplicated in case some of the shipment was lost.[188]

Because some of the needed machinery was not ready, Burton authorized his agent in England, Fraser, Trenholm and Company, to extend the time in the contract with Greenwood and Batley to 1 January 1865, provided Gorgas consented to the new timetable.[189]

Burton's appointment to "the general inspection of all the Armories in the Confederate States" in early June added to his already heavy duties. He asked Gorgas for definite instructions with reference to his responsibilities and wanted to know the list of Armories included in the orders.[190]

In June 1864, as Sherman pressed the Confederate lines at Kennesaw Mountain near Marietta, the war was brought much closer to home. When Colonel D. Wyatt Aiken, commanding the Post of Macon ordered a fifth of the black laborers at the Armory to report to the Post Quartermaster at 8:00 A.M. on 24 June, for shipment to Atlanta to work on that city's defenses, Burton wrote Aiken saying such a move would violate agreements he had with the owners of the Blacks. He wanted Aiken to make his request in the form of a peremptory

---

[186] Maj. Edwin Smith to Burton, Richmond, 18 June 1864, Burton Papers.

[187] Caleb Huse to Burton, London, 11 June 1864, Burton Papers.

[188] Burton to Maj. N.S. Walker, Macon, 28 June 1864, Letters Sent Armory, 1862-65. Running a Federal Blockade which was extremely effective by mid-1864 was uncertain at best.

[189] Burton to Fraser, Trenholm and Company, Macon, 27 June 1864, Ibid. For additional information concerning problems during the summer of 1864, relating to the machinery ordered from Greenwood and Batley see Burton to Caleb Huse, Macon, 13 July 1864; Burton to Fraser, Trenholm and Company, Macon, 13 July 1864; Burton to Maj. Norman S. Walker, Macon, 13 July 1864; Burton to Gorgas, Macon, 15 July 1864; Burton to Gorgas, Macon, 18 July 1864; and Burton to Greenwood and Batley, Macon, 19 July 1864, all in Ibid.

[190] Burton to Gorgas, Macon, 9 June 1864, Ibid. For a list of Ordnance facilities through the Confederacy see Burton to Capt. C.P. Bolles, Macon, 13 July 1864, Ibid. Bolles commanded the C.S. Armory in Tallassee, Alabama.

order, a move which would relieve Burton of any responsibility in the matter. Burton's feeling was that General Joseph E. Johnston, who needed laborers, did not mean for them to come from the Government facilities. In fact, Burton had just received a number of Blacks from Atlanta whom he had hired through a written agreement from the Bartow Iron Works, and who were impressed the day before. The men were afterwards released when the facts became known to the impressing officer. Burton had seventy-five Blacks employed under annual contracts, and twenty-five who worked by the day, and did not want to give any of them up.[191]

On 30 June Burton appealed directly to Joe Johnston asking for the release of the Blacks.[192] But, despite Burton's efforts, Aiken removed twenty-three Blacks, laborers and mechanics, from the Armory. These men were sent to Atlanta on 1 July, a move which seriously disrupted the work. About ten days earlier Aiken had received orders to impress the slaves of private citizens to be sent to the front, a move which caused so much dissatisfaction among Macon slaveholders that many remonstrated with Aiken. Several angry letters were even published in the newspapers. The people bitterly complained because the Blacks employed at the Government establishments were excluded from the order. Burton wrote Gorgas, "The citizens of Macon have enjoyed comparative immunity from the evils and privations of the present war with the U. States, and I could not but regard the opposition manifested by some of them to the simple matter of sending their negroes to the front for a short time, to work on the fortifications, as being not only unpatriotic but exhibiting a feeling which should not only not be encouraged, but, on the contrary should be discouraged in every proper manner." Burton wanted to know if Aiken had exceeded his authority in impressing the Blacks.[193]

The laborers were returned on 4 July after Burton telegraphed Wright, now a brigadier general commanding the Post of Atlanta, stating his operations would be "greatly embarrassed in consequence" of the seizure.[194]

Black laborers were not the only ones conscripted in July. Colonel George C. Gibbs, the new Commandant of the Macon Post, ordered "All detailed men in Macon or vicinity who are capable of duty even in Garrison are hereby ordered to report immediately to Major Michaeloffsky Qr Master for transportation to Atlanta. Exception is made only in case of Hospital attendants who may be unfit for duty." If the ordnance works were suspended, the needs of the case should serve as an excuse. Burton ordered all detailed men who worked at the Armory,

[191] Burton to Col. D. Wyatt Aiken, Macon, 23 June 1864, Ibid.

[192] Burton to Gen. Joseph E. Johnston, Telegram, Macon, 30 June 1864, Ibid.

[193] Burton to Gorgas, Macon, 1 July 1864, Ibid.

[194] Burton to Brig. Gen. Marcus J. Wright, Telegram, Macon, 2 July 1864, Ibid; Burton to Gorgas, Macon, 4 July 1864, Ibid.

or by contractors with the Armory, who could serve on garrison duty to report on 23 July for transportation to Atlanta, and recommended that the organization of Company A, Armory Guards, enrolled to help defend Macon, should be preserved, and that the members of the unit go to Atlanta in a body and offer their services as an organized company.[195] Under this order Burton sent twenty-six men to Atlanta on July 23.[196] Burton was able to secure the exemption of six brick masons he sent to help Mallet work on the laboratory.[197] He also sent a total of twenty-seven carpenters to work on the new laboratory buildings on the same date.[198]

The men sent to Atlanta were men who worked on the new Armory buildings. The remainder of the workforce, especially armorers and machinists, were employed in the repair of arms.[199] Burton was not as fortunate in another matter involving the detail of some of his employees. Lieutenant M.B. Grant of the Engineer Department at Macon, wanted Augustus Schwaab, Civil Engineer and Architect for the new Armory, to help locate the proposed defenses around Macon. Burton sent Schwaab to perform this duty, but stipulated that he would continue to direct, on occasion, the work he had charge of at the Armory.[200]

Burton had other problems during July 1864. He could not comply with a request from Lieutenant Colonel Childs, commanding the Arsenal and Armory at Fayetteville, North Carolina, for 400 gunstocks because the supply of gunstocks at Macon was exhausted in the spring. Since that time the stock machinery had been idle. The reason for his lack of stocks was the lack of walnut wood.[201]

When Colonel Oladowski, Chief of Ordnance, Army of Tennessee asked Burton to repair arms, Burton notified Cuyler on 23 July to send 1,000 or 2,000 muskets so he would begin work on them the following day.[202] Fuss was instructed to pay no attention to appearances, but clean the inside of the barrel, and clear the vent and lock to insure the weapon would fire. Burton simply told Fuss to make certain the "arms shall be made serviceable."[203] Work progressed rapidly, and by the 25th Burton told Walter C. Hodgkins, Superintendent of the

---

[195] Burton, Order No. 31, Macon, 22 July 1864, Order Book, Armories, 1862-1865, Roll 10.

[196] Burton to Col. George C. Gibbs, Macon, 23 July 1864, Letters Sent, Armory, 1862-65.

[197] Burton to Gibbs, Macon, 23 July 1864, Ibid.

[198] Burton to H. Hamlet, Macon, 23 July 1864, Ibid.

[199] Burton to Fuss, Macon, 23 July 1864, Ibid.

[200] Burton to Lt. M.B. Grant, Macon, 29 July 1864, Ibid.

[201] Burton to Lt. Col. F.L. Childs, Macon, 16 July 1864, Ibid.

[202] Burton to Cuyler, Macon, 23 July 1864, Ibid.

[203] Burton to Fuss, 24 July 1864, Ibid.

Armory attached to the Macon Arsenal, to send up a fresh supply of arms for repairs and cleaning.[204]

When Cobb and Gorgas instructed him to organize a military company at the Armory for local defense and for protection in early June 1864 against Federal raids, Burton appointed W.L. Reid as captain and directed all Armory employees who could bear arms to enroll themselves in the company. Burton ordered the drills to be as infrequent as possible. They would be held either in working hours, or outside of them. In the latter case all who drilled would be paid at the same rate as for extra time. In case of an emergency the company would be placed under General Cobb's command. Burton promised to procure arms and equipment, and pledged to help the unit to become as efficient as possible.[205] The unit soon became known as the "Armory Guard" or "Company A." Drill took place on Wednesdays and Saturdays of each week at 4:00 P.M. In case of a Federal attack, the men had to assemble quickly and without special orders.[206]

The drills continued through June with Burton pleased that they took "a lively interest in the efficiency of the company." Absentees were not paid for drill time. If some of them did not report to drill they would be returned to camp and their exempt status revoked. Only Government employees were enrolled in the company.[207]

There seems to have been some problem with drill, because Burton was forced to issue General Order No. 30 on 29 June ordering every detailed man employed at the Armory to enroll in the company. When the unit was fully organized, and everyone was enrolled, those who had valid reasons for being excused from drill could tell Reid. Those with physical disabilities needed medical certificates. Burton would then excuse those who were entitled to the exemption.[208] Burton asked Cuyler for 100 smoothbore muskets of Caliber .69, and the same number of accouterments, together with one thousand cartridges and fifteen hundred percussion caps for the unit.[209]

During the period when Gibbs called up exempt men at the Government facilities to serve in the defenses of Atlanta, Burton ordered the Armory Guards

---

[204] Burton to Walter C. Hodgkins, Macon, 25 July 1864, Ibid.] By 27 July, 200 muskets were ready to turn over to Cuyler. Burton to Maj. J.G. Michaeloffsky, Macon, 27 July 1864, Ibid.

[205] Burton, Order No. 29, Macon, 14 June 1864, Order Book, Armories, 1862-65.

[206] Burton to Capt. W.L. Reid, Macon, 14 June 1864, Letters Sent, Armory, 1862-65.

[207] Burton to Capt. W.L. Reid, Macon, 23 June 1864, Ibid.

[208] Burton, Order No. 30, Macon, 29 June 1864, Order Book, Armories, 1862-65.

[209] Burton to Cuyler, Macon, 18 July 1864, Letters Sent Armory, 1862-65.

to muster at the Pistol Factory on the morning of the 23rd for further orders.[210] However, the order was countermanded later in the day.[211] Then, on 29 July, as Stoneman's raiders approached Macon, Burton ordered Reid to muster his company at the Pistol Factory, march to the Arsenal armory, and report to Lieutenant Colonel Mallet for further orders.[212]

On 30 July the Armory Company, together with the two companies from the Arsenal, helped to repulse Stoneman's Division as it tried to capture Macon. The call was received at 4:45 P.M., while the men were at work, and in a few minutes they mustered in the Armory enclosure. The roll was called, and Captain Reid received his orders. The company then marched down to the Arsenal, received infantry accouterments and ammunition, and joined the two Arsenal Companies commanded by Mallet. The men quickly marched to the expected scene of action, and were at their posts before sundown. They remained on the field until Monday morning, 1 August at which time they were mustered out of service, and allowed to go home and rest. No one in the Armory company was killed or injured in the fight with Stoneman, and the Armory workforce resumed their task of repairing rifles on Tuesday, 2 August. Burton was elated with the performance of his men during Stoneman's Raid, reporting "I feel great pleasure in stating that all of my men who were physically able responded promptly and with alacrity to the call...everyone performed his duty manfully and to my entire satisfaction."[213]

After their participation in repelling Stoneman's attack during which the members of Company A, Armory Guards "felt the want of rifled arms to compete with those of the enemy," Burton decided to arm them with better weapons. The Armory was repairing a large number of Austrian and some Enfield Rifles from which he hoped to use 100 for his men. He asked Gorgas for authorization to issue 100 .54 caliber Austrian rifles to Cuyler in exchange for the .69 caliber smoothbore weapons issued to the Armory Company earlier.[214]

When rumors arrived of another Federal cavalry raid, Burton ordered the members of Company A, Armory Guards, to hold themselves in readiness for

---

[210] Burton, Order No. 32, Macon, 23 July 1864, Order Book, Armories, 1862-65. See also Burton to Capt. W.L. Reid, Macon, 23 July 1864, Letters Sent Armory, 1862-65.

[211] Burton, Order No. 33, Macon, 23 July 1864, Ibid. For a detailed summary of Burton's activities during July see Burton to Gorgas, Macon, 26 July 1864, Letters Sent Armory, 1862-65.

[212] Burton to Reid, Macon, 29 July 1864, Letters Sent, Armory, 1862-65.

[213] Burton to Gorgas, Macon, 2 August 1864, Ibid.

[214] Burton to Gorgas, Macon, 8 August 1864, Ibid.

possible active duty. When they heard three guns fired in rapid succession at the Arsenal they would muster at the Pistol Factory as quickly as possible.[215]

Later in August, Burton issued Order No. 36 which directed the company to assemble for drill on Tuesdays and Fridays at 4:00 in the Pistol Factory enclosure.[216] On August 24, he returned 2,200 rounds of ammunition for the old .69 caliber smoothbore muskets in exchange for ammunition for the new .54 caliber Austrian rifles with which his men were now armed.[217] He also equipped his company with cap boxes, cartridge boxes and belts, bayonet scabbards, canteens, and 4,000 cartridges for the .54 caliber Austrian Rifles together with the necessary percussion caps.[218]

Despite the repair work accomplished on arms for the Army of Tennessee, and the excellent showing his men made in helping to defeat Stoneman and his raiders, work on the new Armory buildings was severely hindered by Army of Tennessee commander John B. Hood's need for men to work on the fortifications around Atlanta. By August Sherman's three field armies closely invested the North Georgia city, causing Hood to call for more men. Burton told Gorgas, on 3 August that he greatly regretted "this as I have collected the force of laborers and negro mechanics at the expense of much trouble and effort," and added, "I can only await their return from the front."[219] By 19 August Burton's anxiety grew to have eighty-four of his men, who labored on the Atlanta fortifications, returned, and wrote Hood, "the operations of this Armory are very much embarrassed in consequence of the want of them."[220] He wanted Gorgas to allow him to hire laborers at the rate of $4.00 a day to make up for the Blacks impressed by Hood to dig fortifications around Atlanta. The bricklayers who worked on the new buildings were idle because the black laborers were unavailable to help them.[221]

The impressment of his black laborers caused Burton to issue Order No. 37 to keep his detailed men at their jobs of repairing arms. The order permitted the absence of detailed men from duty only when they were on leave granted by Burton or by an Army surgeon's certification of disability which entitled them to receive medicines, medical attention, and hospital accommodations. Burton would not permit absences on the "plea of sickness" without the proper surgeon's certificate. Men who were seriously ill had to report the reason to him. Burton would excuse the absent man or not according to the details of the

---

[215] Burton, Order No. 35, Macon, 14 Aug. 1864, Order Book, Armories, 1862-65.
[216] Burton, Order No. 36, Macon, 23 August 1864, Ibid.
[217] Burton to Cuyler, Macon, 24 August 1864, Letters Sent, Armory, 1862-65.
[218] Burton to Cuyler, Macon, 29 August 1864, Ibid.
[219] Burton to Gorgas, Macon, 3 August 1864, Ibid.
[220] Burton to Hood, Macon, 19 August 1864, Ibid.
[221] Burton to Gorgas, Macon, 24 August 1864, Ibid.

case. Punishments for repeated absences would be a reduction of wages for the first offense and the return to field service for repeat offenders. In extreme cases, the absent individual was treated as a deserter. Leaves were limited to cases of absolute need or to those who earned the privilege through their work. Such leaves would be granted as many times as were consistent with the public interests. All Government employees who served in the field received the same pay and allowances as those who remained at their jobs. All absences had to be authorized, and all pay ceased when the man was absent from duty for whatever reason. All applications for leave had to be made in writing to Master Armorer Fuss, and approved by the applicant's foreman.[222]

Hood's evacuation of Atlanta on 2 September which opened the way for Sherman's possible advance against Macon, threw the Ordnance establishments in Macon into a near panic. Mallet, Cuyler, and Cobb advised Burton to pack up all the stock machinery and the machinery of the Pistol Factory at once and ship it to Savannah. All of the other machinery and stores would follow if it proved necessary. Burton told Gorgas, "As neither the stock machinery or the pistol machinery is at present employed- no interruption to the work in hand (repairs of arms) will result- at least for the present." Mallet had gone to Savannah, and reported that he had secured suitable storehouses in which to store the machinery and stores from the Macon Ordnance facilities. By 5 September most of the stock machines and pistol machinery was packed ready for shipment. Cuyler planned to confer with Hood at Lovejoy's Station on the Macon and Western Railroad on the following day. When he returned, Burton hoped to act more deliberately concerning the removal of additional machinery.[223]

His men packed the machinery so rapidly that by 6 September Burton was ready to send it to Savannah for safekeeping. He ordered Lieutenant Selden, his Military Store Keeper, to obtain ten box cars for the purpose from the Post Quartermaster and teams, to help those already assigned to the Armory, to haul the machinery to the cars.[224] Because cars were not immediately available, Burton asked Gorgas if he should ship the items when transportation was at hand.[225] Gorgas telegraphed Burton on the 9th not to remove the machinery. Upon receipt of this directive, Burton decided to await news of Sherman's movements. He planned to keep the machinery packed and send the stock machinery to Columbia, South Carolina, where it could be placed in operation.

---

[222] Burton, Order No. 37, Macon, 1 Sept. 1864, Order Book, Armories, 1862-65.

[223] Burton to Gorgas, Macon, 5 September 1864, Chapter IV, Vols. 20, 29, and 31 Letters Sent Armory, 1862-65.

[224] Burton to Lt. Charles Selden, Jr., Macon, 6 September 1864, Ibid.

[225] Burton to Gorgas, Macon, 8 September 1864, Ibid.

This would make it cheaper to obtain stocks because much of the wood for stock making came from the South Carolina Piedmont.[226]

On 13 September when Sherman's movements were still a matter of conjecture, Burton recommended that the Pistol Factory at Columbus, Georgia, also be moved to Columbia. The latter city was, Burton believed, safer than Macon, and nearer to what sources of raw materials were still available in the rapidly-shrinking area controlled by the Confederacy. A few of the special pistol-making machines might be used in the Pistol Factory at Macon.[227]

The employees in the stock machinery area were sent to the Columbia Armory on 24 September. There they would work under the supervision of Captain C.S. McPhail, Armory Superintendent.[228] In preparation for the move, Burton notified McPhail that five carloads of stock making machines would be sent to Columbia by early October. Only two workmen could be sent, however, although seven or eight had worked in the stock machinery area. The rest had either deserted, died, or had otherwise become unavailable.[229]

When Major F.F. Jones, commanding the Richmond Armory, asked for gunstocks, Burton told him that none were available. The machinery had been idle for four months because the supply of wood to make stocks was exhausted, and every effort to secure additional supplies was unsuccessful. Furthermore, the machinery was all removed and packed ready to ship to Columbia.[230]

Fifty-six cases of stock machines with shafting were sent to Columbia on 6 October. The two mechanics who worked on gunstocks, G.W. Weston and Aaron Stevens, also left for the South Carolina capital. Plans called for the pistol machinery from Columbus, considered a more exposed position than Macon, to be quickly set up in Macon.[231] The pistol machinery from Columbus was installed at the Macon Pistol Factory by 13 October.[232]

Burton was also concerned about the machinery he had purchased from Greenwood and Batley, some of which reached the Confederacy in September and October 1864. Invoices and receipts were sent for fifteen cases of machinery which arrived at Wilmington aboard the steamer *Helen* in early September. Another twenty cases aboard the *Hope* was unloaded on 2 September.[233] News

---

[226] Burton to Gorgas, Macon, 10 September 1865, Ibid.

[227] Burton to Gorgas, Macon, 13 September 1864, Ibid.

[228] Burton to Fuss, Macon, 24 September 1864, Ibid.

[229] Burton to Capt. C.S. McPhail, Macon, 29 September 1864, Ibid.

[230] Burton to Maj. F.F. Jones, Macon, 23 September 1864, Ibid.

[231] Burton to Gorgas, Macon, 6 October 1864; and Burton to Capt. McPhail, Macon, 7 October 1864, both Ibid.

[232] Burton to Gorgas, Macon, 13 October 1864, Ibid.

[233] Lt. John M. Payne to Burton, Ordnance Office, Wilmington, 2 September 1864, Burton Papers.

reached Burton that the *Hope's* crew had run the steamer ashore under the guns of Fort Caswell, near Smithville, North Carolina. Burton feared for his machinery, but, in case it was saved he asked Gorgas for directions where he should send it.[234] His uncertainty evaporated when he received a letter from Lieutenant John M. Payne in Wilmington that the cases, which he described as numbering twenty-five, were on their way to Columbia for storage under orders from Lieutenant Colonel de Lagnel, Assistant Chief of Ordnance.[235]

Another shipment of machinery, sixty-four pipes, sixty-eight packages and pieces of machinery, and three cases were shipped from Nassau aboard the steamer *Ella* in mid-September. The Confederate agent in Nassau, L. Heyliger, advised Burton to keep two boilers in Nassau for the moment. A third and final shipment would be sent to Wilmington aboard the *Hope* or the *Colonel Lamb*.[236]

On 10 September Burton, who was still uncertain about Sherman's movements, recommended that boilers and other heavy machinery which arrived in St. Georges, Bermuda, should remain there for the moment.[237]

As late as 16 November Burton was recommending the retention of heavy machinery in Nassau and Bermuda. It should be painted, he urged Gorgas, to "preserve it from the moist climate in both places."[238]

In the fall of 1864, Burton was beset with other problems. He issued Order No. 30 on 1 October which noted that public property had been stolen from the Armory by employees who were then discharged and returned to their camps. In an effort to put a stop to the thefts, he initiated a policy of court-martialing detailed men and trying others by civil process. The guards at the Armory gates were directed to question and search, if necessary, suspected persons. No property, either public or private, was to be taken from the Armory without the written permission of some foreman or superior officer.[239]

Because of conscriptions of his workforce by enrolling officers, the sending of black laborers to the front to work on fortifications, and carpenters needed for work on the new Laboratory buildings, Burton reported the work on the Armory

---

[234] Burton to Gorgas, Macon, 10 September 1864, Letters Sent Armory, 1862-65. See also Burton to Agent J.M. Seixas, Macon, 12 September 1864, Ibid. for Burton's concern about the cases of machinery which were aboard the *Hope*.

[235] Lt. John M. Payne to Burton, Wilmington, 13 September 1864, Burton Papers.

[236] L. Heyliger to Burton, Nassau, 19 September 1864, Burton Papers. For additional information concerning the cargo of the *Ella* see Burton to Maj. N.R. Chambliss, Macon, 7 October 1864, Ibid. The *Colonel Lamb* was named for Colonel William Lamb, a Norfolk, Virginia native, who was commander of both the Thirty-Sixth North Carolina Heavy Artillery Regiment and Fort Fisher.

[237] Burton to Maj. N.S. Walker, Macon, 12 September 1864, Letters Sent Armory.

[238] Burton to Gorgas, 16 November 1864, Ibid.

[239] Burton, Order No. 39, Macon, 1 October 1864, Order Book, Armories, 1862-65.

buildings was "thrown behind hand to an extent, which threatens serious loss to the Govt." All the floor timbers in the main building, and the towers were exposed to the weather from six to twelve months. Due to this factor, they were decaying, and special efforts were needed to quickly cover the building. Burton wanted the exemption of carpenters and brick masons to perform the work.[240]

By mid-November, only half of the Blacks sent to work on the Atlanta Fortifications had returned. The remainder had been assigned to work as cooks and teamsters with the Army of Tennessee, or had run away. This posed a problem for Burton because the contracts signed with the slave owners specified the Blacks should be employed only on work pertaining to the Army. Therefore, the owners claimed their contracts were voided because their slaves were ordered to the front without their consent. This caused slave owners to hesitate to hire their slaves to Government establishments in general, a fact which caused Burton to "foresee that the difficulties attending the hiring of negro labor next year will be greater than ever before." He attempted to find a solution to this problem by suggesting that a regular force of black laborers be organized for the exclusive service of the War Department, and a number of these assigned to each manufacturing establishment. The men would be clothed and fed by the Quartermaster and Commissary Departments.[241]

Altogether, Burton had ninety-seven men between the ages of seventeen and forty-five detailed to the Armory on 30 September. Of this number, he received orders to turn over one-sixth of his workforce to the Army.[242] To make matters worse, Cuyler suspended the shipment of arms which needed repair to the Armory in early October. Therefore, Burton ordered Fuss to suspend preparations for manufacturing ramrods to repair the arms. Fuss was directed to repair all the arms still in the Armory as soon as possible. Since Gorgas had ordered the installation of the Columbus pistol machinery in Macon, Fuss was ordered to manufacture pistols "with all the vigor possible."[243]

Burton had problems connected with the construction of the new Armory buildings until the end of the war. When he heard that a large number of Blacks had been captured by Confederate forces at Rome in Northwestern Georgia, he asked Cobb to order some of them to Macon to work on the fortifications. The Blacks impressed by Hood to work on the Macon fortifications could then be returned to work on the new Armory buildings.[244]

Despite these difficulties, Burton reported his men had excavated 726 cubic yards of earth from cutting the railroad siding into the Armory grounds by the

---

[240] Burton to Gorgas, Macon, 5 October 1864, Vol. IV, Letters Sent Armory.

[241] Burton to Gorgas, Macon, 15 November 1864, Ibid.

[242] Burton to Cobb, Macon, 27 October 1864, Ibid.

[243] Burton to Fuss, Macon, 6 October 1864, Ibid.

[244] Burton to Cobb, Macon, 7 October 1864, Ibid.

end of October. This ground was used to grade the premises, filling up gullies, and repairing the main street of the Armory, known as "Armory Street." Thirty-five additional cubic yards had been excavated for the foundations of the columns which supported the gearing at intersections of the wing shafting in the main Armory building. This earth, too, was used as grading material. The entire area under the first floor of the main building was cleaned of rubbish, bricks, etc., and a number of serviceable bricks retrieved for future use and the brickwork on the Central Office Towers of the main building was raised by three feet. This included the ornamental brickwork of the cornices. The towers were ready to receive the heavy stone coping. The front wall between the towers, including the ornamental brickwork cornicing, was raised two feet. This wall was also ready to receive the stone coping. The exterior walls of the Central Office Towers, and those of the office building directly behind them, were cleaned with oil, repointed wherever necessary, and the scaffolding around them removed. The six-foot-high, two brick-thick walls outside the windows in the basement of the Central Office Towers were built up with brick, and were ready to receive the stone coping. These walls were 2' wide and 12' 9/12" long in front of each double window. The walls of the east and west end towers of the main building were raised one foot, or up to the temporary projecting roofs.

The brick foundations for columns which supported gearing at the intersection of the wing shaft with the shafting in the main building were begun and carried up to two feet, or to a height where they could receive the large bottom anchor stones. The brick walls of the second story of the third wing of the main building were carried from the bottom of the second tier of floor joists to ten feet above the top of the joists, for a total height of 11' 3/4". Forty-three stone window sills were completed. One kiln of 400,000 brick was burned, and 150,000 bricks hauled from the brickyard to the Armory grounds.[245]

Besides work completed at the new Armory, the mechanics who built and cleaned small arms, and who made machinery and parts, had not been idle. Fifty revolving pistols were completed; 460 Austrian rifles cleaned and repaired, and a lathe chuck for facing pistol cylinders manufactured, together with eighty large bolts and nuts for the new buildings. Fifty machines in the machine shop were dismantled, boxed, and packed for transportation to a place of greater security if necessary. All of the Columbus pistol machinery was unpacked and assembled, and the manufacture of pistols resumed.[246]

During the period in which the Right Wing of Sherman's army approached Macon, the Armory Company consisted of a hundred officers and men. This number included fifteen light duty men, and nine men in the hospital or on

---

[245] Burton to Gorgas, "Summary Statement of Work done at Macon Armory in the month of October 1864," Macon, November 1864, Ibid.

[246] Ibid.

detached duty. Those available for active duty numbered seventy-six. The unit was well armed, however, with 199 .54 caliber Austrian rifles and 4,000 rounds of ammunition.[247] However, there is no evidence that the unit participated in the repulse of Colonel Smith D. Atkin's cavalry assault upon Dunlap's Hill. Although not posing as great a danger to Macon as that caused by Stoneman's Raid the previous summer, The March to the Sea did affect the Armory. The supply of shingles for roofing the new buildings was interrupted because of the invasion.[248]

Burton also needed granite, since the supply available at Stone Mountain had also been disrupted by Sherman. He wanted to buy the granite owned by I.A. Ralston, proprietor of Ralston Hall, which lay in Second Street between Mulberry and Cherry Streets.[249]

As Sherman's army approached, Burton sent many machines to Savannah, including the greater portion of the machines in the machine shop. He also sent the pistol-manufacturing machinery to Columbia, as well as the machinery received from England. But only half of the pistol machinery, two-thirds of the foreign machinery, and half of the arms machinery fabricated in Macon, was shipped before Sherman's troops cut the Central Railroad. The absence of the machinery from the machine shop would not seriously affect active operations because no workmen were available to operate it. Burton did reinstall two or three lathes, and a drill planer in the machine shop, and had on hand a small portable two-horsepower steam engine which furnished enough power to drive about 60 feet of shafting which enabled the Armory workers to repair machinery. No stores were removed. Hopefully, one of the wings of the new Armory building would soon be ready for use. Burton planned to install the Pistol Factory on the second floor of this wing, and place the machine shop machinery on the first floor. The steam engine and boiler used at the temporary works would be placed under a temporary shed in the yard next to the wing. It would be able to drive both the machine shop and the Pistol Factory. Burton planned to leave the temporary works and concentrate all manufacturing at the new facility. In the meantime, the armorers were repairing arms and working on those pistol parts which did not require machinery for their manufacture.[250]

Although much work was done on the permanent buildings in November, Burton was hindered because he was forced to hold his workmen in readiness for a week or more "subject to a moments call for field duty." Despite this

---

[247] Burton to Maj. L.L. Butler, Commanding Post of Macon, Macon, 17 November 1864, Letters Sent, Armory, 1862-65.

[248] Burton to Maj. J. Taliaferro, Macon, 1 December 1864, Ibid.

[249] Burton to I.A. Ralston, Macon, 7 November 1864, Ibid.

[250] Burton to Gorgas, Macon, 7 December 1864, Ibid.

temporary inconvenience, Armory workers constructed thirty-five revolving pistols.[251]

During December, more work was accomplished on the buildings. Workers also tested the thirty-five pistols manufactured the previous month, and made them ready for issue. They also cleaned and repaired 240 .54 caliber Austrian rifles and 446 Belgian muskets.[252]

The winter of 1864-1865 passed uneventfully with little activity taking place except in the area of repairing arms. On 21 February 1865, Gorgas ordered Burton to direct the operations of the armories at Macon, Athens, Columbus, and Tallassee, Alabama. The directive gave Burton authority to transfer employees, materials, machinery, tools, and public funds from either armory to the others. Gorgas also ordered him to take over the operations of the contract pistol-manufacturing establishments of Rigdon and Ansley at Augusta, and Griswold and Gunnison at Griswoldville. In granting this authority Gorgas wanted to produce as many arms as possible.[253]

On 25 February Master Armorer Fuss, temporarily in charge of the Armory in Burton's absence, complained to General Beauregard about his order to take up the rails of the Macon and Brunswick Railroad. The Master Armorer noted that the road was needed because the Ordnance Bureau intended to make the Macon Armory the great national armory, capable of turning out 1,500 arms a week. Because the sources of supply for raw materials from North Georgia had been disrupted by the Sherman Invasion, the only sources available were from Southwestern Georgia via the Brunswick Railroad. Fuss protested, to no effect, that the road was important to the interests of the Armory, and its loss would "cripple, if not suspend the operations of this establishment."[254]

On 28 March Burton ordered Fuss to repair arms as fast as possible because he did not believe the Macon Armory was repairing as many arms as some of the other armories. "It may be," he wrote, "that the arms now being repaired require more repairs than usual which will account for the small number turned out." But he felt more should be done, and suggested that each man should receive a bonus of a dollar for each arm that he repaired, in addition to his daily wages.[255]

---

[251] Burton to Gorgas, "Summary Statement of Work done at Macon Armory in Month of November 1864," Macon, November 1864, Ibid.

[252] Burton to Gorgas, "Summary Statement of work done at Macon Armory in month of December 1864," Macon, 11 January 1865, Ibid.

[253] Gorgas to Burton, Richmond, 21 February 1865, Burton Papers.

[254] Jeremiah Fuss to Gen. Pierre G.T. Beauregard, Macon, 25 February 1865, Letters Sent, Armory, 1862-65, Reel 9.

[255] Burton to Jeremiah Fuss, Macon, 28 March 1865, Ibid.

At the end of March, as Wilson pushed into Central Alabama, Burton asked General Richard Taylor, then commanding the Military Division of the West with headquarters in Meridian, Mississippi, if he should remove the machinery from the Tallassee Armory, near Montgomery.[256]

The machinery was removed to Macon at the end of the month, at which time, Burton wrote Cuyler that he was vacating the temporary Armory buildings and had plans to sell them. If Cuyler wanted to use them, and had money to pay for them, he could buy them. Burton was now, in the last days of the Confederacy, badly in need of money to keep up his work of repairing arms.[257]

By April 1865, just before Wilson's Cavalry Corps captured Macon, the new Armory facility, which had never come into full production, was impressive. The buildings included a main building of brick on stone foundations, 625' x 40', two stories high, with two flank towers, three stories high, which included a double central tower four stories high, and a wing in the rear with dimensions of 160' x 40', two stories high. The main building was not roofed, with the exception of the wing, and two flank towers, which were temporarily covered with shingles. A one-story brick building, 70' x 50', was covered with slate and used temporarily as a carpenter's shop. Other buildings included:

(1) A one-story brick building, 110' x 80', partially under a temporary shingle roof, located east of the wing of the main building.

(2) Two one-story frame buildings about 30' x 18' each, one of which was used as a lime house and the other as a foreman's office, located in the rear of the center of the main building.

(3) A one-story frame building, 30' x 15', used as a foreman's office and small storeroom, located in the rear of the east end of the main building near the stream.

(4) A one-story temporary frame building, 80' x 40', which served as a carpenters shop, located near the foreman's office.

(5) A frame stable with adjoining sheds which afforded shelter for about thirty horses and mules.

(6) A one-story frame building, 35' x 20', used as a smoke house, located northeast of the main building, near the stream.

(7) A one-story frame building, 25' x 15', used as an engine room, located immediately behind the main building.

(8) A one-story frame building, 25' x 18', used as an architect's office, located on the hill behind the main building.

---

[256] Burton to Gen. Richard Taylor, Telegram, Macon, 28 March 1865, Ibid. See also Burton to Maj. W. Taylor, Telegram, Macon, 28 March 1865, Ibid.

[257] Burton to Cuyler, 30 March 1865, Ibid.

(9) A one-story frame cottage dwelling, 40' x 30', with necessary outbuildings and an enclosing fence. Occupied by Jeremiah Fuss, it was located at the east end of the Armory grounds.

(10) A one-story frame cottage, 40' x 30', occupied by D.N. Perry, Foreman of Carpenters, located at the west end of the Armory grounds near the stream.

(11) A frame cottage, similar to the other cottages, occupied by H. Herrington, Master Machinist, located next to Perry's cottage.

(12) The brick foundations for a cottage, begun by Lieutenant Colonel Mallet, to be used as quarters for himself and assistants.

(13) A number of minor buildings or sheds that were not enumerated.

The facility included twenty-five machines for the manufacture of pistols, erected on the second floor of the wing of the main building, with 160 feet of main line shafting. A one-story frame cottage, 40' x 32', occupied by Oliver Porter, Overseer of Laborers, was located on the four-acre-lot adjacent to the Armory grounds. There were also eight one-story frame buildings, 36' x 18', occupied as quarters for the laborers. The entire four acres was enclosed by a nine-foot high board fence. Six additional houses for laborers were located on land adjacent to this lot which the Government planned to buy from the city. A twelve-acre brick yard was located in the swamp below the City Reserve. There were four brick-making machines and sheds, and one frame building, 30' x 15' feet, which was used as a tool house. In addition to the buildings there were many tools, machines, and piles of building materials scattered about the Armory grounds.[258]

After the war, the *Daily Telegraph* printed an article from the *Cincinnati Commercial* which described the Laboratory and Armory buildings. The Armory and the Laboratory were "on a scale of really admirable proportions." The Armory, particularly, would have been, "if completed according to plan, without a rival in the world." The US Government should take charge of these buildings and complete them. The *Commercial* somewhat disingenuously stated that "Coal is abundant in Ga., and these expensive and elegant structures (built by American enterprise) are too valuable to be thrown away." This view was echoed by the *Telegraph* which called the idea "a good one, and our citizens [of Macon] would do well to bring the matter to the attention of the government."[259] The idea, of course, died very quickly because the Federal Government had no intention of locating ordnance facilities anywhere in the former Confederacy, either at that time or for years to come.

---

[258] Burton to Maj. W. McBurney, Macon, 5 July 1865, Burton Papers.

[259] *Macon Daily Telegraph*, 11 July 1865.

A friend of Burton, then in England, wrote in 1867, that the new Armory buildings were uncovered, and the timbers were rotting very rapidly. No disposition had yet been made of it. The Laboratory, on the other hand, was scheduled for use as a barracks for Federal troops.[260] Today, there are no traces of any of the Confederate ordnance facilities which played such an important role in Macon during the war.

---

[260] A. Goulsby to Burton, Macon, 18 January 1867, Burton Papers.

Chapter 10

Macon as an Ordnance Center: The Central Laboratory

The driving force behind the Confederate States Central Laboratory was a remarkable man, John William Mallet. Mallet was born at Dublin, Ireland, 10 October 1832. His parents were Robert Mallet and Cordelia Watson. The elder Mallet, a noted civil engineer, was a member of the prestigious Institute of Civil Engineers, and was a Fellow of the even more famous Royal Society. He was also a well-known scientific writer. The younger Mallet, therefore, enjoyed rare opportunities. His education was begun at a private school in Dublin taught by Reverend J.P. Sargent. He studied at the University of Dublin's Trinity College, but transferred to the University of Gottingen, Germany, where he received his Ph.D. in chemistry in 1853. Coming to the United States in the same year, he received an appointment as chemist to the geological survey of Alabama, where he began his duties in January 1855. However, in 1856, he was appointed professor of chemistry at the University of Alabama, a position which he occupied until 1860. In that year he received an appointment as professor at the Medical College of Alabama in Mobile. His status in Alabama society was strengthened by his marriage to Mary Elizabeth Ormond, a daughter of Justice Ormond of the Alabama Supreme Court in 1857.[1]

Mallet abandoned his educational career when war came in April 1861. On 16 November of that year he was commissioned a first lieutenant in the Confederate Army, and took a position as aide-de-camp to General Robert E. Rodes. Recalling his arrival in the Confederate Ordnance Service, he observed:

> "I was in the summer of 1862 serving most pleasantly as aide-de-camp on the staff of General Rodes, whom I had known well before the war. Another friend of his was Colonel Briscoe Baldwin, chief ordnance officer on the staff of General Lee, and who had been for a while in

---

[1] Vandiver, *Ploughshares into Swords*, 112-113; Sketch of John William Mallet in CSA Lab file, Middle Georgia Archives, Washington Memorial Library, Macon.

charge of Richmond Arsenal. Colonel Baldwin visited our camp below Richmond at the time of Seven Pines, talked with me about the state of the Ordnance service, and asked me to go with him to the office in Richmond of Colonel Gorgas, who had expressed a wish to see me. The result of several interviews with him was that I was, though with a good deal of reluctance, transferred to the ordnance corps with a commission as Captain of Artillery, and ordered to at once endeavor to bring order out of the confusion."[2]

The recently-appointed Mallet wrote Gorgas on 1 July 1862, that there was not much activity at the fledgling Laboratory in Macon. Cartridges were being manufactured, but the operations of the new facility were jeopardized by already-felt shortages of lead, sheet tin, sulphur, and chlorate of potash. Problems also arose with the caliber of ammunition. It was assumed that the caliber of arms was .75, and moulds had been made for it which yielded balls of caliber .735. However, at the Laboratory in Charleston, South Carolina, the caliber of the same rifle was called .70, and the balls cast, in what Mallet believed were English bullet molds, were only .673.[3] Gorgas replied on July 14, that the calibers of the Belgian and English rifle muskets were .70 and .69 respectively. He also informed Mallet that the Ordnance Department planned to immediately push the Wythe County, Virginia, lead mines to their greatest capacity.[4]

On another front, Mallet believed that the planned Central Laboratory should be established at Macon because the city had the advantages of security, railroad communications, and a central location. If, as Mallet said, Colonel James Henry Burton followed his plan to establish an armory in Macon instead of, as originally planned, in Atlanta, it would probably be best to put the Laboratory there, too. Mallet wrote; "There is urgent need of some central place from which molds, gauges &c may be issued, at which experiments may be made, and where the foundation may be laid for regular work upon a large scale in the future. There is great need too now of some distribution of labor among the various Laboratories, to prevent the excessive manufacture of some things and the neglect of others- at Macon and at Columbus the Ordnance officers really do not know what to go to work upon now that they are opening new Laboratory establishments."[5]

---

[2] Vandiver, *Ploughshares into Swords*, 113.

[3] Mallet to Gorgas, Macon, 1 July 1862, Box 3201, Letters Sent, Superintendent of Laboratories, 1862-64.

[4] Gorgas to Mallet, Richmond, 14 July 1862, Box 3193, Letters and Telegrams Received, Superintendent of Laboratories, 1862-65.

[5] Mallet to Gorgas, Macon, 1 July 1862, Letters Sent, Laboratories, 1862-64.

Mallet wrote T.C. Downie, Superintendent of the Laboratory in the Macon Arsenal, from Atlanta on 4 August that he had asked Captain Marcus J. Wright, Superintendent of the Atlanta Arsenal to manufacture molds for Caliber .54 smoothbore muskets. If, however, Downie made such molds in Macon they had better be exactly .530 inches in diameter.[6]

A little later, on 5 August Gorgas informed Mallet that Ordnance officers had picked up from sixty to eighty tons of lead from the battlefields, and these fields, most of them scenes of Confederate victories, were still being gleaned. Blockade runners had recently brought in thirty-four thousand more pounds of lead at Mobile which was sent by Confederate General Braxton Bragg to Atlanta; Columbus, Mississippi; and Selma, Alabama. Furthermore, Ordnance officers had placed ninety thousand pounds of lead from Texas, on the east bank of the Mississippi River at Woodville, Mississippi. Gorgas had ordered half of this supply sent to Atlanta.[7]

By early September Mallet was planning to manufacture balls for eprouvette mortars. Cast of iron, they had to be carefully turned to the true diameter. Mallet assured Macon Arsenal Superintendent Major Richard M. Cuyler, then at Richmond, that the machinists could be sent from Macon to Richmond, but the best workmen demanded and received $3.50 a day. Second-rate machinists could be hired for $2.50 to $3.00 a day.[8] Cuyler replied on 8 September assuring Mallet that the eprouvette balls would be made of cast iron. He also thanked the noted chemist for the information concerning mechanics and stated he would try to get some. He then turned his attention to badly-needed bullet machines, explaining he had all the drawings of a bullet machine and nearly a whole book concerning them copied. Plans called for these drawings, which were full size, to be sent to Macon and used in the development of a bullet machine favored by Mallet.[9]

For his part, Mallet explained to Gorgas on 22 September that progress made on the bullet machine was slow, partly because of difficulties in following all the details on the drawings sent by Cuyler. Although Mallet believed that in time he would be able to fabricate a workable bullet machine in Macon, it might be better to order such a device in England without abandoning the work in Macon. If a second machine could be purchased the two machines could be used to make bullets of different calibers. Colonel James Henry Burton, who had

---

[6] Mallet to T.C. Downie, Atlanta, 4 August 1862, Ibid.

[7] Gorgas to Mallet, Richmond, 5 August 1862, Letters and Telegrams Received, Laboratories, 1862-65.

[8] Mallet to Maj. Richard M. Cuyler, Richmond, 5 September 1862, Letters Sent, Laboratories, 1862-64.

[9] Cuyler to Mallet, Macon, 8 September 1862, Letters and Telegrams Received, Laboratories, 1862-65.

good connections in England, had given Mallet the name of the firm of Greenwood and Batley, Albion Foundry, Leeds, Yorkshire, which manufactured machinery for the Royal Arsenal at Woolwich. Mallet also believed that machinery for making percussion caps should be purchased in England, because "it is very difficult to get fine work of this sort well done in the South, and it can be both well and cheaply done, in England."[10] During the fall of 1862, Mallet searched for a high pressure steam engine or pair of engines of sixty to sixty-five horsepower each. He learned that at least one engine, owned by G.B. Lamar, President of the Savannah Bank of Commerce, was available in Savannah and asked an associate, A.N. Miller, to examine it. By 27 October Miller, and another associate, M.P. Muller, had examined Lamar's two steam engines and three boilers, and reported that the boilers were walled in so they could not examine them properly. The engines were on timber beds and seemed "very old and very uncouth looking things." Another engine and boilers were shown by Miller which were on a solid iron bed. The dimensions of the engine were a fifteen-inch cylinder with a three-foot stroke. The engine would make at least sixty-five revolutions, and pressure on the boilers was carried from ninety to one hundred pounds to which a pressure of only eighty pounds would generate 66.83 horsepower. The engine was owned by the firm of Wilder, Wheaton and Company who had authorized Miller to serve as their agent for its sale. Miller wanted $10,000 for it.[11] Mallet bought the engine and boilers and directed Miller to disassemble them and send them to Macon through the Quartermaster's Office in Savannah.[12]

As the war continued shortages in chemicals also became apparent. On 11 November Gorgas ordered Mallet to begin the possible manufacture of the principal chemicals needed to manufacture ammunition.[13] Mallet wanted to know if he should try to do this through contracts or whether he should hire a competent chemist to make the needed items in Macon. He informed the Chief of Ordnance that the foundation of all chemical manufactures was sulphuric acid, and recommended the speedy completion of a chemical factory proposed at Charlotte, North Carolina, and the making of some sheet lead available for the purpose. Of course, there was also the possibility of importing many of the

---

[10] Mallet to Gorgas, Atlanta, 22 September 1862, Letters Sent, Laboratories, 1862-64.

[11] Muller to Mallet, Macon, 27 October 1862, Letters and Telegrams Received, Laboratories, 1862-65. See also Mallet to A.N. Miller, Macon, 17 October 1862, Letters Sent, Laboratories, 1862-64.

[12] Mallet to Capt. Stewart, A.Q.M., Macon, 20 November 1862, Letters Sent, Laboratories, 1862-64.

[13] Gorgas to Mallet, Telegram, Richmond, 11 November 1862, Letters and Telegrams Received, Laboratories, 1862-65.

needed items from Europe. If this could be done the laboratories would need three hundred pounds of sulphuret of antimony (in mass not powdered), two hundred pounds of regulus of antimony, two hundred pounds of sulphuret of arsenic (realgar), one hundred pounds of nitrate strontia, fifty pounds of camphor, two hundred pounds of gum arabic, five hundred pounds of shellac, and one hundred carboys of nitric acid.[14]

Of course, the problem of shortages of lead would always be with the Ordnance Department. Mallet believed that the "want of lead could become a serious matter if military operations continued through the winter." Possibly lead could be imported from Havana through Mobile, or possibly from Mexico through Texas. It might even become necessary to seize lead in the houses of the large cities, although this "would excite a good deal of unpleasant feeling." Mallet hoped that a new lead mine opened in Charleston, Tennessee, would help alleviate the shortage. To make matters worse the supply of serge flannel used for making cannon cartridge bags was rapidly diminishing, and should be imported from Europe.[15]

The efforts Mallet made to obtain Laboratory materials and machinery for manufacturing ammunition from Europe is a study in frustration. However, he never gave up these efforts, proving his determination to do his part in achieving a Confederate victory. It also revealed his capabilities as a leader. Throughout his correspondence, Mallet continued to urge the importation of both chemicals and equipment from Europe. When Burton went to Europe in May 1863, Mallet ordered a long list of materials needed for the manufacture of rockets, shells, and bullets. The list included a complete set of apparatus for rocket manufacture; lap welding rolls; knives for making wrought iron tubes for rockets; two machines for sawing the tubes to the needed length; ten selfacting machines for boring out the rocket tubes; ten slide lathes on five beds for turning the outside of the rocket tube with two screw presses for putting on and taking off rockets; and fifty mandrills, among other items. The list included special drilling machines, horizontal drilling machines, slide lathes, hand presses, hand force pumps, and hydraulic apparatus for making pellets for wood fuzes for spherical shells with molds for four sizes of fuses. He also wanted slide lathes for turning shells for rifled cannon, the same as made for Woolwich Arsenal; plug cutting machines for Enfield bullets; a double geared drilling machine; a slotting machine with a rising table; a machine to punch out canister plates; and many other items.[16]

---

[14] Mallet to Gorgas, Macon, 20 November 1862, Letters Sent, Laboratories, 1862-64. A carboy is a large glass or glass bottle used to hold corrosive liquids.

[15] Ibid.

[16] Greenwood and Batley to James H. Burton, "Prices of Laboratory machinery," Leeds, 10 July 1863, Burton Papers.

Besides the above, Mallet ordered a thousand tons of lead from Europe, although as late as the middle of August 1863, only 3,000 pounds had been received. He also needed a thousand pounds of twine for fixing field ammunition from abroad.[17]

By early September 1863, some of the shipments sent by Major Caleb Huse, Confederate Purchasing Officer in London, had arrived, but they included only a six-month's supply of laboratory stores.[18] But it was more difficult to receive machinery from abroad than to order it, partly because of the lack of money needed to purchase it, and partly due to the difficulties involved with carrying heavy shipments such as machinery through the Blockade. When, on 7 September 1863, Mallet received a price list of laboratory machinery, manufactured by Greenwood and Batley for the Royal Arsenal at Woolwich, he doubted that some of the machines were necessary, although "many of them are necessary in a permanent Laboratory establishment, and others very useful." He urged the need for a powerful steam engine and boilers needed to power the new Laboratory buildings then under construction.[19]

Mallet received a list of Laboratory stores shipped from England on board the *Coral Isle*, and asked Gorgas to send him a list of the stores when they arrived in Wilmington, North Carolina. He was also happy to learn about the continued shipment of ever-scarce lead, but also needed a supply of brass wire of "the very best quality."[20]

Despite some success in procuring materials, almost insurmountable problems quickly arose. Greenwood and Batley needed the exact shape and size of the bullet to be manufactured on a machine for making pressed bullets so the firm could prepare the punches and dies.[21]

Furthermore, money was scarce to pay for expensive machinery, no matter how badly it was needed to manufacture laboratory materials. On 15 September 1863, Gorgas, saying "Our funds are very limited at present," authorized Mallet to order machinery of only the most simple character to the amount of five thousand pounds. Mallet would have to await the availability of funds to pay for his steam engine.[22] Mallet disagreed with his chief, especially in regard to the steam engine. He believed that a steam engine could be purchased cheaply in England. Besides, an "engine of some sort is of course essential at the Laboratory from the outset, as without it any other machinery I might order

---

[17] Mallet to Gorgas, Macon, 15 August 1863, Letters Sent, Laboratories, 1862-64.

[18] Mallet to Gorgas, Macon, 7 September 1863, Ibid., 1862-64.

[19] Mallet to Gorgas, Macon, 7 September 1863, Ibid.

[20] Mallet to Gorgas, Macon, 14 September 1863, Ibid.

[21] Mallet to Gorgas, Macon, 15 September 1863, Ibid.

[22] Gorgas to Mallet, Richmond, 15 September 1863, Letters and Telegrams Received, Laboratories, 1862-65. A pound is the British medium of exchange.

would be useless." He requested Gorgas' permission to include a steam engine and boilers as part of the machinery authorized, it being understood that the entire order would not exceed five thousand pounds.[23] Gorgas replied, through Major Thomas L. Bayne, on duty with the Ordnance Department, that the order for machinery must include only such machinery which was unavailable in the Confederacy. Mallet must use steam engines which he could buy in the Southern States.[24]

In mid-September 1863, Mallet sent Huse a new list of Laboratory stores needed for a six-month's-supply for all of the Ordnance establishments. This list included numerous items which reveal the desperate need for supplies in the Confederacy. Cartridge paper for outer and middle wrappers for Enfield cartridges (two thousand reams); cartridge paper for powder liners (five thousand reams; strong twine paper for caps and cylinders of fixed ammunition (five thousand pounds); serge or flannel for cartridge bags (fifty thousand yards); woolen yarn to sew cartridge bags (one thousand pounds); flax thread fort tying small arms cartridges (two strands, five thousand pounds); twine for bundling small arms' cartridges (three thousand pounds), wood screws, tacks, brass wire, tin plate, brass wire cloth, bolting cloth, black tin, lead (one thousand tons), and many other items. The list also included such chemicals as isinglass, lamp black, gum arabic, saltpeter, sulphur, nitric acid, sulphur, sulfuret of antimony, regulus of antimony, chlorate of potash, acetate of lead, acetate of copper, oxy-chloride of copper, alum, sulphate of ammonia, nitrate of soda, nitrate of strontia, nitrate of baryta, and sulfuret of arsenic. Clamp screws, a micrometer for measuring bullets, twelve finely-made spring calipers, twelve small calipers, and twelve standard brass scales were also deemed essential.[25]

Some supplies did arrive by early October just in time to prevent a general suspension of work on small arms cartridges. However, the entire quantity of supplies received at Augusta for all the Arsenals south of North Carolina, Mallet deemed "but a small fraction of the aggregate amount ordered." By October 1863, the scarcity of metallic copper had become very serious. Damage to the copper mines of East Tennessee due to the success of Federal Major General William S. Rosecrans in maneuvering General Braxton Bragg out of Middle Tennessee and into North Georgia caused damage to the copper mines and furnaces at Ducktown and the copper rolling mill at Cleveland.[26]

---

[23] Mallet to Gorgas, Macon, 3 October 1863, Letters Sent, Laboratories, 1862-64.

[24] Thomas L. Bayne, for Gorgas, to Mallet, Richmond, 8 October 1863, Letters and Telegrams Received, Laboratories, 1862-65.

[25] Mallet to Maj. Caleb Huse, Macon, 16 September 1863, Letters Sent, Laboratories, 1862-64.

[26] Mallet to Gorgas, Macon, 9 October 1863, Ibid.

Yet, despite many scarcities, there were successes too. A bullet machine manufactured in England had arrived in Wilmington and might be sent to Macon.[27] Mallet, of course, wanted it, writing to Colonel George W. Rains in Augusta, "Please send it- if it is, I suppose, one ordered by me."[28] Despite this, neither the equipment or the Laboratory supplies ordered by Mallet, had even left England as late as December 1863.[29]

The year 1864—which dawned after the road to the Lower South was opened with Grant's spectacular victories over Bragg at Lookout Mountain, Orchard Knob, and Missionary Ridge had raised the Confederate siege of Chattanooga, coupled with Lee's withdrawal behind the Rapidan River in Virginia—would not prove to be a happy time for the Confederacy. While at the beginning of 1863 it seemed that the bold gamble for Southern independence might still be successful, at the close of the year the notion of an independent Southern nation seemed almost an impossibility even to the most diehard Confederates.

The year also saw Mallet as a desperate man concerning the constant shortage of lead. On 2 January he suggested that lead might be run to the coast of Florida from Havana, a regular stop for English steamers. This shortage of lead had reduced the production of small arms' ammunition. The continuance of even the present supply through Wilmington seemed precarious and, in Mallet's words, "likely to become still more so." To add to the problems faced by Gorgas, the shortage of sheet and pig copper was becoming serious. Other Laboratory stores, which were on hand, would become scarce because of the "probably effectual blockade of the port of Wilmington with the calm weather of early summer an evil full of menace for the future." The eastern coast of Florida might be used to move supplies, which could then be carried by wagon to the Lower Chattahoochee River, above Confederate defenses and obstructions, where they could easily be moved by water to Columbus, Georgia. The building of an ironclad ram at Columbus could be used to protect that important city. Mallet suggested that forty to fifty-ton small boats could be used. The lead might be exchanged for cotton, always needed to supply the textile mills of Lancashire. The operation would require the use of twelve or fifteen wagons to haul goods to and from the coast.[30]

---

[27] Gorgas to Mallet, Richmond, 22 October 1863, Letters and Telegrams Received, Laboratories, 1862-65.

[28] Mallet to Rains, Macon, 28 October 1863, Box 3200 Telegrams Sent, Superintendent of Laboratories, Macon, Georgia, 1863-65, Microfilm, Roll 10, Chapter IV, Vol. 52, NARA, hereafter cited as Telegrams Sent, Laboratories, 1863-65.

[29] Mallet to Maj. Thomas L. Bayne, Macon, 15 December 1863, Letters Sent, Laboratories, 1862-64.

[30] Mallet to Gorgas, Macon, 2 January 1864, Ibid. See also Mallet to Maj. John Blair Hoge, Macon, 8 February 1864, Ibid.

Mallet never gave up on his idea to bring lead in through the ports of Florida, although he admitted the difficulty of defending the elongated coast of that peninsular state.[31] On 8 March 1864, he wrote to Major John Blair Hoge, Quartermaster in Lake City, Florida, that the firm of Lehmann, Durr and Company of Montgomery, Alabama, seemed to have certain advantages in their offer to contract for the bringing of sheet copper, brass wire, chlorate of potash, and sulfuret of antimony through Florida.[32] Even as late as February 1865, in the closing days of the Confederacy, Mallet wrote Gorgas, "Shall I try to contract for importation of lead on coast of Florida, as heretofore proposed?"[33] The answer, which arrived from Richmond on 15 March, even as Sherman was marching into Eastern North Carolina and Lee was planning a final ill-fated sortie against Grant in the trenches before Petersburg, was equally optimistic. Lieutenant Colonel James C. Calhoun, Mallet's assistant administrator in the Laboratory, telegraphed his chief, then inspecting the Arsenal in Selma, Alabama, "Recd today the following telegram, Richmond....Lead & chlorate of potassa may be imported."[34]

Mallet's efforts to secure the supplies and equipment ordered in England the year before did not fare any better as 1864 advanced through late winter into early spring. By early February, Mallet received word from Major Bayne in Richmond that Huse had received his order to purchase five thousand pounds worth of machinery in England.[35] A month later, Mallet abandoned his plan to secure a lever or screw press for driving fuzes from England, hoping to buy one from the firm of Dabney and Somers in Richmond which had made one for the Richmond Arsenal.[36] He was equally unsuccessful in purchasing sheet copper and brass wire for percussion caps and friction primers, and even such common chemicals as shellac, isinglass, and nitrate of strontia. Of course, he always wanted lead and English cartridge paper, both superior to that made in the South.[37]

Unfortunately, the delays seemed endless and may have eventually contributed to the sudden collapse of the Confederacy in the spring of 1865. As late as 3 September 1864, Huse replied to a letter Mallet wrote on 27 July, that he had ordered Greenwood and Batley to prepare full drawings and particulars of

---

[31] Mallet to Gorgas, Macon, 6 February 1864, Ibid.

[32] Mallet to Maj. John Blair Hoge, Macon, 8 March 1864, Ibid.

[33] Mallet to Gorgas, Telegram, Macon, 20 February 1865, Telegrams Sent, Laboratories, 1863-65.

[34] Lt. Col. James C. Calhoun to Mallet, Telegram, Richmond, 15 March 1865, Ibid.

[35] Mallet to Gorgas, Macon, 5 February 1864, Letters Sent, Laboratories, 1862-64.

[36] Mallet to Gorgas, Macon, 9 March 1864, Ibid.

[37] Mallet to Gorgas, Macon, 5 April 1864, Ibid.

the machinery which would enable Mallet to build suitable buildings for the necessary shafting.[38]

Because of the delay in sending letters through the Blockade between the Confederacy and England, details of the ordering of equipment were often confused. For instance, Lieutenant Colonel J.A. deLagnel, one of Gorgas' assistants in the Ordnance Bureau, wrote Mallet on 28 September 1864, that he had written Huse ordering him to obtain a release from the contract with Greenwood and Batley which directed the English firm to dispose of a steam engine ordered earlier.[39] But Burton, commanding the Macon Armory, had written Mallet on 17 September, informing him that he had just received a letter from Greenwood and Batley, dated Leeds, England, 4 August 1864, that "Major Huse has given us the order for Major Mallet's engines, boilers &c. and we are busy with them. They will be pretty nearly counterparts of yours."[40] Huse wrote Mallet on 30 September, that the engines and boilers had been contracted for and he had forwarded all the papers relating to the contract, including cost, to Gorgas.[41]

As the fall of 1864—a bad time for the Confederacy—wore on, Burton again notified Mallet that L. Heybiger, Confederate agent at Nassau in the Bahamas, had received a shipment on the steamer *Ella* of additional machinery for both of them. This shipment included parts of a "Lead Squirting apparatus" for Mallet. The *Ella* was due in Charleston, and Burton had telegraphed Major Norman R. Chambliss, commanding the Charleston Arsenal to hold two cases of equipment for Mallet.[42] As late as 17 November 1864, Greenwood and Batley wrote Mallet to express regret about a misunderstanding over technical specifications concerning steam engines. The firm enclosed photographs of Mallet's ill-fated bullet machines and plug machine (they never arrived in the Confederacy), and promised to send photographs of the percussion cap machine and cloth cutting machine for flannel bags in their next letter. They assured the beleaguered Mallet that they were preparing the plan and particulars of the rocket machinery "which we will send you very shortly."[43] Finally, on 18 November, Huse admitted he had made a mistake in ordering the engines "which I cannot now account for except through my desire to do everything in my power to equip your laboratory as completely and as speedily as possible."[44]

---

[38] Maj. Caleb Huse to Mallet, London, 3 September 1864, Letters and Telegrams Received, Laboratories, 1862-65.

[39] Lt. Col. J.A. deLagnel to Mallet, Richmond, 28 September 1864, Ibid.

[40] Burton to Mallet, Macon, 17 September 1864, Ibid.

[41] Maj. Caleb Huse to Mallet, London, 30 September 1864, Ibid.

[42] Burton to Mallet, Macon, 7 October 1864, Ibid.

[43] Greenwood and Batley to Mallet, Leeds, England, 17 November 1864, Ibid.

[44] Huse to Mallet, 18 November 1864, Ibid.

Despite everything, Mallet conducted many experiments which helped to produce fuses, shells, bullets, and many other items for the Confederacy. He experimented in fitting, pressing, and varnishing percussion caps in December 1862.[45] When Lieutenant Colonel Edward Porter Alexander described a hand-drill for opening the Borman Fuse, he suggested giving the machine a fair test.[46] On 13 December 1862, he wrote William A. Clark and Company of Knoxville, concerning a cap machine for drawing the friction primer tubes, and wanted to see a new arrangement for filling, pressing, and varnishing caps.[47]

One of his most noteworthy contributions lay in the field of testing shells to determine the charge of powder needed to burst them with certainty. To this end, he wrote Gorgas in January 1863, "Recent experiments at Macon Arsenal have shewn that, on abandoning the Borman fuze, the bursting charge of ordinary spherical case is not sufficient to burst the projectile with certainty-wooden fuze plug and paper fuzes being needed." Mallet believed that the Confederacy should have fuse plugs made of lead and tin, screwed into the fuse-hole. These should be put into general use for all paper fuses. He also felt that as much power as might be needed to fill the shell should be used in charging projectiles.[48]

When an explosion at the Jackson, Mississippi, Laboratory, killed a number of people in the fall of 1862, a board of officers was convened to look into the causes. Mallet believed the reason for the tragedy "most probably originated in the opening of shells belonging to the damaged ammunition sent down from [General Sterling] Price's Army."[49]

Another explosion, this time at the Richmond Laboratory, was caused when an employee struck a friction primer out of a varnishing board. The spark caused powder from cartridges being broken up in the same room, to explode. Six people were instantly killed, and forty-one more died of their burns. Twenty-two others were wounded. Gorgas issued orders "To prevent if possible a recurrence of so fearful a loss of life." The orders forbade employees from bringing friction primers and percussion caps into rooms where powder was bundled and ready for packing. The number of people allowed in a room where powder lay loose, and where cartridges were broken up, was limited to ten. Such rooms had to be furnished with four doors which opened outwards. All operatives had to wear dresses made of incombustible cloth. The order also stipulated that bundled or

---

[45] Mallet to Maj. Marcus H. Wright, Macon, 6 December 1862, Letters Sent, Laboratories, 1862-64.

[46] Mallet to Gorgas, Macon, 8 December 1862, Ibid.

[47] Mallet to William A. Clark and Company, Macon, 13 December 1862, Ibid.

[48] Mallet to Gorgas, Macon, 12 January 1863, Ibid.

[49] Mallet to Gorgas, Macon, 15 January 1863, Ibid.

packed cartridges would not be allowed to accumulate in any building occupied by workers, but would be removed to another building.[50]

These orders were pertinent because laboratories, especially the one in Macon, were really testing places for cartridges, shells and other items. By February 1863, it became evident that Confederate artillerists preferred the twelve-pounder Napoleon cannon to the six-pounder. This made it necessary to distribute new sets of twelve -pounder gauges to the different arsenals.[51] Although ring gauges for six-pounders and six-pounder and twelve–pounder cylinder gauges were completed, inspected, and distributed to the various arsenals about the middle of January 1863, ring gauges for twelve and thirty-two-pounder cannon and cylinder gauges for eighteen and twenty-four-pounder artillery were not completed and inspected until early March. Nearly all of the sixty gauges inspected passed the test.[52]

Another testing problem presented itself when it was discovered that some Enfield bullets were too large for the rifles they were to be used with. Mallet recommended the reduction of these oversized bullets to the true caliber by swaging, or placing them in a tool known as a swage, to shape them. It was, of course, necessary to verify the diameter of the swage itself from time to time.[53] Mallet notified Gorgas that the subject was one of great importance which demanded constant attention. Steel swages wore under constant use, and had to be constantly inspected and, occasionally, gauged themselves. Besides, numerous complaints came in from the field that the cartridges the laboratories sent into the field contained bullets too large for the rifles for which they were intended. Mallet wrote, "As it is not certain that the standard measures of length which are used at the Arsenal and Ordnance Depots of the C.S. to verify the size of bullets and gauges agree accurately among themselves, officers commanding such establishments will please forward by express average samples (2 or 3 of each calibre) of the bullets they are using for small arms cartridges to this office, so that they may be gauged and their diameters verified, in reference to a single standard."[54]

In early March 1863, Mallet returned to Macon from a trip to Richmond, and began to prepare complete sets of gun-metal gauges for small-arms bullets of

---

[50] Gorgas to Richard Cuyler, Circular, Richmond, 20 March 1863, Orders and Circulars Received, Arsenal.

[51] Mallet to Maj. Marcus H. Wright, Macon, 25 February 1863, Letters Sent, Laboratories, 1862-64. Gauges determined the exact dimensions of the barrel of the cannon.

[52] Mallet to Gorgas, Macon, 9 March 1863, Ibid. Only two gauges out of a total of sixty gauges (ten sets of six) were rejected.

[53] Mallet to Lt. Cunningham, Macon, 31 January 1863, Ibid.

[54] Mallet to Gorgas, Macon, 31 January 1863, Ibid.

the four calibers commonly used by the Confederate Army. They were .54, .58, .69 (rifled for the Belgian rifle, and .69 smoothbore. He hoped they would be ready in a few days for shipment to all the arsenals except those west of the Mississippi River.[55] Two months later Mallet issued new gauges for the Enfield rifle and rifle musket cartridges of English pattern.[56]

One of the most interesting aspects of the Central Laboratory involved its construction. In early August 1862, Mallet visited Atlanta and Macon examining possible sites for a permanent Laboratory. He studied the advantages of both in regard to position and cheapness and found in favor of Macon. He believed that a good location might be obtained upon reasonable terms. Writing to Gorgas, Mallet observed; "I have been and am still at work upon a plan and estimate for the Laboratory suggested for the presentation of which I have already your permission. I hope soon to lay them before you in Richmond. I may say however that in round numbers, for $75,000 a complete and permanent establishment might be built- this sum including a large piece of land & cost of buildings workshops and magazines boundary wall of brick, wells, steam engines, branch railroad track...all at present prices- no expense has yet been incurred for the erection of even temporary Laboratory buildings at Macon. The advantage would be very great of having one thoroughly efficient and regular Laboratory, where a large supply of uniform and standard ammunition might during the war be issued, and which would enable us to do away with many hastily gotten-up and temporary establishments on the restoration of peace. Geographical position of Macon is excellent and must remain so under all conceivable future contingencies. The location then of the principal national armory would render it, yet more suitable as the site for a permanent laboratory establishment."[57]

Plans proceeded through the summer and early fall of 1862, until Mallet was able to offer the job of architect to T.W. Fulton of Savannah on 17 October. Fulton would receive a salary of $150 a month, but had to devote his whole time to the project under Mallet's direction. Fulton's duties involved supervising the surveying and grading of the land, designing and arranging the machinery, and working with Arsenal Commander Cuyler, with whom he already had a contract to build a permanent Arsenal facility.[58] The following day Mallet offered a position to John Hamlet of Savannah to supervise the burning of the necessary brick and the construction of the brickwork.[59] By 20 October, the

---

[55] Mallet to Gorgas, Macon, 2 March 1863, Ibid.

[56] Mallet to Gorgas, Macon, 14 May 1863, Ibid.

[57] Mallet to Gorgas, Augusta, 12 August 1862, Letters Sent, Laboratories, 1862-64.

[58] Mallet to T.W. Fulton, Macon, 17 October 1862, Ibid.

[59] Mallet to John R. Hamlet, Macon, 18 October 1862, Ibid.

energetic Mallet informed Gorgas that he had succeeded in arranging the purchase of the necessary land. Gorgas had instructed Mallet to buy the property to boundary liens. In order to do this Mallet had to purchase one hundred and three acres, for eleven of which (including a small frame house which could be used to great advantage in the progress of the work) he had to pay $1,800. The remainder of the land was bought at $70 an acre. Fulton was already at work preparing the necessary drawings of the buildings, and Mallet was making preparations to prepare the necessary contracts for materials. The latter believed it would be better to burn brick rather than to contract for it. In order to carry this plan out, he began to procure mules, carts, and laborers. He also planned to rent a small machine shop in Macon, where the simpler machinery could be manufactured.[60]

Mallet also began negotiations with Isaac Scott, President of the Macon and Western Railroad, for permission to build a short branch track or turnout to leave the railroad a little on the Macon side of an old sawmill and to run inside the enclosure of the works. He asked for two or three dirt or platform cars to build the branch track, and for permission to obtain dirt from a nearby cut on the main line in order to make a necessary small embankment for the branch.[61] There were many things needed to get the building underway. These included procuring the necessary nails, glass, brick, brick laying, window fastenings, sashes and doors, the manufacture of laboratory machinery, the payroll for mechanics, the payroll for laborers and brick burners, and surveying expenses.[62] After arranging to pay John R. Hamlet a salary of $5.00 a day,[63] Mallet began to hire sixty or sixty-five black laborers to help erect the buildings. He asked Major F.W. Dillard, Quartermaster of Columbus, Georgia, to clothe these men and furnish them with shoes.[64] He told William C. Dawson of Savannah, who had slaves for hire, that he planned to hire twenty-six black men at the rate of $7.50 per month each, and to feed and clothe them at government expense, or pay $150 a year to their owners with the owner supplying the necessary clothes.[65] At the same time he asked the Savannah *Republican* to advertise for sixty or sixty-

---

[60] Mallet to Gorgas, Macon, 20 October 1862, Ibid.

[61] Mallet to Isaac Scott, Macon, 24 October 1862, Letters Sent, Laboratories, 1862-64.

[62] Mallet to Gorgas, Macon, 27 November 1862, Ibid. See also Maj. Hermann Hirsch to Mallet, Savannah, 20 November 1862, Letters and Telegrams Received, Laboratories, 1862-65; Mallet to Hirsch, Macon, 18 November 1862, Letters Sent, Laboratories, 1862-64; Mallet to Barney Brothers, Mobile, Macon, 20 November 1862; and Mallet to John R. Hamlet, Macon, 8 November 1862; Mallet to Gorgas, Macon, 6 November 1862, all Ibid.

[63] Mallet to John R. Hamlet, Macon, 27 November 1862, Ibid.

[64] Mallet to Maj. F.W. Dillard, Macon, 28 November 1862, Ibid.

[65] Mallet to William C. Dawson, Macon, 28 November 1862, Ibid.

five slaves and for carpenters.[66] In order to house these men and construct stables for the mules needed to haul earth and bricks, Mallet asked Virgil Powers, Superintendent of the Southwestern Railroad, for permission to occupy and use a small triangular patch of ground belonging to the Southwestern Railroad, lying on the inner side of the curve of the track nearest to the firm's passenger depot in Macon.[67]

During December 1862, Mallet searched for castings for parts of a brick molding machine to make bricks, worked to secure commissary stores for the laborers, made an effort to obtain medical attention for the Blacks hired for the project, continued to hire more laborers, and purchased four hundred kegs of nails at $35 per keg.[68]

In late December, he purchased a twenty-seven-acre plot of land for a brickyard, and obtained forty mules for the purpose of making and hauling brick.[69] Gorgas, however, balked at this because Colonel Burton had already established a brickyard. Would two brick yards be necessary?[70] Mallet explained his reasons for making the purchase to Captain Edward B. Smith, Assistant to the Chief of Ordnance, explaining that 35,000 bricks were needed per working day to complete the Laboratory buildings in the summer of 1863. He would need five brick-making machines, to each of which he allocated only one mule. The location of the brickyard, determined by the existence of the suitable clay, did not permit more than five loads a day being hauled by each team. In a complex letter he even informed Smith of how many mules and carts he would need to haul the bricks.[71]

In a report to Major General Benjamin Huger, Inspector of Ordnance, on 2 January 1863, Mallet observed that he had purchased iron, nails, glass, and paints, and was in the process of negotiating contracts for lumber and slate. The laborers were grading the land upon which the buildings would stand, and the building would be adequate to provide ammunition for artillery support for 500,000 men. He believed that adequate arrangements were nearly complete for

---

[66] Mallet to Proprietor of *Savannah Republican*, Macon, 28 November 1862, Ibid. See also Mallet to Gorgas, Macon, 1 December 1862, Ibid.

[67] Mallet to Virgil Powers, Macon, 1 December 1862, Ibid.

[68] Mallet to Christopher D. Findlay, Macon, 15 December 1862; Mallet to Major J.L. Locke, Macon, 15 December 1862, and Mallet to William S. Triplett, Macon, 18 December 1862, all Ibid. Triplett was the President of the Old Dominion Nail and Iron Company in Virginia.

[69] Mallet to Gorgas, Macon, 18 December 1862, Ibid. See also Mallet to the Mayor and Council of Macon, Macon, 22 December 1862, Ibid.

[70] Edward B. Smith, for Gorgas, to Mallet, Richmond, 24 December 1862, Letters and Telegrams Received, Laboratories, 1862-65.

[71] Mallet to Capt. Edward B. Smith, Macon, 29 December 1862, Letters Sent, Laboratories, 1862-64.

the erection of the necessary buildings, and "it may be hoped that the work will progress rapidly as soon as the weather permits of brick being made."[72] Indeed, by early January 1863, full designs for all the buildings were ready, with a first set of drawings. Working drawings were being prepared, and all minor classes of materials purchased. Mallet's workers could manufacture the necessary ten million bricks with a savings to the government of seventy or eighty thousand dollars. The necessary mules were purchased, and the laborers hired and engaged in digging clay and preparing the brickyard for burning the brick as soon as the weather permitted. The remainder of the workforce was employed in grading the site, digging foundations for the new buildings, and clearing off wood. Temporary buildings were being built for the workers as quickly as the availability of carpenters and materials permitted.[73]

By late January Mallet could write Gorgas that he hoped the greater part of the buildings for the permanent Laboratory would be completed during the summer and fall of 1863. However, roofs had to be put on the buildings before the wet weather of the following winter set in, or the structures would be damaged by exposure before the next building season. It might be necessary to use shingles in the absence of slate which was an expensive commodity. After peace was declared, Mallet believed, the shingle roofs could be stripped off and replaced with slate, although he believed that much expense could be avoided by putting on slate roofs at the beginning.[74]

In an effort to speed up the work of grading land, digging foundations for buildings, and digging clay for brick-making, Mallet asked for the authority to pay his workers for extra work after the completion of their daily tasks "if they are able and willing to perform such additional labor, paying for the latter to the negroes themselves at a definite rate per cubic yard." He noted that the Blacks constantly asked for permission to do extra work for which they could be paid. They would cheerfully accept ten or fifteen cents per cubic yard, and the Ordnance Bureau would save much money for all work done at such a low price. However, Mallet could not authorize this without special authority, and asked Gorgas to lay the matter before Secretary of War Seddon.[75] He received authority for this request on 20 February 1863. The rate of pay would be ten to twenty cents per cubic yard.[76] As the winter of 1862-1863 progressed, Mallet was faced

---

[72] Mallet to Gen. Benjamin Huger, Macon, 2 January 1863, Ibid.

[73] Mallet to Gorgas, Macon, 6 January 1863, Ibid.

[74] Mallet to Gorgas, Macon, 19 January 1863, Ibid. See also Mallet to Gorgas, Macon, 19 January 1863, Ibid.

[75] Mallet to Gorgas, Macon, 12 February 1863, Ibid. See also Mallet to Gorgas, Macon, 20 February 1863, Ibid.

[76] Gorgas to Mallet, Richmond, 25 February 1863, Letters and Telegrams Received, Laboratories, 1862-65.

with almost as many problems as the Confederacy whose people now realized they were engaged in a long and desperate war, a war which seemed to be going against them with every passing day, especially in Tennessee, gateway to the Southern heartland. On 30 December 1862, he wrote Major N.R. Chambliss at Selma asking for sixty shovels for grading land.[77] On 17 February 1863, he notified Dr. A.C. Rogers at Oak Grove near Forsyth, Georgia, concerning medical attention for slaves. The surgeon and assistant surgeon in charge of the Macon military hospitals had enough wounded on their hands from such battles as Murfreesboro, and other smaller engagements in Tennessee and Kentucky, to give only limited medical care to the Blacks engaged upon building the Laboratory. Mallet also needed to buy needed medicines and stores on the open market.[78]

Another problem involved nails. On 20 February Captain R.J. Echols, Assistant Quartermaster at Charlotte, wrote that he had shipped one hundred kegs of nails to Macon on 15 February.[79] The beleaguered Mallet also needed railroad transportation for wood for burning brick, "without which brick making will be impossible." Many cars belonging to such railroads now in the hands of the Federals as the Louisville and Nashville, the Mississippi Central, and the New Orleans and Jackson, were in Georgia, but Mallet did not have the authority to use them. If he could seize seven or eight cars and place them on the Macon and Western they could be used to further construction of the Laboratory.[80] Possibly the firm of Suffborough and Timmins in Augusta could procure wheels, axles, and springs to be used in building four or five railroad cars.[81] On 18 April 1863, Mallet wrote William T. Quimby, President of the Etowah Iron Company in Etowah, Georgia, to see if his firm could construct rolled axles to build the needed cars.[82] Finally, on 18 May, Mallet informed Gorgas that the railroad cars for the transportation of bricks could be built at the shops of the Macon and Western Railroad in Macon if an order could be given for enough iron from the Etowah Works to make axles for four cars. Workers

---

[77] Mallet to Maj. N.R. Chambliss, Macon, 30 December 1862, Letters Sent, Laboratories, 1862-64.

[78] Mallet to Dr. A.C. Rogers, Macon, 17 February 1863, Ibid.

[79] Capt. R.J. Echols to Mallet, Charlotte, N.C., 20 February 1863, Letters and Telegrams Received, Laboratories, 1862-65.

[80] Mallet to Col. William M. Wadley, A.A. Genl. In charge of R. R. Transportation, Macon, 21 February 1863, Letters Sent, Laboratories, 1862-64.

[81] Mallet to Suffborough and Timmins, Macon, 11 April 1863, Ibid. See also Mallet to Jesse Osmond, Macon, 11 April 1863, Ibid.

[82] Mallet to William T. Quimby, Macon, 18 April 1863, Ibid.

were hauling brick to the building site using cars borrowed from the Macon and Western.[83]

The problems which Mallet faced seemed at times to be almost insurmountable. But he always stood up to them and solved most of them until the very end. The difficulties included adequate rations for the black laborers;[84] a contract with the firm of Wood and Meador of Stone Mountain, Georgia, to supply a large number of granite window and door sills;[85] the hiring of more laborers;[86] a contract for making a considerable number of window sashes and doors;[87] lumber for building skids, window frames, wheel barrow tines, a carpenter's shop and store house at Vineville, and the lumber for the brickyard;[88] and the acquisition of iron columns for the main building.[89]

Despite the tribulations, Mallet reported on 1 April 1863, that the brickyard was completed, together with brick-making machines. The laborers had produced the first brick a few days before. Much labor had been expended upon the work in early 1863 because two causeways were needed to afford a firm road through two swampy lagoons in the area, and much grading was necessary to obtain the proper slope and smoothness of surface. The laborers had dug and thrown up 19,000 cubic yards of brick clay. These projects, together with such others as building eight brick machines and digging four wells, delayed the completion of the yard until the spring of 1863. However, Mallet needed Gorgas' aid to secure additional cars for the Macon and Western Railroad so that line, so necessary to the completion of the project and its future operations, could haul bricks to the grounds "with certainty or even moderate rapidity." It was essential that the bricklayers were not suddenly thrown out of employment from time to time.[90] Moreover, Mallet needed $50,000 to carry on operations for the second quarter of 1863. This included $10,000 for the purchase of lumber;

---

[83] Mallet to Gorgas, 18 May 1863, Ibid.

[84] Mallet to Gorgas, Macon, 24 February 1863, Ibid.

[85] Mallet to Wood, Meador and Company, Macon, 3 March 1863, Ibid.

[86] J.A. McTruder to Mallett, Midville, GA., 2 March 1863, Letters and Telegrams Received, Laboratories, 1862-65; O.R. Singleton to Mallet, Columbus, GA., 16 May 1863, Ibid.; and Mallet to A.S. Nicholson, Macon, 28 May 1863, Letters Sent, Laboratories, 1862-64.

[87] Mallet to W.H. Goodrich, Macon, 5 March 1863, Letters Sent, Laboratories, 1862-64.

[88] Wadley, Jones, and Company to Mallet, Herndon, GA., 12 March 1863, Letters and Telegrams Received, Laboratories, 1862-65; Mallet to Wadley, Jones and Company, Macon, 30 March 1863, Letters Sent, Laboratories, 1862-64; Mallet to Wadley, Jones and Company, Macon, 3 April 1863, Letters Sent, Laboratories, 1862-64.

[89] Mallet to Gorgas, Macon, 19 March 1863, Letters Sent, Laboratories, 1862-64.

[90] Mallet to Gorgas, Macon, 1 April 1863, Ibid.

$8,000 for wood (used for burning brick); $3,000 for cut stone; $5,000 for sashes, window frames, doors, and door frames; $3,000 to pay clerks and foremen; $9,000 to pay mechanics; $9,000 to pay laborers; and $3,000 for contingencies.[91]

In late April, Mallet was presented with still another difficulty. His architect, Fulton, was ill, a condition which threatened to slow down the work. In an effort to solve this problem, Mallet wrote Albert L. West, Architect of the Augusta Arsenal, offering him a position if Fulton did not recover soon.[92] On 1 May, Mallet offered West the position on a temporary basis, but felt honorbound to restore Fulton when he recovered. The salary of $180 a month would be made permanent if Fulton did not recover his health sufficiently to return to work.[93] West replied on 8 May, accepting the position.[94] By late June 1863, Fulton had sufficiently recovered to return to work, prompting Mallet to write Rains that West could return to Augusta.[95]

By 7 May, the brickyard was in full operation, and about three- quarters of a million bricks had been molded. Mallet believed the quality of the bricks was very good, and the laborers had burned them in half the time with an expenditure of about 2/3 the amount of wood which brick burners in Macon had led Mallet to believe. Mallet hoped to begin laying bricks in two or three days, and the only problem on the horizon was the lack of railroad cars to haul them to the building site. In explaining the matter to Gorgas, he noted, "The distance by railroad is but about 2 miles by the common road about 3 miles. The long sandy hills on the latter route would however render the hauling of bricks by wagon enormously expensive. Many additional teams would have to be bought or hired."[96]

By mid-May 1863, Mallet needed fifty additional laborers to grade land. He could also use five or six women, "provided they are able to work with the shovel or spade," and twelve or fifteen boys from fifteen or sixteen to twenty years old who could carry brick molds, wheel bricks, and drive wagons. The women would grade land and dig foundations. After awhile most of the men could be used as helpers to bricklayers and carpenters in the erection of the buildings. Mallet offered to pay $20 a month for fully grown "stout" men, $16 for boys, and $15 for women and younger boys. The Blacks would be sheltered

---

[91] Mallet to Gorgas, "Budget for Second Quarter for 1863," Macon, 6 April 1863, Ibid.

[92] Mallet to Albert L. West, Macon, 27 April 1863, Ibid.

[93] Mallet to Albert L. West, Macon, 1 May 1863, Ibid.

[94] Albert L. West to Mallet, Augusta, 8 May 1863, Letters and Telegrams Received, Laboratories, 1862-65.

[95] Mallet to Rains, Macon, 27 June 1863, Letters Sent, Laboratories, 1862-64.

[96] Mallet to Gorgas, 7 May 1863, Ibid.

in good frame houses, already erected, fed by the Army's Commissary Department, and have a physician (contracted by the Medical Department) "in constant and exclusive attendance upon them." Ad valorem taxes levied upon the Blacks would be paid by the Government, but the owner had to supply clothing, shoes, and bed covers.[97]

Work had progressed during the spring of 1863 to the point where Mallet made plans to purchase a Confederate flag for the facility.[98] He also asked Gorgas to make suggestions about the inscription over the door of the main tower entrance. The bricks made in the brickyard were satisfactory, and the laborers continued to produce large supplies of both pressed and common brick of excellent quality. The foundations of the main building were all laid, and the greater part of the exterior and partition walls were up to the level of the joists. The temporary buildings needed during construction, including a carpenter's shop, a lime store, and other structures, were completed, and building materials were coming in steadily. The grading of the branch railroad embankment connecting the facility was progressing. Work progressed on the main building to the point that carpenters were preparing the joists to support the ground floor and the granite door sills were all laid.[99] During the summer the stone sills of the principal building and the joists of the first floor were all laid. A number of door frames had been received, and were being erected. The foundations of the one-story-high right wing were laid, and the walls carried up to the level for the joists. The foundations for one of the large chimney stacks were also laid.[100] Despite these achievements the workmen had to stop work on the main building for a week or two in the summer because of a shortage of pressed brick of uniform color for the outside of the structure. The almost constant rains of the wet summer of 1863 had ruined large quantities of unburned bricks, and had also greatly slowed the general progress of the work. However, under orders from Gorgas, Mallet was forced to spend much of his time traveling to the other laboratories to supervise their production, an activity which also slowed construction. On a more positive note, some of the machinery, including a steam engine for driving the wood planer and saws and a boiler, had been installed in the main building. A chimney was completed and a large engine well (for permanent use) was finished and bricked up. The carpenters had framed and prepared all of the second floor timbers and joists, and were working on the

---

[97] Mallet to Hon. O.R. Singleton, Macon, 18 May 1863, Ibid.

[98] First Lieutenant A.T. Cunningham to Mallet, Macon, 15 May 1863, Letters and Telegrams Received, Laboratories, 1862-65.

[99] Mallet to Gorgas, Macon, 27 June 1863, Letters Sent, Laboratories, 1862-64.

[100] Mallet to Gorgas, Macon, 3 August 1863, Ibid.

roof framing for the main building. Workers continued to grade the railroad bank and excavate the remainder of the front line of buildings.[101]

On 24 September 1863, Military Storekeeper William McMain wrote Mallet, then in Selma, that the work continued to progress, but had been slowed due to a great deal of sickness among the brickyard workers.[102] By mid-November Mallet told an anxious Gorgas that he needed to hire more slaves for building purposes because of delays caused by the wet summer. Rain had "fallen to such an extent and so frequently as very seriously to retard all building operations." Still the area had been completely excavated, the site for the front line of buildings leveled, the principal building constructed up to the level of the floor of the second story, and workmen were constructing part of the second floor joists. The foundation of the right and left low buildings was completed and the foundations of one long chimney stack laid. The railroad embankment was graded nearly to its connection with the main track of the railroad, and the temporary buildings completed. Mallet assured his chief, "With proper money means the summer of next year ought to see nearly all the heavy work finished."[103]

During 1864, work continued very slowly. Work on the brick boundary wall was slowly proceeding by mid-February, but inflation had seriously retarded progress on the building, forcing Mallet to request $169,000 to support operations for the first quarter of the year,[104] and another $200,000 for the second quarter.[105] By 18 February, laborers had completed the grading of the branch track, and had laid cross ties for part of it, at least enough to switch off a train from the main line. Furthermore, the Superintendent of the Macon and Western promised Mallet enough old railroad iron to lay this portion, and even planned to lay the track for him. Mallet only needed a few kegs of railroad spikes from Tredegar to finish this initial section of track. He reported. "The laying this little piece of track will greatly facilitate the progress of my work, and will diminish the danger which now results from cars standing to unload upon the main line of R.R."[106] Unfortunately for the Confederacy, the Central Laboratory

---

[101] Ibid.

[102] William H. McMain to Mallet, Macon, 24 September 1863, Ibid.

[103] Mallet to Gorgas, Macon, 16 November 1863, Ibid.; For details about the work in December see William H. McMain to Mallet, Macon, 23 December 1863, Ibid.

[104] Mallet to Gorgas, Macon, 12 February 1864, Letters Sent, Laboratories, 1862-64; Mallet to Gorgas, "Funds Needed for First Quarter of 1864," Macon, 4 January 1864, Ibid.

[105] Mallet to Gorgas, "Funds Needed for Second Quarter of 1864," Macon, 2 April 1864, Ibid.

[106] Mallet to Gorgas, Macon, 18 February 1864, Ibid.

was never completed. The coming of the scene of operations to the vicinity of Macon in 1864 intervened.

As Sherman pushed closer to Atlanta, Mallet was forced to turn over one-fifth of his workforce to work on fortifications.[107] Then, as Sherman began his series of shattering victories over Hood, Colonel Gibbs, Commandant of the Post at Macon, ordered all detailed men to report immediately for transportation to Atlanta to help defend that city.[108] All work on the Laboratory, together with the construction of the Armory, had to be suspended.[109]

As the March to the Sea began in November 1864, Mallet, under orders from Gorgas, sent all Laboratory stores to Savannah for safe-keeping. He sent the cap factory and part of the Laboratory, with its necessary workforce, to Selma. All of the machinery was taken down and prepared for shipment to Savannah.[110] However, as Sherman advanced on that city Mallet received orders to send his stores and equipment on the Savannah, Albany and Gulf Railroad to Thomasville in Southwest Georgia, a then-remote town which was out of the path of Sherman's armies.[111] By 25 December 1864, Calvin Fay, Confederate Agent in Thomasville, reported to Mallet "all your stores, and all of Col Cuylers have arrived here that left Savannah, and are all in store, except one car load of machinery of Col Cuylers which is still on the car." From Thomasville the machinery and stores were transferred to wagons for the long trip to Albany, a point even more remote in Southwest Georgia, and a place which was not on the railroad at that time.[112]

In February 1865, Mallet, desperate for lead to make bullets needed by the Confederate forces to fight Sherman as he advanced through the Carolinas, urged the procurement of lead from city-owned water pipes in Mobile. He wrote Dr J.C. Nott of Mobile College on 11 February, "Our need of lead is very great. Will you sanction the removal of lead water pipes from Mobile College?"[113] He also bombarded such officials as Major Henry Myers, Ordnance Officer in Mobile, and Lieutenant Colonel W.R. Hunt of the Nitre and Mining Bureau, with requests to obtain lead from the water pipes under the stores, houses and

---

[107] William H. McMain, for Mallet, to Gorgas, Telegram, Macon, 23 June 1864, Roll 10, Telegrams Sent, Laboratories, 1863-65.

[108] Col. George C. Gibbs, Order, Headquarters Post, Macon, 22 July 1864, Letters and Telegrams Received, Laboratories, 1862-64.

[109] Gorgas to Mallet, Telegram, Richmond, 22 July 1864, Ibid.

[110] Mallet to Gorgas, Telegram, Macon, 21 November 1864, Telegrams Sent, Laboratories, 1863-65.

[111] Calvin Fay to Mallet, Thomasville, GA., 13 December 1864, Letters and Telegrams Received, Laboratories, 1862-65.

[112] Calvin Fay to Mallet, Thomasville, 25 December 1864, Ibid.

[113] Mallet to Dr. J.C. Nott, Telegram, Macon, 11 February 1865, Telegrams Sent, Laboratories, 1863-65.

streets of the Alabama seaport.[114] On 14 February, he told Captain W.H. Warren at the Arsenal in Macon, then in Augusta, "Can send you one or two hundred thousand caps in a day or two."[115] On the following day he urged T.J. Stanford, Agent for the Rock Island Paper Mills in Columbus, "Make thousand pounds of thin and five thousand pounds of thick paper at once" for cartridges.[116] To summarize Mallet's efforts in that final spring in the life of the young Confederate nation, he tried until the very end to produce musket caps, sheet copper, and musket balls in his partially-completed Laboratory, and in rented quarters on Third Street in Macon, a place in which he had operated since 1862.[117]

By late March, General William W. Mackall, commanding the Post at Macon, ordered officials at the Laboratory to turn over .54 and .58 caliber rifles used by a Laboratory Company organized to aid in the defense of Macon in the spring of 1864, to Confederate soldiers passing through Macon to join the reorganized Army of Tennessee, then opposing Sherman in North Carolina. Colonel Cuyler promised to replace them with smooth bore muskets as soon as possible.[118] Mallet wired Gorgas on 25 March, that, due to the lack of money to continue the work and the general pressure upon ordnance facilities "would it not be well to suspend all work on permanent buildings?"[119] Mallet never received an answer to his question because Richmond fell to Grant on 3 April, forcing Gorgas to flee southward with the Confederate Government. Mallet, however, continued to work to supply the armies in the field in the Lower South.[120] The stage was set for Wilson and the fall of Macon.

---

[114] Mallet to Maj. Henry Myers, Macon, 11 February 1865, and Mallet to Lt. Col. W.R. Hunt, Macon, 11 February 1865, both Ibid.

[115] Mallet to Capt. W.H. Warren, Macon, 14 February 1865, Ibid.

[116] Mallet to T.J. Stanford, Telegram, Macon, 15 February 1865, Ibid.

[117] Mallet to Gorgas, Telegram, Macon, 16 February 1865, Ibid.; Mallet to Col. George W. Rains, Telegram, Macon, 16 February 1865, Ibid; Mallet to John Frazer and Company, Telegram, Macon, 16 February 1865, Ibid; Mallet to Lt. Col. J.C. Moore, Telegram, 18 February 1865, Ibid; Mallet to Lt. Col. J.C. Moore, Telegram, Macon, 20 February 1865, Ibid; Mallet to Gen. Wright, Telegram, Macon, 20 February 1865; Mallet to Lt. Col. J.C. Moore, Telegram, Macon, 21 February 1865; Mallet to Capt. W.H. Warren, Telegram, Macon, 3 March 1865, all Ibid.

[118] Cuyler to Lt. Calhoun, Macon, 20 March 1865, Letters and Telegrams Received, Laboratories, 1862-65; Cuyler to Calhoun, Macon, 21 March 1865, Ibid. Calhoun was commanding the Laboratory during Mallet's absence.

[119] Mallet to Gorgas, Telegram, Macon, 25 March 1865, Telegrams Sent, Laboratories, 1863-65.

[120] Mallet to Lt. Col. J.C. Moore, Telegram, Macon, 29 March 1865, Ibid.; Mallet to Henry Myers, Telegram, Macon, 30 March 1865, Ibid.; Mallet to Gorgas, Telegram, Macon, 30 March 1865, Ibid.

1. Railroad Station, Macon, Georgia. On the second floor of this building were the headquarters of General Marcus J. Wright, commanding the Post of Macon in 1864.

Eugenius A. Nisbet

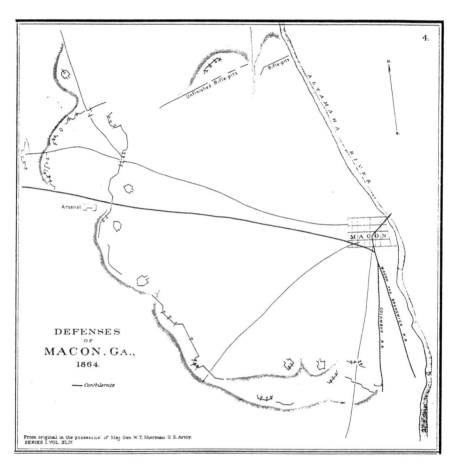

4.

N.

S.

ALTAMAHA RIVER

Unfinished Rifle-pits

Rifle-pits

Arsenal

MACON

MACON and BRUNSWICK R.R.

COLUMBUS R.R.

DEFENSES
OF
MACON. GA.,
1864.

—— Confederate

3. Map of Macon, Georgia, 1864, showing defenses around the city.

4. Brown's Hotel, 1875

5. Cotton Factory, Macon, GA., ca. 1876.

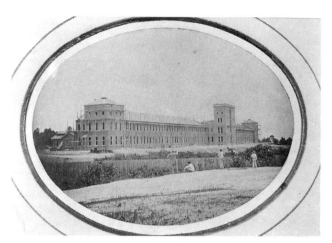

6. Macon Armory, 1865.

7. Residence of William B. Johnston, Macon, GA. Today the building is known as the Hay House.

8. Confederate States Laboratory, ca. 1870's.

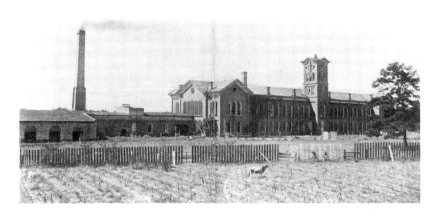

9.Confederate States Laboratory, ca. 1912.

10. Wesleyan Female College, 1868.

11. Railroad Depot, Macon, Georgia ca. 1876.

12. Samuel S. Dunlap House. Used as Stoneman's headquarters on 30 July 1864. The house is now used as the Superintendent's Residence at the Ocmulgee National Monument.

13. Schofield Iron Works, ca. 1876.

14. Group of unidentified Confederate soldiers from Macon.

15. Hendley Varner Napier, ca. 1862. Ocmulgee Rangers (Company A, 19th Georgia Cavalry; then 10th Confederate Cavalry).

16. Mrs. Selina Shirley Poe. Led the women of Macon in support of Confederate soldiers and their families.

17. Brigadier General Edward Dorr Tracy, Jr., ca. 1863.

18. Simri Rose in Masonic dress, ca. 1860.

19. William E. Brice, ca. 1861. Member of the Thomson Guards.

20. Railroad car shed, Macon, GA.

21. Telegraph and Messenger Building, ca. 1876, Macon, Georgia.

22. Fort Hawkins as it might have appeared during the war.

23. Blind Asylum, ca. 1876. Used as a hospital, known as the Blind Asylum Hospital, during the war.

24. Washington Block (built in 1857) ca. 1879. Mulberry Street from Second Street, Macon, Georgia.

25. Stephen Collins, Mayor of Macon 1864-1866.

26. Ovid G. Sparks, Mayor of Macon 1858-1860, 1863.

27. Methven S. Thomson, Mayor of Macon 1860-1862.

28. John J. Gresham, Mayor of Macon 1843-1847 and civic leader during the war.

29. Joseph Clisby, ca. 1860, photograph of a drawing.

30. William W. Carnes, ca. 1862, in Confederate Uniform.

31. Dr. Stanford E. Chaille, 1868, Surgeon in charge of the
Ocmulgee Hospital.

32. Private L.W. Hunt, Macon Guards (Company C, 8th Georgia Regiment).

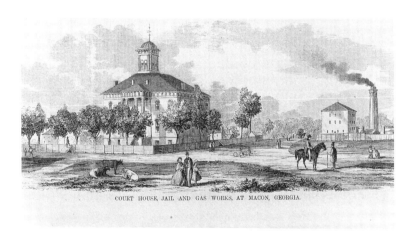

COURT HOUSE, JAIL AND GAS WORKS, AT MACON, GEORGIA.

33. Bibb County Courthouse, ca. 1860s with Macon Gas Company on right.

34. Howell Cobb as Secretary of the Treasury in the Buchanan Administration.

35. Howell Cobb, Jr., after the war.

36. Major John Addison Cobb.

37. Colonel Horace Capron, Massachusetts Commandery.

38. Major General James H. Wilson, Massachusetts Commandery.

39. Colonel Robert H.G. Minty, Massachusetts Commandery.

40. Major General George M. Stoneman, Massachusetts Commandery.
The Loyal Legion and the US Army Military History Institute.

41. General Joseph E. Johnston.

42. Brigadier General Felix Robertson.

43. Colonel Smith D. Atkins.

44. Camp Oglethorpe, Macon Georgia. Federal prisoners spending their leisure time.

45. Prisoners digging escape tunnels at Camp Oglethorpe, Macon, Georgia.

TO THE CITIZENS OF MACON.

HEAD QUARTERS,
Macon, July 30, 1864.

The enemy is now in sight of your houses. We lack force. I appeal to every man, Citizen or Refugee, who has a gun of any kind, or can get one, to report at the Court House with the least possible delay, that you may be thrown into Companies and aid in the defense of the city. A prompt response is expected from every patriot.

JOSEPH E. BROWN.

☞ Report to Col. Cary W. Styles, who will forward an organization as rapidly as possible.

46. Gov. Joseph Brown's message to the citizens of Macon to take up arms in defense of the city.

47. Remains of Confederate breastworks, 1955, in Vineville, near Pio
Nono Avenue. UDC Cross of Honor recipients, L to R: Frank C.
Jones, George M. Nottingham, Jr., and Val Sheridan.

48. Nathan Campbell Munroe, Jr.

49. Mrs. Nathan C. Munroe

Chapter 11

Life in Wartime Macon: 1862-1864

By the spring of 1862, the people of Macon had abandoned their hopes that the war would be short with victory for the Confederacy coming in the first year. Therefore, the tenor of life seemed to reflect the belief that the Confederacy would hope to fight a long war to achieve its independence. When the first reports of the Battle of Shiloh arrived in the city on Monday, 7 April 1862, everyone was ecstatic because they thought it was a Confederate victory. Nathan C. Munroe wrote, "This has been a very exciting day for us in town. When I went into town the flags were flying & soon the bells commenced ringing in joyful exultation of our great victory over the Federal Army in Mississipi [sic]." People rushed through the streets offering congratulations to each other that the tide of a war which had seemed to be going against them in the West had now turned in their favor. The news of the death of General Albert Sidney Johnston, commander of the Army of Tennessee, at Shiloh caused the universal happiness to turn to sorrow at "the loss of so great and good a commander and the deep tone of sorrow which pervades the whole community is a well merited tribute to the gallant man who offered his life so ready a sacrifice upon the alter of his countrys freedom." The people looked hourly for more victories in Virginia and North Carolina. Munroe hoped that God would be merciful toward the Confederacy in the East as he had been in the West, but "with less fatality to the noble officers who lead."[1]

A few days later Munroe's initial optimism was dimmed by news of the Federal attack upon Fort Pulaski. He observed to his beloved daughter, Bannie, that four or five shells a minute were thrown into the fort, causing him to hope the defenders had "escaped without material injury."[2] Munroe learned the news of the surrender of the Fort on 12 April.[3]

---

[1] Nathan C. Munroe, Jr. to Bannie Kell, Sylvan Lodge, 7 April 1862, Kell Letters.

[2] Nathan C. Munroe, Jr. to Bannie Kell, Sylvan Lodge, 11 April 1862, Ibid.

[3] Nathan C. Munroe, Jr. to Bannie Kell, Sylvan Lodge, 12 April 1862, Ibid. The fort surrendered on the afternoon of April 11.

A month later the Federal prisoners captured at Shiloh arrived in Macon and proved, according to Munroe, "the principal topic of interest and excitement just now." Citizens turned out to guard them until units were assigned to perform the chore. This caused the temporary guards to be "very tired and reluctant to perform sustained duty." Munroe went down to see the prisoners at Camp Oglethorpe for an hour's visit. Accompanied by an officer and Presbyterian minister David Wills, Munroe chatted with the prisoners who appeared "contented and cheerful." The entire community felt the prisoners should be paroled and sent home. But the more intelligent Maconites felt the Federal Government understood that the Confederacy was short of food, and, therefore, would not exchange prisoners "but will leave them to help eat us out."[4]

Overall, despite the presence of the prisoners at Camp Oglethorpe, and the activities concerning hospitals, Confederate ordnance facilities, and the fact that the city was a military post, the period from the spring of 1862 until the spring of 1864 was marked by as normal a city life as could be possible in a nation which was waging a life and death struggle with a more powerful enemy along several fronts and on the sea. Macon, to some extent, seemed concerned with showing the world that life might return to some degree of normalcy despite the war. Munroe continued to mourn his wife whom he missed more as time went on. On 10 May 1862, he visited her grave in Rose Hill Cemetery, relating to Bannie that "all is growing beautiful and the vines and roses in fuller bloom than they have been in a long time."[5]

At times Munroe appeared more interested in going to church than in the war. On 12 May he went to the First Presbyterian Church on Mulberry Street to hear his friend Reverend Wills preach, but was disappointed when he heard "a stranger to preach for him," although the sermon was "very good." In the evening he took family members to the country.[6]

This attitude was shared by Macon merchant T. R. Bloom who related to his friend John B. Lamar, gone to be with his brother-in-law, Howell Cobb in Virginia, "There is no news of special interest since you left. Mrs Wm. B. Johnston has had a fine daughter, we have been blessed with abundant rains & the corn crop will be the best ever made in the state, so also pease & potatoes." He then went on to relate that corn was selling at $1.00 a bushel, while cotton was bringing fifteen to seventeen cents a pound.[7]

The period, however, was not without its distractions. Destructive fires continued to provide excitement and concern. An early morning fire on Fourth Street at the residence of Mrs. Newton in early May destroyed several trunks of

---

[4] Nathan C. Munroe, Jr. to Bannie Kell, Sylvan Lodge, 8 May 1862, Ibid.

[5] Nathan C. Munroe, Jr. to Bannie Kell, Sylvan Lodge, 10 May 1862, Ibid.

[6] Nathan C. Munroe, Jr. to Bannie Kell, Macon, 12 May 1862, Ibid.

[7] T. R. Bloom to John B. Lamar, Macon, 15 July 1862, Cobb Papers, 1862.

clothing. Young America Engine Company No. 3 turned out, but, learning that it was out, returned to their homes. The fire, as was usually the case, appeared to be the work of "an incendiary," prompting a reporter for the *Daily Telegraph* to urge the people "to be vigilant and watchful."[8]

In July, another fire caused the destruction of a one-story wooden building, owned by D. B. Woodruff and used as a factory for making friction matches. Again, a *Daily Telegraph* reporter described the blaze as the "the work of an incendiary."[9]

Although a number of fires destroyed stables, the waste house of the Macon Cotton Mills, and an occasional house,[10] one of the worst fires started early in the morning of 20 February 1863, in a large livery stable owned by the firm of Hayden and Goolsby. After destroying the stable, the blaze consumed one half the block fronting on Walnut and Second Streets. The buildings destroyed included Stubblefield's Stables, Hayden and Goolsby's Stables, a warehouse and office occupied by T. R. Bloom, a dwelling occupied by Mrs. Wrigley, another house owned by Mrs. McReynolds, and a large workshop occupied by Nathan Weed which was used to manufacture wooden and iron agricultural implements. The machinery was very valuable because it was driven by a steam engine. The fire also burned a good many outbuildings which belonged to the major structures fronting on the street. Hayden and Goolsby lost sixteen valuable horses together with 5,000 bushels of corn and 150,000 pounds of fodder. They also lost their entire stock of fine carriages and harness, but managed to save their buggies, but were only insured for one-third of the value of the property. Nathan Weed also lost heavily in his buildings, steam engine, tools, and stock. T. R. Bloom did not lose as much because most of his merchandise was removed. The people who lived in the houses also managed to save most of their furniture.[11] A reporter for the *Daily Telegraph* again blamed the fire on an incendiary, observing, "so intense was the heat that the firemen could not approach the burning stables, but succeeded by hard labor in arresting the progress of the fire at a narrow alley, bounded on one side by Weed's Factory and on the other by a small wooden building, occupied as the Law Office of Lanier and Anderson." The paper noted that the inferno was "the most disastrous fire we have had in Macon for several years."[12]

---

[8] *Macon Daily Telegraph,* 7 May 1862.

[9] Ibid., 21 July 1862.

[10] Ibid., 13 Sept, 18 December 1862, 11, 13 February, 14 March 1863, Ibid.

[11] Ibid., 21 February 1863; *Georgia Journal and* Messenger, 25 February 1863.

[12] Ibid. The law offices of Lanier and Anderson were occupied by future poet and musician Sidney Lanier's father, Robert Lanier and his law partner Clifford Anderson. Anderson was the brother of Lanier's wife, Mary Jane Anderson Lanier.

In late March a rash of fires broke out. One of them destroyed the one-story cottage home of Hardin Johnson, along with all of the family's furniture and clothing. A correspondent for the *Georgia Journal and Messenger* reported the Johnson Family barely escaped with their lives. Their house was built on pillars two or three feet high. The out buildings were also burned. A few days earlier Johnson's stable was destroyed by fire. Two days later A. R. Freeman's stable was partially burned in another fire. During the same period Mayor Methvin S. Thomson's smokehouse was set on fire, but was saved through an early alarm. Another building, this time a large wooden storehouse, filled with 1700 bushels of corn, located on Cotton Avenue, nearly opposite the City Hall, was set on fire in the upper story. A small office building adjoining it was also destroyed, together with two brick buildings on the other side. One of these buildings was used as a storehouse for cotton, sixty-five bales of which were burned. The fire was stopped by the efforts of the firemen, aided by a dead wall, next to a one-story wooden house. Fireman stood on the roof of this building, with hoses in hand, and wet blankets. They maintained their position, although they were nearly suffocated by smoke, and in danger of being crushed from the house. The owner of the office was Mrs. Dr. Gorman, and the wooden storehouse and brick storehouse next door belonged to the estate of Marshall Thomas L. Ross. The other brick house was owned by John Hollingsworth, the only person who was not insured.[13] Commenting on these fires, the reporter for the *Journal and Messenger* exclaimed, "These facts show that a bold incendiary is at work, and it becomes our police and others to be specially watchful in that vicinity. No possible object can be imagined that could be attained by these fires, unless to gratify a spirit of revenge or of wanton mischief....Our city seems to be doomed to conflagration. There is an enemy among us who should be sought out and made to pull hemp or cotton."[14]

Fires, of course, made no distinction between prominent buildings and stables or between the rich and the poor. On the morning of 9 July 1863, the attic of the city's leading hostelry, the Lanier House, was badly burned. Since the upper story was seventy feet above the street, the fire engines could not build up enough pressure to reach the area. Furniture was thrown out of the windows of the upper story, and out of adjacent government warehouses. Firemen crawled into the attic area which lay under a flat roof covered with tin, and was only three feet high and very difficult to work in because it was obstructed with many braces and girders. Every fifteen or twenty feet a strong lattice of inch and a half plank ran all the way across. This completely divided the attic into sections. After the fire was extinguished, the building appeared as "a monument of

---

[13] *Macon Daily Telegraph*, 17 March 1863; *Georgia Journal and Messenger*, 18 March 1863.

[14] *Georgia Journal and Messenger*, 18 March 1863.

desolation," stripped of its furniture and with the floors covered with mud and water.[15] Amazingly, only a week later, the hotel resumed full operations, the damages being repaired "as rapidly as the scarcity of building material will allow."[16]

Other fires in 1863 and early 1864, proved more destructive. One of these destroyed the Central Georgia Manufacturing Company's building with a loss of $8,000 to its owner, James Van Valkenburg.[17] Another fire completely burned McEvoy's Warehouse. Used as a government storehouse, the building contained 230 bales of cotton owned by T. L. Harris, who served as agent for other parties. An adjacent building, used as a kitchen, adjacent to the Floyd House Hospital, caught fire from flying cinders. Fortunately, the fire was quickly put out.[18]

On 6 May 1864, a very destructive fire in East Macon began in a cotton warehouse owned by J. A. Nelson. The fire burned the buildings on the north side of Bridge Street, all of which were used to store cotton. These included a new warehouse owned by Lightfoot and Flanders, and numerous dwellings and outhouses behind these buildings. The brick storehouse next to Lightfoot and Flanders also burned. The blaze then swept eastward, consuming everything in its path. The buildings, all constructed of wood, burned quickly. Five thousand bales of cotton were destroyed, including some cotton owned by the Confederacy. The fire department finally stopped the fire on the hill on the eastern corner of the square where it began. The firemen were hindered due to the lack of water because the area's wells dried up as soon as they were broached. The total loss amounted to $74,915. According to a reporter for the *Daily Telegraph*, a "single cistern would have saved much of the cotton and arrested the fire at the alley midway the square."[19] The loss included a small unoccupied two-story dwelling built by William P. Kendall in 1821, and considered the oldest frame building in Macon.[20]

The period also was marked by several attacks and murders. In early January 1864, Maconite John McLane was walking past the Floyd House Hospital when he was attacked and severely stabbed just below his chest. His attacker, a patient in the Hospital named David Johns, a member of the 4th Louisiana Regiment and known "as a desperate character," escaped for a brief time. He was arrested and placed in the Guard House. Two other people were also attacked at the same

---

[15] *Macon Daily Telegraph*, 10 July 1863.

[16] Ibid., 17 July 1863.

[17] Ibid., 15 July 1863.

[18] Ibid., 11 April 1864.

[19] Ibid., 7 May 1864.

[20] Ibid., 11 May 1864. For information on other fires which occurred in Macon during the period see *Georgia Journal and Messenger*, 16 September 1863, and *Macon Daily Telegraph*, 23 September 1863.

time. One of the attackers, another soldier named Thomas Essex, was arrested and also placed in the Guard House. The third culprit, while attempting to strike his victim with a large knife, had his arm caught by a passerby, and was thereby prevented from completing his attack. At the same time the attacks were taking place, a number of bricks were thrown upon people passing in the street. The *Journal and Messenger*'s reporter labeled the attacks as "a preconcerted matter for a wanton attack on the people passing, by sundry soldiers of the hospital." The reporter added there was "No cause whatever...for any disturbance."[21]

Another Maconite, Robert Martin, was not so fortunate as McLane. He was stabbed to death by his attacker, James Burn, at 6:00 P.M., 15 January 1864, on Third Street. The knife entered Martin below his right arm and ranged between his lungs and his liver. Another blow severed the main artery in his left arm near the shoulder, nearly cutting off the arm. Martin staggered along the street shouting, "He has killed me," reached a nearby store, turned in, and died in a few minutes.[22]

On another occasion, two prisoners named Cary and Bryant, who were convicted of assault and robbery and sentenced for terms of nineteen and eighteen years respectively, escaped from the Bibb County Jail on 19 January 1864. The men were chained in the third story, and a guard was stationed below them in the jail yard. They removed their chains, broke or picked the lock of their cell door, and slide down a rope made from their mattresses and blankets. A woman who claimed to be Nellie Bryan, wife of one of the prisoners, helped them to escape. They eluded the guard and ran into the nearby woods. Cary was later arrested a few miles from Macon by a trooper of the Bibb County Cavalry, and sent to the State Penitentiary at Milledgeville. Bryant was recaptured by Sheriff Hodges at a house in the city where he had gone to change his clothes before leaving town. The sheriff's posse surrounded the house, but Bryant disappeared up the chimney. The Sheriff, however, called him down and Bryant surrendered.[23]

Robberies were also committed during the period. One of them netted the thieves eight or nine thousand dollars from the store of Bedingfield and Company. The blame was placed on young men claiming to be soldiers, who managed to make their escape.[24]

Sometimes people were severely injured in accidents. Lucy Knott, daughter of prominent Maconite J.W. Knott, was thrown from a buggy and badly injured

---

[21] *Georgia Journal and Messenger*, 13 January 1864. According to the paper, McLane survived the attack, although he was severely injured.

[22] *Macon Daily Telegraph*, 16 January 1864.

[23] *Georgia Journal and Messenger*, 20 January 1864.

[24] Ibid., 1 June 1864.

in September, 1863, when her horse was frightened by boys flying kites in the streets.[25]

Perhaps two of the most serious losses to the community occurred, however, in the military. One of these was the death of John B. Lamar, Howell Cobb's brother-in-law and one of Macon's wealthiest and most prominent citizens. Lamar was killed at the Battle of Crampton's Gap, part of a larger engagement known as the Battle of South Mountain on 14 September 1862, while serving as a volunteer aide to Cobb who commanded a brigade in the battle. Lamar was trying to rally a portion of Cobb's Brigade in a desperate engagement which Cobb called "the most terrific one of the war." The Confederates were flanked and forced to retreat, although the men fought well. Lamar received a gunshot wound in his left lung and died in a few hours. Cobb tried to comfort his wife, Mary Anne, saying, "The blow which has fallen upon our own family circle in the death of your noble brother is indeed a severe one- well do I know how it will grieve your heart when the news shall reach you." Mary Anne had "however your comforter–who never fails you in the hour of your trials & to that kind Providence must I commend your wounded heart- not doubting he will prove your truest and greatest solace and comfort."[26]

Cobb family friend Lewis Neale Whittle tried to console Mrs. Cobb saying he had begged Lamar not to go to war, that he was of more use to the Cause at home, then he was in the field,; "but after considering the matter some time," Whittle observed, "he said he could remain here no longer & that a sense of duty impelled him to go. Poor fellow! High as he stood with his friends & acquaintances generally, few of them knew how noble & high toned a man he was."[27]

The *Daily Telegraph*'s reporter commented, "It was several days before our community would consent to believe that this gallant soul was no more; but doubt is no longer permitted us. As sad and heavy as is the blow, we must accept it, and mourn the loss of one of our bravest, best and most useful men."[28]

A family friend, M.A. Brantley, wrote Mrs. Cobb from Atlanta that Lamar "was no ordinary brother- with but few other ties he lavished upon his sister and her family a tender fathers love and generosity; not only were you bound to him by a natural sisterly affection,- but his cultivation made him your chosen intellectual companion and your ever judicious adviser."[29]

---

[25] *Georgia Journal and Messenger*, 16 September 1863.

[26] Howell Cobb to his wife, Charlestown, VA., 17 September 1862, Cobb Papers, 1862; *Macon Daily Telegraph*, 1 October 1862.

[27] Lewis N. Whittle to Mrs. Cobb, Macon, 29 September 1862, Cobb Papers, 1862.

[28] *Macon Daily Telegraph*, 1 October 1862. For an initial announcement of Lamar's death see Ibid., 27 September 1862.

[29] M.A. Brantley to Mary Anne Cobb, Atlanta, 2 October 1862, Cobb Papers.

For her part, Mary Ann Cobb bore up well with the stress caused by her brother's death. She revealed her innermost feelings to her husband, "You knew the extent of my devotion to that brother–and was prepared to hear of its overwhelming effect upon me and my family–and perhaps did not expect to hear shortly from me. It was well. For I am so constituted that sorrow strikes deeply into my heart paralyzing in a measure every faculty of the mind, rendering my tongue and pen mute–long-long after the first burst of feeling passes away." She went on to say that she owed "almost all the pleasure I ever enjoyed in childhood and youth–while the last twenty two years have attested his increasing devotion to me and my children in sunshine–or in clouds- in prosperity or adversity he has been to us the ever faithful loving and unchanging brother–uncle and friend. God only knows the depth of my sorrow." Lamar's death was, to her, "the greatest sorrow of my life."[30]

James Mercer Green called Lamar, whom he had served as personal physician before the war, "one of the few men whose good opinion I strongly desired. I have every reason to believe I had both his friendship & his respect- that he valued my opinions both personal & professional & that he reposed great confidence in me generally."[31]

Cobb, who served as executor of Lamar's estate, noted that his assets were valued at the then-enormous sum of $766,753.71. This included his plantation in Bibb County, worth $213,731, and his house, the Bears Den, together with slaves in Macon, $48,830.[32] Cobb, of course, moved to exempt Lamar's overseers from the draft.[33]

In April 1864, Cobb and his wife donated $6,000 to the Christ Church Parish in memory of Lamar. The Vestry invested the money in Confederate bonds.[34] When they received the donation they "Resolved that we the vestry will keep this fund invested until the state of the country is such as to enable them to use it in such manner, that it may be of permanent usefulness to the cause of religion."[35]

Lamar was initially buried at a cemetery in Keedysville, Maryland, at the western foot of the South Mountain. His sister wanted a handsome marble monument placed over Lamar's remains, but wanted to wait until the blockade was raised when the Cobbs could send to Europe for a monument, "one befitting his station and tastes." She added, "No Yankee marble shall ever cover

---

[30] Mary Anne Cobb to her husband, Athens, October 1862, Ibid.

[31] Dr. James Mercer Green to Cobb, Richmond, 17 November 1862, Ibid.

[32] John A. Cobb to his father, Macon, 11 February 1863, Ibid.

[33] J.M. Moore to Cobb, Macon, 22 July 1863, Ibid.

[34] Hart and Payne, *History of Christ Church Parish,* 42.

[35] Vestry of Christ Church to Cobb, Macon, n.d., Cobb Papers, 1864.

his remains. This is my wish."[36] Lamar's body was exhumed after the war and reinterred on December 9, 1866, at Rose Hill Cemetery on a bluff overlooking the Ocmulgee River.[37]

Another prominent Maconite who fell in the Maryland fighting was Major Philemon Tracy. Tracy, brother to Brigadier General Edward Dorr Tracy, was Editor of the *Daily Telegraph* before 1856. As a lawyer and politician he played an active role in the secession movement in Macon. Serving as major of the 6th Georgia Regiment, Tracy was badly wounded in the Seven Days Battles around Richmond. He rejoined his unit and was mortally wounded at the Battle of Sharpsburg, 17 September 1862. Editor Joseph Clisby called him "a man of generous, impulsive character–a brilliant writer–a fine scholar, possessed of natural endowments of the highest order."[38]

Maconites received another shock in May 1863, when another native son fell in battle. This time it was Brigadier General Edward Dorr Tracy, a native of Macon and brother-in-law of prominent Macon citizen William B. Johnston. Tracy fell at the Battle of Port Gibson, Mississippi, on 1 May when his brigade, part of General John Bowen's Division of General John C. Pemberton's Army, attempted to stop Grant's advance into Mississippi at the beginning of the final campaign for Vicksburg. The young lawyer-turned-general was, a reporter for the *Daily Telegraph* eulogized, "a man of most exemplary character, of decided piety, and universally respected and loved wherever known."[39] Tracy was almost instantly killed when a minie ball struck him in the heart.[40]

William Angelo Steele wrote his sister Ellen, Tracy's widow, that he tried to bring her husband's body through the lines in early June 1863. However, the fighting was so intense in that part of Mississippi, that Tracy was taken to the home of a local jurist, Judge Baldwin, dressed, and given a proper burial in Port Gibson in the Baldwin Lot.[41] Family friend Henry M. Smith later wrote giving more details of Tracy's death, and added, "In common with a bereaved nation I

---

[36] Mary Ann Cobb to her husband, Athens, 1 November 1862, Cobb Papers, 1862.

[37] Rose Hill Cemetery Interment Book, p. 164, Rose Hill Cemetery. For additional information concerning Lamar's death see John A. Cobb to his father, Athens, 3 October 1862, Cobb Papers, 1862; John L. Jones, Secretary, Christ Church, to Mary Anne Cobb, Macon, 28 October 1862; John A. Cobb to Mary Ann Cobb, Macon, 29 October 1862; Howell Cobb to his wife, Macon, 1 November 1862, all Ibid.

[38] *Macon Daily Telegraph*, 1 October 1862. For more details concerning Macon's losses in the Battle of Sharpsburg see Clifford Anderson to his wife, near Martinsburg, VA., 21 September 1862, Clifford Anderson Papers, Microfilm, Reel 1, SHC.

[39] Ibid., 2 May 1863.

[40] William Angelo Steele to his sister, Canton, MS., 7 June 1863, Tracy-Steele-Johnston Family Correspondence.

[41] William Angelo Steele to his sister, Ibid.

mourn with you this sad and heavy loss. God alone can enable you to bear it, and while in coming years the memory of the noble and honored Christian gentleman, we now regret shall be a precious heritage to his children, doubt not that the God he served will fulfill his promises to you and be your wise protection and unfailing friend."[42]

In late July, 1863, Tracy's sword was sent to his wife by J. Woodson Smith.[43] The Tracy and Johnston Families attempted to have Tracy's body returned from Port Gibson through the highest levels of the Confederate War Department, but were unsuccessful.[44] Tracy's remains were exhumed in May, 1866, and returned to Macon where they were reinterred in Rose Hill Cemetery on 10 May 1866.[45]

Colonel Robert A. Smith died of wounds received in the fighting during the Peninsular Campaign on 29 June 1862. Starting as Captain of the Macon Volunteers at the start of the war, he died as commander of the 44th Georgia Regiment. Plans called for him to be buried in Macon on 2 July. A writer for the *Georgia Journal and Messenger* praised Smith with the words, "He was a good citizen, and an exemplary and active member of the Methodist church of this city, and has well fulfilled his duty as a soldier and a Christian," and concluded, "He has his reward in the hearts of all who knew him, and in the better world."[46]

The news of the death of Captain Henry J. Menard of the Macon Guards, part of the 8th Georgia Regiment, also deeply stirred Maconites. Menard was mortally wounded at the Battle of Fredericksburg, and died in Richmond on 22 December 1862. His funeral was held at Christ Episcopal Church on 30 December.[47] The *Daily Telegraph*'s correspondent reported Menard was a "gallant young officer," who led "as brave a company as Georgia has sent to the battle-field," and who "has repeatedly distinguished himself for gallantry and good conduct."[48]

The death of so many prominent Maconites in battle naturally turned the thoughts of the people to religion. Statewide church meetings, revivals, and fast days were held in Macon during the period. The Synod of Georgia of the

---

[42] Henry M. Smith to Mrs. Ellen Steele Tracy, Jackson, MS., 5 July 1863, Ibid. This letter gives additional details concerning Tracy's death.

[43] J. Woodson Smith to Mrs. Ellen Steele Tracy, Lynchburg, VA., 28 July 1863, Ibid.

[44] John Archibald Campbell, Assistant Secretary of War, to Lt. Gen. Leonidas Polk, Richmond, 20 January 1863, Ibid.

[45] Rose Hill Cemetery Interment Book, p. 158, Rose Hill Cemetery.

[46] *Georgia Journal and Messenger*, 2 July 1862.

[47] Ibid., 23 and 30 December 1862.

[48] Ibid., 30 December 1862.

Methodist Episcopal Church met in the city in late November. At the meeting Synod received reports of the Board of Trustees of Oglethorpe University, of the Methodist Theological Seminary, and of the Board of Trustees of the Greensboro Female College.[49] During the meeting, presided over by Bishop James O. Andrew, the delegates appointed J. Blakely Smith as Secretary,[50] John A. Cobb told his fiancee Lucy Barrow, "There is a big time here now...the Methodist Conference is in session, about fifteen or twenty ministers were ordained."[51]

The Central Baptist Association met in Macon in late August 1863, and the ministers of the denomination preached sermons at all the churches in the city the following Sunday morning. During Sunday afternoon several interesting lectures were presented by Reverends A. Sherwood, T. Holman, and J. R. Kendrick to the Sabbath School children of the Baptist Church. Superintendent J. DeLoache of the Sunday School presided over the event which included "singing from the many caroling little songsters of the several classes, whose commingled notes discoursed more excellent music."[52]

Revivals were also important during the period. A well-attended revival was held nightly at the City Hall in April, 1863, presided over by Reverend T. R. Christian. A reporter for the *Daily Telegraph* urged the people to attend because "In this the hour of our country's utmost need, it were well if the people generally would unit in acknowledgment of their dependence on a higher power."[53] Another revival was held at the First Street Methodist Church in late April, 1864, during which fifty-five persons were converted.[54]

Fast days were also frequent. One of these days was observed "with great strictness" on 30 March 1863. The streets were silent and deserted as if it were Sunday, and the churches were crowded.[55]

At a Thanksgiving Day, held on 21 August 1864, the event was universally observed. All businesses were closed, and well-attended services were held in all of the churches both in the morning and in the afternoon.[56] Yet another Thanksgiving Day, billed as a "Union Thanksgiving Meeting, was held at the Presbyterian Church on 28 November 1864.[57]

---

[49] *Macon Daily Telegraph*, 24 November 1862.

[50] Ibid., 27 November 1862.

[51] John A. Cobb to Lucy Barrow, Macon, 30 November 1862, Cobb Papers, 1862.

[52] *Macon Daily Telegraph*, 25 August 1863. See also Ibid., 24 August 1863.

[53] Ibid., 22 April 1863.

[54] Ibid., 25, 27 April 1864.

[55] Ibid., 30 March 1863.

[56] Ibid., 24 August 1863. See also Ibid., 18 August 1863 for an announcement of such services held in the Mulberry Street Methodist Church at 10:30 and 5:00.

[57] *Macon Daily Telegraph and Confederate*, 28 November 1864.

As time went on and the war began to go badly for the Confederacy, religious services to pray for God's blessing upon the country increased. By the spring of 1864, daily prayer meetings were held among the city's churches, and businessmen were urged to close their business doors between the hours of 9 and 10 A.M. on Mondays "and unite in the prayers ascending daily in behalf of the country."[58] By late June 1864, City Prayer Meetings were held at the Baptist Church every evening at 5:00 P.M.[59]

Churches were sometimes the scene of farewell sermons such as the one presented by outgoing pastor J. E. Evans of the Mulberry Street Methodist Church on Sunday, 22 November 1864. Commenting upon Evans' departure, a writer for the *Daily Telegraph* reported, "He is, as near as frail humanity often gets to be, a model pastor; and it will be hard to fill his place. We are sorry to part with him, and no doubt this will be the general feeling of the community."[60]

During 1864, as the fortunes of war turned decidedly against the South, speakers gave patriotic speeches designed to raise the spirits of the people. Some of these were delivered at Macon's churches. These occasionally had revolutionary themes because the South considered it was fighting the "Second American Revolution." Reverend C. W. Howard delivered such an address, entitled "Women of the Revolution," at the Presbyterian Church. An admission charge was donated to the Wayside Home of Macon. Music, possibly patriotic, was played upon the occasion.[61]

Another such speech was given by the Reverend Dr. Joseph C. Stiles who spoke upon the state of the country, also in the Presbyterian Church, this time during regular Sunday services. The address was part of a series Stiles gave at Fort Valley, Forsyth, and Griffin, as well as Macon.[62]

A patriotic speech, which was not given in a church, was called "The Present Revolution and Our Obligations to its Martyrs," was presented by Henry M. Law of Liberty County, Georgia, in a building known as the Lecture Hall in May, 1864.[63]

The theme of some of these presentations was historical, reflecting the deep interest many Maconites had in such popular historical periods as that of ancient Egypt. The title of a lecture by Dr. Leybourn was "Egypt, its Ancient Temples,

---

[58] *Macon Daily Telegraph*, 23 May 1864. For dates and times of such meetings held at the Presbyterian and Mulberry Street Methodist Churches see Ibid., 13 May 1864.

[59] Ibid., 21 June 1864.

[60] Ibid., 21 November 1863.

[61] Ibid., 8 March 1864.

[62] Ibid., 24 March 1864.

[63] Ibid., 17 May 1864.

Tombs and Mummy Pits, with the Habits and Customs of the modern Egyptians," which he gave at the Presbyterian Church in early May, 1863.[64]

Presbyterian pastor David Wills performed the 159th marriage ceremony in the Presbyterian Church on Tuesday afternoon, 20 April 1864. The happy couple, Captain Augustus O. Bacon and Miss Jennie Lamar, daughter of John Lamar of Macon, left for Savannah on their wedding trip.[65] Reverend Wills used the Episcopal wedding service, which he read from a book, to marry the couple. During the ceremony, because the light was poor and because he was unfamiliar with the Episcopal service, Wills blundered over the words "the vow of the covenant," and pronounced it "keep the cow and the covenant." When he married another couple on the following day Wills threw aside the Episcopal Prayer Book and, according to Mary Ann Cobb, "went it on the Old Presbyterian style without a book and acquitted himself handsomely." Mrs. Cobb noted, "Every carpenter should work with his own tools and every preacher should read out of his own book."[66]

On occasion, Mrs. Cobb did not find church services quite as amusing. When she attended the Catholic Services on Christmas Day, 1863, she heard "a very good sermon but we got very tired during the long service and faint from the incense.[67]

Talk of church services and religion in general filled the correspondence of Nathan C. Munroe. He wrote his daughter Bannie on 18 August 1862, that Captain Richard Cuyler had served as lay reader at Christ Episcopal Church on Sunday, 17 August. Munroe noted, "the congregation seemed very well pleased, and I hope the service may be continued during Mr Rees' [sic] absence." Although the Misses Conner who served as the church choir, were absent in the country, Cuyler raised the tune and the congregation "sang very well."[68]

The Episcopal Bishop of Georgia, Stephen Elliott, wrote Munroe from Savannah on 29 September 1862, asking the latter's help in obtaining shirtings and sheetings at private sale for societies who worked to clothe Georgia troops. Elliot reported that common unbleached homespun sold for $.75 a yard and sheeting at $1.25 cents a yard in Savannah. Elliott explained that he was writing

---

[64] Ibid., 4 May 1863.

[65] John A. Cobb to Lucy Barrow Cobb, Macon, 20 April 1864, Cobb Papers; *Macon Daily Telegraph*, 21 April 1864.

[66] Mary Ann Cobb to her daughter, Macon, 22 April 1864, Cobb Papers.

[67] Mary Ann Cobb to her cousin, Macon, 26 December 1863, Cobb Papers, 1863.

[68] Nathan C. Munroe, Jr. to Bannie Kell, Sylvan Lodge, 18 August 1862, Kell Letters, 1860-1864. Pastor Henry K. Rees was on a visit to Roswell in North Georgia for his health.

to Munroe because he was a director of the Macon Cotton Factory which produced cloth for the soldiers' uniforms.[69]

Two months later, Munroe reported that Reverend Rees had administered Holy Communion assisted by Reverend Dr. Quintard. He noted, "It was grateful once more amid the many and trying excitement around us to receive in this blessed...our vows to that God who alone can protect and comfort us in times of great trial."[70]

Munroe and his family wrote letters containing the usual news mid-Victorians described either in war or peace. One of his daughters noted a visit by General William W. Mackall and his family in August 1862. Mackall, who had recently been released from a prisoner of war camp at Fort Warren, Massachusetts, said "he was very well treated as prisoner."[71] Munroe discussed sickness among his hands in late September, 1862.[72] Bannie, on a visit to Sylvan Lodge in May 1863, wrote her absent father, "I dissipated by going to Mat Holt's last night to teas where we spent a very pleasant evening. I am to have the pleasure of a 'family tea' this evening with them all."[73] Nearly a month later, Munroe, home again at Sylvan Lodge, informed the now-absent Bannie, "Aunty & I have made you over four gals of Dewbury & 3 of cherry wine. This morning I am preparing to make cherry & plum preserves...Nath is gathering cherries for me."[74] By 15 October he reported "every thing is getting so scarce here now I find it difficult and expensive to keep the household up."[75]

Much of what Munroe reported concerned his health, especially his severe bouts with asthma. He noted, on 12 November 1863, that "My cough troubles me very much and I often have to stop writing to cough as I write this letter."[76] Towards the end of the month he noted that, on occasion, he thought his asthma and cough a bit better, "tho' when the hard paroxysms come on they are not without disagreement."[77] His cough and asthma persisted, however, so much so that five days later he said that they troubled him "so much I have but little comfort of life yet. I try to do the best I can for my dear children and am willing to bear whatever betides me for their sake."[78]

---

[69] Bishop Stephen Elliott to Munroe, Savannah, 29 September 1862, Ibid.

[70] Nathan C. Munroe, Jr. to Bannie Kell, Macon, 30 November 1863, Ibid.

[71] "Little Sis," to Bannie Kell, Sylvan Lodge, 21 August 1862, Ibid.

[72] Nathan C. Munroe, Jr. to Bannie Kell, 18 September 1862, Ibid.

[73] Bannie Kell to Nathan C. Munroe, Jr., Sylvan Lodge, 8 May 1863, Ibid.

[74] Nathan C. Munroe, Jr. to Bannie Kell, Sylvan Lodge, 6 June 1863, Ibid. "Nath" was Munroe's son, Nathan.

[75] Nathan C. Munroe, Jr. to his Sister Martha, Macon, 15 October 1863, Ibid.

[76] Nathan C. Munroe, Jr. to Bannie Kell, Sylvan Lodge, 12 November 1863, Ibid.

[77] Nathan C. Munroe, Jr. to Bannie Kell, Macon, 20 November 1863, Ibid.

[78] Nathan C. Munroe, Jr. to Bannie Kell, Macon, 25 November 1863, Ibid.

When Bannie's children died in September 1863, she wrote her father, "If you sometimes go to the dear enclosure & think of me, go for you & I both! Aunt Bennett promised sometimes to put fresh flowers- that the resting place of my darling[s], may not seem neglected in my absence."[79]

The death of the children affected Munroe and Bannie very much, as it would grandparents and parents at any time. She called the cemetery plot "our precious spot," cut a vine near the graves to press in one of her letters, and believed that the white vines were the prettiest and looked the best in the cemetery.[80] He called the peaceful burial ground "that dear cherished shrine, dedicated to our undying memories of the departed loved ones."[81] When a Confederate camp was moved from near the main gate of Rose Hill Cemetery in September, 1864, Munroe delightedly wrote, "everything in quiet and good order both in & outside of the gateway–nothing was there to disturb its hallowed quiet and if our sweet spirits were hovering round the precious altar we have consecrated to their remains, our words of prayer may be borne by them undisturbed to our dear Father and Saviour in their Heavenly Home."[82]

Disease was always part of life in Macon. In an age when medicine, as we know it today, was in its infancy, sickness was a common place. After a minor outbreak of smallpox in March 1863, a *Daily Telegraph* writer noted, "We are gratified to announce that the last Small Pox case was discharged yesterday, and the city and vicinity are now entirely free from the loathsome disease. We have great reason for gratitude that there have been so few cases, and the community is at last delivered from all fear of the Pestilence."[83]

Nathan Munroe wrote his daughter Bannie that one of her uncle's slaves had spotted fever and would probably live only a short time. When Munroe stopped by the Cotton Factory on his way to town from Vineville he learned the boy had just died.[84]

Sometimes, in the Macon of 1862-1864, after the initial enthusiasm of volunteering had passed and Sherman had not yet penetrated into North Georgia to begin the siege of Atlanta, it seemed that the war was very far away, although articles were not as easy to procure as before. Mary Ann Cobb tried to purchase picnic gloves at Mrs. Dessau's fancy dress shop but Mrs. Dessau couldn't find any, writing her customer "I have been in every shoe store and every dry goods

---

[79] Bannie Kell to Nathan C. Munroe, Jr., Retreat near...., 13 November 1863, Ibid. Bannie lost two children during the war. They are both buried in the Munroe Family Plot in Rose Hill Cemetery, Macon.

[80] Bannie Kell to Nathan C. Munroe, Jr., 27 November 1863, Ibid.

[81] Nathan C. Munroe, Jr., to Bannie Kell, Macon, 2 December 1863, Ibid.

[82] Nathan C. Munroe, Jr., to Bannie Kell, Macon, 11 September 1864, Ibid.

[83] *Macon Daily Telegraph*, 14 March 1863.

[84] Nathan C. Munroe, Jr. to Bannie Kell, Macon, 26 May 1864, Kell Letters.

store. As regards the picnic gloves I do not believe that I have exactly the article you wish, neither could I get them elsewhere."[85]

John A. Cobb wrote one of his brothers from Macon in early October of the same year that there many strangers in Macon, but very few that he knew. He wryly observed, "I saw Miss Leila Powers this morning. She asked where I was stationed I told her in Va. You belong to the fighting army, she said, from that there must be a good many about here who do not belong to the 'fighting army' "[86]

Young John Cobb stayed at the Bear's Den while managing plantations for his parents in Southwest Georgia. In the fall of 1862, he kept house by himself, and lived on meal bacon, coffee, and tea without any milk. He breakfasted on coffee, corn bread, butter, and broiled bacon. Supper was fancier, with bacon and greens, butter beans, corn bread, and sweet potatoes. Lamenting his Uncle John B. Lamar' death, he said that living in the big house was "a dull business staying here...by myself I can tell you."[87]

A few days later he rode out to his uncle's Bibb County plantation, near Swift Creek and found that everything looked very well, although the corn crop was poor. Even so, he would have 2,000 bushels to spare for 1862, and suggested that his parents use the surplus to fatten up hogs. His overseer, Hancock, was making salt at the Bibb Place every day which saved the family much money since salt sold for $145 a sack in Macon.[88]

Cobb believed there were many items locked up in Macon waiting for the prices to go higher and felt the goods should be seized by the Government and sold at reasonable prices. "And these are the men," he scribbled, "who are crying out against the farmers who are trying to put up the price of corn to four & five dollars."[89]

Many items seemed to be available in Macon throughout much of the war. Dr. John S. Baxter of the firm of Jones, Baxter, and Day, General Commission Merchants, wrote his client, the wealthy merchant William B. Johnston who was putting the finishing touches on his magnificent Italianate mansion on Georgia Avenue, today known as the Hay House, that "Your letter was received this morning and as soon as possible I comply with your wishes- and you will find enclosed a diagram of the parlor and of the library which I trust will be sufficiently intelligible to you since you are thoroughly acquainted with the

---

[85] Miriam Dessau to Mary Ann Cobb, Macon, 24 June 1862, Cobb Papers, 1862. She also bought such items as dresses and mantillas, as well as kid gloves, soap, white stockings, and white spool cotton

[86] John A. Cobb to "Dear Brother," Macon, 6 October 1862, Ibid.

[87] John A. Cobb to Lucy Barrow, Macon, 8 October 1862, Ibid.

[88] John A. Cobb to his mother, Macon, 12 October 1862, Ibid.

[89] John A. Cobb to Lucy Barrow, Macon, 28 October 1862, Ibid.

rooms- at the end of my letter you will find the measurements of the fireplaces in the basement parlor and dining room."[90]

Even an occasional good time was enjoyed by the well-to-do during the period. When Mrs. Henry J. Lamar had a party at her home in Vineville in January, 1863, two officers, Lieutenants Colquitt and Ross, escorted Clara Barrow and Lou Brantley to the affair. The party was "a regular frolic $100.00 worth of oysters were to have been present- but no oysters came from Savannah yesterday so said E. Conner who had the ordering of them. Rumor says, oysters are selling in Savannah at $14. per quart! This fact probably accounted for the disappointment. But $100. Worth of turkies- pickle etc. Real coffee made up the defficiency- no cake appeared. sensible when one small pound cake commands $30. at Hornes."[91]

Sometimes a light-hearted article such as the one which appeared in the *Daily Telegraph's* issue for 10 June 1863 made the war seem far away. Its writer urged the young ladies of Macon between the ages of fourteen and twenty-five to form a regiment for the defense of the young men, and urged "All those who wish to join will please enroll their names at the headquarters. The senior class being exempt as over age." The article was issued "by order of Maj. Gen. Cupid commander of the Wesleyan Female College."[92] One of the chief forms of pleasure for the people of Macon during the war years was the theater. The entertainments, which proved a welcome diversion from the grimness of war, included dioramas; music, both singing and instrumental; minstrels; exhibitions; plays; and other presentations. When Burton's Grand Moving Dioramic Panorama came to town in early May 1863, it appeared to a crowded house. These displays, similar to the modern Cyclorama in Atlanta, used either war themes or themes from exotic places like the Middle East. A reporter for the *Daily Telegraph* praised the display noting, "The paints are not mere daubs but fine specimens of art. The scenes on the Bosphorus are gorgeous, and the Turtle Ram fight, and the Manassas Fight, amusing and entertaining."[93]

---

[90] Dr. John S. Baxter to William B. Johnston, Macon, 9 October 1862, Tracy-Steele-Johnston Family Correspondence. The firm was located at the corner of Cotton Avenue and Cherry Street. The dimensions were "Fireplace in basement parlor- Basement dining room width at top 3 ft 1 7/8 in; width at bottom 3' 2 1/4"; Height 2' 7 7/8", Depth- 1' 3 5/8" I [Baxter] give the depth which you did not ask for Windows in parlor front-arch to floor- 12 ft 7/8 in; width- 3 ft 8 1/8", Side arch to floor- 12 ft 5/8, side width- 3 ft 3 1/4, Library windows same as side windows in parlor."

[91] Mary Anne Cobb to her husband, Macon, January 1863, Cobb Papers.

[92] *Macon Daily Telegraph*, 2 June 1863.

[93] *Macon Daily Telegraph*, 3 May 1862. Tableaux are picturesque groups of people or objects.

One such display featured "Our Past," "Our Present," and "Our Future." The performance also featured a Militia Drill, Georgia Scenes, a recitation taken from Edgar Allen Poe's classic poem "The Raven," a declamation, and events simply described as "The Circus," and "the Reliable Gentleman." A play, popular at the time, entitled "The Toodles," was also presented. The reporter for the *Daily Telegraph* described the affair, "Toodles was decidedly on a bust; Mrs. Toodles fully up to her character; Lawyer Glibb was admirably portrayed, George Acorn, Charles Fenton, and the remainder of the characters were generally well sustained." The performance was so good, that the paper gave only light criticism to the actors, relating, "All that is necessary is a more careful study of their characters."[94]

Another tableaux with a war theme was entitled "The Panorama Mirror of the war," which featured thousands of life-like, moving figures. An artist, G. W. Grain of Richmond, executed the panorama which was exhibited in late August, 1863.[95]

The Amateur and War Clubs presented a tableaux at Ralston's on 12 December 1862.[96] Not to be outdone, the ladies of Vineville, assisted by some of the ladies of Macon and "the inimitable wit and wag, Barnes, of Atlanta," displayed a tableaux to raise money for the poor of the city at the end of December 1862.[97] Sandrue's troop, which appeared at Ralston's Hall in December 1863, featured "the most beautiful tableaux, good singing and dancing, by graceful performers." A reporter for the *Daily Telegraph* assured would-be patrons that the "Representations are modest in dress as nothing is represented but will meet the approval of the most religious."[98]

A "Panoptican of the War," also prepared by G.W. Grain, was presented at Ralston's in late June and early July 1864. It dealt with the Bombardment of Fort Sumter and featured five thousand life-like figures. Miss Maggie Southerland, "the Southern Nightingale," sang several beautiful songs, "in which," the *Daily Telegraph*'s writer observed, "we think she could not be surpassed." The performance also displayed the talents of Dan May, a black singer who sang some of his favorite songs.[99]

Minstrels also presented popular entertainments. The Johnson Minstrels performed on the night of 20 May 1862, to a crowded house. A reporter for the

---

[94] Ibid., 19 June 1862.

[95] Ibid., 19 August 1863. A few days later another tableaux featuring "Living Statuary," was shown at Ralston's Hall. It also included magic, mirth, and mystery, and was described as "Chaste and Modest." Ibid., 25 August 1863.

[96] Ibid., 12 December 1862.

[97] Ibid., 30 December 1862.

[98] Ibid., 23 December 1863.

[99] Ibid., 30 June 1864.

Daily Telegraph described the group as "a No. 1 band," adding, "their vocal and instrumental music elicits universal commendation."[100]

One of the most popular actors to appear on the Macon stage during the period was Harry Macarthy, an impersonator as well as a singer who made his fifth appearance in Macon on 7 October 1862. During the performance, presented at Ralston's Hall, and assisted by Miss Lottie Estelle, Macarthy impersonated numerous characters, and sang a number of songs before a large audience. One of the songs, entitled "It is my country's Call," written and composed by Macarthy, "was received with unbounded applause." On the following evening, he gave a benefit to help raise money for the Ladies' Soldier's Relief Society.[101] On the night of 11 October Macarthy presented the "beautiful soul-stirring national song of the South, "The Bonnie Blue Flag," along with a variety of comic songs. "Mr Macarthy is an excellent performer and a most generous man," a correspondent for the *Daily Telegraph* stated, "and is well deserving of public patronage."[102]

The Slomans, a group of singers and musicians composed of a father and his daughters, used a new instrument, the "Alexandre Organ," in Macon for the first time, although it was used, according to a writer for the *Daily Telegraph*, extensively in Europe.[103] During their concert, presented at Ralston's Hall in November 1862, Sloman's comic songs and his troop's performance on the harp, piano, and Alexandre Organ were well-received. A song from the opera Lucia di Lammermoor was also well-received, together with Sloman's "pathetic" ballad of the "Life and Death of King Richard the Third." His renditions of "The Musical Traveler," "Blue Bear," and the "Nervous Family" were "irresistibly comic."[104]

On the following evening, 12 November, the group appeared before a much smaller audience. Lamenting the poor turnout, a writer for the *Daily Telegraph* noted that the group's "entertainment is exceedingly interesting, and well merits the attention and patronage of the public. The young ladies are fine singers and accomplished musicians, and the worthy paterfamilias himself is a host in the way of song and genial mirth."[105] Charles B. Graybill commented laconically about the small turnout, "The Slomans of Charleston gave us several concerts this week, to very small houses."[106]

---

[100] Ibid., 21 May 1862.

[101] Ibid., 8 October 1862.

[102] Ibid., 11 October 1862.

[103] Ibid., 10 November 1862.

[104] Ibid., 11 November 1862.

[105] Ibid., 12 November 1862.

[106] Charles B. Graybill to "Dear John," Macon, 15 November 1862, Cobb Papers, 1862.

Other musicians, such as the Dixie Family Vocal and Instrumental Musicians, performed in Macon during the war years. The admission fee for a concert which they performed at Ralston's Hall on 30 March 1863, was $1.00, and children and servants were admitted for $.50 cents.[107]

Carlo Patti and his company gave several "grand concerts" at Ralston's in mid-April 1863. They were so popular in Columbus that their appearance in Macon was postponed for one night because of the "pressing solicitations of the citizens" of the West Georgia city. After explaining that Patti "comes of the best musical stock," the reporter for the *Daily Telegraph* explained that the members of the company were in Confederate service, and used a furlough to entertain the public "and benefit their finances" at the same time. Patti himself had seen seventeen months of service as a Confederate soldier.[108]

Another concert was presented by Madame Ruhl, who was performing in Macon for the first time, in July 1863. For an admission fee, spectators were treated to Ms. Ruhl's solo soprano in the musical "Kathleen Mavourneen," a performance which was greeted "with deafening applause, and sung with surpassing excellence." The proceeds of $270 received for her one-nights-performance were turned over to the Soldiers Relief Society.[109]

Tom, "the little blind Negro boy Pianist," was also a popular entertainer during the war years. When he presented a concert on the stage of Concert Hall on 22 December 1862, the price of admission was $.75 cents, and $.50 cents for children and servants.[110] He performed again, this time at Ralston's Hall, on 11 April 1863.[111]

Exhibitions, usually given by the students of Polhill's School or Wesleyan Academy, were also popular affairs. When the pupils of Polhill's School appeared at Concert Hall on 23 December 1862, the affair was well-attended by an audience who "were highly delighted with the performances."[112]

Occasionally the entertainment turned to feats of magic. Such a display was shown on 10 February 1863, when Mago Del Mage, "The celebrated southern Wizard and Magician," gave a performance of "MAGIC, MIRTH AND MYSTERY," which was described as "a grand display of skill and dexterity." He also practiced hypnotism, then known as "mesmerism." The admission for the dress circle and parquette was $.75 cents, while gallery seats went for $.50.[113]

---

[107] Ibid., 30 March 1863.

[108] Ibid., 14 April 1863. See also Ibid., 17 April 1863.

[109] Ibid., 16 July 1863.

[110] Ibid., 3 December 1862.

[111] Ibid., 11 April 1863.

[112] Ibid., 24 December 1862.

[113] Ibid., 11 February 1863. See also Ibid., 12 February 1863.

Jean Gilbert, billed as "the unrivalled Wizard of the South!," appeared at Ralston's Hall on 12 and 13 June 1863, offering a performance with his "Mystic Temple of Enchantment."[114]

The people of such an urbane city as Macon enjoyed dramatic productions. Some of these were tragedies, and some were presented as comedies. Many of them, took their themes from past events in England, France, and the Ancient World. The lessee and manager of Ralston's Hall, E.R. Dalton, and his wife, appeared as a "tragedian" and "tragedienne" in one of these, a tragi-comedy called "Ingoma." Other parts were performed by Eloise Bridges, Annie Deland, Jessie Day, Miss Rollins, Dan Russell, O. Nelson, E.W. Blance, F.C. Moreland, George Warren, C. McNinemy, and J. C. Duesberry.[115]

Sometimes the playbill featured two plays in the same evening. Tobin's celebrated comedy in three acts, "The Honeymoon," was shown in early October. This production was following by a "screaming farce, the 'Two Lovers'."[116]

Occasionally, plays were accompanied by such things as a "Grand Fancy Dance," given by J. C. Duesberry on the evening of 8 October 1863. The plays accompanying Duesberry's performance were the "Iron Chest" and "the favorite farce" entitled the "Swiss Cottage."[117]

On 9 October 1863, Ralston's Hall was "filled to overflowing" by a crowd which saw manager E. R. Dalton as Sir Edward Mortimer in the "Iron Chest." Unfortunately, his wife was "razed," although she was usually "quite a favorite," as she attempted to sing without better orchestral accompaniment. On the night of 10 October, plans called for the presentation of Sheridan Knowles' "The Hunchback," in which the popular actress Miss Eloise Bridges, appeared as Julia. On 10 October, a five-act-drama, accompanied by the popular J.C. Duesberry in another "Grand Fancy Dance," entitled "The Robbers of The Forests of Bohemia" by Schiller was presented. A farce entitled "Love in all Corners," was performed on the same evening.[118]

On Friday, 16 October 1863, a large crowd watched the "affecting" drama of "Madaline." This was followed by another drama, "Therese, or the Orphan of Geneva." Another play scheduled for the following week was the classic

---

[114] Ibid., 10 June 1863.

[115] Ibid., 28 September 1863.

[116] Ibid., 5 October 1863.

[117] Ibid., 8 October 1863.

[118] Ibid., 10 October 1863. Possibly the 5-act-drama replaced the "Hunchback." German poet, dramatist, and aesthetic philosopher Johann Christoph Friedrich Von Schiller finished and published "The Robbers" ("Die Rauber") in 1781.

"Camille." A *Daily Telegraph* reporter praised manager Dalton "for his untiring efforts to establish the drama in our city."[119]

Maconites were occasionally treated to such noteworthy performers as Miss Ella Wren, who presented a concert at Ralston's Hall on 2 May 1863.[120]

Opera, too, was popular during the war. White and Beardsley's Opera Troupe performed to crowded houses at Ralston's Hall for eight successive nights in early September 1863. The *Daily Telegraph*'s writer noted the performance enjoyed "splendid success at each performance."[121]

One of the most interesting performances seen in Macon during the war years was a party of Morgan's men, encamped at Decatur, who gave a concert in Ralston's Hall in the winter of 1864. The young men, all Louisianians, whose homes were occupied by the Federals, were all escaped prisoners from Point Lookout Federal Prison in Maryland. They needed money to buy horses for themselves, and had already given one performance in Griffin before they came to Macon. The group sang "all the popular airs and various humorous songs," and were accompanied by Mr. Yeoman, a sixty-one-year-old blind man who performed on the high wire.[122]

Altogether, the people of Macon enjoyed tableaux, minstrels, singing and dancing, and both serious and comic plays during the war years. These were undoubtedly popular because they served as diversions from the grimness of war which, as the spring of 1864 changed to summer, was drawing closer to Macon.[123]

Because of the war, Macon's business community became even more active as the conflict continued. Much of this enterprise was, of course, connected with the production of arms and munitions for the Confederate war effort. In November 1862, a new brass foundry, operated by A. Reynolds and known as the Macon Brass Foundry, located at the corner of Hawthorne and Fourth Streets behind Findlay's Iron Works, advertised for old copper, brass, and sheet zinc. The establishment produced brass castings for steam engines, mill and factory work, sword and gun mountings, spurs, and brass for infantry accouterments.[124] By the fall of 1863, the firm produced brass mill work for railroad locomotives and cars. They also made journal brasses, sword and gun mountings, and plain and finished spears. The firm announced arrangements "by which we are

---

[119] Ibid., 19 October 1863.

[120] Ibid., 1 May 1863.

[121] Ibid., 4 and 10 September 1863.

[122] Ibid., 28 January 1864.

[123] For some other entertainments presented in Macon during the period 1862-1864 see Ibid., 5 July 1862; 29 August and 20 November 1863; 17, 18, and 25 February, 8, 29 March, 3 and 4 May 1864.

[124] Ibid., 13 November 1862.

constantly supplied with the best of BRONZE GUN METEL [sic]–a most superior composition for car journal boxes. Railroad companies can be supplied at short notice and on good terms."[125]

James Taylor Nisbet, brother and law partner of Judge Eugenius A. Nisbet, began the Empire State Iron Works in the fall of 1862, a move which prompted a *Daily Telegraph* writer to report, "We call attention again to this enterprise, which is now happily under way–beyond contingencies–but it is highly desirable that its entire stock should be taken, so as to put it at once into the fullest and largest operation."[126] In early January, five thousand shares of stock were offered, and all were purchased by twenty-six of the most important men in Middle Georgia. By this time the company had installed a 60-horsepower steam engine to drive their machinery. The *Daily Telegraph*'s writer happily announced, "We hope by midsummer they will be producing iron at a great rate."[127]

In April 1863, the firm planned to hire one hundred more able-bodied black laborers, saying "If our people wish iron, the shortest way to get it is to push forward these works." The company offered good wages, certain payment, and "as healthy employment and locality as the world affords."[128]

Thomas Cooper Nisbet, a Nisbet relative, moved his foundry and machine shop to the line of the railroad near the shops of the Macon and Western Railroad, and began to manufacture machinery and castings.[129] Nisbet also offered for sale two new forty-five-horse power engines with cylinders of fourteen-inch diameter and a thirty-inch stroke. He also wanted to sell three boilers with dimensions of forty inches by thirty feet each. The engines and boilers were built by the firm of Harlan and Hollingsworth in Wilmington, Delaware. Nisbet also offered a lot of three-inch shafting and pulleys, leather belting and other machinery.[130]

The business of Farrell and Brother, known as the Enterprise Works and located on the corner of Cherry and First Streets had produced matches during the first part of the war. It was bought by Werner and Company of Canton, Mississippi, and, now known as the Dixie Works, manufactured material for the Confederate Army. When the firm came up to full production, a *Daily Telegraph* reporter predicted the area would be "one of the busiest corners in the city."[131]

---

[125] *Macon Daily Journal*, 14 September 1863.

[126] *Macon Daily Telegraph*, 22 December 1862. Plans called for the completion of the company's organization on January 8, 1863, Ibid., 29 December 1862.

[127] Ibid., 14 January 1863.

[128] Ibid., 22 April 1863.

[129] Ibid., 3 January 1863.

[130] Ibid., 23 January 1863.

[131] Ibid., 8 October 1863.

William J. McElroy continued to produce fine swords as the war continued,[132] while C.W. Brunner and F.W. Maurer produced horn and bone buttons, "such as are used upon pantaloons," at their Macon Button Factory. Their workmen softened, fattened, sawed, turned, and polished the horn, and sawed and turned the bones, a process which the *Daily Telegraph* reporter called "very interesting and expeditious." The reporter boasted, "This is another development of mechanical ingenuity and skill due to Lincoln's blockade. Here substances which had been annually thrown away, for an unknown series of years, are gathered and put to profitable use, and in a month or two form this time, we suppose the Confederacy will be independent of all the world for the supply of horn and bone buttons for pantaloons."[133] Another firm, Truman, Kibb and Wood, produced boot blacking, together with "first rate friction matches in any quantity."[134]

William B. Johnston announced the fact that Macon had become a Public Depository for the Confederacy in March 1863. Appointed Public Depository, Johnston urged the public to come forward and invest their non-interest paying Treasury Notes in eight per cent bonds before 22 April 1863. After that they could only be invested in seven per cent bonds.[135]

Johnston also served as president of the Great Southern Insurance Company, and offered a stock subscription in the firm.[136] George C. Obear served as president of a rival firm, the Empire State Insurance Company, with a capital stock of $500,000.[137] Another firm, the Georgia Chemical Company, organized in 1863, in Griswoldville, offered 500 shares of stock for $1,000 a share. The company's President was E. Parsons, while J.P. Collins served as Treasurer.[138]

For the wealthy, times were not too bad. Nisbet, one of Macon's leading attorneys and a prominent judge and former congressman, could easily afford a two-year subscription to the *Southern Presbyterian,* published in Columbia, South Carolina, for $5.00.[139] Nisbet also bought items from Messrs Johnston and Pile of Macon, wholesale and retail druggists, for $237.99.[140] He also

---

[132] *Georgia Journal and Messenger*, 11 February 1863.

[133] *Macon Daily Telegraph*, 20 February 1863.

[134] Ibid., 19 March 1863.

[135] Ibid., 23 March 1863.

[136] William B. Johnston, Stock Subscription, Macon, 18 July 1863, Eugenius A. Nisbet Letters, 1862-1864.

[137] George C. Obear and Henry L. Fervette, Macon, Stock Subscription, 15 December 1863, Ibid.

[138] E. Parsons and J.P. Collins, Stock Subscription, Griswoldville, 1863, Ibid.

[139] A.A. Porter and Company to Eugenius A. Nisbet, Bill, Macon, 29 December 1862, Ibid.

[140] Messrs. Johnston and Pile to Nisbet, Bill, Macon, 7 October 1862, Ibid. The firm sold drugs, dyes, oils, paints, instruments, perfumery, and patent medicines.

purchased merchandise from the music store of J.C. Schreiner and Sons of Macon, and from hardware dealer Nathan Weed.[141]

During the spring of 1863, there were complaints in Macon about the rise in prices caused by the devaluation of Confederate currency. Goods became scarcer even in prosperous Macon as the war continued and the Blockade became more effective. The Macon Factory, also known as the Macon Manufacturing Company, produced textile goods. When news spread that the business was giving away factory goods to wealthy people the *Daily Telegraph's* correspondent complained, "Change all this gentlemen, make the wealthy pay the market value in cash on produce, and if a compliance with the law requires that 55 cents a yard be given away, let it be in God's name to those who need it." The paper's editor, Joseph Clisby, wanted the Factory to sell for foodstuffs which then could be resold at a price to realize clear of expense the Factory's cost of thirty cents a yard. The Factory should help gather in the produce of the country to Macon, and establish a free market or sell at the cost system. If the Macon City Council would help do this it would do more to control the extortion which caused a rise in prices in Macon, as well as other parts of the Confederacy in 1863. The factory, Clisby believed, should "Supply the poor with plenty as well as the families who have legitimate claims upon their bounty, and do more good generally than they possibly could by giving away the whole product of their looms by the present system."[142]

John A. Cobb complained to his mother that he gave a pound of meat for a yard of cloth. The Factory, by mid-May, was charging $.40 a yard. Young Cobb purchased osnaburgs for the Cobb/Lamar plantations, and had to pay the exorbitant price of $1.35 a yard. "You had better [not] say any thing about your getting this cloth," he advised his mother, "or you will have a thousand & one applications for it, if you let some have it all will want it & the best plan will be to let none."[143]

A small group of women, driven to desperation by the inflation in Macon, tried to replenish their stock of dry goods by seizing articles from a pile of calico in downtown Macon on 1 April 1863. A writer for the *Daily Telegraph* noted that "The proceedings, however, were not conducted with much vigor and determination, and no harm was done so far as we are advised."[144] Furthermore, the mechanics in the city scheduled a meeting for 10 May 1863, for the

---

[141] J.C. Schreiner and Sons to Nisbet, Bill, Macon, 15 September 1862; Nathan Weed to Nisbet, Bill, Macon, 20 May 1862, both Ibid.

[142] Ibid., 28 April 1863.

[143] John A. Cobb to his mother, Macon, 14 May 1863, Cobb Papers, 1863.

[144] *Macon Daily Telegraph*, 2 April 1863.

protection of all mechanical trades, but there were no riots like that in Richmond or other Confederate cities.[145]

Despite these complaints, the Macon Manufacturing Company turned 25,000 pounds of bacon over to the Army of Tennessee, then in North Georgia, and an additional 20,000 pounds to the Post Commissary in Macon. The firm also gave 5,000 pounds of bacon for the benefit of the poor of Bibb County; and traded goods at the rate of a yard of cloth for a pound of bacon in the fall of 1863.[146]

Lewis N. Whittle, prominent Macon attorney, then serving as an aide to Governor Brown, wrote Jefferson Davis on 2 April 1863, that many parts of the Confederacy were suffering from a want of food. Food was scarce, Whittle believed, because of the lack of a proper system to provide it to the people. Government agents were bidding against other persons for available food. Therefore, the price of food was rising so as to put it beyond the reach of the common people. Corn was now selling in Macon for $1.00 to $1.50 a bushel, and meat from $.75 cents to $1.00 a pound. Thousands of bushels of corn and other foodstuffs were carried hundreds of miles further than necessary, because the articles were furnished from parts of states which were far from where they could be just as easily obtained, and just as convenient to the places where they were needed. Whittle believed that much of this food was carried over the Georgia Central Railroad 200 miles, from Macon to Savannah for the forces protecting the latter place, and food was brought from Savannah to Macon destined for the Army of Tennessee, all of which totaled up to 400 miles of useless transportation. Because the railroad had no authority to distribute food. Whittle suggested a central agency or quartermaster should be established in each state from whom all supplies in that state could be drawn by the army, no matter where the army was located.[147]

But, despite these problems, the war had made Macon a prosperous city by the fall of 1862. In December, 1862, a visitor walked about the city and reported, "The first thing which attracted my notice after walking around the corporate lines, on the west side of the Ocmulgee, was the extent of ground included in the limits. This space is large enough for a City of 25,000 people, which...will in time occupy it." The visitor saw "many beautiful situations both in and outside, which require only improvement to equal...any yet built upon." Climbing an eminence known as Troup Hill, named after former Governor George McIntosh Troup, to whom it was presented by the State, the visitor observed the arrival and departure of the various railroad trains. The scene

---

[145] Ibid., 29 April 1863.

[146] Ibid., 23 December 1863.

[147] Lewis N. Whittle to Jefferson Davis, 2 April 1863, Macon, Confederate Secretary of War, Letters Received, Roll 115, December 1862-April 1863, NARA.

before him was of a busy city, with "extensive Government works just beginning to assume form and magnitude." An abundance of pure water was found on the summit twenty-three feet below the surface. The visitor was so taken by the view that he pondered, "this is the place for our nation's capitol, and yonder (looking at another hill just far off) is the one for our Presidential mansion." After discussing the area of 118 acres secured for the Armory, Arsenal, and Laboratory, he noted that "These immense works will doubtless add thousands to your resident population and gradually enhance the value of every acre of land near the city." He also noted the Wesleyan Female College, the Asylum for the Blind, "and other public and private institutions intended to advance the usefulness of those to whom will be trusted in part, the future welfare of our beloved State." He felt that a "Male College" should also be established, and concluded with the observation, that Macon "has more of promise than any other place I have seen. I am sure if your people will but manage right there is no reason to doubt that her display will be the pride and boast of the Confederacy while her population will quadruple in a few years."[148]

Over a year later, in April 1864, another visitor also commented upon Macon's armories, foundries, arsenals, and laboratories. Noting that these "immense works," together with "innumerable Factories, Manufactories of every kind, Brass and Wire Foundries, Mills, etc., the property of private parties, spring up around and about us. These, with numerous other improvements, bid fair to place Macon on a footing with any city in the Confederacy.[149]

All of this prosperity was, of course, based upon a system which is incomprehensible to most modern Americans, slavery. The institution flourished in Macon throughout the war years as noted in other parts of this study. In the summer of 1862, General Hugh Mercer, commanding in Savannah, issued Order No. 13 which directed the impressment of male slaves between the ages of 18 and 60 to work upon the fortifications around Savannah. Under this order, V.A. Menard, agent for Impressment, was sent to Macon to carry out the order. He called upon all slave owners in Bibb, Jones, Houston, and Monroe counties to furnish twenty percent of their male slaves beteen the aforesaid ages by 1 August. If they were not sent by that date, Parsons threatened to press them into service. Even all male free "persons of color" were impressed.[150]

Menard's assistant, W.D. Rainey, asked the people of Bibb County to meet at the Macon City Hall on 30 August to ascertain the number of slaves they planned to send to work on the Savannah defenses.[151]

---

[148] "O" to Joseph Clisby in *Macon Daily Telegraph*, 20 December 1862.

[149] "B" in Ibid., 1 April 1864.

[150] V.A. Menard in *Macon Daily Telegraph*, 26 July 1862.

[151] W.D. Rainey in Ibid., 26 August 1862. See also Ibid., 29 August 1862. No record was available to the author to determine the actual number of slaves sent.

Evidently, not enough slaves were furnished, necessitating another call in November 1862.[152] When the quota of twenty percent was not met, J. Joseph Hodges, Agent of the State for impressing slaves, wrote, "I presume they will be furnished cheerfully, but if any should withhold their quota, I am ordered to report them without delay, that the will of the Legislature may be sustained."[153]

When slave owners still did not produce the necessary quota ordered a large number of them to send their slaves to the Georgia Central Passenger Depot by 5:00 P.M. on Monday, 8 December 1862. The men had to be well clothed with good shoes and blankets. Hodges refused to receive any slaves who were not "strictly sound and healthy.[154]

The *Daily Telegraph* advertised slaves for sale in almost every issue. A few examples will suffice. A "fine negro fellow 25 years old" who was handy with tools was offered for sale by J.B. Smith and Company in the paper's issue for 17 October 1862.[155] Another firm, J.H. Cherry and Company, offered thirty-two Blacks for sale at a public auction in January 1863.[156] Slaves were often used by industries during the war period. The proprietor of the Confederate Match Factory advertised for a black boy in April 1863.[157] Prices were high for slaves during the war. At an auction held by J.B. Smith and Company on October 31, 1863, a black woman and three children sold for $2,950, while another black sold for $2,900.[158]

Despite its central location which placed Macon far from the battlefields of 1862 and 1863, the war was never really far away. In the spring of 1862, new units were being organized in the city, while old ones returned to town to recruit more men to make up for the attrition which is always caused by war. Charles J. Harris, a Macon attorney, raised a new company of infantry, asking recruits to apply at his law office, located over Ells' Drug Store.[159] A reporter for the *Daily Telegraph* wrote about the formation of a corps of Partisan Rangers whose organizers "desired that the corps should be filled immediately with good and true men." Recruits also had to "fond of the daring and adventurous."[160]

---

[152] Ibid., 11 November 1862.

[153] J. Joseph Hodges in Ibid., 29 November 1862.

[154] Ibid., 3 December 1862. The slaveowners included R.F. Woolfolk, Thomas Woolfolk, W.T. Wilburn, A.F. Redding, Mrs. Martha R. Stubbs, Leroy Napier, Dr. J. Myrick, John Bowman, Thomas J. Gibson, Thomas Hill, and others.

[155] Ibid., 17 October 1862.

[156] Ibid., 3 January 1863.

[157] Ibid., 11 April 1863.

[158] Ibid., 2 November 1863.

[159] Ibid., 6 May 1862.

[160] Ibid., 14 May 1862.

Other units returned home to recruit. These included the Bibb County Cavalry which was in Phillips' Legion, stationed at Hardeeville, South Carolina, in early May, 1862.[161] The Thomson Guards offered a bounty of $50, and awaited the completion of uniforms. Applicants were asked to apply at the unit's headquarters on Cherry Street, opposite Subers and Lewis' Store.[162] The Napier Artillery returned home to reorganize. Their battery consisted of four 6-pounders, two twelve-pound howitzers, six caissons, a forge and tools, together with eighty horses. Applicants were urged to apply early at C.A. Ells' drug store.[163] The unit needed eighty more men. A reporter for the *Daily Telegraph* proudly reported, "in column it extends a length of nearly a quarter of a mile, and is an imposing spectacle."[164] On 26 May 1862, the unit moved their encampment from the Academy Square to Camp Oglethorpe, where they planned to remain in camp of instruction for several weeks unless "sooner ordered to the seat of war." On the same day the unit fired a salvo of artillery in honor of General Thomas J. "Stonewall" Jackson's victory over General Nathaniel P. Banks at the Battle of Winchester, May 25, 1862.[165]

Other units which recruited in Macon during the period included the German Artillery and the Gresham Rifles.[166] The Lochrane Guards, in Phillips' Legion, offered a $50 bounty, $25 commutation for clothing and their pay, $.25 per ration, and even $2.00 to each recruit after he was pronounced by a surgeon as fit for the Army. The unit boasted that it had served in the Northwestern Virginia Campaign without losing a man.[167]

When the First Georgia Regiment returned to Macon to recruit on 13 January 1863, having been reduced to about 150 men by such battles as Sharpsburg and Fredericksburg, they were welcomed back with a splendid dinner, served over the Union Depot, then went into camp near the Macon and

---

[161] Ibid., 5 May 1862. The unit was led by Captain Samuel S. Dunlap with A.L. Clinckscales, A.F. Hunter, and G.M. Davis as First Lieutenant, Second Lieutenant, and Ensign respectively. See Gen. Henry C. Wayne to Capt. S. S. Dunlap, Milledgeville, 21 May 1862, Adjutant Generals Letter Book, 10 April to 21 May 1862, p. 575.

[162] *Macon Daily Telegraph*, 7 May 1862. See also Ibid., 21 May 1862.

[163] Ibid., 7 and 8 May 1862.

[164] Ibid. 9 May 1862. By this time, the unit was known as the Macon Light Artillery. It was captained by H.N. Ells, while W.F. Anderson, H.A. Troutman, and C.W. Slaten occupied the positions of First, Second, and Third lieutenant respectively. See Ibid., 20 May 1862.

[165] Ibid., 27 May 1862.

[166] Ibid., 8 May 1862.

[167] Ibid., 7 May 1862.

Western Railroad.[168] On the 16th the unit entered town with their colors streaming and the music of a band, and marched through the streets. They were addressed from the balcony of the Lanier House by Attorney James A. Nisbet. During his remarks, Nisbet "alluded in appropriate terms to the achievements of this glorious corps on the thirteen fields of strife and glory the names of which are emblazoned on their stained and warworn battle flag." The men then went to a hall at the railroad depot and ate "Delicacies and substantials in the greatest variety and abundance" furnished by the women of Macon. Wreaths of evergreen entwined with flowers, and the "bright Stars and Bars of the Confederacy" adorned the table. Presbyterian Pastor David Wills said grace and the men ate. After the meal a number of speeches were made including one by Colonel Thomas Hardeman, Jr. At the conclusion of the fete, a musical club in the regiment "gave some capital songs."[169]

Support for the Confederacy took other forms besides volunteering. Occasional visits by well-known Georgians who had achieved important positions in the Confederate Army were always occasions for celebration. When one of these men, General Ambrose R. Wright visited Macon in late October, 1862, he was serenaded by a large party of citizens at the home of his host, Colonel Washington. The crowd called for a speech, whereupon Wright appeared, leaning on crutches and accompanied by his son, who was also on crutches, having lost a leg at Second Manassas. The general begged to be excused, saying he had been "for near two years engaged with the duties of the camp and field, and felt more like battling with the invader of his country, than indulging in the flowers of rhetoric." However, he thanked the people for the compliment which he believed belonged to the Army of Northern Virginia. The general pointed out that army "had undergone more hardships, fought more battles, and achieved greater successes in the short space of two months, than any other army in the history of the world." It was true that they had suffered loss, but, considering the numbers of their opponents, their casualties were nothing "in comparison with those of the enemy, whom they uniformly repulsed." He defended the army from the "flippant" charges of newspaper reporters and "street corner warriors" who accused them of avoiding their duty and ended his remarks saying "No braver or truer men were ever marshalled on the earth." Wright then urged the people to help the Government provide provisions for the troops during the winter months, and when spring came "all would be well."[170]

---

[168] W.H. Andrews Diary, 13 January 1863, p. 9, Civil War Miscellany, Box 1, Middle Georgia Archives, Washington Memorial Library, Macon. See also *Macon Daily Telegraph*, 13 January 1863.

[169] *Macon Daily Telegraph*, 16 January 1863.

[170] Ibid., 29 October 1862.

A native Maconite, Colonel Thomas Hardeman, Jr., resigned the command of the Forty-fifth Georgia Regiment and returned home in November 1862, to nurse a wound in his lungs which he received during the Seven Days' Battles around Richmond in the early summer.[171]

Macon's highest ranking officer, Brigadier General Edward Dorr Tracy, made a "flying visit" to bring his family away from Huntsville. The *Daily Telegraph* observed that Tracy was "distinguished for his gallantry at the battle of Shiloh ...[and] followed Gen. Bragg through his recent campaign in Kentucky, and has won the distinction of Brigadier."[172]

When President Davis visited Macon on 30 October 1863, he was welcomed at the depot by a huge crowd who gathered under the car shed eager to see him. The Lanier House was prepared for a public reception in his honor, a gala which was attended by a throng of people, many of whom stood in Mulberry Street for a considerable distance in front of the hotel. Driven up to the front door of the hotel in a "neat" phaeton which was drawn by a span of magnificent horses, the President was greeted with loud and enthusiastic cheers which continued at intervals until he appeared on the balcony in front of the hotel, accompanied by his escort, Honorable Eugenius A. Nesbit, and Judge Oliver Lochrane. After Nesbit introduced Davis to the crowd, the President began his speech by thanking his listeners for the reception, and continued to speak in "a clear and fluent style of the valor of Georgia troops upon every battle field, and our future prospects." He closed by praising the devotion and patriotism of the women of Georgia. Davis left Macon on a special train for Savannah at 7:30 P.M.[173]

Not everyone shared the views expressed by Davis. Some tried to avoid military service by taking advantage of every opportunity offered by the Conscription Act. Some offered money to buy substitutes, a legal option under the Conscription Act of 1862. One man offered $2,000 for a substitute to join the Macon Light Artillery, then in Virginia in September 1862.[174]

As early as September 1862, Macon, with a population of 10,000, had furnished twenty-three companies of volunteers for the war. Forty thousand bales of cotton were stored there, with other large government stores belonging to the Quartermaster and Commissary Departments, together with machinery and stores for the Government arsenals and foundries worth "many millions of dollars." Because so few men were left in the city to perform such functions as fire and police protection, Mayor Thomson and other leaders urged Secretary of War George W. Randolph to retain the two volunteer companies, the Macon

---

[171] Ibid., 4 November 1862.

[172] Ibid., 15 November 1862.

[173] Ibid., 31 October 1863. A phaeton was a light, open, four-wheeled carriage, usually drawn by a pair of horses.

[174] Ibid., 6 September 1862.

Volunteers and Floyd Rifles Companies B still in Macon, and authorize these units to fill their ranks with men over forty-five years old to police the city and guard the public stores. The units could also organize the Fire Department and guard the city.[175]

The new mayor, Ovid G. Sparks, together with the city's six alderman, petitioned Secretary of War Seddon on 14 February 1863, to exempt the fire chief and his assistant and twenty men between twenty-five and forty-five years of age for each of the four fire companies, for a total of eighty-two exemptions. Writing, "We cannot believe that the enrollment of these few additional conscripts can be considered by the War Department a matter of sufficient moment to justify it in enforcing an order which exposes the citizens of Macon & the Government...to all the hazards which they must incur by the disorganization of its police & fire department."[176]

Others asked for exemptions for people who occupied certain positions considered crucial for one reason or another. On 12 May 1862, J.M. Boardman, President of the Macon Gas Light Company joined Mayor Thomson; Surgeon William H. Doughty of the Floyd House Hospital; and Arsenal Commander, Captain Richard M. Cuyler, in petitioning Secretary of War Randolph about an exemption for George A. McIlhenny, Manager and General Superintendent of the Company. After pointing out that many private homes and public houses, together with machine shops, iron foundries, flouring mills, railroad depots, and a hospital with several hundred sick soldiers in it were dependent on the Gas Light Company for "the convenience of light." McIlhenny had been thoroughly trained in operating the company, and was "the sole superintendent of all the details of the establishment." They wanted him exempted under the law relating to superintendents and operators in woolen mills and other factories.[177]

The Enrolling Officer for the Fourth Congressional District, F.W. Johnston, wrote to Randolph enclosing another petition concerning McIlhenny, that he was enrolling all Government hands who were not yet detailed together with workers on several railroads, machine shops, and factories. Johnston queried,

---

[175] Mayor Thomson and others to Secretary of War Randolph, Macon, 15 September 1862, Confederate Secretary of War Letters Received, Roll 75, July-December 1862, NARA. As late as May, 1862, one of these units, the Macon Volunteers, Company B, was having difficulty in recruiting men. See *Macon Daily Telegraph*, 29 May 1862.

[176] Ovid G. Sparks and others to James A. Seddon, 14 February 1863, Ovid G. Sparks Papers, 1848-1899, Confederate Misc. Micro. 532, Special Collections Department, Robert G. Woodruff Library, Emory University.

[177] J.M. Boardman, Methvin S. Thomson, Richard M. Cuyler and Dr. William H. Doughty to George W. Randolph, Macon, 12 May 1862, Confederate Secretary of War, Letters Sent, Roll 33, April-June 1862, Book B, p. 517, NARA.

"Are firemen and overseers on rail roads exempt? There are a large number of persons in my district who are evidently invalids, but under my instructions I have no authority to receive the certificates of any but a Confederate surgeon." A few days before fourteen people were sent to a camp nearly two hundred miles from Macon and thirteen returned with discharges. Johnston needed a physician to help him examine all of the people in Macon who desired exemptions. He also noted that "A large no. Of people hired substitutes as soon as the Conscript Act became known," adding he was having trouble enforcing the conscription law in the Fourth District.[178]

Isaac Scott, President of Ocmulgee Mills, located at Seven Islands in Butts County, Georgia, wanted an exemption for the overseer on a nearby plantation owned by the firm. Because the overseer, Stephen H. Johnson, was the only white man on the premises and was between eighteen and thirty-five years old, he should, Scott believed, be exempted.[179]

Even Editor Joseph Clisby of the *Macon Daily Telegraph* urged the Governor to exempt his staff. "Now, if it is understand that all the printers in the newspaper office of the State go," he wrote, "I am patriotically willing to stand my chance with the rest in carrying on business as best I may; but as it is exceedingly difficult to procure skilled labor of this character, I cant well see how we can do business at all." Clisby wanted five printers exempted who had been enrolled.[180]

Another area of exemptions lay in the public sector. Mayor Sparks and others petitioned Secretary of War Seddon on 28 September 1863, to exempt firemen. The Macon Fire Department included four engine companies of fifteen members each for a total of sixty firemen. By the fall of 1863, these men also served as policemen. Eighteen or twenty of the men were subject to conscription, but the remainder would furnish too small a number "for the service which it is reasonable to expect." The Mayor added that the "loss of experienced people would not only greatly impair the efficiency of the corps but...would create vacancies that cannot be filled." Besides, Macon, despite its central location far from the battlefields, was not safe from incendiarism. The North had sent spies to the city "to burn and destroy." The large amount of cotton then in the city was especially vulnerable. After listing the numerous things that made Macon so important, the mills, the large amount of medical stores, provisions, and other supplies for the Army, as well as the Armory,

---

[178] F.W. Johnston to George W. Randolph, Macon, 25 June 1862, Confederate Secretary of War, Letters Received, Roll 55, June-December, 1862, Ibid.

[179] Isaac Scott to George W. Randolph, Ocmulgee Mills, Seven Islands, Butts County, GA., 22 October 1862, Ibid., Roll 73, September-December 1862, Ibid.

[180] Joseph Clisby to Governor Joseph E. Brown, Macon, 26 August 1863, Incoming Correspondence of the Governor, Record Group 1-1-5, Box 38, GDA&H.

Arsenal, and Laboratory, Sparks declared the exemptions were absolutely necessary. Unfortunately, because of the demands for manpower, especially for the Army, Seddon disapproved the petition on 20 October 1863.[181]

Even Superior Court Judge Oliver A. Lochrane was forced to ask for an exemption, informing Governor Brown on 29 July 1863, that he could not discharge his duty and go into a military organization. His argument seemed justified when he wrote, "to be a private under some person who is on your docket would be an anomalous position." The Judge had furnished a man with a horse to go, and had talked to others about doing the same; furthermore his wife was in a delicate condition, his child had whooping cough, and he lived on a plantation with over fifty slaves. Besides, he told the Governor, "I leave it to you how I could well go with my courts commencing next month." Lochrane wanted to join a cavalry company at home when they were called into a fight to protect Macon, but he occupied a position which he felt was incompatible with the army because his duties were "too constant." However, if Governor Brown had to march out to meet the enemy in Georgia, Lochrane would like to accompany him, not as a member of his staff, but with him nevertheless.[182]

Another prominent Maconite, Washington Poe, Macon Attorney and Postmaster, asked for an exemption, this time for his son, Washington Poe, Jr., then sick in a hospital at Petersburg, because he needed him at home as an assistant in the Post Office.[183]

The number of men, including militia officers, who sought exemptions was so large that "A daughter of Georgia (alias Mary Mckinley) wrote to the *Macon Telegraph* urging the paper to publish a list of exempts, together with the reasons for their exemption. She railed against "the militia officers, sheltered by our patriotic Governor; the apothecaries; the pedagogues, fortunate proprietors of twenty scholars; the young and important limbs of the judiciary,- who have availed themselves of their high privilege." She meant "the stout and healthy young men, who have refused to respond to their countrys call, in the hour of her utmost need; suffering our brothers to lay down their lives for a common cause, while they barter fair fame for an inglorious,—a disgraceful safety." These people, she continued, were those who heaped abuse upon President Davis, because the volunteering system was "all-sufficient," when neither that system, nor the Conscription Act was able "to drag them into the field, or at least to

---

[181] Mayor Sparks and others to James A. Seddon, Macon, 28 September 1863, Confederate Secretary of War, Letters Received, Roll 112, July-November, 1863, NARA.

[182] Judge Oliver A. Lochrane to Joseph E. Brown, Macon, 29 July 1863, Incoming Correspondence of the Governor, Record Group 1-1-5, Box 38, GDA&H.

[183] Washington Poe to George W. Randolph, Macon, 1 September 1862, Roll 66, May-October, 1862, Confederate Secretary of War, Letters Received, NARA..

keep them there." She added that "no Southern woman would willingly waste her smiles on such a man."[184]

While volunteering fell off in Macon during 1863—despite the fact that many men sought exemptions—Macon was not remiss in supporting the war. This support was accomplished in two ways: raising money and provisions for the soldiers and their families and providing for local defense. When the Comptroller General for Georgia raised $2,500,000 to distribute among the indigent widows and orphans, discharged soldiers, and the families of indigent soldiers in State and Confederate service, the amount apportioned to Bibb County was about $35,000.[185]

Of course, the Confederacy impressed such provisions in Macon as sugar, molasses, and rice, and took horses from their owners for the artillery service.[186] But during 1863, as war pressures grew more intense, local leaders intensified their efforts to raise food and money for the army. A call was issued in late April 1863 for the planters of Bibb County to meet at the City Hall in Macon on the 29 April to form an organization to furnish food for the military.[187] At the meeting, the planters resolved "To determine the amount of surplus meat" they could spare after reserving a supply for their families.[188]

Another meeting was held, this time at Concert Hall, on 18 May during which a committee consisting of S. DeGraffenreid, E. J. Johnston, Lewis N. Whittle, J.W. Burke, and Virgil Powers was appointed to call upon people for money for the soldiers. Committee members decided to call upon the City Council for additional funds.[189]

Later, in February 1864, a Festival was held at one of the railroad passenger stations to raise money for the Wayside Home, the Macon Soldiers Relief Society, the Ocmulgee Rangers, the Kentucky Soldier's Relief Society, and the poor of the city. The Festival raised $3,090.80.[190]

---

[184] *Macon Daily Telegraph*, 4 July 1862. Mary McKinley, daughter of the merchant- planter, William McKinley, of Milledgeville, married one of General Howell Cobb's sons, Howell Cobb, Jr., after the war. She is buried beside her husband in Oconee Hill Cemetery at Athens, Georgia.

[185] *Macon Daily Telegraph*, 6 March 1863.

[186] Ibid., 3 April 1863 and 28 August 1863. The total value of the 200 hogsheads of sugar seized amounted to $1,500,000 in Confederate money or $14,000 in US currency.

[187] Ibid., 27 April 1863. The names of the leaders of this movement were Leroy Napier, Skelton Napier, S.B. Hunter, Lewis N. Whittle, Thaddeus G. Holt, P.S. Holt, Seth Cason, C.A. Tharp, and W.F. Wilburn.

[188] Ibid., 30 April 1863.

[189] Ibid., 20 May 1863.

[190] Ibid., 11 February 1864. The money was distributed in the following manner: Wayside Home, $500; Macon Soldiers Relief Society, $500; Ocmulgee Rangers,

A Battlefield Relief Association was organized in March, 1864, during another meeting, this time at Concert Hall. The Association asked the Ladies Soldiers Relief Society to furnish whatever supplies they could procure, and to help the committee in its work.[191] The Association began to collect supplies, lint, bandages, garments, cordials, and delicacies of all sorts for the wounded, and planned to send a special committee to the battlefields to distribute the materials.[192]

On 20 March the Battlefield Relief Association met again. During this meeting a committee of fifteen was appointed to go to the battlefields whenever they were called upon, accompanied by the reserve medical corps of Macon.[193]

A Wayside Home was organized in the city early in 1863, which provided free lodging and food, as well as some medical attention to soldiers passing through.[194] The home operated under strict rules which included:

"I. No guests are entertained longer than is necessary to connect with the Trains, en route for their destination, unless detained by sickness, or some other unavoidable cause.

II. While the Home is established for the convenience of transient privates in service, if an officer is in indigent circumstances he is welcome to the hospitalities of the house.

III. Upon arrival, each man is requested to register his name, informing the Superintendent at what hour he desires to leave, and then avail himself of the Bath to be provided.

IV. No one received, or entertained, in a state of intoxication. The House will be closed punctually at 9 o'clock, P.M., and no one will be admitted after that hour, except under special circumstances.

V. Profane language strictly forbidden. No one admitted to meals without the Ticket given by the Superintendent.

VI. No Smoking, except on collonade [sic], till further arrangements are made.

VII. No spitting on wall or floor."[195]

$500; Kentucky Soldier's Relief Society, $500; and the poor of the city, $1,090,80. See also Ibid., 12 February 1864.

[191] Ibid., 15 March 1864.

[192] Ibid. The members of the committee were Dr. James Mercer Green and Samuel Boykin.

[193] Ibid., 22 March 1864. The list of articles was expanded to include stimulants, bandages, lint, crackers, bacon, dried beef, hams, rice, pepper, salt, sugar, coffee, tin plates, pans, buckets, and sponges. See also Ibid., 28 March 1864.

[194] Ibid., 27 April 1863.

[195] Ibid., 24 February 1864.

The second aspect of Macon's war effort (exclusive of the war industries and the volunteering mentioned above) involved preparations for local defense. As early as April, 1862, efforts were made to prepare a full brass field battery to defend the city.[196] In the following October, a writer for the *Daily Telegraph* warned that high water in the Ocmulgee River might afford an opportunity for small Federal gunboats to advance up the river and at least bombard the city. "The river is easily obstructed," the writer cautioned, "and, no doubt, there are many eligible points at which batteries may be erected which could successfully dispute their passage." The writer called on General Pierre G. T. Beauregard to send a competent engineer and a sufficient workforce to obstruct the river and erect batteries.[197]

Governor John Milton of Florida wrote Governor Brown on 5 November 1862 about a joint effort among the governors of Georgia, Alabama, and Florida, to devise a means of defense.[198] Brown replied that he could go no further than Macon until after the legislature adjourned, but would be glad to meet in that city any day Milton set for such a meeting.[199]

During this period other officials in Macon feared a Federal attack upon Macon by way of gunboats ascending the Ocmulgee River. Armory Superintendent James H. Burton asked Ordnance Bureau Chief, Josiah Gorgas to consider the question of obstructing the river at some defensible point. Although Macon was 316 river miles from the mouth of the Altamaha River, which was formed by the Oconee and Ocmulgee, boats which drew only three or four feet of water could ascend the river even when the water was low. "Would it not be advisable to provide against even this possible contingency," Burton questioned, "by obstructing the river and erecting some batteries to cover the obstructions?"[200]

Fears of a Federal ascent up the Ocmulgee River increased when gunfire was heard to the south, although the gunfire probably came from guns sent by Arsenal authorities down the line of the Brunswick Railroad for testing.[201] The following March, Captain Christopher D. Findlay was authorized to raise a company of one hundred men to guard the Confederate property in Macon.[202]

---

[196] Ibid., 3 April 1862.

[197] Ibid., 14 October 1862.

[198] Gov. John Milton to Gov. Brown, Tallahassee, 5 November 1862, GLB 1861-1865, p. 351.

[199] Gov. Brown to Gov. John Milton, Milledgeville, 5 November 1862, Ibid.

[200] James H. Burton to Josiah Gorgas, Macon, 29 October 1862, Letters Sent Armory, 1863-1865.

[201] Ibid., 6 November 1862.

[202] Ibid., 17 March 1863.

Over a year later it was determined to keep the unit, then known as Findlay's Battalion, in Macon for guard duty. Recruits had to be between the ages of seventeen and eighteen and forty-five and fifty.[203] The battalion included an Armory Company commanded by Captain D. E. Stipes, organized in June, 1863.[204]

A committee, chaired by Macon leader John Jones Gresham, met at City Hall in late May 1863, to procure voluntary military organizations for local defense to protect against possible Federal raids into the interior of Georgia.[205] The meeting adjourned until 25 May when Lewis N. Whittle submitted a report urging the raising of six companies of one hundred men each. Four of these would be infantry, one of artillery and one of cavalry. All of the companies would meet at the Courthouse on Saturday, 6 June to elect field officers. The Committee recommended that similar units should be formed in each of the Bibb Militia Districts. The Committee also urged the organizations to "move forward with all dispatch."[206]

In July, when long casualty lists of Macon losses at Gettysburg arrived in the city,[207] Adjutant General Wayne wrote Lewis N. Whittle that "Georgia is now in extreme danger," due to the falling back of Bragg's Army of Tennessee to Chattanooga and the surrender of Vicksburg. Atlanta, Wayne believed, would be "a point of great strategic importance and as [General William Starke] Rosecrans and [Gen. Ulysses S.] Grant can now act in concert we may rationally look for a demonstration on Atlanta and the State Road." If Atlanta fell, Wayne believed that Macon would be the next Federal target, and felt that all Georgians must now rally to defend their common interests. Wayne enclosed copies of laws relating to local defense in his letter.[208]

A company was organized for local defense on 2 August 1863. Called the Macon Manufacturing Guards, and composed of the workers in the Macon Manufacturing Company and Thomas C. Nesbit's iron foundry, the group was led by Captain W. H. Amerson. In recording the advent of this unit, a reporter for the *Daily Telegraph* noted, "Companies formed of such material, as employees in Machine shops and on railroads, can do as effectual service as any we have in the Confederacy in resisting invasion."[209]

---

[203] Ibid., 30 March 1864.

[204] Ibid., 4 June 1863.

[205] Ibid., 20 and 25, May 1863.

[206] Ibid., 27 May 1863.

[207] Ibid., 13, 14, and 15 July 1863. The Macon Guards alone lost four killed and five wounded for a total of nine losses. Ibid., 13 July 1863.

[208] Gen. Henry C. Wayne to Lewis N. Whittle, Milledgeville, 11 July 1863, Adjutant Generals Letter Book, June 15-July 23, 1863, p. 292, GDA&H.

[209] *Macon Daily Telegraph*, 3 August 1863.

All men between the ages of eighteen and forty-five were requested to turn out for the defense of Macon in early August, 1863. An appeal was made for four hundred volunteers for home defense. If the men did not come forward a draft would be made by the military authorities. It was promised that they would not serve in the field except in defense of their homes. Their work involved meeting and repelling raids in certain areas.[210]

By the end of the month, Captain B. D. Lumsden received authorization from Colonel D. Wyatt Aiken, Post Commander, to raise a company to perform provost guard duty in Macon. The company would include exempts and non-conscripts who would be stationed in the city permanently. The men would receive the same pay and allowances as other troops.[211]

Despite these early efforts, little was done to prepare Macon for defense against raids. The reason for this involved the fact that the war, for Maconites, was still far away, even as late as the summer of 1863. Accordingly, few defensive measures were taken in the winter of 1863-1864, even after Andersonville Prison, situated at the village of Andersonville, Georgia, in northern Sumter County, was established in February 1864. It remained for the advent of Howell Cobb to prepare Macon for defense and to lead it through the remainder of the war. Cobb was born at Cherry Hill in Jefferson County, Georgia, on 7 September 1815. He was the son of John Addison Cobb and his wife, Sarah Rootes Cobb. His father, of Welsh descent, was a native of North Carolina who moved as a youth to Georgia where he became a planter and owner of a large acreage. His mother, Sarah Rootes Cobb, was the daughter of Thomas R. Rootes, a lawyer and resident of Fredericksburg, Virginia. His parents had seven children, three boys and four girls. With that many children to educate the Cobbs moved to Athens, Georgia. There, Cobb studied at the school of Mr. Fulton, then attended the University of Georgia where he graduated in 1834. He married Mary Ann Lamar on 26 May 1835. The daughter of Zachariah Lamar and his wife, Mary Ann Lamar, she was born in Milledgeville, Georgia, on 23 April 1818. Upon his graduation, Cobb studied law and was admitted to the bar in 1836.[212]

Born into the planter aristocracy of the Lower South, Cobb's career, in many ways, epitomized the interests and ambitions of that group during the

---

[210] Ibid., 4 August 1863.

[211] Ibid., 26 August 1863.

[212] Samuel Boykin, ed., *A Memorial Volume of the Hon. Howell Cobb of Georgia*, Philadelphia: J.B. Lippincott and Co., 1870, pp. 13-17, 19; Physical remains, Howell Cobb Burial Plot, Cemetery Records, Oconee Hill Cemetery, Athens, GA. John Addison Cobb was born on January 5, 1783, and died on November 23, 1855. Sarah Rootes Cobb was born on September 20, 1792, and died on July 22, 1865. John Addison Cobb Burial Plot, Ibid.

Antebellum Period. In 1837, he became solicitor-general of the Western Circuit of Georgia. Elected to Congress in 1842, Cobb served for several terms in the House, becoming parliamentary leader of the Democratic Party in his chamber in 1848. He sided with the Southern bloc in the fight over the expansion of slavery into the territories, the controversy generated by the annexation of Texas, and the declaration of war against Mexico. Elected Speaker of the House in 1849, Cobb served as Governor of Georgia (1852-1854) and was Secretary of the Treasury in President James Buchanan's Cabinet (1857-1860). He resigned his cabinet post on 6 December 1860, and returned to his home in Athens. In January 1861, Cobb led the fight for secession in Georgia. Although he was not a member of the Secession Convention in Milledgeville When the Confederacy was formed Cobb served as chairman of the convention which met in Montgomery, Alabama. In the summer of 1861 he organized the 16th Georgia Regiment and went to the front as its colonel.[213]

Cobb was a strong candidate for President of the new Confederacy, and he served as presiding officer of the Convention which brought the Confederacy into being. For a time he served as President of the Provisional Confederate Congress after Davis' election. As Colonel of the Sixteenth Georgia, Cobb fought with the Army of Northern Virginia during the early part of the war, and was promoted to brigadier general to rank from 12 February 1862, and major general from 9 September 1863.[214]

On 8 September 1863, Cobb was ordered to organize the militia and other local forces of Georgia, making his headquarters in Atlanta.[215] However, Cobb was unhappy in his new post because, as he explained it, "If the President has done his very best to place me in the most unpleasant position possible he could not have succeeded better than by this order." He had to cooperate with Governor Brown, whom he loathed. However, as he told his wife, "My duty requires me to submit without murmur or complaint and I shall do it."[216] When it became known that Cobb was placed in command of the eight thousand members of the Georgia militia, a reporter for the *Daily Telegraph* opined, "The

---

[213] Ibid., pp. 27, 29, 31; Sketch of Howell Cobb in Duma Malone, ed., *Dictionary of American Biography* 20 volumes (New York: Charles Scribner's Sons, 1936) 4:241-243, hereafter cited as *DAB* with appropriate sketch. An account of Cobb's Confederate career may be found in Horace Montgomery, *Howell Cobb's Confederate Career*, Number Ten of William Stanley Hoole, ed., Confederate Centennial Studies (Tuscaloosa, Confederate Publishing Company, 1959).

[214] Ibid., p. 243; Ezra J. Warner, *Generals in Gray: Lives of the Confederate Commanders* (Baton Rouge: Louisiana State University Press, 1959) 55; Secretary of War Judah P. Benjamin, Order, 13 February 1862, Cobb-Erwin-Lamar Collection; *Macon Daily Telegraph*, 23 September 1863.

[215] *Macon Daily Journal*, 17 September 1863.

[216] Cobb to his wife, Atlanta, 9 September 1863, Cobb Papers, 1863.

troops will doubtless be gratified at being placed under the command of one of Georgia's distinguished sons."[217]

Early in 1864, Cobb wanted to make his headquarters in Macon. The fact that his brother-in-law had lived in the city, and that he had spent many happy hours there caused him to confide to Mary Ann, "I hope the state of things with the army in front may be such that I can feel it to be my duty to make my Head Quarters at Macon. Whilst I will not sacrifice the public interests to my personal comfort, I do feel most anxious to spend more of my time with the loved ones of the home circle."[218]

Cobb wanted Secretary of War Seddon to organize troops for the Confederate service out of the Georgia State Guard. When he did not immediately receive orders from Richmond to this effect he explained that the lack of direction was the cause of a great deal of anxiety to his men, because it left them in doubt as to their future position. Cobb sympathized with them because his own future was equally unsettled. He confided to Mary Ann, "If the application is refused I see nothing left for me to look forward to in the future but to return to the field either in Virginia or with our army at Dalton." He asserted he would be content with either position because his "only ambition is to serve the country where I can best do it, and I am willing to leave others to determine where that shall be."[219] In the meantime he was content to go to Macon, Americus, and other places and make speeches urging the people to continue to resist.[220] The *Daily Telegraph's* reporter was ecstatic about Cobb's address in Macon saying, "Let the people read it and rise to the height of the great argument. Now is the crisis of our fate, and if the people will only meet it in a becoming spirit, we believe the early dawn of a glorious peace will tinge the horizon of the next New Year."[221]

When his application to organize a command for the Confederate service from the Georgia State Guard was refused, it left Cobb, after the State Guard was disbanded, without a command. He felt his superiors had made a mistake because, he wrote, "the action of the Government will lose a large number of these men to the service altogether."[222] Therefore, the uncertainty of his future remained with him, and, as he observed, "I am growing somewhat restless about it. I am ready and willing to undertake any service to which I may be assigned- but at the same time the very uncertainty makes it unpleasant."[223]

---

[217] *Macon Daily Telegraph*, 14 September 1863.

[218] Cobb to his wife, Atlanta, 5 January 1864, Cobb Papers, 1864.

[219] Cobb to his wife, Atlanta, 20 January 1864, Ibid.

[220] Ibid.; *Macon Daily Telegraph*, 12, 15, 16, 1864.

[221] *Macon Daily Telegraph*, 28 January 1864.

[222] Cobb to his wife, Atlanta, 30 January 1864, Cobb Papers, 1864.

[223] Cobb to his wife, Atlanta, 4 February 1864. See also Cobb to his wife, 18 February 1864, Ibid.

In late February Cobb continued to seek a territorial command that would enable him to spend more time with his family, though he still professed a willingness to serve his country "wherever I can best serve & advance her interests." He wanted the position of raising and organizing the reserve corps of Georgia.[224] He finally got his wish on 30 March when he was assigned to the command of the reserve force in Georgia under Special Orders No. 75. His headquarters would be at Macon.[225]

Although his appointment came from the Adjutant and Inspector General's Office in Richmond, he still hesitated to visit his department commander, General Joseph E. Johnston because he feared that, until he had his orders in hand, the latter would insist that Cobb keep his headquarters in Atlanta. "I dont want to see him," Cobb wrote his wife, "until that matter is a fixed fact."[226] Cobb was also fortunate in having his old friend and political ally, General Henry R. Jackson, appointed as his assistant.[227]

An old friend, P. T. Layton in Greensboro, Georgia, sent his congratulations to Mary Ann upon the appointment of her husband, and added, "I congratulate him upon his removal from such a place as Atlanta & especially to so pleasant a point as Macon."[228]

Although John A. Cobb informed his father-in-law, Colonel David C. Barrow that Cobb was expected in Macon on 9 April[229] Mary Ann Cobb wrote Gen. Johnston of her husband's new assignment. "This position accords well with my feelings," she confessed, "as it keeps the General in Georgia and affords me the pleasure of his society of which I have been denied since the war began." Cobb was busily engaged in organizing the Georgia Militia, and expected to raise a "considerable number," despite the obstacles which Governor Brown threw in his path. It was not Brown's intention to merely make Cobb's problems more numerous. He wanted to "continue to interpose to annoy and embarrass the President." Fortunately, Mary Ann believed, Brown was not supported by the people of Georgia when he united with Vice President

---

[224] Cobb to his wife, Atlanta, 23 February 1864.

[225] John Withers, A.A.G., Special Orders No. 75, Richmond, 30 Mar 1864, Ibid. See also Howell Cobb, Jr. to his mother, Atlanta, 1 April 1864, Ibid.; William Rutherford to Cobb, Athens, 4 April 1864, Ibid.; and Cobb to Gen. Samuel Cooper, Atlanta, 5 April 1864, Howell Cobb Letter Book, 1864-1865, pp. 1-5.

[226] Cobb to his wife, Atlanta, 4 April 1864, Cobb Papers, 1864.

[227] John Withers, A.A.G., Special Orders No. 81, Richmond, 6 April 1864, Ibid. See also Samuel Cooper to Cobb, Telegram, Richmond, 14 April 1864, Ibid.

[228] P.T. Layton to Mary Ann Cobb, Greensboro, GA., 9 April 1864, Ibid.

[229] John A. Cobb to Col David C. Barrow, Macon, 8 April 1864, David C. Barrow Papers, Hargrett Library, University of Georgia, hereafter cited as Barrow Papers. Cobb did not assume command until April 16. Cobb to Gen. Samuel Cooper, Macon, 12 April 1864, Cobb Letter Book, 1864-1865, pp. 6-7.

Alexander H. Stephens to create a division among the people and create an anti-administration party.[230]

In preparation for Cobb's arrival, Major C. J. Harris, then commanding Conscripts for Georgia at the Conscript Headquarters in Macon, issued General Orders No. 28 which directed all men between the ages of seventeen and eighteen and forty-five and fifty years to rendezvous at the Enrolling Head Quarters in their Congressional Districts by 16 April. Once they were enrolled, their enrolling officers would organize them into companies of volunteers with the right to elect their own officers.[231]

Pressures crowded upon Cobb to furnish militia to different points as soon as he assumed his new post. When General Jeremy F. Gilmer, the Confederacy's chief engineer, then at Savannah, learned of possible trouble among the prisoners at Andersonville he wired Cobb that troops might be available at the Conscript Camp in Macon or in Atlanta to help guard them.[232]

When Cobb asked for troops to come to Macon from Savannah, General Hugh W. Mercer refused, saying he could not detach regular troops "Unless imperatively necessary."[233] Possibly Cobb could send Georgia Reserves to help guard the Andersonville prisoners?[234] At any rate, Mercer wanted Cobb to organize the Reserves in Savannah quickly because he was ordered to go to Dalton and reinforce the Army of Tennessee. Not only would he take the troops in Savannah, but, most importantly, he would have to take the 57th Georgia Regiment from its post at Andersonville. Therefore, Cobb would have to supply its place with Reserves.[235] As late as 26 April the question of who should guard the Andersonville prisoners remained undecided.[236] However, on the following day, Assistant Adjutant General John Withers issued Special Orders No. 98 directing Cobb to "furnish without delay to the Commandant of prisoners at Americus, Georgia such guards, from the local reserves under his command, as he may deem necessary."[237]

---

[230] Mary Ann Cobb to Gen. Joseph E. Johnston, Macon, 18 April 1864, Cobb Papers, 1864.

[231] Lieutenant. P. Looney, Assistant Adjutant General for Maj. C.J. Harris, Macon, 7 April 1864, Ibid.

[232] Maj. Gen. Jeremy F. Gilmer to Cobb, Telegram, Savannah, 17 April 1864, Ibid. The best study of Andersonville is William Marvel, *Andersonville The Last Depot* (Chapel Hill: The University of North Carolina Press, 1994).

[233] Gen. Hugh W. Mercer to Cobb, Telegram, Savannah, 19 April 1864, Cobb Papers, 1864.

[234] Gen. Hugh W. Mercer to Cobb, Telegram, Savannah, 20 April 1864, Ibid.

[235] Gen. Hugh W. Mercer to Cobb, Telegram, Savannah, 23 April 1864, Ibid.

[236] Gen. Hugh W. Mercer to Cobb, Telegram, Savannah, 26 April 1864, Ibid.

[237] John Withers, A.A.G., to Cobb, Special Orders No. 98, Telegram, Richmond, 27 April 1864, Ibid.

Braxton Bragg, then serving as the Military Advisor to President Davis, ordered Cobb to send two full regiments of Reserves to form a prison guard at Andersonville.[238] By 11 May the two regiments requested for Andersonville had arrived in Macon from Atlanta.[239] Lucius J. Gartrell wired Cobb on 16 May that he had raised ten companies of Reserves in Atlanta, totaling 550 men.[240] General Jackson was also raising Reserves in Savannah.[241] Secretary of War Seddon urged Cobb to collect and organize the Reserves and hurry them into places garrisoned by regular troops. "Every trained soldier," Seddon urged, "that can be spared for service in the field" must be relieved. Seddon observed "we are in the very crisis of our fortunes," and "want every man." He added that Davis had directed this action.[242]

As Cobb readied the Reserves to go to Andersonville to relieve the 57th Georgia, Pope Barrow, one of Cobb's aides, wrote that, although there was not much work to do as yet because the command was not organized, he expected "the workload crowding in on us before long at a great rate."[243] Cobb also directed his son, John A. Cobb, to report to him as aide-de-camp when the younger Cobb was "not engaged in the discharge of the duty as Manager" of five Cobb and Lamar plantations in Sumter and Baldwin Counties.[244]

In late May, Cobb continued to raise troops, many of whom were detailed for the defense of Macon. He was also organizing companies formed of all the men engaged in the different public workshops in the city, including all Government workers, whether details, exempts, or those belonging to organizations in the field. This latter class of soldier was to be designated on the muster rolls, and when they returned to their units in the field they had to be accounted for on the muster rolls. Cobb outlined his policy of providing troops for local defense in a letter to Colonel George W. Rains in Augusta, "It is not proposed to unite this class of companies with any other organization. The

---

[238] Braxton Bragg to Cobb, Telegram, Richmond, 3 May 1864, Ibid.

[239] Lucius J. Gartrell to Cobb, 2 Telegrams, Atlanta, 9 and 11 May 1864, Ibid. Gartrell commanded the Reserves in Atlanta under Cobb's direction. As late as July 9, Brigadier General John H. Winder, at Andersonville, urged Cobb to send Reserves to Andersonville to help guard prisoners. One of the reasons for this was that some of the guards were constantly deserting. On the night of July 8 alone, twelve guards left. See Gen. John H. Winder to Cobb, Camp Sumter, Andersonville, 9 July 1864, Ibid.

[240] Lucius J. Gartrell to Cobb, Telegram, Atlanta, 16 May 1864, Ibid.

[241] Gen. Henry R. Jackson to Cobb, Telegram, Savannah, 10 May 1864, Ibid.

[242] Sec. of War James A. Seddon to Cobb, Telegram, Richmond, 15 May 1864, Ibid.

[243] Pope Barrow to "My Dear Little Sister," Macon, 29 April 1864, Barrow Papers. Barrow was the brother of Lucy Pope Cobb, wife of John A. Cobb.

[244] William M. Browne, Special Orders, Macon, 30 April 1864, Cobb-Erwin-Lamar Collection.

strength of the companies should be known at these Head Quarters and the muster rolls should be forwarded here." These companies, whether in Augusta or Macon, should be enrolled strictly for local defense and only required to drill when it could be done without interfering with their other duties.[245]

Secretary Seddon helped Cobb to raise troops by directing that detailed men already in military service were not liable to perform militia or state duty. Those men who were exempted from service might be subjected to military service if they were detailed men who, in Cobb's judgment, might be used with the Reserves.[246]

Cobb was also pressed by more personal matters during late June and early July. Concerned about Johnston's ability to hold Sherman in North Georgia, he urged his wife to leave Athens and go to *The Hurricane*, the Cobb plantation in Baldwin County below Milledgeville.[247] Some days later he wrote her that two Cobb associates, Major Young and Judge [General Henry] Jackson were with him as delegates to a Methodist convocation in Macon which was charged to take steps to build up an orphanage for the children of deceased soldiers. He also planned to go to Atlanta and argue a case concerning the acquisition of buildings for hospitals in Macon then before the Georgia Supreme Court which was meeting in the North Georgia city. Cobb was also anxious to see Johnston and learn about conditions before Atlanta.[248]

When Cobb's friend, General Johnston, was removed from the command of the Army of Tennessee by Davis, the former came to Macon with his wife and stayed for a time in the Bear's Den. Johnston, however, although feeling hurt by the "unpleasant situation" he was placed in because of his sudden removal, indulged "in no spirit of complaint," but spoke "kindly of his successor and very hopefully of the prospect of holding Atlanta."[249]

On 22 July Johnston was serenaded by over two hundred Maconites who gathered in Walnut Street to see him. However, the General did not appear because he was very tired and his wife was ill. One of Cobb's sons appeared to give Johnston's thanks for the "kind feelings held for him by the people of

---

[245] Cobb to Col. George W. Rains, Macon, 31 May 1864, Howell Cobb Letter Book, 1864-1865, pp. 103-104.

[246] James A. Seddon to Cobb, Richmond, 16 July 1864, Cobb Papers, 1864.

[247] Cobb to his wife, Macon, 22 June 1864, Ibid.

[248] Cobb to his wife, Macon, 9 July 1864, Ibid.

[249] Cobb to his wife, Macon, 20 July 1864, Ibid. For details concerning Davis' removal of Johnston as commander of the Army of Tennessee see James Lee McDonough and James Pickett Jones, *War So Terrible: Sherman and Atlanta* (New York: W.W. Norton & Co., 1987) 205ff. As Johnston's successor Davis placed General John Bell Hood in command of the Army of Tennessee. See also *Macon Daily Telegraph*, 21 July 1864, concerning Johnston's arrival in Macon.

Macon.[250] As Cobb spoke, the tramp of militia could be heard marching to the depot where they entrained for Atlanta. The noise of other trains arriving from the besieged city carried fearful refugees to Macon.[251]

Although most of her people did not then know it, Macon was about to be tested as she never had been before during the forty-one years of her history.

---

[250] *Macon Daily Telegraph*, 22 July 1864. The Johnston's moved into a house opposite Thomas C. Nesbit's residence. R.J. Hallett to Tufts, Macon, 10 September 1864, Howell Cobb Letter Book, 1864-1865, p. 256.

[251] Ibid.

Chapter 12

Assault on Macon:
Stoneman's Raid and its Aftermath

In late July 1864, as he was tightening his grip on Atlanta, Major General William T. Sherman determined to send a cavalry expedition composed of five thousand men against the Macon and Western Railroad, a movement which would correspond with a movement of the Army of the Tennessee under Major General John M. Schofield to East Point, just south of Atlanta. General Kenner Garrard's cavalry division would be placed under Major General George M. Stoneman, Jr., who would take his own division and Garrard's around the left of the Federal line before Atlanta to McDonough. Another body of cavalry commanded by General Edward M. McCook, and consisting of his own division and the division of General Lovell H. Rousseau, commanded by Colonel Thomas J. Harrison of the Eighth Indiana Cavalry, a total force of 4,000 troopers, would move from the vicinity of Fayetteville, Georgia. Both forces were scheduled to unite at Lovejoy's Station on the Macon and Western Railroad on 28 July, which they would destroy "in the most effectual manner." Sherman wrote, "I estimated this joint cavalry could whip all of [Confederate Lieutenant General Joseph] Wheeler's cavalry, and could otherwise accomplish its task...."[1]

George M. Stoneman, Jr. had enjoyed an illustrious career before his assignment to lead the raid on Macon. Born on 8 August 1822 at Busti, Chatauqua County in western New York State. The eldest of ten children of George and Catherine Stoneman, he received his early education at an academy in the nearby village of Jamestown and was appointed a cadet at the United

---

[1] Maj Gen William T. Sherman, Report, Atlanta, 15 September 1864, OR 38: Pt. 2, 75. A thorough account of the campaign may be found in David Evans, *Sherman's Horsemen, Union Cavalry Operations in the Atlanta Campaign* (Bloomington: Indiana University Press, 1996), see especially pp. 304-340. See also Albert Castel, *Decision in the West The Atlanta Campaign of 1864* (Lawrence: University Press of Kansas, 1992).

States Military Academy where he graduated in 1846. Receiving a commission as a brevet second lieutenant in the First Dragoons, Stoneman became quartermaster of the "Mormon Battalion" which formed a portion of General Stephen Kearny's expedition across the Southwest to California. He served in the Southwest until 1855 rising to the rank of captain in the newly-organized 2nd Cavalry. Escaping from Fort Brown, Texas, after refusing to surrender to his immediate superior, General David E. Twiggs, during Texas' secession in 1861, he was assigned to temporary duty at the cavalry school at Carlisle, Pennsylvania. On 9 May 1861, he was promoted to major in the First Cavalry and participated in the campaigns in Virginia. Promoted to Brigadier General of volunteers, he became a major general in November 1862.

Stoneman made a raid upon Richmond at the head of a corps of over 10,000 men during the Chancellorsville Campaign (April 13-May 2, 1863). During the winter of 1863-1864 he was assigned to command the cavalry corps of the Army of the Ohio. With this force he participated in the Atlanta Campaign.[2]

Stoneman and McCook met with Sherman who explained his plans to them. The movement was scheduled to begin on 27 July.[3] However, on 26 July, before the expedition had started, Stoneman asked Sherman if he could take his own division and make a dash on Macon. Stoneman wrote that "by a vigorous stroke" he could release the prisoners in Macon's Camp Ogelthorpe, and "afterward go on to Americus [Andersonville Prison] and release those [prisoners] there." He observed, "I would like to try it, and am willing to run any risks, and I can vouch for my little command. Now is the time to do it before the rebel army falls back and covers that country, and I have every inducement to try it. If we accomplish the desired object it will compensate for the loss as prisoners of us all, and I should feel compensated for almost any sacrifice.[4]

On the same day, Sherman ordered Stoneman to send General Garrard back to the left flank of the Federal army and move against Macon and Andersonville, assuring Stoneman he would keep the Army of Tennessee busy so that the cavalrymen would have nothing to fight but Wheeler's cavalry. "If," Sherman observed, "you can bring back to the army any or all those prisoners of war it will be an achievement that will entitle you and the men of your command to the love and admiration of the whole country."[5] Later, writing in his report,

---

[2] Sketch of George Stoneman in *DAB*, Vol. 18, 92.

[3] Sherman Report, 15 September 1864, 75.

[4] Maj Gen George M. Stoneman to Sherman, Marietta, GA., 26 July 1864, OR, 38, Pt. 2, 264.

[5] Sherman to Stoneman, Marietta, GA., 26 July 1864, Ibid., 265.

Sherman noted, "There was something most captivating in the idea, and the execution was within the bounds of probability of success."[6]

On 27 July Stoneman's command began its movement toward the south; bugles blew in his camps four miles north of Decatur before dawn. By four o'clock the division was on the march.[7] Washington L. Sanford of the 14th Illinois Cavalry, observed "We soon noted a striking contrast between the country hitherto passed over and that portion in the rebel rear carefully husbanded for the supply of the rebel army. Astonishing abundance filled the country. In the afternoon we passed to the right of the romantic 'Stone Mountain,' standing as a lone sentinel keeping watch over a surrounding lovely country."[8]

Stoneman's Division numbered 2,104 officers and men, the general, and seven members of his staff. It consisted of three brigades. The first was commanded by Colonel James Biddle, and included the mounted portions of the 5th and 6th Indiana Cavalry, a total of about seven hundred men. The second brigade, led by Lieutenant Colonel Silas Adams, included five hundred and fifty men of the 1st and 11th Kentucky Cavalry. The 3rd brigade was composed of the 14th Illinois Cavalry, the 8th Michigan Cavalry, and a portion of the 1st Ohio Squadron and numbered 800 men [under Colonel Horace Capron]. Captain Alexander Hardy led a detachment of the 24th Indiana Battery with two three-inch Rodman ordnance rifles and fifty-four men.[9]

The force entered Decatur at sunrise and found Garrard with his command. In Decatur scouts reported that elements of Wheeler's Cavalry were preparing to attack. Therefore, a line of battle was formed and preparations made to fight. However, after sending out scouts to the right and right front, and finding no enemy, Stoneman moved forward, leaving Garrard in Decatur to hold and engage the Confederates to prevent a pursuit. Stoneman's main body continued through the day and most of the night, following the line of the Georgia Railroad until four A.M. on July 28, when it halted two miles north of Covington. There, Stoneman sent Lieutenant Colonel Adams, with his brigade, to Mechanicsburg, on the Ocmulgee River, to observe the movements of the Confederate cavalry. The remainder of the division rested until 8:00 A.M., then resumed its march through Covington. Leaving the railroad in their rear, the troopers crossed the Ulcofauhachee River at 9:00 A.M. At the river Stoneman detached eighty-eight men of McLaughlin's Squadron of Ohio cavalry, under Captain Samuel Wells,

---

[6] Sherman Report, 15 September 1864, Ibid., 76.

[7] Lt Col Robert W.Smith, Report, Marietta, GA., 7 August 1864, Ibid., 915, hereafter cited as Smith Report.

[8] Washington L. Sanford, *History of the Fourteenth Illinois Cavalry and the Brigades to which it belonged* (R.R. Donnelley & Sons Company, 1898) 185.

[9] Smith Report, 7 August 1864, *OR*, 38:2:915.

acting assistant adjutant general on Capron's staff, to destroy the bridge and a large flour mill at Henderson's Mill, and the bridge and factory at Newton's Cotton Factory, all on the river. Wells rejoined Capron at 4:00 A.M. on 29 July after accomplishing his objectives. By nightfall the division had reached the vicinity of Monticello—only forty miles from Macon.[10]

While Stoneman was advancing deep into the heart of Georgia, his Confederate opponents had not been idle. On 27 July General John Hood received information that Federal cavalry had moved around the Confederate right with the objective of breaking his communications with Macon. The following day a large cavalry force (Garrard's) had crossed the Chattahoochee River at Campbellton, moving around the Confederate left. Hood attempted to counter these moves by sending Wheeler to move against Stoneman, while Brigadier General William H. Jackson was sent against the Federal force on the left. Hood also ordered Colonel Joseph C. Lewis's Brigade of infantry to move down the Macon Railroad to try to intercept Garrard. Stoneman was fortunate because the initial Confederate efforts were directed to the area south and west of Atlanta, not towards the southeast.[11]

On the 27th, Hood wired Confederate Secretary of War Seddon that a Federal cavalry raid had begun in the direction of Covington on the Georgia Railroad. Hood reassured the harried Seddon, "Our cavalry in pursuit."[12] At 11:00 A.M. on the 27th, Hood ordered Wheeler to detach what force he could spare to follow Stoneman and try to bring him to battle.[13]

At 5:30 P.M. Hood wired Brigadier General John H. Winder, Commandant of Andersonville Prison, "The raid toward Covington is stronger than at first reported. Destination still unknown. We have a heavy force in pursuit."[14] As the evening of 27 July wore on the Confederates still seemed unaware of the direction, strength, and intentions of the raiders. Hood informed General Braxton Bragg, Military Advisor to President Davis, at 5:30 that a raid was headed toward Covington with ten pieces of artillery; but, although Wheeler was in pursuit, the destination of the raiders was unknown.[15] Fearing Macon might be

---

[10] Ibid.; Col Horace Capron, Report, Marietta, GA., 10 August 1864, Ibid., 925-926, hereafter cited as Capron Report; Maj Haviland Tompkins, Report, Marietta, 12 August 1864, Ibid., 919, hereafter cited as Tompkins Report.

[11] Lt Gen John B. Hood, Report, Richmond, VA., 15 February 1865, *OR*, 38, Pt. 2, hereafter cited as Hood Report; Brig Gen Francis A. Shoup, Journal, Atlanta, 27 and 28 July 1864, Ibid., 38, Pt. 3, 688, hereafter cited as Shoup Journal with appropriate entries.

[12] Hood to James A. Seddon, Telegram, Atlanta, 27 July 1864, Ibid., 38: Pt. 2, 912.

[13] Shoup to Wheeler, Atlanta, 27 July 1864, Ibid., 913. See also the telegrams of Shoup to Wheeler sent at 1:30 P.M. and 5:00 P.M. on 27 July, Ibid., 913-914.

[14] Hood to Brig Gen John H. Winder, Telegram, Atlanta, 27 July 1864, Ibid., 916.

[15] Hood to Gen. Braxton Bragg, Telegram, Atlanta, 27 July 1864, Ibid., 913.

the raider's destination Hood wired Major General Howell Cobb, Commander of the District of Georgia in Macon, "Prepare for it."[16]

Hood's Chief of Staff, General Francis A. Shoup, telegraphed Cobb from Atlanta on 27 July that a small raid was moving towards Covington, but Wheeler's Cavalry was in pursuit.[17] A little later on the 27th Shoup warned "The raid towards Covington is stronger than at first report. Destination still unknown." However, he reassured the by now anxious Cobb: "we have a heavy force in pursuit."[18]

Unfortunately, even as Stoneman began his advance on Macon, Shoup notified Cobb that Hood, aware of the tightening Federal grip on Atlanta, wanted every available man to be sent forward to the besieged city "that can bear an arm unless Andersonville is immediately threatened the regular garrison only should be left there."[19] Under these orders sixteen hundred militia marched down Poplar Street on their way to the Macon and Western Railroad Depot en route to Atlanta.[20] J. William Blackshear noted, "Twelve & fifteen hundred militia go up every day & very wrathy they are, not likely to take many prisoners." He added, "Pity they had not all been in a rage sooner in all these states. These wretchs would not have been among us now."[21]

As Stoneman continued his advance on the evening of 28 July Shoup wired Cobb ordering him to keep the militia at Andersonville for the present, although the Federal raiders were reported across South River [one of the principal tributaries of the Ocmulgee], with one column advancing on the village of McDonough.[22]

With these reports the excitement in Macon greatly increased. On Sunday, 28 July, all of the churches in the city, adjourned upon news that the "Yankees were approaching."[23] On the eve of the raid the people of Macon were still talking about President Davis' removal of Johnston as commander of the Army of Tennessee and replacing him with John B. Hood. Marian B. Blackshear reported she was surprised by the anger of the men on the cars on a trip from

---

[16] Hood to Howell Cobb, Telegram, Atlanta, 27 July 1864, Ibid., 917. See also Shoup to Wheeler, Telegram, Atlanta, 27 July 1864, Ibid., 914 (two Telegrams); and Shoup to Cobb, Telegram, Atlanta, 27 July 1864 (two Telegrams), in Howell Cobb Papers, 1864. Even the usually observant Confederate cavalry believed Stoneman's force to number four thousand, nearly twice its actual size. See Brig Gen Alfred Iverson, Jr. to Cobb, 27 July 1864, Cobb Papers, 1864.

[17] Shoup to Cobb, Telegram, Atlanta, 27 July 1864, Cobb Papers, 1864.

[18] Shoup to Cobb, Telegram, Atlanta, 27 July 1864, Ibid.

[19] Shoup to Cobb, Telegram, Atlanta, 26 July 1864, Ibid.

[20] *Macon Daily Telegraph*, 27 July 1864.

[21] J. William Blackshear to his wife, Macon, 28 July 1864, Blackshear Papers.

[22] Shoup to Cobb, Telegram, Atlanta, 28 July 1864, 5: 15 P.M., Cobb Papers, 1864.

[23] Cobb to his wife, Macon, 28 July 1864, Ibid.

Macon to Savannah. She wrote, "Let us pray that it will be all right in the end." As she passed through the settlement of Griswoldville, she noted the number of refugees from North Georgia who were living in tents and boxcars . From her seat on the train she saw "delicate women [who] looked out sadly as the cars passed. Every body looked troubled but the children who ran about. Servants were cooking breakfast in the open air." She ruefully questioned, "Can it be possible that we will have the same thing to do–& where can we go."[24]

Nevertheless, despite the poor living conditions, and the "thousand and one" refugees in and about Macon, the city which Stoneman was about to attack was "a decidedly busy looking city." With the sounds of industry reverberating around her busy streets, Macon wore a "more active appearance." The *Daily Telegraph*'s reporter recorded "The military departments have all been removed here, adding no inconsiderable number to our floating population." The refugees were safe in Macon "remote," as they were "from the sound of Yankee shells and minnie balls." Despite the relative safety of Macon, the writer asserted: "we trust they will soon be able to return to their homes, a wish, we suppose, they will cheerfully echo in their hearts."[25]

Cobb, determined to defend Macon, sent scouts on the various roads on both sides of the Ocmulgee River leading from Atlanta and Covington. On 27 July he wrote Georgia Adjutant General Wayne at Milledgeville, "It is well enough to be prepared for any emergency."[26] That same evening Cobb issued orders to immediately remove the Federal officers from Camp Ogelthorpe to Charleston.[27] Suddenly, on the 29th, Cobb alerted Georgia Governor Brown that he had received positive information that the Federals had occupied Monticello and were marching on Clinton. While readying a force of cavalry to meet them, Cobb assured the Governor that he was "prepared to cooperate with" him "in any course you may adopt for the protection of" Macon and Milledgeville.[28]

At Monticello on the evening of 28 July, Stoneman received information that the three bridges he thought crossed the Ocmulgee River north of Macon did not exist. He now decided that, instead of advancing on Macon from the direction of Forsyth which had been his original plan, he would march down the east side of the river and destroy the Georgia Central Railroad east of the city. Accordingly, Adams' Brigade moved on the right hand road from Clinton to Macon, Biddle's Brigade on the left hand road, and Capron's Brigade on the far

[24] Marian B. Blackshear to her mother and sister, Savannah, 21 July 1864, Blackshear Papers.

[25] *Macon Daily Telegraph*, 24 July 1864.

[26] Cobb to Maj Gen Henry C. Wayne, Telegram, Macon, 27 July 1864, Howell Cobb Letter Book, 1864-1865, p. 181, Cobb Letter Book, 299.

[27] R.J. Hallett to Col. John B. Cummings, Macon, 27 July 1864, Ibid., p. 179.

[28] Cobb to Gov. Joseph E. Brown, Macon, 29 July 1864, Ibid., p. 184.

left to strike the railroad. On the 29th a few prisoners were taken at Monticello and six pickets captured, while the Federals continued their advance to within twelve miles of Macon.[29]

At 4:00 A.M. on 30 July the column moved forward. Adams' Brigade was sent to the right with orders to reach the Ocmulgee River at some point above Macon, and to look for fords and ferries, or find some other means of crossing. Major Francis M. Davidson of the 14th Illinois Cavalry, with his battalion and Company "H" of the 14th, numbering one hundred and twenty-five men was sent to strike the railroad near Gordon and destroy it east to the Oconee River.[30] When the column was five miles from Macon, Capron's Brigade was sent to the left to strike the line near Gordon. Both parties reached their objectives and burned some small bridges and culverts. They tore up the track at these points for a distance of two or three miles and destroyed three trains of cars and three engines. Twenty-two box cars loaded with commissary and quartermaster stores, and some stock and three passenger coaches with citizens and soldiers aboard were also seized and destroyed.[31] Davidson's men dashed into Gordon and began to destroy the facilities around the railroad depot. The Confederate Government's warehouse there was filled with bacon, meal, and flour together with a large amount of furniture owned by refugees from Charleston, Savannah, and other coastal areas. Davidson's men set fire to the building and destroyed everything. Although efforts were made to destroy one hundred and fifty to two hundred cars and engines, the car shed, and several buildings adjacent to the railroad, much of this was saved through the energetic efforts of the citizens.[32]

One party, commanded by 1st Lieutenant Albert B. Capron of Company "A," 14th Illinois Cavalry, son of Colonel Horace Capron, captured a train, and "seeing another train approaching, loaded with Confederate soldiers, the Lieutenant sprang upon an engine, standing on the track all fired up, and uncoupling it from its train, he seized the level, opened the valve, and sent the engine with terrible speed to meet the incoming Johnnies; there was a terrible crash, but the amount of damage inflicted we never knew, as we moved with alacrity from that position."[33]

Their most successful effort involved the destruction of the bridge across the Oconee River near Emmet (Station No 16). This destruction was completed by a squad of only twelve men. A *Daily Telegraph* reporter lamented, "Why this bridge was left unguarded we cannot conceive. We learn that as late as last Wednesday there was a force of one hundred and fifty men stationed there, and

---

[29] Tompkins Report, 919-920; Capron Report, 926; Smith Report, 915.

[30] Sanford, *History of the Fourteenth Illinois Cavalry*, 189; Smith Report, 915-16.

[31] Smith Report, 916.

[32] *Macon Daily Telegraph*, 2 August 1864.

[33] Sanford, *History of the Fourteenth Illinois Cavalry*, pp. 189-90.

on that evening they were removed and the bridge left unprotected." The reporter declared "for a squad of twelve men to destroy so important a structure is extremely humiliating."[34] Lamenting the destruction caused by Davidson, Adams, and others Cobb wrote his wife on 3 August,

"The amount of property destroyed thru the country where the raiders passed is very great. They stole & robbed indiscriminately [sic] taking horses, mules, provisions, jewelry, and everything of that kind. Burnt all kinds of factorys and mills and what they could not carry away they destroyed—marking their whole track with ruin and desolation. I have heard of no cruelty or outrage to white women in the presence of their witnesses[.] Judge Jackson had started here with Sissy & John's children and were at Gordon when the raiders approached that place. They got off on the train and got to Macon—but lost all their baggage left on the Millegeville [sic] train. Sissy not only lost all of [her] own and the childrens clothing but what she most grieves over—all her family relics--jewelry and silver-breast pins, bracelets etc....indeed all her valuable relics, which had been carefully packed in a valise and...put in a trunk. Her trunks were broken open—and the Yankees [burned] what they did not carry away. They were seen throwing her fine dresses into the fire. The silver pitcher and Jeff's likeness was taken from one of them who was captured at Milledgeville. I hear that they made a visit to our plantation in Baldwin but can learn nothing more nor even confirmation of that. I will let you know as soon as I do hear."[35]

As Stoneman's Division approached Macon, Colonel Capron observed the most terrible panic among the people. He wrote that "train after train of cars came rushing along loaded to their utmost capacity with costly furniture, printing presses and type, private carriages and horses; in fact every conceivable form of movable property," came by. The Federals intercepted these trains, burning the trains. Capron lamented the destruction of all of this valuable property, but consoled himself with the thought that "we were obeying orders." He did what he could, according to his account, to relieve the civilian population from the "barbarities" which usually accompanied such raids as the one led by Stoneman.[36]

Even as this destruction was going on Major A.M. Rowland, commanding Camp Cooper, offered Cobb the services of James W. Blount, formerly a captain in one of the mounted companies connected with the camp, as orderly and guide. Rowland asserted that Blount "understands all about the country and the other side of the river and I have detailed him to report to you for the purpose of

---

[34] Ibid.

[35] Cobb to his wife, 3 August 1864, Cobb Papers, 1864. The underlined words are Cobb's.

[36] Horace Capron, "Stoneman's Raid," in *The National Tribune*, 23 November 1882. p. 1, hereafter cited as Capron, "Stoneman's Raid."

conveying orders to the supporting force."[37] For his part, Cobb, who had received "positive information" that the Federals had captured Monticello and were advancing on Clinton, wrote Governor Brown that he was preparing to send a cavalry force to learn more about the raiders. The politician-turned-general had called upon Adjutant General Wayne in his Macon Office, but not finding him in and knowing that Brown would want to protect Georgia's capital at Milledgeville, assured the Governor he would cooperate with him "in any course you may adopt for the protection of the two points."[38] Brown replied that he could meet Cobb at 3:30 in the Governor's Macon office to "cooperate with you for the defense of this place and Milledgeville against the raid."[39] At the same time a *Daily Telegraph* reporter announced an advertisement by the Sheriff of Bibb County for one–fifth of the able bodied slaves in the county to work on fortifications around Macon.[40]

On the evening of July 29, Stoneman moved Adams' Brigade on the right hand, or River Road, and Biddle's and Capron's Brigades on the left hand or main road. Stoneman accompanied Biddle and Capron. Private Eastham Tarrant of the 1st Kentucky Cavalry in Adams' Brigade, remembered, "We had not gone far before dark came. It was so dark and cloudy that we could scarcely see anything. While marching along, one of our men who had been in advance, came rushing back to us on foot. He told us that he had just escaped from the Rebels, who had captured him a few minutes before. We put out a strong advance guard of select men, and pretty soon they were fired upon by the enemy." One man, Perry J. Porter, of Company I, was killed, and another, Sergeant A.J. Catron, of Company L, was wounded. A heavy skirmish began which, because of the intense darkness of the night, added to the confusion. Adams' men could not determine the position of the Confederates until they saw the flashes of their guns. Two volleys were fired by the Confederates, "and every time they wounded some one, and also killed a horse.[41]

At 5:00 P.M. on 29 July Cobb had sent Major W.S. Wallace with the force of cavalry he had mentioned to Governor Brown for the purpose of obtaining information concerning Stoneman's advance. Accordingly, Wallace rode with his fifty-two men towards Clinton, county seat of Jones County, fifteen miles

---

[37] Maj. A.M. Rowland to Cobb, Hdqrs Camp Cooper, Macon, 29 July 1864, Cobb Papers, 1864.

[38] Cobb to Governor Brown, Macon, 29 July 1864, Cobb Letter Book, 1864-65, p. 184.

[39] Brown to Cobb, Macon, 29 July 1864, Cobb Papers, 1864.

[40] *Macon Daily Telegraph*, 29 July 1864.

[41] Eastham Tarrant, *The Wild Riders of the First Kentucky Cavalry, A History of the Regiment, in the Great War of the Rebellion 1861-1865* (Committee of the Regiment, R.H. Carothers, Louisville, KY., 1894) 361.

north of Macon. Two miles from Macon the road forked. The main road continued on to Clinton while the left hand or River Road passed close to the river. Wallace ordered a detachment of four men to ride up the River Road to see if the Federals were advancing there. With the remainder of his force, he moved up the main road. Five miles from Clinton, Wallace learned that the Federals were advancing in force on the main road. Night came on and Wallace, fearing contact with the Federals, threw a detachment forward under command of a Dr Collins. He ordered Collins to proceed cautiously until he met the Federals. Wallace also directed one of Collins' men to hide near the road and try to determine their strength. Collins agreed to personally supervise this mission. Soon after his advance guard moved forward, Wallace heard a brisk firing. In an effort to meet this new threat he formed his main body on the side of the road in an advantageous position. The advance fell back except for the hidden Dr Collins. Wallace reinforced them and sent them back to the top of the next hill in the direction of Clinton. Federal cavalry soon came up and the skirmishing continued until two hundred Federals advanced within thirty yards of Wallace's line when the Confederates delivered a volley in their ranks which caused numerous casualties. This caused the Federal advance to fall back in considerable confusion. Although Wallace ordered his men to charge, they had not been under fire before and their horses were badly frightened by all of the firing, factors which caused them to fall back. Soon Wallace's men became badly scattered and fled down the road in the direction of Macon. Wallace rallied fourteen men, armed with only six muskets, but withdrew to Macon having suffered the loss of two killed.[42]

When reports began to filter in on the evening of the 29th, the *Telegraph and Confederate's*, reporter announced "Raids are the order of the day." He wrote that Maconites were excited and gathering up their weapons to meet Stoneman.[43] Despite the confusion, Cobb attempted to put up a bold front. He observed, in a letter to his wife written on the 29th, "Raiding parties never go out to fight and hence 500 brave men can defend a place against 5,000 raiders." While admitting there was "some excitement" in Macon for the past two days, he asserted "I have kept out bigots—and have everything ready to meet them [the raiders] if they come." The Confederate General, however, did not believe the Federals would come. He reported "The truth is fears & apprehensions exist everywhere and the safest place is where there [are] troops as the enemy will not

---

[42] Maj W.S. Wallace to Maj Lamar Cobb, Macon, 5 August 1864, Cobb Papers, 1864; *Macon Daily Telegraph and Confederate*, 30 July 1864. The paper reported that "Scouts sent out report that they met the advance five miles beyond Clinton, exchanged shots with them, and left them this side of that village, on the road to Macon. They could tell nothing about the strength of the enemy."

[43] *Macon Daily Telegraph and Confederate*, 30 July 1864.

be apt to come to such places, and if they do come they will be met and whipped."[44]

Nevertheless, Cobb continued to make preparations to oppose the Federal raiders. On 29 July he told Mayor Stephen Collins, that the city-operated ferry established just above the bridge carrying the tracks of the Georgia Central Railroad over the Ocmulgee[45] should be kept ready to pass couriers throughout the day and night. Cobb had great difficulty in getting his pickets across the river on the night of 27 July, and had been unable to get them across on the night of the 28th, even after he had appealed to Collins for help. He cautioned Collins that "As long as raids are threatened upon this place, I deemed it of utmost importance that ferrymen should be kept at the ferry all the time and especially at night." The Confederate Commander wanted to be informed if he could rely "with confidence" upon crossing the ferry at any hour, and warned "You may rest assured that the safety of your city is involved in the question."[46]

As Sunday, 30 July, dawned the editor of the *Daily Telegraph* reported the excitement in Macon was intense as people grabbed their weapons to meet the Federals. He speculated: "What he [Stoneman] is coming here for, is a mystery to us, unless he is coming in heavy force, and there are too many raiding parties out just now to admit of such a supposition." Perhaps, the editor thought, "A few hours…will throw more light on the movement."[47] In fact, on the morning of 30 July confusion reigned even in official circles. On that date Major G.E. Lawson, commanding the garrison in Columbus, sent four twelve-pounder Napoleon cannon to Cobb with three hundred muskets and eighty men to bolster up the forces in Macon. Unfortunately, he could not send more troops since most of his available men had been sent to Hood in Atlanta.[48] After the battle Lawson telegraphed Cobb, "Can you return any of the arms sent you as the raiders have left your city?"[49] Moreover, Brigadier General John H. Winder wired Cobb from Fort Valley, "Where are the raiders & in what force answer at once."[50]

In the morning of 30 July Biddle's Brigade engaged the first Confederate pickets at the forks of the Griswoldville Road seven miles from Macon, driving

---

[44] Cobb to his wife, 29 July 1864, Cobb Papers, 1864.

[45] At the same place it crosses today just below the modern Otis Redding Memorial Bridge.

[46] Cobb to Mayor Stephen Collins, Macon, July 29, 1864, Cobb Letter Book, 1864-65, pp. 183-84.

[47] *Macon Daily Telegraph*, 30 July 1864.

[48] Maj G.E. Lawson to Cobb, Telegram, Columbus, GA., 30 July 1864, Cobb Papers, 1864.

[49] Lawson to Cobb, Telegram, Columbus, GA., n.d., Ibid.

[50] Winder to Cobb, Telegram, Fort Valley, GA., 30 July 1864, Ibid.

them back. Stoneman ordered Capron to picket the Griswoldville Road, and with the balance of his command advance on Macon by following the tracks of the Georgia Central. As he advanced Capron divided his men into detachments which reached the railroad at different points from six and a half to three miles from Macon, and destroyed the line. Five miles of track, two passenger trains, and one stock train loaded with hogs and horses were destroyed with the three locomotives. A machine shop used to manufacture gun carriages was burned three miles outside the city. With Biddle's men, Capron burned the five hundred foot trestle of the Walnut Creek railroad bridge only one and a half miles from Macon. Adams' men moved down the river and one mile above Macon met Confederate forces which they drove back under the cover of their main battery on Dunlap's Hill near Macon, about half a mile above Fort Hawkins. Adams was unable to advance any further because of the firing of a battery of artillery under Major Taliaferro, but continued the battle.[51]

Fortunately for the citizens of Macon, the city was not without her defenders. By the morning of 30 July these included 600 Tennessee regulars under Major John W. Nisbet and 1,000 Georgia Militia, both in route to Atlanta from Andersonville, who arrived in Macon on the evening of the 29th. Cobb quickly conscripted the entire force to defend Macon. Colonel John B. Cumming, commanding the 5th Regiment of Georgia Reserves, commanded the left of the Confederate defense line, placing Peschke's battery of three pieces on the Clinton Road where they composed the extreme left of the Confederate line. Major Taliaferro's battery was stationed on the hill one half mile beyond Fort Hawkins. In the interval between Taliaferro and Cumming were Lieutenant Colonel Christopher D. Findlay's Battalion. Altogether, by 7:00 A.M. on 30 July the Confederates had placed 2,000 men in a defensive line between East Macon and Walnut Creek. About 500 men in Macon's Home Guard units under Colonel George C. Gibbs, Commandant of the Post of Macon and the Federal Officers' prison at Camp Oglethorpe, formed a line of battle west of the river. These troops included Captain B.F. Ross' Macon Volunteers Company B, known as the "Silver Greys"; workers in the Macon cotton factory commanded by Major M.R. Rogers, Lieutenant Colonel Wiley's company of convalescents, Lieutenant Nicoll's Fireman Guards, and Captain J.R. Armstrong's Company. This force was posted some distance from the river on the Vineville Road.[52] At the same time that Adams advanced Colonel G.W. Lee, whose brigade of Georgia Militia was entrusted with the overall defense of the East Macon area, sent Colonel Hooper's Regiment toward Griswoldville. At 5:00 A.M. on 30 July Colonel L. Armstrong's Regiment was sent to the left to strengthen

---

[51] Smith Report, 916; Capron Report, 926; Macon *Christian Index*, 12 August 1864.

[52] John C. Butler, *Historical Record*, pp. 263-65.

Cumming along the Clinton Road. Simultaneously, Lee moved his troops along the Milledgeville Road and formed line of battle on the crest of a hill immediately beyond East Macon. The Second Georgia Reserve Militia under Colonel Holt was placed on the left and the right flank of a detachment of Georgia Militia under Colonel Harris was formed on the right of the Milledgeville Road. Captain Brooks' Company was detached from Colonel Harris' right and thrown forward to Walnut Creek as scouts. When they encountered Stoneman's advance they fired a volley, but were pushed back by superior numbers to the main Confederate line.[53]

Two hours later the Federals advanced to the crest of Dunlap's Hill, site of the Samuel S. Dunlap farm, vacated by the Confederates, and began a strong fire with small arms. Soon afterward one of Captain Hardy's three-inch Ordnance Rifles opened fire upon the Confederate line. This threw part of the reserve militia into confusion, but Lee was able to rally them with the help of his officers. The men were again formed into line "where during the remainder of the day they fought like veterans."[54]

At this juncture Generals Cobb and Joseph E. Johnston arrived on the field. Cobb asked Johnston to assume command, but he declined, instead offering his services as a special aide to Cobb. Cobb later acknowledged his "great obligation" to Johnston.[55] One writer claimed that Cobb, due to his tremendous weight, did not actually ride onto the field, but actually occupied an arm chair of considerable size, located under a large Umbrella-Chinaberry tree in front of a residence on the left side of the main street in East Macon as his troops climbed the hill toward Cutter's Green and advanced on the Federal position on Dunlap's Hill. According to this account

> "At his side stood a small table, on which was a large glass of something iced and a palm-leaf fan." From this position Cobb wrote "his orders and dispatches to the front....Orders generally to fall back to the other side of the river, which could be more easily defended, but orders which were utterly disregarded until finally Colonel Cummins [sic], annoyed by their frequency, returned word in vigorous language that he, Col. Cummins, knew what he was about and would fall back only when he was obliged to do so; that if General Cobb wished to fall back he might go to the other side of the river, or farther."[56]

---

[53] Col G.W. Lee Report, Headquarters Camp Rescue near Macon, 4 August 1864, Cobb Papers, 1864, hereafter cited as Lee Report.

[54] Ibid.

[55] Cobb to his wife, Macon, 3 August 1864, Cobb Papers, 1864.

[56] Arthur E. Boardman to Mrs. Frank F. Jones, Macon, GA., 28 April 1928, in *Confederate Reminiscences and Letters 1861-1865*, Georgia Division United

On the other hand, Governor Brown, while in Macon at the time of the engagement, was not actually present on the field as some of the newspapers, notably the Atlanta *Intelligencer*, stated. Cobb wrote his wife that, if the *Intelligencer* was believed "you would have felt easy about myself...for you would have supposed that Gov. Brown did everything–and was in command of the troops." Cobb observed "that Gov Brown did his duty in turning over the militia who were here to me. That is all that he did...all that he could do."[57]

After burning the bridge over Walnut Creek, Capron attempted to advance along the railroad to Macon.[58] In an effort to block this move, Lee asked Cobb for reinforcements and received Gibbs', Findley's, and Mallett's Battalions. Lee wrote, "These brave officers moved their commands forward in admirable order to my extreme right under a very heavy fire being greatly exposed for a part of the way on passing over a piece of open ground. Taking position and pouring their volleys into the enemy, they soon checked his advance."[59]

Gibbs marched through Macon with his Home Guard, passing down Georgia Avenue and Mulberry Street. As the men advanced through the streets of Macon, mothers sent their sons out with baskets containing bottles of hot coffee, sandwiches, fried chicken, hard-boiled eggs, and biscuits "on their way to East Macon, and to wait upon them as they marched and munched, for no delay was permissible."[60] Gibbs moved across the river with his Home Guard, probably at the ferry immediately above the still-standing bridge of the Georgia Central Railroad. Posting his men on the extreme Confederate right once they reached the east bank of the river, Gibbs marched them through a cornfield at the base of the hills east of the river, but was forced to reform ranks after crossing a rail fence. The home guard was posted on the George W. Adams farm. The Macon Volunteers Company B, along with the Firemen Guards, formed line of battle behind the fence behind another cornfield. Major Rogers placed his cotton factory company to the right as skirmishers while the Convalescent Company was posted in an orchard immediately behind Gibbs' line. This unit was exposed to the severest fire, but because they fought in single file their casualties were not as

---

Daughters of the Confederacy, in six volumes, 1996-1997, Museum of the Confederacy, Archives, vol. 3, 1996, 164, hereafter cited as Boardman Letter. The author has not found any information to substantiate that account which was written years after the battle.

[57] Cobb to his wife, Macon, 3 August 1864, Cobb Papers, 1864; Gov Joseph E. Brown to Cobb, Macon, 29 July 1864, Ibid. Brown had offered troops to held defend the city on July 29.

[58] Capron Report, 926.

[59] Lee Report.

[60] Boardman Letter, p. 162.

high as those of the other Home Guard companies. Part of the Cotton Factory Company was later moved to the extreme right flank of the Confederate defense force, over one mile in advance of any other troops, except a few men of Cummings' Regiment commanded by Major McGregor. From this position they probably saved the Central Railroad bridge from being burned by Capron's men. The Home Guard observed the skirmishers driven in by Adams, retreating in some disorder towards Macon, but when part of Adams' men advanced in their direction the Home Guard stood their ground and opened fire. For about half an hour a furious battle raged. Because of the brave stand made by the Home Guard, the accurate fire of Taliaferro's artillery, and a desperate charge by Nisbet's Tennesseeans, Adams was driven back, although his troopers continued to engage the Confederates while Hardy's two three-inch Ordnance Rifles fired into the suburbs east of the river.[61]

J. William Blackshear, confided in a letter to his wife from his office at the *Daily Telegraph*,

"[W]e could hear the cannonading distinctly[.] I hurried down town as soon as possible, and together with John Stubbs, shouldered my musket and fell in with a company of veteran troops from the west. Marching over to East Macon a Battalion of 4 companies was formed and march[ed] to Fort Hawkins thence to the hill on the left where we lay the balance of the day waiting for the Yankees, thinking they might try to flank us and cross the river above Macon. Our cannon was playing on the enemy from old Fort hill. They began to retreat about the time we reached the hill and by 8 o'clock had retreated two or three miles our men following."[62]

While the battle raged to his right, Lee began to construct earthworks in front of the Federals at Dunlap's Hill. Soon a piece of artillery sent by Cobb was placed in position and began to fire on Capron's men. Faced with the arrival of Confederate reinforcements and under cannon fire Capron began to withdraw. Soon afterwards he attempted to attack Lee's left, but Cumming's Brigade checked Capron's advance. Cumming's left firmly held the key stronghold of Fort Hawkins, and his arrival on Lee's left flank soon forced Capron back.[63]

---

[61] Macon *Christian Index*, 12 August 1864; Carolyn White Williams, *History of Jones County, Georgia*, Macon, J.W. Burke Company, 1957, p. 107; *Daily Telegraph*, 11 August 1864. The city bridge was washed away by a flood in June 1864.

[62] J. William Blackshear to his wife, Macon, 2 August 1864, Blackshear Papers.

[63] Lee Report.

Fort Hawkins proved an especially strong position. The fort, fully garrisoned by militia, was an old US fort standing on a high and steep hill, known as "Fort Hill," on the east side of the Ocmulgee River. It was strengthened by abatis, "so as to make it invincible against attacks of cavalry." Furthermore, Stoneman, about this time, learned that there was a large force of infantry [militia] in Macon.[64] Lee later reported, "Too much praise cannot be given to the various officers commanding bodies of troops under my command and to their brave men, many of whom have never before been in an engagement. By their admirable conduct a force of at least 1200 veterans of the enemy were kept at bay for about seven hours, and finally repulsed. The loss of the troops under my command...was 35 killed 54 wounded and 30 or 40 missing. Most of whom however have since been accounted for. The enemy loss was fully equal to ours."[65]

Though the Federals, from their position at Samuel Dunlap's house, fired upon the city, Stoneman ordered his troops to withdraw. There were two reasons for this. The Federal commander found it impossible to reach the railroad bridge over the Ocmulgee River at Macon,[66] and scouts reported the arrival of a "large cavalry force" on the west side of the river near Macon.[67] Stoneman himself wrote "Before I had completed what I desired to accomplish I learned that a force of the enemy's cavalry was close upon my rear, and the only course for me to pursue to get out was . . . whip this force."[68] He then sent Adams' Brigade south along the east bank of the river, intending to march through South Georgia and on to Pensacola, Florida, then occupied by Federal forces. However, when Adams had marched two miles, a scout reported Iverson's arrival at Macon. Stoneman, fearful that this force would reach a ferry over the river where he intended to cross, ordered Adams to withdraw.[69]

---

[64] Sanford, *Fourteenth Illinois Cavalry*, p. 190.

[65] Lee Report; the *Macon Daily Telegraph and Confederate* gave Confederate losses as sixty, of whom some sixteen were killed. The paper also published a list of those killed and wounded in its issue for 2 August 1864. *Macon Daily Telegraph Confederate*, 2 August 1864. Those killed were J. B. Landrum, 2nd Georgia Militia, Macon; Lt. William Goldsmith, adjutant, 27th Georgia Battalion; James B. Scharpshire, 12th Georgia Battalion; W. J. Vaughn; a man named Morris, and two unknown.

[66] Smith Report, 916.

[67] Tompkins Report, 920. Lieutenant Colonel Robert W. Smith reported the Confederate cavalry number "1,000 to 1,500 strong." Smith Report, 916. The "large cavalry force" was Brigadier General Alfred Iverson's Brigade of Wheeler's Cavalry Division.

[68] Maj Gen George Stoneman, Report, Macon, 6 August 1864, *OR*, 38: Pt. 2, 914, hereafter cited as Stoneman Report.

[69] Ibid., 914.

Eastham Tarrant of the 1st Kentucky Cavalry, noted, "If we had only hurried a little, we could have released nearly 1,500 of our officers confined in prison at Macon [they had all been moved by this time], and so materially injured the Atlanta and Macon railroad as to have caused the enemy to evacuate Atlanta. We were twelve hours behind time. They had only 500 men in Macon twelve hours before, guarding the Union prisoners, and we could have defeated them easily. We had delayed so long-giving the enemy time to gather from Augusta and other places a force sufficient to withstand us—that we could do nothing more. We had not been interrupted on our march to Macon by any forces in our rear. We well knew that Wheeler's Cavalry would soon be after us, and it was best for us to make our way out."[70]

During the battle the noise of the Federal bombardment could be heard all over the city. Mary Ann Cobb then at the Cobb home in Athens, noted that the people "could hear the musketry and cannon and thought we could see the smoke from the bombs. A bomb fell behind the Ocmulgee Hospital right across the street, and a ball or a bomb one or the other struck in front of Mr [Asa] Holts house and rebounded or ricocheted went through one of the posts or pillars and the window smashing the upper part of the window sash and shattering the window panes. I believe that was the only damage done in this part of the City." Mrs. Cobb was proud of one of the "souvenirs" of the battle, a piece of a fence rail which Stoneman's men had used as a fortification. She was equally ecstatic about the fact that "We beat the Yankees of course and have spirit, ardour, determination and 'Melish' enough two or three times as many more."[71]

Johnston, for his part, was highly complimentary of Cobb's conduct and the men under his command. Writing in his memoirs, he observed, "General Cobb met the Federal forces on the high ground east of the Ocmulgee; and repelled them after a contest of several hours, by his own courage and judicious dispositions, and the excellent conduct of troops, who heard hostile shot then for the first time."[72] Thwarted in his efforts to capture Macon, due in part to his own hesitancy and lack of determination, Stoneman decided to retreat towards Milledgeville. Accordingly, his men marched through the late afternoon, approaching Clinton at dusk.[73]

During the engagement several homes on the edge of Macon were struck by Federal balls and shells. One house, according to the *Daily Telegraph and Confederate*, "was perforated with bullets and now presents a battle-scarred

---

[70] Tarrant, *First Kentucky Cavalry*, p. 362.

[71] Mary Ann Cobb to her mother, Athens, GA., 31 July 1864, Cobb Papers, 1864.

[72] Joseph E. Johnston, *Narrative of Military Operations, Directed, During the late War Between the States*, Introduction by Frank E. Vandiver (Bloomington: Indiana University Press, 1959) 369.

[73] Smith Report, 916.

appearance." The Dunlap house suffered by having its stable torn down, and its lawn scarred by a temporary entrenchment thrown up by Stoneman's men.[74]

When Capron's men advanced to within a mile of Clinton they found fifty Confederates posted in line of battle blocking their line of retreat. Capron charged them and drove them back. Thirty-three Federals who had been captured during the Federal advance and held in the Jones County Jail were freed. Capron's men captured their guards, and burned the jail. The troopers continued their retreat on the Hillsborough Road with orders to charge and drive the Confederates whenever they met them. At 9:00 P.M. the Federals began to skirmish with numerous Confederates, and the retreat slowed to a crawl. When Capron reached a point three miles from Clinton he found a strong advance guard of the Confederates. Charging them, he drove them back for half a mile, when he met a larger force posted behind barricades. Capron ordered the 8th Michigan Cavalry to charge them. They did, driving them from their position. In a second charge the Michiganders drove them back again to their main line situated eight miles from Clinton. At this point, Confederate militia attacked Capron in front and on his left flank. Heavy skirmishing continued all night.[75]

At daylight on 31 July Stoneman ordered Capron to advance. Capron's men pushed forward one and a half miles when very general and heavy skirmishing began. The Confederates, Iverson's Brigade and local militia units, were drawn up in line of battle in front of and on Capron's left near a house of worship called Sunshine Church. They had two pieces of artillery with them with which they opened fire as Capron advanced.[76]

Brigadier General Alfred Iverson, Jr.—Stoneman's opponent at the Battle of Sunshine Church, as the engagement came to be called—was the son of Senator Alfred Iverson and Carolina Goode Holt. Born at Clinton, Georgia, on 14 February 1829, he spent his time in Washington, D. C. where his father was a US Senator, and in Columbus, Georgia. He was at the Tuskegee Military Institute in Tuskegee, Alabama, at the outbreak of the Mexican War, and, though only seventeen years old, he received permission from his father to leave school and enter a Georgia regiment that the elder Iverson had largely equipped. After service in Mexico, the younger Iverson began to study law in his father's law office in Columbus, but soon grew tired of that profession. He then began contracting on railroads in Georgia. He received an appointment as First

---

[74] *Macon Daily Telegraph and Confederate*, 2 August 1864.

[75] Ibid.; Capron Report, 926; Tompkins Report, 920.

[76] Capron Report, 927. Sunshine Church was located near the settlement of Round Oak in northern Jones County. The church was burned by the Right Wing of Sherman's Army in November, 1864, during the March to the Sea. The present Sunshine Church, known as New Sunshine Church, is located on top of a hill immediately west of Round Oak.

Lieutenant in the First United States Cavalry in 1855, recruiting a company mostly from Georgia and Kentucky, and served with distinction, especially in the troubles in Kansas Territory in 1856. Marrying Harriet Harris Hutchins, daughter of Judge N.L. Hutchins of Gwinnett County, Georgia, he soon saw service in the Mormon Expedition of 1858, and against the Indians in Indian Territory, especially taking part in expeditions against the Comanches and Kiowas. When the Confederacy was organized he offered his services to the new republic, receiving an appointment as captain in the Provisional Confederate Army. By 1864, he was a brigadier general commanding a brigade of cavalry in Wheeler's Division.[77]

Stoneman soon reached the battlefield and formed his entire division in line of battle with Adams' Brigade and the 8th Michigan Cavalry of Capron's Brigade on the left, and the balance of Capron's men on the right. Biddle's Brigade and one piece of artillery was held in reserve. The other three-inch Ordnance Rifle was placed in the center of the line. According to one account both of Stoneman's three-inch Ordnance Rifles were placed just outside the churchyard of Sunshine Church. Stoneman's men used the church as a hospital during the battle.[78]

Lieutenant Colonel Smith described Iverson's position, "the enemy was there in force, upon ground of his own selection, with strong works and barricades, on an elevation in the road in our front, with his lines of battle extending out from this point in the shape of a V, completely covering and enfilading our right and left flanks."[79]

Upon learning that a strong force of Confederates was in their front, some of Capron's men urged "A lot of negroes, who had followed us...to escape while they could, as their fate would be severe if captured with us and unarmed they could not aid us." Some of the Blacks followed this advice, while many more decided to stay with the Federals at their own risk.[80]

As the battle developed neither commander knew much about the strength of his opponent. Despite some cleared land, most of the area consisted of rolling ground covered by thick woods. First Lieutenant Albert B. Capron, who served as an aide to his father, noted that "This first movement of the rebels was partially intended to develop our strength and to draw us forward within range of

---

[77] Sketch of Iverson by Joseph T. Derry in Clement A. Evans, ed., *Confederate Military History*, in 12 volumes (Atlanta, GA.: Confederate Publishing Company, 1899) 6:425-26.

[78] Capron Report, 927; Captain J. M. Wells, *With Touch of Elbow' or Death Before Dishonor, A Thrilling Narrative of Adventure on Land and Sea* (Philadelphia, Chicago, and Toronto: The John Winston Company, 1909) 213.

[79] Smith Report, 916.

[80] Sanford, *Fourteenth Illinois Cavalry*, 194.

their artillery which appears to have been placed in battery." Although Capron's line was on elevated ground which commanded a clear view of the entire Federal line, intervening woods prevented him from seeing the Confederates. A road entered on Capron's rear, exposing the Federals to an attack from that direction. To prevent this, Capron placed a squadron of the 14th Illinois under Captain Sanford, about a mile out on this road. However, the firing had hardly begun, in the first advance of Iverson's line when Sanford was driven back by a force of Confederate cavalry. Capron, anticipating such an attack, had kept two companies of the 14th Illinois mounted to counter such a move. He personally led a charge with this force, while Sanford, observing the movement for his relief, wheeled his command in an open gallop in one of the few open fields in the area, and charged the Confederates completely routing them.[81]

When Stoneman ordered an advance, his whole line moved forward and engaged Iverson. The Confederates met the advancing horsemen in seemingly superior numbers, and with a yell charged the Federal lines, causing the left of the 8th Michigan to swing a quarter of the way around. The right of the regiment held its position. Some Confederate cavalry charged Capron's extreme right and rear but were repulsed. During his counterattack Capron drove Iverson's men two and a half miles to new positions behind barricades. In the melee Iverson used his single cannon with extreme accuracy. The fight continued with Capron bringing up four companies of the 14th Illinois who checked another Confederate charge, again driving them back to their barricades. At the same time the 14th Illinois and McLaughlin's Ohio Squadron held Iverson in check in Capron's front. Capron then fell back a short distance from his original position, and held his ground until 12:30 P.M. He was then ordered to strengthen his lines and prepare to make a heavy charge on foot. In order to do this, he brought every available man to the line including his provost guard. At 1:00 P.M. Stoneman ordered an advance, holding one regiment of Adams' Brigade in reserve. As the Federals charged, the Confederates rose up in force and rushed at the Federal lines, cutting off Capron's communication with Stoneman. This sudden charge caused Adams' Kentucky Brigade to break and run for their horses. Capron's men, nearly surrounded, also fighting dismounted in the broken, heavily wooded ground, were forced to fall back to their horses, a move which created some confusion because the Confederates pursuit was so vigorous that many of Capron's troopers could not mount their horses, which were captured and mounted by the Confederates. Using the captured horses, the Confederates repeatedly charged Capron's rear as his men continued to retreat.

---

[81] Albert B. Capron, "The Stoneman Raid to Macon, Georgia in 1864," n.d., typescript, pp 9-10, Horace Capron Papers, Manuscript Division, LC, hereafter cited as Capron, "The Stoneman Raid to Macon." Iverson actually had only one cannon, favorably a 12-pounder, with him.

Although Capron tried to contact Stoneman, the staff officers sent to make contact were cut off and could not report. Stoneman, for his part, tried to communicate with Capron but failed for the same reasons.[82]

At 4:00 P.M. Stoneman discussed the situation with his staff and most of his brigade commanders. It was decided to attempt to cut through the Confederate lines on the Federal right rear because it seemed to be the weakest point of Iverson's line. As final preparations were made the Confederates opened fire with their cannon on both the Federal right and left. They continued their fire and charged Stoneman's line which gave way, resulting in a general withdrawal. Lieutenant Colonel Smith received orders to rally a portion of the line, but while he was doing this he became separated from Stoneman. The line gave way again, and the Confederates advanced to within fifty yards of the Federal line, both in front and on the flank. Stoneman prepared to surrender, but gave permission to all who could escape to do so. Capron and Adams did so. Stoneman determined to fight as long as possible in order to give most of his men a chance to escape. About two-thirds of the command or 1,300 men succeeded in escaping. Most of them retreated through Eatonton.[83]

Albert Capron grimly remembered the plight of his Father's brigade at this juncture: "Cut off from Gen. Stoneman and surrounded by the enemy, it required no time for us to decide that our only hope was in the desperate attempt to cut our way through the enemy. At this juncture, I was sent, in hot haste, to call in Capt. Lord from his outpost. Of course, we were left in the rear and did not overtake our shattered command until several hours afterward."[84]

Capron and Adams began their escape. Capron hastily rallied all available men, and "companies formed without regard to regiments, and officers available placed over them. We were now cut off from General Stoneman and surrounded by the enemy. The column was put in motion along the woods about one-eighth of a mile from the road leading to our right rear, being on foot and behind barricades. A cavalry charge...made an opening, but within a short distance we encountered a force of cavalry, who fought bravely and gave us a running fight several miles that cost us dearly in men. A recount showed nearly one-half missing." Capron's ranks, however were hourly reinforced. Regaining their horses, Capron's men broke up into detachments and "With a yell and with sabers flashing," dashed upon the enemy's left flank, led by a number of brave and skillful officers. The Confederates fought fiercely with carbines, revolvers, and muskets. One observer remembered that the reports of weapons fired at close range "mingled in a loud roar; while flashing sabers crossed blades in the sharp conflict; but nothing could long impede the force of a charging column of

---

[82] Capron Report, 927.

[83] Ibid., 927; Smith Report, 917.

[84] Capron, "The Stoneman Raid to Macon," 11.

desperate men, each of whom preferred death on the battlefield to incarceration in Andersonville." The Confederate lines finally broke and "woods and underbrush, usually great impediments to the passage of mounted men, are dashed through by these maddened troopers, as though they were dashing over a plain." Capron, later joined by Adams and his men, withdrew over the Hog Mountain Road to Eatonton. So desperate was the retreat that Adams' Brigade came upon a number of horses, ridden to death and lying in the road.[85]

Federal losses in the Battle of Sunshine Church were 200 killed and wounded and 500 taken prisoner. They also lost their two three-inch Ordnance Rifles, over one thousand Sharps Rifles (8-shot), and a large number of horses. The Confederates lost 100 killed and wounded.[86]

Stoneman's conduct at the end of the Battle of Sunshine Church has since been the source of some controversy. Major Tompkins wrote that the Federal commander "saw no other way for the lives of the men to be respected but for him to surrender, which he would do only as a last resort." Tompkins asserted that Stoneman had little regard for his personal safety as long as he could save his command. "He was not," Tompkins observed, "in the whole day scarcely from under the most severe fire of the enemy."[87] Stoneman wrote, "I insisted on continuing the contest and, if taken prisoner at all, upon being taken fighting, but the officers with me protested that, being without ammunition and surrounded, our escape was next to impossible; that there was no use in fighting longer; that we had accomplished our object in covering the retreat of the rest of the command until it was well under way, and that in justice to all concerned we should surrender."[88]

The Federal Commander believed that surrender was the only option left open to him. He could not save his two three-inch Ordnance Rifles; his horse had been shot from under him; he could barely mount the worn-down horse he found to replace it; and the chances of escape for his remaining force were so small that he decided to surrender, and blamed his action on what he termed the bad conduct of Adams' Kentuckians during the attack in the morning and throughout the entire day.[89] A participant in the engagement agreed with

---

[85] Sanford, *Fourteenth Illinois Cavalry*, pp. 197-99, Tarrant, *First Kentucky Cavalry*, p. 366.

[86] *Macon Daily Telegraph and Confederate*, 3 August 1864. General Iverson also reported that 500 Federals had been captured with Stoneman. See Hood to Seddon, Atlanta, 1 August 1864, *OR*, 38: Pt. 5, 937; Hood to Maj Gen Joseph Wheeler, Atlanta, Ibid., 938; Hood to Lt Gen William J. Hardee, Atlanta, 1 August 1864, Ibid., 937; Hood to Brig Gen William H. Jackson, Atlanta, 1 August 1864, Ibid., 939.

[87] Tompkins Report, 920.

[88] Stoneman Report, 914.

[89] Ibid.

Stoneman's assessment declaring "Whatever may be the decision of military critics upon Stoneman's course, in the great heart of the loyal American people Stoneman will stand approved and honored for his brave attempt to liberate our thousands of poor, suffering comrades at Andersonville."[90] Another veteran stated it more succinctly: "There can be but one explanation for the course pursued by Gen. Stoneman: he had conceived the idea of releasing the Union prisoners held at Macon and Andersonville....This idea took possession of him, and controlled him."[91]

Stoneman, however, was not without his critics. Lieutenant A. B. Simmons of Company C, 5th Indiana Cavalry, remembered the entire raid as a big blunder, observing, "Now I must say that were it possible I would rather blot from memory all knowledge of that egregious blunder and its disastrous outcome."[92]

Certainly the most scathing commentary upon Stoneman's actions before Macon and at Sunshine Church was written by no less a figure than Sherman himself. Lieutenant Isaac M. Brown, 6th Indiana Cavalry, wrote an account of the raid in the Columbus (Ohio) *Republican*, published 22 July 1875, in which he cited Sherman's official after action report of the raid. In his article Brown noted that, as Stoneman advanced past Stone Mountain, "there was not a rebel to be seen." When Stoneman and his command reached Macon they "found some State militia ready to dispute our passage into the city." According to Brown, the Federals opened fire upon them, and in the exchange only one trooper was killed, with a loss of eighteen killed and thirty-two wounded for the Confederates. Stoneman then precipitously gave the order to withdraw on the Milledgeville Road, "some three or four miles, where the command came to a halt, and after remaining in our saddles for near an hour, during which the hardest rain fell I ever saw." The troopers were then ordered back upon the same road over which they had advanced two days before.[93] Brown sent Sherman a copy of the paper. After carefully reading Brown's comments, Sherman wrote that Stoneman did not obey his orders "which looked to the destruction of the Railroad below ATLANTA FIRST [the capital letters are Sherman's]: & going afterwards to Macon & Andersonville to rescue our prisoners." Sherman observed that "Others must write the free history of the Stoneman Raid. I have

---

[90] A participant, "Stoneman Raid," in *The National Tribune*, 5 September 1895, p. 3.

[91] General Green B. Baum, "With the Western Army The Stoneman Raid," in *The National Tribune*, 9 October 1902, p. 6.

[92] Lieutenant A.B. Simmons, "With Stoneman on his Macon Raid," in *The National Tribune*, 28 February 1924, p. 7.

[93] Isaac M. Brown, "The Stoneman Raid to Macon," in The Columbus *Republican*, 22 July 1875, Isaac M. Brown, Account of Stoneman's Macon Raid," in USAMHI.

not attempted it, only as an incident to other events connected with it."[94] In retrospect the raid upon Macon and Andersonville was ill-conceived and poorly conducted. It could have been successful if Stoneman and his commanders had been more aggressive and more dedicated to the capture of Macon and the relief of the Andersonville prisoners. However, the determination to inflict as much damage as possible to the Central Railroad, ordered by Sherman, and Stoneman's reticence in front of Macon were the principal reasons for his failure. When he began his poorly conducted withdrawal through Clinton to Sunshine Church he lost the initiative to Iverson who seized upon it to achieve the most noteworthy success to Confederate arms accomplished in Georgia during the summer of 1864. Stoneman's defeat also reveals a flaw in Sherman's strategy of concentrating on the destruction of railroad facilities. While this objective seemed desirable in view of the overall Federal war effort, it obviated Stoneman's goal of capturing Macon and freeing the Camp Ogelthorpe and Andersonville prisoners.

The lot of the prisoners, as it is in all wars, was especially hard. Charles W. Homsher of the 5th Indiana Cavalry was captured and taken, together with his entire regiment, to the rear about four miles and put into a mule pen fence, ten rails high. Here the officers were separated from the men and taken to a nearby house which temporarily served as a headquarters for the Confederates. About 8:00 P.M. a blowing rain began, making the plight of the prisoners even more miserable. They had nothing to eat that night, and then extreme weariness set in. The following day the prisoners were formed into a line and marched back to Macon. They marched through the battleground and saw one of their regiment lying dead on the ground, unburied. Fortunately, their captors seemed to be honorable men, although some of them insulted their captives. The column stopped near a cornfield and some of the guards pulled off the corn and threw it over the road. The Indianians grabbed it "like so many hogs." They reached a bridge eight miles from Macon and stopped for the night, after a forced march of nearly twenty miles. Homsher did not get any supper, but got some corn in the morning. The column then proceeded to Macon. On their way they passed by a farm house, and a lady, standing at the gate called out to them "that is the way I like to see you all come." Some of the Hoosiers retorted that "old Billy Sherman will be along in a few days." At the edge of Macon the Georgia militia took over as guards. The streets were lined with women who said "I wish the last one of them was kill[ed]."[95]

---

[94] William T. Sherman to Isaac M. Brown, Headquarters Army of the United States, St. Louis, MO., 26 July 1875, photocopy, in Isaac M. Brown, "Account of Stoneman's Macon Raid," USAMHI.

[95] Extracts from the Diary of Charles W. Homsher, 5th Indiana Cavalry, in Civil War Times Illustrated Collection, 1864-65, USAMHI.

Another member of the Fifth Indiana, Joseph Clouse of Company M, remembered, "It was a good thing for those who escaped, but hard for those who were kept back. It was a hard thing to do, to reverse our guns and turn them over to the enemies of the Stars and Stripes." The Confederates stripped everything of value and comfort from Clouse and his fellow prisoners, then moved them to the rear. Noting that the guards took two prisoners to a corn field for food, Clouse remembered that a number of men escaped while in the field: "One would suddenly make a dash for liberty and the guard could not leave the other prisoner to pursue the fugitive." The following day the prisoners moved through Macon and were put on board a freight train for Andersonville. "Here," Clouse exclaimed, "we were taken in charge by the inhuman Gen. Wirtz." [sic] [96]

William Blackshear reported that the prisoners were brought through the streets of Macon in squads. Sixty-eight Federals marched into the city on the morning of 3 August prompting Blackshear to write "I wish every mother's son of them had been 'lost' in other words killed–the miserable wretches. Have you seen accounts of the atrocities committed by them?"[97]

When Stoneman was brought back to Macon as a prisoner and marched through the streets, the city was in a state of intense excitement. Women stopped a visitor, Lieutenant David Champion, of Company G, Fourteenth Georgia Regiment, to show him bullet marks on the houses, and where cannon balls had knocked the bark off trees.[98]

Some efforts were made to pursue the raiders, especially Brigadier General William W. Allen's Brigade of Wheeler's Cavalry Corps. Allen reached Eatonton on the night of 1 August, but found "further pursuit hopeless," the Federals having exchanged their exhausted horses for fresh mules and horses which they impressed from the people along their route. Allen decided to move to Shady Dale in Jasper County, and planned to cooperate with any cavalry sent out by Hood and Wheeler to intercept them. He stopped there to await further orders.[99]

---

[96] Joseph Louis Co. M, 5th Indiana Cavalry Regiment Memoirs, Reunion Programs, July 27, 1864-October 9, 1919, in John Sickles Collection, USAMHI. Henry Wirz was a major, not a general.

[97] J. William Blackshear to Marian Blackshear, Macon, August 3, 1864, Blackshear Papers.

[98] Lieutenant Randolph E. Champion, Reminiscence, n.d., in *Confederate Reminiscences and Letters 1861-1865*, in 6 volumes (Georgia Division United Daughters of the Confederacy, 1996-1997) 5:19.

[99] Brigadier General William W. Allen, Report, 2 August 1864, in Lewis Leigh Collection, USMHI.

The relieved Confederates began congratulating themselves upon their victory. Hood wrote in his memoirs, quoting from General Shoupe's diary "the 1st day of August deserves to be marked with a white stone." The Confederate commander breathed an almost audible sigh of relief when he thought about the damage that might have been done to the Confederacy if Stoneman had succeeded in capturing Macon and proceeding on to lightly-defended Andersonville, observing "Fearful indeed would have been the consequences had they [the Andersonville prisoners] been turned loose upon the country in its unprotected condition."[100]

Cobb wrote his wife on 1 August that everyone was safe in Macon, and "Genl Stoneman is now here a prisoner."[101] *Daily Telegraph* Editor Clisby congratulated the men who defended the city while excoriating the Federals who "exhibited their mean brutality in throwing shells in the eastern portion of the city." Fortunately, no civilian was injured. The Confederate artillery was ably manned forcing Stoneman's men to leave their position on the left of the Central Railroad. The militia, for their part, behaved with great gallantry and showed considerable spirit and patriotism in their quick response to the call to arms. Clisby praised the convalescent and detailed soldiers who were out and "acted with the usual valor of veterans." The defenders included several companies made up mostly of officers in the Confederate army from colonels to lieutenants who "had thrown aside their stars and bars and shouldered muskets." However it would be impossible to single out any man or group of men, because they all acted with "the most gratifying spirit of determination and bravery." "We take pride," Clisby continued, "in the manner in which the citizens of Macon emulated the heroic example of Petersburg and Richmond, and can safely promise that a raid on this city in the future will be met in the same manner as this first has been."[102] Upon learning of some of the original depredations caused by Stoneman and his men, Dolly Sumner Burge confided to her journal "Is this the way to make us love them & their union?"[103]

---

[100] John Bell Hood, *Advance and Retreat: Experiences in the United States and Confederates States Armies* (New Orleans, Published for the Hood Orphan Memorial Fund, 1880) 197.

[101] Cobb to his wife Macon, 1 August 1864, Cobb Papers, 1864.] The following day Cobb confided that "the late experience of Yankee raiders in this state will put a stop for a while to that kind of business." Cobb to his wife, Macon, 2 August 1864, Ibid.

[102] *Daily Telegraph,* 2 August 1864.

[103] Dolly Sumner (Lunt) Burge, 29 July 1864, Dolly Sumner (Lunt) Burge Diary, 1864, in Burge-Gray Family Papers, Emory University.

The pastors of the various churches in the city called for a day of prayer and thanksgiving on Friday, 5 August, "to thank God for Stoneman's defeat."[104] Services were conducted by the Reverend David Wills at the First Presbyterian Church, but Cobb was not pleased. He considered Wills' remarks "were personally offensive to me and all other officers charged with the defense of the city." Cobb believed that Wills intended to be offensive, and promised that he would not give the Presbyterian minister another opportunity of repeating these remarks because "I shall attend no more of the meetings unless I know that he will not be there."[105]

After the raid, the authorities in Macon devoted their attentions to repairing the damage caused by the raiders and recovering as much stolen property as possible. One of the major problems involved repairing the Georgia Central Railroad whose tracks and trestles had been destroyed by the raiders in various places west of the Oconee River. The major problem, of course, involved rebuilding the great bridge over the Oconee River which had been burned by the raiders. By 5 August Cobb reported to his wife that cars would run on the Central by the "first of next week." However he predicted that it would be two weeks before laborers could complete repairs on the Oconee bridge. In the meantime, the eastbound and westbound trains would meet on opposite sides of the river and move passengers across in flatboats.[106]

Cobb received a great deal of support from his superiors in the Confederate military hierarchy. General Braxton Bragg, telegraphed the Macon commander from Columbus on 1 August asking information about the destruction to the railroad and telegraph lines on Stoneman's line of march, and urging the use of every means to immediately repair the damages.[107] Shoup urged the importance of building a wagon bridge over the Oconee, and offered a pontoon bridge but wanted to know how many pontoons would be needed.[108]

Fortunately for the prosperity of Macon and the defense of Atlanta trestles on the Central Railroad, although fired in many places, did not burn sufficiently to cause any substantial damage.[109] However, Cobb told his wife as late as 10 August that the Oconee Bridge would not be repaired for two or three weeks.[110]

---

[104] *Daily Telegraph,* 5 August 1864.

[105] Cobb to his wife, Macon, 7 August 1864, Cobb Papers, 1864.

[106] Cobb to his wife, Macon, 5 August 1864, Ibid.

[107] Braxton Bragg to Cobb, telegram, Columbus, 1 August 1864, Cobb Papers, 1864.

[108] Shoup to Cobb, Telegram, Atlanta, 2 August 1864, Ibid. See also Hood to Cobb, Telegram, Atlanta, 1 August 1864 and Shoup to Cobb, Telegram, Atlanta, 2 August 1864, both in Ibid.

[109] *Macon Daily Telegraph,* 8 August 1864.

[110] Cobb to his wife, Macon, 10 August 1864, Cobb Papers, 1864.

The aftermath of the raid left Cobb with other problems possibly of equal importance with railroad repair. One of these involved the Blacks who left their owners to fight with the raiders. Other slaves acted as guides and in a number of ways were guilty, in Cobb's eyes, "of conduct which demands summary punishment." He expressed concern that, since civil law procedures were too slow and cumbersome, the Black population "may become very troublesome on occasion of these raids." "If I had the power, Cobb exclaimed, "I would at once organize a Court and have the cases summarily disposed of." He hoped that Hood [who had enough problems of his own] would organize such a tribunal. Nothing ever came of Cobb's efforts, however.

Still another difficulty lay in the return of horses and mules taken from their owners by the raiders. These, Cobb directed, had to be identified and claimed by their owners. If they were not claimed they would be turned over to the Confederate Government. All horses belonging to the Federals and found in the possession of private individuals must be surrendered and turned over to the Confederacy. All Federal stragglers and wounded left in the area of military operations, as well as arms and horses had to be turned over to the Quartermaster in Macon.[111]

Despite the good fortune of Macon and its people in escaping capture by Stoneman and his men an even bigger test of their courage and determination lay just ahead. As the days of summer began to pass and the land lay ready for another autumn, Sherman continued to tighten his grip on the gate city of Atlanta. This boded ill for a Confederacy that faced a twilight period of defeat. The question was simple. Would Macon and its citizens be up to the test?

---

[111] Cobb to Captain Tufts, Macon, 2 August 1864, Cobb Letter Book, 1864-65, p. 185. For more information concerning the return of captured horses see Cobb to Captain Samuel S. Dunlap, Macon, 4 August 1864, Ibid., p. 186 and Lamar Cobb to Col A. Young, Macon, 15 August 1864, Ibid., pp. 210-11.

Chapter 13

Macon and the March to the Sea

After the repulse of Stoneman's Raid brought home the fact that the war was literally at Macon's doorstep, the attention of its defenders and citizens turned to defense and Sherman's movements. On 5 August Cobb wrote Shoup revealing a plan to defend the city, after receiving Bragg's tacit approval. Under Cobb's plan, a small guard would be placed at each of the railroad bridges in Georgia "as it is the only mode of protecting our rail roads from raids." Cobb explained that he would have used this plan to defend Macon by using troops from the Georgia Reserves, but every man he could raise was called to defend other important points. Cobb needed Hood's support for such a force because Macon might have enough troops to defend it in the future as it had in the trying days of late July. Already, efforts were underway to build earthworks around Macon, and Cobb was attempting to secure some pieces of artillery to place in them. He also needed sufficient cavalry to repel raids. He concluded: "The important public interests here require that every possible arrangement should be made for the proper defense of this place."[1] On 11 August R. J. Hallett, Cobb's Assistant Adjutant General, ordered Colonel Cumming to take charge of the Georgia Central Railroad Bridge across the Ocmulgee and place a proper guard on constant duty there.[2]

In the following days Cobb placed Macon in a state of defense. On 6 August he wrote General Wayne that a militia force was needed to defend Macon.[3] Wayne replied on 15 August that rumors of cavalry raids in Middle Georgia were being spread by the Confederate cavalry.[4] On 13 August Cobb had written

---

[1] Cobb to Shoup, Macon, August 5, 1864, Cobb Letter Book, 1864-65, p. 189. See also Cobb to Shoup, Macon, 24 August 1864, Ibid., p. 224.

[2] R.J. Hallett to Col. John B. Cumming, Macon, 11 August 1864, Ibid., 202.

[3] Cobb to Wayne, Macon, 6 August 1864, Ibid., 196-97.

[4] Wayne to Cobb, Milledgeville, 15 August 1864, Cobb Papers, 1864.

Secretary of War Seddon, stating he did not have enough troops to defend Macon.[5]

In an effort to counter Wayne and Brown, who believed that the militia should either be sent to support Hood in Atlanta or to defend Milledgeville in case of another cavalry raid, Cobb wrote Shoup on 15 August urging him to "consider the importance of this place [Macon], not only as a depot of arms and provisions but as the connection of our rail road communications I am sure you will not think that I overestimate the importance of providing for its sure defense."[6]

Cobb needed cavalry, and asked Colonel W.M. Browne, Commandant of Conscripts at Augusta, to send both Captains Tufts' and B.H. Wise's cavalry companies for temporary duty in Macon.[7] On 24 August Cobb ordered Captain B. H. Wise to move his cavalry unit to Clinton, stationing a picket consisting of at least one lieutenant and ten men, at Monticello. Wise was directed to keep pickets between Clinton and the Ocmulgee River and on the Eatonton road as far as Blountsville. The pickets were ordered to inform Wise of any Federal advance, and received instructions not to molest private property. Cobb wanted Wise to make semi-weekly reports of the strength and condition of his company, and of the operations of his pickets.[8]

Cobb's earnest entreaties to protect Macon did not go unheeded. Even though the pressure by Sherman's three field armies was intense. Responding to a question by Governor Brown of 7 August that the militia garrisoned at Andersonville might be needed in Atlanta, on 19 August Hood ordered Brigadier General Winder to immediately send the militia to Macon.[9] However, Cobb, in mid-August, did not seem too concerned about raids when he tried to reassure Governor Brown that a raid was not imminent against either Macon or Milledgeville.[10]

During early August the authorities began to call for slaves to build fortifications around the city.[11] By 11 August Captain M. B. Grant, Assistant Engineer in charge of the fortifications around Macon, had almost 500 slaves

---

[5] Cobb to Seddon, Macon, 13 August 1864, Cobb Letter Book, 1864-65, pp. 209-10.

[6] Cobb to Shoup, Macon, 15 August 1864, Ibid., 213.

[7] Lamar Cobb to Colonel W.M. Browne, Commandant of Conscripts, Augusta, Macon, 16 August 1864, Ibid., 215.

[8] Lamar Cobb to Captain B.H. Wise, Macon, 24 August 1864, Ibid., 222.

[9] Brown to Hood, Telegram, Milledgeville, 7 August 1864, Governors Letter Book, 1861-65, p. 675; Hood to Brown, Telegram, Atlanta, 19 August 1864, in Ibid., p. 685.

[10] Cobb to Brown, Macon, 16 August 1864, Ibid.

[11] *Macon Daily Telegraph,* 3 August 1864.

working on the fortifications. Cobb asked Dr. Samuel H. Stout, Medical Director of the Army of Tennessee, then in Macon, to provide a medical officer to report to Grant to provide medical care for the laborers.[12] Chief of Staff Shoup also agreed to allow Grant the necessary tools to construct earthworks around Macon to remain there until the work was completed.[13] By 29 August with the fall of Atlanta imminent, Cobb ordered Captain O. Tufts at Macon to detail four men from his company of militia to report to Sheriff J. Joseph Hodges of Bibb County to help impress slaves to work on the fortifications.[14]

During August, the major impediment to the building of fortifications around Macon was General Hood himself. Hard pressed by Sherman's building pressure against Atlanta, Hood needed all the troops and black laborers he could get to help in the defense of that city. Hood informed Governor Brown on 7 August that he needed 2,000 Blacks. How, the beleaguered commander asked, could "he get them most speedily?"[15] Brown replied that the speediest way was to impress them from their owners. However, the Governor, although he did not have the power himself, assured Hood that he would "be glad to aid you as far as I can."[16] On 28 August when the pressure on Atlanta was at its greatest and Sherman was about to cut the Macon and Western Railroad connecting Atlanta with Macon, Shoup ordered Cobb to send the militia on to Atlanta, although some organized troops might be sent to Winder to guard the prisoners at Andersonville.[17] On 28 August General Alfred Iverson, Jr., victor of Sunshine Church, wired Cobb from Griffin that he needed six six-pounder cannons with ammunition immediately.[18]

As August ended, a correspondent for the *Daily Telegraph* issued the ominous report that heavy firing was heard "just north of Macon from the fighting at Jonesboro."[19] As if this news was not bad enough, on 2 September 2, the worst possible catastrophe occurred for the defense of Macon–Hood evacuated

---

[12] R.J. Hallett to Dr. Samuel H. Stout, Macon, 11 August 1864, Cobb Letter Book, 1864-65, pp. 202-03.

[13] Shoup to Cobb, Telegram, Macon, 18 August 1864, Cobb Papers, 1864. Cobb was in Atlanta to confer with Hood about the deteriorating military situation in Georgia, Hood to Cobb, Telegram, Atlanta, August 17, 1864, Ibid.

[14] R.J. Hallett to Captain O. Tufts, Macon, 29 August 1864, Cobb Letter Book, 1864-65, p. 230.

[15] Hood to Brown, Telegram, Atlanta, 7 August 1864, GLB, 675.

[16] Brown to Hood, Telegram, Milledgeville, 8 August 1864, Ibid.

[17] Shoup to Cobb, Telegram, Atlanta, 28 August 1864, Cobb Papers, 1864. There were 553 militia at Camp Rescue in Macon, although many of them were without arms. See Frank E. Sushe, Assistant Adjutant and Inspector General to Gen. Wayne, Telegram, Macon, 28 August 1864, Ibid.

[18] Iverson to Cobb, Telegram, Griffin, GA., 28 August 1864, Ibid.

[19] *Macon Daily Telegraph,* 2 September 1864.

Atlanta. Upon receipt of the news that the evacuation was planned Cobb called for every man capable of bearing arms to enroll to defend Macon.[20] So many messages arrived at the telegraph office that Cobb ordered militia Captain Tufts to send two men to serve as couriers to carry messages to headquarters.[21] On 5 September Cobb, always concerned about the smallest details, ordered Quartermaster Major Morgan to provide forage for the large force of horsemen Cobb expected to come and help in the defense of Macon.[22]

Sherman had won more than just the city of Atlanta when he occupied that crucial position on 3 September. He had cut the vital arteries of the Confederacy and opened its heartland to invasion. Now, the *Daily Telegraphs* reporter gloomily asserted: "all Georgia is open to him–and Macon, Columbus, and Augusta can be seized whenever Sherman should advance." The paper noted that the question for the Confederate Government, sitting in the besieged city of Richmond, was "whether the State of Georgia is necessary to the achievement of our independence?" If it was, then steps should be immediately taken to drive Sherman out, but if it was not, the sooner Hood's Army of Tennessee was sent elsewhere the better it would be. For, as the reporter concluded his assessment of the situation, "it will only fritter away in a hopeless contest with superior numbers aided by advantages of position."[23]

While these events unfolded to the north of Macon Cobb issued Special Orders No. 98 ordering the immediate impressment of five hundred additional slaves for a period of thirty days to complete Macon's fortifications. The impressing officer was directed to immediately impress as many as he could in Macon, and the remainder from Bibb and neighboring counties. Cobb noted: "The importance of the immediate completion of these works should silence any complaints that might other[wise] be made."[24]

Cobb considered the matter of building fortifications so important that when General Marcus J. Wright, Post Commander, asked Cobb to impress enough slaves to dig soldiers' graves, he replied that no hands could be spared. Instead,

---

[20] R.J. Hallett, Special Orders No. 85, Macon, 2 September 1864, Howell Cobb Special Orders Book 1865, Hargrett Library, University of Georgia.

[21] Lamar Cobb to Capt. O. Tufts, Macon, 5 September 1864, Cobb Letter Book, 1864-65, pp. 242-243.

[22] Lamar Cobb to Maj. Morgan, Macon, 5 September 1864, Ibid., 242-44.

[23] *Daily Telegraph,* 9 September 1864.

[24] R.J. Hallett, Special Orders No. 98, Macon, 19 September 1864, Cobb Special Orders Book, 1865, 66-7.

Cobb asked Bibb Sheriff Joseph Hodges to impress twenty-five additional slaves to dig the graves.[25]

After Atlanta fell a near panic came over the people of Macon and Bibb County. Reflecting these fears, Nathan C. Munroe, Jr. informed his beloved daughter, Bannie, on 17 September that Macon was kept in a constant uproar by rumors about Sherman's movements spread by the Atlanta and North Georgia refugees. Many Macon families, he observed, "speak of removing and are preparing for it." He was glad that Bannie was in a place of comparative safety and urged her to be in no hurry to come to Macon until Sherman's future movements became better known.[26] A few days later Munroe reported the people were in constant fear of a raid, or a forward movement of Sherman's army on Macon which appeared as their logical target. Many were moving or preparing to move. Munroe wrote, "I think most of those who can get away will do so." Hood was moving toward Newnan on the LaGrange Road, leaving the Macon and Western Railroad unprotected. "What the object of this move is," Munroe exclaimed, "is yet unknown to us."[27] Munroe felt that since the Army of Tennessee had moved on the LaGrange Road toward Newnan, all of Georgia south of Atlanta was now open, although he did not believed "that Sherman would leave Atlanta with his main army while Hood is so near him." If this were the case, Munroe opined Macon would only be open to raids "which we have a force here to meet if they should come." The excitement and fear of a Federal invasion was so widespread by late September that many people in Vineville and north of Macon were moving or preparing to move away.[28] A writer for the *Daily Telegraph* took up the cry about the number of people leaving Macon in early September noting, "What is the matter with the people that they are running from their homes? Sherman is not yet on the march for Macon, and we do not believe he will be here for at least six months, if ever."[29]

Depredations caused by Confederate cavalry against their own people added to the general unrest. When complaints arrived that men of Captain Stark's cavalry were robbing citizens around the cavalry camp near Macon, Cobb directed Major Hallett to threaten the arrest of the offenders, and promised to

---

[25] R.J. Hallett to Gen. Marcus J. Wright, Macon, 9 September 1864, Cobb Letter Book, 1864-1865, p. 252; R.J. Hallet to Joseph Hodges, Macon, 9 September 1864, Ibid., p. 252.

[26] Nathan C. Munroe, Jr. to Bannie Kell, Sylvan Lodge, 17 September 1864, Kell Letters.

[27] Munroe to Bannie Kell, 20 September 1864, Ibid.

[28] Nathan Munroe, Jr. to Bannie Kell, Macon, 22 September 1864, Ibid.

[29] *Daily Telegraph,* 10 September 1864.

hold their officers responsible for the conduct of their men.[30] By 24 September rumors circulated that Sherman's army was on the march, but no positive information had arrived. Hood, in an attempt to make it more difficult for Sherman to invade Middle Georgia, had ordered the officials of the Macon and Western Railroad to take up their rails and bring them as far down the line as Barnesville. Georgia Railroad officials had also been directed to take up their rails as far down as Greensboro. This, Munroe hoped, "will cut off the enemys movements on both roads until they relay the tracks, which will take some time."[31] A large public meeting was held in Macon on 23 September to raise money for the support of the Atlanta exiles. Macon, however, were so quiet that when Jefferson Davis passed through on 23 September on his way to meet with Hood and the army there was no great public demonstration. Munroe hoped that Davis "will be able to inspire that confidence and enthusiasm in the country which will enable us to regain that [territory] which we have lost. He says that means are ample if the people will but make the effort."[32]

When Davis arrived in the city on the Georgia Central Railroad at 4:00 A.M. on 23 September "no one in the city had the least intimation of his coming." The morning newspapers advertised a public meeting to take place at the Baptist Church at 11:00 A.M. to provide relief, as mentioned above, for the Atlanta refugees. When news of Davis' arrival became generally known, the organizers of the relief meeting decided to ask him to speak. A committee composed of Clifford Anderson, Cobb, and H.B. Troutman, was sent to the Cobb residence on the corner of Walnut and Second Streets to give Davis a formal invitation. Soon the committee returned to the church with Davis in tow. When the Confederate President arrived at the head of the right hand aisle of the church there was prolonged applause. Davis turned to the audience and repeatedly bowed very low. After an introduction by Cobb, Davis addressed the people. He talked about adversity, being the son of a Georgian, and that the cause was not lost. He noted that Sherman could not maintain his long line of communications for long, and must retreat sooner or later. Sherman, Davis asserted, would be destroyed "and escape with only a body guard as an escort," just as Napoleon had done at the conclusion of the Russian Campaign in 1812. He then explained, "I know the deep disgrace felt by Georgia at our army falling back from Dalton to the interior of the State, but I was not of those who considered Atlanta lost when our army crossed the Chattahoochee. I resolved that it should not and I then put a man [Hood] in command who I knew would strike an

---

[30] Hallett to Capt. Stark, Macon, 12 September 1864, Howell Cobb Letter Book, 1864-1865.

[31] Nathan Munroe, Jr. to Bannie Kell, Sylvan Lodge, 25 September 1864, Kell Letters.

[32] Nathan Munroe, Jr. to Bannie Kell, Macon, 24 September 1864, Ibid.

honest and manly blow for the city, and many a Yankee's blood was made to nourish the soil before the prize was won."[33]

By the end of September, things had quieted down somewhat. Munroe wrote that the neighbors were not leaving as fast as they had been, although many seemed anxious to leave.[34] Vineville seemed quieter than it had been because the alarm of an early raid by Sherman's forces was suspended and people did not believe that the Federals would come soon.[35]

The changed military circumstances caused by the fall of Atlanta, did not outwardly affect Macon. Nurse Kate Cumming passed through the city in late September and confided to her journal that "Macon is a beautiful place; the streets are very wide, and the buildings lofty. It is the third town in importance in Georgia, and is one hundred miles southeast of Atlanta." She believed the city was very patriotic, and "the citizens have done much for the cause." She observed that the Wayside Home for soldiers was entirely supported by the people of Macon, and wished "there was one at every place where our soldiers are likely to be detained." She felt that the home was indispensable in its efforts to furnish food and lodging to poor soldiers who had no money, and who were waiting for trains to take them to their homes.[36]

The city which Nurse Cumming visited had changed, by the summer of 1864, from a quiet place "noted for the ease and elegance of its inhabitants and but seldom disturbed by the rush and bustle of commercial thoroughfares" into a busy city where "The streets are daily thronged with citizens, soldiers, exiles and refugees, drays and omnibuses, Government wagons, Huckster's carts, carriages, buggies and cavaliers on prancing steeds." This gave a lively air to the place. Editor H. L. Flash of the *Daily Telegraph and Confederate* believed that Macon had turned into another Atlanta "previous to its investment by the enemy."[37]

In view of the changed military circumstances caused by the fall of Atlanta, Cobb continued to prepare for the worst. On 30 September he ordered the arrest of all deserters, and offered a reward of $30 for each man apprehended or returned to his command.[38] This was followed on 6 October by General Order No. 21, issued by General Wayne, which required all detailed men not in service to join

---

[33] *Daily Telegraph and Confederate,* 24 September 1864.

[34] Nathan Munroe, Jr. to Bannie Kell, Macon, 29 September 1864.

[35] Nathan Munroe, Jr. to Bannie Kell, Macon, October, 1864, Ibid.

[36] Entry for 19 September 1864, in Richard Harwell, ed., *Kate Cumming, The Journal of a Confederate Nurse, 1862-1864,* Savannah: The Beehive Press, 1975, pp. 216-217.

[37] *Macon Daily Telegraph and Confederate,* 24 September 1864.

[38] Ibid., 30 September 1864.

the State Militia commanded by Major General Gustavus W. Smith.[39] Another decision, one which would affect the future of the city when Sherman did begin his March to the Sea, involved the establishment of a "camp of convalescence" at Macon commanded by General Wright. The camp, known as "Camp Wright," was established at the Georgia School for the Blind. All convalescent soldiers were ordered to report there.[40]

Cobb's duties were expanded in late September when he was assigned to the command of the District of Georgia, a district, which as Hood explained, "will embrace all the posts in the state of Georgia."[41] Howell Cobb, Jr., writing to his mother from Athens, noted that "Pa's new command...accmulates office work. I shall endeavour to leave here next Monday [to help him]."[42] Over a month later, Cobb's duties were greatly increased when he received the authority to appoint and remove Post Commandants and Provost Marshals in his district.[43]

The seemingly ever-present threat of drafting public officials affected Macon's leaders in the fall of 1864. In October, Mayor Stephen Collins wrote Governor Brown that the alderman of cities were not exempted from service under Brown's reorganization of the militia. If these men were drafted, Collins explained, Macon "will be deprived of such a number of her alderman as will leave me entirely powerless in the premises." Macon was a military post, almost an outpost, because of the large number of people passing through the city every day. This caused an unsettled condition of affairs which, in turn, created a burden on city officials. "Cities," Collins warned, "should be allowed to have their officers & more especially this the case with Macon."[44]

Two weeks later Collins wrote Brown again, this time in regard to exemptions from militia duty for Macon's firemen who were being ordered out for militia duty by the Governor. Collins made the point that Augusta had three hundred firemen and could spare some of them for militia duty. But Macon had too few to have any left, "if the small force we now have are ordered away, as they are to leave tomorrow." Collins wanted Brown to arrange with Cobb to allow the small number of firemen to remain. Presumably Brown exempted some of the men because they fought fires until the end of the war.[45]

---

[39] Ibid., 20 October 1864.

[40] Ibid., 7 October 1864.

[41] Hood to Cobb, Telegram, Headquarters, 28 September 1864, Cobb Papers, 1864.

[42] Howell Cobb, Jr. to his mother, Athens, 9 October 1864, Ibid.

[43] Col. E.J. Harris, Inspector General, Army of Tennessee to Cobb, Telegram, HdQrs. Army of Tennessee, 15 November 1864, Ibid.

[44] Mayor Stephen Collins to Brown, Macon, 17 October 1864, Incoming Correspondence of the Governor.

[45] Mayor Stephen Collins to Governor Brown, Macon, 31 October 1864, Ibid.

By early October Cobb grew frustrated because work on the fortifications was hindered by the lack of wagons and mule teams to haul earth. He also needed wagons and ambulances for Camp Wright. In desperation, he asked Major A.P. Mason, Assistant Adjutant General for the Army of Tennessee to furnish eleven wagons and two ambulances to fill the need.[46] Of course, Cobb had constant problems procuring labor to build the fortifications.[47] Fortunately, by 12 October Cobb could write Major Mason asking for a bonded officer to pay off the Blacks, and to impress additional hands. He confided, "At present we have large numbers of negroes employed and as far as I know, not the first [step] taken to provide for the payment of the hands, supplying their wants beyond the mere feeding of them." "This is an important matter," he added, "and I beg early attention to the subject."[48]

By early October, in large part because of Cobb's efforts, progress was being made to build the fortifications and provide in other ways for the defense of the city. The fortifications, which eventually stretched along the length of modern Pio Nono Avenue from present Pierce Avenue to below Montpelier Avenue, then the Columbus Road, included several forts, one on Rogers Avenue east of Vineville Avenue in the vicinity of the Munroe-Goolsby House (156 Rogers Avenue), another on a high bluff overlooking the Ocmulgee River in Riverside Cemetery, and one behind the present Superintendent's residence at the Ocmulgee National Monument.[49]

By this time Macon also contained a number of camps. These included Camp Oglethorpe; Camp Rescue, opposite the gate of Rose Hill Cemetery near modern Riverside Drive; Camp Cobb [not located], which served as headquarters of the 5th Regiment of Georgia Reserves under Colonel John B. Cumming; Camp Cooper [not located], the Headquarters of the Camp of Instruction, commanded by Major A.M. Rowland; and Camp Wright, located near Fort Hawkins, commanded by Colonel S. M. Colmes, and headquarters of the 5th Tennessee Regiment.[50]

---

[46] Cobb to Major A.P. Mason, Macon, 5 October 1864, Cobb Letter Book, 1864-65, p. 269.

[47] G.W. Lay to Cobb, Telegram, Richmond, 5 October 1864, Cobb Papers, 1864.

[48] Cobb to Maj. Mason, Macon, 12 October 1864, Cobb Letter Book, 1864-65, pp. 276-77.

[49] Observation of the physical remains by the author; Mary Callaway Jones, "Some Historic Spots of the Confederate Period in Macon," p. 14, in Genealogy and Archives Room, Washington Memorial Library, Macon, hereafter cited as Jones, "Some Historic Spots; Thomas Yoseloff, ed., *The Official Atlas of the Civil War*, Plate 135, No. 4, 1958 from Captain Calvin D. Cowles, comp., *Atlas to Accompany the Official Records of the Union and Confederate Armies* (Washington, D.C.: Government Printing Office, 1891-95).

[50] Jones, "Some Historic Spots," 14.

The building of these fortifications and encampments did not occur without some hardships on the part of Macon's people. Nathan C. Munroe wrote his daughter, Bannie, that 800 men were encamped at Sylvan Lodge, destroying the fences and timber, and desolating the property very much, but, he added, "I suppose it is inevitable & I bare [sic] it as well as I can."[51] The soldiers camped around Munroe's home had destroyed all of the wood pasturage in the vicinity and a large part of the fences and timber by September 27.[52] By the evening of 7 October Munroe temporarily laid aside any feelings of patriotism, and paid a call to the commandant of the battery and camp of artillery which was just below the large road gate which led to Sylvan Lodge. The officer, Munroe noted, "seems quite a gentlemen & promises to allow no more injury to our place then military necessity requires." But other encampments in Munroe's field were "doing us much damage."[53] By 12 October the authorities were building some of the Macon fortifications in an area which adjoined the yard fence of a Mrs. Tibbes, inside of the Vineville Hospital yard. Some of the officers frightened Mrs. Tibbes by telling her that they might have to extend the line of fortifications into her yard and move away one of her out buildings. But, Munroe confided, "as yet it has not been done," but added, "The encampments in our grounds are constantly encroaching upon us and have now got up to our stable lot fence."[54] Despite assurances to Munroe, work continued on the fortifications. He complained to Bannie on 18 October: "There is a large force at work on our fort near the wood gate- and the work progressing rapidly- and great destruction to our timber."[55] The desolation of Munroe's property continued although he had sent his slave Ned to the market for a leg of mutton and a soup bone and invited a Captain Yates and a Surgeon Baxley, camped at the wood gate to "Sylvan Lodge," for dinner "which they very kindly did and we had a pleasant dinner, Aunt Jane furnishing the custard & pickles."[56]

As the fall progressed and the military situation continued to deteriorate, Munroe complained that the people had heard nothing from Hood's army for sometime. There was no direct mail or telegraphic communication between the front in northwest Georgia and Macon.[57] Nearly two weeks later Munroe still had heard no news from the army, although "Our place is much more quiet all apprehension of raids for the present passed away." Although there was still no

---

[51] Nathan Munroe, Jr. to Bannie Kell, Sylvan Lodge, Kell Letters.

[52] Nathan Munroe, Jr. to Bannie Kell, Macon, 27 September 1864, Ibid.

[53] Nathan Munroe, Jr. to Bannie Kell, Macon, 8 October 1864.

[54] Nathan Munroe, Jr. to Bannie Kell, Macon, 12 October 1864, Ibid.

[55] Nathan Munroe, Jr. to Bannie Kell, Macon, 18 October 1864, Ibid.

[56] Nathan Munroe, Jr. to Bannie Kell, Macon, 14 October 1864, Ibid.

[57] Nathan C. Munroe, Jr. to Bannie Kell, Macon, October 3, 1864, Ibid. Munroe was concerned because his son, Nathan, was with the Army of Tennessee.

news from the front, Munroe had learned that the militia were rendezvousing in Macon, "and we learn the turnout is very general."[58] Trains leaving Macon were crowded with people escaping from Sherman, prompting Munroe to exclaim, "there is very great difficulty in getting through on the trains-they go off so crowded."[59]

In early November another morale-boosting visit by President Davis gave the people of Macon a brief respite from the problems generated by Sherman's occupation of Atlanta. Davis, realizing the impact of Sherman's victory, was greeted by Mayor Collins and two or three other gentlemen who met him at the railroad station to perform escort duty, but the male population of the city had organized itself into a committee of the whole for the same purpose, and crowded around the railroad cars, from which Davis and his party were "extricated by some process unknown." The same crowd, or much of it, went with the carriages of the presidential party to the Lanier House, walking "both a quick and double-quick to the music of vociferous shouts and cheers." After the cavalcade reached the hotel, Davis appeared on the balcony and greeted the people in what was for him a rousing speech, complimenting Georgia and its soldiers in a brief exposition of the issues involved in the war. He contrasted these issues "with those of the first war of independence- in glancing at its present aspects and certain fruition in complete political and commercial independence." The Confederate president thought the "signs of the times justified him in saying to every one 'be of good cheer'. But the Confederate cause still demanded the greatest energies of the people. Every man, he asserted, who could bear arms should be in the army, "and those who could not should labor in the common cause by sustaining the armies in every way possible." He ended his address by thanking the ladies for their support of the Confederate cause, and made "an impressive invocation of the smiles of Heaven upon the hearth-stones made desolate in this cruel and unjustifiable war, and upon the cause and the country." Davis then received the greetings of the men and women of Macon in the parlors of the hotel, "which were thronged with the beauty of the city." After a private supper, he concluded his two-hour-visit by a speedy departure. The people, according to the *Telegraph and Confederate's* reporter, gave Davis proof of his strong popularity in Macon, and Davis, for his part, seemed much pleased with both the informality and warmness of his reception.[60]

After leaving Macon, Davis passed through Griswoldville on his way to Savannah. About forty black women who worked in the Armory there gathered around him wanting to see him. A writer for the *Journal and Messenger* noted that "With true politeness he alighted from the car and gave them a hearty shake

---

[58] Nathan Munroe, Jr. to Bannie Kell, Macon, 14 October 1864, Ibid.

[59] Nathan Munroe, Jr. to Bannie Kell, 15 October 1864, Ibid.

[60] *Macon Daily Telegraph and Confederate,* 2 November 1864.

of the hand." After making a few appropriate remarks, Davis continued on his journey.[61]

In October 1864, Hood decided to move upon Sherman's communications and destroy as much of the Atlantic and Western Railroad between Atlanta and Chattanooga as he could. Sherman pursued the unlucky Confederate General who withdrew into northeastern Alabama hoping that Sherman would follow him. If not, Hood determined to draw Sherman away from Georgia by invading Middle Tennessee and capturing Nashville. If all of his plans were realized, Hood planned to carry the war into Kentucky as far as the Ohio River as Generals Braxton Bragg and Edmund Kirby Smith attempted to do in the ill-fated Kentucky invasion of the summer and fall of 1862. Hood's plans effectively removed the Army of Tennessee from Georgia and gave Sherman a free hand in the State. Sherman promptly burned Atlanta on 15 November and, dividing his army into two wings, began his destructive March to the Sea. The troops remaining under his immediate command were the Army of the Tennessee and the Army of the Ohio, together 60,000 strong. Sherman had sent General Georgia H. Thomas' Army of the Cumberland back to Middle Tennessee to deal with Hood.

The only organized troops left in Georgia to oppose Sherman were Major General Gustavus Woodson Smith's Georgia Reserves, then based at Lovejoy's Station, joined by two small regiments of Georgia State Troops and several detachments of home guards who were ordered to report to him by General Cobb, and Lieutenant General Joseph Wheeler's Cavalry. Smith commanded 2,800 infantry, 3 batteries of artillery, and 250 local reserve cavalry. Wheeler's forces numbered 2,000. With these small forces it was impossible for Wheeler and Smith to make an effective defense against Sherman's immense army.[62]

The Federal Right Wing consisted of the Army of the Tennessee, commanded by Major General Oliver Otis Howard. It was composed of the 15th and 17th Corps commanded by Major Generals Peter J. Osterhaus and Francis P. Blair, Jr., respectively. These two corps, which mustered a total of seven divisions, pushed Wheeler's cavalry and Smith's force back to Griffin and Forsyth. Wheeler, then the senior officer in the field in Georgia, ordered Smith

---

[61] *Georgia Journal and Messenger,* 4 November 1864.

[62] Gustavus W. Smith, "The Georgia Militia During Sherman's March to the Sea," in Robert U. Johnson and Clarence C. Buel, eds., *Battles and Leaders of the Civil War* (New York: Thomas Yoseloff, 1956) 4:667; W.C. Dodson, ed., *Campaigns of Joseph Wheeler & His Cavalry 1862-1865 From Material Furnished by Gen. Joseph Wheeler To Which is Added His Concise and Graphic Account of The Santiago Campaign of 1898* (Atlanta: Hudgins Publishing Company, 1899) 286; Jacob D. Cox, *The March to the Sea Franklin and Nashville* (New York: The Blue & The Gray Press, n.d.) 28.

to march rapidly and concentrate his forces at Macon, and prepare the fortifications there for "vigorous" defense. Wheeler also placed small parties of cavalry on Sherman's flanks and rear, and kept his main force in his front to engage his advance.[63]

As Sherman's large force began its march toward Macon Confederate Congressman Clifford Anderson, fearing for the people of his congressional district, telegraphed Cobb from Richmond "Is any movement in progress against Macon or Augusta?"[64] General Beauregard, for his part, wired General M.L. Smith from Tuscumbia, Alabama, on 14 November to urge Cobb to complete the fortifications around Macon at once.[65]

First reports indicated that Sherman was moving from the Coosa River Valley in Northeastern Alabama where he had pursued Hood towards Kingston and Marietta, Georgia. Beauregard, then in command of the Military Division of the West which included large portions of Mississippi, Alabama, and Georgia, warned Cobb from his post in Tuscumbia, Alabama, that "Sherman may contemplate advancing into Georgia to check movement of this army [Hood's] into Tennessee." If this should happen, Lieutenant General Richard Taylor, then in Georgia, would hold Baker's Brigade for Cobb's use, if needed for the defense of Columbus, Macon, or Augusta, while Wheeler would operate in Sherman's rear. Cobb was then in Griffin, in charge of a military buildup to attempt the recapture of Atlanta or at least make a demonstration before that important city.[66] Beauregard continued to bombard Cobb with information about what little he knew of Sherman's movements. At 7:00 P.M. on the 16th he ordered Cobb to move all extra supplies at Augusta or Macon "intended for Military Division of West to Columbus and Selma[.] you must look also to safety of prisoners at Millen."[67] The indefatigable Creole general followed this message with another at 10:00 P.M. with a report from Wheeler that Sherman was about to march with three corps from Atlanta to Augusta or Macon. Beauregard urged Cobb to be ready with all available forces and those of Georgia to defend either place to the last extremity cutting and blocking up the roads in front of the Federals. Wheeler's Cavalry would harass Sherman's flanks and rear, and Cobb was again

---

[63] Orlando M. Poe Report, *OR* 44:56; Dodson, ed.,*Campaigns of Wheeler & His Cavalry,* 287; Smith, "Georgia Militia," 667; Gustavus W. Smith to Joseph Wheeler, Forsyth, GA., 18 November 1864, *OR,* 44:868.

[64] Clifford Anderson to Cobb, Telegram, Richmond, 15 November 1864.

[65] Beauregard to M.L. Smith, Telegram, Tuscumbia, AL., 14 November 1864, Ibid.

[66] Beauregard to Cobb, Telegram, Tuscumbia, 7 November 1864, Cobb Papers, 1864; Colonel George W. Brent to Cobb, Telegram, Tuscumbia, 7 November 1864, Ibid. Brent was Beauregard's Assistant Adjutant General.

[67] Beauregard to Cobb, telegram, Tuscumbia, 7 P.M., 16 November 1864, Cobb Papers, 1864.

ordered to remove or destroy supplies of all kinds before Sherman could capture them. Cobb had to notify Governor Brown and South Carolina Governor Millard Bonham, as well as General William Joseph Hardee and Taylor for help in case Sherman advanced. Beauregard added: "should this movement occur Lt Genl Taylor will assume immediate command of all troops operating against Sherman–I will join you should it become necessary."[68]

Cobb himself knew more about Sherman's movements than Beauregard. He confided to his wife from Griffin on 16 November that the Federals had burned Atlanta, destroyed the railroad from Atlanta to the Chattahoochee River and burnt the railroad bridge over the Chattahoochee. Rumors circulated that Sherman had ordered the railroad to Marietta burned, and had begun the movement of his army toward Griffin. Wheeler very accurately estimated the force, which included all of the right wing, to number 30,000 men, while Kilpatrick's cavalry mustered 6,000. An advanced detachment of Confederate cavalry fell back from Jonesboro to Lovejoy's Station, and Cobb and Gustavus W. Smith, commanding a force of infantry and artillery at Lovejoy's Station, ordered a retreat on the evening of 15 November to Griffin. Their men marched all night. Cobb noted that he and Smith remained in the rear and "were the last to get into camp. Cobb felt that Sherman intended to advance into Middle Georgia, but did not know where. He believed that the destination was Macon and felt that his small force could do little to stop the Federals, but hoped he would be reinforced in time to impede Sherman's progress. Cobb hoped that his wife would move down with his family to Americus in Southwest Georgia, but concluded that he had "no serious fears now that Macon can be taken–still it will not be so comfortable to be there with a Yankee army around it."[69]

As Sherman prepared to advance into Middle Georgia, Confederate officials sent a flurry of telegrams to each other reporting the move. On 16 November Cobb wired Brigadier General Robert Toombs: "Sherman has burned Atlanta and destroyed the Rail Road to Altoona [Georgia] burned bridge over Chattahoochee. Has moved as far as Jonesboro and McDonough in very large force. It requires every man that Confederate and State authorities can put in the field, to meet this force. He is evidently moving on Macon." Governor Brown assured Beauregard on 17 November, that he would do everything in his power to aid Cobb. Realist that he was, the Governor admitted that "we have not force to stop the movements of the enemy." Brown wired Wheeler on 17 November that Sherman was evidently marching on Macon, and urged the cavalryman to

---

[68] Beauregard to Cobb, Tuscumbia, Telegram, 10 P.M. 16 November 1864, Ibid.

[69] Cobb to his wife, Camp near Griffin, 16 November 1864.

keep him advised of each important movement, and would "do all I can to rally force to aid you."[70]

Jefferson Davis, anxious to prevent a Federal invasion of the rich agricultural and industrial areas of Georgia, urged Cobb to "get out every man who can render any service even for a short period." The Macon Commander should use Blacks to obstruct roads by any means possible. He should also obtain "shells prepared to explode by pressure" from Colonel George W. Rains. Davis told Cobb that Lieutenant General Hardee would reinforce him, and Lieutenant General Taylor would help him to oppose Sherman.[71]

In preparing to defend Macon Cobb took stock in the men and arms that he had available to him. He asked Major A. M. Rowland, Commander of Camp Cooper, for information concerning these needs. Cooper counted arms and men and found he had 125 .75 caliber muskets on hand, but needed 175 for a total of 300. He also needed 250 cartridge boxes and belts, 300 canteens and haversacks, and 6,000 cartridges. Rowland believed that he would have 300 men fit for duty in a couple of days through the return of absent squads and the receipt of new materials. He assured Cobb that he would arm absentees and deserters and put them into the trenches, but cautioned "most of the men reported for duty are light duty' men and unable to march far, but capable of manning the works."[72]

On 17 November an aroused Cobb, aware of the danger to Macon posed by Sherman's invasion, issued Special Orders No. 139 which called for all able-bodied men to join military units during the emergency. The units available to defend Macon included a brigade under Brigadier General William W. Mackall; Lieutenant Colonel Hollinguist's Reserve Artillery of the Army of Tennessee who served as infantry; Colonel S.M. Colmes' wounded soldiers at the Convalescent Camp (Camp Wright); the detachment from the Macon Arsenal under Lieutenant Colonel John W. Mallett, known as the Arsenal Battalion; Major Rowland's Engineer Company; Major Green's Engineer Company; Captain Winston's City Battalion; Captain Bass's force from the Dixie Works; units from the Bulkley Steam Works; hospital employees; and troops from the Commissary Department. Although records are not available to give precise numbers they probably numbered altogether less than 2,000 men. Cobb ordered Assistant Quartermaster Captain John T. Brown to take charge of all trains

---

[70] Cobb to Toombs, care of Brown, Telegram, Griffin, 16 November 1864, 1861-65, 730; Brown to Beauregard, Telegram, Milledgeville, 17 November 1864, Ibid., 730; Brown to Wheeler, Telegram, Milledgeville, 17 November 1864, Ibid., 730.

[71] Davis to Cobb, Telegram, Richmond, 16 November 1864, Cobb Papers, 1864.

[72] Major A. M. Rowland to Cobb, Camp Cooper, November 17, 1864, Ibid.

arriving and leaving Macon. No train could arrive or leave the city without a permit from Cobb.[73]

Major J.T. Burns, commanding a small detachment of scouts sent by Cobb to learn Sherman's route, wired Cobb on 18 November that he crossed the Ocmulgee River early that morning and halted his force after moving four miles on the Monticello Road. Burns sent a scout of citizens and soldiers up the river who had returned. They "report the enemy to be crossing in heavy force," he wrote, "mostly infantry at Buttons factory [on the Ocmulgee] & moving in the direction of Macon by way of Monticello." Burns assured his chief that he would attempt to pass through their line of march on the night of the 18th and report as soon as possible. He would send cavalry to Macon and Milledgeville on the morning of the 19th and try to learn if the Federals were marching toward Augusta. Only about a hundred cavalry had crossed the river by the morning of the 18th, but there were few citizens to report their movements "as all have taken [to] the forest."[74]

As the Federals began their march reports came into Macon concerning their whereabouts. A writer for the *Daily Telegraph and Confederate* reported on 18 November, "The city was considerably excited, owing to various reports of the advance of the enemy." It was known "positively" that the enemy was near Griffin. But, the paper assured the excited people, "There is no doubt that the military authorities will do every thing in their power to stay the advance of the enemy, and we trust they will receive the cordial support of the entire community."[75] On the following day, a correspondent for the paper urged the people to come to the defense of Georgia. If the citizens refused to fight for their State "woe be unto them. For the day is near at hand in which the cepter will depart from Judah and they and their possessions be left to the mercy of an aspiring foe."[76] A thousand and one rumors were afloat in the excited city. These tales received some credence when a traveler reported seeing several large fires in the vicinity of Griffin, which lent support to reports that the enemy was burning in their rear. Stories circulated that the towns of Monticello and Hillsboro were burned, but the paper reported "if this be true we think that the outrage must have been committed by small detachments of cavalry."[77]

---

[73] Major R. J. Hallett, Special Orders No. 139, Macon, 17 November 1864, in Howell Cobb Special Orders Book, 1865, Hargrett Library, University of Georgia, hereafter cited as Cobb Special Orders 1865 Book.

[74] Major J.T. Burns to Cobb, Telegram, 14 miles southwest of Monticello, 1 P.M., 18 November 1864, Cobb Papers, 1864.

[75] *Macon Daily Telegraph and Confederate,* 18 November 1864.

[76] Ibid., 19 November 1864.

[77] Ibid.

Various political and military leaders urged the people to stand fast and oppose the invaders. Julian Hartridge, a member of the Georgia delegation in the Confederate Congress, assured the citizens of Middle Georgia that President Davis and Secretary of War Seddon were doing all they could to meet the emergency. Hartridge exclaimed, "Let every man fly to arms, remove your negroes, horses, cattle and provisions away from Sherman's army and burn what you cannot carry, burn all bridges and block up the roads in his route."[78]

Beauregard, then at Corinth, Mississippi, issued a proclamation to the people of Georgia asking them to "Arise, for the defense of your native soil: rally around your patriotic Governor and gallant soldiers. Obstruct and destroy all roads in Sherman's flanks and rear, and his army will soon starve. Be confident and resolute. Trust in an overruling providence, and success will crown your efforts." He assured the people he would soon join them in defense of their homes. The paper asserted, "The clarion voice of this gallant Louisianian, like the blast of Roderick's bugle, will be worth a thousand men."[79]

Governor Brown added his voice to the chorus of leaders who urged the people to resist, issuing a proclamation for all men between the ages of sixteen and fifty-five to report to General Smith at Macon for forty days service in the field.[80] The *Daily Telegraph and Confederate's* reporter warned, "If the people of Georgia do not come down upon Sherman like wolves on a sheepfold, they are unworthy of themselves. Fight him in the front, fight him in the flank, fight in the rear. Remove everything valuable in his path throw every obstruction in his way." Rumors were widely circulated that Sherman's Right Wing was about thirty miles east of Macon, but the direction of their march was uncertain. The Federals were reported to be so numerous that they had a wagon train eight miles long. Some believed that Sherman intended to bypass Macon because of "a large force gathered here" and "splendid fortifications" which surrounded the city. At any rate, the paper asserted "Macon is to be defended to the last, and those best informed believe it can be held against any force Sherman can bring against it."[81] Reporters for the paper continued to arouse excitement in the people as Sherman's March to the Sea progressed.[82]

Fortunately, the paper could report more positive views when its editor noted: "We are glad to notice the determination to defend Macon to the last extremity, and should the Yankees attempt to take the city they will find a lion in the path, to obstruct their passage."[83] Cobb, despite the rumors afloat

---

[78] Ibid., November 21, 1864.
[79] Ibid.
[80] Ibid.
[81] Ibid.
[82] Ibid.; Ibid., November 18, 1864.
[83] Ibid., 19 November 1864.

everywhere, kept a cool head. He told his wife on the 19th that, although Sherman "still keeps us in doubt as to his movements," he would probably make a feint upon Macon, but his real objective was Augusta. "We shall probably," Cobb thought, "have a small brush with him here–but he will then march on Augusta en route for Charleston."[84]

To add to the confusion, Wheeler received directions from several Confederate generals. On 18 November Taylor, then at Selma, Alabama, urged Wheeler to keep him advised of Sherman's movements. If the enemy moved east towards Augusta, Wheeler had to inform Hardee at Savannah and the Confederate authorities in Richmond. Beauregard telegraphed on the 18th, directing the cavalry leader to employ his cavalry to the best advantage, interposing his men in Sherman's advance and destroying supplies to keep them from falling into Sherman's hands. Hood notified Wheeler from Florence, Alabama, that "It is very important that you should not allow any portion of your mounted forces to be shut up in a besieged city, but keep them constantly harassing the enemy." Wheeler should destroy Sherman's trains and cut off his foraging parties.[85]

So great was the confusion among the Confederate high command that Wheeler urged the Confederate War Department to issue definite orders to the officers in command in Georgia concerning the policy to be followed "particularly as to defending Macon, Augusta, or Columbus." If these places were not to be defended, Government stores should be removed upon Sherman's approach, if possible. Someone, Wheeler believed, should be sent to command in Georgia, who knew the plans of the Government.[86] Diarist Mary Boykin Chestnut, writing in her diary, observed, "I sit here [in Richmond] and listen for Sherman's bugles. I know we have nothing to put in his way but a brigade or so of troopless, dismantled Generals."[87]

As Sherman prepared to march, the leaders of the State, realizing that Milledgeville would probably be one of his objectives, prepared to evacuate the town. Anticipating this move the Macon City authorities asked Dr. C.B.

---

[84] Cobb to his wife, Macon, 19 November 1864, Cobb Papers, 1864. For information concerning Sherman's advance and Wheeler's efforts to oppose Sherman in the vicinity of Macon see Wheeler to Cobb, Telegrams (2), Forsyth, 18 November 1864, Ibid.; Wheeler to Cobb, Telegram, Forsyth, 19 November 1864, Ibid.; Brigadier General B.D. Fry to Hardee, Telegram, Augusta, 19 November 1864, Ibid.; Governor Brown to Cobb, Telegram, 19 November 1864, Ibid.; and Brigadier General S.W. Ferguson to Hardee, Telegram, Crawford, Georgia, 8 P.M., 20 November 1864, Ibid.

[85] Dodson, ed., *Campaigns of Wheeler & His Cavalry*, p. 287.

[86] John B. Jones, *A Rebel War Clerk's Diary*, Earl Schenck Miers, ed. (New York: Sagamore Press, Inc., 1958) 450.

[87] Mary Boykin Chestnut, *A Diary From Dixie*, Ben Ames Williams, ed. (Boston: Houghton Mifflin Col., 1949) 453.

Gamble, Medical Director of the Army of Tennessee in the absence of Dr. Samuel H. Stout, to return the City Hall to them so they could offer it to the State for use as the temporary State capitol. Gamble wrote Dr. James Mercer Green, Surgeon in Charge of Confederate Hospitals in Macon, that he had agreed to their request, and wanted the patients transferred to the Ocmulgee and Floyd House Hospitals. The furniture would be stored in an outbuilding. Gamble believed that the lower rooms, which had served as storage rooms for medical supplies belonging to the Stout Hospital, had been returned to the quartermaster. With Green's approval, the City Hall Hospital would be permanently closed. In a short time, the Stout Hospital would also be closed. This would leave three hospitals open in Macon: the Floyd House Hospital, the Ocmulgee Hospital, and the Blind School Hospital.[88]

Mayor Stephen Collins formally offered Brown the use of the City Hall, describing the building as containing "two large rooms suitable for the Legislature and five smaller rooms for offices, besides a large enclosed and covered space for store room." The Mayor believed that the building could be used by the State and wrote: "I am gratified to be the medium of tendering it to you. It can be turned over," he added, "in complete order and ready for immediate occupation."[89] Brown accepted Collins' offer, and added that at the moment, he did not need all the space offered, "and trust I may not be in the way of any use the Council may wish to continue to make of the rooms needed by them."[90]

The problems of Macon's Confederate hospitals at this time included the temporary disruption of medical facilities for the sick and wounded soldiers; the disastrous campaign in North Georgia; the hurried evacuation of Atlanta; the crowding of the sick and wounded into closed box cars; the hygienic condition of the hospitals in Macon; the sudden transfer of the gangrene-infected patients from other Macon hospitals to the Empire Hospital, a large collection of tents in Vineville; the unsuccessful efforts of the Empire Hospital's Surgeon in charge, William P. Harden, to procure proper medical facilities in Vineville; the arduous duties and the unhealthy atmosphere of the Empire Hospital which added increased stress to both nurses and medical officers; and "the miserable & even dying condition in which many of the patients were received." These conditions prompted Surgeon Joseph Jones of the Medical Board, then inspecting Macon's hospitals, to urge Surgeon Harden to write down his experiences which "will

---

[88] Dr. C.B. Gamble to Dr. James Mercer Green, Macon, 7 November 1864, Samuel H. Stout Papers, EU.

[89] Collins to Brown, Macon, 19 November 1864, in Incoming Correspondence of the Governor. The same letter is found in GLB 1861-65, p. 732.

[90] Brown to Collins, Macon, 23 November 1864, Incoming correspondence of the Governor.

not only prove interesting to the profession as a part of the Medical History of the Army of Tennessee, but will also prove (I think) of value to your professional reputation."[91]

The advance of Sherman's two armies prompted Cobb to ask Governor Brown for a train belonging to the Georgia Central Railroad, then loaded with cotton, for use to remove the sick and wounded soldiers from Macon.[92] Brown concurred and ordered E.B. Walker, the Georgia official in charge of State Railroads, to support Cobb.[93] However, Cobb ordered Chief Surgeon Gamble to "retain one hospital at this Post."[94] Some of the hospitals were sent into the Smithville area of Southwest Georgia, considered by many as the safest region of the State. Others, as mentioned above, stayed in Macon.[95]

As the Right Wing of his army approached the vicinity of Macon, Sherman's strategy was working perfectly. His first objective was to place his army "in the very heart of Georgia," interposing between Macon and Augusta, and forcing Wheeler, Cobb, Smith, and other Confederate generals to divide their forces to defend these places, as well as Millen, Savannah, and Charleston.[96]

Sherman's 5,500-men cavalry division, known as the 3rd Cavalry Division and commanded by Brigadier General Hugh Judson Kilpatrick, was given the task of spearheading the march of the Right Wing. Accordingly, Kilpatrick made a feint against Forsyth, thirty miles north of Macon, then rapidly marched to Planter's Factory Ferry on the Ocmulgee River below Jackson and crossed the river. Sherman ordered Kilpatrick to make a feint against Macon by sending his troopers to strike the Georgia Central Railroad as close to the city as possible. Plans called for the cavalry to then retire towards Gordon, thoroughly destroying the railroad as they went. Kilpatrick reached Clinton, fifteen miles north of Macon, on 19 November. Learning that some of Wheeler's cavalry had also crossed the river near Macon to oppose him, Kilpatrick advanced on the Clinton-Macon Road.[97]

---

[91] Dr.Joseph Jones to Dr. William P. Harden, Macon, 8 November 1864, Samuel H. Stout Papers, Manuscripts Department, Tulane University Libraries, New Orleans.

[92] Cobb to Brown, Telegram, Macon, 17 November 1864, Incoming Correspondence of the Governor.

[93] Brown to E.B. Walker, Milledgeville, 17 November 1864, GLB 1861-1865, p. 732.

[94] R.J. Hallett to Gamble, Macon, 19 November 1864, Cobb Letter Book, 1864-65, p. 330.

[95] Dr. Stanford E. Chaille to Dr. Samuel H. Stout, Ocmulgee Hospital, Macon, 30 November 1864, Samuel H. Stout Papers, EU.

[96] William T. Sherman's Report, *OR,*, 44: Pt. 1, 8.

[97] Hugh Judson Kilpatrick's Report, *OR*, 44: Pt. 1, 362-63; James *Moore, Kilpatrick and Our Cavalry; Comprising a Sketch of the Life of General Kilpatrick*

Wheeler, hindered by the confusion in the Confederate high command, had sent Colonel Robert H. Anderson's Brigade to Cobb to observe Kilpatrick's movements. On 19 November Wheeler also sent Crews' Brigade of Georgians to Cobb who placed the new arrivals on the Milledgeville Road with orders to engage any enemy forces who might threaten the Georgia Central Railroad. On the evening of the 19th Wheeler came to Macon after ordering the remainder of his command, except Colonels Samuel W. Ferguson's and William C.P. Breckinridge's Brigades to follow.

At 11:00 P.M., Wheeler arrived in Macon to find General Hardee, the new commander of the Department of Georgia, already there. Hardee ordered Wheeler to move at daylight on 20 November with all of his available troops, except Crews' Brigade, to the Macon-Clinton Road. Wheeler's objective was to find Kilpatrick's force and oppose him. As he advanced, Wheeler was delayed by small squads of Kilpatrick's Cavalry, which the Confederates drove off. The Confederate cavalryman joined his advance guard, riding with it to the edge of Clinton only to observe Osterhaus' 15th Corps marching through toward Gordon. The Federals were unable to see Wheeler because of dense fog. Six of Wheeler's troopers dashed into the small Jones County seat and captured Osterhaus' personal servant, an enlisted man, within twenty feet of the General's headquarters. Then a regiment of Federal cavalry charged Wheeler and his escort, driving them back. Wheeler, however, was reinforced by two regiments from his main body who charged Kilpatrick's men pushing them back to the protection of Osterhaus' infantry.

Wheeler then learned from his scouts that the Federals were moving in considerable force toward Griswoldville, eight miles east of Macon on the Gordon Road. He hurried to meet this new threat with a portion of his men, but soon met a courier from Crews with a message that some of Kilpatrick's men had moved to the Georgia Central Railroad. Crews moved to pursue the enemy under Hardee's orders, but this move left the Macon-Milledgeville Road open to the Federal advance. Wheeler, fearing that the enemy would slip into Macon behind him, quickly marched to a point on the Milledgeville Road east of the City, in the area known as East Macon.[98]

At 12:00 noon on the 20 November Colonel Smith D. Atkins, commanding the 2nd Brigade of the 3rd Cavalry Division, marched from Clinton,

---

With An Account of the Cavalry Raids, Engagements, and Operations Under his command from the Rebellion to the Surrender of Johnston (New York: W.J. Widdleton, Publisher, 1865) 176-178.

[98] Joseph Wheeler's Report, *OR*, 44:1:406-07. Osterhaus, noting Wheeler's presence at Clinton, wrote, "Some rebel cavalry kept hovering around Clinton, and repeatedly attacked our pickets without making any impression." Peter J. Osterhaus' Report, Ibid., 82.

accompanied by Kilpatrick. Atkins' force included Lieutenant Colonel Matthew Van Buskirk's 92nd Illinois; the 3rd Indiana led by Captain Charles U. Patton; Colonel George S. Acker's 9th Michigan; Colonel Thomas T. Heath's 5th Ohio; the 9th Ohio under Colonel William D. Hamilton; the 10th Ohio under Lieutenant Colonel Thomas W. Sanderson; McLaughlin's (Ohio) Squadron under Captain John Dalzell; and the Ninth Pennsylvania commanded by Colonel Thomas Jordan. Atkins' force was accompanied by Captain Yates V. Beebe's 10th Wisconsin Battery.[99]

While at Clinton, Companies B and L of the Ninth Pennsylvania were detached from Kilpatrick's Division and ordered to cover the direct road from Clinton to Macon. The remainder of Kilpatrick's troopers marched down a more easterly road.[100]

Spearheaded by the Ninety-second Illinois, Atkins' Brigade encountered Crew's men four miles from Macon on the Milledgeville Road. The Confederates were dismounted and posted behind barricades. A battalion of the Ninety-second under Captain Becker of Company I, dismounted, and pushed through the woods to within a short distance of Crews. The Confederates, preparing to charge, were met by a portion of Atkins' force; but the charging column of Confederates did not come far. Becker's dismounted men fired on the charging men. A member of the 92nd reported: "Starting with a yell, Rebels rushed out of their rail barricade, and came toward Captain Becker, with his battalion of Spencers concealed in the brush, when the Captain ordered the boys to fire, and the head of the Rebel column was surprised and halted; and it was now our turn to charge, and the 10th Ohio Cavalry started for the enemy with a shout and flashing sabres; and then the entire brigade of graycoats, like frightened birds, scattered, in confusion, through the woods and fields, in terror and dismay." According to this account, the Confederates lost five killed and six wounded.[101] Atkins wrote that Becker's Battalion numbered two hundred men, all armed with Spencer rifles.[102]

Atkins ordered his men not to pursue Crews, but to continue their advance to Macon. The command soon reached the railroad bridge over Walnut Creek, two miles east of Macon. Here a Confederate picket guard was posted. The 92nd

---

[99] *OR*, 44: Pt. 1, 25.

[100] John W. Rowell, *Yankee Cavalrymen Through the Civil War with the Ninth Pennsylvania Cavalry* (Knoxville: The University of Tennessee Press, 1971) 207.

[101] Ninety-Second Illinois Reunion Association, *Ninety-Second Illinois Volunteers,* Freeport, Illinois: Journal Steam Publishing House and Bookbindery, 1875, 176-177, hereafter cited as Reunion Association, *Ninety-Second Illinois Volunteers.*

[102] General Smith D. Atkins, *With Sherman's Cavalry Marching Through Georgia* (Chicago: Samuel Harris & Co., n.d., p. 10.

Illinois dismounted, and drove the Confederates from the creek, and crossed over. They moved up the hill, and drove the Confederates from the hill beyond.[103]

The Confederate force, which was placed on the crest and Eastern slope of Dunlap's Hill, consisted of the 1st Convalescent Regiment, commanded by Lieutenant Colonel Brooks of the 15th Tennessee Regiment, the 2nd Convalescent Regiment under Captain Walker of the 16th Tennessee Regiment, and about 375 men from Captain Albrough's Company. The artillery units included troops from Curry's, Bellamy's Guist's, Howell's, Palmer's, Rivers', and Captain Edmund D. Baxter's Light Artillery Companies, deployed as infantry. These men were commanded by Captain Albrough. Other forces consisted of a detachment of seven companies under Colonel T.S. Howe of the 24th Tennessee Regiment and a volunteer company from the Blind School Hospital commanded by Captain Aikens. The whole force did not exceed 1,000 or 1,200 men. They were supported by Captains Rivers' and Howell's Batteries consisting of four guns each. Rivers' Battery included four twelve-pounder howitzers, while Howell's Battery consisted of four twelve-pounder Napoleons.[104]

The defense was fortunate to have four battalions of artillery, known as the Reserve Artillery, from the Army of Tennessee which were left by Hood to help protect Macon as he began his advance into Tennessee after the fall of Atlanta. These units included Waddell's Battalion with the batteries of Barret, Emery, and Bellamy; Palmer's Battalion, with Yates', Lumpkin's, and Harris' Batteries; and Martin's Battalion which included Baxter's, Howell's, Rivers', and Pritchard's Batteries. Waddell's men had a full compliment of ammunition for their guns, but no horses to pull them. Palmer's force had both ammunition and horses; while Martin's Battalion had a full compliment of ammunition, but no horses. That is why most of the artillerymen fought as infantry—they had no horses to pull their batteries. The entire force of Reserve Artillery was commanded by Lieutenant Colonel J.H. Hallonquist.[105]

---

[103] Reunion Association, *Ninety-Second Illinois Volunteers*, p. 177; Smith D. Atkins' Report, *OR*, 44:1:389-90.

[104] *Macon Daily Telegraph and Confederate*, 28 November 1864; Lt. Col. J.R. Waddy, Report of the Reserve Artillery of the Army of Tennessee, Macon, n.d., Army of Tennessee Papers, DU, hereafter cited as Reserve Artillery Report. Waddy was Chief of Ordnance, Military Division of the West.

[105] Reserve Artillery Report. The batteries of Rivers and Pritchard were consolidated. The guns assigned to each battery included: Barret's- three 12-pounder Napoleons, Emery's-four 10-pounder Parrotts, Bellamy's-four 12-pounder howitzers, Yates'-four 12-pounder Napoleons, Lumpkins'-four 12-pounder howitzers, Harris'-two 12-pounder Napoleons and two unidentified cannon, Baxter's-four 12-pounder howitzers, Howell's- four 12-pounder Napoleons, Rivers

Colonel S. M. Colmes, Commander of the 50th Tennessee Regiment and Commander of Camp Wright, led the Confederate force. Ordered to report to Brigadier General Marcus J. Wright at Macon on 29 September 1864, Combs received his appointment as commander of the camp on 4 October 1864. He was also placed in charge of the defenses of Macon on the north or east side of the Ocmulgee River. Many of Colmes' men were from Camp Wright which was the convalescent camp. They were disabled Confederate soldiers, who were "fit for garrison and guard duty, and who are temporarily disabled for field duty on account of wounds, or disease, received or contracted in the service."[106]

Colmes had been told that he had cavalry in his front which was advancing on the north side of Walnut Creek, on all the roads leading to East Macon. Assured that he would have sufficient notice of any approach of the enemy, the Colonel had taken the precaution of stationing a picket, consisting of one officer and ten men, at each crossing of Walnut Creek, including the bridge which carried the tracks of the Georgia Central Railroad. At 3:30 P.M. the 92nd Illinois, deployed on foot, rushed forward to cross the creek. At the same time, Beebe's guns opened fire on the Confederate line, a fire which was answered by Rivers' and Howell's guns. The *Daily Telegraph and Confederate* reported that

---

and Pritchard's (consolidated)-four 12-pounder howitzers, and Jeffrey's-four 12-pounder Napoleons. The total number of guns in these batteries was 39. As late as 9 January 1865, Lieutenant Colonel Richard M. Cuyler, Arsenal Commander, wrote Cobb's Adjutant, Captain R.J. Hallet, "I am of the impression that several pieces of artillery were sent by Genl Hood to Macon. Cuyler to Hallet, Macon, 9 January 1865, Cobb Papers, 1865. Chief of Ordnance Gorgas, in a note enclosed with Cuyler's letter, commented: "It is thought that Genl Hood, previous to his late movements sent to the rear some pieces of artillery &c. Please find out and let me know how many and where these pieces are. They were left by him somewhere as a 'reserve' I believe." Gorgas to Cuyler, Richmond, 28 December 1864, enc. in Cuyler to Hallet, Macon, 9 January 1865, Telegrams Sent, Arsenal, 1862-65.

[106] *Macon Daily Telegraph and Confederate,* 28 November 1864; Eugenius A. Nisbet, "Statement of Colonel S.M. Colmes, commanding Camp Wright, near Macon Georgia, to the petition of Elbert B. McBurnett for writ of Habeas Corpus to Judge Oliver A. Lochrane," Macon, 27 February 1865, Eugenius A. Nisbet Letters, 1864, July - 1866, February, DU; "Statement of Colonel S.M. Colmes to Petition of William L. Murray for writ of habeas corpus to Judge Oliver A. Lochrane," Macon, 16 March 1865, Ibid. On September 28, 1864, Captain Robert L. Barry had been ordered to turn over his battery, horses, and equipment of the Mississippi Artillery and report with his men to General Wright, commanding the Post at Macon. Captain Edmund D. Baxter's Tennessee Light Artillery Company was stationed at East Macon on the Clinton Road during the period November-December 1864. Civil War Centennial Commission, *Tennesseans in The Civil War A Military History of Confederate Union Units with Available Rosters of Personnel,* In two Parts, Part 1, Nashville: Civil War Centennial Commission, pp. 125, 184.

"Col. Colmes, now properly aroused to the imminent danger threatening his position, rushed to the scene of action. The old Hero, having seen the smoke of other battles, and heard the booming of other guns, and crack of other rifles, was not alarmed, but he was surprised."[107]

Colmes threw his whole force into line of battle. Major Thorpe of the 31st Tennessee Regiment deployed and advanced a line of skirmishers under his command while Colmes, "with his hat off, seeming to forget his years, his gray hairs and white beard, sprang to the front, waved his hat and cheered on his advancing lines."[108] At this juncture Atkins ordered the 10th Ohio to charge the Left Section of Rivers' Battery which was placed in the road just west of Walnut Creek on the East slope of Dunlap's Hill. Atkins placed the 92nd Illinois in line to hold the creek crossing and the road. The 5th Ohio was held in reserve to support the 10th Ohio if the latter regiment gained a sufficient advantage. The 10th, supported by two squadrons of the 92nd, crossed the creek "in a most difficult place," and the regiment, consisting of about 450 men, "charged in column of fours" up the road. This dashing charge, in which the cavalrymen used their sabers, drove Thorpe's pickets back upon the main Confederate line.[109] Sanderson described the charge, "The distance to reach the guns was something over half a mile along a road through deep woods which concealed the enemy's guns and their works. The regiment…charged along the road, [and] reached the enemy's guns." The main Confederate line stretched behind the guns with long lines of breastworks and rifle pits filled with Combs' infantry.[110]

The Left Section of Rivers' Battery, two twelve-pounder howitzers commanded by Lieutenant Shea, was placed in a redoubt which completely blocked the Cross Keys Road, known as the Old Garrison Road, directly in front of the gate which led to Captain Samuel S. Dunlap's house. The artillerymen tried desperately to fire their cannon at the advancing troopers but one of Shea's guns was equipped with faulty friction primers, five of which failed to fire when the gun was charged with canister; this caused the cannon to fall into the hands of the 10th Ohio. Some of the Federal troopers even charged into the redoubt and temporarily captured it. Sanderson wrote that his men could have spiked Shea's howitzers if they had possessed the proper equipment. Some of the Confederate militia broke when Sanderson's men entered the redoubt, but others rallied to prevent the Federals from entering the main Confederate fortifications. At this crisis Captain Howell's four Napoleons, stationed at Fort Hawkins, in rear of the Confederate line, poured a continuous and well-directed fire into the right flank of the charging 10th Ohio. The Confederate infantry,

---

[107] *Daily Telegraph and Confederate,* 28 November 1864.
[108] Ibid.
[109] Smith D. Atkins' Report, *OR,* 44: Pt. 1, 390.
[110] Thomas W. Sanderson Report, Ibid., 404.

consisting of six or seven convalescent soldiers under Lieutenant McCartley, and a number of men from Captain Bellamy's battery who were serving as infantry, fired a volley into the advance of the Federals. Bellamy's men, commanded by Lieutenant W.D. Hooper, had just arrived on the field, and did not have time to form a line of battle. Hooper wrote "but notwithstanding the disadvantage, we drove them in a few minutes."[111]

The Federals withdrew across Walnut Creek in good order to a position two or three hundred yards from their point of greatest penetration, leaving several dead horses and Captain J.H. Hafford, commanding Companies C and M of the 10th Ohio who led the charge, a prisoner. His horse had been shot and killed a few yards from the Confederate fort on Dunlap's Hill by a fifteen-year-old boy named Asa Clark, a member of Rivers' Battery who had, like most of the Confederate defenders, fought on foot.[112] Atkins praised the conduct of his men, exclaiming "The charge was made under the fire of nine pieces of artillery, and was gallantly and well done."[113] Atkins noted that the 10th Ohio temporarily captured the Confederate outer works and nine pieces of artillery. However, "a steadier line was back of the militia, and the 10th Ohio, not without loss, withdrew. The Federal objective, however, was to hold the Confederates in place while they tore up the tracks of the Georgia Central Railroad. Sherman, Atkins believed, "never intended to make" an assault upon Macon.[114]

Wheeler, who arrived on the field soon after the charge of the 10th Ohio was repulsed, found the intervals between the railroad bridge, the Dunlap's Hill fort, and Fort Hawkins unprotected. He quickly placed Harrison's and Akins' Brigades in line to cover these unprotected areas.[115]

During the attack on Dunlap's Hill, the ten-man force guarding the strategic railroad bridge over Walnut Creek, was forced back, by some of the 92nd Illinois fighting on foot. Captain E. S. Hance of the 24th Tennessee, observing the withdrawal of the bridge guard, rushed to the bridge with a force of twelve or fourteen men. Forming line of battle, Hance and his men fired a few volleys into the Federals, drove them back, and held the troopers in check, preventing the bridge from being burned.[116]

---

[111] Ibid.; *Macon Daily Telegraph and Confederate,* 22 November and 1 December 1864.

[112] *Daily Telegraph and Confederate*, 22 November, 1 December 1864; Thomas W. Sanderson's Report, *OR*, 44: Pt. 1, 390.

[113] Smith D. Atkins Report, Ibid., 404.

[114] Atkins, *With Sherman's Cavalry,* pp. 10-11.

[115] Joseph Wheeler Report, *OR*, 44: Pt.1, 407.

[116] *Macon Daily Telegraph and Confederate,* 28 November 1864; Reunion Association, *Ninety-Second Illinois Volunteers,* p. 177.

While the fighting was in progress the 9th Ohio Cavalry, with portions of the 5th and 10th, tore up the tracks of the Georgia Central Railroad and the adjacent telegraph wire for about two miles. Other units who participated in destroying the railroad towards and through Griswoldville to Gordon included the 9th Pennsylvania and a detachment from the 92nd Illinois.[117] Colonel William D. Hamilton of the 9th Ohio sent a battalion under the command of Major Bowlus to burn the Georgia Central Railroad bridge over the Ocmulgee River at Macon. This detachment slipped by the embattled Confederates on Dunlap's Hill, and approached the crucial bridge. However, Bowlus found the bridge to be heavily defended by artillery, which opened fire upon him and prevented him from carrying out his mission. Bowlus, however, succeeded in destroying the railroad to within several hundred yards of the bridge.[118]

Casualties for the battle on 20 November included one man killed and two wounded in Bellamy's Battery, two wounded in the 92nd Illinois, seven wounded and twelve horses killed in the 10th Ohio, and, according to a Confederate account, the "leg of a Yankee on the bank of Walnut Creek."[119]

The *Daily Telegraph and Confederate* noted that the Confederate defenders, because of their resistance had "Saved the Government an immense value in public buildings and in manufacturing interest and munitions of war, all of which, but for the daring and intrepidity of the men would now have been in ashes and ruins."[120]

In commenting upon the sharp demonstration before Dunlap's Hill the historian of the 92nd Illinois noted: "The cavalry had demonstrated so strongly upon Macon, that the enemy was effectually deceived, and massed all his cavalry and available forces to guard that point." The destruction of the Central Railroad east of Macon gave Sherman's troops "an open road, uninterrupted by any of the enemy's troops," as the Federal commander continued his March to the Sea. Unfortunately, the demonstration was not without its cost, "Many of our troops were wounded, especially by the Rebel shell, for their nine pieces of artillery kept up incessant fire until dark, our guns replying." The Federals loaded their wounded into ambulances and carried them away with them because they had no hospitals available.[121]

---

[117] Reports of Smith D. Atkins, Thomas J. Jordan, and Matthew Van Buskirk, *OR*, 44: Pt. 1, 390, 386, 394.

[118] William D. Hamilton Report, *OR*, 44: Pt. 1, 401.

[119] *Macon Daily Telegraph and Confederate* 22 and 28 November 1864, Matthew Van Buskirk's Report, *OR*, 44: Pt. 1, 394; Thomas W. Sanderson's Report, Ibid., 404.

[120] *Macon Daily Telegraph and Confederate,* 28 November 1864.

[121] Reunion Association, *Ninety-Second Illinois Volunteers,* 177-78.

Howell Cobb, Jr., Cobb's son and one of his staff, proved more adept at guessing Sherman's intentions than many of the Confederate high command. He noted that Atkins' troopers had succeeded in capturing one of the cannon, "but held it only five minutes." The artillerists had driven them back with clubs, and no farther advance was made upon Macon. Concerning Sherman's objectives, the younger Cobb commented: "I think their object was, not to destroy Macon, but a portion of the Central Rail Road. They have torn up the track as far as McIntire, [Station] No. 16. I suppose ten or fifteen miles is effectually destroyed."[122]

After night had fallen Atkins withdrew his troopers, and Wheeler moved his command to Griswoldville. Smith moved his Georgia Reserves into the lines on Dunlap's Hill after briefly occupying a portion of the defenses west of Macon. Atkins left Van Buskirk's 92nd Illinois behind Walnut Creek throughout the night of the 20th-21st, and some skirmishing occurred, but the major fighting swirled toward the east, with constant skirmishing on 21 November and a pitched battle fought at Griswoldville on the 22nd. The fight there cost the Confederates "51 killed and 472 wounded," according to General Smith. These losses were due to the rashness of the Confederate field commander, Brigadier General Pleasant Phillips.[123]

Howell Cobb, Jr. noted that, at Griswoldville, the Federals opposed General Phillips' militia with both infantry and artillery, with one brigade of cavalry. His figures were close to those given by General Smith, five hundred killed, wounded, and missing. However, Cobb laconically commented: "The enemy lost not one fifth that number." The affair was badly managed by Phillips, and no one knew who gave the order to charge. Cobb believed that the officer [who gave the command] should be shot."[124]

The *Daily Telegraph and Confederate's* correspondent commented upon the gallantry of the militia at Griswoldville, saying they "behaved with distinguished gallantry, advancing upon the enemy's breastworks in perfect order and no straggling. They charged through an open field within fifty yards of the Yankee works and maintained their ground until ordered to withdraw."[125]

---

[122] Howell Cobb, Jr. to Mary McKinley, Macon, 24 November 1864, Cobb-Erwin-Lamar Collection. For a brief account of the Battle of Griswoldville see Ibid.

[123] Smith D. Atkins' and Matthew Van Buskirk's Reports, *OR*, Vol. 44: Pt. 1, 390, 394; Gustavus W. Smith's Report, Ibid., 413; Smith, *Georgia Militia*, 667; Atkins, *With Sherman's Cavalry*, p. 11; Reunion Association, *Ninety-Second Illinois Volunteers*, 177.

[124] Howell Cobb, Jr. to Mary McKinley, Macon, 24 November 1864, Cobb-Erwin-Lamar Collection.

[125] *Macon Daily Telegraph and Confederate*, 24 November 1864.

As the fighting receded to the east Macon gradually returned to normal. By 24 November the Southern Express Company had resumed business, and freight was being shipped from all points except Augusta and Savannah and destinations to the east. Refugees who had fled the city earlier were returning, and the community was considered safe. By the end of November many stores had reopened "and the city has resumed something of its business appearence [sic]."[126] A reporter for the *Daily Telegraph and Confederate* succinctly concluded, "By the beginning of next week, Macon will look as it did before Sherman's scoundrels threatened the city."[127]

Sherman's men failed to capture a city which they did not really intend to take. By the November 1864 Macon had been saved twice. Would the luck of the city and her people hold in the twilight days of the Confederacy?

---

[126] *Macon Daily Telegraph and Confederate,* 25, 26, and 28 November 1864.
[127] Ibid., 1 December 1864.

Chapter 14

Macon in the Final Winter of the War

After the departure of Kilpatrick and Atkins and their men life in Macon slowly returned to some degree of normalcy, although much excitement continued, as it had, throughout the war years. Nathan C. Munroe, Jr. wrote his daughter Bannie that the times in Macon were exciting, but, by 24 November the community was becoming quieter. He hoped that the Federals would make no further demonstration against Macon. "There seems," Munroe asserted, "to be no enemy this side of the Ocmulgee." Trains on the Macon and Western Railroad were running again as far up the line as Griffin. Vineville was nearly deserted, but the encampments were still nearby, and the officers occasionally ate at Sylvan Lodge. Munroe pitied the soldiers who "are calling for something to eat all the time." He tried not to turn any of them away. The crisis, however, was not over for Georgia because Sherman approached the seaboard. "If we allow the Federals," he wrote, "to reach the seaboard I fear there is much trouble for us." However, all was in God's hands. After all, God had answered the prayers of the people and prevented, Munroe believed, the Federals from overrunning Macon.[1] On 26 November Munroe wrote Bannie "the town is getting more quiet-and our village but for the militia would seem about like a 'devoted village' so many have gone away."[2]

Unfortunately, Wheeler's troopers had scattered around Macon stealing mules and committing other depredations. General Richard Taylor had issued an order requiring all stock taken by Wheeler's men to be returned to its owners if identified by proof of ownership.[3] Brigadier General B.D. Fry, commenting upon the outrages committed upon civilians by Wheeler's troops, observed: "The whole country from here to the Ocmulgee appears to be full of stragglers

---

[1] Nathan C. Munroe, Jr. to Bannie Kell, Macon, 24 November 1864, Kell Letters, 1860-1864.

[2] Nathan Munroe, Jr. to Bannie Kell, Macon, 26 November 1864, Ibid.

[3] Ibid., Nathan Munroe, Jr. to Hendley Varner, Sylvan Lodge, 24 November 1864, Ibid.

from the cavalry commands. Complaints are made here almost daily from the surrounding counties of their depredations."[4]

Some good news arrived from the various battle fronts. Hood was "steadily progressing in Middle Tennessee and the Yankees are evacuating many of the towns," and the Confederates had reoccupied Atlanta where people were returning to their homes. Prayer meetings were held at Munroe's own Christ Episcopal Church, but they were very poorly attended and, he noted, there seemed to be "a want of gratitude for our deliverance which may bring upon us a still further punishment."[5]

After Sherman bypassed Macon with the bulk of his force, there was much speculation in the city about his route. One of Cobb's sons, Howell, Jr., wrote his fiancee, Mary McKinley, then refugeeing from Milledgeville, that her home town was spared much destruction although the penitentiary, arsenal, and railroad depot were burned. The Federals had burned everything at "The Hurricane, a large plantation owned by the Cobbs in Baldwin County near Milledgeville, while the Mayor of Milledgeville had called upon Mayor Collins for assistance. It was as yet uncertain where Sherman would go, although the younger Cobb believed that "Augusta and interior cities are in no danger." Sherman would "be afraid to risk an attack upon any place when resistance would be made." Howell, Jr. felt that was the case with Macon. One defeat and Sherman's army "would become demoralized. And like Stoneman; his entire force would be scattered–and most of it captured." Cobb, had met General Taylor who was in Macon during the crisis caused by Sherman's approach and the Kilpatrick-Atkins Attack, and was favorably impressed with the Louisianian. He felt Taylor "was a man of fine mind & good judgment. He would make a bold but prudent commander, hence a successful one."[6] Lucy Barrow Cobb, wife of John Addison Cobb wrote, "The Yankees visited Genl. Cobb's plantation in Baldwin- & burnt & destroyed everything there. Fortunately Johnny moved the negro men & stock off in time to save them- everything else was lost- but the negro cabins- which were left standing."[7]

As Sherman's March proceeded toward Southeastern Georgia the danger to Macon receded. First Lieutenant Edmund D. Baxter, commanding his battery in East Macon, asked Major Lamar Cobb, who served as his father's Assistant Adjutant General, for permission to requisition some twelve-pounder howitzers

---

[4] B.D. Fry to Cobb, Augusta, 16 December 1864, Cobb Papers, 1864.

[5] Nathan Munroe, Jr. to Bannie Kell, Sylvan Lodge, 1 December 1864, Ibid.

[6] Howell Cobb, Jr. to Mary McKinley, Macon, 26 November 1864, Cobb-Erwin-Lamar Collection.

[7] Lucy Cobb to "Cousin Bessie," Americus, GA., 28 November 1864, Barrow Papers. For additional details concerning the burning of the Cobbs' Baldwin Plantation see Lucy Cobb to David C. Barrow, Americus, 28 November 1864, Ibid.

from the Macon Arsenal with the necessary ammunition and equipment so he could man a stationary battery in a section of the defensive line in East Macon.[8] By 30 November Pope Barrow, brother of Lucy Cobb and one of Howell Cobb's aides, noted, that the closest Federal was at least fourteen miles east of Macon [they were much farther].[9] By 1 December it was known that they had crossed the Oconee. "Their destination," Lucy Cobb opined, "is now thought to be Savannah, Port Royal, or Brunswick." She added: "When will we see the end of all this?"[10] As Sherman's troops moved farther away from Macon Nathan C. Munroe breathed a strong sigh of relief. Vineville was quiet again, most of the military had gone, and many of the refugees were returning.[11]

The officers responsible for the defense of Macon were concerned about Sherman's route and the fact that Hood had taken the Army of Tennessee into Middle Tennessee. Beauregard informed Cobb on 2 December of his plans to go from Opelika, Alabama, to Savannah.[12] The following day, Beauregard ordered Cobb to assume control and direct administration of the Georgia District without reference to Hood. All communications must be sent directly to Beauregard.[13]

During the next two or three weeks the military situation remained fluid and uncertain. On the 13th Beauregard wanted Cobb to repair the telegraph line between Macon and Augusta.[14] Two days later Beauregard wanted an update on the repair of several railroads and telegraph lines. It would be advisable, the Creole General decided, to concentrate all available resources on a single telegraph line from Milledgeville to Maxfield and Augusta.[15]

While the military authorities were attempting to assess the damage caused by Sherman's advance through Middle Georgia, life in Macon continued on a somewhat tense but even keel. Even while Sherman's troops approached the city the theater continued to function. On 4 November Miss Fannie Kemble, one of the most famous actresses of the day, appeared in a play entitled "The Spectre Bridegroom."[16] Plays continued even during the March to the Sea. On November 23, the *Daily Telegraph and Confederate* advertised the presentation

---

[8] First Lieutenant Edmund D. Baxter to Major Lamar Cobb, Baxter's Battery, East Macon, 25 November 1864, Cobb Papers, 1864.

[9] Pope Barrow to "My Dear Betsey," Macon, 30 November 1864, Barrow Papers.

[10] Lucy Cobb to "Dearest May," Americus, 1 December 1864, Cobb-Erwin-Lamar Collection.

[11] Nathan C. Munroe to Bannie Kell, Sylvan Lodge, 5 Dec. 1864, Kell Letters.

[12] Beauregard to Cobb, Telegram, Montgomery, 2 Dec. 1864, Cobb Papers, 1864.

[13] Colonel George W. Brent to Cobb, Telegram, Montgomery, 3 December 1864, Ibid. See Beauregard to Cobb, Telegram, Charleston, S.C., 10 December 1864, Ibid.

[14] Beauregard to Cobb, Telegram, Charleston, 13 December 1864, Ibid.

[15] Beauregard to Cobb, Telegram, Charleston, 15 December 1864, Ibid.

[16] *Macon Daily Telegraph and Confederate,* 4 November 1864.

of a "Grand Musical Olio," and "The Prison of Monterey–and Nan."[17] A few days later a writer for the paper noted the presentation of two "Splendid Pieces for Saturday Night." This included singing and dancing on the stage and "Korn Kobb in his Comicalities."[18]

Other portents were not as favorable to municipal happiness during this period. Fires, always the fear of people in a city built largely of wood, became more newsworthy as the memory of the battles fought around Macon receded. On 13 December 1864, a reporter for the *Daily Telegraph and Confederate* described the burning of the Vineville Academy in Vineville, a two-story wooden building. A drunken soldier carelessly made a fire in a fireplace of one of the rooms on the second story of the building, and then fell asleep. A reporter for the paper intoned: "There is too much drinking among the soldiery quartered around Macon, to say nothing about civilians. Let all take a lesson from this awful penalty for a single debauch."[19] Nathan C. Munroe, who witnessed the fire from the upper floor of Sylvan Lodge, saw circles and sparks of fire flying from the top of his house into the yard. Running into the sitting room, he found it was the nearby Academy, and sent one of his servants to the room to make certain that the cinders did not catch his house on fire. However, he wrote, "we have had so much wet and rainy weather the last 3 days that nothing caught & no building was consumed except the Academy." Munroe heard that the drunken soldier went to one of Dr. William Low's slave houses, got some fire, and went to the Academy to start a fire. The soldier then lay down by the fire which reached the floor and burned the building down along with himself. The authorities found his rifle and his remains near the chimney.[20]

In early February the home of former mayor Dr. Methvin S. Thomson was set on fire, undergoing considerable damage. Thomson's servants discovered the blaze at 3:00 A.M. and put it out without alerting the Fire Department. Investigation showed the blaze was started under the house. It destroyed almost all the furnishings of one room, including many valuable books. A reporter for the *Journal and Messenger* complained, "It is time that some one was caught and hung without ceremony."[21]

During this late period of the War, religious services continued. Captain Thomas J. Key, an artillery officer from Alabama, arrived in Macon on the morning of 5 February 1865, and without resting from a long journey, went to the First Presbyterian Church since it was a Sunday. On entering the edifice he

---

[17]Ibid., 23 November 1864.

[18] Ibid., 26 November 1864.

[19] Ibid., 13 December 1864.

[20] Nathan C. Munroe, Jr. to Bannie Kell, Sylvan Lodge, 11 December 1864, Kell Letters.

[21] *Georgia Journal and Messenger,* 1 February 1865.

found "everything done up in order-but such as I think is out of place in a house of worship." Many of the pews, to Keys' consternation, were rented, a custom which he disliked because, as he said, "the house of God should be free to every individual and there should be no reserved seats to bar the stranger when he attends worship." A Black youth served as sexton, but he refused to be seated by anyone, and looked for his own seat. In a few moments some ladies came into the pew, and told Keys it belonged to them. He left the building, later confiding to his diary that "the rental of seats is a degenerate innovation upon Christianity."[22]

The following Sunday, 12 February Key attended the Episcopal Church, but arrived later than he planned and found the building crowded with well-dressed men and women. He noted the building had a beautiful interior "and the stained glass windows gave out many rays of different hues." Key did not like the sermon as well as he did the building, noting it was "fair, but cold and unfeeling." However, he revisited the Presbyterian Church the same day for Sunday evening services and discovered "that at that service the seats were free to all."[23]

On 19 February Key attended services at the Methodist Church, and was greatly impressed by the sermon because the pastor's words "far surpassed his appearance." The sermon, the artillerist felt, "threw entirely new light upon Christian faith, hope, and charity, and delivered an exposition different from any that I had ever heard." Every Sunday, Key noted, the churches were thronged with attractive and well-dressed women, and there were also many men "who are fixed up in a style too rich for such a crisis as this."[24]

Key attended one of the churches on 5 March and, for the first time in three years, saw the Lord's Supper administered. This led him to exclaim: "Oh, how many more privileges we are now enjoying, stationed here, than we have had at any time during the war! Macon is truly a church-going city."[25]

The Alabama artillerist and the men of his company remained in camp about a mile east of Macon in a pine grove during February 1865, waiting for fresh horses for their artillery battalion. The weather of early February was extremely cold and the wind slapped around the campsite so "keenly that there is no such thing as comfort around our fires in the open air." In an effort to keep from freezing, he found a large box with the top off, placed it near the fire and got into

[22] Thomas J. Key Diary, 5 February 1865, in Wirt Armistead Cate, ed., *Two Soldiers The Campaign Diaries of Thomas J. Key, C.S.A., December 7, 1863-May 17,1865 and Robert J. Campbell, USA., January 1, 1864-July 21, 1864* (Chapel Hill: The University of North Carolina Press, 1938) 187.

[23] Ibid., 12 February 1865, 190-191.

[24] Ibid., 19 February 1865, 194-195.

[25] Ibid., 5 March 1865, 199.

it. That kept him warm, although he felt like a "smoked rabbit." Despite the discomfort, he read about seventy pages of a novel entitled *Joseph II and His Court* by Frau Klara Mundt.[26]

Key amused himself by visiting in private homes and being entertained with music and conversation. On one of these occasions he played "an amusing game or play called 'scissors', also a very laughable one called 'the third man'." Key "laughed over these innocent amusements until my sides were sore." Later that night he returned to his cold campfire and bed on the damp ground, "longing for the happy day when we should be allowed to mingle with dear ones at home in the felicities of the family circle."[27]

On the morning of 16 February Key visited Macon to see "the legislative talent of the State," but, unfortunately, the Legislature did not meet due to the lack of a quorum. Therefore, upon the invitation of Maconite Captain C. Freeman and a Sergeant Bailey, he went up to the Wesleyan Female Seminary on College Street [where the Macon Post Office is currently located] to look at the city, including the Village of Vineville to the North. "Macon," Key noted, "is dotted with some residences as fine as can be found in any large city, and the evergreens and the taste in the arrangement of the yards are beautiful beyond description. The residences are palace like and superbly furnished." After dining with Captain Freeman the party went to Rose Hill Cemetery. Key described the burial ground, even then a Macon showplace, as the home of "the sacred dead" which was "adorned and beautified to an extent that is surprising." The graves were excavated and walled with brick before the deceased were interred, and the lots were enclosed, in hundreds of cases, "with rock basement and cast-iron railings of the finest pattern." The Alabamian was impressed by the costly and beautiful monuments, and by the extent of the cemetery, then covering an area of twenty acres and laid off with neat walks, "with here and there fresh springs gurgling from the hillside." At one point the land was excavated to form an artificial grotto floored with crystal rocks. The area contained a beautiful spring with a strong flow of water, and included several artificial ponds in which fish "sported gleefully, giving life to the city of the dead." Key's attention was drawn to one vault in which the long metal coffin, "which had not been affected in the least by the ravages of time," could be plainly seen.[28]

The commonalties of life were changed on occasion during this wet, dreary winter, by speeches intended to arouse the enthusiasm of the people and increase

---

[26] Ibid., 9 February 1865, 190. Joseph II, the son of Empress Maria Theresa, was Emperor of the Austrian Empire during the late 18th Century. Supported by the British and the Prussians, he launched an abortive invasion of Revolutionary France in 1792 which ended in the defeat of his troops at the Battle of Valmy.

[27] Ibid., 13 February 1865, 191.

[28] Ibid., February 16,1865, 192-93.

their desire to continue the war despite constantly-bad news from the battlefront. In mid-February a writer for the *Georgia Journal and Messenger* announced a forthcoming speech by General Cobb "on the state of the country."[29] Cobb spoke at City Hall to an immense crowd. His theme was the avarice of the people, the question of whether the Confederacy had the strength left to conquer the peace, and the methods by which all the Confederate forces might be brought into the field. Key scribbled in his diary: "His remarks were received with the utmost attention and he was often interrupted by immense applause. He said that there are annually 50,000 young men arriving at the age of military duty." Cobb's speech, Key believed, helped to calm the dissatisfaction arising in the people of Georgia.[30]

On the following evening, 17 February, Georgia Senator Benjamin Harvey Hill, one of Davis' champions in the Confederate Senate, gave a speech that "was eloquent and created great enthusiasm." Hill, Key believed, was "a chaste and beautiful speaker," who presented his points with force and effectiveness. Hill told the people that he could "assure them that Virginia and North Carolina have an abundance of provisions to feed Lee's army until harvest." The moderate Georgia Senator noted that the Confederate States produced 50,000 arms, exclusive of pistols, each year, and that if "the enemy were to take all our principal cities we would have enough machinery and powder and ball to continue the war for ten years." Hill criticized Governor Brown whose course was "obstinate, selfish, unfounded, and ambitious."[31]

The principal interest Key showed in Macon, however, were the meetings of the Georgia General Assembly. During the meeting of 17 February Key listened to a message from Governor Brown in which he discussed military matters and "harped almost exclusively upon President Davis and the management of the government." The address was, Key felt, a tirade against certain persons which was "unworthy of a patriot," and asserted, "it was an invitation for Georgians to desert their country and join the foe who is destroying and invading their homes." Brown, Key believed, hated Davis so much that he wanted the legislature to call a convention to change the Confederate Constitution so that a general might be appointed to command all the armies and deny Davis this authority. In conclusion, Key opined "the Governor is an ambitious demagogue

---

[29] *Journal and Messenger*, 15 February 1865. M. J. Crawford wrote Cobb on 16 February that "I am glad to hear that you speak in Macon tonight." M. J. Crawford to Cobb, Columbus, 16 February 1865, Cobb Papers, 1865.

[30] *Macon Daily Telegraph and Confederate*, 17 February 1865; *Key Diary*, 17 February 1865, p. 193.

[31] *Key Diary*, 18 February 1865, p. 194.

who is willing to destroy his country in order to accomplish his wicked and seditious purposes."[32]

On 20 February the Alabama artillerist listened to a discussion in the House on some resolutions from Senator Hill which commended Brown's call for a State constitutional convention, "and announcing to [President Abraham] Lincoln that Georgia- on view of the dishonorable terms he has offered the South-is for the war to the last." The discussion which followed caused much animosity because Confederate Vice President Alexander H. Stephens' faction supported the "narrow and unpatriotic views" of Governor Brown. Key believed that trouble would arise in Georgia from the Brown faction because the Governor was "another ambitious Aaron Burr."[33]

Eliza Andrews had an experience of a different kind while traveling to Macon in late December. Her train suddenly stopped within two miles of Macon, when it reached the bridge over Walnut Creek which had been damaged by Stoneman's troopers in July. A heavy storm had so weakened the damaged structure that it threatened to collapse under the weight of the engine. Many of the men on the train, some of them returning from a Federal military prison, decided to walk into the City, but Eliza was forced to stay on the train. The conductor broke into a supply of hardtack he kept on the train to feed the workmen. By daybreak no arrangements had been made to take the passengers and their baggage into town. An argument broke out because no provisions were made for bringing the passengers into Macon, and a fight appeared about to break out. At 8:00 A.M. an engine and a single boxcar arrived at the other end of the bridge, but had to unload its freight before the passengers could board. Eliza had a difficult time in crossing the bridge which was eighty feet high and half a mile long over a swamp. The creek was fearsome, having been swollen by heavy rain to a torrent. Part of the flooring of the bridge was washed away and the only crossing was a narrow plank, barely two hands wide. The frightened young woman confided to her diary that "Strong-headed men walked along the sleepers on either side, to steady any one that might become dizzy." The porters followed the procession with the trunks, and it seemed a miracle "how they contrived to carry such heavy loads over that dizzy, tottering height." The party reached the Georgia Central Railroad depot only ten minutes after the Southwestern train had left, so they went to the Lanier House where they were placed in comfortable rooms. Charles Day, father of Mary Day, future wife of Sidney Lanier, called on Eliza and other friends. She noted his striking appearance, "with his snow-white hair framing features of such a peculiar dark complexion that he made me think of some antique piece of wood-carving." Her

---

[32] Ibid., pp. 193-94.
[33] Ibid., 20 February 1865, p. 195.

impression of the elder Day was heightened by a "certain stiffness of manner that is generally to be noticed in all men of Northern birth and education."[34]

After the military hospitals returned to Macon from their brief hiatus to keep them from falling into Sherman's hands, the confidence of the surgeons responsible for the care of the sick and wounded men was badly shaken. Surgeon Stanford E. Chaille, in charge of the Ocmulgee Hospital, wrote Medical Director Stout: "In my opinion Macon will not long remain one of the safest places in the Confederacy, and will soon be emptied of troops & hence so given little Hospl. accomodation." Chaille, however, believed it was necessary to keep one or two hospitals in Macon including, hopefully, his own. By the end of November, 1864, Chaille had expanded the Ocmulgee Hospital to house six hundred patients, chiefly through the use of existing buildings and tents. However, the facility had been originally designed to hold only three hundred, a number which Surgeon Chaille asserted he would be glad to get to as soon as the needs of the service permitted.[35]

Surgeon C.B. Gamble wrote Surgeon S.M. Bemiss, the Assistant Medical Director for the Army of Tennessee, that the hospitals were being reestablished in Macon, and all the bunks, stoves, and other hospital property left in the threatened city was being gathered together for use. The Floyd House Hospital was crowded almost to capacity, and Gamble agreed with Surgeon Chaille that at least two hospitals should be kept in Macon, preferably the Blind School Hospital and the Ocmulgee Hospital since military operations might require them. All of the wounded cavalrymen from the battles in Eastern Georgia could be moved into these hospitals as soon as the Central Railroad was opened since 1200 beds would be ready in Macon.[36]

When the Polk Hospital was moved to Macon in late February 1865, Medical Examiner Gamble told Dr. Stout that "it would be impossible to procure buildings in Macon." However, Stout might order the consolidation of the Polk and Blind School Hospitals. If the medical authorities placed the Polk Hospital in Vineville they would have to place the patients in tents. Wards then being built for the patients in Macon would not be ready for patients for six weeks, and only two at that time. Surgeon Parker, Gamble believed, might be an excellent choice to place in charge of both hospitals.[37]

---

[34] Entry for 24 December 1864, in Spencer Bidwell King, Jr., ed., *The War-Time Journal of a Georgia Girl 1864-1865* (Macon: The Ardivan Press, 1960) 49-55.

[35] Chaille to Stout, Ocmulgee Hospital, Macon, 30 November 1864, Stout Papers.

[36] C.B. Gamble to S.M. Bemiss, Macon, 25 November 1864, Stout Papers, EU. The two hospitals were needed because of the actions at Dunlap's Hill and Griswoldville.

[37] C.B. Gamble to Samuel H. Stout, Macon, 24 February 1865.

In the winter of 1864-1865 a period of quiet descended upon Macon. On 18 December Howell Cobb, Jr. wrote his fiancee, Mary McKinley, that there was "no news from any quarter." About the only news that seemed worth recording was the fact that the telegraph was once again in operation from Macon to Charleston via Millen.[38] However, Nathan C. Munroe wrote about the same time that "The public mind is becoming much exercised about the state of our affairs." "But," he added "God knows and will I trust make us to see that his doings are all for the best."[39]

For Howell Cobb, the time was one of uncertainty, although January began on a pleasant note. On the 6th the Cobbs entertained two distinguished guests, General Beauregard and Commodore Raphael Semmes. Howell, Jr. described the latter as a man who possessed "a very fine eye, dark hazel." He was an able man who, unfortunately, spread morale-boosting rumors common among the Southern leadership at the time. The commercial interest of the North, Semmes reassured his listeners, was badly crippled, and felt it was "ridiculous" for the Confederate Government to create a navy. He felt, accurately, that the object of the Confederacy should be to destroy the North's commerce vessels "And not endeavour to meet their war vessels." Beauregard, the younger Cobb, believed, had "nothing remarkable about him- except his agreeable manners." He might be "a fine engineer" but should not be considered a great man. Young Cobb reported 'We have but three great generals Lee, Johnston & Dick Taylor.'[40]

In mid-January, Cobb received an unpleasant surprise in the form of a message from Adjutant and Inspector General Samuel Cooper which threatened his future plans to defend Macon to the last extremity. Cooper wrote, "it is thought best that your HdQrs should be at Augusta heretofore to the place at which the conscript service has been administered and whence the commandants of conscripts have been withdrawn for service in the field as the point in Georgia [Augusta] most immediately threatened. Your presence and command may serve to collect there a large number of the reserve forces. You will therefore establish yourself there with all practicable dispatch."[41] Brigadier General W.L. Browne in Augusta wired Cobb on 17 January: "Your presence here is vitally important the condition of affairs requires immediate and authoritative action."[42]

---

[38] Howell Cobb, Jr. to Mary McKinley, Macon, 18 December 1864, Cobb-Erwin-Lamar Collection.

[39] Nathan C. Munroe, Jr. to Hendley Varner, Sylvan Lodge, 5 January 1865, Kell Letters.

[40] Howell Cobb, Jr. to Mary McKinley, Macon, 6 January 1865, Cobb-Erwin-Lamar Collection.

[41] Cooper to Cobb, Telegram, Richmond, 11 January 1865, Cobb Papers, 1865.

[42] Browne to Cobb, Telegram, Augusta, 17 January 1865.

Although Cobb dutifully began the transfer of his headquarters to Augusta,[43] he wrote Cooper a diplomatic letter disagreeing with the transfer. Cobb felt "it is still more important that I should keep my Head Quarters at Macon. The defense of South Western Georgia (*the granary of the Confederacy*) is left without troops, and at Augusta I could take no steps in time to meet a raid."[44] Cobb did not like the assignment at all, confiding to his wife that "The order was very unexpected to me and I am at a loss to account for it. There is no sense in it- and is not only a great sacrifice of my personal comfort & interest but is equally unfortunate for the public service." He informed Mary Anne that he had written the War Department about the order, "& if they have not lost all their senses at Richmond–or become uncurably perverse and obstinate–the order will be countermanded & I shall return to Macon in a few days." He left the house in charge of Major Lamar Cobb, one of his sons. He also wanted his son John Addison Cobb, in charge of most of his private business affairs on his plantations, to come up to Macon from Augusta for a day or two and see that everything was in order. Mary Anne, Cobb felt, should return to Macon from a home they had purchased in Americus (a safer place for her at the time], and might want to move to Athens so they could be closer to each other.[45]

Cobb waited for several days to receive an answer from Richmond to his letter of 16 January, but as late as 25 January no answer had arrived, although the politician-turned-general expected to receive one in the near future.[46] While in Augusta Cobb received the news that Lieutenant General D.H. Hill had been ordered to command the District of Georgia with headquarters in Augusta. Cobb, who did not like Hill, was relieved to receive word from Lieutenant General William J. Hardee that Hill's new assignment did not affect the Georgian's position as Commander of Reserves for Georgia.[47] Howell, Jr. wrote one of his brothers on 26 January that there was still no news from Richmond concerning the elder Cobb's appointment.[48] However, on the same date Cobb received a telegram from Cooper informing him that, "As Maj Gen D H Hill is in command of the District at Augusta you can return to your former position."[49] Cobb, despite the order which sent him back to Macon, remained in Augusta

---

[43] Cobb to Brent, Macon, 16 January 1865, Cobb Letter Book, 1864-65, p. 449.

[44] Cobb to Cooper, Macon, 16 January 1865, Ibid., p. 447. Italics authors.

[45] Cobb to his wife, Macon, 16 January 1865, Cobb Papers, 1865.

[46] Pope Barrow to Howell Cobb, Jr., Augusta, 25 January 1865, Ibid.

[47] Ibid., William J. Hardee to Cobb, Telegram, Charleston, 25 January 1865, Ibid.

[48] Howell Cobb, Jr. to "Dear Brother," Macon, 26 January 1865, Ibid.

[49] Cooper to Cobb, Telegram, Richmond, 26 January 1865, Ibid.

until 29 January. He returned to Macon by the end of the month, and was once more established in his old headquarters at the Bear's Den.[50]

During the period that Cobb was temporarily assigned to Augusta, a number of important changes had occurred in the command structure of Georgia and the Lower South. On 20 January, Brigadier General William T. Wofford, a veteran of the Army of Northern Virginia, was assigned to command the Reserve Forces of Northern Georgia, under Cobb at Macon.[51] Asher Ayres, a prominent Macon merchant, wanted to send a steamboat down the Ocmulgee River to bring up rosin and other supplies "much needed by the Government & people," but needed Cobb's written authority to do this.[52] At the end of January, General D.H. Hill wired General William W. Mackall, in charge at Macon in Cobb's absence, to send Palmer's Artillery Battalion, then at Macon, to Augusta because it was thought Sherman [who was still confusing his opponents concerning his movements] was moving on the latter city.[53] Even such a mundane matter as the seizure of tobacco in Macon was brought to Cobb's attention.[54]

However, more important matters demanded Cobb's attention during this period. C.B. Duffield, in Secretary of War Seddon's Office, wired to say: "The Secty of War directs that the impressment of slaves be hastened as rapidly as possible their labor is greatly needed by order."[55]

While he was temporarily assigned to Augusta Cobb received a copy of Special Field Orders from Beauregard announcing General Hood's resignation "at his own request." General Richard Taylor, then commanding the Department of Alabama, Mississippi and East Louisiana, was ordered by the War Department to temporarily assume command of the Army of Tennessee.[56]

Cobb was also troubled by the withdrawal of units from Macon to serve in other areas even more threatened than Middle Georgia. One of these withdrawals involved the transfer of some of the artillery batteries around Macon. Several residents of East Macon Precinct petitioned Cobb to retain Captain Howell's Battery of Major Martin's Battalion in its position protecting the raid-prone area

---

[50] Howell Cobb, Jr. to his mother, Macon, 28 January 1865, Ibid.; Cobb to his wife, Macon, 31 January 1865, Ibid.

[51] H.L. Clay, A.A.G., Special Orders No. 16, Richmond, 20 January 1865, Ibid.

[52] "Syd" [nephew of Cobb] to Cobb, Macon, 21 January 1865, Ibid.

[53] General D.H. Hill to William W. Mackall, Telegram, Augusta, 29 January 1865, Ibid.

[54] Major Norman W. Smith, Chief Inspector, to Cobb, Augusta, 3 February 1865, Ibid.

[55] C.B. Duffield to Cobb, Telegram, Richmond, 28 January 1865, Ibid.

[56] Beauregard to Cobb, Special Field Orders, Hdqrs., Military Division of the West, 23 January 1865, Ibid.

around the bridge over Walnut Creek and the approach to Dunlap's Hill and Fort Hawkins. "This battery has been for several months camped in this immediate neighborhood," they noted, "& it is with pleasure that we state no better behaved set of men have been camped in Macon since the War." The unit had been engaged in patrol duty, and protected the homes of citizens from thieves. These latter individuals included soldiers from the various camps about the City. The petitioners concluded: "East Macon will be exposed to the thieving rascals around us, that will no longer have any fear of apprehension or restraint & will give a loose rein to their vandalism." Such a unit, which had proved its "great usefulness in the community," should be retained.[57]

Another problem involved a newspaper published in Macon called *The Southern Confederacy,* which Colonel George C. Gibbs—then commanding at Camp Sumter at Andersonville—believed contained articles which incited both the prisoners and the soldiers who guarded them. Gibbs assured Cobb that he would prevent the circulation among both groups if he could do so. Cobb concurred and suppressed the paper.[58] It was no wonder that Cobb wrote his wife on 16 February that his table was crowded with letters and his office with visitors. His head, Cobb explained, was crowded "with matters & things in general so you will excuse this pretext for a letter."[59]

Another of Cobb's problems involved personnel matters. Whether it was the detail of Private Henry G. Ralston of Company "D," Blount's Battalion to the Nitre and Mining Service because Ralston was assigned to "light duty;" the desired resignation of Assistant Adjutant General and District Provost Marshal Charles M. Peden; the arrival of Brigadier General Hugh W. Mercer in Macon to assist in its defense; the assignment of Colonel Leon Von Zinken of the 20th Louisiana Regiment to command a sub-district in West Georgia; or his own assignment to temporarily command the Department of Tennessee and Georgia, Cobb was overwhelmed by paperwork.[60]

---

[57] W.S. Brantly, W.J. Lightfoot, J.B. Lightfoot and others to Cobb, East Macon, 1 February 1865, Ibid.

[58] Colonel George C. Gibbs to Cobb, Camp Sumter, Andersonville, 15 February 1865, Ibid.; Cobb to Gibbs, Macon, 16 February 1865, Cobb Order & Letter Book, 1865, 8.

[59] Cobb to his wife, Macon, 16 February 1865, Cobb Papers, 1865.

[60] Henry A. Farrow to Cobb, Office Nitre & Mining Bureau, District of Georgia, Macon, 24 February 1865, Ibid.; Charles M. Peden, Macon, 28 February 1865, Ibid.; R.J. Hallett, Special Orders No. 55, Macon, 14 March 1865, Howell Cobb Special Orders Book, 1865, p. 158; Cobb, Special Orders No. 59, Macon, 20 March 1865, Ibid. Von Zinken's subdistrict was composed of Troup, Merriwether, Harris, Talbot, Taylor, Muscogee, Macon Chattahoochee, and Schley Counties.; Kinloch Falconer, A.A.G., Army of Tennessee, Special Orders No. 12, Headquarters near Smithfield, N.C., 27 March 1865, Cobb Papers, 1865.

Cobb was also concerned with the illegal exportation of cotton down the Ocmulgee River, and eventually to Europe. A men named N. McDuffie wrote Cobb from Hawkinsville that "The true men of this section are determined that the Ocmulgee River shall not be used for an illegal trade with the enemies of our country, and they care very little whether the effort is made by high officials, or the lowest characters in the land." McDuffie believed that the laws governing the export of cotton should be enforced. Did Cobb have the authority to grant permits to "engage in such a traffic?" If so, the people of Hawkinsville should be told. In any regard the people of the area were "determined to prevent this traffic on this river." Cobb disagreed with McDuffie's position, but assured the disgruntled Georgian that he had the authority to grant such permits. On 31 March Cobb received official permission to issue such permits for the export of cotton on Governor Brown's certification that the cotton belonged exclusively to the State of Georgia. Cobb also received authority to import salt for the use of the State.[61]

Another of Cobb's problems involved either repairing or destroying railroads. On 19 December 1864, Beauregard ordered Cobb to use ten wagons then in Atlanta to support work on repairing railroad lines disrupted by Sherman. George H. Hazelhurst wired Cobb from Columbus on the 29th that he had "received no orders about repairing any Rail Road." Beauregard also wanted Cobb to have the railroad from Atlanta towards Chattanooga destroyed as far up the line as possible. A bridge blown down on the Macon and Western Railroad needed repair because "material for reconstructing Georgia Roads are transported over that line." General William J. Hardee, however, wanted the harried Cobb to "take immediate measures to have the rail road & other bridges over the Altamaha destroyed."[62]

Another problem confronting the harassed politician-turned-general involved rumors of raids, talk which was sparked by The March to the Sea. At the end of December, Cobb received a message from H.W. Fielden, A. A. G. to Hardee in Charleston, that Hardee had no information about a Federal force moving toward

---

[61] N. McDuffie to Cobb, Hawkinsville, Georgia, 23 March 1865, Cobb Papers, 1865; Cobb to McDuffie, Macon, 30 March 1865, Cobb Order and Letter Book, 1865, pp. 64-6; Samuel Cooper to Cobb, Telegram, Richmond, 31 March 1865, Cobb Papers, 1865.

[62] Major Norman W. Smith to Cobb, Telegram, Augusta, 19 December 1864, Ibid.; George H. Hazelhurst to Cobb, Telegram, Columbus, 29 December 1864, Ibid.; Beauregard to Cobb, Telegram, Charleston, 30 December 1864, Ibid.; J.M. Hattle to Cobb, Telegram, Columbus, 30 December 1864, Ibid.; Hardee to Cobb, Telegram, Charleston, 31 December 1864, Ibid.. See also John M. Otey, A.A.G., to Cobb, Telegram, Charleston, 20 December 1864, Ibid. and Beauregard to Cobb, Telegram, Charleston, 23 December 1864, Ibid.

Andersonville. Major A.M. Allen, District Commissary for the Columbus District, wrote Cobb that a large amount of corn in the vicinity of Albany should be moved immediately to Macon and Columbia because of possible raids. If "there be any prospect of raids upon that section soon," Allen exclaimed, "I would most respectfully suggest that authority be given to the receiving officers to impress wagons and teams...to secure the prompt removal of the corn." In late February, General Taylor reassured a by then anxious Cobb, to warn him "in time should Columbus be threatened it will be after Montgomery is attacked or threatened."[63]

In early February 1865, Taylor began to move the remnants of the shattered Army of Tennessee through Macon en route to South Carolina to oppose Sherman. On the 3-4 February General Benjamin F. Cheatham's Corps passed through the City by rail. General William B. Bate's Division also went through. Howell Cobb, Jr. confided to his fiancee, Mary McKinley, that "The same train that brings the troops from Columbus- carried them in to Milledgeville, sometimes without stopping." If the troops needed rations, arms, and ammunition, they remained in Macon for an hour or two, otherwise they continued on their way.[64]

It depressed Cobb to observe the remains of the once-powerful Army of Tennessee. Of the 35,000 men that Hood took into Tennessee, Cobb believed, "we cannot now count upon twenty thousand, and I hear that not five thousand will get to Augusta in time to take part in the fight." The principal blame for the destruction of the army, Cobb believed, had to be placed on President Davis' shoulders because he had removed Cobb's friend, General Joseph E. Johnston, from command. But, Cobb felt, "It is too late to correct the evil, and there is too much obstinacy to palliate it by his restoration." Cobb had Cheatham in for lunch earlier that day and sent the well-fed corps commander on his way to fight Sherman.[65]

As the movement of troops continued, Beauregard ordered Cobb to direct all commanding officers to march their troops to wherever rail transportation was available without waiting for trains to pick them up in Macon.[66]

Cobb took his responsibilities seriously. He felt, in early February, that "It is an important time for me to be here [Macon]." But, unless Davis gave up his

---

[63] H.W. Fielden, A.A.G., to Cobb, Telegram, Charleston, 31 December 1864, Cobb Papers, 1865, A.M. Allen to Cobb, Office District Commissary, Columbus, 31 December 1864, Ibid.; Richard Taylor to Cobb, Telegram, Meridian, MS., 25 February 1865, Ibid.

[64] Howell Cobb, Jr. to Mary McKinley, Macon, 4 February 1865, Cobb-Erwin-Lamar Collection.

[65] Cobb to his wife, Macon, 6 February 1865, Cobb Papers, 1865.

[66] Brent to Cobb, Telegram, Augusta, 8 February 1865, Ibid.

long-held opposition to Johnston, Sherman, Cobb believed, "is destined to go wherever he pleases." It was the "common talk" of both officers and men as they passed through Macon that they "never could be got to fight until Johnston was restored to them." One officer told Cobb that if Davis restored Johnston to command it "would bring back the absentees at once and the army would be as large as when he left it."[67]

He got his wish on 25 February when Johnston, then at Charlotte, under the authority of the War Department, issued Special Orders No. 1 assuming command of the Army of Tennessee, and of all troops in the Department of South Carolina, Georgia, and Florida.[68]

As the wet, cold winter of 1864-1865 slowly drew to a close Captain Key received an order from General Beauregard ordering his battery, greatly reduced in numbers because of constant service and many battles, to remain in Macon. Key was told that Captain W.C. Jeffries would take his place in the field, but the former officer missed serving with the now-dead General Patrick R. Cleburne's Division. Key applauded that unit when he confided to his diary: "I had stood by these gallant men in so many heroic charges, and the booming of my guns had cheered and inspired them in so many instances, that alike we shall miss each other." On February 23, he received an order to move his camp to the position vacated by Captain Jeffries on the Columbus-Macon Road. At the new encampment Key and his men found good cabins, "and gladly and for the first time in twelve months did we find shelter from the snows and storms, not even having had tents heretofore." On the following day Key visited Colonel James H. Hallonquist, commander of the Tennessee artillery units then in Macon, and Brigadier General Mackall to learn what orders in the way of papers, reports, and other items he needed for his new position.[69]

During the next two days Key and his men stayed in their little cabins "with the tenacity that a groom adheres to his beautiful young bride." On 26 February he watched the wagon trains of Johnston's army as they passed through Macon towards South Carolina. Key mustered his company on the 28th under orders from Colonel Hallonquist. He also received several foreigners, prisoners whom the Confederates had captured, who came to the artillery camp and asked to be enlisted in the Confederate Army. Key swore in two of them, a Hungarian and an Irishman, "to the cause of independence and the South." During early March, Key captured a Black man who had left his owner, and rode

---

[67] Cobb to his wife, Macon, 9 February 1865, Ibid.

[68] Joseph E. Johnston, Special Orders No. 1, Charlotte, NC, 25 February 1865, copy in Ibid.

[69] *Key Diary,* 22-24 February 1865, Ibid., 196-97.

into Macon to advertise him for sale. On the following day he picked up a young black who had left his owner, and also advertised him.[70]

However, despite these interludes, Key presided over a meeting of his company during which resolutions were passed proclaiming the reenlistment of the entire company for an additional period of four years; denouncing Georgia Governor Brown as simply another Aaron Burr; appealing to the people of Georgia to support the Confederacy; and deploring Lincoln's reelection. Copies of these resolutions were sent to the newspapers in Macon, Augusta, and Columbus, and to the *Memphis Appeal* which was then being published in Columbus.[71]

Captain John McIntosh Kell also disagreed with Confederate Vice President Alexander H. Stephens and Georgia Governor Brown. The now-famous Executive Officer of the "Alabama" who, through his wife "Bannie" had close connections with Macon, wrote his Mother from Richmond on 2 March 1865, that Stephens and Brown were stirring up dissatisfaction throughout Georgia against the Confederate Government. He observed: "I cannot for my life understand why the people at home do not appreciate our true position & understand that peace is only to be obtained when the enemy are satisfied that we can not be conquered, then only will we have peace & independence, for I can not believe that we are so craven as to desire peace upon any other conditions."[72]

The concerns of Key and his men about the adherence of Georgians to the Confederate cause were alleviated when Maconites observed a fast day on 10 March. Businesses were closed and, Key believed, "everyone appeared to be in earnest in his petitions to God to bless our cause, give victory to our arms, and restore us to our homes and dear ones."[73] However, at this time not all Southerners felt as hopeful as Key. Bannie Kell wrote her husband on 28 February that "It is believed here [Macon] that Richmond will be evacuated ere long. If so & your vessel has to be destroyed, I trust and pray you will come home & stay till after my confinement."[74]

Key rode into Macon on 13 March to get a recruit from the barracks, but finding there were charges against the man, he abandoned his mission. Taking advantage of his time in the city, he met with Lieutenant John Yerley and Captain Ewing of Arkansas who sat on a board to examine the matter of rations.

---

[70] Ibid., 25 February-2 March 1865, Ibid., 197-98.

[71] Ibid., 3 March 1865, 198.

[72] John M. Kell to his mother, 3 March 1865, E. A. Nisbet Letters, 1864.

[73] *Key Diary*, 10 March 1865, 199.

[74] Bannie Kell to her husband, Sylvan Lodge, 28 February 1865, Kell Letters, 1865-1869. Kell, a captain in the Confederate Navy, was then stationed at Rocketts, the Confederate naval base just below Richmond; Bannie was pregnant.

For three days each week the government issued each soldier a ration of one third of a pound of bacon. For the remaining four days the men received about a gill of sorghum in place of meat. However, Key accepted this with good grace, believing that the Confederate officials had the interest of the country at heart "and intend doing the best they can for all parties." But, even though he wrote brave words, the ration was not sufficient for Key. On 14 March he ate a limited quantity of corn bread and sorghum, and then called on a friend to go to the country with him for two reasons: to become acquainted with the people of the region and to find something to eat. After traveling for seven miles at a slow trot through a "desperately poor country," Key and his companion arrived at the neatly painted home of a Mr. Hollingsworth. Hollingsworth met the two men at the gate and invited them into the parlor. The invitation was extended to dinner during which they "ate heartily, as hungry men will do." Returning to the parlor, the three men discussed politics and Governor Brown. Key described his host as "an intelligent, whole-souled gentleman who is for prosecuting this struggle until we shall become free and independent of the North."[75]

On 19 March Key returned with Dr. Hannum to Hollingsworth's where they met their friend's two daughters who were home from school. The conversation, as usual, turned on politics and the tremendous efforts made by the US Government to conquer the Confederacy. There was some anxiety in the area caused by a smallpox epidemic which caused several deaths. Mrs. Hollingsworth prepared a dinner, and, as Key wrote in his diary, "we aided in dispatching the first turkey that we had seen on the table in a long while."[76]

However, much of Key's activity during late March did not concern eating, but the outfitting of his battery. On 17 March he addressed a letter to General Mackall asking for twenty horses and some rifles to enable his men to capture some deserters who were hiding in the country around Macon. Mackall did not have the horses, but the Brigadier ordered thirty troopers from Lieutenant Colonel Blount's cavalry battalion to report to Key for duty.[77] On 23 March sixteen troopers reported to Key who added ten of his artillerists on foot, "as I had no horses to mount them." The expedition went into the country five miles from Macon and captured some deserters.[78]

This activity around Macon would soon be interrupted by events which began to absorb the attentions of the people of the beleaguered community in the form of another invasion in a completely unexpected direction. This attack would have far-reaching effects upon the busy community along the banks of the Ocmulgee.

---

[75] *Key Diary,* 14 March 1865, p. 201.

[76] Ibid., March 19, 1865, p. 203.

[77] Ibid., 15 and 19 March 1865, pp. 202-03.

[78] Ibid., 23 March 1865, pp. 204-05.

Chapter 15

Wilson's Raid

In March 1865 General George H. Thomas, Commander of the Department of the Cumberland with headquarters at Nashville, Tennessee, sent a mounted cavalry raid against Confederate facilities in the Lower South. The force was commanded by a remarkable young brevet major general named James Harrison Wilson. Wilson was born on 2 September 1837, near Shawneetown, Illinois, a river town located on the Ohio. He attended McKendree College in St. Clair County, Illinois, and entered West Point in 1855. Graduating sixth in his class in 1860, Wilson served as assistant topographical engineer of the Department of Oregon at Fort Vancouver. He was chief topographical engineer of the Port Royal expedition and of the Department of the South. He also participated, in his latter capacity, in the capture of Fort Pulaski at the mouth of the Savannah River in April 1862. During the Maryland Campaign in the fall of 1862 he served as aide-de-camp to Major General George B. McClellan, and participated in the Battles of South Mountain and Sharpsburg. He then served at Grant's headquarters in the West with the rank of staff lieutenant colonel. However, his duties with Grant were primarily concerned with engineering. During the campaign against Vicksburg he was inspector general of the Army of the Tennessee, taking part in all the battles before and after the capture of the city. He became the only officer ever promoted to troop command from Grant's regular staff when he was made brigadier general of volunteers. He continued on staff duty during the Chattanooga Campaign, and served as chief engineer of the army under Sherman which was sent to raise Confederate Lieutenant General James Longstreet's siege of Knoxville. On 17 February 1864 he was appointed Chief of the Cavalry Bureau in Washington. While in this post he showed his outstanding talent for organization and administration. These attributes, together with the tactical sense he later demonstrated, made him an important leader in the War. In the overland campaign against Richmond Wilson was assigned to command a division of cavalry under Sheridan, and led this force with great ability in the many fights of the summer of 1864, both on the way to Petersburg and in the Shenandoah Valley. However, just before the battle of Cedar Creek in late October, his mentor Grant, had him transferred to the Western Theater as

Chief of Cavalry of Major General William T. Sherman's Military Division of the Mississippi. This position placed him on a par with Sheridan in the East.

Wilson prepared Brigadier General Hugh Judson Kilpatrick's Division for Sherman's March to the Sea, and recruited, equipped, drilled, and organized the remainder of the cavalry in the West into a powerful corps of 17,000 men. He commanded this force in the victories over Hood at the battles of Franklin and Nashville in November and December 1864.[1]

As Wilson led his 17,000-man force, known as the Cavalry Corps of the Military Division of the Mississippi, from Gravely Springs, Tennessee, on the morning of 22 March 1865 the young cavalry commander was about to embark on the most successful expedition of his military career. His personal appearance was not imposing. He was described as being five feet eight inches tall, fair-faced, square-headed, with curly sandy hair, and a reddish mustache and imperial. He had large blue-gray eyes. He was a complex man who could be either full of fun or full of fire "as the case might be." His face could assume a grim aspect because his mouth was slightly undershot. He had large white teeth on his lower jaw with some overlapping, and with large white uppers. According to a Confederate account there was no regularity of his features. A reporter for the *Macon Daily Telegraph* noted "there were yet few young faces...that one's eyes dwelt upon with more pleasure. It had health and fire in it, ambition and resolve; high self-appreciation, not allied to conceit, and the wholesome air of one generally determined to make his mark in the world before quitting it."[2] A Northern account, written after Wilson's death, stated he was erect, with a military bearing which made him seem a bit taller than he was. Even when he was in middle and later life, he "stood and walked like a cavalryman who never forgot that he had served with distinction under Grant, Sherman, Sheridan, and Thomas, and as an independent commander had led the longest and greatest single cavalry movement in the Civil War." Wilson possessed "bold initiative, an adventurous and dauntless spirit, aggressive temper and invariable confidence." This same account described him as the "striking personification" of the so-called 'Old Army,' was reserved, on occasions blunt and occasionally imperious. He was, at the same time, but more rarely, sentimental.[3]

---

[1] Sketch of James Harrison Wilson in Ezra J. Warner, *Generals in Blue: Lives of the Union Commanders* (Baton Rouge: Louisiana State University Press, 1964) 566-67.

[2] *Daily Telegraph,* 15 July 1865.

[3] James Edward Kelly, "Two Noted Federal Cavalry Leaders," in United States Army Recruiting News, the Recruiting Publicity Bureau, US Army, Governors Island, NY, 1939, in Bill Frank Collection, Delaware Historical Society, Wilmington, Box 11, Folder 39.

Wilson's command consisted of three divisions: The 1st, 2nd, and 4th. The 1st Division, commanded by Brigadier General Edward M. McCook, included two brigades. The 1st Brigade, under Brigadier General John T. Croxton included the 8th Iowa, Fourth Kentucky Infantry (mounted), the 6th Kentucky, and the 2nd Michigan. The 2nd Brigade under Colonel Oscar H. LaGrange included the 2nd Indiana (battalion), 4th Indiana, 4th Kentucky, 7th Kentucky, and 1st Wisconsin. The artillery attached to this division, commanded by Captain Moses M. Beck, was the 8th Battery of Indiana Light Artillery. Brigadier General Eli Long's Second Division, commanded by Colonel Robert H.G. Minty in Long's absence, was composed of Colonel Abram O. Miller's 1st Brigade, commanded by Colonel Jacob G. Vail. Its units included the 98th Illinois, 123rd Illinois, 17th Indiana Mounted Infantry, and the 72nd Indiana. Colonel Robert H. G. Minty's 2nd Brigade was composed of the 4th Michigan, Third Ohio, 4th Ohio, and 7th Pennsylvania. Artillery support was furnished by Captain George I. Robinson's Illinois Light Artillery Battery, known as the Chicago Board of Trade Battery.

Brevet Major General Emory Upton's 4th Division included two brigades: the 1st led by Brevet Brigadier General Edward F. Winslow with the 3rd Iowa, 4th Iowa, and 10th Missouri; and Brevet Brigadier General Andrew J. Alexander's 2nd Brigade. This latter unit included the 5th Iowa, 1st Ohio and 7th Ohio. The artillery unit attached to this brigade was Lieutenant George B. Rodney's Battery "I" of the 4th United States Artillery.[4] The total number of men in Wilson's force was 13,480 with fifty medical officers.[5]

This force left its camps near Gravely Springs, Tennessee, on 22 March 1865 and advanced south toward Selma, Alabama. After crossing the black Warrior River, Wilson's force defeated Lieutenant General Nathan Bedford Forrest near Plantersville, and captured Selma and Tuscaloosa. In early April Montgomery fell, and the force advanced toward Columbus, Georgia. Wilson sent Oscar LaGrange's Brigade to capture strategic Fort Tyler on the Chattahoochee River opposite West Point, Georgia. He then attacked Columbus on 16 April 1865.[6]

---

[4] Organizational Chart of the Cavalry Corps, Military Division of the Mississippi, in *OR*, 49: Pt. 1, 402.

[5] Report of Surgeon Francis Salter, Medical Director, Ibid., 403. This number included 4,096 in the 1st Division, 5,127 in the 2nd Division, and 3,923 in the 4th Division. There were also 334 men in the 4th US Cavalry attached to the command.

[6] The best study of Wilson's Raid is James Pickett Jones, *Yankee Blitzkreig Wilson's Raid through Alabama and Georgia* (Athens: The University of Georgia Press, 1976).

When Wilson approached Central Alabama, Cobb urged General Richard Taylor to give him all the help he could to defend Georgia.[7] In response to a message from Colonel Leon Van Zinken, commanding the post at Columbus, asking Cobb to send the Georgia State Line to Columbus and General Wofford's Cavalry towards General Robert Tyler's threatened position at Fort Tyler,[8] Cobb directed Mayor T.G. Williams of Columbus to defend that city against Wilson because Governor Brown would not "call out the militia from their homes sooner than necessary."[9] However, Georgia Adjutant and Inspector General Wayne, desirous of protecting Macon, issued Special Orders No. 36 ordering the two regiments of Georgia State Line troops to go to Macon with all their wagons and equipment ready for field service.[10]

Even as reinforcements for Cobb were on the way, efforts were made to arrest deserters and "skulkers" in Central Georgia to aid in Macon's defense.[11] Cobb assured President Davis, then fleeing with the Confederate Government in Danville, Virginia, that "The spirit of our people is better than you would have probably looked for. The true men are bold defiant and hopeful." Davis' address to the people of the Confederacy urging them to continue the struggle, Cobb believed, was "unsurpassed by any paper you have issued." Cobb hoped that the speech would rally Virginians to keep fighting, while suggesting that Davis establish a new Confederate capital in Georgia.[12]

When Wilson approached Columbus in mid-April, Cobb moved there with all the force he could spare to defend the line of the Chattahoochee. He estimated Wilson's force at 10,000, and believed that 3,000 defenders were available to resist him. Cobb assured his wife that he had just inspected his lines and planned to give Wilson "as warm a welcome as is in my power." He believed Wilson's force was a very large and well organized raiding party, which "do not expect to hold the country but intend to destroy & devastate." If Wilson succeeded in capturing Columbus, Cobb believed he would destroy Southwestern Georgia. If the Confederates succeeded in defending Columbus the Federals would flank that position and invade the rich southwestern portion of

---

[7] Cobb to Taylor, Telegram, Macon, 4 April 1865, Cobb Order & Letter Book, 1865, pp. 78-9.

[8] Colonel Leon Van Zinkin to Cobb, Telegram, Columbus, 5 April 1865, Cobb Papers, 1865.

[9] Cobb to Mayor T.G. Williams, Macon, 5 April 1865, Cobb Order & Letter Book, 1865, p. 81.

[10] Henry C. Wayne, Special Orders No. 36, Milledgeville, 5 April 1865, Cobb Papers, 1865. See also Wayne to Cobb, Milledgeville, 5 April 1865, Ibid.

[11] Second Lieutenant H.J. Cooper to Major Lamar Cobb, Camp near Macon, 6 April 1865, Ibid.

[12] Cobb to Jefferson Davis, Macon, 8 April 1865, Cobb Order & Letter Book, 1865, p. 88.

the state anyway. Cobb showed a knowledge of strategy unusual in a non-professional soldier when he wrote that "Macon is an important point with them and though it is not in immediate danger–I do not think it will remain there after you know that Columbus has fallen, or been flanked, provided either of these events should transpire." Like many other people, Cobb believed that Forrest was at Wilson's rear. If that was true, Cobb believed that Wilson would be defeated. Unfortunately for Macon's defenders, Columbus fell on 16 April.[13]

At Columbus on the afternoon and evening of 16 April Wilson's men made several charges but were "handsomely repulsed." However at 9:00 P.M. Cobb's lines were broken. During the darkness of late evening many of Wilson's men dismounted and serving as infantry, crawled to within a few yards of the Confederate line. Wilson then used small bodies of cavalry to charge the defenses at several points. When the defenders rose to fire at the mounted troopers, the dismounted men poured a deadly fire into them. Cobb and most of his staff, however, successfully made their escape.[14]

As Wilson's force advanced a correspondent for the *Daily Telegraph and Confederate,* urged the people of Middle and Southwestern Georgia to fight for their homes and property. "Woe be to them," the writer warned, "if by their supineness and inactivity, they permit this city to fall into the hands of the foe." The paper assured the people that "As certain as the sun shines we can whip the enemy if the men within easy distance of this city will hurry to the rescue. If all come who can and should, there will be no fight." Wilson, the reporter noted, would not dare to attack such an army as could be concentrated here [in Macon] in the next three days. The paper reminded the people that "When Stoneman attacked Macon, our people turned out en masse, and the result was that this celebrated raider and a large portion of his band were brought captives into town." The people could defend themselves just as well now. Three companies were organizing. A notice appeared in the same issue that Colonel J.W. Avery and Captain T.G. Hout planned to raise a cavalry command to help defend Macon. The two officers, using the same approach employed by President Davis in the fall of 1864, urged Maconites to fight the Federals at every step, harass him on his march, strike on his flanks, and impede his advance.[15]

When Wilson's troopers began their march on Macon the military authorities began to concentrate more troops to defend the city. The defenses on the Columbus Road needed buttressing. On 17 April Colonel John B.

---

[13] Cobb to his wife, Columbus, 15 April 1865, Cobb Papers.

[14] Howell Cobb, Jr. to Mary McKinley, Macon, 19 April 1865, Cobb-Erwin-Lamar Collection.

[15] *Daily Telegraph and Confederate,* 18 April 1865.

Cumming was assigned to command the fortifications in that area.[16] Captain Gillespie in the Quartermasters Office was directed to send his company of employees to report at the Battery commanded by Captain Key on the Columbus Road.[17]

On 19 April Cobb issued General Orders No. 7 ordering all detailed and furloughed soldiers, except those assigned to the Quartermaster, Commissary, Ordnance, and Engineers, to join some organization. Arrangements were made to fire an alarm of two guns from the City Hall which would serve as a signal for the gathering of the local defense forces. Cobb appealed to the citizens of Macon, able to bear arms, to resist Wilson. He told the people that "It requires united and vigorous effort on the part of every one; and this appeal is made with perfect confidence that a prompt response will be made to it." He added that Wilson's defeat before Macon "would be attended with the happiest results."[18]

While these arrangements were in progress, every effort was made to improve the fortifications. On the 18th Cobb ordered the impressment of all able-bodied slaves and turned them over to Lieutenant Colonel Frobel in charge of the fortifications.[19] Captain Key needed men to work on the palisading and abatis in front of his line which was located between the Houston and Columbus Roads about two miles west of Macon. He wrote, "I have a long line to prepare and defend around the city, and have no axes and few laborers. Will not the citizens send me, at once, their negroes with axes to make palisade and abatis." The men were instructed to report to Key at the fortifications.[20] Hopefully, with only a few days' labor, slaves might strengthen the defenses, already in good condition, and make them impregnable if held by only a few determined soldiers. Besides the militia was mobilizing, and they would probably be enough to defend the city. Furthermore, Macon's defenders would be greatly aided if the authorities would take the large amount of cotton in town and haul it into the streets to serve as barricades. If Wilson breached the outer fortifications, the cotton barricades would help to keep him out with the help of "trusty sharpshooters behind," and the city's defenders might possibly defeat Wilson.[21] Because of the shortage of tools, efforts were made to impress all available axes and shovels.[22] Orders were also issued to impress all horses and mules in front of Wilson's

---

[16] Colonel R.J. Hallett, Special Orders, Macon, 17 April 1865, Cobb Special Orders.

[17] R.J. Hallett to Captain Gillespie, Macon, 17 April 1865, Ibid., n.p.

[18] *Macon Daily Telegraph and Confederate,* 20 April 1865.

[19] Hallett to Captain C. Armstrong in charge Impressment, Macon, 18 April 1865, Cobb Special Orders.

[20] *Macon Daily Telegraph and Confederate,* 20 April 1865.

[21] Ibid., 19 April 1865.

[22] Hallett to Major John L. Morgan, Macon, 18 April 1865, Ibid.

advance.[23] Another directive called for the impressment of all mules in the city to be used in strengthening the defenses.[24]

Efforts were also made to remove stores from the city. George S. Obear, then a captain in the militia, was relieved from the command of the Macon Militia Battalion and placed in charge of Government property. Obear received directions to take the property to a point where it would be safe from Wilson's troopers.[25] Cobb ordered Colonel John H. Colmes to guard various points on the Ocmulgee River because some men were leaving to avoid participating in the defense.[26]

On the following day the editor of the *Daily Telegraph and Confederate* admitted that rumors were plentiful "and so diverse that it is impossible to arrive at the truth." A train bound for Atlanta on the Macon and Western returned, and the engineer reported that the Federals were at Thomaston. Another force, reported to be near LaGrange earlier in the week, had presumably turned back before reaching that town. On the 18th an engineer and conductor traveled to within eighteen miles of Columbus, where they heard that there was heavy fighting in progress. They said they could hear the reports of cannonading. The paper hopefully reported: "It was also stated that it was thought General Forrest was there, and that he was driving the enemy." Of course, as the paper admitted, "It is too late for us to investigate these statements and ascertain their credibility. Whatever needed to be done either in strengthening the defenses or in placing troops in them had to be done quickly. If, the paper opined, "the enemy does not exceed six thousand, we are of the opinion that, with the men and means at our disposal, we can successfully defend the city." But if the city could not be defended, if the liquor was destroyed and the people did not show unnecessary bitter feelings or language during the Federal occupation, there should be no cause for alarm. The paper, trying to put the best face on things, observed that Wilson's force was only a raiding party, "whose business it is to destroy everything that belongs to the government, that will subsist our army; and that, unless exasperated [sic], private property will escape [destruction]. Only public property would be destroyed and the raiders would leave as soon as they have rested, in a few days."[27]

Not all Maconites were as optimistic as the editor of the *Daily Telegraph and Confederate*. Some of the women continued to urge the military authorities

---

[23] Hallett to Captain James Anderson, Macon, 18 April 1865, Ibid., n.p.

[24] Hallett to Captain James Anderson, Macon, 18 April 1865, Ibid., n.p.

[25] William W. Mackall to...Macon, 17 April 1865, Howell Cobb Order & Letter Book, 1865, n.p.

[26] R.J. Hallett to Colonel John H. Colmes, Macon, 17 April 1865, Ibid., n.p.

[27] *Macon Daily Telegraph and Confederate*, 19 April 1865.

to destroy all the whiskey in the city, including liquor in private homes. This radical proposal was voiced because of the proximity of the Federals, who were rumored as being at Thomaston and Barnesville, and because there were fears that the small garrison of the city could not hold out against an invasion by a force the size of Wilson's.[28]

Even as the paper spread many rumors concerning Wilson's advance, the superintendents of the Arsenal, Armory, and Laboratory labored to remove as much of their equipment and products as possible. On 5 April Colonel Richard Cuyler, Arsenal Superintendent, notified Colonel George W. Rains, commanding ordnance facilities in Augusta, that Cobb wanted ordnance stores removed from Columbus. The most important of these, Cuyler thought, "might be removed at once without stopping the work."[29] On the following day Cuyler wired A. M. Laughlin of the C. S. Naval facility in Columbus that he could furnish the latter with eight-inch siege carriages, but none for other heavy guns.[30] On the same date Cuyler received a telegram from Brigadier General Josiah Gorgas, Chief of the Ordnance Bureau, then fleeing with the Confederate Government at Danville, presumably notifying him of his whereabouts.[31] By 17 April after Columbus had been captured and even as Wilson approached Macon, Cuyler had prepared a train of ammunition under directions from Rains which consisted of sixteen cars containing ammunition. Cuyler ordered these stores sent to several points, preferably Covington, Madison, and Greensboro on the Georgia Railroad. Hopefully by the time his Special Messenger, J. H. Levy reached Atlanta the Georgia Railroad would be open. "You will use every exertion," Cuyler asserted, "to push your cars through to Covington & on reaching that place, stop one half of them, remaining with them."[32]

On the same day, the harried Arsenal superintendent ordered Special Messenger W.G. Ward to accompany Levy. When the train reached Covington, Levy would stop with half of the cars, and Ward would go to Madison where the latter had to "make every exertion" to obtain storage. This storage would have to suffice for the protection of the ammunition in Ward's care, and also other stores which would be sent later "if possible."[33]

Finally, even as Wilson pushed toward the excited city, Cuyler announced the dispatch of yet another train containing ammunition and the lead and cap

---

[28] Ibid., 20 April 1865.

[29] Cuyler to Rains, Telegram, Macon, 5 April 1865, Telegrams Sent, Arsenal, 1862-1865.

[30] Ibid., Cuyler to Laughlin, Telegram, Macon, 6 April 1865.

[31] Cuyler to Colonel Wright, Macon, 6 April 1865, in Records of Confederate Ordnance Facilities, Macon, Box 3191, Letters Sent Arsenal, April, 1865.

[32] Cuyler to J.H. Levy, Macon, 17 April 1865, Ibid.

[33] Cuyler to Ward, Macon, 17 April 1865, Ibid.

factory to Milledgeville. He had received orders from Cobb, however, to send no more on the 19th, although, as he told Rains, "We may ship more to Milledgeville & haul them to Greensboro." These were the only two shipments that Cuyler was able to send.[34]

Colonel James H. Burton, Superintendent of the Armory, behaved as coolly as did Cuyler. He telegraphed Gorgas on 6 April advising the ordnance chief to send all the machinery saved from the Richmond Arsenal to Macon. It would be advisable, Burton explained, to send all the armorers along.[35] On the same day Burton informed Gorgas that General Mackall had recently refused several applications for the detailing of men whose services were badly needed to work on the unfinished buildings at the Armory. Determined to complete the new facility, Burton noted: "[I]t will be necessary for the Govt. to adopt a more liberal policy with reference to the granting of details essential to the completion of the buildings." More black laborers were also needed, possibly as many as 100, which Burton could not get by hiring. Possibly, Burton suggested, some slaves could be detailed to him by the Engineer Department. Housing additional workers was also a problem, but Burton promised to do the best he could to resolve this difficulty, possibly by using the vacated temporary armory building for that purpose.[36]

On the following day Burton informed Mackall that Gorgas planned to remove the machinery saved from Richmond to Macon. Therefore, Mackall should reconsider his position on the detailing of deferred laborers to the Armory. The buildings had to be completed. In order to do this, carpenters and some other types of mechanics were badly needed, as well as seventy-five to 100 additional black laborers. Burton had not been able to hire more slaves because "owners do not respond to my advertisements." The probable reason for this was because the owners did not want to lose their slaves if Wilson captured Macon.[37] Mackall relented on the 8th, and agreed to detail any men who were needed as carpenters.[38]

Burton continued his assignment in an optimistic tone even as Wilson pushed into Central Alabama. On 7 April he proceeded with arrangements for the removal of the pistol machinery from the temporary arsenal facility to the new buildings, and "for the construction of new machines to replace those" burned by Sherman at Columbia, South Carolina. The pistol machinery was

---

[34] Cuyler to Rains, Telegram, Macon, 19 April 1865, Telegrams Sent, Arsenal, 1862-65.

[35] Burton to Gorgas, Telegram, Macon, 6 April 1865, Letters Sent, Armory, 1863-65.

[36] Burton to Gorgas, Macon, 6 April 1865, Ibid.

[37] Burton to Mackall, Macon, 7 April 1865, Ibid.

[38] Burton to B.F. Perry, Foreman of Carpenters, Macon, 8 April 1865, Ibid.

being placed in position and the counter shafting erected in the new facility. On 1 April Burton's men had started a temporary steam engine at the new Armory. The machines which Sherman had destroyed at Columbia were fortunately of simple construction, and could be manufactured at the Arsenal foundry. Burton informed Gorgas that "Every effort will be made to resume the finishing of pistols at the earliest moment possible. In the meantime some portions of the work on pistols is being performed."[39]

By mid-April, as Wilson approached Columbus, Mackall directed Burton to give him the number of Armory military company men who might be relied on in the event that Wilson attacked Macon. Burton noted one hundred and one on the muster roll, but ten were absent on special duty or on leave. Twenty were in the hospital or unfit for duty, leaving an effective strength of seventy-one. However, the men were well drilled with their organization complete, and were fully armed with .54 caliber Austrian rifles.[40]

Then, on 15 April Burton wired Colonel Marcus H. Wright, commanding the Columbus Arsenal: "If in your judgement Columbus cannot be held if attacked send pistol machinery, tools and stores to Macon."[41]

By the 17th, after Columbus had fallen, Burton followed a similar course to Cuyler's when he directed one of his staff, Lieutenant Charles Selden, Jr., to take the official books and papers of the Arsenal, Armory, and Laboratory to Greensboro through Atlanta. Wilson's approach dictated this course. Burton urged Selden to "try to get them to Athens or such other safe point–as in your judgement, may seem safe for the time being." If the enemy pressed Selden too closely Selden's instructions included the destruction of Confederate money in his charge.[42]

Colonel John W. Mallett, Superintendent of Laboratories, like his counterparts, pursued a course of business-as-usual as March 1865, drew to a close. On the 31st he informed Colonel Rains in Augusta, "I have half a million caps ready for you." Unfortunately, getting them to Augusta would be difficult because Sherman had cut the railroads in the eastern portions of Georgia, and the Confederates, pressed on many fronts, could not repair them.[43] On the following day Mallet reported to Rains that he had 11,000 pounds of lead in Macon, but feared it would not reach Augusta safely. The determined Mallet asked, "Shall I send it?"[44]

---

[39] Burton to Gorgas, Macon, 7 April 1865, Ibid.

[40] Burton to Mackall, Macon, 14 April 1865, Ibid.

[41] Burton to Wright, Telegram, Macon, 15 April 1865, Ibid.

[42] Burton to Lieutenant Charles Selden, Jr., Macon, 17 April 1865, Ibid.

[43] Mallet to Rains, Telegram, Macon, 31 March 1865, Telegrams Sent, Laboratories, 1863-65.

[44] Mallet to Rains, Telegram, Macon, 1 April 1865, Ibid.

Mallet continued to attempt to furnish supplies to the army to the end.[45] Writing to Rains on 14 April he recorded, "Columbus stores are moved. Macon will probably soon be seriously threatened. Shall I take any steps to move cap factory? It is now our only source of this supply, but its removal would entail considerable delay in again getting to work. To what point shall I move if at all?"[46]

On 15 April Mackall urged Mallet to move the cap factory because Wilson was approaching Columbus.[47] Two days later, 17 April, Mackall ordered everything moved at once because Columbus had fallen to Wilson on the 16th.[48] To expedite the movement of ordnance stores Mackall placed all railroad transportation under Cuyler on the 17th "for the purpose of removing Government Property."[49] Cobb directed that eight wagons and teams be turned over to Mallett, but assured Quartermaster Captain Brown that "they will only be called for in case of great emergency."[50] By 17 April all of the ordnance facilities in Macon were either moving their material or preparing to do so. By the following day Cobb underscored the great danger Macon was in by arranging to send an ammunition train to Milledgeville for safety.[51]

While these preparations were underway Wilson, flushed with success after the fall of Columbus, prepared to advance against Macon. He commenced his march from the Chattahoochee industrial center on the morning of 17 April with Colonel Robert H.G. Minty's Second Division in the advance. On the following day, Minty, accompanied by Wilson, made a forced march, seizing the important Double Bridges across the Flint River, fifty-four miles from Columbus. The Federals camped at Waverly Hall on the evening of 18 April where they found five abandoned field guns and twelve wagons laden with machinery, probably the machinery sent by Wright in an abortive attempt to reach the authorities in Macon. Minty also captured forty prisoners and burned two cotton factories.[52]

---

[45] Mallet to M.H. Wright, 2 Telegrams, Macon, 5 and 14 April 1865; Mallet to W.J. Page, Telegram, Macon, 5 April 1865; Mallet to Rains, 3 Telegrams, Macon, 8, 11, and 12 April 1865, all in Ibid.

[46] Mallet to Rains, Telegram, Macon, 14 April 1865, Ibid.

[47] Mallet to Rains, Telegram, Macon, 15 April 1865, Ibid.

[48] Mallet to Rains, Telegram, Macon, 17 April 1865, Ibid.

[49] R.J. Hallett to Captain J.T. Brown, Macon, 17 April 1865, Cobb Order & Letter Book, 1865, n.p.

[50] R.J. Hallett to J.T. Brown, Macon, 17 April 1865, Ibid., n.p.

[51] R.J. Hallett to Major J.M. Hottle, Macon, 18 April 1865, Ibid., n.p.

[52] James Harrison Wilson Diary, 17, 18 April 1865 in James H. Wilson Papers, Diaries of James Harrison Wilson, in Delaware Historical Society, Wilmington, hereafter cited as Wilson Diary, 1865 with appropriate entry; Wilson to Brigadier

As the Federals progressed toward Middle Georgia from Columbus and from Fort Tyler, which also fell on the 16th, the more northerly column, part of LaGrange's Brigade, marched through LaGrange which Surgeon Nathaniel S. Robinson of the 1st Wisconsin Cavalry described as "a fine town of about 1500 inhabitants. Many very fine residences."[53]

While Wilson's force approached Macon and the military authorities began initial preparations to evacuate the city, Eliza Frances Andrews, a young Georgia refugee from Washington, Georgia, noted in her diary on 17 April that she had seen some "poor fortifications" thrown up along the line of the Southwestern Railroad, with only a few men to man them. That was the only preparation for defense that she saw. "We are told that the city is to be defended, but if that is so," she observed, "the Lord only knows where the men are to come from." The prevailing opinion, the young refugee noted, was that the authorities planned to evacuate Macon, and every preparation seemed to proceed toward that goal. The Confederate authorities had impressed every available horse to remove government stores, so much in fact, that, Eliza complained, "we had great difficulty in getting our baggage from the depot to the hotel. As she proceeded to the Lanier House she saw Mulberry Street in front of the hotel filled with officers and men "rushing to and fro, and everything and everybody seems to be in the wildest excitement." Seeing Macon about to be deserted to its fate, Eliza exclaimed: "I used to have some Christian feeling towards Yankees, but now that they have invaded our country and killed so many of our men and desecrated so many homes, I can't believe that when Christ said 'Love your enemies', he meant Yankees." Eliza did not want to see their souls lost, for that, as she said, "would be wicked, but as they are not being punished in this world, I don't see how else they are going to get their deserts."[54]

When Eliza arrived at the depot of the Macon and Western Railroad to refugee in Atlanta on the following morning—Tuesday, 18 April—she found such a crowd of people waiting to leave the city that "we could hardly push our way through, and when the ladies' car was opened there was such a rush that we considered ourselves lucky to get in at all." Many people were unable to get their trunks aboard, and, many of them being poor, they decided to stay with their baggage. The trains that left in the confusion of the morning were supposed to be the last that would leave because Wilson was expected before nightfall. Many people predicted that Eliza's train would be captured. She looked out the

---

General William D. Whipple, A.A.G., Department of the Cumberland, Macon, 3 May 1865, Report, *OR*, 49: Pt. 1, 352, hereafter cited as Wilson, 3 May Report.

[53] Wilson Diary, 1865, 17 April 1865; Nathaniel S. Robinson Diary, 17 April 1865, *Civil War Times Illustrated Collection*, USAMHI, hereafter cited as Robinson Diary.

[54] Andrews Journal, 17 April 1865, pp. 148-49.

window and saw a terrible rush of people to get on all the outgoing trains. Her train had on board some government specie and the assets of four banks, besides much private property, and heard that the total value of the cargo carried was over seventeen million dollars. There were also over 1,000 passengers on the train. People who could not get inside the cars were hanging on wherever they could find a place to hold on to. She scribbled in her journal, "the aisles and platforms down to the last step were full of people clinging on like bees swarming round the doors of a hive. It took two engines to pull us up the heavy grade around Vineville, and we were more than an hour behind time in starting, at that." To make matters even worse, rumors filled the air. Rumormongers spread a tale that the Macon and Western was cut at Jonesboro; still another circulated that some of Wilson's troopers were in Barnesville and had cut the tracks there. Yet another story was spread that a large force of the enemy was at Thomaston with plans to capture the train upon which Eliza was a passenger. Eliza vividly described the scene when these rumors floated about the cars. "I never saw such wild excitement in my life," she wrote. "Many people left the cars at the last moment before we steamed out, preferring to be caught in Macon rather than captured out on the road, but their places were rapidly filled by more adventurous spirits." One group of refugees from the fighting at Columbus, who seemed nearly crazy with excitement, sat near Eliza and her party. One of Eliza's former classmates, Mary Elizabeth Rutherford, always, according to Eliza, a great scatterbrain, was among the group. She jumped up on her seat, tore down her back hair and went into hysterics at "the idea of falling into the hands of the Yankees." Such antics seemed natural enough in the beginning of the war, when the people were new to wartime tensions, but now that we are, as Eliza pointed out, "all old soldiers, and used to raids and vicissitudes," people should know how to face such alarums quietly.

Despite these problems the train finally left the station and proceeded as far as Goggins's Station, four miles from Barnesville. There it was stopped by country people who said the train from Atlanta had been captured by Wilson and the Federals were only five miles beyond Barnesville waiting for more trains to come from Macon. Thereupon a decision was made to return to Macon to prevent much valuable property from falling into the hands of the Federals. As the train returned to Macon Eliza saw excited crowds gathered at every station. The news the passengers brought with them only increased the excitement. The report related that Wilson's cavalry were advancing on Macon in three columns, and would be in the city in the next two days. Eliza noted, upon her return to the Lanier House, that the demoralization was complete. She wrote: "We are whipped, there is no doubt about it. Everybody feels it, and there is no use for the men to try to fight any longer, though none of us like to say so." The young Georgia girl found an immense crowd at the depot on her return, and when she saw what an uproar the approach of Wilson created, she lost all hope and realized the Confederacy was doomed. She observed, "The spell of invincibility has left us and gone over to the heavy battalions of the enemy."

Along her route from the depot to the hotel she saw that the authorities were preparing to evacuate Macon. Government stores were piled up in the streets and all the horses and wagons that could be seized for government use were being hurriedly loaded in the effort to take the stores away. The rush of men, she noted "had disappeared from Mulberry St. No more gay uniforms, no more prancing horses, but only a few ragged foot soldiers with wallets and knapsacks on, ready to march–Heaven knows where." She walked about the streets while waiting for a room, and found everything in the wildest confusion. Many businesses were closed, and sad little knots of people were standing on the street corners talking about the situation. All liquor that could be found in the stores, barrooms, and warehouses, had been taken by the authorities and emptied in the streets. In some places the streets smelled like a distillery. Eliza observed the disgusting spectacle of men and boys of both races on their knees lapping the liquor up from the gutter. Little children were "staggering in a state of beastly intoxication." There was, Eliza felt, no more dreary scene in the world than a city about to be evacuated, "unless it is one that has already fallen into the hands of the enemy." She returned to her hotel with a heavy heart, for when she was walking about the city, she heard new rumors about Lee's surrender. No one seemed to dispute it, and everyone felt ready to give up hope. The common cry in Macon was "It is useless to struggle longer," and the poor wounded soldiers were hobbling about Macon with despair written all over their faces. Eliza confided to her diary: "There is a new pathos in a crutch or an empty sleeve, now, that we know it was all for nothing."

On the following day, Wednesday, 19 April, the Confederates began to evacuate Macon. All through the night, from the safety of her hotel room, Eliza could hear the tramp of men and horses, together with the rattle of artillery and baggage wagons down Mulberry Street. The group traveling with Eliza tried to keep their spirits up by singing some of the favorite war songs, but they seemed "more like dirges now." Finally, they gave up the effort and went to their rooms. Matters were made even worse later in the night when a terrific thunder storm arose. A bolt struck one of the lightening rods of the hotel and "made such a fearful crash that many of the guests, suddenly roused from their sleep, took it for a Yankee shell." People in the wildest state of excitement ran about the halls. The following morning, the party did not wait for breakfast at the hotel but started off for the depot on foot with cold biscuits in their hands. They reached the Georgia Central Railroad Depot and found enough people waiting there with their baggage to fill a dozen trains. As the excited crowd scrambled for places next to the track, Sidney Lanier, a friend of one of the party, approached trying to get on one of the trains. He was introduced, but everyone soon lost each other in the crowd. Lanier, who "looked as thin and white as a ghost," was just recovering from a bout with typhoid fever. Finally, a train backed up and the party boarded it. Senator Robert Toombs, who was from Eliza's home town of Washington, and who was traveling with Eliza's party, introduced the group to Governor Brown, who was a passenger on the train. Eliza noted that the Governor "looked at me with a half-embarrassed expression and poked out his hand with no pretense at cordiality." The young girl did not know whether this was due to resentment at the political preferences of Eliza's family who were political opponents of the governor, or merely a preoccupation about the Governor's "own rather precarious affairs."   On the way to Milledgeville, Eliza observed Georgia's chief executive very closely and noted that he was "a regular Barebones in appearance, thin, wiry, angular, with a sallow complexion and iron-gray hair. His face wears an expression of self-assertion rather than obstinacy and I couldn't help thinking how well he would have fitted in with Cromwell's Ironsides." The Governor's clothing did nothing to offset the negative impression which Eliza had formed. He wore a rusty, short-tailed black alpaca coat that looked decidedly homemade. Eliza completed her journey to Milledgeville amid this distinguished company.[55]

At 6:00 A.M. on 20 May, Minty's 2nd Division continued its march toward Macon. The advance unit, Lieutenant Colonel Frank White's 17th Indiana Mounted Infantry, of Colonel Abram O. Miller's 1st Brigade, marched rapidly toward the city. Four companies armed with sabers formed the advanced guard under Major John J. Weiler. White, who commanded the remaining companies, reported, "From our camp of the preceding night, from whence we started in the morning, it was forty-five miles to Macon. After marching about twenty-four miles, and when near Spring Hill, the advance guard first met a small force of the enemy and drove them off, capturing a few." White moved forward with the remaining companies and assumed control of the march. After resting near Spring Hill for an hour or so, the march continued. Near Montpelier Springs White again encountered the Confederates, charging them and driving them up to and through a strong barricade of rails and brush erected across the road. The Federal troopers captured a dozen men including three officers, and a few horses. White continued his advance, pushing forward rapidly to prevent the Confederates from burning the important bridge over Tobesofkee Creek by Mimm's Mills. At the creek, White found three hundred Confederates in line of battle. He attacked them, and his advance charged on horseback over the bridge which had been set on fire. Dashing across the bridge, the troopers were stopped because Confederates had removed some of the planking. The men dismounted, together with the two advance companies, E and H, of the 17th. After a sharp fight of about five minutes the Confederates were driven back in confusion. White, meanwhile, ordered portions of his other companies to put out the fire on

---

[55] Ibid., 18, 19 April 1865, pp. 149-56.

the bridge, "the men carrying the water in their hats, caps, and everything else available." He sent two companies across a ford below the bridge to pursue the Confederates. The troopers pushed forward around a bend in the road, keeping the retreating Confederates under fire for about two hundred yards. Firing very rapidly the troopers caused the Confederates to abandon over a hundred guns, blankets, and haversacks, and forcing them to "fly as for their lives." White moved forward until he was two miles east of the bridge and about thirteen miles from Macon when he was met by a flag of truce under Brigadier General Felix Robertson who was carrying an important message from Howell Cobb.[56]

Earlier on 20 April, Cobb received a message from General Beauregard, then in Greensboro, North Carolina, which the Creole commander had sent the day before. It read: "Inform Gen commanding enemies forces in your front that a truce for the purpose of a final settlement was agreed upon yesterday between Genl Johnson & Sherman applicable to all forces under their commands. A message to that affect from Genl Sherman will be sent him as soon as practicable. The contending forces are to occupy their present positions forty eight (48) hours notice being given in the event of resumption of hostilities."[57]

White declared, "I know nothing about 'truces, armistices or final settlements.' All I can do is to send this letter back to General [actually Colonel] Minty my division commander, and wait for further orders." Minty, riding close behind White, opened the envelope and read its contents. He realized that he was also a subordinate, and sent it to Wilson. Minty, believing the message might be a ruse, ordered White to give Robertson's party five minutes to get out of the way, and then to continue his march to Macon. White, who was already getting inpatient, pulled out his watch and interrupted a "pleasant" chat with Robertson, saying, "Orders require me to push for Macon as rapidly as possible, and I'll give you just five minutes to get out of the way with your flag of truce and escort." Robertson promptly wheeled about and rejoined his escort, starting for Macon at a brisk trot to report to Cobb. Minty and White actually had no authority from Wilson to continue their advance until Wilson had received Cobb's message.[58]

Wilson received the message at 6:00 P.M. and sent a staff officer to stop the advance and inform Cobb that he would see him, and then rode forward

---

[56] Lt. Col. Frank White Report, Macon, April 21, 1865, *OR*, 49: Pt. 1, 457-58, hereafter cited as White Report. General Long, was riding with Wilson further to the rear. The division was temporarily commanded by Colonel Minty.

[57] Beauregard to Cobb, Telegram, Greensboro, N.C., 19 April 1865, Cobb Papers, 1865.

[58] James Harrison Wilson, *Under the Old Flag* (Greenwood Press: Westport, Conn., 1971) II:276-77, hereafter cited as Wilson, *Under the Old Flag II*; Howell Cobb, Jr. to Mary McKinley, Macon, 24 April 1865, Cobb-Erwin-Lamar Collection.

rapidly.[59] However, in his after action report, Wilson noted, "I declined without questioning the authenticity of the armistice or its applicability to my command, upon the ground that my subordinates were not authorized to act in such matters," and hurried to overtake Minty and White.[60]

White began "to drive everything before me and save the bridge over Rocky Creek at Bailey's Mill." Placing Adjutant W. E. Doyle in charge of an advance guard of fifteen men, White ordered him forward at a trot, supporting him closely with the regiment. About two miles down the road Doyle saw the flag of truce party in the rear of a cavalry battalion of two hundred and fifty men under Colonel Blount. Blount was moving forward slowly, trying to delay White's troopers. Doyle charged the Confederates, causing Robertson and his party to run into the woods. Doyle captured three officers in the flag of truce party, and drove Blount's troopers toward Macon at a gallop. Despite their withdrawal, the Confederates kept up a steady fire upon Doyle, although the Federals suffered no casualties. When Doyle arrived at the bridge over Rocky Creek he discovered Blount's men trying to burn the structure. Doyle pushed the Confederates back, pursuing them closely to some palisading which protected the crossing of Rocky Creek. He paused here and sent word to White that he needed reinforcements. White quickly sent Major John J. Weiler and Lieutenant James H. McDowell with Company E of the 17th Indiana forward as reinforcements.

The advance party resumed their march, but were slowed down by a force which fired at them, but soon began to retreat in confusion through some gardens on the right. Weiler and Doyle led their troopers through the palisading which they tore down and rode up to and over the earthworks defending Macon on the west. The Federal officers ordered the defenders, composed of militia, to surrender, telling them that "we had two divisions of our cavalry in their rear."[61]

Colonel Cumming, in charge of defending the works was not present, and the men believing that they were cut off, were surrendered by subordinate officers. Upon these orders Cumming came up and ordered the surrender of 500 militia under his command. These troops threw down their arms and marched down to the road, where Lieutenant McDowell took charge of them and formed them into a line. The advance was slowed down when Weiler and Doyle learned that there were at least a thousand Confederates on each side of the road behind

---

[59] Wilson Diary, 1865, 20 April 1865.

[60] Wilson, 3 May Report, 352.

[61] Lieutenant Colonel Frank White to Capt. O.F. Bane, Acting A.A.G., First Brigade, Second Division, Macon, 21 April 1865, *OR*, 49: Pt. 1, 457-58, hereafter cited as White Report. John C. Butler reported the defenders included citizens, invalids from the various hospitals and artisans in the various workshops, the whole not exceeding 2,500 men. John C. *Butler, Historical Record of Macon and Central Georgia*, p. 285.

good substantial works and well-armed who might close ranks behind their force.[62]

Sergeant Benjamin F. McGee of Company I in the 72nd Indiana Volunteer Infantry, believed the works around Macon were twelve or fifteen miles long, and of "very substantial character." However, there were defects connected with their construction. The engineers had placed the ditches on the inside instead of the outside, and, McGee felt, "we could have just charged right over them on horseback."

McGee believed the Confederates made the work of receiving the surrender of the militia tedious at best. He wrote, "the Johnnies still stood in their places behind the works, and when ordered to throw down their guns, would one at a time, as they were ordered, standing their guns up against the works in proper shape to be speedily taken up again, and then marched out, while all those not very near our men would still stand their ground and hold on to their guns."[63] Despite this, as darkness was gathering, the 17th collected all the Confederates on both sides of the road for a distance of 100 yards, taking altogether about 2,000 prisoners. According to McGee, Long sent five men, including McGee, into the city. "It was quite dark," McGee remembered, "and we could not tell where we were going to, or what danger we were in; but on we went till near the heart of the city, where we halted, and for three hours waited in a great deal of suspense." McGee observed there were between seven thousand and ten thousand Confederates in Macon, and only the 17th and 72nd Indiana available to capture the city. It would be at least two hours before the remainder of Miller's 1st Brigade arrived. Minty's 2nd Brigade would not arrive before the following morning. The 1st and 4th Divisions were twenty-five miles away, and, McGee remembered, "so far as any help they could give us in case we should get into a fight was concerned, they might as well be a hundred miles off."[64]

As dusk was gathering, White pushed through the works and met some officers at Tattnall Square under another flag of truce under Colonel Richard M. Cuyler, Superintendent of the Arsenal, sent by General Cobb with a note asking

---

[62] Ibid., 458; John McElroy, "The Wilson Expedition," Chapter XII, in *The National Tribune,* 7 August 1913, p. 5, hereafter cited as McElroy, "The Wilson Expedition."

[63] Benjamin F. McGee, comp. and William R. Jewell, ed., *History of the 72d Indiana Volunteer Infantry of the Mounted Lightning Brigade,* Lafayette, Indiana: S. Vater & Company, *The Journal,* Printers, 1882, pp. 586, 591, hereafter cited as McGee, *History of the 72d Indiana Volunteer Infantry.* McGee served as the Regimental Historian for the 72nd Indiana. The remainder of the Confederate troops about Macon surrendered on the afternoon of April 21. Ibid., pp. 591-92.

[64] Ibid., pp. 586-587; White Report, 459. Wilson entered Macon with half a dozen staff officers and a small escort after White had occupied the city. Wilson, *Under The Old Flag,* II, 278-79.

what terms would be given for the surrender of Macon and the troops in and around the city. Cobb had instructed his men not to fire on the Federals because he considered the war at an end and had disbanded his forces. He also insisted that Wilson stop in the position he was in when he first received Robertson's party. White disagreed, saying the surrender had to be unconditional, and gave the flag of truce five minutes to get out of the way. White continued into town for a distance of four or five blocks and met another flag of truce stating that Cobb agreed with his terms, surrendering the city and everything in it. He then pushed forward, going to Cobb's headquarters on the second floor of the Lanier House on Mulberry Street where he took formal possession of the city. White quickly placed patrols on duty and camped his regiment on the courthouse square and the adjoining street. The 72nd Indiana, in the meantime, had been ordered to leave the city and go into camp just inside the western defenses.[65] For his part, Wilson was very pleased with White's action noting that both White and Minty "had displayed such sound judgment and such unusual enterprise on the march and in forcing the city to surrender without waiting for me that I felt under special obligation to them." Wilson noted that White had marched one hundred and four miles from Columbus to Macon from 6:00 P.M., 18 April to 6:00 P.M. 20 April. The Federal commander was especially impressed with White who had received the surrender of the city, confined his prisoners, and taken all proper precautions to post videttes, patrol the streets, and place Macon's people under perfect safety and control without waiting for orders. "When I reached there [Macon] two hours and a half later," Wilson noted, Macon "was as quiet as a country village that had never heard a harsher tone than a flute note."[66]

According to initial estimates, the prisoners captured numbered between 1,500 and 3,500 men. General officers captured included Cobb, Major General Gustavus W. Smith, Brigadier General William W. Mackall, Brigadier General Hugh Mercer, and Brigadier General Felix Robertson. There were 300 officers of all grades below the rank of brigadier general; five stand of colors, about sixty pieces of artillery of all calibers, and about three thousand stand of arms. There were also large quantities of quartermaster's, commissary, medical, and ordnance stores captured in the city. White also captured the unfinished Arsenal, Armory, and Laboratory. Federal losses were one killed and two wounded, while a picket at the City Hall turned State Capitol, was killed by one of White's men in an

[65] White Report, 459; Butler, *Historical Record*, pp. 285-286; McGee, *History of the 72d Indiana Volunteer Infantry*, p. 587. A good account of White's entry into Macon is found in Spencer B. King, "April in Macon," in *The Georgia Review*, Summer 1960, XIV, no. 2, pp. 147-53, "April in Macon."

[66] Wilson, *Under The Old Flag*, II:282.

exchange of gunfire.[67] Many caissons and limbers were also captured, although many of these were unserviceable.[68]

White, extremely proud of his capture of Macon, was lavish in the praise he gave to the officers and men under his command including Major Weiler, Adjutant Doyle, and Lieutenant McDowell. The Indiana officer, flushed with his success, reported, "I have also to return my thanks to every officer and man in the regiment for the cheerfulness with which they endured the hardships incident to the march, for the alacrity with which they obeyed every order, and for the gallant manner in which they have gone at the enemy wherever they have found him since the opening of the campaign."[69]

Wilson, in his autobiography, explained his actions. He felt his "situation was a peculiar one." He was separated by many miles from Sherman in North Carolina and Thomas in Nashville, Tennessee; was conducting an independent campaign through the Lower South; and "had the ample latitude of an independent commander." He felt that he would have "cheerfully obeyed" either Sherman's or Thomas' orders to stop his advance, but believed it was his first responsibility, while looking out for his men, to support the best interests of the United States in Middle Georgia. "With this thought uppermost," he wrote, "I pushed on toward Macon as rapidly as I could," arriving at the fortifications at 8:30. Everything by this time was controlled by White.

When he arrived at Macon, Wilson was met at the City Hall by the impatient Cobb, accompanied by Smith, Mackall, Mercer, and Robertson with their staffs. He was informed that Cobb was unconditionally surrendering under protest to a force which he and the forces under his command could not resist. Cobb correctly believed that both the Federal and Confederate Governments had an equal responsibility to uphold the armistice. Wilson disagreed, asserting that Cobb was "proud and imperious by nature," and could not understand that, while Beauregard had informed him of the preliminary agreement between Sherman and Johnston, Wilson's officers doubted the disinterestedness of the Confederates. The Federal officers could neither be persuaded nor bullied into obeying any directions except Wilson's. Once Minty and White captured and

---

[67] White Report, 459; King "April in Macon," 148-49. Wilson reported the number of prisoners as 1500, Wilson, May 3 Report, 353. King gave the number of prisoners as 1,995, which White herded into the former officer's prison at Camp Ogelthorpe. He also reported that White burned three large warehouses near the railroad depot which contained 20,000 sacks of corn. White burned the buildings, but saved the corn for his horses. It was impossible, given the small amount of time his men had to do this, that White had time to save all of the 20,000 sacks of corn. Author's note. This was corn badly needed by Wilson's horses.

[68] Major Charles L. Greenoh Report, Macon, 28 June 1865, OR., 49: Pt. 1, 413.

[69] White Report, 459.

disarmed the garrison and confined it in Camp Ogelthorpe the two officers went to Wilson, who was at the western fortifications near Tatnall Square and conducted him directly to the City Hall. Here he met Cobb, and had "a most interesting interview with him and his officers." Cobb received Wilson with "lofty politeness," but renewed his argument against his capture, feeling that Wilson should not only agree to the armistice, but that Wilson should withdraw his troopers from Macon "to the point at which my advance guard met his flag of truce." Wilson refused this request asserting that no one could stop the Federal cavalry except Wilson. The argument continued, with both officers refusing to yield.

The exasperated Wilson finally turned to Cobb's second-in-command, Smith, whom the Illinoisan had met when he was a cadet at West Point. Wilson said, "General Smith, I am going to ask you the question I have just asked General Cobb and hope you feel at liberty to answer it fully and frankly. Have General Lee and his army surrendered." Smith replied, "Yes, sir, Lee and his army have surrendered!" Upon receiving this information Wilson turned to Cobb and assured the Georgian that he no longer doubted that an armistice existed, but could not place his command under it until he received confirmation from General Sherman. However, he assured Cobb that the fighting was at an end. He then paroled a sullen and dejected Cobb and his officers to their quarters with instructions to report to the City Hall at 9:00 each morning until further orders. Cobb reluctantly accepted Wilson's decision as the best answer he could get and left.

By the time the meeting was over it was nearly midnight. Wilson realized "that the last campaign, as well as the war, was ended." He confessed, "I was heartily glad of it." He then went to the Lanier House, where his staff had established headquarters. Through the remainder of the night he received reports and gave instructions to maintain order and protect persons and property.[70]

Late on the night of 20 April Wilson wired Sherman in cipher with an account of the occupation of Macon, and asking for orders. He concluded "I shall remain here a reasonable length of time to hear from you."[71]

---

[70] Wilson, Under the Old Flag, II, 278-82. For Wilson's official report of the capture of Macon see Wilson Report, 29 June 1865, OR, 49, Pt. 1, 365-69. For additional information about the Confederate view of the surrender, see Cobb to Beauregard, 24 April Letter, Telegram, Macon, 20 April 1865, Cobb Papers, 1865 and Howell Cobb, Jr.

[71] Wilson to Sherman, Telegram, Macon, 20 April 1865, appended to Wilson Report, 29 June 1865, OR, 49: Pt. 1, 367. Wilson sent this message to Sherman in cipher because he feared "that it might be tampered with by the rebel telegraph operators. Ibid.

Sherman replied later that night that Johnston had agreed to a "universal suspension of hostilities looking to a peace over the whole surface of our country." The Ohioan believed that the peace would "be made perfect in a few days," and ordered Wilson to stop hostilities unless he learned they would be resumed. He suggested that Wilson contract for supplies about Fort Valley or Columbus or about Rome and Kingston in Northwest Georgia. Amazingly, Sherman ordered Wilson to report his position through Confederate General Johnston.[72]

Even as the rest of his command entered Macon during the next few days,[73] Wilson took steps to secure the city. This task was made possible because, at least for the present, the Federal commander's difficulties with Cobb were resolved. He assigned Colonel Jacob G. Vail, commander of the 1st Brigade in Minty's/Long's 2nd Division to command Macon, and appointed Colonel Mitchell of the 98th Illinois Cavalry as provost marshall. He also saw Cobb again and asked him to report his staff officers and generals. At 5:00 P.M. Sherman's telegram announcing an armistice and directing Wilson to stop military action, arrived. Wilson followed Sherman's instructions, and sent a message to General Edward R.S. Canby, commanding the Military Division of West Mississippi, then in the field near Mobile, Alabama, and a messenger to Sherman presumably to relate events leading up to the occupation of Macon.[74]

At 8:00 P.M. on 21 April Wilson wired Sherman asking if he could release the prisoners.[75] Later that evening Sherman replied, ordering Wilson to occupy his position and contract for supplies for his men and horses. Once again, Sherman directed his subordinate to cease hostilities until he heard otherwise. However, Sherman also felt that the Confederate positions "must not be altered to our prejudice." The commander of the Military Division of the Mississippi informed Wilson of Lee's surrender, and assured him that he only awaited the approval of President Lincoln [news of the assassination had not yet arrived] to make terms of peace within the United States.[76]

Even as a number of Confederate citizens and soldiers, as Wilson confided to his diary, felt "disposed to question our rights to Macon,"[77] Wilson announced

---

[72] Ibid., 367.

[73] See reports of Emory Upton, Edward McCook, Robert H.G. Minty, and others in *OR*, 49: Pt. 1.

[74] Wilson Diary, 1865, 21 April 1865.

[75] Wilson to Sherman, Telegram, Macon, 8:00 P.M., 21 April 1865, OR, 49: Pt. 2, 425.

[76] Sherman to Wilson, Telegram, Raleigh, N.C., 21 April 1865, Ibid., 426. Because of communication difficulties Sherman did not know that Lincoln had been assassinated on the night of April 14, and had died on the morning of the 15th.

[77] Wilson Diary, 1865, 21 April 1865.

the armistice and ordered them to stop further acts of war. He assured them that supplies were to be contracted for "and everything done to secure good order." The Illinois cavalryman then commended his officers and men for their gallantry, steadiness, and strength in battle throughout the hard marches of the campaign. He also asked them "to remember that the people in whose midst they are now stationed are their countrymen, and should be treated with magnanimity and forbearance, in the hope that, although the war which has just ended has been long and bloody, it may secure a lasting peace to our beloved country."[78]

Cobb, for his part, wired General William T. Wofford, then in North Georgia, telling him of the Sherman-Johnston Convention, and that all military operations had ceased for the time being, and would not be resumed except on forty-eight hours notice, adding "In my opinion they will not be resumed at all."[79]

During the next week word of the armistice spread from Macon across Georgia. However, despite the cessation of fighting, confusion reigned. State officials wondered if the terms of the armistice extended to state officers or would they be taken prisoner? Could they exercise their authority outside the area controlled by Wilson or would a few days notice be given if hostilities resumed?[80]

When Georgia Adjutant and Inspector General Wayne asked him for orders, Cobb replied that Macon was captured, and its garrison held as prisoners of war on their parole not to leave the limits of the city. Wayne received Cobb's assurance that Wilson was waiting further orders from Sherman in regard to future movements of his command.[81]

While the city was occupied and he was a prisoner, Cobb reassured his wife the situation was as pleasant as it could be considering the outcome of the war. How long the armistice would continue, he added, he couldn't say although, he believed "in my opinion hostilities will not be renewed." Wilson and his men were behaving well, and treating the citizens with great courtesy. Overall, Cobb felt that Wilson's force was "the best disciplined army of the enemy that I have come in contact with."[82]

Cobb busied himself during the next few days arranging for the parole of his officers and men. He wrote Wilson on 25 April answering a verbal proposal concerning the prisoners made by Wilson on the 24th, that the prisoners at

---

[78] Maj. E.B. Beaumont, A.A.G., for Wilson, Special Field Orders, No. 22, Macon, 21 April 1865, *OR*, 49: Pt. 2, 426.

[79] Cobb to Wofford, Telegram, Macon, 21 April 1865, in Ibid., 49: Pt. 2, 428.

[80] Comptroller General of Georgia to Cobb, Milledgeville, 24 April 1865, Cobb Papers, 1865.

[81] Cobb to Wayne, Macon, 23 April 1865, Ibid.

[82] Cobb to his wife, Macon, 23 April 1865, Ibid.

Macon, Columbus, and West Point, should be paroled. Cobb, ever the lawyer, believed that the parole would be binding "if the capture is held to be legal," but if his protest was upheld and the capture of Macon illegal, then everyone should be released from their parole. Cobb told Wilson that a portion of the garrison included convalescents, and invalids who couldn't leave, and whom Cobb felt obligated to support during Wilson's occupation. Those individuals who lived in Macon might want to remain in the city until the armistice was concluded. Their wishes, Cobb believed, should also be taken into consideration.[83]

By 27 April Cobb had arranged for the parole of all of the officers and men held prisoner by Wilson, and most of them planned to leave Macon on the following day. He did not know how long he would stay in Macon, but had to make certain that his command would be taken care of before he left for home. He also felt he had to stay in Macon to "protect the people & country, as far as I can from the depredations and impressments of the enemy." This he tried to do by furnishing Wilson with supplies without the Federal commander resorting to the impressment of private property. He surprisingly had a high regard for Wilson, believing that the victorious cavalryman was "courteous and gentlemanly." Wilson, Cobb observed, went so far as to say that he answered any request made to him through [Cobb] that did not violate his positive orders." In fact, Cobb's position was "as pleasant as it could be under the circumstances." Nevertheless, the Georgian wanted to leave for home as soon as possible, and expressed disappointment that he knew so little of events that were transpiring out of Macon. Nothing was known of the continuing negotiations between Sherman and Johnston, but most people believed that hostilities would not resume.[84]

While Wilson busily consolidated Georgia under Federal control, the troopers who had followed him through one of the most successful and arduous campaigns in American history, were making themselves as comfortable as possible while resting in the vicinity of Macon. In fact, the horsemen of the Cavalry Corps soon made Macon into as large a camp as it had been in the early days of volunteering during the spring of 1861. At daylight on 21 April the men of the Chicago Board of Trade Battery swam in the millpond on the bank of which they camped, then slept until noon. At 2:30 P.M. the men broke camp and marched toward Macon trying to find a camp. However, the 4th Division got into the city ahead of them, so the unit halted in the woods one mile from town, and went into camp at a place where there was neither wood nor water.

---

[83] Cobb to Wilson, Macon, 25 April 1865, Ibid.

[84] Cobb to his wife, Macon, 27 April 1865, Cobb Papers, 1865. Cobb left Macon for Athens on the night of 29 April, Howell Cobb, Jr., to Mary McKinley, Macon, 28 April 1865, Cobb-Erwin-Lamar Collection.

The following day, the 22nd, the battery marched through Macon and went two miles out on the Columbus Road going into a "fine camp shady and plenty of wood & water." By Sunday the men cleared their campsite, amid rumors that Lee had surrendered the Army of Northern Virginia. However, their camp, being on the side of the road, was covered with dust.[85]

James Nourse of the Chicago Board of Trade Battery described the camp in a letter to his father on the 25th: "We have a good camp, shady, some dust, could not get along without a little." All of the battery's wounded had been sent on to Savannah, and black laborers worked to repair the Georgia Central Railroad.[86]

Sergeant Benjamin F. McGee of the Seventy-second Indiana Volunteer Infantry marveled at the artillery captured with the city. The cannons included sixty pieces, all mounted and in the very best condition. There was, he thought, enough ammunition to "supply all the armies in the Confederate states." The ammunition had been hauled out of the arsenal in great loads and piled on the ground beside the guns. Some of the siege guns were 64-pounders which needed a gallon of powder for each load. The powder was tied up in flannel sacks, and, when examined, the Federal troopers found the grains were as large as hulled walnuts.

The 98th and 123rd Illinois of Vail's First Brigade in Long's 2nd Division when into camp on the night of the 20th just outside the western defenses. Minty's 2nd Brigade camped on Tobesofkee Creek, three miles west of the works. At noon on 21 April the 1st and 4th Divisions began to arrive, and went into camp on the northeast and northwest sides of Macon.

As they proceeded into Macon, The men of the 72nd Indiana found everything quiet, with the city government continuing to operate. The *Daily Telegraph and Confederate,* soon to revert to the *Daily Telegraph,* continued to publish, which seemed a treat to Wilson's men, who had been without news for so long, even though the news was "rebel news."[87]

Late in the afternoon of 21 April some of the members of the 72nd Indiana determined to relieve the monotony caused by the easy capture of Macon. They

---

[85] James Nourse Diary, 21-24 April 1865, 1862-1878, typescript, pp. 283-84, in John Emory Bryant, Maine and Georgia Letters; 1851-1863, DU.

[86] Nourse to his father, Camp of Chicago Board of Trade Battery, Macon, 25 April 1865, Lewis Leigh Collection, DU.

[87] McGee, *History of the 72d Indiana Volunteer Infantry,* pp. 590-91. The reason for such large grains of powder was that a 64-pound gun threw a conical shell which weighed at least one hundred and twenty pounds. This tremendous weight, when it started from the gun, would start very slowly. A gallon of musket powder behind one of these shells would explode instantly, and burst the gun before starting the shell. As McGee said, "Coarser grained powder would ignite and explode slowly, and start the ball with less force." Ibid., p. 591.

decided to set fire to the piles of ammunition around the cannon. "This made things lively for a few minutes," McGee asserted, "as the bursting shells sent the old iron flying in every direction, and the burning powder sent up volumes of smoke, and you would have thought a volcano had broken loose."[88]

James W. Latta of McCook's 1st Division described Macon as a beautiful city located in a valley "& containing some of the most handsome private residences in the south." The churches were open on 22 April and the cool and pleasant weather accentuated by "the ringing of the bells," reminded Latta of a "piping bowl of peace." Latta noted the summer-like weather in Macon had its good and bad points. Although annoyed by flies and the heat, the men feasted on strawberries, salad greens, radishes, and green peas. Like Key, a month or two earlier, Latta was impressed by Rose Hill Cemetery which had only a few artificial adornments added except for a handsome entrance. "The natural situation & conformation of the ground on the banks of the Ocmulgee," he scribbled in his diary, "render the spot quite picturesque & romantic."[89]

Each trooper in Wilson's command seemed to have a different observation about Macon as they became acquainted with it. C. D. Mitchell reported that everyone in the city recognized the armistice, except the women who lived in, what he termed, "the "brown stone fronts" who didn't seem either pleased nor happy. Mitchell said Macon would be "a beautiful little city" except "in that prison pen [Camp Ogelthorpe] our poor prisoners have been jeered, cursed and starved."[90]

E.N. Gilpin of the 3rd Iowa Cavalry in Winslow's 1st Brigade of Upton's 4th Division had a fine view of Macon from his office in a confiscated tent on a beautiful greensward near the Fair Ground. On the 25th Gilpin saddled his horse and rode into town, visiting the Arsenal and other government buildings. During a second visit to Macon on 27 April Gilpin described the city as "one of the most magnificent in the South, parks, lakes, statuary; outside of Tempe's Vale, one would hardly expect to see anything more beautiful." On a third visit, he observed that the people were friendly, including most of the paroled soldiers, "though some of them are moody and cherish resentment."[91]

---

[88] Ibid., p. 592.

[89] James W. Latta Diary, 22-23 April 1865, in James W. Latta Diary, The Papers of James W. Latta, LC.

[90] C.D. Mitchell, Field Notes, 22 April 1865, Extract from Field Notes of the Civil War C.D. Mitchell, March 15–May 14, 1865, LC, hereafter cited as Mitchell, Field Notes.

[91] E.N. Gilpin Diary, 22, 23, 27, and 29 April 1865, in E.N. Gilpin, 3d Iowa Cavalry, "The Last Campaign. Diary of E.N. Gilpin March 11-May 14, 1865," Reprint from *The Journal of the US Cavalry Association* (Leavenworth, KS: Press of Ketcheson Printing Co, n.d.) 657-59.

Gilpin shrewdly observed one trait which was "very noticeable in these Southern people." Certain families in each State, he felt, held themselves with a "kind of superiority above the others." They were, he believed, "different from Northerners, who think Smith is just as good as Jones, and so is Robinson."[92]

Many of the paroled Confederates, who were 11,000-strong by 21 April told Alva C. Griest of the 72nd Indiana Infantry that the war was over and "they are glad of it and are tired of it and want to be at home." The Southerners mingled freely with their Federal counterparts, with the former rebels even carrying their side arms, which Griest considered as "curious." He noted that the Confederates seemed to be "warm friends" who talked freely about the war and its terrible ravages.[93]

Dr. W. H. Barker of the 3rd Iowa Cavalry, pitied the ragged Confederate soldiers who overran the country about Macon. These "footsore and weary-ragged-dirty[,] unkempt[,] hungry[,] penniless, discouraged[,] and hopeless" men, as he described them, were "cowed[,] humbled[,] and crestfallen." Many of them were homeless, and scorned by their own people, "especially by the wealthy-former slave holding class." This latter group, Barker, asserted, often refused them food or shelter, and utterly ignored them. On the other hand, Barker reported, these same soldiers were treated in the kindest manner by the Federal troopers, and "not even upbraided for the gallant fight" they had made for the fallen Confederacy. However, Barker's charitable attitude toward the defeated Confederates changed over time. He recorded that, after the new President Andrew Johnson inaugurated generous Reconstruction policies toward the defeated South, the former soldiers "became quite impudent–and would loudly boast–'You alls did not lick we uns–Youns only overpowered weuns'."[94]

Despite their impressions of Macon as a beautiful city, many troopers remained in a bad mood. As early as 12 April while they were still in Alabama, the men had received the news of Lee's surrender. On the 22 April news arrived of the armistice between Sherman and Johnston which surrendered the Army of

---

[92] Gilpin Diary, 30 April 1865, p. 659.

[93] Alva C. Griest Journal, 21-22 April 1865, "Three Years in Dixie Personal Adventures, Scenes and Incidents of the March. The Journal of Alva C. Griest, Company B, 72d Regiment, Indiana Volunteer Infantry First Brigade, Second Division, First Cavalry Corps. M.D.M. July 26, 1862-July 6, 1865," in Eli P. Long Papers, USAMHI, hereafter cited as Griest Journal. Major C.L. Greeno, Provost-Marshal of Wilson's Cavalry Corps, reported that 14.985 Confederate prisoners were paroled in Macon in April and May, 1865. Of course, the majority of these were men from Lee's Army of Northern Virginia and Johnston's Army of Tennessee who passed through Macon on their way to their homes in the Lower South. See *OR*, 49: Pt. 1, 415.

[94] W.H. Barker, M.D., "My Memories of the Civil War," Harvey, Iowa: n.p., 1926, in USAMHI, p. 144, hereafter cited as Barker, "Memories."

Tennessee, but, as Sergeant McGee wrote, "all the news we get comes from the rebels, and the men say 'it will not do to tie to'." Wilson's men took all of this with stoical indifference. Many in the army believed that "the rebels have not been half whipped, and in proof of this point...the citizens are chafing at our occupation of the city, and swearing we have no right to be here, and that we have violated the armistice or we could never have gotten inside the city." This type of talk goaded the Federals many of whom threatened to burn Macon. Yet these remarks were made mostly by non-soldiers, "who bitterly curse the leaders of the rebellion and the soldiers, for not holding out longer." Most of the privates were happy to lay down their arms.[95]

Soon a report arrived which greatly agitated the feelings of most of the men. Shortly after breakfast on the morning of 23 April news arrived of the assassination of President Lincoln. McGee declared, "Oh, what a terrible national calamity is this! Can it be that this nation has not yet suffered enough? O, God! can this be the precursor of more war and bloodshed? How this fills us with gloom and strange forebodings. But, oh, Lord, may Thy will be accomplished and peace speedily proclaimed!" The news struck the men "like a thunderbolt," and several fires broke out later on the 23rd, while on the evening of 22 April two city blocks were burned. During an inspection the men were checked to learn the exact number of cartridges and their exact fighting trim in anticipation of the renewal of hostilities after Lincoln's assassination. The members of the provost guard were especially vigilant to keep the city from being burned, and several fires set about the city were put out by the soldiers.[96]

C. D. Mitchell observed that the murder of Lincoln had "spread a cloud over the camps."[97] Dr. W. H. Barker wrote "the low mutterings of his [Wilson's] troopers-boded no good to the defunct Confederates-an awful vengeance threatened–to fall on both the army–and the country–as well." Barker believed that only the rejoicing over the end of the war held the vengeful feelings in check until "better councils prevailed–and normal conditions were again established."[98]

Alva C. Griest confided to his diary that the news of Lincoln's murder was "sorrowful news if true and it will be worse for the Rebels for Lincoln was their friend if they only knew it." Griest had no confidence in Vice President Andrew Johnson, however, believing him to be a "Rebel sympathizer at heart," but added, "I hope I am mistaken." Shortly afterward Griest proclaimed that Lincoln was murdered by a man named Wilkes Booth.[99]

---

[95] McGee, *History of the 72d Indiana Volunteer Infantry*, pp. 592-93.
[96] Ibid., p. 594.
[97] Mitchell, Field Notes, 24 April 1865, p. 47.
[98] Barker, "Memories," p. 143.
[99] Griest Journal, 24 and 26 April 1865.

The anger of many officers and troopers was redirected from their vanquished foe to their commander on 28 April when their officers marched the men out about three miles, halted them, and searched for private property. This property, which included gold, silver, watches, and jewelry, was purportedly stolen by some of the men during the campaign. Unfortunately, some property was found in the first company of the 3rd Ohio Cavalry which was searched. Other men who had taken private property hid it in the sand under their feet until the search ended. The 3rd Ohio returned to camp at 4:30.[100]

Alva Griest explained that the search was conducted because a Macon bank was robbed on the night of 26 April and some $30,000 to $40,000 stolen. His unit, the 72nd Indiana Infantry, was told it was being marched to Augusta on 27 April. Their officers halted the column three and a half miles from Macon, formed the men in a hollow square and searched them. Despite this effort the money was not found by evening.[101]

Dr. W. H. Barker reported the men of his unit, the 3rd Iowa Cavalry, were told they were going on a long and dangerous expedition, marched for over an hour, and then halted in an open field next to a creek known as Silver Creek. They were dismounted and ordered to unsaddle their horses, and place the saddles on the ground in front of them. The men stood at the heads of their horses, while officers searched them thoroughly, Confiscating watches, money, pocket books, and pocket knives. Barker reported the men regarded the search "as a most disgraceful–and humiliating indignity–and it was resented as such." He added that the search "came near causing a mutiny." The officers mollified their men by promising to return the confiscated valuables. To make matters even worse, when the unit returned to camp they found it despoiled of everything leaving only the bare ground.[102]

The 3rd Iowa remained in their desolate camp for several days, half-starved and with nothing to do. Everyone was left alone to come and go as they pleased. One of Barker's squadron, "a restless-mischievous recruit," decided to have some fun. Near the camp was an abandoned Confederate battery with the guns and ammunition chests standing just where they had been placed before the

---

[100] Sergeant Thomas Crofts, *History of the Service of the Third Ohio Volunteer Cavalry in the War for the Preservation of the Union from 1861-1865. Compiled from the official records and from Diaries of members of the Regiment,* pp. 203-04.

[101] Griest Journal, 27 April 1865. Griest was possibly more concerned with the dangers which might be found in the Ocmulgee River than in being searched, however. He noted that Macon was "surely a very unhealthy place situated as it is along the banks of the Ocmulgee River, which is a still muddy stream and has alligators in it." He gloomily added, "One was killed here last June 13 feet long after he had eaten a man who was bathing in the river." Ibid.

[102] Barker, "Memories," 143.

surrender. The trooper went to the ammunition chests, opened one, uncapped a number of fixed shells, collected a quantity of powder, and scattered it all through the battery which stood in a pine grove where the ground was thickly covered with pine needles. He made long trails of powder, and then touched it with a match. Barker wrote: "a wild scene followed, and an explosion that aroused the whole camp." Luckily, no one was hurt. The Confederate officers had hidden their swords in a nearby brush pile, and when they came to reclaim them they found them ruined by the fire.[103]

Another unit, the 1st Ohio Cavalry, destroyed a large amount of Spencer ammunition on the night of 3 May by throwing the cartridges in the fire. This outfit was punished when Wilson fined each commissioned officer in the regiment $10 to pay for the ammunition. The enlisted men were also punished with a $5 fine for each man on the muster and pay rolls. In his Special Field Orders No. 30, issued on 4 May Wilson explained, "This order is found to be necessary to protect the Government of the United States from losses on account of willful destruction on the part of enlisted men and gross neglect on the part of the officers."[104]

The stern manner in which he punished his troopers for violating orders not to destroy ammunition set the tone for Wilson's military regime in Macon. He hoped that a combination of firmness in dealing with his men and kindness of the type that a strict father meted out to his children in dealing with civilians would pave the way for an early return to normalcy in Middle Georgia.

---

[103] Ibid., 144.

[104] E. B. Beaumont, Special Field Orders No. 30, Macon, 4 May 1865, *OR*, 49, Pt. 2, 601.

Chapter 16

Macon Under Wilson

On 3 May Wilson issued Special Field Orders No. 29 announcing the firing of a 200-gun salute at noon the following day "in honor of the victories gained by the armies under the command of Lieutenant-General Grant and the peace resulting to our country." Lieutenant Rodney of the 4th US Artillery was directed to fire the salute.[1] During the morning of the 4th Wilson's troopers made the necessary preparations to raise the US flag on Mulberry Street in front of the Lanier House at the moment when Rodney's guns fired their salute "in honor of the victories gained by Federal armies of late." The *Macon Evening News* noted, "Although we deem this rather bad taste in the authorities, under the circumstances, we trust it will not produce a bad effect.[2] Despite the possibility that the action might "produce a bad effect," the stars and stripes was formally raised in front of the Lanier House where Wilson had his headquarters at 2:00 P.M. on 4 May accompanied by the roar of cannon, by this time an unfamiliar sound in Macon.[3] Laura Boykin confided to her diary, "A few days ago the Yankees fired 200 guns...and reared the old and hated US flag in the middle of the town, but I closed my doors to shut out the sound and bowed my head and wept."[4]

Federal commanders followed this victory celebration by heaping lavish praise on the men who had followed Wilson from the Tennessee River, through Alabama, and into the heart of Georgia. Thomas wired Wilson from Nashville on 14 May to express his "entire satisfaction with [the operations of Wilson's command] from the time of its first concentration at this place," on 2 November 1864 to the present. The men had "the proud satisfaction, Thomas believed, "of knowing that they have eminently done their part toward the suppression of this

---

[1] E.B. Beaumont, Special Field Orders No. 29, Macon, 3 May 1865, *OR*, 49: Pt. 2, 587.

[2] *Macon Evening News*, 4 May 1865.

[3] Ibid.; Crofts, *History of the Third Ohio Cavalry*, p. 204; Wilson Diary, 1865, 4 May 1865.

[4] Boykin Diary, 1 May 1865.

gigantic rebellion and that their deeds will be recorded among the honorable and glorious in the history of their country."[5] Minty, whose men had actually captured Macon, told them that their march from the Tennessee River was "a triumphal one, and now forms a bright page in the history of our country." Urging his men to behave in an "honest and honorable" manner, Minty wanted each man to be the protector and defender of "the weak and helpless and that the honor of the command is in his hands, not be tarnished, but to have fresh luster added to it, and that every man will so act that all must acknowledge that the division is great in peace as in war."[6]

Wilson himself boasted his men had made the last campaign and fought the last battle of the war. His troopers, he noted, were "a close, compact, and efficient organization of three divisions and six brigades with from three to five regiments to a brigade and a battery of horse artillery to each division, the whole capable of marching easily and indefinitely at the average rate of thirty-five miles per day."[7]

Anxious to rejoin the people of Georgia and Florida to the Union, Wilson began a series of actions designed to accomplish these goals. He sent several of his subordinates to receive the surrender of the Confederate garrisons at Atlanta and Augusta. General Emory Upton was sent to Atlanta and Augusta to receive the surrender of the garrisons at those places, and General Edward McCook to Tallahassee, Florida, to receive the surrender of the Confederate troops garrisoned there. Major M. H. Williams was ordered to receive the surrender of the Confederate troops at Milledgeville. Another subordinate, Wilson's ordnance officer, Major McBurney, was directed to go to Milledgeville and receive the ordnance, ordnance stores, and others stores there and send them to Macon.[8]

Another important problem which confronted Wilson was the surrender of the state troops under Governor Brown's command. On 3 May Wilson wrote Brown ordering him to surrender the soldiers to him as the officer designated to receive it. One of the points which Wilson emphasized was the officers must give their individual paroles not to take up arms against the United States until

---

[5] Thomas to Wilson, Telegram, Nashville, 14 May 1865, 12:00 noon, *OR*, 49:2: 763.

[6] Captain T.W. Scott, Acting A.A.G., for Minty, Circular, Macon, 22 May 1865, Ibid., 872.

[7] Wilson, *Under The Old Flag*, II:295.

[8] Wilson to Thomas, Macon, 3 May 1865, *OR*, 49: Pt. 2, 583, hereafter cited as Wilson to Thomas, 3 May 1865; Wilson to Commanding Officer, Richmond, VA., Telegram, Macon, 4 May 1865, Ibid., 598; Beaumont, Special Orders No. 67, Macon, 2 May 1865, Ibid., 568; Wilson, *Under The Old Flag*, II:306. Upton left Macon on May 1 and arrived in Augusta on the 3rd. Wilson to Thomas, 3 May 1865.citation?

properly exchanged, with each company, battalion, or regimental commander to sign a similar parole for the troops under his command. The governor had to surrender all arms and public property, although this directive "will not embrace the side-arms of the officers nor their private horses or baggage.[9]

Georgia Adjutant and Inspector General Wayne told Wilson that Brown was in Milledgeville and planned to be in Macon on Friday afternoon on 5 May to meet with the Federal commander.[10] The meeting between Brown and Wilson, held on 6 May became an early test of President Andrew Johnson's determination to restore the Union. Wilson and Brown had a long discussion in which Brown, who had already called a meeting of the Georgia General Assembly for 22 May and who had met with Cobb and other leading Georgians on the night of 5 May asked for Wilson's support. The Federal commander forbade the meeting of the legislature on the ground of inexpediency. Instead, Wilson urged "quietude, improvement of municipal law and discouraged political meetings of all kinds as not calculated to restore peace and good feeling."[11]

In a letter to his immediate superior, General George H. Thomas, Commander of the Department of the Cumberland at Nashville, Wilson outlined his policy of forbidding public meetings. "I have discountenanced everything like political meetings and discussions," Wilson wrote, "and counseled the people to defer all political action till the excitement of the recent events has abated." Wilson did not believe that the Georgia General Assembly and State officials, all of whom were elected because of their support for the Confederacy, should be allowed to control the future policies of the State. He would, therefore, forbid any meeting of the legislature or the assembly of any state or county convention until the proper authority was obtained from Washington. The young cavalry general, who showed many statesmanlike qualities by his conduct of affairs at Macon, felt that "when the soreness necessarily felt at defeat has been allayed, and the people have had time to think dispassionately," there would be no difficulty in reestablishing the relations between Georgia and Alabama and the rest of the United States.[12]

Thomas replied on 9 May that Wilson was correct in his decision not to permit the meeting of the General Assembly. It would be up to President Johnson to decide what steps were necessary to place Georgia in a proper relation with the rest of the United States. Wilson, in the meantime, should encourage the people in their efforts to reestablish civil law in Bibb and

---

[9] Wilson to Brown, Macon, 3 May 1865, *OR*, 49:2, 585-86.

[10] Wayne to Wilson, Telegram, Milledgeville, 4 May 1865, Ibid., 599.

[11] Wilson Diary, 1865, 6 May 1865; William Harris Bragg, *Joe Brown's Army The Georgia State Line, 1862-1865* (Macon: Mercer University Press, 1987) 109-10.

[12] Wilson to Thomas, Telegram, 3 May 1865, *OR*, 49: Pt. 2, 584.

surrounding counties "in accordance with the Georgia code in force prior to January 1861, except that in all matters the negro must be regarded as a free man."[13]

After the meeting Brown, with Wilson's knowledge, asked Johnson to allow the General Assembly to meet "because of great destitution of provisions and with a view to the restoration of peace and order by accepting the result which the fortunes of war have imposed upon us." Brown wanted to know if Wilson had the support of the Government. Would Johnson, Brown asked, order Wilson to let the Assembly meet?[14]

On 6 May Wilson telegraphed Secretary of War Edwin M. Stanton, a leader of the Republican Radicals, asking for instructions.[15] Wilson explained to a sympathetic Stanton that Brown, without the cavalry commander's knowledge, had issued the call for the General Assembly to meet. However, Wilson believed it was improper for either Brown or the General Assembly to exercise any power, directly or indirectly, in shaping policy or opinion in regard to reestablishing Georgia as a state within the Union. Wilson told Stanton he would not permit the Assembly to meet, unless ordered to do so by Federal officials in Washington, believing there was no need for such meetings, "certainly none when controlled by prominent secessionists."[16]

Stanton, acting for Johnson, replied on the evening of 7 May ordering him not to allow the General Assembly to meet because the collapse of the currency and the great destitution of provisions among Georgia's poor were caused "by the treason, insurrection, and rebellion against the authority, Constitution, and laws of the United States, incited and carried on for the last four years by Mr. Brown and his confederate rebels and traitors, who are responsible for all the want and destitution now existing in that State." The war and its attendant destitution, Stanton felt, was brought on by Brown and his compatriots, who continued fighting to "the last extremity," until forced to surrender. Stanton told Wilson that the legislature could not meet to "set on foot fresh acts of treason and rebellion," concluding with instructions to "take prompt measures to prevent any assemblage of rebels as a Legislature or under any other pretext within your command."[17]

On the same evening, Stanton ordered Wilson to arrest Brown, "who pretends to act as Governor of Georgia," and send him to Washington as a

---

[13] Thomas to Wilson, Telegram, Nashville, 6 P.M., 9 May 1865, Ibid., 680.

[14] Brown to Johnston, Telegram, Macon, 6 May 1865, Ibid., 630.

[15] Wilson Diary, 1865, 6 May 1865.

[16] Wilson to Stanton, Macon, 6 May 1865, *OR*, 49: Pt. 2, 628.

[17] Stanton to Wilson, Telegram, Washington, 6:00 P.M., 7 May 1865, Ibid., 646-47.

prisoner.[18] Wilson sent Captain G.H. Kneeland of his staff to Milledgeville to arrest Brown on the evening of 9 May.[19] This order was sent even though Wilson paroled Brown in the latter's capacity as commander-in-chief of the military forces of Georgia, while forbidding him to act in his capacity as governor.[20] Captain Kneeland arrested Brown in Milledgeville on Tuesday evening, 9 May, and returned to Macon early in the morning of 10 May. The Governor was sent to Washington at 9:00 A.M. on the same day with an escort commanded by Lieutenant William Bayard and a contingent from the 4th US Cavalry.[21]

Grant, Wilson's powerful patron, observed these proceedings from his post in the War Department at Washington. He advised the Secretary of War on 19 May that if Brown's call for the meeting of the Georgia General Assembly happened after Brown's parole, there was no question that the governor had violated his parole. But, if the call came before the parole, Grant believed that the Government should observe their part of the contract, although he would not advise Stanton to send Brown, who by this time was imprisoned in Washington, back to Georgia "under any circumstances." However, Grant felt that Brown should be subject to arrest as long as he observed his parole "without giving him notice first that he is absolved from further observance of it."[22]

Brown's stay in Washington was relatively short, possibly due in part to Grant's position regarding his parole. By 2 July Georgia's former chief executive had returned from Washington and issued an address to the people of Georgia in which he resigned his position as governor.[23]

Another of Wilson's tasks, possibly the most important, involved feeding his men. Wilson soon learned that his large force could not long subsist unless extraordinary measures were taken to feed them. Sherman directed his subordinate to purchase supplies in Southwest Georgia, a move which Wilson

---

[18] Stanton to Wilson, Telegram, Washington, 7:00 P.M., 7 May 1865, Ibid., 647; Wilson Diary, 1865, 9 May 1865.

[19] Beaumont, Special Orders No. 73, Macon, 8 May 1865, Ibid., 683; Wilson Diary, 1865, 9 May 1865.

[20] Wilson Diary, 1865, 8 May 1865.

[21] Ibid., 10 May 1865; Wilson to Brown, Macon, 9 May 1865, *OR*, 49: Pt. 2, 681-82; Wilson to Stanton, Telegram, Macon, 10 May 1865, 10 A.M., Ibid., 702; *Macon Daily Telegraph*, 11 May 1865. Brown was incarcerated in a cell in Washington's Carroll Prison. Bragg, *Joe Brown's Army*, 110.

[22] Grant to Stanton, Washington, 19 May 1865, *OR*, 49: Pt. 2, 836.

[23] Wilson to Thomas, Macon, 2 July 1865, Ibid., 1060. Wilson, angered because Brown did not ask for permission to take these actions, noted, "Unless he has done this by direction and permission of the President, I think he should be arrested and removed to a Northern prison." Ibid.

considered "both kindly and considerate, and so far as it was necessary and practicable his instructions were carried into effect." All foraging, Wilson observed, was discontinued as soon as the war ended.[24] As early as 1 May Sherman announced that he was sending supplies to Wilson from Savannah to Augusta by boat, and thence via rail, but felt that Wilson should move his troops to Decatur, Alabama, partly because of supply problems.[25] Wilson believed that it would be "impracticable to make the march which you direct" because the country between Macon and Decatur was "utterly denuded of forage." Besides, Wilson could buy enough corn in Southwest Georgia to last his men and animals four weeks. After that time the supply would have to come from Savannah.[26] Wilson had 17,000 soldiers, including his three black regiments, and 21,000 animals to feed. He told Thomas on 7 May that he could subsist in Macon for another twenty to twenty-five days.[27]

One of Wilson's problems lay in the fact that, while enough corn might be shipped via rail to subsist his corps until the end of May, the people did not have the capability to haul it to the nearest line for any distance due to the lack of available capital. To make matters worse the Savannah River at Augusta, the principal connection between Wilson and the outside world, had only three and a half feet of water in it and was falling and the Ocmulgee was no better.[28]

When Wilson asked Montgomery C. Meigs, the Union's able Quartermaster General on 11 May about repairing railroads in Georgia, Meigs replied that Federal policy prohibited spending money on railroad repairs in any part of the former Confederacy, except when needed to supply posts and garrisons. Money could be spent only on military necessities. Hay for horses and mules, for instance, had to be transported by water from Savannah to Augusta, and thence by rail to Macon.[29] Grant, on the other hand, was more helpful, authorizing his protégé to use captured money to buy supplies, and felt it was unnecessary to repair the railroads around Atlanta because all of Wilson's communications with the rest of the country would be by sea.[30]

---

[24] Wilson, *Under the Old Flag*, II, 298.

[25] Sherman to Wilson, Telegram, Savannah, 1 May 1865, *OR,* 49: Pt. 2, 550.

[26] Wilson to Sherman, Telegram, Macon, 4 May 1865, Ibid., 598.

[27] Wilson to Thomas, Telegram, Macon, 6 P.M., 7 May 1865, *OR*, 49: Pt. ?, 648-49. Wilson suggested that, if Thomas and Sherman wanted him in Northern Alabama badly enough, the former officer would have to send him forage "as far below Dalton as possible," and repair the railroad from Atlanta to Chattanooga to enable him to move. Ibid.

[28] Wilson to Brevet Major General John A. Rawlins, Chief of Staff, Washington, Telegram, Macon, 7 A.M.. 11 May 1865, Ibid., 762.

[29] Meigs to Wilson, Telegram, Washington, 17 May 1865, Ibid., 816.

[30] Grant to Wilson, Telegram, Washington, 430 P.M., 18 May 1865, Ibid., 829.

By 19 May after the military authorities made plans to send some of the Cavalry Corps north to the Tennessee River, Wilson wired General Canby in Alabama, that he needed supplies of long forage and grain for 6,000 animals.[31]

By July Wilson was buying corn from former Confederates, including the Cobbs who sold five hundred bushels through a government contractor at eighty cents a bushel. The family had two thousand more bushels to sell from their plantations in Worth and Sumter Counties, Georgia. The Federal Government was paying them $.75 a bushel in greenbacks or $.50 in gold. However, John A. Cobb, who managed his father's plantations, believed he could get $.55 to $.60 a bushel in gold for the corn if it were delivered at the Southwestern Railroad Depot in Americus.[32]

While he was in Macon, Wilson used the city as a base to track down and capture some of the Confederacy's most important officials, including the South's most famous refugee, Jefferson Davis. In early May, Wilson took precautions to capture Davis by sending some scouts and detectives to watch the line of the Savannah River and the roads leading through northern Georgia. More troops were alerted in the eastern portion of the State, and the famed cavalry raider, General Benjamin Grierson who had recently arrived at Eufaula, Alabama, was directed to move toward the Mississippi River by way of Union Springs, Tuskegee, Montgomery, and Selma, Alabama to head Davis off if he should escape Wilson's dragnet in Georgia. Wilson did not believe Davis could escape if he had wagons and a large escort, but felt it "will be quite difficult to apprehend him if he attempts it well mounted with one or two attendants.[33]

Davis was captured by Federal troopers of Colonel Robert H. G. Minty's 2nd Division near the hamlet of Irwinville in South Georgia on 10 May and brought to Macon. He arrived on 12 May and had dinner with Wilson at the Lanier House. The conversation between the two men was cordial concerning their experiences at the US Military Academy; some of the professors both men had studied under, especially the famed teacher, Dennis Hart Mahan; some of Davis' generals, particularly Lee and Johnston; the events leading up to Davis' capture; and the charges which might be raised against him. The Confederate president, accompanied by a 150-man guard, left Macon on an evening train bound for Atlanta on 13 May. General Emory Upton accompanied Davis and his party to Augusta on 14 May.[34]

[31] Wilson to Canby, Telegram, Macon, 19 May 1865, Ibid., 840.

[32] John A. Cobb to Howell Cobb, Macon, 10 July 1865, Cobb-Erwin-Lamar Collection.

[33] Wilson to Thomas, 3 May 1865, *OR*, 49: Pt. 2, 584.

[34] Wilson Diary, 1865, 12, 13, and 14 May 1865; Wilson to Robert H.G. Minty, Macon, 12 May 1865, *OR,* 49: Pt., 2. 735. For a more detailed account of Davis' capture see Wilson, *Under the Old Flag*, II, 305; and Burke Davis, *The Long*

Laura Boykin described Davis' entry into Macon on the afternoon of 12 May. She went to church that afternoon to meet the choir, and sat alone for an hour before anyone came. Someone called her to the door to witness a great event. From this vantage point she saw excited crowds in the street, and witnessed the arrival of Davis and his party guarded by 600 Federal troopers who "filled the street, up to the church." She added, "I fairly writhed in agony."[35]

Wilson also used Macon as a base to snare other high-ranking Confederate officials. One of these men, Alabama Confederate Senator Clement C. Clay, surrendered to Wilson at Macon on 12 May. On 17 May Wilson received orders from Secretary of War Stanton to arrest Confederate Vice President Alexander H. Stephens. Wilson had, however, precipitated the order by arresting Stephens on the 11th.[36]

During his march through Alabama, Wilson ordered each of his three divisions to recruit and organize a regiment of former slaves. Minty began to organize the regiment assigned to his 2nd Division, and assigned Major Martin Archer to command it. Eight troopers from the division were detailed to help Archer take charge of the men as they were organized into companies. As Minty proceeded more slaves joined the regiment until, upon the arrival of the 2nd Division at Columbus, the regiment numbered 1,400 of whom about 1,200 were mounted on horses and mules. Difficulties arose in obtaining provisions for the men and forage for their animals, but enough was obtained. By the time Wilson reached Macon, on 21 April, his regiment and the black regiment assigned to the 4th Division totaled 2,700 men. On 24 and 25 April, the men were examined by the surgeon and the two regiments were each reduced to 1,000 men. Wilson ordered each regiment to report to their division commanders on 1 May although there was a shortage of arms and accouterments. While they were camped in Macon, the men had enough tents and sheds to protect them from the weather, and most of them were well-clothed in captured Confederate uniforms. Minty wrote: "The most difficult part of the organization of the colored troops was that of subsistence, as we were compelled to subsist entirely upon the country and when we take into consideration that a large cavalry force were constantly in our advance, nearly clearing the whole country of subsistence, it made the procuring of rations for the regiments a difficult matter indeed, which

---

Surrender (New York: Random House, 1985) 140-58. For a full account of Davis' flight and capture see William C. Davis, *Jefferson Davis; The Man and His Hour* (New York: Harper Collins Publishers, 1991) 604-42.

[35] Boykin Diary, 13 May 1865.

[36] Wilson Diary, 1865, 12 and 17 May 1865.

was only accomplished by industry and perseverance on the part of officers and men."[37]

On 18 May Stanton sent a message to Wilson approving the organization of the three black units and directing him to muster them in for three years.[38] Wilson soon asked Rawlins for regimental numbers to give to these units.[39] Rawlins designated the unit assigned to the 1st Division as the 136th US Colored Troops [USC.T.]. The regiment assigned to the Second Division was designated as the 137th Regiment USC.T., while that assigned to the 4th Division received the designation of the 138th USC.T.[40] The three regiments were soon organized into a brigade which Wilson called the "African Brigade." On 21 May Stanton told Wilson to place General Andrew J. Alexander, commanding the 2nd Brigade in Upton's 4th Division, in command of the new organization, an order which Wilson complied with as soon as Alexander consented to assume the additional responsibility.[41]

The most interesting part of Wilson's administration, headquartered in Macon's Lanier House, concerned his relations with Howell Cobb. Although, as Wilson said, "Cobb was not only one of the largest slaveholders, but an original secessionist, whose proudest boast was that his state followed him, not he his state." Although Cobb had, from the first, thrown his "whole heart and fortune" into the Confederacy, but, as a shrewd lawyer he quickly realized that when Lee and Johnston surrendered and Davis became a fugitive, the end had come. From that time the Georgian did everything he could to restore order and public confidence, and to help Wilson. Wilson heaped lavish praise upon him as "a man of austere manners and great dignity, who scorned to ask favors for himself, but did his utmost to ameliorate the condition of his fellow-citizens." The acquaintance of the two officers, started under such trying conditions, "ripened into a friendship" which lasted until Cobb's death over three years later. Wilson asserted, many years later, that he remained on good terms with the Cobb family.[42]

Cobb proved his willingness to support Wilson by helping him collect badly-needed supplies for his large corps. The Georgian ordered his quartermasters and commissaries throughout Georgia, especially in the relatively untouched region of Southwestern Georgia, to ship grain, corn, and other provisions to the Federals. Wilson noted that this was done "before any terms of capitulation had been made known to him or myself." Of course, Cobb had

[37] Major Martin Archer Report, near Macon, 17 May 1865, *OR*, 49: Pt. 2, 818-19.

[38] Stanton to Wilson, Telegram, Washington, 18 May 1865, Ibid., 828.

[39] Wilson to Rawlins, Telegram, Macon, 830 A.M., 22 May 1865, Ibid., 870.

[40] Edward P. Inhoff, General Orders, No. 29, Macon, 27 May 1865, Ibid., 919.

[41] Wilson Diary, 1865, 21 and 22 May 1865.

[42] Wilson, *Under The Old Flag*, II, 284-85.

another motive for doing this, because, as Wilson observed, "to have been compelled to forage for them [provisions] would have resulted in the devastation of the entire country in the vicinity of the city."[43]

Unfortunately, the War Department dropped a bombshell on Cobb on 19 May when Assistant Secretary of War Charles A. Dana ordered Wilson to arrest Cobb and send him as a prisoner to Fort Lafayette in Boston Harbor.[44] In obedience to this order Wilson reluctantly issued Special Orders No. 85 directing his aide-de-camp, Captain William W. van Antwerp, to go to Athens, where Cobb then was, and arrest him.[45] Wilson promptly informed Dana's superior, Secretary of War Stanton, that Cobb was protected by a parole, but Stanton replied, "If Howell Cobb is protected by any parole, it [his arrest] is not designed to violate it." However, the War Secretary asked Wilson to send a copy of Cobb's parole to Washington so that Judge Advocate General Joseph Holt might review it to "determine its legal effect." In the meantime, Stanton assured Wilson, "you may retain him in Macon until the question is settled."[46]

Cobb, however, was not in Macon when this telegram was sent. Instead, he was in Atlanta awaiting transportation to Chattanooga, Tennessee, from which point he would proceed north to Boston. He arrived in Atlanta on the evening of 24 May and prepared to leave the following morning for the Tennessee city. While not happy about his arrest, he confided to his wife that Wilson and his officers had given him "every courtesy & attention." It, however, didn't raise Cobb's spirits much to learn that his travelling companions would be Confederate Secretary of the Navy Stephen R. Mallory and Georgia Confederate Senator Benjamin H. Hill.[47]

Fortunately, because of Wilson's influence, Cobb was released upon his arrival in Nashville. By 4 June, he was back in Athens under orders to remain in Georgia subject to Johnson's orders. He assured Wilson he would "Promptly respond to any orders or summons that I may receive; and in the meantime shall strictly conform to my parole." "For this act of personal kindness and confidence," Cobb told the young cavalryman, "I am indebted in a great measure to yourself," assuring him that neither he or Johnson "shall have cause to regret the confidence that has thus been manifested." Cobb wanted most of all

---

[43] Wilson Report, Macon, 29 June 1865, *OR*, 49: Pt. 1, 367- 68. Of course, Cobb, in all his dealings with Wilson, cleverly won the appreciation of the young Federal cavalryman, knowing that his relationship with Wilson would benefit him when he sought a pardon. It might also help him if he was arrested.

[44] Charles A. Dana to Wilson, Telegram, Washington, 19 May 1865, *OR*, 49: Pt. 2, 839.

[45] Wilson, Special Orders No. 85, Macon, 21 May 1865, Ibid., 861.

[46] Stanton to Wilson, Telegram, Washington, 24 May 1865, Ibid., 889.

[47] Cobb to his wife, Atlanta, 25 May 1865, Cobb Papers, 1865.

to have a personal interview with Wilson on matters of public interest, and planned to come to Macon at any time Wilson could see him.[48] Mary Ann Cobb also had a good word to say to Wilson, which by the tone of her letter, must be genuine, expressing her thanks for Wilson's "kindness and...marked courtesy towards my husband."[49]

Wilson replied he would be happy to see the Georgian whenever he came to Macon, and observed, the two men could discuss both public and private matters.[50] Cobb arrived in Macon in mid-June, and conferred with Wilson. Upon the latter's advice, he wrote a remarkable letter to Johnson on 14 June, which Wilson promptly sent to the President. The letter was printed and widely circulated throughout the country, but, Wilson noted, "it was not received in any part of the country with the favor to which its moderate and statesmanlike views entitled it." Cobb opened with a declaration that he was an original secessionist who advised the people of Georgia to secede, asserting that he had served in the army until the close of the war, and that his course since the collapse of the Confederacy had "conformed to the obligations of the surrender." Cobb, Wilson believed, realized the South was defeated, and using that for a basis, set down the principles which he believed should guide the policy of both North and South. In a covering letter Wilson called Cobb's letter, "this weighty and dignified contribution to the question of reconstruction," and considered the Georgian had rendered "a public duty, the wisdom of which has been amply justified by the course of subsequent history."[51] A writer for the *Macon Daily News* noted that Cobb believed that slavery was forever dead, but was not at all sad. The reason for Cobb's confidence lay in the fact that he believed "a bright future lay ahead" for the South and expressed confidence in the President's ability and integrity, "and thought his course towards us would be conciliatory."[52] The *Daily Telegraph* noted Cobb's visit to Macon, reporting the former Confederate leader seemed "to be in excellent health and fine spirits." His stay in Macon would be brief because he was in the city only on private business.[53]

Cobb was also highly thought of by the officers who served under him. One of them, Brigadier General William W. Mackall, informed Cobb on 19 July 1865, that he was leaving the following morning for Baltimore where he

---

[48] Cobb to Wilson, Athens, GA, 4 June 1865, Ibid. Cobb had been, according to a newspaper reporter, "treated with much consideration and kindness by the military authorities ever since his arrest." *Georgia Journal and Messenger*, 7 June 1865.

[49] Mary Ann Cobb to Wilson, Athens, 30 May 1865, Cobb Papers, 1865.

[50] Wilson to Cobb, Macon, 6 June 1865, Ibid.

[51] Wilson, *Under the Old Flag*, II, 361-62.

[52] *Macon Daily News*, 14 June 1865.

[53] *Macon Daily Telegraph*, 13 June 1865.

intended to live. Before he left, however, he wanted to thank Cobb "for all the many acts of kindness you have shown me and assuring you of my hopes that you will yet be enabled to serve your state for its great benefit."[54]

During May 1865, Cobb remained in Macon, not only to cooperate with Wilson, but also to rent his wife's house, the Bear's Den. Cobb had used the residence as both home and headquarters during the period 1863-1865, but now made arrangements to rent it and the furniture which came with it for $50. a month to George M. Logan with two stipulations: (1) Cobb's son, John A. Cobb, might use it during his frequent visits to Macon on Cobb family business, and (2) "the three servants Louisa[,] Mary[,] and Robin to retain the use of their rooms."[55]

Things seem to have run smoothly under this agreement until late July when an officer called on Logan and told him to be prepared to vacate the premises if needed by Brigadier General John T. Croxton, commander of the 1st Brigade in Brigadier General Edward M. McCook's 1st Division. Croxton told Logan he could make an inventory of the furniture, but that none of it was to be moved. Lewis W. Whittle, Macon businessman, lawyer, and friend of Cobb who had served as the latter's agent and attorney, protested the matter to Wilson but was told that nothing could be done because the property did not belong to Cobb, but was the separate property of his wife. By the end of July, Croxton had moved into the house. When Whittle protested to Croxton he was informed that the property had been seized on the grounds of military necessity because Croxton could not find another house in Macon. He tried to tell Croxton that the Planters Hotel was available for rent, and explained that Mrs Cobb inherited the house from her only brother [the deceased John B. Lamar]. The sister had preserved the house and its contents just as Lamar had left it. The Cobbs had allowed Logan to rent the property because he had been a close friend of Lamar. When he learned these facts, Croxton regretted that he had taken the house, but refused to vacate the premises. To make matters worse, some of the property was destroyed by Croxton and his men, especially some of the trees which Federal troopers cut down to make room for tents. Moreover, the servants had been forced to leave.[56]

In an effort to force Croxton to move out, Cobb wrote General James Steedman, Military Governor of Georgia with headquarters in Augusta, asking for his help in restoring the property to Logan. Cobb pleaded his wife's anxiety that the property be restored, saying that he held the property only as trustee since the house and lot were the property of his wife. Croxton had taken possession of the residence by force against the protests of both Whittle and

---

[54] Mackall to Cobb, Macon, 19 July 1865, Cobb Papers, 1865.
[55] George M. Logan, Agreement, Macon, 1 May 1865, Ibid.
[56] Whittle to Cobb, Macon, 3 August 1865, Ibid.

Logan. The seizure, furthermore, was made in time of peace on the plea of military necessity, "which necessity," Cobb informed Steedman, "did not exist as at the time another house more convenient more central and in every respect better suited to the wants of Genl. Croxton was offered for rent and his attention was called to it by Mr. Whittle." Private property, Cobb believed, could not be seized in this manner in time of peace. Croxton had also refused to allow Logan to remove some of the articles which were held in high esteem by Mrs. Cobb. Furthermore other contents of the house were also taken, some of the trees were cut down to make room for tents, and the Freedmen whom Cobb had furnished with a house on the lot were forced to leave.[57]

Croxton still occupied the Bear's Den in late September.[58] Despite this seeming setback, Cobb joyfully told his wife on 26 October that Wilson had rented Mrs. Henry G. Lamar's house, and planned to "give up ours" when the Federal commander returned from Milledgeville.[59] Two days later, Cobb wrote his wife that "We are once more in possession of our house. A great feat has been performed- the lawful owners have been permitted to take possession of their own property." By the evening of the 28th the Federals had left the Bears Den, but not without some loss to the Cobbs. Cobb noted that the residence was badly in need of a good cleaning, but was "unable to say what is the extent of the damage- but not so great as I expected." Unfortunately, the greatest damage occurred in the library where many of the books were missing. On a more positive note, the furniture looked dingy, but none was missing. The pictures were all saved although the Federals had rearranged them.[60]

During the fall of 1865, Cobb was occupied with even more important matters than his efforts to secure the return of the Bear's Den. In September, he approached several of his friends in Macon to help him obtain a pardon. One of them, William B. Johnston, met with President Johnson, and reported that the Tennesseean had inquired about Cobb's whereabouts and his health. Johnston replied that Cobb was in Athens and well, and that he wished to get a pardon. Johnson then asked whether Cobb had applied for a pardon. Johnston said that he had not, and would not apply for one until he "had some assurance that it

---

[57] Cobb to General James Steedman, Athens, 10 August 1865, Ibid. See also Cobb to Steedman, Athens, 27 August 1865, Ibid.

[58] Cobb to his wife, 19 September 1865, Ibid.; Mary Ann Cobb to her husband, Athens, September 1865, Ibid.

[59] Cobb to his wife, Macon, 26 October 1865, Ibid. Presumably, Croxton occupied the house during this period.

[60] Cobb to his wife, Macon, 28 October 1865, Ibid.

would be granted." The President replied that Cobb must first apply for a pardon before anything could be done.[61]

Cobb followed Johnson's advice and quickly filed an application for a pardon, and asked General Steedman for his support in securing it. He also fervently defended himself against charges that he was cruel to Federal prisoners in Macon and Andersonville, assuring Steedman that the charges were false, and added he had "never spoke an unkind word–much less do an unkind act to a prisoner during the war." The Georgian had repeatedly supplied the needs of prisoners from his own means. This included clothing and feeding them and giving them money. He believed that, if he had no other claim upon Johnson for a pardon, he felt it [the pardon] was "due to me for my uniform kindness to prisoners–whenever the occasion occurred." Besides, Cobb looked upon the war as over immediately upon his receipt of the news that Johnston had surrendered, and since that time he had advised the people to submit to the Federal victory, and conform "to the new state of things." Cobb believed, since he was badly hurt by the war in a pecuniary way, it was important to him and to his family that he should be restored as soon as possible to his status and rights as a citizen.[62]

During October Cobb continued his efforts to secure a pardon,[63] until, by the end of the month he met with his friend, Judge Oliver Lochrane, who assured him that, during a meeting with Johnson, "my name was the subject of a part of the conversation & that I might look confidently for a pardon."[64] Cobb apparently never received an individual pardon.[65]

---

[61] William B. Johnston to Cobb, Washington, 27 September 1865, Ibid. During this period Cobb was asked to appear as a witness in the trial of Henry Wirz for alleged crimes committed while he was commandant of Andersonville Prison. General James B. Steedman, Headquarters, Department of Georgia, Augusta, Orders, 3 October 1865, Ibid.

[62] Cobb to Steedman, Athens, 11 October 1865, Ibid.

[63] W.N. Mitchell to Cobb, Milledgeville, 12 October 1865, Ibid. ; W.N. Jackson to Cobb, Washington, 13 October 1865, Ibid.; and Cobb to William H. Seward, Athens, 17 October 1865, Cobb-Erwin-Lamar Collection.

[64] Cobb to his wife, Macon, 28 October 1865, Cobb Papers, 1865. A typescript copy of this portion of Cobb's October 28 letter is also on file in the Cobb-Erwin-Lamar Collection.

[65] Leroy P. Graff, Ralph W. Haskins, and Paul H. Bergeron, eds., Cobb to Andrew Johnson, Macon, 20 November 1865, *The Papers of Andrew Johnson*, 14 vols. (Knoxville: University of Tennessee Press, 1967-1997) 9, September 1865-January 1866, 410 fn. See also Cobb to Andrew Johnson, Athens, GA., 17 October, 1865, Ibid., 254-55. In January, 1867, Johnson extended Cobb's parole so he could visit any place in or out of the United States. Johnson to Cobb, Washington, 7 January 1867, Ibid., Vol. 11, August 1865-January 1867, 545.

Not all Maconites joined Cobb in stolidly accepting their Federal conquerors. Laura Nisbet Boykin, daughter of Judge and former Congressman Eugenius Aristides Nisbet, briefly described Wilson's advance through Alabama, and admitted, on the night of 1 May 1865, "This night in bitterness of spirit, I acknowledge that Southrons are a subjugated people." She wrote of the "wretchedness" of the initial stages of the Federal occupation. Describing the events of April 20, she ruefully confided to her diary, "That fearful night, we felt for the first time the iron heel, and the merciless power of the Vandals. Almost every house was entered. Four ruffians after vainly attempting to steal my horses, came to the door and threatened to burst it down. Came in and searched the house - demanded watches, threatened to hang and shoot my husband, and forced him, after threatening to forcibly enter my room, to show and deliver to them the concealed watches. They took mine and his and $3,000, and left." She noted "The crushing sense of humiliation weighed me to the earth. It took hope from my heart - lustre from my eye–smiles from my lips, and elasticity from my step. I wept in bitterness and anguish." She felt the people of Macon and the South were "without any army without arms, and in very truth are forced back into the old Union. [66]

On another occasion, when it seemed that her father might be arrested, Laura scribbled, "I despise this contemptible and cringing twaddle of the press about the Union restored - brother love - laudation of Yankee Generals and the like! True Southerners hate the Yankees and always will. The Union is restored by a compulsory welding; there is no cement of love. But I will not sleep, if I think more of the Yankees."[67]

Yet, two days later, she reluctantly played some "Yankee songs from a Yankee Glee book." However, on 5 June the unreconstructed young woman, reluctantly visited Wilson's headquarters with a friend who planned to return to New Orleans and who needed permission from Wilson to leave. But she could not make up her mind to see Wilson on behalf of her father, and called the young general, a "military dictator" and "his Highness." Later that day, after being persuaded by friends that she needed to see Wilson, Laura seriously considered seeing him "and swallow my imprecations against the Yankee ruler."[68]

An early historian of Macon and Central Georgia, John C. Butler, himself a Confederate soldier, described Wilson as a "tyrant." The young cavalry commander, Butler felt, "was not possessed of a single magnanimous quality of liberal sentiment." Butler heard that Wilson, in the Eastern Theater, was known

[66] Boykin Diary, 1 May 1865. The underlining in this and other quotations from her diary are Mrs. Boykin's.

[67] Ibid., 3 June 1865.

[68] Ibid., 5 June 1865.

as 'spoony' Wilson', and believed that from "his seizures of private property here, which he appropriated to his own individual use, he sustained the reputation he had won in Virginia." Butler described Wilson as having "boasted ...of the capture of Macon as the grand achievement of his military career," and concluded: "If there be any glory in it, there is certainly no true soldier who would envy him in its enjoyment." Wilson departed from Macon, according to Butler, "leaving not a regret or a friend behind him."[69]

Macon, as an occupied city, was subject to depredations by the Federal troopers as is the case with all occupied cities throughout history. However, despite the fears of Maconites, although Wilson allowed enlisted men to enter Macon without passes, he forbade them to ride their horses in the streets.[70] In short, he did what he could to protect people and property. To that end, he issued General Orders No. 30 on 28 May forbidding soldiers to tear down fences, or in any way to interfere with civilian property "or with the negroes in their service or employ. Troopers could not graze their horses in cultivated, enclosed fields. When they were sent out to graze, a commissioned officer accompanied them. These officers would be held responsible for the conduct of the men.[71] Colonel Vail, Post Commander at Macon, issued orders on 30 May forbidding anyone from carrying away lumber and brick from yards and from the fortifications which surrounded the city. Persons caught violating this order would be arrested and turned over to the Post Provost Marshall for trial.[72] By his actions, Wilson reminded everyone, military and civilian alike, who was in control. By 31 May, he completed plans to establish a military court to examine civilian misdemeanors, and to adjudicate private squabbles. All persons who violated both civil law and military regulations would be brought before this tribunal.[73]

Such a court was badly needed. A little chapel was desecrated in East Macon, and every pane of glass and every seat except one was broken. A brass band which belonged to the 17th Indiana Mounted Infantry, stationed nearby, was just leaving the building. The people of the area hoped the damage would be speedily repaired "so as to permit divine services to be resumed."[74]

Some of the soldiers committed desecrations in the cemeteries. Laura Boykin reported, on 1 June that Federal troops were encamped all around Rose

---

[69] John C. Butler, *Historical Record,* 287.

[70] *Macon Daily Telegraph*, 7 July 1865.

[71] Capt Edward P. Inhoff, Acting A.A.G. for Wilson, General Orders No. 30, Macon, 28 May 1865, *OR*, 49:2, 923; *Georgia Journal and Messenger*, 31 May 1865.

[72] *Macon Daily Telegraph*, 1 June 1865.

[73] Ibid., 31 May 1865.

[74] Ibid., 29 June 1865.

Hill cemetery and, to make matters worse "the sanctity and quiet was disturbed by a brass band playing before the gate."[75] Over a month later, Federal troops, in an effort to escape the heat of a Macon summer, used the lakes in the vicinity of Rose Hills "Crystal Spring," for bathing. That, in itself, might have been permissible, since the weather was hot, but the men bathed in the nude in full view of many people. To make matters worse, the men performed their ablutions on a Sunday. The *Daily Telegraph* noted: "The Cemetery is visited every day by mourners and others, and on no time more than on Sabbath afternoons. We understood from persons near the spot, that these lakes are the resort of soldiers on other days for the same purpose. This practice should be stopped. The river is near enough, and secluded enough, for bathing."[76] Since nothing was done to prevent the continued use of Rose Hill's lakes by the soldiers, the practice of bathing continued through the summer. By mid-August troopers stationed in the neighborhood of Rose Hill and Oak Ridge Cemeteries were cutting down shrubbery, trees, and fences in both burial grounds. The situation became so bad that the City Council's Committee on Rose Hill Cemetery reported crowds were seen in the lakes daily "regardless of decency and the presence of visitors." However, there is no record that anything was done to stop the practice of bathing.[77]

Macon was also a place where trials were held and prisoners were incarcerated. By 4 August Wilson ordered Captain McFeety, Judge Advocate of the Post at Macon, to adjourn the military court which he headed, and ordered General John T. Croxton to try future cases.[78] However, fights between soldiers and civilians and soldiers against each other persisted. In late August, a fight broke out between a trooper and a Macon civilian when the soldier, who had taken a ride on the Maconite's mule without his knowledge returned the animal.[79]

In early September, another court-martial was organized to try offenders against military laws and regulations. Captain W. W. Badger of the 176th New York, part of Macon's permanent garrison, presided over the tribunal as Judge Advocate. Thomas J. Musgrove, a civilian from Randolph County, Georgia, aided by R. W. Snell of the same place, killed W. Armstrong, a soldier in Company E, 145th Indiana Volunteer Infantry near Cuthbert. Both Musgrove

---

[75] Boykin Diary, 1 June 1865.

[76] Ibid., 4 July 1865.

[77] Simri Rose and J.L. Jones, Report of Committee on Rose Hill Cemetery, Council Minutes, 15 August 1865, Book F, p. 100.

[78] Capt. Edward P. Inhoff, A.A.G., Orders, Macon, 4 August 1865, Cobb Papers, 1865.

[79] *Macon Daily Telegraph*, 24 August 1865.

and Snell were taken to Macon and confined there. However, while Musgrove was tried, Snell was released due to a lack of sufficient evidence.[80]

Of course, Wilson received the strong support of the commanders of the Post of Macon. When Post Commandant Colonel Jacob G. Vail was assigned to command the Columbus District in Georgia, Wilson assigned Lieutenant Colonel Frank White, who had served as Provost Marshal, as Post Commandant. Lieutenant H. H. McDowell was named as White's successor.[81] White, whose 17th Indiana Mounted Infantry, had ridden ahead of Minty's Division and occupied Macon on the evening of April 20, was described as a "gentlemanly soldier" who had "won the confidence of the people" in the discharge of his duties as Provost Marshal. An order, issued by White, prohibiting the sale of whiskey to soldiers and Blacks, drew the praise of the *Journal and Messenger,* which expected the interests of the city to be more closely promoted now that White had assumed the more important post.[82] Unfortunately, White was relieved by Wilson in late July, when his regiment prepared to leave the city. He was succeeded by Colonel Johnston of the 2nd Michigan Cavalry.[83] Johnston's tenure did not last long. On 4 August Colonel Martin R. Archer, commander of the 137th United States Colored Troops, assumed the position of Post Commandant.[84]

As 4 July approached, Wilson and his staff planned an elaborate ceremony for the nation's most important holiday. The troops scheduled to participate in a parade were ordered to assemble on Tattnall Square at 4:00 P.M. on the 4th. Plans called for the procession to start there and march down Cotton Avenue to Oak Street, then down Oak to Second Street and on to Mulberry. The parade would continue down Mulberry by the courthouse to the Trotting Track below the city [located on the grounds of the present Central City Park]. Orders went out for the soldiers to march dismounted but armed. All regimental bands were directed to march. Plans called for speeches by Judge Lochrane, Thomas Hardeman, Jr., and others. Everyone in Macon and vicinity was invited, and most of them were expected to attend. The various fire companies were expected to turn out, bringing with them at least one fire engine. The preparations included a salute of thirty-six guns, one for each state in the Union [including the former Confederate states]. The announcement concluded: "Let all who can be present, and let us celebrate the day as it should be celebrated."[85]

---

[80] Ibid., 5 and 6 September 1865.

[81] Ibid., 23 June 1865.

[82] *Georgia Journal and Messenger,* 28 June 1865.

[83] *Macon Daily Telegraph,* 29 July 1865.

[84] Ibid., 9 August 1865.

[85] *Macon Daily Telegraph,* 1 July 1865.

The editor of the *Daily Telegraph* disagreed saying "we see the land draped in mourning, the maimed soldier hobbles through the streets, the cry of the widow and the orphan is heard. Many, very many, sleep their last sleep and will never again celebrate this anniversary of American independence."[86] Judge Lochrane declined the invitation to speak explaining "the condition of our people...precludes me from engaging in public festivity." He promised, however, to speak upon the subject of the defeated South, and report to them the opinions and positions of the highest officials of the Federal Government which they gave him during their recent meetings.[87]

The Fourth of July began with a thirteen-gun salute in honor of each of the original States. All business was suspended in the forenoon. At 10:00 A.M. a large crowd, mostly freedmen, headed by marshals and a brass band marched through Macon to a grove near the Methodist Episcopal Colored Church. Two speeches were given by black leaders in which they opposed the idea of sending Blacks back to Africa. They were Americans and should remain here. The procession then reformed and moved down Second Street to the old fair grounds, and had dinner. A military display followed at 5:00 P.M., with troops marching down Second Street to Mulberry, and down Mulberry to the race track, now Central City Park. There the ceremonies commemorating the 4th were held, with the seats mostly filled with soldiers. The white citizens did not attend. A Colonel Kelly of the 4th Kentucky Cavalry read the Declaration of Independence, and Colonel White pointed out that several white leaders who had been invited to speak had declined. Not having another speaker, White himself made a speech in which he complimented the soldiers for their bravery and urged them to go home and resume the responsibilities of civilian life. The Georgians attending were advised to accommodate themselves to the new order of things, and live in obedience to the laws and constitution of the United States. White told the freedmen they were now free, but must now work harder than ever. He told them they must not come to Macon where there was no work for them, but remain on the farms and make crops. Both General Wilson and Colonel Kelly refused to speak, but Judge Lochrane, when called upon, reluctantly agreed. He expressed pride in being an American citizen and reverence for the occasion.[88]

One of the most ticklish problems facing Wilson as Military Governor of the Macon District was that of the freedmen. On 13 May he wrote Superior Court Judge Iverson L. Harris of the Ocmulgee Circuit, that no obstacle would be thrown in the way of the enforcement of the law and the punishment of crime by the civil authorities but Blacks must be considered free men. In his letter, Wilson expressed his desire to see the courts continue to enforce the law and the

---

[86] Ibid., 4 July 1865.

[87] Ibid.

[88] Ibid., 5 July 1865.

punishment of crime according to the "penal code of the State as it existed on the 1st of January 1861." This held true except in cases involving the freedmen who must now be considered free. However, with this one stipulation, Wilson promised Iverson that "No obstructions will be thrown in the way of your holding your sessions or in the enforcement of your sentences." The Federal commander hoped that all good people would help to restore "peace, order, and the enjoyment of life, liberty, and property under the laws."[89]

The influx of Blacks into the city following the Federal occupation, created a situation where many former slaves lounged on street corners in idleness.[90] Many of them were destitute, without either food, clothing, or a place to sleep.[91] The Macon City Council passed an ordinance ordering all idle freedmen arrested and held in the guardhouse for trial by Mayor Collins, as well as such penalties as ball and chain, bread and water, work on the streets, public works, confinement in the guardhouse and stocks, according to the type of offense committed.[92]

This situation led to Wilson's issuing orders concerning the freedmen on 5 July 1865. Part two of these directives constituted former masters as guardians of minors and of the aged and infirm in the absence of parents or other near relatives who could support them. Part four ordered able-bodied freedmen not to leave their homes to live in idleness. Former masters could not turn away or drive from their plantations faithful hands without paying for the labor already performed. Freedmen would have to obey civil and criminal law, and could be punished for violations of the law just like white people. However, in no cases could their former masters brutalize them. With the end of slavery all laws and customs which were formerly necessary for its preservation ceased to exist. Furthermore, employers and servants had to agree upon the wages to be paid, and Wilson promised not to interfere with any just arrangements or contract. However, he advised the freedmen that for the present they could expect only moderate wages. When employers could not pay money, scarce in Middle Georgia at the time, the freedmen had to be satisfied with a fair share of the crops.[93]

This order was reinforced by General Steedman, appointed Military Governor of the Department of Georgia with headquarters at Augusta by President Johnson on 20 June 1865. Steedman, in his General Order No. 4, directed that the aged and helpless and women and children who lived in their

---

[89] Wilson to Judge Iverson L. Harris, Macon, 13 May 1865, *OR*, 49: Pt. 2, 745-46.

[90] *Macon Daily Telegraph*, 19 May 1865.

[91] Ibid., 23 May 1865.

[92] Council Minutes, 13 June 1865, p. 94.

[93] Captain Edward P. Inhoff, Acting A.A.G., Orders, Macon, 5 July 1865, *OR*, 49: Pt. 2, 1068.

former slave cabins would not be taken from these places until the State or Federal Government had provided for them. This help would not be given to those who could work. These people would not be allowed to remain idle.[94]

By September a writer for the *Daily Telegraph* reported the freedmen were returning to the countryside on every train.[95] Those who remained in the city cleaned up the streets,[96] and Federal troops collected all idle freedmen and took them before the Provost Marshall who placed them in an enclosure at the Court House where anyone desiring hands could get them.[97]

The indefatigable Laura Boykin experienced a sense of shock when her driver flatly refused to drive her carriage. The former slave, 'Sam', said he was free. Laura believed otherwise. He could of course, leave her premises, "but," she wrote, "as long as he remains here he is my slave and should be made to obey." She added, almost as an afterthought, "This is only a beginning of troubles we are to have with the 'institution'."[98]

A few days later, Laura wrote of the excitement and worry caused by the emancipation of the slaves. "Last night," she wrote,"Yankee Chaplains went to the colored churches and proclaimed the negro free. The consequence is many families are today without a servant, and doing the work themselves. This was premature on the part of the Chaplains, but it soon will come."[99]

On May 22, "after tea," Laura called her female servants, and asked them what they planned to do. They told her they would remain with her. Whereupon, she agreed to allow them to stay, and assured them she would pay them wages "as soon as the 'Freedman's Bureau' establishes the rates." She noted that she could now sleep in peace because "for the present, my kitchen status is fixed."[100]

During this period the Freedmen's Bureau, officially known as the Bureau of Freedmen Refugees and Abandoned Lands, was just getting organized. On 20 June 1865, Brevet Major General Rufus Saxton, Assistant Commissioner of the Bureau for South Carolina and Georgia, with headquarters at Beaufort, South Carolina, appointed Brigadier General Edward A. Wild as acting assistant commissioner for all that portion of Georgia lying west of the Altamaha,

---

[94] Brevet Colonel Seth B. Moe, A.A.G., General Order No. 4, 14 July 1865, Headquarters, Department of Georgia, Augusta, in *Georgia Journal and Messenger*, 19 July 1865. For Steedman's appointment see Major General George H. Thomas, General Order No. 1, Nashville, 20 June 1865, *OR*, 49: Pt. 2, 1017.

[95] *Macon Daily Telegraph*, 8 September 1865.

[96] Ibid., 19 September 1865.

[97] *Georgia Journal and Messenger*, 20 September 1865.

[98] Boykin Diary, 14 May 1865.

[99] Ibid., 22 May 1865.

[100] Ibid., 27 May 1865.

Ocmulgee, and Yellow Rivers, and north from a line to Sheffield and Lawrence to Cumming. Wild, whose headquarters were at Macon, received directions to establish agencies at Columbus and Atlanta. "The freedmen should understand their status as freemen at once," Saxton wrote, "and must be protected in their newly acquired rights. The former owners must be informed that slavery is not recognized by the US Government." Saxton wanted Wild to settle freedmen on abandoned lands, and placed him in charge of their educational, industrial, and other interests. Wild was also instructed to issue army rations to them "as may be necessary to prevent starvation."[101]

Wild placed Colonel Howland of the 2nd Ohio Cavalry temporarily in charge of Bureau activities at Macon in mid-July.[102] However, Second Lieutenant John G. Barney of the 187th Ohio Volunteers was permanent agent of the Bureau at Macon by 26 August.[103]

By 1 September Barney reported there were five schools with twelve teachers and 725 black students enrolled in Macon. The schools in both Macon and Atlanta were started by Professor John Ogden, sent out by the Western and Northwestern Freedmen's Aid Commission.[104]

On 17 May Wilson wired Thomas informing him he had received an order from Grant to leave a force of four thousand men to garrison places in Georgia, and to move with the remainder of the Cavalry Corps to the Tennessee River. Wilson believed that 1,000 infantry in Macon and one thousand at Atlanta would be sufficient, with those already at Augusta. Wilson wished for his entire corps to leave Georgia, and hoped that General Steedman could leave enough men to garrison the state. He cautioned Thomas that "This is no country for stock, and therefore the Government cannot well afford to keep cavalry here." At any rate it would be some time before he could begin his movement because Wilson's men were scattered throughout Georgia and Florida.[105]

A few hours later Wilson sent another message to his superior urging him to make certain that sufficient supplies were deposited, including a depot of grain at the Etowah in Northwest Georgia. The Illinoisan said he might leave Croxton's Brigade, except the 8th Iowa whose term of service ended in eighteen months, in Georgia if the latter officer received an appointment as military governor of the State. Wilson felt that Croxton's Brigade of 2,000 troopers

---

[101] Brevet Major General Rufus Saxton to Brigadier General Edward A. Wild, Beaufort, S.C., 20 June 1865, Edward A. Wild Correspondence, DU.

[102] Wild to Saxton, Augusta, 14 July 1865, Ibid.

[103] Wild to Saxton, Macon, 26 August 1865, Ibid.

[104] John G. Barney, Roster of Employees at Macon, 1 September 1865, Ibid.

[105] Wilson to Thomas, Telegram, Macon, 10:30 A.M., 17 May 1865, OR, 49: Pt. 2, 814.

would be sufficient to garrison all of Georgia.[106] Thomas replied at 11:00 P.M. on the 17th that Grant wanted him to remain with the portion of his corps still in Georgia.[107]

Wilson replied to a message Thomas sent him on 18 May assuring the latter that he would send a portion of his corps to the Tennessee River as soon as they could be concentrated. He was ordered to remain in Macon. If those men who went to the Tennessee River were mustered out, he could create a new division of veterans under Upton, Croxton, Alexander, Winslow, or LaGrange.[108]

The exchanges between Wilson and Thomas resulted in the retention of ten veteran regiments in Macon with Brevet Major General Emory Upton being placed in command of the division. Croxton, Winslow, and LaGrange were placed in charge of the three brigades that composed Upton's command.[109]

Wilson directed two brigades, a battery of artillery, and the entire train of one division to leave Macon on the morning of 23 May, at 7:00 with reveille sounded at 4:00 A.M. As this force marched through Macon, the men were ordered to march by fours, and no one could leave the ranks for any reason.[110]

In commenting on the movement of a portion of Wilson's command, the *Daily Telegraph's* writer observed many troopers had "expressed to us the warmest sentiments of friendship towards the citizens of Macon, from whom they have so generally experienced the most considerate treatment during their sojourn in our midst for a month, and the satisfaction of knowing they are going home alone allays their regrets at leaving." The troopers had generally conducted themselves well while in the city. It was, the writer believed, "universally acknowledged that the city has not enjoyed so quiet a season for years, or that which has marked the presence of the Union forces among us, which fact speaks strongly as to the excellent discipline maintained among his troops by the Major General [Wilson] commanding, and the morale of the men themselves." The strength of the garrison, the writer believed, would not be effectively decreased, because plans called for the replacement of those who left with others belonging to a different branch of the service.[111]

---

[106] Wilson to Thomas, Telegram, Macon, 1:00 P.M., 17 May 1865, Ibid., 815.

[107] Whipple (for Thomas) to Wilson, Telegram, Nashville, 1100 P.M., 17 May 1865, Ibid., 815.

[108] Wilson to Thomas, Telegram, Macon, 1:30 P.M., 18 May 1865, Ibid. This message did not arrive in Macon until 1:00 P.M. on May 22.

[109] Wilson to Thomas, Telegram, Macon, 22 May 1865, Ibid., 870. See also Capt T.W. Scott to Col Howland, commanding Second Brigade, Macon, 21 May 1865, Ibid., 862 and Wilson to Thomas, Telegram, Macon, 21 May 1865, Ibid., 850.

[110] Capt T.W. Scott, Circular, Macon, 22 May 1865, Ibid., 872.

[111] *Macon Daily Telegraph*, 23 May 1865.

On 22 May Thomas ordered Wilson to muster out only that portion of the corps whose term of service ended before 31 October 1865. Wilson should remain in Macon with a division of 4,000 men, and send the rest of his troops to Tennessee. Only those men whose term of service expired after 31 October would be retained in Macon.[112]

Wilson wanted an assignment to go to the Mexican border and serve under his old cavalry chief, Major General Phil Sheridan, a desire which Thomas was prepared to grant, provided Grant was willing.[113] Wilson wired Thomas on the 22nd that "The men have got the idea from newspapers that they are to be mustered out. Please inform me as soon as possible what is the policy in this matter."[114] Thomas passed on Wilson's recommendations to Grant on the 23rd, asking him if he had received orders about the disposition of the three regiments of black troops recruited by Wilson.[115]

Grant replied that he wanted Wilson to remain in Georgia, "which State I contemplate giving him command of." The young officer would need some cavalry, and, Grant assured Thomas, he planned to send some infantry from Washington to help Wilson to carry out orders for mustering out those troops whose time expired before 1 October 1865. Grant hoped Wilson could send 5,000 cavalry to the Mississippi River where they might be available if Sheridan, on the Mexican border, needed them. Two thousand more of Wilson's men could go to South Carolina. Grant insisted that those men who remained in the South should be troopers whose time of service did not end before 31 October. Wilson must move on this matter at once.[116]

Thomas, for his part, wired Wilson on 26 May ordering him to keep two thousand men in Georgia, send some to Texas, and one thousand to South Carolina. The remainder of Wilson's Cavalry Corps must go to Tennessee, where they would be mustered out and reorganized. Some of these men, those whose terms of service did not expire before 31 October 1865, would be sent to help restore law and order in Kentucky, Alabama, and Mississippi.[117] Wilson replied on 29 May assuring Thomas he would carry out his orders as soon as possible.[118] In order to accomplish his mission Wilson proposed to reorganize

---

[112] Thomas to Wilson, Telegram, Nashville, 5:00 P.M., 22 May 1865, Ibid., 671.

[113] Thomas to Grant, Telegram, Nashville, 11:00 A.M., 23 May 1865, Ibid., 882-83; Wilson Diary, 1865, 24 May 1865.

[114] Wilson to Thomas, Telegram, Macon, 22 May 1865, OR, 49, Pt 2, 870-71; Wilson Diary, 1865, 25 May 1865.

[115] Thomas to Wilson, Telegram, 11:00 A.M., 23 May 1865, *OR*, 49: Pt. 2, 883.

[116] Grant to Thomas, Telegram, Washington, 9:10 P.M., 23 May 1865, Ibid., 882.

[117] Thomas to Wilson, Telegram, Nashville, 26 May 1865, Ibid., 909-10.

[118] Wilson to Colonel Thomas M. Vincent, A.A.G., Telegram, Macon, 29 May 1865, Ibid., 928.

those men who remained in the army into brigades and divisions and returned with the troops of other arms by districts.[119]

On 26 June Thomas issued Special Orders No. 3 dissolving the Cavalry Corps, Military Division of the Mississippi.[120] Wilson acknowledged receipt of the orders on 1 July.[121] On the following day he told his men that their corps had ceased to exist. In announcing the order Wilson, who had a flair for the dramatic, wrote, "The rebellion has terminated in the establishment of your country upon the basis of nationality and perpetual unity." He noted that their "deeds have contributed a noble part to the glorious result. They have passed into history and need no recital from me." After reciting a list of their victories he told them they had "learned to believe yourselves invincible, and contemplating your honorable deeds may well justly cherish that belief. You may be proud of your splendid discipline no less than your courage, zeal, and endurance." He concluded: "Peace has her victories no less than war. Do not forget that clear heads, honest hearts, and stout arms guided by pure patriotism, are the surest defense of our country in every peril. Upon them depend the substantial progress of your race and order of civilization, as well as the liberty of all mankind."[122]

On the same day he explained to Thomas the disposition of troops in Georgia. After urging favorable consideration of Major General Gustavus W. Smith's application for a pardon, he noted that Georgia, west and south of the Ogeechee and Altamaha Rivers, was quiet. All that was needed to protect the interests of the Federal Government was an ample force to manage the Treasury Department in the area and proper representatives to operate the Freedmen's Bureau.[123] Wilson also received orders on 2 July to report to General Steedman.[124]

During the following weeks more of Wilson's men left Macon. In late July, the 17th Indiana Mounted Infantry was ordered to Nashville for muster out, but

---

[119] Wilson to Brigadier General William D. Whipple, Telegram, Macon, 5 June 1864, Ibid., 960. Whipple served as Chief of Staff to Thomas. Two days later Wilson complained to Chief of Staff Rawlins that "The muster out is depriving me of my best officers." Wilson to Rawlins, Telegram, Macon, 7 June 1865, Ibid., 967. Also see Wilson to Major General Quincy A. Gillmore, Telegram, Macon, 8 June 1865, Ibid., 970.

[120] Whipple to Wilson, Telegram, Special Orders No. 3, Nashville, 26 June 1865, Ibid., 1035.

[121] Wilson to Whipple, Telegram, Macon, 1 July 1865, Ibid., 1057.

[122] Wilson to the Officers and Men of the Cavalry Corps, Military Division of the Mississippi, Orders, Macon, 2 July 1865, Ibid., 1059.

[123] Wilson to Thomas, Telegram, Macon, 2 July 1865, Ibid., 1059-60.

[124] Wilson Diary, 1865, 2 July 1865.

the order was rescinded and the unit left the service at Macon.[125] By 23 August the last volunteer regiment of cavalry, the 17th Pennsylvania, was mustered out, leaving on the 24th.[126] Nine companies of the 4th US Cavalry left on 25 August. Seven companies went to Augusta and two to Hawkinsville. The remaining three companies of the regiment stayed in Macon.[127] By the end of September only three regiments remained in Macon: the 187th Ohio, the 176th New York, and the 137th USC.T.,one of the three black regiments recruited by Wilson in Alabama and Georgia. All of these units were infantry.[128]

Prosperity returned to Macon, but very slowly. Shortly after he captured the city, Wilson urged the people to resume their peaceful occupations.[129] On 13 May many stores were open, and a reporter for the *Daily Telegraph* commented: "and considerable evidence of returning vitality was shown." The paper expected to see the auction houses reopened soon "and to hear again the stentorian voices of auctioneers crying off their goods."[130] However, on 16 May, a writer for the paper noted the idleness in the city. Many people were offering their services, but "there is no one to employ them."[131] Toward the end of May an article in the paper stated, "It is a matter of extreme regret to see so much idleness in the city. This is not from choice but rather from the fact that there is no work to do. Men and women are everywhere seeking employment, and are willing to accept anything, soever small, as compensation. The fewest number are successful in the finding of situations." Many businessmen were not making enough money to pay their rents, and therefore, had no money to employ anyone.[132]

Unfortunately, Wilson and his men had not been able to restrain some of the criminal elements in the community. Nathan C. Munroe reported "There are so many horrible murders & robberies here every day & night that Nathan [his son] or indeed nobody scarcely goes out at night." The area around Vineville was much quieter by late August, however, because, Monroe explained, "the troops are gone from the camp in the rear of us."[133]

---

[125] *Macon Daily Telegraph*, 29 July 1865. On July 30, a report in the *Daily Telegraph* stated that plans called for many of the men to be mustered out in the city. Ibid., 30 July 1865.

[126] Ibid., 24 August 1865.

[127] Ibid., 26 August 1865.

[128] Ibid., 27 September 1865.

[129] Ibid., 13 May 1865.

[130] Ibid., 14 May 1865.

[131] Ibid., 16 May 1865.

[132] Ibid., 23 May 1865.

[133] Nathan C. Munroe, Jr. to Bannie Kell, Sylvan Lodge, 18 August 1865, Kell Letters, 1865-1869. The troops mentioned were Federals who occupied some of the old camps along the fortifications.

On 8 October, Munroe reported to Bannie his doctor's horse was stolen from the gate to Henry Lamar's house in the middle of the preceding day, while the doctor was in the house. The theft, Munroe believed, was committed by a Federal soldier who "was seen by several persons to ride him off about 5 minutes after the Doctr. Got off of him." The frustrated doctor pursued the soldier, evidently one of Macon's permanent garrison, nearly to his camp, but could not find him. Reverend Rees's horse was also stolen from its stable, when the locked door was removed from its hinges. People tracked the thief to the City Bridge, but lost the trail at that point.[134]

However, there were signs everywhere that things were gradually returning to some degree of normalcy. For one thing, the demand for houses, both for business and residences, became far greater than the supply. Second class store rooms rented for $100 per month, and first class for one-fourth more. Everyone who rented expected to do business enough in time to justify their paying these prices. Dwelling houses brought all kinds of prices. These were determined by the quality of the dwelling and its locality.[135] F.W. Simms wrote from Sylvan Lodge that Colonel Dent, one of Munroe's neighbors, looked for mules to purchase, but could find none worth buying. Sims, himself, attended a sale sponsored by the Federal authorities, and was astonished to find no cheap horses sold, and "how dear the mules were." Sims wrote horses brought from $10 to $30, while mules commanded even more- $60 to $110. No two-horse-wagons were available because Federal troops used only wagons drawn by teams of four or six animals.[136]

Another good sign was the fact that the city market was again prospering.[137] A reporter for the *Journal and Messenger* observed, "Glancing round the market ...we saw that there was nothing on sale but meat- no vegetables nor products of the barn-yard or dairy. We trust, however, that the market will improve in these latter respects, so soon as country dealers get the hang of things."[138]

---

[134] Nathan C. Munroe, Jr. to Bannie Kell, Macon, 8 October 1865, Ibid.

[135] *Macon Daily Telegraph*, 17 May 1865.

[136] F.W. Sims to Captain John M. Kell, Sylvan Lodge, 20 August 1865, Kell Letters.

[137] *Macon Daily Telegraph*, 14 May 1865.

[138] *Georgia Journal and Messenger*, 7 June 1865. The same article gave the price of bacon from 8 to 12 cents a pound; lard, 8 to 10 cents; fresh beef, 10 to 15 cents; fresh pork and mutton, 15 cents; butter, 15 to 25 cents; eggs, per dozen, 15 to 20 cents; chickens, 20 to 30 cents; flour, per pound, 4 to 5 cents; meal per bushel, 85 cents to $1.00; corn 75 cents to $1.00; fodder, 75 cents to $1.25; cane syrup, per gallon, 35 cents to 40 cents; sorghum, per gallon, 20 cents; salt, 2 to 3 cents per pound; good quality New Orleans sugar, 20 to 25 cents; common qualities of sugar at lower rates; and wheat, per bushel, $1.25 to $1.50.

By mid-summer life had returned almost to normal in Macon. A ferry, established by order of City Council, operated over the Ocmulgee River just above the Georgia Central Railroad bridge,[139] while work crews pressed forward with the reconstruction of the City Bridge.[140]

In late May, the courthouse was in a "sad state of dilapidation" which needed "renovation from top to bottom." A writer for the *Daily Telegraph* noted, Bibb County needed a new courthouse because the old one was too small, too architecturally outdated, and lacked many features needed if Macon was to rise from the ashes of defeat. He reported, "The old house is now hardly any thing but a pile of filth- the halls, rooms and yard having recently been desecrated by men and horses to such an extent as to make them positively offensive."[141] The fence around the building was destroyed and livestock grazed upon what was left of the beautiful lawn and damaged the fine shade trees.[142]

On 21 October the Bibb County Jail was burned to the ground, presumably by some of the prisoners who had deliberately set it on fire. The city owned a guard house located on Third Street, but it was not large enough to accommodate the demands made upon it.[143] The jail, a well-built structure, was three stories high with eighteen cells, all of which were, with the halls, inlaid with eighteen inches of solid pine. The strong walls resisted the heat for fourteen hours, but finally three sides of the building crashed to the ground. The Ocmulgee Fire Company, which had fought the blaze for hours, stood by until the fire completely burned the remains of the building. The men constantly poured water upon the buildings which belonged to the Gas Company, and other buildings in the area in order to prevent further destruction. However, the Bibb Superior Court planned to order the immediate construction of a new and more substantial jail.[144]

Other buildings were being erected, or were being put to other uses. On 22 August W.T. Nelson's petition to construct a wooden storehouse on his lot, No. 3, on Square 43, was granted by the City Council upon the condition that he get the written consent of all the property holders and insurance agents who might be affected in case of fire.[145] In mid-August Federal troops stored cavalry equipment in a building on Cherry Street. The equipment was turned in to the quartermaster by those cavalry regiments scheduled to be mustered out.[146] In

---

[139] *Macon Daily Telegraph*, 3 August 1865.
[140] Ibid., 6 September 1865.
[141] Ibid., 25 May 1865.
[142] Ibid., 9 August 1865.
[143] Ibid., 22 October 1865.
[144] Ibid., 24 October 1865.
[145] City Council Minutes, 22 August 1865, p. 101.
[146] *Macon Daily Telegraph*, 15 August 1865.

October the Post Office was moved from its location on Second Street to a new location at the corner of the alley on Third Street, midway between Cherry and Mulberry.[147] The new postmaster, J.H.R. Washington, was appointed to that position by Wilson on May 16.[148]

Vendors charged $.50 for meals at the City Market House, showing the inflation rampant throughout large areas of the post war South.[149] Ordinary houses rented for $40.00, about three times as much as they rented for before the war.[150] Street hands were busily engaged redraining the gutters and filling up holes on Cherry Street, one of Macon's principal thoroughfares.[151] Cotton was being shipped down the Ocmulgee River to the Altamaha and on to the seaport of Darien. The going price was $.21 cents to $.28 cents a pound.[152] Joel Branham's Female Academy resumed operations on 4 September.[153] A reporter for the *Daily Telegraph* commented on the quietness of Macon. The streets wore the same quiet, orderly appearance as they had before the war. The business climate was enhanced by "the familiar sound of the auctioneer's bell, the rattling of innumerable dray wheels drown all other noises; and the arrival of wagons from the country, heavily loaded with cotton, and other produce, the hurrying to and fro of the man of business."[154]

The theater, too, resumed productions within a month after the Federal occupation. By late May, Crisp's Company presented "Macbeth" to a large and appreciative audience. The *Daily Telegraph's* reporter noted "the order and decorum maintained throughout the whole performance...." and added "The theater of late is favored by the fair sex and is a favorite place of resort."[155]

In late October a troupe performed "The Hunchback of Notre Dame," at Ralston's Hall. Commenting on the production, the *Journal and Messenger's* writer regretted "to see such a meagre attendance of the fairer portion of creation." He added, "The ladies can take our word for it, that they run no risk in visiting Ralston Hall now, under the present management." Strict order would now be observed, and the theater would become a place of innocent, intelligent amusement.[156]

---

[147] *Georgia Journal and Messenger,* 18 October 1865.
[148] *Macon Daily Telegraph,* 16 May 1865.
[149] Ibid., 24 August 1865.
[150] Ibid., 26 August 1865.
[151] Ibid., 31 August 1865.
[152] Ibid., 2 September 1865.
[153] Ibid., 5 September 1865.
[154] Ibid., 7 September 1865.
[155] Ibid., 23 May 1865.
[156] *Georgia Journal and Messenger,* 18 October 1865.

Lectures were also well attended. Colonel C.C. Henderson, formerly of the Confederate Army, planned to deliver a lecture at the City Hall on 26 May. Plans called for his subject to be true courage and its attributes. Henderson also intended to discuss the "present state of affairs in the country." The price of admission was fifty cents in US currency.[157]

Despite seeming progress, the loss of so many Macon men in the war hung like a cloud over the city. Their deaths left 487 widows and 913 children who lost their husbands and fathers.[158] By the end of May nearly all of the young men who went forth to fight had returned. But, of the twenty-three companies furnished by Macon to the Confederacy, not more than five companies of men, all told, were still alive. A writer for the *Daily Telegraph* noted, "This is indeed a fearful mortality." But, he added, "they have left on the historic page deeds of heroism that their children's children in the lapse of rolling years will treasure in memory. And the living will oft recount the marches, the battles, and the sieges they have gone through–forgetting nothing- ashamed of nothing that they did in fighting for what they believed to be the liberties of mankind."[159] So great was the loss suffered by Macon that the *Daily Telegraph's* reporter exclaimed, "Truly has the war cost our city many noble youths. A list of the dead ought to be prepared by some one and published."[160]

Despite their sacrifices, it was obvious that the Southern troops, for all their valor and sacrifice, had lost the war. The 14,985 men paroled in Macon during April and May 1865,[161] had certain penalties attached to their status as surrendered troops. They could not wear any stars, bars, straps, stripes, cords, tassels, buttons, or any insignia of rank, position or office in the former Confederate Army after 10 June 1865. All persons who continued to wear these items after that date would be considered as still bearing arms against the US Government, and would be treated accordingly.[162]

Confederate soldiers also faced additional problems. Since many of them were short of food to take home with them the *Daily Telegraph* urged its readers to furnish rations and some kind of lodging for the many paroled soldiers then passing through Macon on their way home from Northern prisons.[163] Efforts were made by Federal officials to provide one pair of shoes each to paroled

---

[157] *Macon Daily Telegraph*, 25 May 1865.

[158] Ibid., 20 September 1865.

[159] Ibid., 31 May 1865.

[160] Ibid., 16 May 1865.

[161] *OR*, 49: Pt. 1, 415.

[162] Adjutant W.E. Doyle for Colonel J.G. Vail, Headquarters Post, Macon, 3 June 1865, in *Georgia Journal and Messenger,* 30 June 1865. See also *Macon Daily Telegraph,* 4 June 1865.

[163] *Macon Daily Telegraph*, 25 June 1865.

Confederate soldiers who were barefooted.[164] The *Daily Telegraph* asked for special assistance for such disabled soldiers who needed help like as Private Thomas Jones, a double amputee, formerly of the Macon Guards.[165]

By 3 September in addition to the paroled soldiers, about 1,450 citizens of Bibb County had taken the required oath of allegiance to the United States. The *Daily Telegraph's* writer recounted "this is very nearly the number of votes usually polled in the county previous to the war."[166]

It became more difficult to secure medical attention at the end of the war. In October 1865, doctors raised their fees.[167] To make matters worse, only two hospitals continued to operate in the city: the Ocmulgee and the Blind Asylum. All other hospital facilities were closed. These two housed only twenty patients, a few Confederate soldiers who lived at great distances from Macon. Some of these men could travel, but many did not have the money to go to their homes. A writer for the *Daily Telegraph* urged Maconites to raise money so these men could finally return home.[168]

The lives of private individuals had returned to some degree of normalcy. Laura Nisbet Boykin, who had hated the very name of Wilson when Macon capitulated in late April, finally met the Federal commander on 14 June and wrote, "He impressed me very favorably, as a courteous and educated gentleman. He is only 25 yrs of age, and his promotion has been wonderfully rapid." The young officer influenced Laura even more favorably when he promised to send her some new books he had ordered from Boston. The spirited young Southern woman and the dashing cavalry commander still disagreed about many things, but they parted, Laura confided to her journal, "very good friends." He had flattered her about her playing the piano, which pleased her. She learned that Wilson was "a connoisseur of music," who even promised to help her father get a pardon.[169] Laura had written earlier that she was "considering whether or not to recant and swallow my imprecations against the Yankee ruler" because she feared for her Father's safety, and wanted to secure a pardon for him.[170] By 17 June Laura was "quite fascinated with the Yankee General," and blushed when she wrote this because she had denounced him as a thief and murderer. She did not apologize for her changed attitude, merely noting "It is curious, these revolutions in sentiment!" Instead, she went to see Wilson,

---

[164] Captain P.C. Simpson to Major Armstrong, Quartermaster's Office, Macon, 10 July 1865, in *Records of East Tennessee Civil War Records*, III, 340.

[165] *Macon Daily Telegraph*, 11 July 1865.

[166] Ibid., 3 September 1865.

[167] Ibid., 20 September 1865.

[168] Ibid., 5 September 1865.

[169] Boykin Diary, 14 June 1865.

[170] Ibid., 5 June 1865.

accompanied by Reverend David Wills. Alluringly dressed in a Grenadine dress trimmed with crape on the skirt and waist she went to Federal headquarters. During what turned out to be "a delightful visit," Wilson proved very affable, assuring Laura that her Father would not be sent a prisoner to Washington, and promising to recommend him for a pardon if his arrest was ordered. He even offered her one of his horses to go on a ride with him, saying he would accompany her, but that it would "create a 'stir' among the gossips of the town." Laura scribbled in her diary about the "Many pleasant things he said," noting she "came away very light-hearted and relieved, and very kindly disposed towards the Genl."[171]

After seeing Wilson in church on 18 June and 25 June Laura, dressed "in the luxury of a very few linen garments," was taking tea on the back balcony of her home on the afternoon of the 25th, when Wilson entered the house. She hurriedly dressed and "spent a very pleasant evening" with the young cavalryman.[172] A few days later she even gave a breakfast in his honor with only a few other guests.[173]

On 3 July Laura wrote her father, temporarily out of town, discussing among other things, their relations with "our Northern brethren, and the disposition of our towns people to nurse their hostility towards them, and refuse all intercourse with the officers among us, and absent themselves from the table of the Lord for fear Yankees might be there." She noted that such conduct was "all useless, impolitic and unchristian."[174] During the following weeks Laura's relations with Wilson improved to the point that, by 20 July she received an invitation to take a carriage drive with him. She "deliberated upon braving the gossiping spinsters of Macon," but finally agreed to go. She had a "charming drive, which invigorated me much," and retired immediately upon returning home in a condition which she described as "quite invalidish."[175]

Life for Nathan Munroe returned to a condition of near-normalcy. He continued to douse himself with such things as a chloroform mixture to help his chronic cough–"and to try to breathe." He also continued to attend his beloved Christ Episcopal church, and listen to the sermons of his good friend Reverend Rees. He went to Rose Hill Cemetery to visit the graves of his wife and grandchildren. At the conclusion of one such visit he wrote Bannie that he "found all quiet and in good order as usual there," and sent her a flower from the

---

[171] Ibid., 17 June 1865.
[172] Ibid., 18 and 25 June 1865.
[173] Ibid., 29 June 1865.
[174] Ibid., 3 July 1865.
[175] Ibid., 20 July 1865.

head of the graves of her two children. He was also happy to see the encampment of Federal troops gone from the neighborhood of the cemetery.[176]

A few days later Munroe was still trying to breathe, this time by inhaling the fog from the boilers of his cane mill, which he hoped would help his asthma.[177] In early October, Munroe attended church where he heard a lay reading by Lewis N. Whittle, also a member of the church. But there was only a moderate audience to hear Whittle's eloquence.[178] The following Sunday Whittle read a "very good sermon on the 'Sins of the Tongue' very appropriate & proper." During the service an announcement was made that Mrs. Flint, wife of the proprietor of the Flint House, had died the night before. Indeed, sickness was rife that autumn.[179] Munroe told Bannie on 14 October that twelve of the Blacks who worked at the Ocmulgee Mills were sick with fever. The prominent Macon editor and businessman Simri Rose was also sick with the same ailment. Munroe himself had a bowel complaint for which he took a solution known as Bryan's mixture. Episcopal services were read by lay reader Whittle who took his text from David's penitential Psalm 51. Munroe believed that Whittle presented "a most excellent illustration of sin & its consequences & more without which we can have no hope." Fortunately, a larger number of people attended church and exhibited a greater interest in lay reading.[180]

During the fall of 1865, Munroe's letters to Bannie chronicled much of what happened in the civil life of Vineville and Macon. On 22 October he informed her that a small child, Lu Logan, fell out of a third story window at the Lanier House, "and was literally mashed to death- her skull and almost every bone in her body fractured[.] she lived about 3 hours."[181] A few days later he noted that corn meal cost $1.25 a bushel at the mill, while bacon was very scarce and expensive.[182] On the evening of 27 October he jubilantly informed her, "I got my pardon from the president today."[183]

But, despite this bit of good news, Munroe's asthma continued to trouble him. By the end of October he was forced to take chloroform at least twice a day to get much comfort. He told Bannie that he disliked getting into the habit, but

---

[176] Nathan C. Munroe, Jr.. to Bannie Kell, Sylvan Lodge, 27 August 1865, Kell Letters, 1865-1869.

[177] Nathan C. Munroe, Jr. to Bannie Kell, 29 August 1865, Ibid.

[178] Munroe to Bannie Kell, Sylvan Lodge, 1 October 1865, Ibid.

[179] Nathan C. Munroe, Jr. to Bannie Kell, Sylvan Lodge, 8 October 1865, Ibid.

[180] Munroe to Bannie Kell, Sylvan Lodge, 14 October 1865, Ibid. Whittle was lay reading because of the continued absence of Reverend Reese who had gone away for his health. Ibid.

[181] Nathan C. Munroe, Jr. to Bannie Kell, Sylvan Lodge, 22 October 1865, Ibid.

[182] Munroe to Bannie Kell, Sylvan Lodge, 25 October 1865, Ibid.

[183] Nathan C. Munroe, Jr. to Bannie Kell, Sylvan Lodge, 27 October 1865, Ibid.

excused it on the ground that "but what little time I may be spared to my children I must try & be as comfortable as I can."[184]

Sickness continued to plague the community. When the child of one of the workers at the Ocmulgee cotton factory developed smallpox it caused a panic among the other workers, some of whom decided to flee the area. Munroe wrote that the sick person "being a child it is difficult to send it off to the hospital and our people dont appear to be satisfied to have the house [where the sick child was] quarantined & stay near it so I dont yet know what the result will be." To make matters worse, a number of Maconites who had gone to New York for a visit returned sick. Munroe observed they "all look skeleton like and were confined to their beds several weeks." He breathed with great difficulty because he had not had time to take his usual dose of chloroform, and confided to Bannie that he never ventured "to take it at night for fear it might make me sleep too hard." Munroe was so preoccupied with the fear of a smallpox epidemic that he noted the return of his beloved pastor in a single sentence: "Mr Rees arrived unexpectedly yesterday looking apparently in quite good health and says he feels very well."[185]

As early as July 1865, the City Council voted to appropriate $150 to Dr. L. Carter, the surgeon in charge of the Macon Small Pox Hospital, for attending to several smallpox cases then in his establishment.[186] Carter had proposed to treat all pauper smallpox cases for $10 each.[187]

The City Council directed Dr. A.P. Collins, the City Physician, to organize a smallpox hospital in July. With his own money Collins bought suitable furniture including bunks, mattresses, bedding, and cooking utensils to serve a hospital of sixty beds, reporting "The hospital supplies did not cost the city one farthing not even hauling to the hospital." Colonel White, then Commandant of the Post, had allowed Collins the use of an army ambulance to carry smallpox cases from the city to the hospital. Collins, under the authority of the Mayor and City Council, employed three hospital attendants. One of these individuals served as steward and ward master for $60 a month, and had previously served in these capacities for three years in a smallpox hospital. Another employee, a black man, was paid $8.00 a month as an ambulance driver. The third attendant, a black woman, received compensation at $5.00 a month. The City Council authorized Collins to make twenty tables and the same number of benches, and also have work done on one of the buildings to serve more patients. The Council paid $50 for these improvements. By December, through careful management, Collins and his staff had spent only $60

---

[184] Munroe to Bannie Kell, Sylvan Lodge, 28 October 1865, Ibid.

[185] Nathan C. Munroe, Jr. to Bannie Kell, Sylvan Lodge, 30 October 1865, Ibid.

[186] Council Minutes, 11 July 1865, p. 97.

[187] Ibid., 18 July 1865, p. 98.

of public money to purchase provisions. Only two cords of wood were provided by the city because, Collins explained, "I have managed to surmount it [the scarcity of wood] by making the convalescent patients and attendants go to the rear of the hospital and cut old logs and brush." After being forced to turn over the ambulance to the Freedmens Bureau on 27 November Collins used his own team to carry smallpox cases out of Macon to the hospital free of charge to the city.

Since the hospital was organized Collins had admitted and treated about 300 smallpox cases, 275 Blacks and twenty-five whites, treating all of these with medicine, food, nursing, and bedding, and had not received pay or compensation for one third of those he cared for. He had also furnished medicine and medical treatment to about twenty-five patients among the white paupers, and planned to make out a bill for these cases and present it to the City Council. His bill included $330 for the steward and ward master, $44 for the ambulance driver, and $27 for the cook. The physician's bill, including medicine amounted to $250. Rations for 45 days totaled $60. Including the expenses for making tables and benches and repairing them and providing wood, Collins' total compensation amounted to $771.50.

By the end of December, the Council's Committee on Public Property arranged with Federal Lieutenant H.P. Webb to use a building on property taken over by the US Army near the new Arsenal at a moderate rent.[188]

In early November Munroe recorded the advent of very heavy rains which filled the rivers of Middle Georgia. He then abruptly turned to the church service for Sunday, 5 November, which was preached by the returned Reverend Rees. The text was from Revelation 11:12, "And they heard a great voice from Heaven saying unto them come up hither." This had a peculiar effect on Munroe who noted that Rees buried three people in the congregation during the week: Miss Joyce, Miss Mary Ann Taylor, and an old lady of about seventy whom Munroe did not know. To make matters worse, one of his former slaves, a man simply known as "Ned" became ill with smallpox. Munroe stopped by the man's cabin on his way to church and tried to get a doctor to help him, but none would come to treat the aged man.[189] In his letter, Munroe also mentioned the scarcity of cars on the Macon and Western Railroad which he helped to manage.] On the following day he visited Ned again, found him very ill, and sent for two doctors, but neither of them came. He finally got Dr. Holt to come to see the sick man. Munroe described Ned's condition: "when I saw his miserable condition and the miserable place he was in–I could not but feel it was her [Emma, Ned's wife]

---

[188] Ibid., 26 December 1865, p. 115.

[189] Nathan C. Munroe, Jr. to Bannie Kell, Sylvan Lodge, 5 November 1865, Kell Letters.

who had brought it upon him–but I said not a word of reproach."[190] By 7 November Munroe had secured the services of Dr. Hammond, another Macon physician, to attend to Ned. Hammond suggested they feed Ned a milk punch which, Munroe noted, "has already brightened him up a little–but I think recovery extremely doubtful." The smallpox epidemic continued to rage, especially among the Blacks, some of whom had already been placed in the hospital. The disease threatened to spread among the general population because the Blacks moved about freely now that slavery had ended.[191]

On the following day, 8 November, Munroe went by Ned's quarters but found him so confused under the influence of morphine which Dr. Hammond had prescribed for him, that the old man did not know anything at all. As Munroe approached Ned's shack he went through the quarter of Macon in the upper part of Cotton Avenue where he noticed so many conspicuously placed little red flags denoting smallpox cases that he imagined he smelled the disease, and observed "the air fairly stank with it."[192]

However, despite these problems, many of which resulted from the Southern defeat in the War, peace had returned to Macon, and much of the reason for the relatively easy transition from war to peace was due to Wilson's capable administration. When the City Council learned on 15 August that Wilson would probably leave Macon in the near future its members offered a resolution of thanks to the Federal commander and his officers for the preservation of order in and around their city, resolving, "the best wishes of this Council accompany Genl Wilson in his retirement from this post."[193]

---

[190] Nathan C. Munroe, Jr. to Bannie Kell, Sylvan Lodge, 6 November 1865, Ibid.

[191] Nathan C. Munroe Jr. to Bannie Kell, Sylvan Lodge, 7 November 1865, Ibid.

[192] Nathan C. Munroe, Jr. to Bannie Kell, Sylvan Lodge, 8 November 1865, Ibid.

[193] Council Minutes, 15 August 1865, p. 100. Wilson had received orders to take command of the District of Columbus and the 2nd Division, Department of Georgia on October 13. He did not leave the State until December 19. Wilson Diary, 1865, 13 October and 19 December 1865.

Epilogue

In March 1868, Trueman G. Avery, a partner in the firm of Bennett and Avery, Produce Commission Merchants of Buffalo, New York, passed through Macon on business. He arrived in the city on an evening in late March, and went immediately to Brown's Hotel, and then ordered a carriage and rode through the streets viewing the city. Avery found the thoroughfares to be very broad, and noted General Howell Cobb's residence—John B. Lamar's former Bear's Den—on Walnut Street, which he described as "a square wooden house, with large grounds." Avery reserved high praise for Brown's Hotel, which was clean, well operated, with a fine table. The waiters were very obliging, and did not delay serving dinner. The proprietors were Eliphalet Brown and his son, with the son doing the work. The charges of the hotel were moderate. All along the route of the Georgia Central Railroad from Savannah Avery had viewed the ruins of depots, freight houses, and mills, at almost every station. All of these facilities were replaced by the time of his visit. The Georgia Central Railroad was well-equipped, and was doing a very good freight business, averaging 3,500 bales of cotton a day. In fact the line was doing such a good business that it was paying its stockholders dividends of ten percent.[1]

The famous American writer Bret Harte presented a more sombre view of Macon when he visited the city on a lecture tour in November 1874. Macon was, according to Harte, the "principal city of the old cotton-planting aristocracy, and on the heights around are still standing some of the lordly houses of the great slave-owners." The homes were "often very beautifully equipped and have a certain broad ease and munificence...the streets are like public squares, the houses are low and large!" He noted that the bedroom in the Lanier House in which he was writing was "as large as our parlour." Yet the town had a "deserted, kind of heart-broken air."

There was much ivy about which contributed to the scene. The gardens were nearly all neglected. He described Joseph Bond's former residence as a fine house which "belonged to a young man who owned thirteen hundred slaves and was the largest cotton autocrat in the district." Bond had been killed, Hart noted, by an overseer with whom he was arguing "for the overseer's ill-treatment of a slave!" On a drive to Rose Hill Cemetery, Harte was impressed by

---

[1] Trueman G. Avery, Diary, 20 March 1868, pp. 23-24, in Charles Samuel Spencer and Uriah N. Parmelee Correspondence, 1845-1911, Diaries, 1864-1865, Typescripts of Correspondence and Diaries, DU.

the tombs which were "ivy-shrouded, and black with age, but always showing some sign of recollection in a bouquet of yesterday or an attempt to restore the half-concealed inscription." Although the cemetery was overgrown with bushes and other growth, it was the burial place of the Confederate dead of Macon; "a thousand on the hillside, each name recorded on the little headboard." As Harte and a friend drove back to the hotel the friend pointed out the different signs of progress, a new cotton mill, a new church, a new driving path, the State Fair Grounds, and a new cottage. But Harte noted that Rose Hill Cemetery seemed "to cover the whole town–the planters' sombre houses were mausoleums, the few listless people we met who looked up were only ghosts of their dead selves wandering around aimlessly, and waiting to be covered up again." The city seemed to be covered with an atmosphere. "It is an intoxication," he observed, "but an intoxication without exaltation, without levity, without hopefulness. It is the resignation, the silence, the sweetness, the tenderness, of death."[2]

And yet, in its way, Macon, like the immortal phoenix, was slowly beginning to rise from the ashes of defeat, to resume its rightful place among the foremost cities in the South.

---

[2] Bret Harte to his wife, Macon, 7 November 1874, in Geoffrey Bret Harte, ed., *The Letters of Bret Harte* (Boston and New York: Houston Mifflin Company, 1926) 44-47. Joseph Bond's fine mansion is now owned by Mercer University. Author's note.

APPENDIX A

Some Macon Leaders During the War

Eugenius A. Nisbet

Eugenius A. Nisbet, one of Macon's most prominent citizens, was born in Greene County, Georgia, on 7 December 1803. He was educated at Powelton Academy in Hancock County, attended Columbia College, and transferred during his junior year to Franklin College, part of the University of Georgia, with the highest honors in his class. He studied law in Judge Gould's law school at Litchfield, Connecticut, and was admitted to the bar by a special act of the Georgia Legislature. He began the practice of law in Madison, Georgia, served four terms in the Georgia House, and three in the State Senate. While in the Senate in 1830, he led the fight for the establishment of a State Supreme Court. He ran for Congress in 1838, and again in 1840, but resigned before the end of his term. He was elected to the State Supreme Court for a two-year-term in December, 1845, was reelected in 1847, but was defeated for reelection by Judge Henry L. Benning in 1853. He returned to private practice in Macon in partnership with his brother, James. He served as a member of the Secession Convention, and drew up the ordinance under which Georgia seceded from the Union.

He represented Georgia in the Confederate Provisional Congress, and also served as President of the Board of Trustees of Oglethorpe University and of the University of Georgia. Because of his achievements, Nisbet received the degree of Doctor of Laws from the University of Georgia in 1868. He also served as an elder in the First Presbyterian Church of Macon, was the superintendent of the Sunday School there, and teacher of the Bible Class. He represented his church as a delegate to numerous Presbyterian Synods and General Assemblies. He received a pardon from President Andrew Johnson after the war. Nisbet died on 18 March 1871, and is buried at Rose Hill Cemetery in Macon. He married Amanda Battle on 15 April 1825. Twelve children were born to this union.[1]

---

[1] Biography/Obituary Files, Middle Georgia Archives, Washington Memorial Library, Macon.

George S. O'Bear

George S. O'Bear was born in Salem, Massachusetts on 15 April 1822, and died in Birmingham, Alabama at the home of his son, George S O'Bear, Jr. on 23 December 1888. He was buried at Rose Hill Cemetery in Macon. O'Bear became a resident of Macon in 1841, associating himself with the firm of E. V. Johnson and Company, Jewelers. He served as Chief of the Macon Fire Department from 1865 to 1877 and as Mayor of Macon for three years. He also served as a Bibb County Commissioner and as a Trustee of the Public Schools in Bibb County.[2]

John S. Schofield

John S. Schofield was born in England in 1820, and was a self-made man. He came to Georgia in 1844, and worked for the Central and Monroe Railroads (the Monroe Railroad was later renamed the Macon and Western Railroad). In 1850 he and his brother opened a small foundry in a log shed which employed only six men. By 1855 the firm of Schofield and Brother supervised an establishment which offered such items as saw milling machinery, steam engines, iron store fronts, and pipes for gas or water. In 1859 the Schofields built their large iron shops and foundry on Fifth Street, near the Union Depot. They amassed a considerable fortune in their business and survived the war with their shops intact and their business so prosperous that Schofield owned property valued at over $20,000, a considerable sum for that time. Schofield left a wife and four sons. He died on 23 January 1891, and was buried in Rose Hill Cemetery.[3]

Lewis Neale Whittle

Lewis Neale Whittle was born on 15 May 1818, in Norfolk, Virginia. As a youth he became a surveyor, and was employed by railroads in Virginia and Georgia. He married Sarah M. Powers of Monroe County, Georgia, studied law, and came to Macon to be admitted to the Bar. He had a prosperous career, served two terms in the Georgia State Legislature, was a senior warden and leader in Christ Episcopal Church on Walnut Street in Macon, and was a director of both the Macon and Western and Macon and Brunswick Railroads.

---

[2] Ibid.

[3] Sketch of John S. Schofield in Ibid.; Robert S. Davis, Jr., "Confederate Machine Toolmaker: John S. Schofield of Macon, GA," *Tools and Technology the newsletter of the American Precision Museum, Windsor, Vermont,* in Middle Georgia Archives, Washington Memorial Library.

During the war he served as an aide to Georgia Governor Joseph E. Brown. Some of his greatest contributions came in the field of education, serving on the boards of the Georgia Academy for the Blind; the Bibb County Board of Education; the Macon Free School; and the University of the South in Sewanee, Tennessee. He was the first president of the Georgia Bar Association in 1883 the same year in which he died. Whittle School in Macon was named after him.[4]

Washington Poe

Washington Poe, the son of William Poe, a Revolutionary War soldier from Lancaster County, Pennsylvania, and his wife Frances Winslow, was related to the famous American writer, Edgar Allen Poe. He was born in Augusta, Georgia, on 13 July 1800, and was orphaned early due to the death of his mother on 22 July 1802, and his father on 13 September 1804. He and his three siblings became wards of Thomas Cumming, a close friend of the Poes, a prominent banker and the first mayor of Augusta. Cumming raised and educated the children. Poe was educated at Sand Hill Academy in Augusta, then sent to a private school in New Jersey which specialized in preparing students for Princeton. He returned to Augusta where he entered in a warehouse and commission business with his brothers, Robert and William. He then returned north and enrolled in Judge Gould's law school in Litchfield, Connecticut. He remained there in 1824, and returned to Macon where he was admitted to the Bar in May 1825. He entered private practice with Oliver Prince, the Intendant of the new town of Macon. In January 1827, he succeeded Edward Dorr Tracy, Sr. as Solicitor-General of the Macon Circuit. On 24 December 1829, he married Selina Shirley Prince, the fourteen-year-old sister of Mary Prince. During the war Selina was instrumental in organizing the women of Macon in support of the soldiers and their families. Poe joined the Presbyterian Church in November 1828, and became a ruling elder in 1829. He served as mayor of Macon in 1840.

In November 1841, he was appointed legal guardian of Virginia and Frances Prince, children of Oliver Prince who, with his wife, was drowned in an accident at sea. He settled Prince's extensive estate. In 1840 Poe served as a delegate from Bibb County and speaker at the convention held in Macon to ratify the anti-Van Buren presidential slate. Poe, a Whig, admired and supported Henry Clay and was elected President of Macon's Henry Clay Club in 1844. He was also elected in that year to the US House of Representatives. In November 1860, Poe presided over a meeting called in Macon on the day of the 1860 presidential election. He cautioned the people of Macon to be calm and deliberate in their response to Lincoln's election. In January 1861, he was elected as a Union

---

[4] Sketch of Lewis Neale Whittle, Biography/Obituary Files.

delegate to the Georgia Secession Convention in Milledgeville. He served in that body as one of three members from Bibb County.

When the war came he was appointed Postmaster of Macon. He participated in public life both during and after the war. In 1870 he delivered the main address at the cornerstone laying ceremony for the new Bibb County Courthouse at the corner of Mulberry and Second Streets. Two years later he served as a Bibb County delegate to the September 1872, state-wide Democratic Convention. Poe cut an impressive figure as a lawyer and a politician. He was erect, tall, stately, and was impressive, with a slender figure. He was gracious in manner and filled "the full measure of the term 'a perfect gentleman'." He died on 7 October 1876, and was buried in Rose Hill Cemetery.[5]

Simri Rose

Born at Branford, Connecticut in 1799, Simri Rose served an apprenticeship as a printer in New Haven, Connecticut, and in the New York Office of Harper's Publishing Company. In 1819 he moved to Georgia where he located in the frontier post of Fort Hawkins, across the Ocmulgee River from the future town of Macon. He published a little newspaper there called *The Bull Dog*, and later joined Marmaduke J. Slade in purchasing an interest in the Georgia Messenger, one of Macon's earliest newspapers. Rose later added another newspaper, the *Journal*, which he merged into a paper known as the *Macon Journal and Messenger*. Subsequently, he sold the newspaper to the Macon Telegraph which became known as *The Telegraph and Messenger*. However, the paper later dropped the word *Messenger* and became known as *The Macon Telegraph*.

In 1828 he married Lavinia E. Blount, the daughter of Colonel James E. Blount and his wife Elizabeth de Roulhac of Blountville in Jones County, Georgia. They had nine children. Rose organized and became superintendent of Macon's first Sunday School at Christ Episcopal Church, where he also served as a vestryman. He provided beautiful shade trees and parks for the city of Macon, and even developed the Botanic Garden at the head of Magnolia Street. Another park, known as Rose Park, which fronted his home was laid off and planted by him. He also gave Rose Hill Cemetery to the City. His home on Beall's Hill, next to the home of Governor George W. Towns, was later owned and occupied by Eliphalet E. Brown, long-time proprietor of Brown's Hotel. Rose was a mason, a Whig, and a strong supporter of the Union. However, he supported the Confederacy when war was declared.[6]

---

[5] Sketch of Washington Poe in Ibid.
[6] Sketch of Simri Rose in Ibid.

Reverend David Wills

Reverend David Wills, the Pastor of the First Presbyterian Church in Macon during the war period, was born at Gettysburg, Pennsylvania, on 7 January 1822. Educated at Washington College, Tennessee, and Columbia Theological Seminary, he received the degrees of Doctor of Divinity and Doctor of Literature. He served as pastor at the Presbyterian Church in Laurens, South Carolina, from 1850 to 1860, and in Macon from 1860 to 1870. Later (1870-1874), he was President of Oglethorpe University and Pastor of the Western Presbyterian Church of Macon (1874-1879). In 1879 Wills served as a chaplain in the US Army, retiring from that position in 1886. He then became Pastor of the Disston Memorial Church in Philadelphia where he retired in 1901. He died in Washington, D.C. in January 1916, and was buried out of the New York Presbyterian Church in Washington. His body was interred in Glenwood Cemetery. Wills married Frances Rebecca Watt of Fairfield, South Carolina, before the war. They had four sons and two daughters. Wills was described as "over 6 feet in height[,] well proportioned, with a most amiable disposition, as well as an eloquent speaker, he soon became known and admired by the people of all denominations."[7]

Marcus Wright

Marcus Wright was born at Purdy in McNairy County, Tennessee, on 5 June 1831. He became an attorney in Memphis, and joined the 154th Tennessee Regiment, a militia unit. Early in the war Wright became Colonel of the 154th Senior Tennessee Regiment which evolved from the militia unit of the same name. He was promoted to Brigadier General on 13 December 1862, and was assigned to duty as Post Commander of Macon where Camp Wright, one of the many military encampments in the city, was named for him. He surrendered to Federal troops at Grenada, Mississippi, on 19 May 1865. Wright returned to Memphis where he resumed his law practice. In 1878, he was appointed as an agent of the US War Department for the collection of Confederate records by the Government at Washington, D.C. He retired in June 1917, and died on 27 December 1922.[8]

---

[7] Sketch of Reverend David Wills, *Macon Daily Telegraph*, 15 Jan. 1916, in Ibid.

[8] Ezra J. Warner, *Generals in Gray* (Baton Rouge: Louisiana State University Press, 1959) 346-47.

APPENDIX B

Some Civil War Historic Sites in Macon

There are many historic sites in Macon including a number that played a role in the history of Macon during the Confederacy. Of these, probably the most significant is Rose Hill Cemetery. Located on Riverside Drive only a few locks from the center of the business district, this beautiful cemetery is the final resting place for many of Macon's Confederate leaders. On the south side of the cemetery, close by the Ocmulgee River, 602 men who died in Macon's Confederate hospitals, primarily in 1864, rest amidst quiet hills and a lovely stretch of river. Most of the men were badly wounded in the battles for Atlanta, especially Peachtree Creek, the Battle of Atlanta, Ezra Church, and Jonesboro. Some of the men were killed defending Macon in the repulse of Stoneman's Raid on 30 July 1864. Others fell at Sunshine Church in Jones County where Stoneman and hundreds of his men were forced to surrender after a fierce engagement on 1 August 1864. In addition to these men, a number of leaders who led Macon during the war years have found their final resting place at Rose Hill. These include Simri Rose, Dr. James Mercer Green, John B. Lamar, Washington Poe, Eugenius A. Nisbet, Nathan C. Munroe, Jr., William B. Johnston, Edward Dorr Tracy, Jr., George O'Bear, and many others.

Little remains of the extensive Confederate fortifications around Macon. A small portion of the original works along the military road which later became **Pio Nono Avenue** may be seen on the northwest corner of the intersection of Vineville Avenue and Pio Nono Avenue.

A large 10-gun fort is located behind the Superintendent's house at the **Ocmulgee National Monument** on Emory Highway in the eastern part of the city. Another impressive fort is located on a bluff above the river in **Riverside Cemetery** which is located on Riverside Drive near the bridge which carries that highway across Interstate Highway 75.

Probably the most impressive building remaining from the Confederate Period is **Macon's City Hall**. This historic structure, located on Popular Street near its intersection with First Street, and converted from a cotton warehouse in 1860, became a Confederate hospital, known as the "City Hall Hospital," in 1863. The building was returned to the city in November 1864, and offered to Governor Joseph E. Brown as the temporary capitol of Georgia when Sherman's March to the Sea forced the evacuation of nearby Milledgeville. It served as headquarters for Brown, Georgia Adjutant General Henry C. Wayne, and a meeting place for the General Assembly for its last session under the Confederacy early in 1865.

The final shots of the war in Macon resounded here when Wilson's Cavalry Corps captured Macon in the evening of 20 April 1865. A guard, standing on the porch of the building, exchanged fire with members of the 17th Indiana Mounted infantry. The guard was killed. Another reminder of the war in and near Macon are the foundations of the bridge carrying what was formerly the **Georgia Central Railroad** over Walnut Creek near the boundary of the Ocmulgee National Monument. This bridge was one of the primary objectives of both George Stoneman's raiders on 30 July 1864, and the assault of Colonel Smith D. Atkins's troopers on 20 November of the same year. The site is just a few yards west of the present crossing of Walnut Creek by the Emory Highway. The visible remains of Confederate Macon include many of the old and beautiful buildings which abound in the city. These encompass homes, churches, and places of business of some of Macon's most prominent Confederate leaders.

The **home of John B. Lamar** at 577 Walnut Street, now used for offices, was willed by Lamar to his sister, Mary Ann Cobb, wife of General Howell Cobb. General Cobb used the home, then known as **"the Bear's Den,"** as a residence and headquarters during the period 1862-1865. It is located on the southeast corner of Second and Walnut Streets.

Near the "Bear's Den" on Walnut Street is **Christ Episcopal Church**, presided over during the war years by Reverend Henry Rees. The building, constructed in 1852, included among its members Nathan C. Munroe, Jr., Increase C. Plant, Simri Rose, Lewis Neale Whittle, and many others prominent during the war.

Another church which played an important role in civic life during the war is the **First Presbyterian Church**, located on Mulberry Street on the southwest corner of Mulberry and First Streets. The church, built in 1858, was presided over by Reverend David Wills during the war. Its membership included Clifford Anderson, Washington Poe, Eugenius A. Nisbet, Colonel John B. Lamar, John J. Gresham, and John C. Butler, author of the postwar History of Macon and Middle Georgia.

The **Washington Block** on Mulberry Street at the corner of Mulberry and Second Streets was one of the centers of business activity during the war. The Macon Volunteers used the building's third floor as their armory at the time. Macon is filled with many homes of prominent wartime leaders.

The **Hay House** at 934 Georgia Avenue was built for William Butler Johnston, a prominent Macon businessman and Confederate Depository for Macon, and is probably Macon's finest home although it is now used as an historic site open to visitors throughout the year. Johnston married Anne Clark Tracy, sister of Brigadier General Edward Dorr Tracy, Jr. who was killed in the

Battle of Port Gibson, Mississippi, at the onset of the Vicksburg Campaign on 1 May 6 1863.

Nearby is the **Cannonball House** which was the residence of Judge Asa Holt and his family. The house, now maintained by Macon's United Daughters of the Confederacy, was hit by a shell fired from Dunlap's Hill in what is now the Ocmulgee National Monument by one of Stoneman's two 3-inch ordnance rifles on 30 July 1864, during the Stoneman Raid. The Holt Family barely escaped injury. In front of the house is a bronze, 12-pounder Napoleon cannon cast at the Macon Arsenal in April 1864. The cannon was captured by Sherman's forces at Rocky Face Ridge in North Georgia during the opening phases of the Atlanta Campaign of 1864.

Nearby, at **974-81 Magnolia Lane** is the former residence of the **Tracy Family**. Edward Dorr Tracy, his son, Edward Dorr Tracy, Jr., and other members of the family lived there. Edward Dorr Tracy was a judge and a political leader and his son, mentioned above, was the highest ranking Maconite to serve in the Confederate Army.

A reconstructed blockhouse of **Fort Hawkins** marks the site of the old fort, constructed in 1806, and used as a fortification to protect the approaches to Macon in the two battles fought in 1864. The Superintendent's residence on the Ocmulgee National Monument was the home of Captain Samuel S. Dunlap during the war. It was used briefly as Stoneman's Headquarters during the Stoneman Raid.

The **Confederate Monument**, located on Second Street and Cotton Avenue, was constructed in 1879. It consists of a 10-foot tall statue of a Confederate soldier looking north. The monument originally stood at the intersection of Mulberry and Second Streets, but was moved to relieve traffic congestion at that place.

The **Monument to the Women of the Confederacy**, built in 1911, is located at the First Street terminus of Macon's Avenue of Flags in Poplar Street Park.

Dr. James Mercer Green, Director of Macon's Confederate hospitals, lived at **841-845 Poplar Street**. The house was built in 1840.

The former home of one of Georgia's wealthiest cotton planters, Joseph Bond, located at 988 Bond Street on top of Coleman Hill, was used as the headquarters of Major General James H. Wilson during the occupation of Macon in 1865. It is now known as the **Woodruff House** and is owned by Mercer University.

Isaac Scott, President of the Macon and Western Railroad, lived at **1073 Georgia Avenue**. It was later the residence of another of Macon's wartime leaders, John J. Gresham. In 1864, Colonel Lewis N. Whittle purchased the residence located at 1231 Jefferson Terrace from Dr. Richard H. Randolph.

Colonel Edward H. Hugenin of Savannah lived in the house located at **1261 Jefferson Terrace** during the war. The home was built in 1843-1844. Hugenin raised a company for Confederate service known as the Hugenin Rifles.

John Jones Gresham, mentioned often in the pages of this book, lived at **353 College Street**. Twice mayor, Gresham was president of the Bibb Manufacturing Company. The house, completed in 1842, now serves as an elegant bed and breakfast inn.

A structure located at **641-661 Monroe Street**, served as part of a Confederate hospital on Vineville Avenue. Nurses and military personnel lived in the structure during the war. Another building used as a hospital is located at 688 Monroe Street.

Sterling and Sarah Lanier lived in the cottage at **935 High Street**. They were the grandparents of famous Georgia poet and writer Sidney Lanier who was born in the house. Lanier, a Confederate soldier, was captured while running the Blockade out of Wilmington, North Carolina. He was taken to Point Lookout Prison in Maryland where he spent much of the remainder of the war. The building is now the headquarters of the Middle Georgia Historical Society which has offices on the second floor.

John Hill Lamar, Confederate colonel and civic leader before the war, lived at **544 Orange Street**. Lamar fell in battle on 12 July 1864. Judge Clifford Anderson, a member of the Confederate Congress and captain of the Floyd Rifles, lived at 642 Orange Street.

Federal troops camped in **Tattnall Square Park** after Wilson captured Macon on 20 April 1865. However, Confederate forces did not surrender in the park, but in the earthworks located a short distance west on Montpelier Avenue, known in 1865 as the Columbus Road.

Leroy Napier, another of Macon's wartime leaders, lived in a splendid mansion located at **2215 Napier Avenue**.

Joseph Clisby, editor of the Macon Telegraph, lived at **201 Clisby Place**. Federal officers in McCook's Division, occupied the house in 1865.

The residence located at **159 Rogers Avenue** was owned by Nathan C. Munroe, Jr. He wrote many of the letters to his daughter, Bannie Kell described in this book, from this house. Some of the fortifications built to protect Macon, including a large fort, were built near this home. The building is now owned by the Pilot Club of Macon. The fort and adjoining breastworks were destroyed many years ago.

These physical remains serve as a constant reminder of what Macon was like during the Confederacy.[9]

---

[9] Much of the information in this appendix is taken from Calder W. Payne, James E. Barfield and others, *Macon: An Architectural Historical Guide* (Macon: Williams & Canady, 1996).

Index